Disaster Management Handbook

PUBLIC ADMINISTRATION AND PUBLIC POLICY

A Comprehensive Publication Program

EDITOR-IN-CHIEF

EVAN M. BERMAN

Huey McElveen Distinguished Professor
Louisiana State University
Public Administration Institute
Baton Rouge, Louisiana

Founding Editor

JACK RABIN

Professor of Public Administration and Public Policy
The Pennsylvania State University—Harrisburg
School of Public Affairs
Middletown, Pennsylvania

Available Electronically

Principles and Practices of Public Administration, edited by Jack Rabin, Robert F. Munzenrider, and Sherrie M. Bartell

PublicADMINISTRATION*netBASE*

Disaster Management Handbook

Edited by

Jack Pinkowski
Nova Southeastern University
Fort Lauderdale, Florida, U.S.A.

CRC Press
Taylor & Francis Group
Boca Raton   London   New York

CRC Press is an imprint of the
Taylor & Francis Group, an **informa** business

CRC Press
Taylor & Francis Group
6000 Broken Sound Parkway NW, Suite 300
Boca Raton, FL 33487-2742

Library of Congress Cataloging-in-Publication Data

Disaster management handbook / editor, Jack Pinkowski.
     p. cm. -- (Public administration and public policy)
  Includes bibliographical references and index.
  ISBN-13: 978-1-4200-5862-8 (alk. paper) 1. Emergency
  management--Handbooks, manuals, etc. 2. Disaster relief--Handbooks,
manuals, etc. 3. Crisis management--Handbooks, manuals, etc. I. Pinkowski, Jack.

HV551.2.D55 2008
363.34--dc22   2007034449

**Visit the Taylor & Francis Web site at
http://www.taylorandfrancis.com**

**and the CRC Press Web site at
http://www.crcpress.com**

Dedication

To the memory of Jack Rabin, the executive

editor of the Public Administration and Public

Policy book series, whose leadership and

inspiration will certainly be missed by

our community of practice

Contents

SECTION VI: PLANNING, PREVENTION, AND PREPAREDNESS

Preface

The first decade of the twenty-first century has considerably raised an awareness of the potential danger to modern civilization from disasters, both natural disasters and those resulting from intentional human activities. The 2003 hurricane season was the sixth most active on record. The hurricane season of 2004 was one of the deadliest and costliest ever for the Atlantic Ocean basin. Four hurricanes raged across the state of Florida with two of them making landfall near the same spot within a few weeks of one another. And in 2005 there were seven major hurricanes including Hurricane Wilma, the most intense storm ever recorded. When it was in the Gulf of Mexico, its winds were documented at 185 miles per hour and its pressure was 882 millibars, the lowest ever. And Hurricane Katrina caused devastating flooding in New Orleans, displacing tens of thousands, and basically destroyed the coastline along the state of Mississippi.

The decade did not see new records in just hurricane destruction. In 2004 there were 1717 tornados, an all-time record.[*] And on December 26, 2004 a magnitude 9.0 earthquake off the coast of Sumatra triggered a tsunami that killed hundreds of thousands and left millions homeless in Southern Asia including Thailand, Indonesia, Sri Lanka, and India. The damage was estimated to be as great as $2 billion.[†]

Adding to the natural disasters were the terrorist attacks of September 11, 2001 on the United States by Islamic extremists that destroyed the World Trade Center in New York and resulted in nearly 3000 deaths. This added to the death and destruction at the other terrorist targets at the Pentagon in Washington, DC, and at the downed attack-airplane in Shanksville, Pennsylvania, and constituted a clarion call to do something substantially different about disaster management and preparedness in America.

---

[*] NOAA Reports Record Number of Tornadoes in 2004. NOAA 04-126, U.S. Department of Commerce News. Available at http://www.norman.noaa.gov/publicaffairs/releases/tornadoes2004.shtml.

[†] 2004 Global Register of Major Flood Events, Dartmouth University Flood Observatory. Available at http://www.dartmouth.edu/~floods/Archives/2004sum.htm.

The direct costs of these recent disasters in terms of lives lost, families dispersed, property damaged, economic impact, and future increases in insurance premiums added to the direct cost of response and rebuilding and constitute one of the seminal periods in history. It provided the motivation for this handbook on disaster management. My intention was to collect scholarly articles from academics around the world that were interested in an analytical critique of the issues involved and the various proposals for improvement. But I also felt that it was important to solicit personal accounts from the practitioner community involved with these various scenarios to add their perspectives and lessons learned to the dialog, which is frequently left out of such work.

In my formal book proposal to Jack Rabin, then executive editor of the Public Administration and Public Policy book series, I originally proposed a single volume on disaster management and homeland security. But after much discussion and refinement of the approach, we reached a conclusion that two separate volumes would be appropriate: one dedicated to homeland security, the *Homeland Security Handbook*; and this one, more broadly focused, the *Disaster Management Handbook*. Unfortunately, Jack will not see the eventual publication of these two volumes. As executive editor of the Public Administration and Public Policy book series since 1980, he marshaled the development of nearly 200 new titles until his death on November 13, 2006. His influence on the literature of public administration was widely felt and his passing will be missed by so many whom he inspired in the development of this discipline.

The result of nearly two years of effort is this reference work that is intended to serve our understanding of the interrelated, multidisciplinary issues of preparedness, response, recovery, and mitigation in dealing with prevention and rebuilding relating to disasters. We rely on the concept of "praxis," which combines theory and practice resulting in the practical application of learning from experience and applied theoretical scenarios. This handbook is a valuable means to communicate lessons learned among professionals in the field as well as a library resource.

I am most grateful to the contributors of the handbook not only for their valuable contributions to this work and their individual expertise but also for their considerable patience over the extended time since the call for proposals. I am grateful for the assistance of Mary Fenney, my assistant, who helped immensely with the organization of the database and Excel spreadsheets relating to the distribution of the call for manuscripts. The financial support from my associate dean, J. Preston Jones, of the H. Wayne Huizenga School of Business and Entrepreneurship at Nova Southeastern University has really truly been invaluable. And I am grateful above all for the consideration, patience, understanding, and encouragement that I have consistently received during the project from my publisher, Rich O'Hanley, at Taylor & Francis.

It was only with all of their help and the valuable contributions from so many experts that I was able to finally finish editing this handbook. I want to express my sincere appreciation to all of the contributors, for the enormous amount of time that they spent concerning their individual contributions, and for the high quality of their effort. It is our collective desire that through this *Disaster Management Handbook* we can share informed ideas, make important improvements, and become better prepared for the challenges of disaster management in the twenty-first century.

Jack Pinkowski

Introduction

Disasters have been a natural reoccurring fact of life on Earth as long as we know. In fact, the scientific literature suggests that the earth and all life-forms on it developed only after a disaster on a cosmic scale, i.e., the big bang. And according to the theory of evolution, this eventually led to our lives today that followed another worldwide disaster, a collision, or near miss with an asteroid, which precipitated the extinction of the dominant predators of the day, the dinosaurs. So, contrary to the current dialog about global warming, increasing frequency of major disasters like hurricanes, climactic changes, and other crises are part of life on this planet. Nevertheless, modern humankind is compounding the dangers inherent with Mother Nature. The complete proof regarding the frequency of widespread disasters and their long-term trend is beyond us because we have very limited records, geologically speaking. Still, it is important that we understand that disasters have a profound impact on life and the direction that future events take.

Of course, life today and the impact of contemporary disasters are very different than those of prehistoric times. Now we have developed societies (as well as lesser developed areas that may be in jeopardy because of the activities of the developed world), we have the complexity of modern life, we have a built environment that is more vulnerable because we have allowed development even where we know danger exists. For example, we know that volcanoes erupt repeatedly. Yet, with the record of devastation from the eruption of Krakatoa in Indonesia in 1883 when 36,417 people died, mostly from tsunamis generated by the explosion, we have increasingly allowed coastal development throughout the world. This had a great deal to do with the 283,106 lives lost from the Indian Ocean tsunami in 2004. Development has substantially increased the casualty count from a similar cataclysmic event in nature. In another example, the ancient cities of Pompeii and Herculaneum were covered by ash and volcanic debris almost instantly when Vesuvius erupted in AD 79, burying an estimated population of 20,000. Today, more than four million people are estimated to live in metropolitan Naples, in the shadow of that volcano.

We, as humans, with our intelligence, memories, emotions, affiliations, aspirations, and legacy may be arrogant in that we ignore such risks or are naïve in thinking that it will not affect us. But certainly humans care about the future, we believe that we can plan to make it better, and we think that we are smart enough to do something about it. The great earthquake and fire that destroyed San Francisco in 1906 resulted in 700 deaths and leveled a great city. A similar catastrophe was the Chicago fire in 1871 that destroyed about four square miles of a major city's center, killing hundreds. Yet, our response in both cases was to rebuild on the same geography. But we rebuild with new requirements, in these cases for local building codes, building materials suitable to the inherent risks of urban areas or moving ground in fault zones, new and better evacuation plans and fire suppression equipment, monitoring devices and early warning systems, etc. Now we are facing another great challenge in rebuilding the city of New Orleans, which is below sea level. The floodwaters that covered nearly 80 percent of the city following Hurricane Katrina in 2005 were the result of our not planning well enough for potential disasters that we know can happen and not properly executing the plans that were made. In all of these examples, including those resulting from natural phenomena, intentional destruction, and human error or negligence, the result has been great loss of life and property initially and even greater numbers at risk afterward.

Maybe we cannot avoid the occurrence of natural disasters and their impact on human civilizations because of our still imperfect ability to predict the weather and when and where geological or climactic events will occur. But we can do something about their effects. Man-made disasters are another thing altogether. Intentional destruction of other human beings, property, buildings, their societies, culture, economic systems, and the natural environment has its roots in human behavior. The clash of civilizations and the attempt at domination of one group by another is rooted in the study of political science. Extremist movements, religious zealotry, autocratic leaders, and institutionalized aggressive behavior must look to sociology and psychology for greater understanding of the causes and motivation. But when it comes to the consequences of disasters and incident management, we are dealing with the same issues. In that case, we can learn from the past and use that understanding to help us prepare for the future. It starts with sharing what we have learned and contributing to our collective understanding of how to deal with the potential for damage and destruction from disasters.

Disaster management is rooted in the fundamental belief that we can do something about avoiding disasters and lessen the potential for substantial loss of life and property, or destruction of the environment on which human beings depend. It involves planning and preparedness to avoid catastrophes and mitigation to lessen the consequences from disasters. Response and disaster relief concern our ability to help our fellow men under trying circumstances as a result of disasters. Recovery, rehabilitation, and reconstruction are indicative of the indomitable human spirit to come back from adversity even better and stronger. The expanded scope of disaster management then extends to recovery and preparing better for the next challenge, and getting daily life back to a state of development before the disaster and making it even better in the future.

This handbook serves as a single point of reference that is useful for sharing accounts and lessons learned. It meets the need for a publication where practitioners, academics, and the general public may share their real-world experience and learn from each other. It is substantially different from any other collection in the past in that it includes contributions from many disparate quarters, in particular the practitioner community that must deal with such real-world issues every day. We will all greatly benefit from sharing experiences and approaches across disciplines. Even if we cannot control all of the causes of disasters, we can prepare and respond based on the present state of development in the science of disaster management. This will enable us to thwart possibly destructive forces and craft constructive, workable policies that will contribute to the prevention of needless loss of life, destruction of the environment, and enormous financial impact.

The chapters in the handbook are divided into six sections. In Section I, Introduction, Theoretical Constructs, and Conceptual Foundations, we present chapters on the relationship of modern development to disaster vulnerability, the politics of disaster management, the presidential leadership in the United States, and the role of coordination in disaster management.

The Indian Ocean tsunami of December 2004 and the resultant great loss of life is attributed to the growth of coastal development in "Coastal Development and Disaster Preparedness: The Delusion of Preparedness in Face of Overwhelming Forces." Another chapter that addresses the rise in man-made (technical) as well as natural disasters over the past century, and identifies causes for increasing vulnerability is "Rising Disasters and Their Reversal: An Identification of Vulnerability and Ways to Reduce It."

The practical challenges of responding to disasters in a framework of multilayered, multi-jurisdictional responsibility is viewed as ultimately a political problem in the context of the evolution of the Federal Emergency Management Agency (FEMA) in "The Politics of Disaster Management: The Evolution of the Federal Emergency Management Agency." "Katrina and Her Waves: Presidential Leadership and Disaster Management in an Intergovernmental Context" is another chapter that addresses political leadership and intergovernmental performance regarding Hurricane Katrina in 2005. And coordination of intergovernmental aid along with private sector and public sector actors as constituting the essence of disaster preparedness and response is the subject of the concluding chapter, "The Role of Coordination in Disaster Management," in the section.

Section II, Case Studies and Lessons Learned: U.S. Natural and Environmental Disasters, covers the experience with various natural disasters in the United States including hurricanes, floods, and wildfires.

A comparison of the response to an earthquake in 1964, in Alaska, during the Johnson administration with the Bush administration's performance during Hurricane Katrina in 2005 is evaluated in "A Different Approach to Disaster Recovery: Alaskan Earthquake Disaster Recovery." Another comparison of two southern states, regarding Hurricane Hugo in 1989 in "Hurricane Hugo: Two States' Responses to the Disaster" leads to the conclusion that the effectiveness of response arises from the priority given to the potential threat on behalf of the political leadership.

"Hurricanes Katrina and Rita: The Critical Role of the Nonprofit Community in the San Antonio Disaster Response" brings to our attention the significant role of nongovernmental resources in disaster response. Of special significance regarding what small jurisdictions can do about major disasters when they are dwarfed by larger intergovernmental powers in terms of resources and attention is treated in "Small Town Disaster Management: Lessons Learned from Katrina in Mississippi." A significant aspect of small town challenges includes the availability of cash and accounting systems with which to pay its bills in addition to accounting for reimbursement for expenses from the federal government. Another chapter, "Emergency Contracting for Hurricane Katrina in New Orleans Gulf Area" specifically addresses emergency procurement in disaster response. The final chapter in this section, "Debris Disposal and Recycling for the Cedar and Paradise Wildfires in San Diego," in this section presents data on recycling material from disaster cleanup concerning the accounts of wildfires in California. It concludes that it is an overlooked way that the cost of cleanup can be reduced by emphasizing recycling from the debris.

We highlight several international case studies in Section III, Case Studies and Lessons Learned: International Disasters. These include avalanches in the Alps, flooding in Canada, disaster management and response in Turkey, resilient communities in India, and the HIV/AIDS pandemic in Africa.

"Disaster in the United States and Canada: The Case of the Red River" looks at similarities and differences between the two countries in disaster planning and outcomes. It is an example leading to the necessity and benefits from greater cooperation but reinforcing a need for an international standard.

The chapter "Variability of Natural Hazard Risk in the European Alps: Evidence from Damage Potential Exposed to Snow Avalanches" points to how communities may change due to socioeconomic transformation of conservation or wilderness areas into recreational enclaves, which has repercussion for increased vulnerability from disasters. The natural environment has normal, relief-of-pressure points into which humans have interjected their presence. It is at their peril but with seasonal variation and short-term fluctuations in the potential for damage, which can be monitored. Vulnerability of communities from disasters and disaster management with an approach to make them able to cope better with hazards and disasters that they are exposed to is discussed in "Toward Disaster Resilient Communities: A New Approach for South Asia and Africa." The contention is that we always need to learn from past disasters.

Changes in disaster management in Turkey following a major earthquake is the subject of "Disaster Management Structure in Turkey: Away from a Reactive and Paternalistic Approach?" The shift is from the central state as being responsible for all phases of disaster response to more dependence on private sector providers and homeowner self-sufficiency. Provincial and local governments have more control but this has resulted in the lack of a comprehensive national-level disaster plan.

Disaster in terms of decimation of the population from pandemic disease is the subject of "HIV/AIDS in Africa: Botswana's Response to the Pandemic" with its far-ranging repercussions extending to the supply of labor, availability of health care workers, and the growing number of orphans across much of sub-Saharan Africa.

Section IV, First Response and Emergency Management, is about the people, methods, and issues in on-the-scene disaster response and preparation.

Attempts to establish multi-jurisdictional and multi-organization coordination and collaboration in the Department of Homeland Security paradigm are covered in "National Incident Management System: Bringing Order to Chaos." It is rooted in basic command and control hierarchy under conditions of substantial uncertainty and the need for immediate action and accountability.

Another sector charged with life and death responsibilities during disasters is the health care institutions whose needs and issues for disaster preparation are the subject of the chapter "Hospital Emergency Preparedness." All sectors share a challenge as how to deal with the public's need for information regarding any crisis as it proceeds through its various stages. "Media Relations and External Communications during a Disaster" provides insight into this important responsibility and expands the consideration of outlets for information dissemination to Wi-Fi, Internet, wireless telephony, and broadband cable outlets.

Finally, in this section, two chapters focus on the involvement of the military in civilian disaster response. "Responding to Natural Disasters: An Increased Military Response and Its Impact on Public Policy Administration" explores the integration of the military in such scenarios with its various implications. It concludes that apparently it is one way to improve effectiveness when faced with an overwhelming magnitude of the disaster. But it advises that caution is warranted regarding the continuing permanent authority of the military, which has great potential for the abuse of power. The other chapter on this topic, "Military Involvement in Disaster Response," reminds us that disaster response agencies have few if any full-time personnel because most disaster employees are involved at the planning level. In this case, the military is a means of providing auxiliary forces quickly who are trained in many emergency response areas and have stores of equipment at their disposal. Still, the recommendations advise caution and calculated decision making to weigh the pros and cons, especially regarding the issue of relinquishing command control.

Under Section V, Human, Personal, and Interpersonal Issues, the impact of disasters on the personal lives of victims and emergency services personnel is discussed.

A frequently overlooked component of disaster plans that requires special attention and commitment of resources is the group of citizens who have limited mobility such as hospital populations and others with logistical challenges. The chapter "Disaster Management and Populations with Special Needs" provides a perspective by focusing on this component of disaster plans.

The individual needs and pressures on first responders is the subject of several chapters in Section V. "Disaster Psychology: A Dual Perspective" treats the subject of competing emotions including fears, exhilaration, and depression as felt by those on the front lines. And "Managing the Spontaneous Volunteer" provides advice for dealing with well-intended volunteers who are a challenge because they are not knowledgeable regarding the pre-established disaster plans. "First Responders and Workforce Protection" discusses the mental health of the responders and attempts to manage the dilemma of competition, envy, and hostility among response teams. It also makes several suggestions for utilizing victims and evacuees as useful and productive volunteers for their own mental health benefit.

The need for counseling and stress management rehabilitation is addressed in "Disaster Rehabilitation: Towards a New Perspective," which suggests gender differences should be considered. A sustainable livelihood framework is offered as a key to disaster rehabilitation efforts to promote environmental protection and reduce long-term vulnerability in India and elsewhere. And "The Half-Full Glass: How a Community Can Successfully Come Back Better and Stronger Post-Disaster" suggests that disaster recovery and rehabilitation can present substantial opportunities for community redevelopment.

In Section VI, Planning, Prevention, and Preparedness, we look at planning for the future. This includes training, intergovernmental relations, preparedness by the medical care disciplines, and basic strategic planning. As training in disaster management is an essential component of being prepared for the effective execution of the plan, a case study on training in Hawaii is included in "The Role of Training in Disaster Management: The Case of Hawaii." It presents a good catalog of necessary components of such training to respond to environmental and man-made disasters.

Mutual aid, coordination, and collaboration are included in the considerations in the chapter "Disaster Management and Intergovernmental Relations" with the conclusion that intergovernmental cooperation amounts to shared governance in disaster scenarios with shared responsibilities. But it begins with a well-prepared local government for leading the first response. The obstacles that still need to be overcome to bring the hospital community up to readiness for their role are the focus of "Issues in Hospital Preparedness." The conclusions reached include a call for hospital leadership to innovate efforts to safeguard communities by assuring appropriate funding and training to meet its vital role in disaster response.

We conclude the section with a chapter on basic strategic planning in "Strategic Planning for Emergency Managers." It brings together the perspective that plans need to incorporate many different skill sets, stakeholders, and physical components, which should be informed by an overall direction including where you eventually want to be and how you will get there.

Editor

Jack Pinkowski is a professor of public administration at the H. Wayne Huizenga School of Business and Entrepreneurship at Nova Southeastern University in Fort Lauderdale, Florida. He teaches many courses for masters students as well as candidates in the doctoral curriculum. His teaching assignments include courses in government budgeting, public financial management, organization theory, ethics, economic systems, economic development, and comparative government and economic systems. Jack is also the principal instructor for the capstone course in the master of public administration (MPA) program, which culminates the coursework for the MPA degree. Professor Pinkowski combines real-world experience with academic credentials that enhance teaching in the classroom and applied research.

Before beginning his academic career, Jack was a successful business entrepreneur with more than 30 years of experience in global trade and real estate development. Today he shares his experience in the classroom and by consulting for the betterment of our communities. He contributes to several economic development initiatives, serves on local government and nonprofit boards, and consults for local governments on these issues. He is the editor of the *Homeland Security Handbook* and, along with Ali Farazmand, is coeditor of the *Handbook of Globalization, Governance, and Public Administration.*

Jack received his PhD in public administration from Florida Atlantic University in Boca Raton, Florida, an MPA from Georgia Southern University in Statesboro, Georgia, and a BA from Temple University in Philadelphia, Pennsylvania.

Contributors

George Bass
Long Beach Fire Department
Long Beach, Mississippi

Laurence J. Berger
New York-Presbyterian
  Healthcare System
New York, New York

Randolph Burnside
Department of Political Science
Southern Illinois University-
  Carbondale
Carbondale, Illinois

Nicholas V. Cagliuso, Sr.
New York-Presbyterian
  Healthcare System
New York, New York

David B. Cohen
Department of Political Science
The University of Akron
Akron, Ohio

Grant Coultman-Smith
Sergeant of Police
Victoria, Australia

and

School of Social Sciences and
  Liberal Studies
Charles Sturt University
Bathurst, Australia

Mark R. Daniels
Department of Political Science
Slippery Rock University of Pennsylvania
Slippery Rock, Pennsylvania

Orelia DeBraal
Department of Public Works
San Diego, California

Alka Dhameja
School of Social Sciences
Indira Gandhi National Open University
New Delhi, India

Mary M. Dickens Johnson
Villanova University Continuing
  Studies Faculty
Fort Lauderdale, Florida

Sven Fuchs
Institute of Mountain Risk Engineering
University of Natural Resources
  and Applied Life Sciences
Vienna, Austria

Brian J. Gallant
Barnstable County Sheriff's Office
Sandwich, Massachusetts

N. Emel Ganapati
School of Public Administration
Florida International University
Miami, Florida

Brian J. Gerber
Division of Public Administration
School of Applied Social Sciences
West Virginia University
Morgantown, West Virginia

Paula J. Havice-Cover
Disaster Preparedness and Response
Colorado State Division of Mental
    Health
Denver, Colorado

Dwight Ink
Senior Fellow
National Academy of Public
    Administration
Washington, DC

Margreth Keiler
Department of Geography
    and Regional Research
University of Vienna
Vienna, Austria

Donna R. Kemp
Department of Political Science
California State University-Chico
Chico, California

Pam LaFeber
Division of Public Administration
Northern Illinois University
Naperville, Illinois

Andrew N. Lazar
Cornell University
Ithaca, New York

Eliot J. Lazar
New York-Presbyterian
    Healthcare System
Ithaca, New York

Mordecai Lee
Professor of Governmental Affairs
University of Wisconsin-Milwaukee
Milwaukee, Wisconsin

Jay Levinson
Division of Identification & Forensic
    Science
Israel Police (retired)
Jerusalem, Israel

Nancy S. Lind
Department of Political Science
Illinois State University
Normal, Illinois

David McEntire
Emergency Administration and
    Planning
University of North Texas
Denton, Texas

Uma Medury
School of Social Sciences
Indira Gandhi National Open University
New Delhi, India

DeMond S. Miller
Department of Sociology
Rowan University
Glassboro, New Jersey

Raymond Misomali
Emergency Administration and
Planning
University of North Texas
Denton, Texas

Bruce J. Moeller
Sunrise Fire Rescue
Sunrise, Florida

Sandra A. Palomo-Gonzalez
San Antonio Area Foundation
San Antonio, Texas

Matthew Pavelchak
Department of Civil and
Environmental Engineering
Rowan University
Glassboro, New Jersey

Susan J. Penner
School of Nursing, Graduate Division
University of San Francisco
San Francisco, California

Jack Pinkowski
H. Wayne Huizenga School of Business
and Entrepreneurship
Nova Southeastern University
Fort Lauderdale, Florida

Robert Powers
Emergency Services Disaster
Consulting and Research
Raleigh, North Carolina

Ross Prizzia
Department of Public
Administration
University of Hawaii-West Oahu
Pearl City, Hawaii

Dianne Rahm
Department of Public Administration
The University of Texas at San Antonio
San Antonio, Texas

J. Norman Reid
Federal Emergency Management
Agency
Fairfax, Virginia

Jason D. Rivera
Liberal Arts and Sciences Institute
Rowan University
Glassboro, New Jersey

David W. Sears
U.S. Department of Agriculture
Bethesda, Maryland

Thabo Lucas Seleke
Department of Political and
Administrative Studies
University of Botswana
Gaborone, Botswana

Keshav C. Sharma
Department of Political and
Administrative Studies
University of Botswana
Gaborone, Botswana

Rhonda Sturgis
City of Newport News
Newport News, Virginia

Christine Wachsmuth
San Francisco General Hospital
USF School of Nursing
San Francisco, California

Wayne T. Williams
Department of Public Works
San Diego, California

INTRODUCTION, THEORETICAL CONSTRUCTS, AND CONCEPTUAL FOUNDATIONS

I

Chapter 1

Coastal Development and Disaster Preparedness: The Delusion of Preparedness in Face of Overwhelming Forces

Jack Pinkowski

CONTENTS

Introduction

Only during the first half-decade of the twenty-first century we have witnessed around the world astounding incidents of disaster with great human impact on a magnitude rarely matched during recorded history. These include the intentional disaster forced on the United States on September 11, 2001 by terrorists' attacks on the World Trade Center in New York and the Pentagon in Washington, DC when nearly 3,000 people of all nationalities perished; the sudden and unexpected Indian Ocean tsunami on December 26, 2004 that resulted in 283,106 known fatalities (USGS 2006) although it impacted far less developed coastal regions of the world; and, Hurricane Katrina flooding that destroyed an American city as a result of rising waters with 1,280 known deaths recorded in Louisiana alone (Ringle 2006). The hurricane's winds destroyed much of the gulf coast region of the United States that had seen considerable coastal development over recent decades, and it put more citizens at risk than the previously remote, barrier-islands conditions.

It is an understatement to say that we cannot control Mother Nature. Although we are ultimately at the mercy of natural forces, emergency management and disaster planning initiatives are intended to mitigate loss of life and destruction of property through prior planning and public policy aimed at preventing people from putting themselves needlessly in harm's way. Presumably this allows us to develop areas for economic advantage while planning for the worst-case scenario. Counter-intelligence and surveillance programs are intended to monitor and interdict potential criminal elements and combatants to protect innocent citizens from terrorists who want to inflict economic pain on developed societies to perpetuate their own culture free from Western influences. Despite substantial national budgets devoted to these tasks, we still suffer horrific outcomes like we have seen from 2001 through 2004. Is it therefore unreasonable to assume that we are collectively under the delusion of preparedness?

Delusion of Preparedness

This chapter will attempt to summarize these natural catastrophic events and what led to "successful" development that ultimately failed society by leaving the potential for such enormous economic destruction and loss of life. Hopefully this will lead to the identification of areas of effort that show the most promise in preventing such losses in the future and possibilities for sustainable development with reduced exposure to natural catastrophes. It will be limited to natural disasters because intentional and man-made disasters, including wars and civil conflict, will be addressed elsewhere. They involve simultaneously planning from both sides: for destruction by terrorists and combatants, and for prevention by community planners and the disaster management community.

Perhaps preparedness is ultimately at best a hunch and fortuitous. But studying past events can serve as valuable learning lessons to prevent future calamities. In this context, the definition of "lessons learned" includes the knowledge and first-hand experience gained by participation in actual events, training, simulations, and exercises. It is also informed by after-action reports, consultation with subject matter experts, and from additional research on the incident and participants. Although this contribution is one step removed from the actual events, it relies on studying after-action accounts, as well as contemporaneous reports of activities, to attempt to identify where emergency management and disaster planning professionals, along with community planners, could have done better. Once-in-a-lifetime events and 100-year floods, albeit infrequent, still should be part of the planning process to inform intelligent and sustainable development.

Indian Ocean Tsunami

Tsunamis are seismic sea waves that result from earthquakes on the ocean floor. Landslides, volcanic eruptions, and meteorites can also generate them. In fact, one theory on the sudden mass extinction of the dinosaurs' reign as masters of the earth, along with 70 percent of the flora and fauna species at the time, is that they succumbed to massive tsunamis generated by either an asteroid impact or volcanic activity. Besides the inundation of coastal regions, the climatological ecology was altered by cosmic dust or iridium spewing from volcanoes that resulted in blocking sunlight necessary for plant life and breathable air for all aerobic life forms (Abell et al. 1988; Gardom and Milner 1993). Although no one today was here when the dinosaurs were alive, the possibility for great destruction from infrequent events can have history changing implications. Historically, tsunamis are probably a lot more frequent than we think but their impact has become more pronounced because of coastal development that has been built in their way.

The December 26, 2004 tsunami was the result of a magnitude 9.0 on the Richter scale submarine earthquake between Aceh, Indonesia, and Sri Lanka. According to the USGS National Earthquake Information Center, this was the third strongest earthquake ever recorded. The strongest quake ever instrumentally documented was magnitude 9.5 in southern Chile resulting in up to 5,700 fatalities. More than 280,000 deaths of the December 2004 make this tsunami and earthquake second only to one reported in 1556 in China with an estimated 830,000 fatalities. In fact, there have only been a little over 20 earthquakes with 50,000 or more deaths since earthquake records have been kept (USGS 2006). Yet the scale of the December 2004 tsunami was considerable and worldwide as it made four million people homeless in 12 countries (Stone 2006). As of January 2005, only one month after the crush of the waves, reports already included more than 160,000 deaths in Indonesia, 31,000 in Sri Lanka, 10,000 or more in India, and 5,000 in Thailand (Bardalai 2005). The number of fatalities was later increased including deaths in Sumatra, Java, Malaysia, and Myanmar. One issue with tsunami deaths, especially in remote regions of the world, is knowledge about who is even missing and where survivors, as well as casualties, can be located.

Earthquakes are well-known geological phenomena that result from the sudden relief of pressure caused by compression of the earth's 12–13 tectonic plates at their boundaries. Considerable modern development continues directly over the subterranean faults in California and elsewhere around the developed world. The energy released in the earthquake is due to the pent-up forces under compression. Buildings and public infrastructure must be able to withstand the anticipated short-duration shock wave. But as the plates continue to move and compress at their boundaries, a new buildup of energy begins, and the threat from future shocks although temporarily diminished is never eliminated.

Earthquakes are not necessarily uncommon. The U.S. National Earthquake Information Center estimates that there are about 50 earthquakes every day somewhere on earth, or about 20,000 per year. Since 1900, there has been an average of 17 major earthquakes of magnitude 7.0–7.9 per year and one magnitude 8.0 and higher-order earthquake annually. According to the records since 1900, the number of earthquakes of magnitude 7.09 or greater is relatively constant. Development to withstand this metric is at least reasonable, but is it enough? Each whole number of magnitude on the Richter scale represents a logarithmic progression and consequently a more than tenfold increase in strength.

Regarding coastal or undersea earthquakes and resulting tsunamis, there is already a system of advanced warnings for tsunamis in the Pacific Ocean basin. But it has not been deployed in the Indian Ocean because tsunamis are more common in the Pacific. Over the past 500 years there have been three to four Pacific basinwide tsunamis, and the December 2004 event was the first Indian basinwide destructive tsunami ever recorded. Yet, although rare in the Indian Ocean, tsunamis are not unheard of in that part of the world. Over the past 100 years, there have been seven recorded tsunamis as the result of earthquakes near Indonesia, Pakistan, and India alone. In 1883, the Krakatoa (Krakatau) volcano eruption led to a tsunami in Sri Lanka that inundated districts of Java and Sumatra. In fact, Indian Ocean tsunami records date to the year 416 when a tsunami was recorded in Java, Indonesia. And Banda Aceh, near the epicenter of the 2004 tsunami, has recorded tsunami events as far back in the records as 1837 (NGDC 2006). But due to development, coastal areas and the tourists and residents who are attracted to them have resulted in the new potential for catastrophic loss of life and property. A flaw in our thinking about local economic development is the fact that these potentially destructive forces are regionwide or ocean basinwide events which cannot be planned or responded to only on a decentralized, local level. It takes not only national cooperation, but also international.

The most important measure to prevent loss of life resulting from the "great waves" of tsunamis has to be advanced warning. The parting of the seas exposing the seabed as a result of the water initially subsiding and pulling away from the coastline and then covering up the curious who become mortally trapped by the subsequent tremendous waves is very similar to the biblical account of Moses parting the Red Sea, which subsequently engulfed legions of soldiers. This has also been reported in ancient historical accounts such as by Ammianus Marcellinus regarding the loss of 50,000 in Alexandria Egypt in AD 365 (*Readers Digest* 1989). The trap is created because the time between successive wave crests can vary from five to ninety minutes.

The long length of the waves is one of the distinguishing characteristics of tsunamis. Although the wavelength is long, in the open ocean the wave heights are short, approximately 2–3 feet, which makes them unnoticeable on ships. Many tsunamis of the past have not been noticed or recorded because they dissipated before striking immovable objects in their way. Now coastal development presents a barrier to these long waves that result in much more noticeable results. Consequently, seismic and wave monitoring buoys and satellite observation offer the only advanced warning systems that provide promise as society continues to develop our coastlines. Such systems are beyond the capability of local authorities acting alone.

Tsunami waves can travel at speeds up to 600 miles per hour in the open ocean with amplitude of only a few feet until they reach the coastal shelf when the combination of compression of the water piling up and shallow depths generate onshore heights of 30 feet up to 100 feet. Like volcanic eruptions, the time when the energy release of tectonic plate slippage will occur cannot be predicted precisely in advance. However, once detected, there is a probable three-hour window for advanced warning of a potential tsunami. Of course, nearest the site of origin times are very short. But at great distances away the devastating affects can be expected and mitigated with additional time for warnings to the local population. Local notice is the responsibility of local authorities, but it must be both informed by international organizations and the warning heeded, not countermanded, by in-country administrative or procedural roadblocks. With a major earthquake, a tsunami could reach the beach in a few minutes, even before a warning is issued. The December 26, 2004 tsunami off western Sumatra caused waves that reached Indonesia in just 15 minutes, Sri Lanka in two hours and crossed the entire Indian Ocean, arriving at the shores of Kenya in nine hours (ITIC 2006b). With these speeds, local authorities should not wait to issue warnings. In the December 26, 2004 tsunami six waves pummeled the coast in Thailand. It was reported that officials in Thailand had been informed about the Indonesian underwater earthquake and the potential for seismic sea waves an hour before the waves came ashore on the tourist-filled beaches of Southern Thailand. Yet Thai authorities chose to not issue an evacuation warning (Kurlantzick 2005).

Even the typical 10–20 ft wave heights are very destructive, and the areas at greatest risk are those less than 25 ft above sea level within one mile from the shoreline. This makes most modern coastal development at risk in tsunami susceptible areas. Besides potential loss of life, potential devastation from tsunamis comes from pollution of community drinking water and loss of infrastructure, such as police and fire service buildings, medical facilities, pipelines, and electrical transmission lines (ITIC 2006a). During the 1990s property damage from tsunamis was nearly US$1 billion. The property damage from the December 2004 Indian Ocean tsunami by itself was in the multiple billions of dollars (ITIC 2006b). The risk and expense of such outcomes is increasing with coastal development.

Although we cannot predict when underwater earthquakes will occur, and consequently, where a tsunami will be generated by studying the historical data, we can determine where they are most likely. Local development has to take this data into account, and it should be monitored by international agreements if we are to avoid devastation when they do occur. The ability to detect and locate earthquakes once they happen has improved due to the substantial increase in the number of seismograph stations across the globe, from only 350 in 1931 to 8,000 today. The improvement in communications and satellite technologies also has improved the speed and ability to detect and provide instantaneous information about earthquakes. The key remains greater measurement instruments to add to the database that is studied and monitored. Past tsunami height measurements, for example, are useful in predicting future tsunami impact and flooding inundation; this should be useful for future planning and restrictions on coastal communities.

The response to tsunamis that can save lives relies mostly with local citizens and family members. There is little that the international community or external aid workers can do to save lives if they do not even know who is missing, the local territory, or even understand the local culture. The time to mobilize international aid and response is probably beyond the window of opportunity for triage and lifesaving. However, foreign aid is definitely valuable in terms of financial support, medical assistance, heavy equipment, food, water, and comfort supplies in the recovery phase. Then the international assistance has to work in concert with local efforts that remain primary. This working in concert still has to be coordinated by some overarching authorities above the local level. There was, however, a great deal of confusion and congestion owing to the lack of any coordination of the relief efforts in the December 2004 tsunami (Stone 2006).

The new breed of "citizen journalists" on the Internet came of age in the wake of the December 2004 tsunami as bloggers carried the message of needs for supplies and whereabouts of loved ones to anxious relatives around the world, including photos of missing or found children (O'Grady 2005). The traditional news media did not have staff or facilities in these remote areas, but bloggers proved superior in actually providing essential communications swiftly where there was Internet access (Pinkowski 2006). Although information sharing is productive and needed, there was nothing like an Incident Command System established as a clearinghouse for information and to direct resources to specific local needs (Pinkowski 2001a).

Preparedness for earthquake-generated tsunamis does not suffer from lack of historical information. The U.S. National Geophysical Data Center (NGDC) of the National Oceanic and Atmosphere Administration (NOAA) maintains a tsunami database with information on events from 2000 BC to the present in the Atlantic, Indian, and Pacific Oceans, as well as the Mediterranean and Caribbean Seas. As 80 percent of tsunamis occur in the Pacific, the Pacific Tsunami Warning Center (PTWC) was established to monitor seismological data and water levels from stations throughout the Pacific Ocean. It is augmented by regional centers in Japan, French Polynesia, and Chile, in addition to those in the United States. As a result of the 2004 tsunami, new warning systems are being implemented in the Indian Ocean, the Caribbean Sea, the Atlantic Ocean, and the Mediterranean Sea. This should contribute to improved capacity in providing advanced notice to vulnerable areas, but it does not address the need to reconsider local community planning that continues to mine the coast for new population centers.

From Delusion to Illumination?

Future improvement must continue the expansion of the recording and monitoring instruments including greater use of satellite observation, perhaps including geostationary orbit. Just as effective is a need for a worldwide public education program so people will know how to get out of harm ways in the advance of tsunamis. In Indonesia, although animals were observed moving to higher ground, local people and tourists ventured out onto the laid-bare sea floor to observe the curiosity and subsequently perished. Local populations should adopt new programs of instruction in schools to teach tsunami threat avoidance behavior, as well as warning signs. This should include hotel and resort personnel. The awareness activities and educational programs must be ongoing and supported by political support, public policy, laws and regulations, and funding to implement the necessary programs.

A network of local tsunami warning stations must be established especially in the developed tourist resorts along the coast. These need to be tied to government agencies and Internet automated warning announcement to alert the resident population. This warning system should include evacuation route maps for pedestrians posted in conspicuous public places. Real-time monitoring of earthquake activity and sea-level monitoring should enhance the risk assessment.

There are several lessons learned from the Indian Ocean December 2004 tsunami response that may reduce future suffering and save lives from any future disaster. One is that international aid is most effective only when coordinated by experienced international humanitarian organizations. Second, relief programs must relate to the actual needs of the victims and not be imposed upon them by distant uninformed decision makers. Rehabilitation of survivors takes teams of social and psychological counselors and is an important component of disaster response. This is especially true when families do not know the fate of their loved ones or are mourning their loss (Stone 2006).

Considering coastal resources when siting population centers can mitigate environmental impacts of tsunamis. Natural barriers offshore, such as coral reefs, mangroves in the nearshore, and sand dunes onshore, considerably lessen the impact of tsunami waves on the coastal environment. Mangrove forests in Thailand buffered buildings from the massive waves of the December 2004 tsunami. Sand dunes in Sri Lanka's national parks prevented seawater from penetrating inland and washing the shore away when it retreated (Mastny 2005). Because of the long wavelength and shallow height of the tsunami wave, most of the onshore height of the wave results from the welling up of the seawater as it approaches shore. Coral reefs dissipate that energy. Of course now, in addition to man, the tsunami has contributed to the damage of the coral reefs, dunes, and mangroves and has increased the likelihood of coastal erosion.

Coastal development that degrades the natural coastal assets, such as mangrove clearing, coral mining, shrimp farming, and reef destruction due to port traffic, along with accompanying beach erosion, work to put the coast and its residents at greater risk from tsunamis. We can do little about most previous destruction of the environment. Nevertheless, coastal restoration projects could protect against tidal surges and would be invaluable. These could include planting or replanting mangroves, banning further mangrove and coastal dunes destruction, and the establishment of artificial reefs offshore.

Ultimately, no infrastructure can withstand the extreme force of a direct hit from a powerful tsunami. Well-planned and well-constructed public infrastructure can substantially help with the sheltering of people and distribution of resources to people who are affected by disasters (Cho 2005). This includes local government centers that serve multiple purposes including serving as shelters, for the storage of supplies, and as information clearinghouses or staging areas. Schools and other public buildings should be constructed with these alternative uses in mind. And they should be backed by building codes suitable for their environmental conditions.

After the disaster, the sooner the economy can return to normal the less will be the non-human cost of the disaster's impacts. Clearly the lessons from the December 2004 tsunami lead to greater local–national–supranational cooperation in the planning and recovery of coastal communities. Coastal development does not have to stop, but business as usual cannot continue if we are to learn from our delusion of preparedness.

Hurricane Katrina

Despite tabletop planning exercises and days of advance warning as the slow moving storm approached the American Gulf Coast, the city of New Orleans appears to have been caught off guard by Hurricane Katrina. There were very accurate predictions of the storm's track in addition to extensive preplanning and disaster modeling that foresaw just such an outcome as being likely (White and Whoriskey 2005). Emergency managers knew that they were vulnerable but were under the delusion that they were prepared.

The storm highlighted many latent defects in the American readiness fabric. These same potential liabilities may exist in many other developed regions that face atmospheric or man-made phenomena with potentially catastrophic consequences despite apparent planning and emergency preparedness. In the case of Hurricane Katrina, the previously established administrative procedures actually impeded the response in its early stages. Critically focused atmospheric events frequently have the power to overwhelm local response capabilities.

Deteriorating Infrastructure

In New Orleans, we have learned that the levees had been poorly maintained for decades. In many cities, old sewage and drainage systems are in disrepair. Many communities depend on drinking water from ground sources that could become contaminated by flooding that is predictable, and to which, they would be susceptible (Pinkowski 1997). Wetlands, nature's own safety valve mechanism to accommodate storms and flooding had been filled-in for new development of luxury condominiums (Young 2006). All across the United States transportation systems, bridges, dams, sea walls, wastewater treatment facilities, and hazardous materials storage and handling sites have been similarly poorly maintained and pose threats to public safety if they fail (Pinkowski 2001b). Development guidelines that may have been appropriate for a bygone era are no longer consistent with the current state of development. The evolution in uses of property and facilities has disparate affects on subsequent residents and stakeholders that is not equally shared and generally falls on lower socioeconomic groups. Unfortunately, this phenomenon, although well known, is not in the general consciousness of most local leaders sufficiently for them to have corrected it.

Emergency Response, Poverty, and Racism

Tevye said in *Fiddler on the Roof*, "It's no sin to be poor; but it's no great honor either." The nexus of poverty in cities and disparate racial composition of local residents in certain areas is neither intentional, nor is it even a conscious fact for legislative or administrative elites. In 1968, two African-American activists, Stokely Carmichael and Charles Hamilton, described the results of government actions that have the effects on certain groups as "institutional racism." Institutional racism is described as the condition where, "The overall structure of our society and some of its most mundane habits produce racialized oppression" (Young 2006, p. 42).

In New Orleans, local government did not provide transportation for the citizens without their own vehicles to evacuate. As it turns out, most of them were in predominately black neighborhoods. Racial and economic demographics in disaster-prone zones has been shown to be common adjoining hazardous materials sites, noxious chemical plants, and low-lying, environmentally dangerous areas such as the Ninth Ward of New Orleans (Pinkowski 2001b). The people who suffered most in New Orleans after Hurricane Katrina were those who did not evacuate because they were unable to leave due to lack of money, transportation (their own or publicly provided), and no real place to go (White and Whoriskey 2005). Almost 30 percent of the people who did not evacuate did not own cars (Kotkin 2006).

In July 2005, monsoon rains flooded the Indian city of Mumbai (Bombay) and eight million of India's poorest were the victims. The floods wiped away the shantytowns where half of the 16 million people in Mumbai were living and left them with absolutely nothing (*New York Times* 2005). As in the wake of devastation in New Orleans that seems to have affected mostly its poorest residents, accusations of selective treatment were aimed at the government on the premise that slow and inept response was due to the fact that those most affected were the poor.

Although often cited as one of the richest countries on Earth, poverty is not uncommon in the United States. According to the U.S. Census in 2004, 12.7 percent of the population lives at or below the federal government definition of poverty (Census 2004). In eastern New Orleans, more than 74 percent of the people were living below twice the poverty threshold, which is a proxy for a "living wage." Roughly one in four in New Orleans were poor. There were 100,000 people living in "high poverty zones." In the case of New Orleans, the economic decline was long and steady. The tourism industry in many American cities, although world-class, does not pay high wages. The industrial, commercial, and professional sectors of the economy in New Orleans are much smaller than other cities of its size. "It has long been among America's poorest and most crime-ridden cities" (Kotkin 2006). This was accompanied by a history of inept and corrupt local government including a police force considered among the worst in the country for convictions and serious crime (Kotkin 2006). The image of a successful city was largely an illusion.

New Orleans is not unlike many cities in other liberal industrial nations around the world considering the struggle with serious underclass problems. But it is different in that the urban underclass is not due to an influx of immigrants with radically different cultures. The poor in New Orleans are largely native-born as curiously, few immigrants are making the city their permanent destination (Kotkin 2006).

Not to belittle the poor victims of Hurricane Katrina and the many citizens who have been spread across the United States as a result of losing everything in the storm, but these victims are not exclusively black or poor. Communities all along the Gulf Coast from Alabama to Texas were ravaged, and small towns were wiped out.

Neighboring communities who took in evacuees found their local social services overburdened. Baton Rouge, Louisiana reported a population increase of 250,000, with corresponding financial strains on local government budgets and school resources (Preston 2005b).

As the placement of evacuees from New Orleans and other Gulf Coast communities across the country began, the issue of race rarely came up. There were 24,000 from the New Orleans Superdome alone (Chan 2005). A testament to the character of Americans was their willingness to take in evacuees even though it imposed new financial and logistic constraints on their own communities. Across the country communities, even private citizens, offered housing to homeless families among the hurricane evacuees. More than 200,000 people have taken up temporary residence in Texas in temporary shelters, hotels, and private homes (Preston 2005a). The city of San Antonio, Texas even received help from the Mexican Army in feeding its tent city of evacuees. According to Nim Kidd (personal communication, January 26, 2006), Emergency Management Coordinator for the city of San Antonio Office of Emergency Management, the Mexican army, disregarding treaties and international protocol, just sent mess crews across the border to provide cooking and dining services because they knew the Texans could use the help. The real issue with the shortcomings of the Hurricane Katrina response lies in the nature of local and overall authority and decentralized decision making.

Shortcomings of the Federal System

The federal system of government is one where the subnational units cede to the national government certain powers and only those powers that it chooses to give up for mutual advantage and security. The U.S. Constitution was founded on the premise that any powers not given to the national government in the Constitution are retained by the states. In addition, the Constitution memorializes strict separation of powers in the government (Farazmand 1997). The U.S. model has also firmly established through doctrine of Home Rule and legal status of cities the hierarchy of state and local government such that local governments are creatures of the state (Morgan and England 1999).

The problems with the federal system during disasters relate to the limitation of those powers especially where the national level of government has amassed enormous stockpiles of relief supplies, financial resources, and other assets that include the military, yet is powerless to act unless called in by the state government. Local city and town administration is also required to appeal through the state level. Established procedures for mobilizing disaster aid proceeds from the bottom up, beginning at the local level, working through the states, and only then passing on to the federal government (Schneider 2005). In New Orleans, the local government was apparently overwhelmed by the magnitude of the disaster that they faced.

Instead of taking steps to mobilize greater resources up the governmental food chain, they were themselves adrift in the chaos that ensued when the levees broke, flooding the city (Treaster and Sontag 2005).

The governor of Louisiana, Kathleen Babineaux Blanco, did her part by asking the federal government for resources, but she stopped short of declaring martial law or even a state of emergency which would have greatly expanded police and military powers. Nonetheless, the federal government tried to be proactive in offering assistance but was rebuked as the governor declined the offer to place the National Guard under federal government control (Luo et al. 2005). The mayor of New Orleans, Ray Nagin, pleaded for federal help directly but was put off with promises of "vast assistance" but not immediate action. When federal troops eventually arrived they were preoccupied with lifesaving responsibility and rescuing stranded people from rooftops.

Illumination from the Dark Lessons of the Storm

One of the lessons learned from Hurricane Katrina is that all levels of government must fully understand the emergency response plan and follow it. This includes the elected officials and not just the emergency responders (O'Connell 2006). Full-scale rehearsals of the emergency plan are also useful. According to Tony Carper (personal communication, November 29, 2005), former director of the Broward County, Florida Emergency Management Agency, a stronger message needs to be disseminated that no one should expect any help for the first three days following a storm. Citizens need to be prepared and self-sufficient as governmental resources are mobilized in the storm's aftermath. The mayor of Gretna, Louisiana, Ronnie Harris, reported that his city was basically on its own in the response with no other help available. He recommends other jurisdictions tell their people to be prepared for "no assistance from anyone for a minimum of five days" (O'Connell 2006, p. 16). This includes for cities, food, water, ice, and transportation for its Emergency Operations Center (EOC) workers.

Although much of the media reports have been on the shortcomings and failures of the Hurricane Katrina response, there was also a great deal of effective aspects of the response. These included the skilled and compassionate professionals who manned shelters. The National Response Plan model worked well and volunteers proved to be very beneficial for feeding and housing duties. Mobile career centers were set up and linked by satellite to ensure that people with disabilities could reenter the workforce (Millington 2005). Service agencies collaborated across borders. In Beaumont, Texas, an emergency response plan that had been created to respond to a bioterrorism attack or hazardous material release was put into action in the hurricane aftermath. Everyone involved with the response was familiar with it because they had practiced through a full-scale rehearsal six months earlier. But the Beaumont, Texas Mayor, Guy Goodson, said that they never expected "the enormity of people coming to us and the absence of knowledge about the special needs that those people would have" (O'Connell 2006, p. 16).

Police officers, firefighters, and other emergency responders mobilized across the country to spend weeks at a time in the devastation zone to help with response, triage, and cleanup efforts. Mutual aid agreements and local government compacts to offer mutual assistance in disasters enable many jurisdictions to mobilize staff and material quickly and effectively.

We have already seen the lessons learned from heeding the call for evacuation and dismissing complacency concerning approaching storms. Cyclone Larry, a Category 5 storm with 180 mile per hour winds hammered the northeastern coastal area of Australia on March 19, 2006 with considerable damage to crops and wildlife areas but less impact on the civilian population due to sparse development (CBS 2006a). It was the most powerful storm to hit Australia in more than 30 years and resulted in hundreds of millions of dollars in damages. But already taking a lesson from Hurricane Katrina in the United States, residents evacuated early or went to shelters resulting in very few casualties from the storm (CBS 2006b).

The next steps must be reevaluation of development decisions that allow increased density in hazard prone zones around the world. Local governments need to be more prepared to serve on their own for the initial period after storms and cannot expect the mobilization of higher levels of government until administrative procedures work through the steps.

The pattern of decentralized political and administrative power should be modified to allow for the national level of government to use its breadth of resources to aid victims across jurisdictions instead of waiting in the wings as if it were some thespian understudy. This can be accomplished within the federal system and under the strict separation of powers doctrines without sacrificing local and state autonomy by pre-event declarations and intergovernmental compacts. Such prearranged agreements should allow for immediate mobilization after events conditional upon actual catastrophic impact. Israel's disaster response depends on quick intervention by its military (Levinson 2007). Quick mobilization of military resources aided the federal response in Australia in the wake of Cyclone Larry and was welcomed by local governments there whose own resources were quickly overwhelmed in the face of overwhelming force of nature (CBS 2006b).

References

Abell, G.O., Morrison, D., and Wolff, S.C., 1988. *Realm of the Universe*, 4th edition. Philadelphia: Saunders College.

Bardalai, A., 2005. In the Tsunami's Wake. *National Interest*, 79, Spring, 108–112.

CBS, 2006a. CBS News. Available from: http://www.cbsnews.com/stories/2006/03/19/world/main1419446 [Accessed March 26, 2006].

CBS, 2006b. CBS News. Available from: http://www.cbsnews.com/stories/2006/03/20/world/main1419544.shtml [Accessed March 26, 2006].

CENSUS, 2004. U.S. Bureau of the Census, Housing and Household Economic Statistics Division. Available from: www.census.gov.

Chan, S., 2005. Superdome had an hour of fuel before a potentially deadly panic. *New York Times*, 8 September, p. A.24.

Cho, J., 2005. In the wake of the tsunami. *UN Chronicle*, 42 (1), March/May, 40–41.

Farazmand, A., 1997. *Modern Systems of Government*, Thousand Oaks, CA: Sage.

Gardom, T. and Milner, A., 1993. *The Natural History Museum Book of Dinosaurs*. London: Virgin.

ITIC, 2006a. International Tsunami Information Centre. Available from: http://ioc3.unesco.org/itic/categories.php?category_no=4 [Accessed March 25, 2006].

ITIC, 2006b. International Tsunami Information Centre. The Great Waves. Available from: http://www.prh.noaa.gov/itic_pr/The%20Great%20Waves/tsunami_great_waves_5.html [Accessed March 25, 2006].

Kotkin, J., 2006. Ideological hurricane. *The American Enterprise*, 17 (1), 24–29.

Kurlantzick, J., 2005. Man-made disasters. *American Prospect*, 16 (2), 15–16.

Levinson, J., 2007. Military involvement in first response and emergency management. In: J. Pinkowski, Ed., *Disaster Management Handbook*. New York: Taylor & Francis, pp. 413–422.

Luo, M., Alford, J., and Lipton, E., 2005. The embattled leader of a state immersed in crisis. *New York Times*, 8 September, p. A.26.

Mastny, L., 2005. Healthy coastlines mitigate disasters. *World Watch*, 18 (3), May/June, p. 7.

Millington, M., 2005. Disability, poverty, and Hurricane Katrina. *Journal of Rehabilitation*, 71 (4), 3–4.

Morgan, D.R. and England, R.E., 1999. *Managing Urban America*, 5th edition. New York: Chatham House.

New York Times, 2005. As toll rises to 749 in India monsoon, Mumbai goes back to work. *New York Times*, 30 July, p. A.6.

NGDC, 2006. National Geophysical Data Center. The NGDC tsunami database contains information on tsunami events from 2000 B.C. to the present in the Atlantic, Indian, and Pacific Oceans; and the Mediterranean and Caribbean Seas. Available from: http://www.ngdc.noaa.gov/seg/hazard/tsu_db.shtml [Accessed March 25, 2006].

O'Connell, K., 2006. Cities heed lessons from 2005 storms: Many reassess disaster preparedness, response. *American City and County*, 121 (2), 12–16.

O'Grady, P., 2005. A new medium comes of age. *New Statesman*, 134, 10 January, 14–15.

Pinkowski, J., 1997. A study of wellhead protection for community drinking water in Chatham County, Georgia, Savannah, GA: Chatham County-Savannah Metropolitan Planning Commission.

Pinkowski, J., 2001a. Potential for disaster: Case study of the Powell Duffryn chemical fire and hazardous material spill. In: A. Farazmand, Ed., *Handbook of Crisis and Emergency Management*. New York: Marcel Dekker, pp. 433–450.

Pinkowski, J., 2001b. Planning for prevention: Emergency preparedness and planning to lessen the potential for crisis. In: A. Farazmand, Ed., *Handbook of Crisis and Emergency Management*. New York: Marcel Dekker, pp. 723–736.

Pinkowski, J., 2006. Globalization and information and communications technology influences on democratic governance. In: A. Farazmand and J. Pinkowski, Eds., *Handbook of Globalization, Governance, and Public Administration.* New York: Taylor & Francis, pp. 189–206.

Preston, M., 2005a. Communities cross the line to provide aid: Governments across country help Gulf Coast. *American City and County,* 120 (11), 8, 10.

Preston, M., 2005b. Please send money: Hurricane-torn coastal communities call for help to rebuild. *American City and County,* 120 (11), 32.

Readers Digest, 1989. Great disasters. Readers Digest Association.

Ringle, K., 2006. The search for Katrina's victims finds some missing by choice. *The Washington Post,* 24 March, p. A.03.

Schneider, S.K., 2005. Administrative breakdowns in the governmental response to Hurricane Katrina. *Public Administration Review,* 65 (5), 515–516.

Stone, M., 2006. How not to respond to a crisis. *New Statesman,* 135, 9 January, p. 14.

Treaster, J.B. and Sontag, D., 2005. Despair and lawlessness grip New Orleans as thousands remain stranded in squalor. *New York Times,* 2 September, p. A.1.

USGS, 2006. U.S. Geological Survey. Largest and deadliest earthquakes by year, 1990–2005. Available from: http://earthquake.usgs.gov/regional/world/byyear.php [Accessed March 25, 2006].

White, J. and Whoriskey, P., 2005. Planning, response are faulted. *The Washington Post,* 2 September, p. A.01.

Young, I., 2006. Katrina: Too much blame, not enough responsibility. *Dissent,* 53 (1), Winter, 41–46.

Chapter 2

Rising Disasters and Their Reversal: An Identification of Vulnerability and Ways to Reduce It

Raymond Misomali and David McEntire

CONTENTS

A portion of this chapter appearing on pages 32–33 was published in "Triggering agents, vulnerability, and disaster reduction," in *Disaster Prevention and Management* 10 (3): 189–196.

Introduction

Regardless of location, mankind is threatened by hazards of many types. This has been especially evident during the previous five years when terrorists attacked the United States on September 11, 2001, a tsunami hit Asia in 2004, and a record number of hurricanes hit U.S. coasts. In addition, over the previous century, hazardous events have occurred with increasing frequency around the world, impacting a greater number of people. Therefore, more must be done to address disaster vulnerability. This paper examines this concept as a way to identify how to safeguard life and property in the future. The paper seeks to provide a holistic approach to emergency management based on McEntire's model of disaster vulnerability.[1] It consolidates some of the major concepts of vulnerability that scholars have posed in prior research. To reach this goal, the chapter will review the rise of disasters over the previous century, the nature of the concept of vulnerability, the causes of vulnerability, and alternative approaches for addressing it.

The approach suggested in this chapter provides a comprehensive approach to emergency management. It recommends consideration of the variety of factors that lead to an increase in vulnerability. Doing so will enable a community to better prepare for the threats it faces. The approach suggested in this chapter also provides for an inclusive emergency planning process that requires the involvement of the public, private, and nonprofit sectors to identify and address major weaknesses in the emergency management program.

Disasters on the Rise

During the previous century, disasters emanating from natural and technological hazards have occurred with increasing frequency. Although the occurrence of such hazards has increased, deaths from them have been steadily declining worldwide. Nevertheless, there has been an increase in the resulting financial impacts of such occurrences. This section will discuss disaster trends, covering the previous century up to the present time. Specifically, this section will discuss how both natural and technological hazards have caused human loss and destruction.

The data available from the World Health Organization's Collaborating Center for Research on the Epidemiology of Disasters (CRED), the Emergency Events Database (EM-DAT), shows that hazardous events have been on the rise around the world (Figure 2.1). These include natural and technological hazards.

EM-DAT identifies natural disasters as the following: drought, earthquake, epidemic, extreme temperature, famine, flood, insect infestations, slides, volcanoes, waves/surges, wild fires, and windstorm. To date, the available data shows that over 37 million people around the world have died from 4922 natural hazards. The data also shows that although more people died during the first half of last century, there were fewer occurrences of natural hazards than during the latter

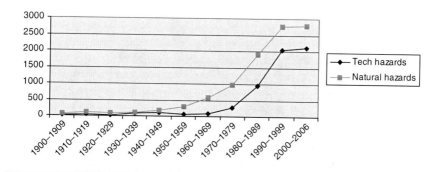

Figure 2.1 Trend showing frequency of natural and technological hazardous events since 1900. (From EM-DAT: The OFDA/CRED International Disaster Database, Université Catholique de Louvain, Brussels, Belgium. Available at www.em-dat.net. With permission.)

half of the century. For example, between 1900 and 1959, there was an average of 141.5 natural hazards, although the following five decades saw an average of 1806 natural hazard occurrences. Between 1900 and 1959, an average of 5,379,229 people died; whereas, between 1960 and 2006, only 993,058 people died as a result of such hazards.[2]

Although the most recent natural disasters, such as the tsunami in South Asia and Hurricane Katrina, show disastrous impacts on human life, data shows that more people have actually died as a result of droughts than any other hazard recorded by EM-DAT (Figure 2.2).

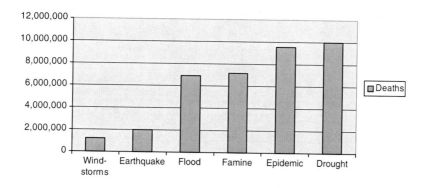

Figure 2.2 Number of individuals killed from the six deadliest natural disasters. (From EM-DAT: The OFDA/CRED International Disaster Database, Université Catholique de Louvain, Brussels, Belgium. Available at www.em-dat.net. With permission.)

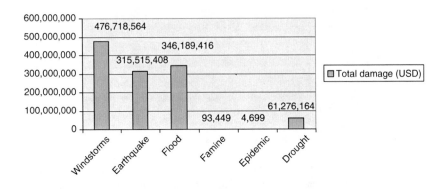

Figure 2.3 Total damage (USD000) caused by the five deadliest natural disasters. (From EM-DAT: The OFDA/CRED International Disaster Database, Université Catholique de Louvain, Brussels, Belgium. Available at www.em-dat.net. With permission.)

The second deadliest hazard of the previous century was epidemics. Such epidemics include malaria, cholera, dengue fever, typhoid, etc. Statistic reveals that natural hazards that emanated from windstorms caused the greatest amount of damage (Figure 2.3). Such hazards include cyclones, hurricanes, storms, tornadoes, tropical storms, typhoons, and winter storms.[2]

As the chart indicates, windstorm-related hazards caused more than $476 million damage over the previous century. The second most destructive hazards were floods that caused close to $350 million damages.[2]

Research shows that the financial impact of natural hazards peaked during the previous decade, while the least costly disasters occurred between 1910 and 1919 (Figure 2.4). Increased development and infrastructure over the years has led to the

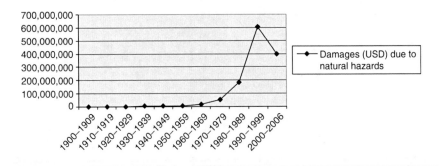

Figure 2.4 Trend showing damages (USD000) due to natural hazards since 1900. (From EM-DAT: The OFDA/CRED International Disaster Database, Université Catholique de Louvain, Brussels, Belgium. Available at www.em-dat.net. With permission.)

increased losses. Although the trend appears to be reversing at the moment, it is evident that disasters have had a major financial impact on the world—especially over the last decade.

Besides natural disasters, it is worth mentioning that technological hazards also account for a considerable number of deaths, destruction, and financial loss. According to the EM-DAT database, a technological hazard is any event or accident originating from the following modes of technology: transportation, boat, rail, industrial, road, and miscellaneous accidents such as any technological accident of a nontransport and nonindustrial nature. Several notable technological events include the sinking of the Titanic in 1912, the Chernobyl nuclear accident in 1986, and the Trans World Airlines (TWA) airplane explosion in 1996. Over the last century, technological hazards have caused a total of 287,520 deaths and over $24 billion in damages.[2] They, too, are very serious hazards.

The trends in natural and technological disasters clearly demonstrate that there has been a rise in disasters over the years. This data also shows that many livelihoods and economies have been adversely impacted. However, this research does not provide a complete picture of disasters because it fails to indicate the impact of vulnerability on such occurrences.

The Concept of Vulnerability

When scholars discuss vulnerability, it is usually from two vantage points: disaster proneness and insufficient capability.[3,4] Some scholars note, for instance, that individuals residing in Florida are vulnerable (or prone) to disasters triggered by hurricanes. When discussing proneness, authors usually look at vulnerability as it relates to one's risk or susceptibility. The other view of vulnerability is in terms of insufficient capability. This relates to an entity's lack of capacity to mitigate, prepare for, respond to, and recover from a disaster. A recent example is Hurricane Katrina, where the city of New Orleans experienced a disaster because it had not adequately prepared to deal with a hurricane of this magnitude. In this instance, scholars look at the ability of individuals to protect themselves from a hazard, and to cope with a disaster effectively, mainly resistance and resilience. This section will look at these definitions of vulnerability from the academic literature, concluding with a discussion of the importance of both views on proneness and views on capability.

In "Disaster mitigation: The concept of vulnerability revisited," Juergen Weichselgartner reviews the concept of vulnerability and concludes there are two distinct themes within the literature. The first theme identified is vulnerability as "risk/hazard exposure."[5] This theme can be summarized as proneness. The second theme identified by Weichselgartner is "vulnerability as social response."[5] He suggests that, "vulnerability as tempered response—focuses on coping responses including societal resistance to hazards."[5] This can be summarized by capability. Combining both these perspectives, McEntire views vulnerability as a blend of the two concepts above.[1,3,4] This final theme can be summarized by the holistic approach to emergency management suggested here.

Many other scholars share similar views about vulnerability. Downing discusses vulnerability in terms of proneness, and defines it as "a measure, of a given population or region, of the underlying factors that influence exposure to the hazardous event and predisposition to the adverse consequences."[6] The International Panel on Climate Change defines vulnerability as, "the extent to which a natural or social system is susceptible to sustaining damage from climate change."[6] David E. Alexander states "human vulnerability is a function of the costs and benefits of inhabiting areas at risk from natural disasters."[7] According to Susan L. Cutter, vulnerability is the "likelihood that an individual or group will be exposed to and adversely affected by a hazard. It is the interaction of the hazards of place (risk and mitigation) with the social profile of communities."[7] Others see vulnerability as a function of poverty, powerlessness, and discrimination.[8] The argument here is that poor people are most likely to live in the most hazard-prone locations.

The underlying theme in the definitions mentioned above concerns how people, places, or property/infrastructure are exposed to a level of risk because of location and the likelihood of a natural hazard occurring in a community. Social/political circumstances are also related to proneness. Individuals are also prone to disasters because, as Weichselgartner states, their susceptibility is increased when they are exposed to a risk or a hazard.[5]

The other perspective of vulnerability concerns insufficient capability. When a person is vulnerable, he or she lacks, the quality of being capable—or the ability, skill or competence to deal effectively with disasters.[9] Some examples of vulnerability discussed in this perspective are given below, and they primarily refer to the ability of an individual, group or community to cope during a hazard event. For example, Wisner et al. define vulnerability in terms of an entity's "capacity to anticipate, cope with, resist, and recover from the impact of a natural hazard. It involves a combination of factors that determine the degree to which someone's life and livelihood are put at risk by a discrete and identifiable event in nature or in society."[8] Bohle et al. define vulnerability "as an aggregate measure of human welfare that integrates environmental, social, economic, and political exposure to a range of potential harmful perturbations. Vulnerability is a multilayered and multidimensional social space defined by the determinate, political, economic, and institutional capabilities of people in specific places at specific times."[7] Kelly and Adger define "vulnerability in terms of the ability of individuals and social groupings to respond to, in the sense of cope with, recover from and adapt to, any external stress placed on their livelihoods and well-being."[10] Anderson and Woodrow assert that vulnerability is "the capability to protect one's community, hole and family and to re-establish one's livelihood."[11] Timmerman provides a similar definition. He states that vulnerability is "the degree to which a system acts adversely to the occurrence of a hazardous event. The degree and quality of the adverse reaction are conditioned by a system's resilience (a measure of the system's capacity to absorb and recover from the event)."[5]

In summarizing these definitions of vulnerability, one common theme is apparent. Vulnerability consistently relates with capacity. Most disasters occur because an individual, society, or infrastructure lacks the capability to withstand the force of a hazard or deal with it effectively.

Although the literature provides two distinct perspectives on vulnerability, there is a third perspective on the matter.[1] This view is that vulnerability cannot be studied by exclusively looking at proneness or capability. One must acknowledge that the two terms are not mutually exclusive. Proneness is increased when there is insufficient capacity. Capacity is often a reflection of the degree of proneness. The relation of these two concepts is exemplified by the events of Hurricane Katrina. During this event, it was abundantly clear that people were prone to disasters not only because of their location, level of poverty, and the weak condition of the levies, but also due to the inability of citizens as well as local, state, and federal officials to mitigate and adequately prepare. For example, if the city was built in a safer area and if the levies were able to resist the strength of the floodwaters that followed the hurricane, the citizens of New Orleans might not have suffered as they did during Hurricane Katrina. Also, if all levels of government and citizens had increased their capacity by adequately planning for worst-case scenarios, the proneness to the disaster could have been tremendously decreased.

Therefore, understanding proneness and capability as determinants of vulnerability is essential for emergency management personnel. An effective emergency management program must adequately incorporate the perspectives of those who regard vulnerability in terms of proneness to disasters and those who view it as insufficient capability. Doing so is imperative as policy may be limited if only one view is considered. Concentrating on both perspectives of vulnerability will provide a more complete approach to the rising disaster problem.

Causes of Vulnerability

To better understand vulnerability, it is important to look at the various sources that create or augment it. Prior disasters have resulted from several factors. For example, social economic factors (such as poverty) and demographic patterns (such as growing populations, gender, children, and elderly populations) have all increased vulnerability in disasters. Other factors that have augmented vulnerability include policy failures, weak emergency management institutions, environmental degradation, and cultural attitudes. This section will discuss these six factors and how they each contribute to vulnerability.

The first factor, poverty, increases an individual's proneness to disasters and decreases his or her capacity to cope with a hazardous event in a number of ways. For example, poor people usually live in substandard conditions, including "inadequately maintained housing."[12] Poverty is also a source of vulnerability because impoverished individuals lack the financial resources to prepare for and respond to a hazardous event. During a hurricane, for example, a poverty stricken individual might not be able to board up his or her home. This increases the household's likelihood of being adversely affected by the hazard.

Indigent populations are also least likely to have adequate transportation during an emergency. This complicates their ability to evacuate. This was exemplified during Hurricane Katrina. Although some did not heed the warning to evacuate New Orleans, others were simply unable to do so because they lacked the means of transportation. The scenario above also occurred in Hurricane Andrew where many poor individuals lacked personal transportation to evacuate and were "left to walk or hitchhike out of evacuation zones."[12] Another factor that increases the vulnerability of poor individuals and is related to transportation is the fact that they are unable to access "relief supply depots and disaster-assistance centers."[12] In addition, because the poor population does not have adequate reserves to recover from a hazard event, they are more likely to suffer greater consequences during a disaster.[12] This occurs because a disaster increases the impoverished person's burden to overcome their predicament.

Demographics, such as growing populations, are a second factor of increased vulnerability. Growing populations lead to an increase in vulnerability as more people are concentrated in one location, there is a higher likelihood of disastrous consequences when the area is faced with a hazard. For example, on September 11, 2001, nearly 3000 people died when hijacked airplanes crashed into the Twin Towers at the World Trade Center in New York city. On the other hand, fewer individuals died in Virginia and in the rural fields of Pennsylvania. This demonstrates how populated areas can be more vulnerable to disasters than less populated areas. Also, where there is a higher concentration of individuals, there is a higher likelihood that the emergency response system could be overwhelmed, as was the case with Hurricane Katrina. There were too many individuals who required assistance when this disaster occurred.

Other demographic factors, such as a larger number of elderly, single mothers, and children, also increase vulnerability. The elderly are vulnerable for many reasons. One reason is they lack the agility to respond to a hazard. During Hurricane Rita, 23 elderly individuals died when a bus that was evacuating them from the threat of the hurricane caught on fire. These individuals were unable to escape the burning bus because they lacked the health and physical ability to do so. The elderly are also less likely to possess the financial resources needed to respond to, or recover from, a hazardous event.

Women, especially single mothers, are also vulnerable during hazard events. The reason for their proneness or inadequate capability is that they, in most cases, lack the resources to adequately respond during an event.[12] Single parent mothers generally have more limited funds than men because they use almost all their money to support their children. As women in such conditions raise children without the assistance of a spouse, they can barely meet the challenges of caring for their children on a day-to-day basis, let alone providing for them during an emergency or disaster. Women are also vulnerable to disasters because "they are more likely to remain with family members in emergencies to nurture, assist, and protect them."[13]

Children are vulnerable to disasters because they lack the family support to cope with the effects of a disaster. For example, when children are forced into temporary shelters or disaster-assistance centers, they have to endure the psychological pain of being displaced from their homes. In some cases, they endure the pain of losing a parent or being temporarily separated from a parent. Such moments can prove difficult for a child causing them to experience major psychological setbacks.[12]

A third factor that increases vulnerability is policy failure. Policy shortcomings were evident in the terrorist attacks on September 11, 2001, when the hijackers were able to commandeer technology, such as airplanes, to attack the United States. Although policy makers had identified the eastern and western coasts of the United States as natural buffers against foreign enemy aggression, they failed to recognize that hijacked airplanes could be used as weapons on the homeland. Therefore, the attacks of September 11 illustrated that policy makers and intelligence officials did not identify the potential sources of threats that faced the United States. Perhaps the current policy of proactively engaging terrorists on foreign soil will prove to be the answer to the policy failure that enabled terrorists to attack New York, Washington DC, and Pennsylvania on September 11, 2001.

Another example of a lapse in public policy occurred after September 11 when the terrorist attacks on the World Trade Center occurred in 2001, the federal government understandably increased its focus on terrorism hazards by creating a new department responsible for homeland security. However, because the focus shifted to terrorism after September 11, some have concluded that this downplayed the significance of natural hazards. For example, Federal Emergency Management Agency (FEMA), which used to be a stand-alone department headed by a cabinet level director, became buried in the bureaucracy of a new department, Homeland Security. It also lost a great deal of funding for mitigation and its function of preparedness. As a result, many have concluded that the lack of independence by FEMA has limited its ability to respond to natural disasters. These views have been more widely accepted, especially after the government failed to adequately prepare for, and respond to Hurricane Katrina.

Policy failures can also be seen in developing countries. For example, in Malawi, where heavy rains cause flooding and human suffering during the rainy season, the government has failed to establish a policy that mitigates human loss and suffering, or adequately prepares for impending flood conditions. Rather, when a flood occurs, the government reacts after human loss and suffering has already occurred. A reactive disaster management policy fails to address the most prevalent forms of vulnerability and, as a result, people die and property is lost.

A fourth factor of increased vulnerability is weak emergency management institutions. Again, Hurricane Katrina provides an example of how weak institutions are ineffective during a disaster. Although the city of New Orleans possessed an emergency operations plan, it was clear after the hurricane had passed that the planning process was incomplete. This was plain to see when the media provided images of individuals stranded in their homes or on rooftops of buildings, and yet, there was a parking lot full of flooded school busses. These busses could have been used to evacuate citizens before the storm had hit New Orleans, but officials failed to coordinate with drivers and provide information to citizens on where they should seek shelter. This oversight by New Orleans illustrates the paper plan syndrome, where one has a very well-written emergency operations plan because of a state or federal mandate, but does not take the time to ensure operability, and as a result, disastrous consequences occur.

Another example of a weak emergency management program was evident during the September 11 attacks. Although the city and the mayor of New York were praised for their response efforts, there were elements of their program that were weak. For example, after the New York City Office of Emergency Management had acquired radios for the city's fire and police departments in 1996 and 1997, the agencies never resolved their differences regarding their interagency communications. As Dwyer and Flynn report, "the fire chiefs kept them in the trunks of their cars. As for the police chiefs, the radios never left the shelves."[14] An existing rivalry between the police department and the fire department impeded communication among the two organizations during the September 11 terrorist attacks and people died as a result.

Environmental degradation, a fifth factor, causes vulnerability in a variety of ways. Degradation of the environment usually occurs when pressure to accommodate an increasing population increases and land is sacrificed to make way for human development. Therefore, "flood plains and unstable hillsides become sites for housing, often informal and low-quality housing, because there is not other land available at reasonable cost, sufficiently close to employment opportunities."[15] The idea of changing the environment to accommodate human needs is not new. "More than 9,000 years ago, the Sumerians of Mesopotamia started irrigating land to meet increased demand for food from a growing population but their civilization eventually collapsed partly because of the water logging and salinization that resulted."[16] The examples above demonstrate that there are very dire consequences to poor environmental management. To limit the impact of disasters that occur as a result of degradation, mankind must exercise better stewardship of this earth.

A sixth, and final factor that causes vulnerability is people's attitudes and culture. In a study, conducted by Turner et al., it was discovered that "blacks were much more fatalistic about earthquakes than Anglos, and felt that there was little or nothing one could do to protect against them."[17] This could be due to limited funds or it may result from socialization. Regardless, it can therefore be concluded from this study that blacks could be more vulnerable to earthquakes than Anglos.

Language is also a cultural factor that increases vulnerability. When other cultural groups immigrate to the United States, and do not fully assimilate by learning English, their vulnerability is exhibited during a hazard event because this barrier prevents them from understanding emergency messages. It is evident that cultural attitudes are important to consider during emergencies. Emergency managers must be aware of the cultural make up of their communities to ensure that every individual is able to understand warning messages and act accordingly during a hazard event.

The six factors mentioned above are not the only sources of vulnerability. Vulnerability can also be increased by other variables that require further study by scholars. Some of these factors are

1. *High illiteracy rates.* Lack of education is closely related to people who are unable to respond effectively during a hazardous event.
2. *Decline in the health status of a country or region.* For example, the growth of human immunodeficiency virus/acquired immune deficiency syndrome (HIV/AIDS) in sub-Saharan Africa complicates disaster response as more and more people are in a weak state of health. Not only are HIV-positive individuals susceptible to opportunistic diseases, they are also vulnerable to other hazards.
3. *Migration to new communities.* Families that move to a new community, increase the vulnerability of that community because they do not share the same disaster history as other residents in the area. Whereas long-standing residents who have history in the community might know how to respond to a particular hazard, new families must learn about the hazards that threaten the community and how to build a capacity to respond to, or cope with them.
4. *Lack of adequate human resource allocation to emergency management.* Many emergency managers in municipalities hold dual roles such as fire chief and emergency management coordinator. As a result, one area suffers at the expense of the other.

It is clear that vulnerability originates from many sources. What is also clear is that emergency managers need to address vulnerability to prevent disastrous outcomes during hazard events.

Reducing Disaster Vulnerability

Thus far, this chapter has discussed disaster trends and the concept and causes of vulnerability. The ever-important question remains: how does an individual, organization, community, or nation address vulnerability to disasters? The answer to this inquiry lies in two important principles: "liability reduction (i.e., the diminution of risk and susceptibility) and capacity building (i.e., the augmenting of resistance and resilience)."[1] This section will discuss the concepts of risk, susceptibility, resistance, and resilience, as well as how these approaches interact to facilitate a reduction in disaster vulnerability.

Several scholars discuss the impact of risk on disasters. Dennis Mileti defines risk as "the probability of an event or condition occurring."[13] Alwang et al. define risk as "a known or unknown probability distribution of events."[19] According to Weichselgartner, "highly complex, interdependent, and interactive" decisions "may create increased risks, to potential hazards."[5] These definitions therefore demonstrate that risk is the physical result of the decisions that expose humans or their property to a hazard, whether known or unknown. For example, families that chose to reside in coastal regions or on fault lines are at risk of incurring damage or injury due to a hurricane or earthquake hazard. Therefore, to reduce the potential for harm or disruption, these families can move to locations that have a lower level of risk from known hazards. Another way to reduce risk is through the development and careful use of warning systems. Giving advanced notice does much to decrease the potential for physical harm. Therefore, the first way to address vulnerability is by reducing risk.

There are advantages and disadvantages to viewing vulnerability reduction through the concept of risk. The advantage of the risk reduction approach is that it is proactive, looking to the future to anticipate impending threats. Also, this approach focuses on the physical consequence of risky decisions that lead to an individual's increased exposure to a hazard. Therefore, a risk reduction approach to emergency management will focus heavily on safeguarding human life, property, and physical infrastructure. However, viewing vulnerability through this concept also has shortcomings. When one considers vulnerability through risk reduction, they fail to acknowledge nonphysical factors that increase vulnerability. Such factors are a poor economy, cultural values and traditions, politics, and poor emergency management policies and practices.

Reducing susceptibility is the second approach to dealing with vulnerability. An important aspect to vulnerability reduction is a proper understanding of the social, cultural, political, economic, psychological, and organizational variables related to disasters. For example, as Hurricane Katrina demonstrated, impoverished individuals are most susceptible to a disaster because they lack the resources to respond and recover. The elderly are another social group that is susceptible to disasters because, in most cases, they lack the mobility, health, and financial resources to avoid hazards. Culturally, some individuals or communities are more susceptible to disasters than others because they are more culturally fatalistic.[17] Politics also determines susceptibility as politicians, in response to the public and media, direct resources for mitigation, preparation, response, and recovery efforts. In so doing, they can increase funding or manpower before, during, and after a disaster and, as a result, minimize a community's susceptibility to a disaster. It is also important to understand how the economy interacts with susceptibility. Strong economies are able to withstand the impact of a disaster, and, as a result, are able to quickly recover from a hazard event. On the other hand, countries or communities with weak economies are more susceptible to a disaster because they do not have the financial infrastructure to enable them to quickly recover. Psychological variables of a community also impact susceptibility because a country's mindset during a disaster determines how quickly it can recover. For example, Israel, a country that has experienced regular terrorist attacks, has consistently been able to continue functioning because her people have developed the psychological capacity to withstand the threat of terrorism. Finally, organizational variables impact a community's susceptibility because an organization's ability to mitigate and prepare for a disaster could either increase or decrease a community's susceptibility.[18]

To minimize loss during a hazard event, communities must reduce their susceptibility by addressing the previously mentioned variables that lead to disasters. This requires significant social change as well as an emergency management organization, which is aware of the demographic composition of their community.[19] Such information will enable an emergency manager to provide training and public education to increase the community's disaster awareness. Therefore, an advantage of this approach is that it is possible to prepare citizens for hazard events by reducing poverty or by increasing their awareness. A disadvantage is that even if a citizenry is wealthy or informed, that does not guarantee they will minimize further death and destruction. Steps still have to be taken to reduce physical risk.

Another way to address vulnerability is by increasing resistance to a hazard. "Resistance suggests the ability of structures and infrastructure to withstand the forces of powerful agents, minimizing damage."[4] According to Donald Geis, who discusses the disaster resistant communities in "By design: The disaster resistant and quality-of-life community," the concept was specifically developed to provide "the overarching guidance that informs development in hazard-prone areas."[20] Geis adds, "its purpose is to provide the direction essential to our core mission of minimizing the growing human and property losses from extreme natural events."[20] The idea behind this approach is to "resist the disaster" through proactive prevention and mitigation measures.[20] It implies ameliorating structural problems in advance of a hazard event to minimize the impact of a disaster. Disaster resistance is accomplished by utilizing building codes and technology to ensure safe and disaster resistant structures.

As with the risk reduction approach, this concept is forward thinking and seeks to implement known strategies to minimize loss of life and property during a hazard event. However, a drawback of the resistance concept is that it supposes all mitigation activities will withstand the force of hazards. Also, building disaster resistant communities relies upon construction practices for known hazards. Knowledge about hazards may be limited at times as the world continues to change and different threats are introduced. Another disadvantage to this approach is that building code enforcement is expensive and socially unpopular. Therefore, it is possible the resistance concept could lead to high construction costs or lead people to reside in a less expensive, but more vulnerable home.

Enhancing resilience is another way to build capacity to effectively deal with a disaster. "Resilience includes the individual's and community's ability to respond and recover based on preparedness and other measures."[4] "Resiliency to disasters means a locale can withstand an extreme natural event with a tolerable level of losses"[13] and without significant outside assistance. Reducing vulnerability through the resilience approach requires raising the capacity of an individual, organization, community, or nation to cope with a disaster and recover as quickly and effectively as possible. Increasing resilience can be accomplished by possessing the following qualities: shared community values, aspirations, and goals; established social infrastructure; positive social economic trends; sustainability of social and economic life; partnerships; communities of interest; established networks; and resources and skills. According to Buckle et al., these are all the factors that enable individuals, families, and communities to minimize the impact of disasters and increase their resilience during disasters.[21]

The main advantage of this concept is that it accepts the reality that disasters occur; therefore, it advocates planning response and long-term recovery activities. However, this strength is also a weakness in that the focus is less on mitigation and more on preparedness measures. Also, because the focus is more on social and cultural values, this concept negates the value of strengthening the physical infrastructure.

These components, risk, susceptibility, resistance, and resilience, comprise the four approaches to vulnerability reduction.[1] They are not mutually exclusive, however. To provide a better understanding of these concepts, McEntire furnishes the following explanation:

> Risk, susceptibility, resistance, and resilience influence our degree of vulnerability in a convoluted fashion. As an example, our risky choice of location can be exacerbated by construction that does not take into account disaster resistance. Our susceptibility owing to political and economic factors may limit our resilience (or ability to respond and recover) after a disaster has occurred. Policies that increase susceptibility because of cultural preferences may also jeopardize the efforts to harness technology and build disaster resistance. A risk-prone infrastructure may degrade individual and community resilience because it is unable to withstand the powerful forces of hazards. Policies that make people susceptible to disaster often result in an intentional or unintentional transfer of risk. If a society is not resilient after a disaster (due to its

failure to plan adequately for disasters), it may also be less likely to promote resistance during recovery operations.[22]

Therefore, "risk and susceptibility, as well as resistance and resilience, often interact in mutually reinforcing ways."[22] For this reason, these factors cannot constitute an efficient and effective emergency management program when applied individually. To help an emergency management program succeed, one needs to apply all four factors so that all liabilities can be minimized and all capabilities can be enhanced. These components demonstrate the complicated nature of vulnerability and the need to understand all the components it comprises to construct a comprehensive approach to emergency management. This approach also acknowledges the interaction between physical and social environments. Risk and resistance, which focus more on infrastructure, including the natural and built environments, must not be separated from susceptibility and resilience, which address culture, economic, and political landscape.

The holistic approach posited in this chapter is therefore worth the consideration of emergency management organizations. It also seems to be supported by scholars when the literature is viewed from a cumulative prospective. For example, scholars such as Peter Timmerman,[23] Dennis Mileti,[13] Don Geis,[20] James Kendra and Tricia Wachtendorf,[24] Weichselgartner[5] and many others have all collectively touched on the four approaches discussed in this chapter. As scholars are focusing on these concepts presented here, it might be wise that practitioners should also follow suit.

Conclusion

Although the approach suggested in this chapter is highly advantageous, it has three drawbacks. First, this process requires that a community invest many hours of planning to identify liabilities and capabilities in any given community. Second, as this approach is more comprehensive than others that have been proposed in the past, its implementation requires many resources, both financial and human. For example, this strategy will require large amounts of funds to adequately assess risks, susceptibility, resistance, and resilience. This process will also require competent human resources to ensure the processes of liability reduction and capacity building are thoroughly implemented. Third, and finally, there needs to be more discussion and debate regarding the approach posed in this chapter to better refine the ideas suggested. Additional studies will be needed to understand vulnerability and how to reduce it.

Even though the suggestions made in this paper are not without criticism, it is likely that their implementation will ensure that more lives and property are safeguarded in the future. Although the occurrence of hazardous events may continue in the future, the loss of life and property need not always rise as a result.[25]

References

1. McEntire, D.A., Why vulnerability matters: Exploring the merit of an inclusive disaster reduction concept, *Disaster Prevention and Management*, 14, 2, 2005.
2. EM-DAT: The OFDA/CRED international disaster database, Université Catholique de Louvain, Brussels, Belgium. Available at www.em-dat.net.
3. McEntire, D.A., A comparison of disaster paradigms: The search for a holistic policy guide, *Public Administration Review*, 62, 3, 2002.
4. McEntire, D.A., Tenets of vulnerability: An assessment of a fundamental disaster concept, *Journal of Emergency Management*, 2, 25, 2004.
5. Weichselgartner, J., Disaster mitigation: The concept of vulnerability revisited, *Disaster Prevention and Management*, 10, 85, 2001.
6. Green, C., The evaluation of vulnerability to flooding, *Disaster Prevention and Management*, 13, 323, 2004.
7. Cutter, S.L., Vulnerability to environmental hazards, *Progress in Human Geography*, 20, 529, 1996.
8. Wisner, B., Blaikie, P., Cannon, T., and Davis, I., *At Risk: Natural Hazards, People's Vulnerability and Disasters*, Routledge, New York, 2004.
9. Friend, J.H. and Guralnik, D.B., *Webster's New World Dictionary of the American Language*, World Publishing, New York, 1960, p. 215.
10. Kelly, P.M. and Adger, W.N., *Assessing Vulnerability to Climate Change and Facilitating Adoption*. Working paper no.GEC-1999–07. The Centre for Social and Economic Research on the Global Environment (CSERGE), Economic and Social Research Council (ESRC), United Kingdom, 1997.
11. Sapountzaki, K., Coping with seismic vulnerability: Small manufacturing firms in Western Athens, *Disasters*, 29, 195, 2005.
12. Morrow, B.H., Identifying and mapping community vulnerability, *Disasters*, 23, 1, 1999.
13. Mileti, D., *Disasters by Design: A Reassessment of Natural Hazards in the United States*, Joseph Henry Press, Washington, DC, 1999, Chapter 4.
14. Dwyer, J. and Flynn, K., *102 Minutes: The Untold Story of the Fight to Survive Inside the Twin Towers*, Henry Holt, New York, 2005, p. 60.
15. Boullé, P., Vrolijks, L., and Palm, E., Vulnerability reduction for sustainable urban development, *Journal of Contingencies and Crisis Management*, 5, 179, 1997.
16. Clarke, R., Lamb, R., and Ward, D.R., *Global Environment Outlook 3: Past Present and Future Perspectives*, Earthscan Publications, London, 2002, Chapter 3.
17. Fothergill, A., Maestas, E., and Darlington, J.D., Race, ethnicity and disasters in the United States: A review of the literature, *Disasters*, 23, 156, 1999.
18. McEntire, D.A., Revolutionary and evolutionary change in emergency management: Assessing the need for a paradigm shift and the possibility of progress in the profession. Presented at the FEMA Higher Education Conference, 2005, p. 1.
19. Alwang, J., Siegel, P.B., and Jorgensen, S.L., Vulnerability: A view from different disciplines, Social Protection Discussion Paper, June 2001, p. 1.
20. Geis, D.E., By design: The disaster resistant and quality-of-life community, *Natural Hazards Review*, 1, 151, 2000.
21. Buckle, P., Mars, G., and Smale, S., New approaches to assessing vulnerability and resilience, *Australian Journal of Emergency Management*, 15, 8, 2000.

22. McEntire, D.A., Triggering agents, vulnerabilities and disaster reduction towards a holistic paradigm, *Disaster Prevention and Management*, 10, 189, 2001.
23. Timmerman, P., Vulnerability, resilience, and the collapse of society, Institute of Environmental Studies, University of Toronto, Toronto, 1981.
24. Kendra, J. and Wachtendorf, T., Elements of resilience after the World Trade Center disaster: Reconstituting New York City's emergency operations centre, *Disasters*, 27, 1, 2003.
25. Merriman, P.A. and Browitt, C.W.A. (Eds.), *Natural Disasters: Protecting Vulnerable Communities*, Thomas Telford, London, 1993, Chapter 7.

Chapter 3

The Politics of Disaster Management: The Evolution of the Federal Emergency Management Agency

Mark R. Daniels

CONTENTS

During testimony before a U.S. House of Representatives committee, former Federal Emergency Management Agency (FEMA) Director Michael Brown gave lawmakers a lesson in federalism. Brown expressed his perception that FEMA is a coordinating agency for state and local emergency responses. "We don't own fire trucks, we don't own ambulances," he explained (Fox News, 2005). He laid the blame for the poor response to Hurricane Katrina on Louisiana Governor Kathleen Blanco and New Orleans Mayor Ray Nagin, and described state and local government in Louisiana as "dysfunctional." When his poor performance was compared with the response of Rudy Guiliano after the September 11 World Trade Center attacks, Brown responded by rhetorically asking, "So I guess you want me to be the superhero, to step in there and take everyone out of New Orleans?" (Jordan, 2005).

This testimony exposed the lack of agreement between House members and Brown over the role of FEMA in meeting the challenges posed by natural disasters. The role and scope of power of federal agencies over state and local governments has been a topic of debate in electioneering, including Presidential debates. FEMA is a federal agency with wide powers over hazards, disasters, and emergency management. Under previous Director James L. Witt, FEMA was transformed into a mission oriented, customer service agency that conducted studies of hurricane evacuation traffic in the Southeast United States. During 1999s category IV Hurricane Floyd, FEMA coordinated the largest evacuation of a major geographic region in the history of the United States. Witt saw FEMA's role as a fast, first responder of emergencies in contrast to Brown's perception of FEMA as a coordinating organization for state and local response.

This chapter examines the evolution of FEMA during the past 75 years focusing on the different approaches to federalism and management that have characterized FEMA's history. The chapter will explore the evolving role of FEMA in emergency management, the intergovernmental strategy, and management style adopted for it by the executive branch. Finally, the chapter will conclude with observations about the emergency management outcomes reflected by the type of leadership and federalism approach adopted by the executive branch.

History of FEMA

Politics is both the process by which community decisions are made and the exercise of power in government decision making. In this sense, the politics of FEMA include the processes by which FEMA makes decisions and exercises power along with other governments. Over time, the politics of FEMA has changed, in large part consistent with the growth of the country and the increased scope of the federal government. Mankind's concern and interest in emergency management can be traced back to the early civilization, as seen by hieroglyphics that depict cavemen trying to deal with disasters (Haddow and Bullock, 2003: 1). FEMA's roots can be traced back to a 1803 Congressional Act that provided assistance to a New Hampshire town that suffered an extensive fire (ibid.: 2). Over the next 100 years, Congress passed legislation on a case-by-case basis more than a hundred times in response to natural disasters including hurricanes, earthquakes, and floods. In the 1930s the Reconstruction Finance Corporation and the Bureau of Public Roads were authorized by the Congress to make disaster loans for repairs, and the U.S. Army Corps of Engineers were authorized to control flood projects (ibid.). The 1950s and 1960s were decades of unprecedented natural disasters, including Hurricane Hazel, a category IV storm in 1954 that hit Virginia and North Carolina, Hurricane Diane that hit the mid-Atlantic states in 1955, Hurricane Audrey that landed in Louisiana and Texas in 1957, Hurricane Carla in 1962, the Alaskan earthquake in 1964, Hurricane Camille in 1969, the Southern California earthquake of 1971, and Hurricane Agnes in 1972. These disasters were accompanied by the passage of the National Flood Insurance Act of 1968 and 1972, and the passage of the Disaster Relief Act of 1974, which established the process of Presidential disaster declarations (FEMA, 2005). FEMA became the main agency for disaster recovery (Haddow and Bullock, 2003: 5).

Finally, the National Governor's Association sought to decrease the number of federal agencies with which state and local governments had to interact and coordinate recovery efforts. One of President Jimmy Carter's more successful initiatives was to reorganize the executive branch of the federal government, and in 1979 Carter created FEMA as an umbrella organization housing numerous federal emergency and disaster recovery programs (ibid.: 6). Included under FEMA in this reorganization were the National Fire Prevention Control Administration, from the Department of Commerce; the Federal Insurance Administration program from the Department of Housing and Urban Development (HUD); the Federal Broadcast System from the Executive Office of the President; the Defense Civil Preparedness Agency from the Department of Defense (DoD); the Federal Disaster Assistance Administration from HUD; and the Federal Preparedness Agency from the General Services Administration.

With the election of President Ronald Reagan, the cold war arms race accelerated and the focus of FEMA drifted from earthquake, hurricane, and flood programs to nuclear attack preparedness (ibid.: 8). The early emergency management directors were civilians, but during the Reagan administration this shifted to political appointees (Waugh, 2000: 29). FEMA became known during this period as a dumping ground for political appointees with little experience. The criteria for appointing individuals to FEMA was summed up by one of Reagan's advisors: "Was he a Reagan man? Two, a Republican? And three, a conservative?" (Wamsley, et al., 1996: 267). The most crucial concern, this advisor added, was to ensure that conservative ideology was properly represented. Of course, one way to obtain ideological control of a bureaucracy is to make political appointments starting at the top, continuing downward all the way to the lower levels of the bureaucracy. In a study conducted by Paul Light, he noted that when Bill Clinton became President he needed to find appointees for 15 layers of government, compared to the only 6 layers of government encountered by President Kennedy's administration (ibid.: 269). FEMA became crowded with more than 30 political appointees, a number surpassed only by the Office of Management and the Budget (ibid.: 271). These deep appointments in FEMA and elsewhere in the executive branch bureaucracy were perceived as "fourth echelon slots" to be filled by mid to lower level political operatives: for example, a campaign advance man, or a regional political organizer. As Elliot Richardson explained, although it is difficult for a career administrator to be preempted by an outsider who has little or no experience, eventually career bureaucrats get driven away from decision makers as the number and depth of political appointments are made, and these politically appointed "deputy assistant secretaries" become gatekeepers to higher-level political executives, slowing and possibly distorting communication (ibid.: 274, 281).

At the same time, however, political appointees who are qualified for their appointments can be a valuable asset to the bureaucracy. Within FEMA, regional directors have to work with mayors, county executives and boards, and governors and politically appointed directors have turned out to be the best because of the political comfort level they brought with them to the job (Maranto, 2005: 34). These politically appointed regional directors have often served as local or state elected officials, and understand the political pressures that officials often face during a natural disaster. As Robert Maranto observes, "in a political system politicians tend to be better at politics" (ibid.: 70). Political appointees work in a "gray zone" where they have to balance the demands of their organization's mission with the demands of their party, their interest groups, and their political benefactors. On the other hand, careerists live in the "black and white" world of policies and procedures. Both political appointees and careerists are needed to make an agency function effectively within a technical and political environment.

FEMA descended into scandal during the Reagan administration, and was investigated by a subcommittee of the House Committee on Science and Technology, the Department of Justice, and a grand jury. These investigations concluded that there were inappropriate relationships with private contractors and a misuse of federal monies. In response, the director and top aides resigned (Waugh, 2000: 29). FEMA's poor response to Hurricane Hugo in 1989 was followed by an even worse response to Hurricane Andrew in 1992 where 61 people were killed and 160,000 people were left homeless along with $26.5 billion in damages. FEMA's poor response led Senator Ernest Hollings (Democrat, South Carolina) to call FEMA top executives "the sorriest bunch of bureaucratic jackasses" (Haddow and Bullock, 2003: 9). The election of Bill Clinton ushered in a new era in FEMA history. President Clinton appointed James Lee Witt as Director, an appointment based on Witt's experience as Director of Emergency Management in Arkansas, and his appointment was considered one of the success stories in the Clinton administration (Waugh, 2000: 31). President Clinton also elevated the director of FEMA to a cabinet level position (Haddow and Bullock, 2003: 12). Under Witt, FEMA became more collaborative and cooperative and embraced aspects of total quality management. On his first morning on the job, Witt was reported to have stood in the lobby of the FEMA headquarters greeting employees as they came to work.

He also asked career employees to rotate jobs to provide fresh perspectives on what the agency did (ibid.). Witt also brainstormed with agency workers to develop a mission statement: "Reduce the loss of life and property and protect our institutions from all hazards by leading and supporting the nation in a comprehensive risk-based emergency management program of mitigation, preparedness response and recovery" (ibid.: 32). Related to the mission statement were three goals: (1) "to protect lives and prevent the loss of property from all hazards; (2) reduce human suffering and enhance the recovery of communities after disasters strike; (3) ensure that the public is served in a timely and efficient manner" (ibid.). Witt emphasized mitigation, which is reducing or eliminating risks to people and property. For example, Witt implemented programs to move houses out of flood plains along the Mississippi River. In addition, Witt emphasized terrorism preparedness in response to the Oklahoma City bombing of 1995 and the first bombing of the World Trade Towers in 1992. Often referred to as the Witt Revolution, Witt's tenure with FEMA witnessed sweeping reforms including customer service training, mitigation, risk avoidance, and strengthened relations with local and state emergency managers (Haddow and Bullock, 2003: 10). Witt included vertical integration, linked FEMA with local and state emergency managers, and horizontal integrated FEMA's programs with one another, such as linking temporary housing programs with low interest disaster loans for property losses, crisis counseling, unemployment assistance, and many other disaster programs administered by FEMA (Waugh, 2000: 55).

Witt also developed the Integrated Emergency Management System (IEMS) based on intergovernmental agreements (Waugh and Sylves, 1990: 51). This system was intended to strengthen state and local responses, and to make sure that they received maximum possible support (ibid.: 52). FEMA also encouraged states and territories to adopt interstate compacts regarding emergency responses, and expanded training programs for local and state governments.

Witt's transformation of FEMA paid off during the response to Hurricane Floyd in 1999. When this category IV hurricane was aiming at Cape Fear, North Carolina, FEMA coordinated the evacuation of 2,350,000 people, the largest peacetime evacuation in the history of the country (Alexander, 2002: 152, 153).

President George W. Bush's first director of FEMA was Joe Allbaugh, campaign manager of the 2000 presidential race. Allbaugh's previous experience included an appointment as Oklahoma's Deputy Secretary of Transportation, and serving as chief-of-staff to Governor George W. Bush. The staffing of FEMA reverted to the patronage system that was in place before the Clinton years. After the second World Trade towers attack on September 11, 2001, the Homeland Security Act of 2002 merged over 22 federal agencies and offices, and 180,000 employees, into a single department responsible for immigration enforcement, border and transportation security, information analysis and infrastructure protection, science and technology research development for security, and emergency preparedness and response (Sauter and Carafano, 2005: 53). FEMA is now part of the largest executive department ever created, a vast bureaucracy with many different programs and past administrative allegiances, facing a challenging task of adequately communicating within itself. With Allbaugh's departure from FEMA in 2003, Michael Brown, FEMA's legal counsel, was appointed director. Brown's qualifications were exclusively political; he knew Allbaugh from Republican politics in Oklahoma. Brown ran unsuccessfully for the U.S. House of Representatives in 1988 (he received 27 percent of the vote) and worked with Allbaugh in many local races. Brown was Commissioner of the International Arabian Horse Association, and resigned to become counsel to FEMA when President Bush appointed his friend Allbaugh in 2001. Brown resigned after the Hurricane Katrina controversy, and was replaced by R. David Paulison, the former head of the U.S. Fire Administration. The Bush administration took care in finding a replacement who had solid credentials. Paulison by training was a firefighter, and was formerly chief of Miami-Dade Fire Rescue and President of the International Association of fire chiefs.

FEMA: Federalism and Ideology

The U.S. Constitution divides power between the national and state governments giving defined functions to each. This legal arrangement is referred to as "federalism." The nature of the relationship between the national and state governments has been debated over the course of the country's history, and federal courts have often intervened to further assist in defining the jurisdictional powers of the national and state governments. There are many theoretical approaches to analyzing the relationship between the national and state governments over time, however, three broad perspectives can be identified: (1) dual federalism, (2) cooperative federalism, and (3) new federalism (Walker, 1981: 19–107). Dual federalism views the relationship between the national and state governments as two spheres of influence, each with its own jurisdiction, power and authority. Examples of dual federalism are the early Supreme Court cases of *McCulloch v Maryland* (1819) and *Gibbons v Ogden* (1824). In the McCulloch case, the Supreme Court ruled that the national government had used implied powers to create a National bank, and that the Supremacy Clause prohibited the state of Maryland from taxing the bank. In the Gibbons case, the Court ruled that the commerce clause gave the National government the power to regulate commerce between and within states, and that state governments' power of regulating commerce cannot interfere with National authority. Both cases involved the Court interpreting the Constitution to establish jurisdictional boundaries between the national and state governments. Perhaps the most defining case of this era was *Dred Scott v Sanford* (1857), a case involving an American slave's claim of freedom because he lived with his owner in a state designated as "free" by the Missouri Compromise of 1820. The Court ruled, among other things, that the Missouri Compromise was unconstitutional, because the Constitution does not give the power of regulating slavery to the national government. Instead, the power of regulating slavery is reserved for the states by the tenth Amendment.

Again, the Court delineated separate spheres of authority for the national, state, and local governments. The metaphor for this era of federalism is a "layer cake," with the large bottom layer the state governments and their sphere of authority, and the smaller but top layer the national government with its own, supreme, sphere of authority.

The cooperative era of federalism began after the Civil War during a period characterized by a severe approach to reconstruction and an assertion of national authority. The aftermath of the Civil War produced the thirteenth, fourteenth, and fifteenth amendments, all imposing federal authority upon the states and their people. During this period, the national government emerged as the authority over the regulation of commerce, and also emerged as the authority on taxation culminating with the income tax in 1913. The national government eventually became a major funding source for states and localities, and along with the growth of grants came a growth in national influence over states and localities. Cooperative federalism matured by the 1960s and was viewed symbolically as a "picket fence." The pickets represented policy areas (education, transportation, housing, and so forth) and the horizontal boards that held the pickets upright were the three levels of government (national, state, and local). It was within public policy that the three levels of governments cooperated to accomplish goals.

The third era of federalism combines the approaches of recent Presidents to control federal spending and to return policy initiatives back to state governments. Starting with President Nixon's "New Federalism" and extending all the way to President George W. Bush's "devolution revolution," executive branch action has intended to devolve the authority of the national government and return more policy discretion and control to states. Greater decentralization in policy making and implementation has been desired, along with a reduction in the commitment of funding from the national government. Under President Clinton, aid to families with dependent children became a block grant run by states named Temporary Assistance to Needy Families, and the traditional medicaid program could be replaced by state managed "demonstration projects." These programs continued to receive federal funding, but the intent was to gradually have state governments pick up a bigger piece of the budget while assuming greater responsibility for how the programs would be run. This era is characterized by a nostalgic return to the era of dual federalism and the concept of the reserved powers of states, and the limited, specific powers of the national government.

FEMA's position in intergovernmental relations has always rested upon how emergencies are initiated by state and local governments. Federal law actually permits FEMA to respond only when the capacities of state and local governments have been exceeded (Waugh and Sylves, 1990: 48). Even the cost of emergency response is set by federal law, and according to the Stafford Act of 1988 the federal government is limited to 75 percent of the cost of Presidential declared emergencies, with the remaining 25 percent of the cost split between local and state governments (ibid.: 53).

One of the reasons for FEMA's poor response to Hurricane Hugo in 1989 was that a state government had to request the assistance of FEMA before FEMA could respond. The same situation arose in 1992 with the response to Hurricane Andrew. Clinton's FEMA director, James Lee Witt, wanted a more horizontal, proactive agency. He audited the disaster fund and found $800 million in unused money to send back to the U.S. Treasury. He emphasized mitigation, or prevention, by taking sustained action to reduce and eliminate risk to people and property. He also emphasized a close relationship among the federal, state, and local emergency management providers. FEMA's state and local training programs eventually saw the transition of these governments to the FEMA model (Waugh, 2000: 193). One author described FEMA under Witt's leadership as an example of "picket fence federalism" (ibid.). For example, during Hurricane Floyd in 1993, Witt called every governor and every member of Congress in each of the states affected on the weekend preceding the storm. He set up video conferencing with all of the hurricane-risk states, talking to mayors, asking them to talk to their governors about their needs. FEMA helped to evacuate four million people before the flooding from the Hurricane could get to them (Witt, 2005). According to one FEMA employee, acting preemptively, even before the governors could request assistance, was not permitted by the law, "but when was the last time Clinton obeyed the law?" the employee joked (Bovard, 2005: 1). On a television news broadcast, Witt explained how FEMA had an informal, cooperative arrangement to assist state and local governments with the evacuation, an almost perfect case study example of picket fence federalism.

In contrast, Michael Brown's explanation of what went wrong during Hurricane Katrina was a return to terminology of dual federalism. Brown explained that he was waiting for Governor Kathleen Blanco of Louisiana and Mayor Ray Nagin of New Orleans to act and request assistance from FEMA, and that the emergency management agencies at the state and local level did not function well (Fox News, 2005). Brown continued

> Guess what, FEMA doesn't own fire trucks; we don't own ambulances; we don't own search and rescue equipment. In fact, the only search and rescue or emergency equipment that we own is a very small cadre to protect some property that we own around the country. FEMA is a coordinating agency. We are not a law enforcement agency.

Brown was both right and wrong. FEMA does not own fire trucks, but there were federal assets not used during Katrina. The Interior Department offered FEMA 500 rooms, 119 pieces of heavy equipment, 300 dump trucks and other vehicles, 300 boats, 11 aircraft, and 400 law enforcement officers (Meserve, 2006). Senator Susan Collins, chair of a committee with jurisdiction over Homeland Security Administration (HSA) and FEMA, said "now you might be able to understand if it came from outside of government, but this is another federal agency, an agency that was offering trained personnel and exactly the assets that the federal government needed to assist in the search-and-rescue operations" (ibid.). Brown also explained that he felt "personal regret that I was unable to persuade Gov. Blanco and Mayor Nagin to sit down, get over their differences and work together. I just couldn't pull it off." Both Blanco and Nagin disagreed with Brown's accusations that they were "dysfunctional" and did not request federal assistance promptly.

The delay in obtaining a request for help from the governor and mayor should not have prevented Brown from moving ahead quickly to bring federal assistance to the disaster area if he had been operating within a cooperative federalism model. Brown should have realized that the capacity of state and local authorities had been exceeded and should have ordered an evacuation. As mentioned previously, James Lee Witt moved ahead with the 1993 evacuation of the east central Atlantic coast before any formal request for assistance. Cooperation among governments was stressed under Witt's picket fence approach to emergency management. In contrast, Brown stressed the state and federal boundaries involved in emergency management. Brown's reliance on the reserved power of states and the limited role of the federal government is consistent with the Bush administration's decentralized approach to federalism and its desire to give greater recognition to the powers reserved to the states.

FEMA: Management and Ideology

The election of George W. Bush in 2000 can be seen as the continuation of the Reagan administration, after the interruption of the George H.W. Bush and Bill Clinton presidencies. The return of a true conservative to the executive branch meant a return to the principles of privatization that had characterized the 1980s. This can be best seen in the executive branch response to the terror attacks of September 11: The creation of HSA by executive order. President Bush combined 22 agencies and over 180,000 employees into the largest bureaucracy in the federal government (Sauter and Carafano, 2005: 53). At the same time, the Bush administration made a commitment to privatize as many government services as possible. Outsourcing on homeland security programs has topped $130 billion since the creation of HSA (Klinenberg and Frank, 2005: 44). When the Bush administration compared the creation of HSA with the creation of the DoD in 1947, a European diplomat expressed surprise. "I'm struck," the diplomat said "that in devising a new strategy for the future that the nation focused on a model from the past" (Kettl, 2005: 4).

The creation of HSA came from political, not administrative imperatives (ibid.: 5). President Bush needed to embrace a symbolic act that would show the country was responding effectively to the terrorist menace. At the same time, the conservative administration took the opportunity to force Congressional democrats to accept a personnel system for the Transportation Safety Administration (TSA) that would be exempt from collective bargaining. The antiunion provision for TSA officers was swallowed by Congressional democrats who did not want to vote against HSA and appear to be "soft" on terrorism.

When asked about the creation of HSA and the reorganization of 22 agencies within it, James Lee Witt responded that "it will be 10 years before it's functional" (Witt, 2005: 4). Witt also reported that the reorganization led many FEMA employees to take early retirement, and actually took resources away, in particular, preparedness training and exercise. The political appointees that flooded FEMA at the beginning of the Bush administration now extended throughout HSA.

Protecting Americans from the threat of terrorism became the guiding mission of HSA, and emergency management and FEMA were down played. FEMA was no longer a cabinet level position. James Lee Witt would often telephone the Secretary of Defense to ask for assistance with disaster response, but Witt questioned whether current Secretary of Defense Donald Rumsfeld ever heard of Michael Brown prior to the Katrina controversy. Witt expressed surprise that FEMA did not work more closely with DoD during Katrina, because while Witt was the director of FEMA, DoD had a colonel as a liaison at FEMA headquarters and worked with him in the operations center (Witt, 2005: 6).

The threat of terrorism was translated into no bid contracts, and much of the money spent was directed to predominantly Republican states with a low risk of terrorism (Klinenberg and Frank, 2005: 46). Iowa bought traffic cones and wall clocks with hidden cameras, Columbus, Ohio, bought bulletproof vests for dogs in the fire department, and the District of Columbia paid students in a summer jobs program to develop rap songs about emergency preparedness (ibid.). Mason County, Washington, spent $63,000 for a biochemical decontamination unit that no one has been trained to use. "We're tying to figure out how to use it," said a county deputy, "the state and feds said, 'you all need one of these,' we said 'why?'" (ibid.: 52). And Bennington, New Hampshire, spent almost $2,000 for five chemical weapons suits. "I don't see no specific threats," said the police chief, "it was just something they offered, so we figured we'd get on the bandwagon" (ibid.).

The no bid contracts also translated into sweetheart deals for former HSA executives. Former deputy administrator, Carol DiBattiste, took an executive position with ChoicePoint, a company that provides background investigations, for a combined compensation package of $950,000. FEMA's former director, Joseph Allbaugh, obtained a $100 million contract for the Shaw Group to pump water out of the flooded city. Allbaugh's previous private sector job was as a lobbyist for reconstruction contracts in Iraq. And, Mike Parker, a former government of the people (GOP) congressman from Mississippi who directed the Army Corps of Engineers, agreed to consult for the Ash-Britt company just days before it obtained a $550 million contract for municipal solid waste removal. Not coincidentally, the contract was with the Army Corps of Engineers.

Conclusions on Federalism, Management, and Ideology

Before James Lee Witt came along, FEMA's reputation was so bad that it was the target of vaudeville type jokes: "Every hurricane, earthquake, tornado and flood brings two disasters: one when the event occurs, the second when FEMA arrives" (Kettl, 2005b). For decades, FEMA had a reputation as a dumping ground for political appointees who had minor roles in campaigns and therefore deserved a minor, relatively unimportant job somewhere in the bowels of the federal bureaucracy.

What makes for good emergency management? A best selling emergency management textbook explains that

> Good leaders are necessary for emergency management. They will have the knowledge, experience and training to do the job unselfconsciously. They are dependable, reliable, and usually not given to unpredictable mood shifts. A combination of rigidity and flexibility is valuable. They recognize the abilities and limitations of colleagues. They have an adaptive management style. (Alexander, 2002: 139)

Despite knowing the ingredients for good emergency management, the Bush administration strayed from the Clinton administration's successful FEMA model and reverted back to the past practices of both Democratic and Republican Presidents who saw emergency management as an opportunity to fill patronage positions for marginally qualified minor political operatives. President Bush's first FEMA director, Joseph Allbaugh, was marginally qualified and his second director, Michael Brown, had no qualifications. Both, however, are now well-qualified lobbyists for contractors who are seeking lucrative government contracts for emergency services. Most damaging for FEMA during the Bush Administration was demoting the agency from Cabinet level rank, and putting it deep into the new Homeland Security mega-agency. An executive branch management ideology that perceives emergency management as a patronage opportunity and as a source for lucrative no bid contracts for companies aligned with its political party has put politics before administration.

At the same time, adopting a federalism model that stresses the reserved powers of states and the limited role and power of the national government also contributes to poorly coordinated emergency management efforts and a slow response time to evacuation and disaster assistance. How do we reduce the danger to human life during disasters? Again, a best selling emergency management textbook states that "The most effective means of reducing danger to human lives is evacuation" (Alexander, 2002: 149). According to a popular saying, "When you are hanging upside down from your seatbelts in a rolled-over SUV, the last thing you care about is the name on the decal on the side of the emergency vehicle" (Kettl, 2005: 9). Evacuation is critical when a category IV hurricane is approaching a city situated below sea level and protected by dikes that were designed for only a category III hurricane, and citizens who are in harms way do not care about government boundaries or theories of federalism. "FEMA doesn't evacuate communities, FEMA does not do law enforcement, FEMA does not do communication," Michael Brown defiantly told Congress (Gardner, 2006). Brown was wrong: FEMA worked with state and local officials during the Hurricane Floyd evacuation, and James Lee Witt was personally at the scene.

When you are being taken out of harms way, the last thing you care about is the decal on the side of the rescue bass boat. The picket fence model of federalism, where the national, state, and local governments all cooperate on public policy programs, gave way to a nostalgic return to decentralized national government, and a concern for the reserved power of states. Michael Brown's statements about what FEMA "does not do" indicates a concern for ideology over coordination of services among three levels of government. It is true that FEMA does not own fire trucks, ambulances, and does not do law enforcement, communications, or evacuations: however, it does coordinate these services on a regional basis during disasters and emergencies.

In Donald Kettl's research report entitled, "The worst is yet to come," his title refers to a test of our country's homeland security system. Kettl concludes that September 11 and Katrina show that there are deep problems in the performance of American government (Kettl, 2005a: 16). The conclusions are that FEMA's performance problems were due to a nostalgic, ideological embrace of an inter-governmental relations federalism model that undermines the cooperation among national, state, and local governments during emergencies and disasters. At the same time, the Bush administration abandoned the best practices model of the Clinton administration and allowed FEMA to once again descend into a trash heap of unqualified and marginally qualified minor political operatives who destroyed the morale of career employees, drove career employees to early retirement, and were human obstacles when action had to be taken to save lives during our nation's greatest natural disaster. Unless FEMA has a political purge, undergoes management reform and embraces once again a picket fence approach to federalism and inter-governmental relations, most certainly "the worst is yet to come."

References

Alexander, D. 2002. *Principles of Emergency Planning and Management.* Oxford University Press, Oxford, England.

Bovard, J. 2005. The Floyd Fiasco. American Spectator. www.jimbovard.com.

FEMA. 2005. Federal Emergency Management Agency, About FEMA. www.fema.gov/about/history.

Fox News. 2005. Brown defends FEMA response, September, 28. www.foxnews.com.

Gardner, T. 2006. Brown accepts more blame on Katrina. Associated Press, January 19. www.yahoo.news.

Haddow, G.D. and Bullock, J.A. 2003. *Introduction to Emergency Management.* Butterworth Heinemann, Boston, Massachusetts.

Jordan, L.L. 2005. Brown blames dysfunctional Louisiana, Associated Press, www.breitbart.com/news.

Kettl, D.F. 2005a. The worst is yet to come: Lesson from September 11 and Hurricane Katrina. Fels Government Research Service, Report 05-01, University of Pennsylvania, Fels Institute of Government.

Kettl, D.F. 2005b. Bush longs for James Lee Witt. www.slate.com.

Klinenberg, E. and Frank, T. 2005. Looting Homeland Security. *Rolling Stone,* Issue 990/991.

Maranto, R. 2005. *Beyond a Government of Strangers: How Career Executives and Political Appointees Can Turn Conflict to Cooperation.* Lexington Books, Lanham, Maryland.

Meserve, J. 2006. FEMA failed to accept Katrina help, Documents Say. Cable News Network, January 30. www.cnn.com.

Sauter, M.A. and Carafano, J.J. 2005. *Homeland Security: A Complete Guide to Understanding, Preventing, and Surviving Terrorism.* McGraw-Hill, New York.

Walker, D.B. 1981. *Toward a Functioning Federalism.* Winthrop Publishers. Cambridge, Massachusetts.

Wamsley, G.L., Schroeder, A.D., and Lane, L.M. 1996. To politicize is not to control: The pathologies of control in Federal Emergency Management. *American Review of Public Administration.* September 26, 263–285.

Waugh, W.L. and Sylves, R.T. 1990. *Cities and Disasters: North American Studies in Emergency Management.* Charles C. Thomas, Springfield, Illinois.

Waugh, W.L. 2000. *Living with Hazards, Dealing with Disasters: An Introduction to Emergency Management.* M.E. Sharpe, Armonk, New York.

Witt, J.L. 2005. Interview with Frontline, September 16, 2005. www.pbs.org.

Chapter 4

Katrina and Her Waves: Presidential Leadership and Disaster Management in an Intergovernmental Context

Brian J. Gerber and David B. Cohen

CONTENTS

Introduction: Presidents, the Federal Government, and the Politics of Disasters

> I don't think anybody anticipated the breach of the levees.
>
> —President George W. Bush, September 1, 2005, ABC's *Good Morning America*

> There currently is no defense against a surge from a major storm, a category 4 or category 5 hurricane. . . . Such storms can generate surges of 20 to 30 feet above sea level—enough to top any levee in south Louisiana.
>
> —*The Times-Picayune Special Report*, June 23, 2002

Hurricane Katrina was the worst natural disaster in modern American history. The slow-moving category 3 hurricane came ashore on August 29, 2005, pummeled the Gulf Coast and, due to the flooding that followed, drowned a major American city. When the rain ended and the flood waters eventually subsided, Katrina killed around 1500 people and caused immense damage to the Gulf Coast states of Louisiana, Mississippi, and to a lesser extent Alabama. When completed, the cleanup and recovery will be unprecedented in terms of scale and cost.[*] Katrina also resulted in the largest emergency migration in American history—over 1.2 million residents of the Gulf Coast moved just days and hours before the storm made landfall (Nigg et al. 2006). Many of the casualties from Katrina came from among those underprivileged populations who did not have the means to leave. If they survived, many were left homeless (Cutter and Emrich 2006).

As tragic as the initial casualties were from the winds and storm surge, perhaps more shocking about the entire Katrina episode is the poor government response—at all levels—in the aftermath of Katrina's landfall.[†] When President George W. Bush told a national audience on *Good Morning America* three days after Katrina came ashore that "I don't think anybody anticipated the breach of the levees," he was simply wrong. For years, researchers, journalists, and even the U.S. Army Corps of Engineers had predicted the flood that would destroy New Orleans (see Select

---

[*] The Bush White House estimates that Katrina caused $96 billion in damage (Townsend 2006: 7), but other independent estimates reach as high as $200 billion (Burby 2006).

[†] The sustained winds from Katrina were measured at 121 mph upon landfall creating a storm surge that reached 27 feet (Select Bipartisan Committee 2006).

Bipartisan Committee 2006). The Bush administration's lack of foresight on the levee issue is emblematic of a greater disconnect between the Bush White House and the tragedy of Katrina. Bush failed in his role as symbolic leader during the Katrina crisis. The appearance of a president woefully out of touch with the events of the Gulf Coast could not be revived even after he cut short his extended vacation in Crawford, Texas. By then, the damage, both to the Gulf Coast and to Bush's leadership image, had already been done (see Barnes 2005).

Bush's failures on the symbolic leadership front are important, but extend well beyond that. Perhaps even more significant are larger issues of managerial competence and decisions over key policy questions.

Since local governments are the first entities to respond to a natural calamity disaster management is often viewed as primarily a local and state responsibility. The progression of responsibilities of local-to-state-to-federal is the model applied for most disaster events (e.g., tornadoes, floods, chemical spills/releases). But hurricanes, particularly those on the size and scale of Katrina, produce so much damage, both in terms of human and economic costs, that there is an expectation that the federal government intervene in the response and recovery effort. According to the National Response Plan (NRP), events like Hurricane Katrina are supposed to be classified as an incident of national significance (INS) thus triggering a federal response. The fact that the secretary of Homeland Security, Michael Chertoff, waited until two days after Katrina stuck to designate Katrina an INS significantly delayed the federal response and exacerbated the image of a White House that was clearly not paying attention to the events on the Gulf Coast (Select Bipartisan Committee 2006).

While Bush, Chertoff, and Federal Emergency Management Agency (FEMA) Director Michael Brown all have been thoroughly criticized for their lack of leadership and managerial competence, there is also a broader policy-making context that bears great relevance to the inadequate federal response to Katrina. Recognizing the presidential role in federal disaster management and wishing to make the emergency management system more efficient, President Jimmy Carter issued Executive Order 12148 on July 20, 1979, creating FEMA as a stand-alone executive agency (Sylves and Cumming 2004). Recognizing the significance of both the presidential role in disaster management and the importance of an effective federal response to presidential power, President Bill Clinton elevated the FEMA director (James Lee Witt at the time) to cabinet-level status. Demonstrating FEMA's standing in the Clinton administration, President Clinton is reported to have told cabinet members to give Witt "anything he wants" (Cannon and Harris 2005). The prominence afforded FEMA under Clinton abruptly evaporated with the incoming Bush administration—a policy shift that was made even more pronounced when, following the events of 9/11, FEMA was rolled into the new Department of Homeland Security (DHS). This was a conscious policy choice that has resulted in FEMA being significantly downgraded in status, especially regarding disaster preparedness efforts that became well established under Witt. The decision, which we describe below as a move to something quite similar to the pre-Carter civil defense approach to disaster management, was made despite concerns from academics, journalists, and homeland security specialists alike about potential adverse consequences (see Cannon and Harris 2005; Hollis 2005). Early assessments of the Katrina response suggest that altering FEMA's mission focus in this way has hampered its effectiveness in dealing with a natural disaster such as Katrina (Schneider 2005).

We use the Hurricane Katrina disaster as a vehicle for addressing presidential performance on disaster policy and disaster management. We are specifically interested in this question: What factors explain presidential performance on disaster policy and disaster management? We argue that it is necessary to link presidential disaster management performance to a president's approach to governance generally and to the more focused issue of how presidents define the mission of federal disaster management. We highlight the utility of considering these two critical factors in how a president approaches three key functional roles in disaster politics and policy: president as symbolic leader, as policy initiator, and as administrative manager. Before examining how and why presidents perform as they do in those functional capacities, we also provide a general overview of a president's power potential can be as a policy-making leader.

Giving attention to presidential performance is justifiable because while disaster management policy making and implementation in the United States encompass a vast array of local, state, federal, nonprofit, and key private stakeholders, presidents critically shape disaster policy and management in three key ways. First, while the disaster management system in the United States is enormously complex and decentralized, atop it sits the federal government with FEMA, as a part of DHS, functioning as the lead agency. While disaster response is in the first instance a local and then a state responsibility, if a disaster of sufficient magnitude occurs, the federal government provides coordination and material resources that localities and states are often unable to manage or produce themselves. The president is ultimately responsible for the federal government's ability to guide and direct the intergovernmental disaster management system. Second, as an elaboration of the first point, it is important to note that FEMA is best understood as a mostly presidential agency (Sylves and Cumming 2004). As such, presidents have direct influence over specific activities of the lead federal agency in all phases of disaster management. Third, while critical resources flow to state and local governments from presidential decisions, most obviously in the instance of a disaster declaration, presidents can have a much broader impact on the disaster management system by initiating policies and programs that shape not only the actions internally to key federal agencies, but also more importantly by shaping incentives for preparedness and mitigation planning and response and recovery coordination throughout the entire intergovernmental system.

These three reasons are even more significant when one considers two important trends that suggest that presidents will become even more, not less, directly relevant to disaster management in the United States, at least for the foreseeable future. One trend is the widely acknowledged steady pattern of increasing federal importance across all phases of the management of natural or man-made disasters (see Platt 1999). Although the creation of DHS complicates the core mission of FEMA, the focus on terrorism as an element of all-hazards management has two key implications. One is an even greater relevance of federal priorities in hazards planning at the state and local level. For better or worse, hazards planning activities are influenced by a federal interest in terrorism preparedness in that key grant programs have made such considerations tied to funding. Another is that post-9/11, 2001, the NRP, and the National Incident Management System (NIMS) place federal officials at the center of planning and response efforts to deal with catastrophic incidents, including potential terror attacks, and natural or technological disasters. As a result, recent changes to the national disaster management system have strengthened the importance of federal officials in coordinating response and recovery efforts.

A second trend is that vulnerability to natural hazards is likely to increase in the foreseeable future (see Burby 2006; Cutter and Emrich 2006; Steinberg 2000). Because of this, disaster politics are likely to become woven into presidential politics even more than is the case presently. The troubles that the response to Hurricane Katrina represent for the Bush administration make it likely that other major natural disasters are going to require a more vigorous presidential response and that failure to respond adequately will be a political issue.

Disaster Management and Presidential Policy-Making Power

Our goal is to develop a framework for assessing presidential performance on disaster policy and disaster management. In our view, the most useful way to understand presidential performance on disasters is to consider the intersection of two key factors. The first is the general approach to governance taken by a given presidential administration. By "approach to governance" we mean how a president views the appropriate level of federal government activity in shaping private sector activities, the distribution of governmental authority across the federal system, the possibility of reforms in public sector management, the approach to managing the specific office of the presidency, and the priorities within the president's overall policy agenda. A president's perspective on governance is relevant to disaster management because it directly affects how the federal responsibility for disaster management is viewed. It also indicates how willing a president might be to support critical principles such as policy-forcing behavior in the area of initiating planning mandates at the state and local level, how an agency like FEMA is managed administratively, and how much a priority disaster issues might represent to a particular administration.

Although the passage of the Disaster Relief Act of 1950 is commonly viewed as a watershed moment in terms of initiating an ever-expanding level of direct federal involvement in disaster management, the Carter Administration's Reorganization Plan No. 3 of 1978 is perhaps the key benchmark in terms of an increasing importance of presidential control over federal disaster management policy. During the period from Presidents Carter to G.W. Bush, in broad terms we see two basic, competing, views of governance. Among other things, both Presidents Carter and Clinton pursued more effective and efficient public management practices as major initiatives in their presidency. These reform efforts indicate, in part, an optimistic view of the capacity of the federal government to affect positive policy change and help explain Carter's interest in creating FEMA in the first place, as well as Clinton's reinvention of it some 15 years later. This is in sharp contrast to the much more pessimistic view of federal authority from the three Republican Presidents, but Reagan and G.W. Bush especially. For instance, G.W. Bush's efforts at civil service reforms have been designed not only to improve federal administrative capacity but also to limit the policy influence and standing of public employees by increasing the amount of federal work outsourced. In that light, the Bush administration's interest in promoting more outsourcing of various program functions at FEMA and a disinterest in enhancing existing preparedness programs—efforts that may have had at least some indirect effects on the Katrina response—are not surprising.

The second factor, which traverses the first, is how presidents have approached the specific issue of defining the federal government's mission with respect to disaster management. Examining precisely how a president defines that mission for the federal government generally, and for FEMA, as the lead disaster management agency specifically, is critical. As Wilson's (1989) seminal discussion of bureaucracy makes clear, the way in which an agency's mission is defined or framed is essential to its substantive performance.

Just as there are two broadly coherent but competing views of governance between the Democratic and Republican presidents, there is a similarly distinct view of what the federal government's primary functional role in disaster management policy specifically should be. This encompasses the issue of where primary policy making and administrative responsibilities should lie. The disaster management system in the United States that we see today largely grew out of the civil defense preparedness system developed in the 1950s and 1960s. Not surprisingly then, one view of the core mission of the federal government on natural or technological disasters closely parallels the original civil defense perspective. The logic of the Civil Defense Act of 1950 was that the responsibility for civil defense in the event of an attack from an external enemy* would be vested in state and local government. The federal government would take on the more limited role of mobilization in the event of a major attack. In its historic origins, the civil defense perspective conceives of the federal government as a limited partner for catastrophic events with respect to state and local responsibilities (May 1985).

The Reagan administration adopted the view that the mission and scope of federal actions on disaster events should be limited in scope—with the exception that particular attention should be paid to how the federal government would respond to a military attack and how the federal government could promote state

---

* With a nuclear attack from the Soviet Union being the paradigmatic threat.

and local preparedness for such an event. This view has resurfaced in the G.W. Bush administration. The Bush approach to FEMA has been to de-emphasize or alter key activities initiated during the Clinton administration. With the transition of FEMA into the development finance institutions (DFIs), the agency has moved away from a focus on promoting preparedness and mitigation in the area of natural and techno-logical hazards. FEMA's preparedness functions have been largely eliminated under DHS Secretaries, Tom Ridge and Chertoff, and shifted to other areas of DHS. In essence, the G.W. Bush administration, post-9/11, has returned to the civil defense model where the federal government's lead disaster management agency is geared toward dealing with an external attack threat, with a catastrophic terrorist event replacing the Soviet nuclear attack threat. In other words, building its antiterrorism capabilities has occurred at the expense of promoting preparedness for natural disasters, as evidenced by a dramatic shift in the substantive focus of FEMA preparedness grants to antiterrorism efforts (see Schneider 2005).

However, while using the civil defense model as a means of orienting the national emergency management system, and especially its lead agency, it is important to recognize that from 1950 to the mid-1970s, the civil defense model functioned poorly in terms of achieving its stated purpose. Specifically, there was limited capacity for, and commitment to, civil defense preparedness at the state and local level (May and Williams 1986). Without adequate resources (financial and administrative expertise) many subnational governments lacked the ability to effectively develop and implement policies such as crisis relocation planning (May and Williams 1986). Moreover, many subnational governments did not necessarily agree with various civil defense policy objectives, making policy commitment uneven across the United States (May 1985). In the early 1970s, civil defense officials began informally promoting the idea of a dual-use approach where civil defense program funds could be utilized for nonattack-related disaster preparedness. Although the Ford Administration actually curtailed this practice on the grounds that state and local government should shoulder the financial responsibilities of natural disaster preparedness, Congress acted by amend-ing the Civil Defense Act to codify the dual-use approach and permit civil defense program hinds to be used in disaster response and recovery (May and Williams 1986).

Recognition that the existing civil defense model as an approach to promoting state and local emergency/disaster preparedness could be made more effective by explicitly promoting a dual-use perspective contributed to the Carter reorganization plan that created FEMA. As one of the core principles motivating the creation of FEMA through the reorganization, defining the mission of FEMA and other federal agencies as one of promoting what is today referred to as an all-hazards management approach across local, state, and federal governments is a competing view to the civil defense model.* Carter's emphasis on dual-use, or all-hazards, received a much fuller

---

* Other core principles included a desire for greater executive control over any federal response to a civil emergency or disaster as well as a desire for greater efficiency in the use of federal resources.

expression in the Clinton presidency.* Moreover, the all-hazards emphasis of Clinton included a greater emphasis on mitigation and preparedness; along with a stronger intergovernmental framework and development of closer public–private partnerships (see Schneider 1998). Under the leadership of Director Witt, FEMA was a strong positive example of the Clinton administration's reinvention approach to governance.

Presidents as Policy Makers

Presidential scholars have often debated the role of the president in the policy-making arena. Some have argued that, as a consequence of being embedded in the institutional framework of the U.S. system, presidential power is shared and dependent upon other institutional actors. This emphasis on institutional constraints on presidential policy making can be termed a shared power model. The thesis of this model is that because a president's power is shared with, or constrained by, other institutional and noninstitutional actors such as Congress, the judiciary, state and local governments, public opinion, the media, and the constitution, presidential policy-making power is quite circumscribed.

Neustadt's (1960) assertion that "presidential power is the power to persuade" is perhaps most illustrative of this approach. In his seminal work, Neustadt notes that a president's persuasion power is contingent on a president's Washington credibility and professional reputation. Thus, presidents are, at times, at the mercy of both Washington elites and public opinion. Though Kernell's (1997) "going public" thesis is often juxtaposed with Neustadt's, Kernell also sets forth a model in which presidential power and policy success are impacted by a president's ability to move public opinion. Thus, both Neustadt and Kernell, and others in the shared power school, project an image of presidential power that is contingent on acquiring assent from other institutional actors—presidents are constrained in what they can do on their own and unilateral executive policy making is quite limited (see also Edwards 1983; Jones 1999; Light 1999; Rose 1991; Seligman and Covington 1989).

In contrast to the shared power model of presidential policy making is the unilateral actor model. This school of thought argues that presidents have an impressive arsenal of formal powers which can be used unilaterally—i.e., with either minimal input or without the consent of other institutional (e.g., Congress) or noninstitutional (e.g., public opinion) actors. Though some unilateral powers of the president can be overturned subsequent to their use[†] such authority allows

---

* To be clear, we are not arguing that *only* Carter and Clinton subscribed to an all-hazards approach, For instance, Reagan essentially accepted the dual-use premise—but his administration was much more focused on the traditional Cold War external military threat and emphasized a limited policy responsibility for the federal government for nonmilitary disasters (see May 1985).

[†] For instance, executive orders can be overturned by the courts or Congress.

presidents to make policy quickly and decisively. Nathan's (1976, 1983) work suggests the possibilities for unilateral action through administrative procedures like reorganization initiatives or central clearance. The literature examining unilateral tools has tended to focus on somewhat higher visibility actions such as executive orders (see Gleiber and Shull 1992; Krause and Cohen 1997; Mayer 1999, 2001; Morgan 1987). Cooper (1986, 2002), however, has tended to emphasize administrative actions that generally produce less attention, such as signing statements, proclamations, internal agency memoranda (that instruct policy actions), and presidential directives, arguing that those powers give a president direct control over policy making.

Durant (1992) and Waterman (1989) show that even with the potential for unilateral policy making via administrative actions, the use of those tools is meaningfully shaped by political contingencies such as the preferences (and their relative intensity) of other important actors in a policy domain. This raises a general question: what are the conditions under which presidents are likely to use some combination of persuasive and unilateral policy-making tools at their disposal? It also raises the particular question: how and why do presidents combine such tools in the pursuit of disaster management policies?

It is essential to recognize that the two lines of argument on the shared power and unilateral power perspectives are not mutually exclusive. In fact, the policy-making resources (encompassing both formal and informal powers) of the presidency can be located on a continuum ranging from a relatively high degree of autonomy over the policy action taken (such as appointments) to a relatively low degree of autonomy (such as introducing legislation or tackling a policy question through the courts). In other words, there are significant constraints on a president's ability to control policy making when presidents attempt to use certain channels (e.g., legislation, gaining public support for policies) that also happen to be quite visible to the public.* But other channels of policy making, while less visible (i.e., typically drawing little, or at least less, public attention), are equally important because they afford presidents a greater level of control over the nature of the policy action undertaken.

The alternatives to securing passage of new legislation or public support can be thought of as "under-the-radar" tactics in shaping policy because only the most attentive of publics are aware of their substance and use. These tools include judicial actions, such as an administration initiating a lawsuit to enforce a regulatory statute or an administration settling an existing lawsuit on terms favorable to the regulated private interest. Enforcement or implementation decisions signified by internal agency memoranda that instruct an agency to behave in a particular way, or efforts to "counter-staff" an agency through political appointments of individuals to change the mission and task orientation of a bureaucracy, are also critically important

---

* Those two policy-making channels typically have been the focus of much research on the president as policy actor.

tactics for policy change. Although some rulemaking proposals garner significant public attention, most rulemaking efforts that interpret or reinterpret a statute garner little mass public attention and sometimes only limited attention by affected interests (see Kerwin 1994; Martino-Golden 1998). The use of executive orders, on the other hand, is sometimes promoted by an administration as a major policy-making initiative—sometimes controversially so. The furor over President Clinton's proposed executive order to allow openly homosexual individuals to serve in the military makes evident that some administrative tactics such as executive orders are neither absolute, politically costless, nor free from public scrutiny. In general, though, most executive orders do not invite significant amounts of public attention. We take up the question of how presidents utilize their policy-making resources in terms of influencing the politics and policy of disasters next.

Presidents as Policy Makers on Disaster Management

Natural disaster management system in the United States is structured, in its ideal form, as a bottom-up model where local governments are in charge of first response. Because a natural or technological disaster occurs in a specific geographic area, the local government of jurisdiction has the primary responsibility for managing the event. A defined series of steps occur before state, and then federal, agencies become involved if local authorities are unable to adequately manage the situation. State governments provide a policy framework within which local governments develop response plans; they also provide a large framework for coordination of resources across a state to deal with a disaster. When state and local governments are overwhelmed by a disaster, the federal government likewise provides financial resources and other assets relevant to response and recovery. Schneider (1995: 35–37) points out that the disaster response system operates with six key assumptions: natural disaster events are limited to relatively specific geographic areas; all three levels of government will work together in concert to manage a disaster event; all governmental units take their response obligations seriously; the broader response system, the network of responsibilities, is apparent and understood by all parties; FEMA will hold state and local governments accountable for their response and recovery decisions; and finally, other relevant parties, such as aid-providing nonprofits, understand the operation of the disaster response system.

This is an ideal characterization of how the system should function. Schneider (1995: 37) points out that in reality, the governmental response system is "disconnected, uncoordinated, underfunded, and discredited." There are a variety of reasons for this negative characterization, but as Burby and May have discussed in a variety of settings (Burby 2006; May 1985; May and Burby 1996; May and Williams 1986) developing a combination of adequate administrative capacity at all levels of government, especially among subnational actors, and commitment to policy goals such as preparedness and hazard mitigation is an enormously difficult challenge. There exist a variety of disincentives that face subnational governments in accepting the responsibility of adopting serious hazard management programs, such as pressures to promote development in hazard-prone areas or the belief that federal assistance will make up for gaps in funding emergency/disaster management systems.

In this context presidential efforts at shaping the policy direction of not only a few select federal agencies but also the intergovernmental disaster management system become important. From a historical perspective, over 200 years, the federal government has increased its visibility and responsibilities in the area of emergency management. Since 1803, when the U.S. Congress authorized federal resources to assist the city of Portsmouth, New Hampshire recover from a deadly fire, the federal government has been assisting state and local governments respond and recover from disasters. The Great Labor Day Hurricane of 1935 demonstrated that even a popular president like Franklin D. Roosevelt could not escape criticism if the federal government appeared slow to react in the face of a calamity (Glover 2005). The category 5 storm, the strongest hurricane ever recorded, killed over 400 people, most of whom were unemployed World War I veterans who were sent by the Roosevelt administration to build a highway in the Florida Keys. Franklin D. Roosevelt and his administration were excoriated by critics for being slow to react to warnings and failing to get the veterans out in time (Steinberg 2000).

By 1950, the federal government had provided resources to states and localities over 100 times for the purposes of natural disaster response and recovery (Townsend 2006). Though case-by-case in nature, the federal role during this era became rather obligatory. In 1953, President Dwight Eisenhower formalized the presidential role in emergency management when he issued the first presidential declaration of a disaster regarding damage from tornadoes in Georgia. From 1953 to 2002, there have been 1448 presidential disaster declarations and from 1974 to 2002, 178 emergency declarations, demonstrating that presidents and the federal government do indeed exercise their authority in disaster management (Sylves and Cumming 2004). The key issue then is to examine the specifics of the presidential role in disaster management. As noted above, there are three key functional roles that characterize presidential actions in this policy area.

Presidents as Symbolic Leader

President George W. Bush received high marks for his actions in the immediate aftermath of 9/11 from journalists and citizens alike. This despite the circuitous route Air Force One traveled to return to Washington and despite lingering in Emma Booker Elementary School in Sarasota, Florida reading *My Pet Goat* to grade school children in the midst of the tragic events of that day. Bush's speech to the nation that evening from the Oval Office was his first real test as a symbolic leader during a crisis. He reassured the public that the "The functions of our government continue without interruption. Federal agencies in Washington which had to be evacuated today are reopening for essential personnel tonight, and will be open for business tomorrow."* Bush passed his first test with flying colors: his approval rating soared and the country was unified in the belief that the United States would respond to terrorism and would survive and thrive in the aftermath of the deadly attacks (Hetherington and Nelson 2003).

The events of 9/11 highlighted the president's symbolic management role. Eulau and Karps define symbolic management (or what they term symbolic responsiveness) as "public gestures of a sort that create a sense of trust and support in the relationship between representative and represented" (Eulau and Karps 1977: 241). Thus, one of the many challenges for a president during a crisis is to "project an image that the President is truly the people's representative and ready to be responsive to them" (Eulau and Karps 1977: 247).[†] We argue that the president's symbolic role is actually composed of two significant leadership responsibilities during a crisis: *captain of the ship* and *mourner-in-chief*. We examine both roles below in the context of the Katrina crisis.

The president as captain of the ship is a symbolic leadership role which demonstrates that a president is fully in charge of the federal government during times of crisis. His task is to build confidence in the public-at-large, as well as within the federal bureaucracy and other levels of government, that he has everything under control and will ensure that the federal government's response will be swift, efficient, and effective. The captain's role requires that the president appear engaged, focused, and willing to make quick but good decisions.

The mourner-in-chief role, on the other hand, is "part preacher, part psychologist, a kind of comforter-in-chief-that falls within the job description of modern presidents" (Cannon 2003). Particularly in the television age, presidents are expected to comfort or calm the nation during times of crisis and to put the specific tragedy in perspective for a grieving nation.

During 9/11, Bush mastered both the captain and mourner roles. Bush played the mourner role well, placing the 9/11 tragedy into context, and vowing a rapid and sustained American response. Bush as captain was focused, engaged, and not shy of making quick decisions with little regret. This management style was appreciated by an American public desperate for fast action and a decisive leader. The federal bureaucracy responded to Bush's symbolic leadership as the country as a whole, swept up in a wave of patriotism, rallied around their leader (Hetherington and Nelson 2003).

The same cannot be said for Bush as symbolic leader during the Katrina crisis. Though Bush had essentially the same resources at his disposal at his Crawford,

---

* "Statement by the President in His Address to the Nation." September 11, 2001. http://whitehouse.gov/releases/2001/09/20010911–16html. Viewed April 15, 2006.

† Though their research focuses on congressional representation, the typology Eulau and Karps (1977) develop can easily apply to presidents and other chief executives as well.

Texas ranch as he did at the White House, the fact that Bush stayed on his month long vacation as Katrina was driving toward the Gulf Coast was a huge public relations error. In fact, Bush made only one public statement about Katrina before the hurricane made landfall in a speech dedicated to Iraq's draft constitution. Bush spent only three short paragraphs of the fifteen paragraph speech discussing Katrina; he quickly discussed the steps he had taken to allow federal disaster assistance to begin flowing and then moved to reassure a jittery American populace:

> Yesterday, I signed a disaster declaration for the state of Louisiana, and this morning I signed a disaster declaration for the state of Mississippi. These declarations will allow federal agencies to coordinate all disaster relief efforts with state and local officials. We will do everything in our power to help the people in the communities affected by this storm.*

Katrina struck on August 29. Just a few hours after Katrina made landfall and at the very time that the levees in New Orleans were failing, Bush was participating in a town hall meeting in Arizona on the topic of Medicare. During the lengthy session, Bush briefly tried to reassure residents of the battered Gulf Coast: "Our Gulf Coast is getting hit and hit hard. I want the folks there on the Gulf Coast to know that the federal government is prepared to help you when the storm passes."†

The following day Bush traveled to San Diego to commemorate the 60th anniversary of V-J Day. Again, in another lengthy address, Katrina merited two paragraphs. Bush did not return to Washington until the following day, August 31. On his way back, he ordered the pilot to fly over the Gulf Coast so he "could see firsthand the scope and magnitude of the devastation."‡ This brief flyover and the president's delayed return to Washington, DC resulted in a great deal of criticism. Emblematic of the criticism, Cannon (2005: 2722) observed:

> Bush had been in office only months on 9/11, and Americans set partisanship aside and rallied behind him...When the levees failed late Monday morning, Bush was heading to California from Arizona in the final week of a long working vacation. As New Orleans filled with water on Tuesday, Bush delivered a speech commemorating the anniversary of V-J Day, then headed back to Crawford ahead of schedule.

---

* "President Discusses Hurricane Katrina, Congratulates Iraqis on Draft Constitution." August 28, 2005, http://www.whitehouse.gov/news/releases/2005/08/20050828–1.html. Viewed April 15, 2006.

† "President Participates in Conversation on Medicare." August 29, 2005. http://whitehouse.gov/news/releases/2005/08/20050829–5.html. Viewed April 15, 2006.

‡ "President Outlines Hurricane Katrina Relief Efforts." August 31, 2005, http://www.whitehouse.gov/news/releases/2005/08/20050831–1.html. Viewed April 15, 2006.

White House press secretary Scott McClellan announced that Bush's vacation was being cut short. The following day, Wednesday, Bush ordered Air Force One to fly low over the damaged areas as he flew back to Washington. Bush's two subsequent trips to the Gulf Coast didn't dampen the developing consensus: Bush was out of touch, FEMA was back to its bureaucratic ways, and the federal government, despite ample warning, had not responded rapidly, efficiently, or humanely enough to an unprecedented disaster on America's own shores.

On the day of his arrival back in Washington, Bush gathered the Cabinet together and addressed the media in the Rose Garden. It was the first major address Bush gave on the topic of Katrina. With his Cabinet surrounding him Bush began by describing the devastation to the Gulf Coast. He then commented

> The people in the affected regions expect the federal government to work with the state government and local government with an effective response. I have directed Secretary of Homeland Security Mike Chertoff to chair a Cabinet-level task force to coordinate all our assistance from Washington. FEMA Director Mike Brown is in charge of all federal response and recovery efforts in the field. I've instructed them to work closely with state and local officials, as well as with the private sector, to ensure that we're helping, not hindering, recovery efforts. This recovery will take a long time. This recovery will take years.*

By the time Bush arrived back at the White House, his reputation as a decisive, engaged leader, fully in charge during times of crisis, had suffered an enormous hit. Barnes (2005: 2807), a journalist for the *National Journal*, observed at the time that

> What's been really weakened by the inadequate government response to Katrina and by Bush's own reaction to the crisis is the public's perception of his leadership qualities—arguably the calling card of his presidency. Measured against the resolve that Bush demonstrated after the 9/11 attacks, his performance in the immediate aftermath of Katrina seems, to much of the public, like a faint echo.

Public opinion data supports the proposition that the public was disappointed with Bush's symbolic leadership. Shortly after 9/11, two-thirds of respondents in a CBS News poll expressed a lot of confidence in President Bush contrasted with just

---

* "President Participates in Conversation on Medicare." August 29, 2005, http://www.white house.gov/news/releases/2005/08/20050829–5.html, Viewed April 15, 2006.

one-third in a CBS News poll conducted one week after Katrina (Barnes 2005). A Pew Research Center poll conducted on September 6–7, 2005, echoes this sentiment as only 28 percent of respondents believe that Bush "did all he could to get relief efforts going quickly" and only 38 percent approved the way Bush was handling the Katrina crisis.

In perhaps his most significant speech about Katrina, Bush traveled to Jackson Square in New Orleans to deliver a prime time nationally televised address. Bush began the speech utilizing the rhetoric of the mourner-in-chief:

> In the aftermath [of Katrina], we have seen fellow citizens left stunned and uprooted, searching for loved ones, and grieving for the dead, and looking for meaning in a tragedy that seems so blind and random. We've also witnessed the kind of desperation no citizen of this great and generous nation should ever have to know—fellow Americans calling out for food and water, vulnerable people left at the mercy of criminals who had no mercy, and the bodies of the dead lying uncovered and untended in the street. These days of sorrow and outrage have also been marked by acts of courage and kindness that make all Americans proud Across the Gulf Coast, among people who have lost much, and suffered much, and given to the limit of their power, we are seeing . . . a core of strength that survives all hurt, a faith in God no storm can take away, and a powerful American determination to clear the ruins and build better than before. Tonight so many victims of the hurricane and the flood are far from home and friends and familiar things. You need to know that our whole nation cares about you, and in the journey ahead you're not alone. To all who carry a burden of loss, I extend the deepest sympathy of our country. To every person who has served and sacrificed in this emergency, I offer the gratitude of our country. And tonight I also offer this pledge of the American people: Throughout the area hit by the hurricane, we will do what it takes, we will stay as long as it takes, to help citizens rebuild their communities and their lives. And all who question the future of the Crescent City need to know there is no way to imagine America without New Orleans, and this great city will rise again.[*]

The rest of the speech was filled with a laundry list of steps the federal government had taken at the behest of the President, as well as various tasks Bush hoped to achieve in the next several months. Most of the items on the laundry list remain unfinished. Two years later much of the city of New Orleans, for example, remains

---

[*] "President Discusses Hurricane Relief in Address to the Nation." September 15, 2005. http://www.whitehouse.gov/news/releases/2005/09/20050915–8.html. Viewed April 15, 2006.

covered by debris and rubble. Despite Bush's goal "to get people out of the shelters by the middle of October," thousands of Gulf Coast residents are still living in government housing (see Singer 2006).

Presidents as Policy Initiator

As we discussed earlier, a president has a long list of tools by which to shape policy—beyond the role of providing symbolic leadership or simply trying to persuade the Congress on a legislative proposal. A president can utilize a variety of formal mechanisms to initiate policy changes that affect the federal government's ability to manage the preparedness, mitigation, response, and recovery phases of a disaster. These include defining new policy goals or revisions of existing policy via executive orders, regulatory changes, agency reorganization, budgetary changes, and making key appointments to influence agency behavior.

The power of reorganization can lead to significant, substantive policy changes. Three cases of reorganization illustrate the extent to which a president can influence the direction of the federal role in disaster management. The importance of Carter's reorganization creating FEMA in the first, discussed briefly above, is obvious in that it helped create a clearly defined lead federal agency, as opposed to the uncoordinated set of programs across a variety of departments and agencies. A similarly important reorganization occurred when G.W. Bush made the decision to include FEMA within DHS. Two consequences of that decision are likely to have adverse long-term consequences for FEMA's ability to manage federal disaster responsibilities. First, as noted above, placing FEMA within a department whose mission is focused primarily on antiterrorism complicates FEMA's own sense of mission, to the detriment of natural or technological preparedness activities. Second, the loss of prestige and operational control by reducing the FEMA director's status from its previous cabinet-level is an impediment to a director's ability to motivate other administrative agencies to work cooperatively to coordinate actions.

While the creation of FEMA and its relocation are major illustrations of the importance of a president's ability to shape policy through reorganization, other reorganization efforts that are not widely known can produce major policy shifts. For example, after President Clinton appointed James Lee Witt director of FEMA, Witt created a new mitigation directorate that became responsible for directing and coordinating most of FEMA's mitigation programs across a wide range of hazards (Platt 1999). Creating that unit was important because it provided a stronger administrative framework for launching a more proactive effort on promoting mitigation strategies throughout the intergovernmental system. The mitigation directorate produced a National Mitigation Strategy in December of 1995, which represented at least a major symbolic step forward in using a federal agency to promote behavioral changes on disaster issues among state and local governments as well as key private sector stakeholders. While a shortcoming of the strategy was a deficiency in moving beyond broad principles, it did set the stage for another Clinton Administration effort, Project Impact, whose aim was to promote disaster-resistant communities through a more extensive use of public–private partnerships than had previously been attempted (see Platt 1999).

Presidential appointments represent another mechanism by which a president can choose to pursue specific policy goals. Two points about appointments are key: first, political appointments signal the relative degree of priority that an agency or policy domain represents to an administration—which is also reiterated by the type of political support afforded those appointees; second, as noted above, FEMA is an agency that historically has been highly/primarily responsive to the White House directly, rather than Congress. As to the latter point, this is significant in that it gives a president much greater leverage over the actual operations of the lead federal agency on disasters as compared to other administrative agencies that may have strong legislative constituencies that might complicate efforts at presidential control. As to the former point, the type of symbolic and substantive priority given to a FEMA director and top staff is essential to how effectively FEMA might function in working with other federal agencies, especially given its lack of size (relatively few employees and small budgets) and its lack of direct regulatory authority.

For instance, FEMA under Director Witt is widely acclaimed as having achieved a great deal of success in transforming the capacity of FEMA to operate as an effective agency. In part this success can be attributed to the fact that because of President Clinton's known support, the "White House political office and key staff regularly protected and defended FEMA, something seldom done by White House staffs of previous presidents" (Sylves and Cumming 2004). By contrast, given that the Reagan and G.H.W. Bush administrations general approach to disaster management could be labeled "passive federal governance" (May and Williams 1986), it is not surprising that they did not place a high priority on previous emergency management expertise in their top appointees.* Schneider (1998) notes that FEMA historically, before the Clinton administration's appointment of Witt, has had major reputational problems in terms of internal leadership, brought about in part because of the lack of appointees with actual emergency management expertise in an agency that was instead seen as a "dumping ground for political appointees" (43). The passive governance approach, where the federal government is not seen as having an appropriately proactive role to play on disasters resurfaced in the G.W. Bush administration. While the much embattled Michael Brown had no real relevant emergency management experience, perhaps an even more telling appointment was Joe Allbaugh, Bush's first FEMA director. Similarly lacking in expertise, Allbaugh pursued several organizational changes at FEMA and

---

* Indeed, for the bulk of the first Bush presidency, FEMA did not even have a permanent director.

explicitly sought to de-emphasize the Clinton-era efforts on disaster mitigation (Sylves and Cumming 2004).*

Another avenue by which a president can initiate or change policy is through the use of executive orders or other similar formal directives to an administrative agency. While some executive orders represent important policy initiatives, such as Carter's order creating FEMA, most are relatively narrow in scope and as a result draw low levels of public attention. And though the Congress might act to reverse an executive order, as might a federal court, neither event happens with any frequency, giving a president a great deal of control over the use of that tool.[†] At the same time, a president can pursue policy change by issuing a policy instruction memorandum, written to direct an administrative agency to take specific actions. Such statements guide operational activities at an agency and receive extremely limited public scrutiny. While such memoranda can have very significant policy impacts, they are also subject to virtually no constraints from other institutional actors.

In terms of disaster politics and policy, presidents frequently have used executive orders to specify policy responsibilities in terms of a particular type of hazard (see Sylves and Cumming 2004). For example, Reagan issued E.O. 12656 which spelled out the functional lines of authority for federal agencies for particular types of disaster events. Similarly, Clinton and G.W. Bush issued a series of executive orders and presidential decision directives on homeland security that have defined how the federal government should prepare for and respond to a terrorist incident.

Presidents as Administrators

The president also can serve a direct or indirect administrative management function. An obvious action in this area is disaster declaration. But presidents can also help direct incident response by using the weight and prestige of the office to guide behavior of federal subordinates, or to guide the behavior of key state or local officials. As for the latter, state or local officials might appeal directly to the White House—beyond the formal request of a disaster declaration—for direct assistance to mobilize resources throughout the intergovernmental disaster response system. Similarly, for reasons such as electoral imperatives, presidents are able and willing to make their priorities known during disaster recovery efforts, including helping speed the delivery of recovery aid. May (1985) suggests the possibility that presidents have demonstrated a greater willingness to make disaster declarations in presidential election years.

The immediately preceding discussion highlights just several ways in which presidents use specific policy-making tools to direct FEMA specifically and federal

---

* Allbaugh was Bush's Chief of Staff in Texas and 2000 Campaign Manager. He had no emergency management experience.
† Deering and Maltzman (1999) suggest, however, that presidents issue orders strategically to avoid congressional reversal, which mitigates the level of autonomy to some extent.

disaster policy more generally. But as noted earlier, a third functional area in which presidents shape disaster management is their performance of administrative tasks, which includes activities such as being involved in the federal response to a disaster. Katrina and G.W. Bush's administrative managerial performance in this regard provide a compelling negative illustration of how presidential involvement—or in this case noninvolvement—has an impact on the federal government's disaster response.

George W. Bush's management of the Katrina response cannot be characterized as anything but a failure. As Katrina struck, Bush was on vacation, as was Vice President Richard Cheney. Emblematic of the delayed response to Katrina, and indicative of a chief executive wholly out of touch with the situation in the Gulf, Bush's counselor Dan Bartlett produced a DVD with news footage for the president to watch on Air Force One before his first post-Katrina visit, so he would understand the magnitude of the devastation (Thomas 2005). For a week, while people baked in the Gulf Coast sun in places like the I-10 Cloverleaf or suffocated in the unbearable stench and humidity inside shelters like the New Orleans Superdome and Convention Center with little food or water, little federal presence on the ground could be protected. Evan Thomas succinctly summed up the national mood about the federal response three weeks after Katrina:

> How this could be—how the president of the United States could have even less "situational awareness," as they say in the military, than the average American about the worst natural disaster in a century—is one of the more perplexing and troubling chapters in a story that, despite moments of heroism and acts of great generosity, ranks as a national disgrace. (Thomas 2005)

A proactive federal response to the impending Katrina disaster was in order. A reactive federal response to disasters, known as a "pull" system, in which the federal government waits for states to make specific requests about what they need before the federal government acts, is the norm. However, a "push" system whereby the federal government preempts state government requests for assistance and pre-places resources before the crisis commences is not unprecedented (Select Bipartisan Committee 2006). Bush, Chertoff, and Brown had ample warning that Katrina would be catastrophic. Max Mayfield, director of the National Hurricane Center, bluntly warned the White House and the relevant state and local leaders about the impending doom they faced (Townsend 2006). The National Weather Service office in Slidell, Louisiana, similarly warned that levees in New Orleans would be overtopped, airborne debris would be widespread, windows would be blown out, and power and water shortages would "make human suffering incredible by modern standards" (Townsend 2006: 28). Had the White House heeded the warnings of the National Hurricane Center and the National Weather Service and initiated a push system while Katrina was still in the Gulf of Mexico—as it did a few weeks later before Hurricane Rita hit—the federal response would have been exponentially faster. Fully two days passed until DHS Secretary Chertoff declared Katrina an INS thus setting the wheels of the federal government, through the NRP, slowly grinding. Chertoff, however, never activated the Catastrophic Incident Annex (CIA) portion of the NRP that would have quickly shifted the federal response mode from a reactive pull response to a proactive push response (Select Bipartisan Committee 2006). The irony remains that the NRP-CIA was written specifically for an incident such as Katrina, yet was never activated.

The DHS had recently completed the NRP and the NIMS—blueprints for how the federal government would lead an intergovernmental response to whatever type of calamity was faced. Katrina was the first major test of the NRP, a test that failed miserably. Four days after landfall, on September 2, Bush flew to the Gulf region, ostensibly to tour hurricane damage and meet with victims, but also to powwow with Louisiana Governor Kathleen Blanco and New Orleans Mayor Ray Nagin to work out the command and control problems afflicting the intergovernmental response. A heated discussion took place aboard Air Force One at Louis Armstrong International Airport, New Orleans, in which Mayor Nagin suggested that Bush "federalize" the Louisiana National Guard troops. Although there is some disagreement over whether Bush could federalize those troops without permission, Blanco resisted the suggestion and Bush dropped the idea (Thomas 2005). A temporary takeover of state National Guard troops during a crisis is not unprecedented in American history as President Eisenhower's and Kennedy's actions during the civil rights era demonstrate. The Bush White House in this instance, however, demonstrated uncharacteristic cautiousness about legal definitions and intergovernmental jurisdictions thus slowing the governmental response even further.

Conclusion

A effective way to assess presidents and how the federal government has approached and executed disaster management practices is to consider the closely related factors of how a president's general approach to governance interacts with the more specific decision of how a president defines the policy mission of FEMA and other key federal agencies. These two factors should not be considered redundant. For instance, while G.W. Bush is conventionally understood to be a conservative president who generally favors circumscribing federal policy authority to the benefit of state government, there are many instances where he has not actually followed that approach consistently. One illustration is the No Child Left Behind Act that represents a significant expansion of the scope of federal authority into the management of education policy (see Peterson and West 2003). Another illustration more relevant to our discussion is the fact that in the aftermath of the administration's dismal performance in response to Katrina, the White House has offered a proposal to dramatically expand the federal government's role in disaster first response. Specifically, Bush's Homeland Security

Adviser Frances Townsend announced that in revising the federal response guidelines for a catastrophic event, that a larger and sometimes leading role for active duty military troops would be encompassed (see Townsend 2006: 94–96; see also Vande-Hei and White 2005). The key point is that while in a governance sense Bush is not committed to public management reforms designed to enhance federal administrative capacity, he seemingly is willing to redefine dramatically the scope of federal control in terms of disaster response.

The irony of the Bush administration's post-Katrina actions is that the White House is seeking greater federal control of disaster management, whereas pre-Katrina, natural disaster preparedness had been an afterthought. Though ostensibly dedicated to an all-hazards approach to disaster management, the Bush White House clearly favored pre-Katrina, through grant policies, administrative reorganizations, and rhetoric, a focus on terrorism preparedness and response at the expense of natural disaster preparedness and mitigation. The administration's decision not to support funds requested by the U.S. Army Corps of Engineers to improve New Orleans' levee system illustrates this point. This despite ample warnings of future levee failure by experts, including those that took part in the Hurricane Pam exercises of 2004 (see Select Bipartisan Committee 2006).

Inattention or downsizing of a federal disaster management role has been a characteristic of Republican administrations since FEMA's creation on Carter's watch. FEMA withered under the leadership of Presidents Reagan and George H.W. Bush as a reactive federal role in the disaster management policy system became institutionalized. This at a time when the beginning of the 24 hour news cycle, or what Wamsley and Schroeder (1996) term the "CNN Syndrome," began to focus a national spotlight on most disasters, no matter how local in nature. The chaos and disorder surrounding the G.H.W. Bush administration's efforts to respond to Hurricane Hugo in 1989, and to a much greater extent Hurricane Andrew in 1992, provided a valuable lesson to incoming President Bill Clinton who responded by elevating the FEMA director to Cabinet status in both formality and practice (Hollis 2005). Given the criticism George H.W. Bush received after his lackluster performance guiding the response to Andrew, it would make sense to expect George W. Bush not to have repeated the same mistakes. However, Bush's selection of an under-qualified Joe Allbaugh to initially head FEMA, along with the selection of an even more under-qualified, political-crony to replace Allbaugh in the person of Michael Brown is as clear an indication that FEMA under George W. Bush had been downgraded and politicized.

Conducting a comparative assessment of the policy priorities and actions of presidential administration over the last 30 years should be the focus of future efforts. But it is important to note that such assessment work is useful because future presidents seem likely to play an even larger role in disaster policy and politics. We have limited our efforts here to highlighting several key features of presidential policy-making power and how it can affect the disaster management system in the United States to suggest a means of providing a comparative assessment of presidential disaster management performance.

References

Barnes, J.A. 2005. A disillusioned public. *National Journal*, September 17 (38), 2806–2809.

Burby, R.J. 2006. Hurricane Katrina and the paradoxes of Government Disaster Policy: Bringing about wise governmental decisions for hazardous areas. *Annals of the American Academy*, 604 (March), 171–191.

Cannon, C.M. 2003. The mourner-in-chief. *National Journal*, February 8, (35), 6.

Cannon, C.M. 2005. Learning from mistakes. *National Journal*, September 10 (37), 2720–2722.

Cannon, C.M. and Harris, S. 2005. FEMA may work best standing alone. *National Journal*, September 10 (37), 2725.

Cooper, P.J. 1986. By order of the president: Administration by executive orders and proclamation. *Administration and Society*, 18, 233–262.

Cooper, P.J. 2002. *By Order of the President: The Use and Abuse of Executive Direct Action.* Lawrence, Kansas: University Press of Kansas.

Cutter, S.L. and Emrich, C.T. 2006. Moral hazard, social catastrophe: The changing face of vulnerability along the hurricane coasts. *Annals of the American Academy*, 604 (March), 102–112.

Deering, C.J. and Maltzman, F. 1999. The politics of executive orders: Legislative constraints on presidential power. *Political Research Quarterly*, 52, 767–783.

Durant, R.F. 1992. *The Administrative Presidency Revisited: Public Lands, the BLM and the Reagan Revolution.* Albany: SUNY Press.

Edwards, G.C. III. 1983. *The Public Presidency: The Pursuit of Popular Support.* New York: St. Martin's Press.

Eulau, H. and Karps, P.D. 1977. The puzzle of representation: Specifying components of responsiveness. *Legislative Studies Quarterly*, 2 (3), 233–254.

Gleiber, D.W. and Shull, S.A. 1992. Presidential influence in the policy-making process. *Western Political Quarterly*, 45, 441–468.

Glover, K.D. 2005. Policy storms of the century. *National Journal*, September 17 (38), 2815–2816.

Hetherington, M.J. and Nelson, M. 2003. Anatomy of a rally effect: George W. Bush and the war on terrorism. *PS: Political Science and Politics*, 36 (1), 37–44.

Hollis, A.L. 2005. A tale of two Federal Emergency Management Agencies. *The Forum*, 3 (3), Art. 3 (March). http://www.bepress.com/forum/vol3/iss3/art3.

Jones, C.O. 1999. *Separate but Equal Branches: Congress and the Presidency*, 2nd edition. Chatham, New Jersey: Chatham House Publishers.

Kernell, S. 1997. *Going Public: New Strategies of Presidential Leadership*, 3rd edition. Washington, District of Columbia: CQ Press.

Kerwin, C.M. 1994. *Rulemaking: How Government Agencies Write Law and Make Policy.* Washington, District of Columbia: CQ Press.

Krause, G.A. and Cohen, D.B. 1997. Presidential Use of Executive Orders, 1953–1994. *American Politics Quarterly*, 25, 458–471.

Light, P.C. 1999. *The President's Agenda: Domestic Policy Choice from Kennedy to Clinton*, 3rd edition. Baltimore, Maryland: Johns Hopkins University Press.

Martino-Golden, M. 1998. Interest groups in the rule-making process: Who participates? Whose voices get heard? *Journal of Public Administration Research and Theory*, 8, 245–270.

May, P.J. 1985. *Recovering from Catastrophes: Federal Disaster Relief Policy and Politics*. Westport, Connecticut: Greenwood Press.

May, P.J. and Burby, R.J. 1996. Coercive versus cooperative policies: Comparing intergovernmental mandate performance. *Journal of Policy Analysis and Management*, 15 (2): 171–201.

May, P.J. and Williams, W. 1986. *Disaster Policy Implementation: Managing Programs Under Shared Governance*. New York: Plenum Publishing.

Mayer, K.R. 1999. Executive orders and presidential power. *Journal of Politics*, 61 (2) May, 445–466.

Mayer, K.R. 2001. *With the Stroke of a Pen: Executive Orders and Presidential Power*. Princeton, New Jersey: Princeton University Press.

Morgan, R.P. 1987. *The President and Civil Rights: Policy-Making by Executive Order*. Lanham, Maryland: University Press of America.

Nathan, R.P. 1976. The administrative presidency. *The Public Interest*, 44 (Summer), 494–520.

Nathan, R.P. 1983. *The Administrative Presidency*. New York: Wiley.

Neustadt, R.E. 1960. *Presidential Power: The Politics of Leadership*. New York: Wiley.

Nigg, J.M., Barnshaw, J., and Torres, M.R. 2006. Hurricane Katrina and the flooding of New Orleans: Emergent issues in sheltering and temporary housing. *Annals of the American Academy*, 604 (March), 113–127.

Peterson, P.B. and West, M.R. 2003. *No Child Left Behind?: The Politics and Practice of School Accountability*. Washington, District of Columbia: Brookings Institution Press.

Platt, R.H. 1999. *Disasters and Democracy: The Politics of Extreme Natural Events*. Washington, District of Columbia: Island Press.

Rose, R. 1991. *The Post Modern President: George Bush Meets the World*, 2nd edition. Chatham, New Jersey: Chatham House Publishers.

Schneider, S.K. 1995. *Flirting with Disaster: Public Management in Crisis Situation*. Armonk, New York: M.E. Sharpe.

Schneider, S.K. 1998. Reinventing public administration: A case study of the Federal Emergency Management Agency. *Public Administration Quarterly*, 22 (Spring), 36–57.

Schneider, S.K. 2005. Administrative breakdowns in the governmental response to Hurricane Katrina. *Public Administration* Review, 65 (5), 515–516.

Select Bipartisan Committee to Investigate the Preparation for and Response to Hurricane Katrina. 2006. A Failure of Initiative. *United States House of Representatives*. February 15. http://katrina.house.gov/.

Seligman, L.G. and Covington, C.R. 1989. *The Coalitional Presidency*. Chicago, Illinois: The Dorsey Press.

Singer, P. 2006. Camp FEMA. *National Journal*, March 11, 20–26.

Steinberg, T. 2000. *Acts of God. The Unnatural History of Natural Disaster in America*. New York: Oxford University Press.

Sylves, R. and Cumming, W.R. 2004. FEMA's path to homeland security: 1979–2003. *Journal of Homeland Security and Emergency Management*, 1 (2), Art. 11.

Thomas, E. 2005. How Bush blew it. *Newsweek*. September 19.

Townsend, F.F. 2006. The federal response to Hurricane Katrina: Lessons learned. *The White House*, February. http://whitehouse.gov/reports/katrina-lessons-learned/.

VandeHei, J. and White, J. 2005. Bush urges shift in relief responsibilities. *Washington Post.* September 26.

Wamsley, G.L. and Schroeder, A.D. 1996. Escalating in a Quagmire: The changing dynamics of the emergency management policy subsystem. *Public Administration Review*, 56 (3), 235–244.

Waterman, R.W. 1989. *Presidential Influence and the Administrative State.* Knoxville, Tennessee: University of Tennessee Press.

Wilson, J.Q. 1989. *Bureaucracy: What Government Agencies Do and Why They Do It.* New York: Basic Books.

Chapter 5

The Role of Coordination in Disaster Management

Ross Prizzia

CONTENTS

Coordination and Disaster Preparedness

Coordination and collaboration in disaster management among public and private sector agencies and organizations at the community, city, local, state, national, and even international levels have become increasingly urgent. Technological advances of early warning systems and the continuous improvement of these systems have facilitated and supported agency coordination in the management of man-made and natural disasters in the State of Hawaii (HGICC, 2006). Disaster preparedness requires an understanding of various hazards, planning, coordination, an investment in continuous training involving national standards, and leadership that supports collaboration at all levels of the existing decentralized system of governance (Bentley and Waugh, 2005; Cigler, 2006).

On September 11, 1992, when the eye of Hurricane Iniki passed directly over the island of Kauai as a Category 4 hurricane, emergency managers of the State of Hawaii experienced their version of a 9/11 attack by mother nature. Iniki remains the most powerful hurricane to strike the State of Hawaii in recorded history, causing $1.8 billion in damage. However, coordination among emergency managers at the local level in Kauai and Oahu counties as well as at the state and federal levels of government prior to, during, and after Iniki minimized the number of deaths to a total of six. This stands in stark contrast to the number of casualties of Hurricane Katrina in 2005. The Central Pacific Hurricane Center (CPHC) issued tropical cyclone warnings and watches for the hurricane well in advance, and accurate forecasts allowed for wide-scale evacuations. A hurricane watch was issued for Kauai early on September 9 and was upgraded to a hurricane warning later that day (CPHC, 1992). Prior to Iniki's arrival in Kauai, 8000 people were housed in shelters, many of who remembered Hurricane Iwa in 1982. Rather than sending tourists to public shelters, two major hotels kept their occupants in the buildings during the storm's passage. During the evacuation of the island, people left days before to either family, friends, or to shelters. Because schools were canceled, traffic was light and evacuation was well executed (USACE, 1993). Among those on Kauai was filmmaker Steven Spielberg, who was preparing for the final day of shooting of the movie Jurassic Park. He and his 130 cast and crew remained safely in a hotel during Iniki's passage (Kamen, 1992). Roughly one-third of Oahu's population participated in the evacuation to public shelters, while many others went to a family or friend's house for shelter. The evacuations went smoothly, beginning with the vulnerable coastal areas. For those in need, vans and buses provided emergency transportation, while police directed traffic in certain overused intersections. The two main problems during the evacuation were lack of parking at shelters and inadequate exit routes for the coastlines (Kamen, 1992).

Immediately after the storm in Kauai, many were relieved to have survived the worst of the Category 4 hurricane. However, relief soon turned to apprehension due to lack of information, as every radio station was out and there was no news available for several days. Using food from battery powered refrigerators and freezers, communities held lavish parties to cope with the situation. Though food markets allowed those affected to take what they needed, many Kauai citizens insisted on paying. Because the hurricane destroyed much of their belongings, many groups gathered for video parties powered by portable generators. In addition, entertainers from all over Hawaii, including the Honolulu Symphony, provided free concerts to the victims (Sommer, 2002). Although looting occurred in the aftermath of Iniki, it was minor. A group of Army Corps of Engineers, who experienced the looting after Hurricane Andrew just weeks prior to Iniki, were surprised at the overall calmness and lack of violence on the island.

Kauai citizens remained hopeful for compensatory monetary aid from the government or insurance companies (Sommer, 2002), while the military effectively provided aid for their immediate needs, even before local officials requested aid (Peach, 1993). However, in the months after the storm, many insurance companies left Hawaii. In response, State Governor John D. Waihee III enacted the Hurricane Relief Fund in 1993 to help unprotected Hawaiians. The fund was never needed for another Hawaii hurricane, and it was terminated in 2000 when insurance companies returned to the islands (Harris, 2001).

In contrast to Iniki, when Hurricane Katrina ravaged Louisiana and Texas in 2005, it exposed a failure of policy and leadership at the federal level which paralyzed managerial and administrative capacity at the local level, resulting in a lack of coordination and an effective command system (Cigler, 2006; Farazmand, 2005). Katrina was one of the worst natural disasters in U.S. history. The storm killed more than 1200 people in Louisiana, Mississippi, and Alabama, left hundreds of thousands homeless, and caused tens of billions of dollars in damage. The government's inadequate response to this disaster spawned several studies and even a special hearing of the U.S. Senate Homeland Security and Governmental Affair Committee (Jansen, 2006). One post-Katrina study, "Political Appointments, Bureau Chiefs and Federal Management Performance," suggests that government executives are better managers in time of crisis in general than politically appointed bureau chiefs (Lewis, 2005). The study finds that politically appointed bureau chiefs get systematically lower management grades than bureau chiefs drawn from the civil service. Findings indicate that programs administered by appointed managers get grades five-to-six points lower than those administered by careerists even when controlling for differences among programs, substantial variation in management environment, and the policy content of programs themselves (Lewis, 2005).

The study further reveals that career managers have more direct bureau experience and longer tenures and these characteristics are significantly related to management performance. Apparently, although political appointees have higher education levels, more private or nonprofit management experience, and more varied work experience than careerists, these characteristics are uncorrelated with management performance (Lewis, 2005). Lewis therefore concludes that some combination of structural changes to reduce the number of appointees or increased sensitivity to appointee selection based upon certain background characteristics could improve federal bureau management (Lewis, 2005).

Problems of Coordination

Terrorist Attacks on the World Trade Center

Coordination became of critical importance to disaster management in the wake of the attacks on the World Trade Center on September 11, 2001. It is recognized that coordination is essential not just for detecting and preventing terrorist attacks, but also for ensuring an effective local response to terrorist events. When terrorist-related events occur, coordination is critical among police officers, firefighters, emergency medical technicians, public health workers, and other similar emergency personnel. Terrorist attacks, like the ones on the World Trade Center and the Pentagon, require extraordinary levels of coordination. Such catastrophes are not simply fires, crime scenes, or emergencies with injured people, and they can happen instantaneously all at once overwhelming the ability of any agency or jurisdiction to respond. Therefore, the effectiveness of a community's response to a terrorist attack is dependent upon coordination among first responders and their ability to implement response plans.

The attacks on the World Trade Center created overwhelming coordination problems. Emergency supervisors in the lobbies of the two towers lacked reliable information about what was happening above them or outside the buildings. Television viewers around the country had better information on the spread of the fires than the lobby emergency supervisors, who had no access to the television broadcasts. Moreover, radio communications were sporadic throughout the towers. First responders raced into burning buildings without regard for their own safety, but the scale of the New York attacks overwhelmed the system. A New York City Police Department (NYPD) helicopter circled overhead, but the fire chiefs had no link to the police information. There were no senior NYPD personnel at the fire department's command posts—and vice versa. Further, the New York City Fire Department (FDNY) lacked an established process for securing mutual aid from surrounding communities. Nassau and Westchester counties supplied ad hoc assistance, but the FDNY had no procedure for integrating the reinforcements into its own effort. With half of the FDNY force at the World Trade Center, and with no established mutual aid agreement with neighboring communities, the rest of the city lacked adequate protection. Moreover, coordination problems within and between the NYPD and FDNY were compounded by bureaucratic competition, especially among those in the intelligence community whose responsibility was to interpret conflicting reports on the hijackers' activities (Kettl, 2003).

In an attempt to address some of the problems of coordination exposed in response to the World Trade Center disaster, many emergency planners recommend that local officials should follow an "all risk" strategy that involves building a strong, basic capacity for local emergency response and deploying that capacity to respond to natural and man-made disasters including terrorism (FEMA, 2003). This recommendation is especially poignant because most cities cannot afford to create a special team devoted solely to terrorism. The FDNY discovered during 9/11 that responding to a building collapse requires the same fundamental techniques regardless of the cause. Effective response to terrorism depends on an effective first-response system that can handle a wide range of emergencies. The catastrophic destruction of the terrorists' attacks on September 11 revealed that even the best trained and equipped first responders can find themselves overwhelmed.

In response to disasters, local governments typically rely on mutual aid agreements with neighboring communities under which reinforcements can be brought in quickly. Because of its size, the FDNY had no formal mutual aid agreements with surrounding jurisdictions. Such agreements are often difficult to achieve because of the dilemma of smaller communities not wanting to join larger communities in a regional approach, thus sacrificing their right to separate funding, whereas larger communities are not willing to guarantee that they would respond to problems in smaller towns for fear that serious events would overwhelm their own capacities (Robinson et al., 2003).

A 2003 Council on Foreign Relations (CFR) study found that two years after September 11 "the United States remains dangerously ill prepared to handle a catastrophic attack on American soil" (Rudman et al., 2003). The council found that fire departments often could supply radios to just half of the firefighters on a shift and that only 10 percent of the nation's fire departments had the personnel and equipment to rescue people trapped in a building collapse. Police departments lacked the gear to protect their officers following an attack with weapons of mass destruction, and most states did not have adequate equipment, expertise, or capacity to test for biological or chemical attacks. The CFR study noted that "America's local emergency responders will always be the first to confront a terrorist incident and will play the central role to deal with the immediate consequences," and concluded that the first responders were "drastically under funded" and "dangerously unprepared" (Rudman et al., 2003). Under close examination, even the best prepared communities showed dangerous gaps in equipment and training. First responders everywhere discovered that the coordination with neighboring communities was often inadequate. Some of the problems were technical, like radios with different frequencies. Other problems were political and bureaucratic, as was the case at the federal and local levels, where individual departments and local governments struggle to maintain their autonomy. The problems of coordination exposed deficiencies in readiness and response to the terrorist man-made disasters of September 11, 2001. Unfortunately, the lessons learned from this experience did not translate into an improved capability in response to the natural disaster, Hurricane Katrina, in August 2005.

Problems of Coordination in Response to Katrina

Hurricane Katrina was a natural disaster that overwhelmed the existing capability of the federal, state, and local response system and became a regional catastrophe. This was rather surprising because emergency planning had taken place after the man-made disaster on September 11 and the natural disaster caused by Hurricane Pam in Louisiana in July 2004. In coordination with state, local, and community-based emergency managers, the Department of Homeland Security (DHS) and Federal Emergency Management Agency (FEMA) collaborated and developed a number of strategic planning initiatives to support an "all hazards approach" in the preparation for and response to disasters. Critical assessments were made and kept up-to-date of the real and potential response capability of the federal, state, and local disaster response systems. The assessments include but are not limited to the following (Wells, 2006):

- Magnitude of the disaster
- Situational awareness on the part of designated emergency managers and affected citizens
- Continuity of government operations
- Mass evacuation operations and potential use of hotels and cruise ships as shelters
- Security issues

Apparently, the assessments of response capability and the ability to implement the new all hazards initiatives of disaster readiness and response systems failed when put to the test by a disaster of Katrina's catastrophic proportions. There were major problems of coordination with the communications, security, evacuation, and supply systems in response to Katrina that eventually led to a collapse in the command system and widespread chaos and loss of life. According to one FEMA, federal coordination officer who was on the scene and part of the response effort to Katrina, the major problems included the following (Wells, 2006):

- Inadequate existing emergency management systems to cope with catastrophic disasters
- Limited capability at the state and local levels of government in terms of equipment, supplies, and distribution system
- Inadequately trained, staffed, and equipped federal response teams

- Leadership and emergency managers with little or no emergency management training or experience with limited decision-making skills in time of crisis
- Inadequate competent financial management before, during, and after the disaster

Critical to the effective response capability was the coordination of the federal and other response teams. However, many team members were meeting for the first time and never trained together prior to the disaster. Moreover, for many of the team members their participation as an emergency responder was not their primary job function, but rather a temporary, part-time, secondary responsibility. Moreover, many of the upper and mid-level emergency managers designated to network with and assist in coordinating the deployment of rapid response teams remained in their offices in Washington, DC and other locations remote from the scene of the disaster. This resulted in the response teams functioning more like a loosely organized group rather than a well-trained rapid response team (Wells, 2006). Even where teams did coordinate effectively, because their response training focused more on the symptomatic lessons learned from the last disaster (i.e., Hurricane Pam), their disaster readiness capability was inadequate to address the fundamental problems and new challenges of Katrina (Wells, 2006).

Coordination and Organizational Theory

Coordination within the Department of Homeland Security (DHS) with 22 agencies proved to be very difficult, especially in determining which agencies should be linked and how. Because homeland security includes many different agencies performing many different functions, drawing clear lines of responsibility is difficult. Figuring out how to make all the agencies work together is even more difficult. As journalist Sydney J. Freedberg Jr. observed, "The US government was just not designed with terrorists in mind" (CBS NEWS, 2002). Effective homeland security requires tailoring coordination to the special nature of homeland security problems, and each incident requires a response tailored to the special needs it presents (Kettl, 2003).

Political leaders and theorists have traditionally relied on organizational structure to solve coordination problems. For theorists like Gulick, "wherever many men are thus working together the best results are secured when there is a division of work among these men. The theory of organization, therefore, has to do with the structure of coordination imposed upon the work-division units of an enterprise" (Gulick, 1937). Accomplishing difficult jobs requires the division of labor among workers and that organization requires effort at establishing coordination. Gulick emphasized only four ways of organizing: according to purpose or function, process (or the way things are done), clientele (the individuals served), or place (the location being served). Organizational leaders must choose one of the four and none of the choices is ideal, with each having advantages and disadvantages. Leaders must make the necessary choice of one alternative, with the knowledge that the choice brings clear benefits and certain costs.

Gulick concluded that organization by purpose or function was most often the best choice because "purpose is understandable by the entire personnel down to the last clerk and inspector" (Gulick, 1937). Organizing by function also was emphasized by Frederick W. Taylor in his pursuit of scientific management and his focus on division of labor (Taylor, 1911). When organizations had a difficult time finding highly skilled people to accomplish difficult jobs, Taylor's response was to redesign the job through "job simplification," focus on a narrow set of skills, separate the job into each of these skills, and increase the number of workers. Thereafter, each worker was directed to perform one skill in a mechanized sequence. This process eventually evolved into the assembly line of production in the private sector.

However, because it is usually difficult to divide work neatly, organization by function involves fundamental problems that can create gaps, service problems, and inefficiencies. Organization by function also tends to strengthen top-down managers, whose job is to define functions and allocate responsibilities. Christopher Hood pointed out that when disasters occur, a common response is to suggest that "the problem (whatever it was) could have been averted if only there had been more coordination, better procedures, more planning and foresight, clearer assignment of authority, more general 'grip' on the part of experts, professionals, or managers." The typical solution is "to tighten up the rules and authority structures to prevent a recurrence" (Hood, 1998). However, coordination is often a "problem of contingency, and what works best depend on the problem to be solved" and existing structures are rarely able to adapt easily and quickly enough to many of the most difficult problems presented by man-made and natural disasters (Kettl, 2003b). First responders and officials could better be able to adapt to the unpredictability of a specific emergency and address problems common to coordination during disasters if there were more nonstructural approaches, including interorganizational networks (such as mutual aid agreements), improved information technology, and stronger political leadership (Kettl, 2003b). Moreover, process theories of motivation, and other nonstructural, process-oriented approaches such as total quality management (TQM), and "best practices" may prove to be more relevant and applicable in addressing the problems of coordination in disaster management.

Coordination and Technology

The problems that emerged in the response to September 11 reinforced Herbert Simon's argument about the need for contingent coordination, especially when dependent on technology (Simon, 1947). For example, when New York City divided its public protection operations along the traditional functional lines of

and monitoring a developing threat; notifying appropriate federal, state, and local agencies of the nature of the threat; and deploying the requisite advisory and technical resources to assist the lead federal agency (LFA) in facilitating interdepartmental coordination of crisis and consequence management activities (Prizzia and Helfand, 2006).

The actions each agency or department must perform during each phase of the response include crisis management and consequence management actions that are necessary to control and contain chemical, biological, nuclear/radiological, and conventional materials or devices. Prescribed actions will continue to be refined to better clarify the mission, capabilities, and resources of supporting departments and agencies.

The CONPLAN establishes local agencies and defines their responsibilities. The departments and agencies listed below agreed to support the overall concept of operations of the CONPLAN to carry out their assigned responsibilities under PDD-39 and PDD-62. The departments and agencies also agreed to implement national and regional planning efforts and to conduct appropriate activities to maintain the overall federal response capability.

Primary Federal Agencies

The response to a terrorist threat or incident within the United States will entail a highly coordinated, multiagency local, state, and federal response. In support of this mission, the following primary federal agencies will provide the core federal response:

- Department of Justice (DOJ)/Federal Bureau of Investigation (FBI)
- Federal Emergency Management Agency (FEMA)
- Department of Defense (DOD)
- Department of Energy (DOE)
- Environmental Protection Agency (EPA)
- Department of Health and Human Services (DHHS)

The Department of Justice and the Federal Bureau of Investigation will be the lead agencies for crisis management. The Federal Emergency Management Agency has been designated as the lead agency for consequence management.

Although not formally designated under the CONPLAN, other federal departments and agencies may have authorities, resources, capabilities, or expertise required to support response operations. Agencies may be requested to participate in federal planning and response operations, and may be asked to designate staff to function as liaison officers and provide other support to the LFA (Prizzia and Helfand, 2006). The CONPLAN defines the responsibilities of the various federal agencies in the event of a terrorist attack.

Plans to Improve Coordination

In March of 2006, Homeland Security Secretary Michael Chertoff announced several new measures designed to strengthen the FEMA's essential functions so it can more effectively respond to manmade or natural disasters, particularly during catastrophic events. These new measures are designed to match the experience and skills of FEMA employees with twenty-first century tools and technology, maximizing the agency's performance regardless of disaster size or complexity. However, it should be noted that in April 2005 the U.S. Senate Homeland Security and Governmental Affairs Committee proposed that FEMA, which floundered in the wake of Hurricane Katrina, should be abolished and replaced with a new organization better equipped to respond to disasters (Jansen, 2006). While acknowledging "significant failures" in how he and FEMA handled the storm, Secretary Michael Chertoff assured the committee that he made changes to ensure that the government would not be caught off guard by the next hurricane. Those changes include the creation of the rapid response teams that can be deployed quickly to threatened regions and better communications (Jansen, 2006).

The DHS fiscal year 2007 budget request asks for increased funding to begin strengthening FEMA—specifically a 10 percent increase in FEMA's budget over this fiscal year. In total, funding for FEMA's core budget will grow 40 percent since fiscal year 2004. This budget request also provides additional resources to update FEMA's Emergency Alert System, increase FEMA's procurement staff and overall capabilities, improve capital infrastructure and information technology; and strengthen overall mitigation, response, and recovery capabilities.

Together, these new measures and additional resources are intended to improve DHS's ability to build integrated homeland security capabilities, eliminate unnecessary bureaucracy, serve disaster victims more effectively, and empower FEMA to act with efficiency and urgency when fulfilling its historic and critical mission of response and recovery particularly before the next hurricane season (PA Times, 2006).

Other changes instituted to improve coordination include the following:

■ Improve coordination and efficiency of operations. A new director of operations coordination will enable DHS to more effectively conduct joint operations across all organizational elements; coordinate incident management activities, and utilize all resources (PA Times, 2005).

■ Enhance coordination and deployment of preparedness assets. The Information Analysis and Infrastructure Protection Directorate will be renamed the Directorate for Preparedness and consolidate preparedness assets from across the department. The Directorate for Preparedness will facilitate grants and oversee nationwide preparedness efforts supporting first responder training, citizen awareness, public health, infrastructure and cyber security, and ensure proper steps are taken to protect high-risk targets. The directorate will be managed by an undersecretary and include

1. A new assistant secretary for cyber security and telecommunications, responsible for identifying and assessing the vulnerability of critical telecommunications infrastructure and assets; providing timely, actionable, and valuable threat information; and leading the national response to cyber and telecommunications attacks.
2. A new chief medical officer, responsible for carrying out the department's responsibilities to coordinate the response to biological attacks, and to serve as a principal liaison between DHS and the Department of Health and Human Services 2001, the Centers for Disease Control, the National Institutes of Health, and other key parts of the biomedical and public health communities:
   - Assistant Secretary for Infrastructure Protection
   - The Office of State and Local Government Coordination and Preparedness responsible for grants, training, and exercises
   - U.S. Fire Administration
   - Office of National Capital Region Coordination.

FEMA Reengineering for Catastrophe Readiness and Response

FEMA began several initiatives to improve coordination after Katrina exposed problems of coordination of readiness and response in communications, evacuation, and understanding of the national response plan and relevant state and local response plans. Prominent among these initiatives is the FEMA reengineering for catastrophe readiness and response initiative that includes but is not limited to the following (Shea, 2006):

- Develop and implement advanced logistics and supply tracking system similar to that of the private sector.
- Improve communications by training and deploying five-person "communication teams."
- FEMA collaboration with state and local governments to identify wide gaps in the existing response capability and to establish effective methods to close these gaps.
- FEMA/DHS collaboration to address legal and social issues to improve evacuation plans by improving the relationship with Red Cross in the effective use of volunteers before, during, and after evacuations.
- Improve understanding of National Response Plan among all emergency managers and responders at all levels of governments including the private sector and community-based volunteers.

Disaster Management in the State of Hawaii

The primary government agency for disaster response is the Oahu Civil Defense Agency (OCDA), a department in the city and county of Honolulu. The mayor acts as the CEO of OCDA and has the power to declare a disaster. Disasters are county specific. Each county (i.e., Honolulu, Maui, Kauai, and Hawaii) individually determines what constitutes a disaster. For example, the island of Hawaii may have volcanic eruptions listed as natural disasters, whereas Honolulu would not. Disasters can also be localized to certain areas within a county and designated to the Local Emergency Planning Committee (LEPC), which is part of the city and county of Honolulu, as opposed to the State's Emergency Response Commission, which oversees the Hawaii State Civil Defense System. The state's primary responsibility is to provide leadership in rapid assistance during a disaster, with a full range of resources and effective partnerships. To strengthen its leadership role, the State of Hawaii hosted leaders from the public and private sectors to meet and develop innovative response strategies at the Inaugural Asia-Pacific Homeland Security Summit in Honolulu in November 2003 (Mangum, 2003).

All city departments follow the directive outlined in the city and county of Honolulu's Emergency Operations Plan (EOP). Once the EOP draft is approved by the mayor and city council, all county departments and coordinating county agencies follow suit accordingly.

Most of Oahu's medical centers play a crucial role in disaster preparedness and response (Griffith and Oshiro, 1999). In particular, Queen's Medical Center (QMC) with its 560 beds is the largest and oldest hospital and main trauma center in Hawaii. QMC is instrumental in the coordination of disaster response and it plays an active role in Honolulu's Disaster Committee (Prizzia, 2004).

Coordination of Public and Private Sector Organizations

It has been proposed that emergency management is both proactive and reactive. This realization applies to QMC in its efforts to coordinate with outside agencies (Sensenig, 1999). The primary means by which QMC achieves its coordination is through the Healthcare Association of Hawaii (HAH).

The HAH is a nonprofit organization representing the State of Hawaii's acute care hospitals and two-thirds of the long-term care beds with a total of 41 facilities. HAH also represents community-based providers and many supporting organizations that provide services and supplies to the healthcare industry. This includes the HAH Emergency Preparedness Committee (EPC), which is responsible for providing hospital services in support of the state civil defense system as cited in Hawaii's Disaster Relief Act (Hawaii Revised Statutes, Chapter 127) and various federal, state, and county emergency response plans. The chair of the EPC is appointed by the chief executive officer (CEO) of HAH. Members are appointed by the CEO of their respective healthcare organization. EPC coordinated Island Crisis, a full-scale chemical terrorism response drill in May 1999 in which fourteen hospitals participated and five of these facilities demonstrated their ability to provide emergency casualty decontamination.

The Honolulu-based EPC is unique in the nation. Its strength is the ability to bring key stakeholders involved in healthcare emergency response into one well-aligned and well-coordinated system. Improvement opportunities include the need to further incorporate nonhospital organizations into the network more effectively and to provide ongoing professional development of hospital emergency coordinators. According to former Vice President of Kaiser Permanente Medical Center, Toby Clairmont, who has worked over 250 emergencies in the last 25 years ranging from multifamily structural fires to hurricanes, three critical factors in successfully responding to emergencies are

- Family emergency preparedness
- Local community emergency response teams
- Well-trained organizational coordinators

HAH includes among its affiliate members other organizations that support coordination in emergency response efforts, such as Hawaii Air Ambulance and International Life Support, Inc. Moreover, a Web site was developed by the Emergency Preparedness Program (EPP) of the HAH. It is designed to provide information and data management services to healthcare facility emergency managers of organizations such as the American Red Cross, Hawaii State Civil Defense, OCDA, and hotels that are also members of Honolulu's disaster committee at the city and county of Honolulu's EOC. This coordination extends to the neighboring islands. For example, in June 2001, the West Hawaii branch of the American Red Cross provided disaster response training to community-based volunteers in Kona.

Other organizations in the network are Kaiser Medical Center, Kuakini Medical Center, St. Francis Medical Center, Queen's Medical Center, Tripler Army Medical Center, and Blood Bank of Hawaii. The Blood Bank of Hawaii plays a vital role and designates 10 percent of all donated blood to disaster victims suffering from trauma.

The OCDA facilitates agency coordination through communication, training, procedures, and information within the city and county of Honolulu. OCDA also coordinates disaster responsibilities among various private organizations and educates the public about emergency preparedness. Interviews with OCDA personnel revealed that they are continuously reviewing, revising, and testing procedures outlined in the EOP. The administrator of the OCDA works closely with the mayor and acts as an advisor for disaster preparedness and emergency management. OCDA also has hundreds of volunteers.

The EOC is designed to facilitate agency coordination emergency response including establishing operational policy, providing logistical and resource support, and communications. Specifically, the EOC houses the communications system for the Emergency Broadcast System and a meeting place for the city and county of

Honolulu's Disaster Committee. During a real disaster or training exercise, the city and county of Honolulu's Disaster Committee gathers on a rectangular table equipped with a telephone for each seat. The mayor sits on one end of the table and the OCDA administrator on the other. Other representatives from various city and county of Honolulu departments occupy the rest of the table (e.g., fire, police, public works, etc.). The EOC also houses the communications and radio devices for emergency medical services (EMS), hospitals, police, fire, utility companies, and federal, state, and other county agencies.

Advanced warning systems located at disaster and research centers in Hawaii also aid agency coordination in response to a wide range of natural disasters that threaten Hawaii and the Pacific region. The Pacific Tsunami Warning Center (PTWC) was established in 1949 in Ewa Beach, Hawaii, to provide advance warnings of likely tsunamis to most countries in the Pacific Basin. It is continually upgraded with the most sophisticated technology, including access to NASA's Earth Observing System (EOS) data. The PTWC also plays a crucial role in agency coordination in disaster response in Hawaii and throughout the Pacific. The PTWC monitors a real-time reporting deep-ocean system that communicates with weather resistance surface buoys that surround the Hawaiian Islands, and are sensitive enough to detect tsunami vibrations throughout the Pacific (EOSDIS, 2005).

The Pacific Disaster Center (PDC) located in Kihei on the island of Maui in Hawaii enhances agency coordination by assisting emergency managers to network in Hawaii and throughout the Pacific region to make informed decisions in times of crisis (Shirkhodai, 2003). The Research Corporation of the University of Hawaii (RCUH) in coordination with the PDC, Hawaii State Civil Defense, Pacific Command for DOD, FEMA, and other disaster organizations has begun development for the automatic production of cloud-free base images using full-resolution Landsat 7 data. This advance technology and Landsat 7 data will enable users at remote sites to evaluate the quality and coverage of images using browse data prior to ordering the full resolution scenes. This technology will also enable disaster managers to obtain an essentially cloud-free high resolution satellite image of their geographic area of interest. The image will be generated on demand using the most recent data available for the area, which extends over much of the Pacific and Indian Oceans (Mouginis-Mark, 2005).

Survey of Emergency Managers on Role of Coordination

The role of the coordination in emergency management in Hawaii is of special importance. The impact of coordination on emergency management is a topic of great concern during all phases of a disaster, but is particularly critical during the final phase of disaster preparedness and the initial phase of disaster response. Coordination helps emergency managers to prepare and respond to disasters, especially in the immediate post-impact stage of a disaster. To obtain firsthand data on the role of coordination during the critical phase of final disaster preparedness and initial disaster response, a sample of 50 emergency managers which represents about 20 percent of the emergency managers in the State of Hawaii with ten years or more of emergency management experience was surveyed during the months of November and December of 2005. The emergency managers were contacted by e-mail and telephone and asked the following questions.

- Do you feel coordination among community, local, county, state, and federal agencies is adequate to meet the challenge of a major natural and man-made disaster? How might coordination be improved?
- In your opinion, how can coordination with the private sector be improved to assist your efforts before, during, and after a major natural or man-made disaster?
- In your opinion, how best could you utilize the media to assist in coordinating your efforts before, during, and after a major natural or man-made disaster?

Results of the 2005 Survey

Adequacy of Coordination

In response to the question about the adequacy of coordination among community, local, county, state, and federal agencies to meet the challenge of major natural and man-made disasters, over 90 percent of the Hawaii emergency managers responded that they were adequately prepared. The main reasons given by respondents for the adequacy of coordination in Hawaii included the following:

- The emergency management community regularly conducts exercises together. They work together and participate in coordinated planning and operations meetings.
- County, state, and federal agencies in Hawaii are working together to address the issue of coordination to achieve the goal of interoperability.
- The Honolulu Police Department (HPD) through the DHS, State Civil Defense as well as CERT conducts training regularly with other agencies including personnel with military-based unified and incident commands.
- The Hawaii Fire Department (HFD), HPD, EMS, and Ocean Safety have adopted UHF radios that allow interagency communication. The new system eliminates the past problems of different radio frequencies and related deficiencies highlighted in the 9/11 disaster by providing for quality, short range, line of sight communications and are far superior in convoy situations than CB radios.
- The established network among the HPD, military, U.S. Coast Guard, EMS, and FEMA, National Guard Units, and DOD Affiliations functions extremely well with an excellent working relationship.

■ Many civilian emergency personnel working for public agencies at the state and local levels also serve in some capacity in military National Guard or reserve units so there are great opportunities to share ideas.
■ Emergency personnel at the state and local levels are well trained and train annually in all types of hazards.

Some emergency managers expressed that they believed that disaster coordination in Hawaii is the best in the nation and noted that "many emergency preparedness instructors on the mainland commented on the excellent networking within the state of Hawaii." Another emergency manager noted that "Whenever I travel to the mainland for training or conferences it never ceases to amaze me how far ahead are we in terms of internal and external coordination and communication. We are lucky that our county boundaries are separated by water and this fact has eliminated the problems that many communities face in regards to turf battles and county jurisdiction."

Improving Coordination

In response to the question as to how coordination might be improved, 93 percent of emergency managers responded that training is the most important means to improve coordination. All aspects of training were cited by emergency managers including increased frequency, increased funding for replacement emergency personnel while those in place are in training, and more "hands-on" training. Typical responses on improving coordination among emergency managers included the following:

■ Coordination is currently adequate. However, if like in the World Trade Center disaster, the community loses its leaders; other people will need to rise to the occasion to coordinate. To improve, ensure lower level managers know the system and can take command.
■ I do believe that coordination is adequate, but can always be improved. And this can be done through more drills which involve all levels of government.
■ To take someone off of their primary assignment to participate in training or tabletop exercises requires a replacement. This replacement costs money in overtime to ensure that public safety is not compromised during the training and coordination exercises.
■ Coordination can be improved by achieving common communications protocols, real-time field training and brief and concise written policies and procedures that are Web-based shared and are updated at least once a year.
■ As for the community, I think improvement can be achieved by the CERT program. This training is designed to prepare the community in the event of a catastrophic disaster and residents are trained to help their family and neighbors in a disaster.

Improving Coordination with the Private Sector

In response to the question as to how to improve coordination with the private sector, 85 percent of the emergency managers responded that there should be more proactive approaches to include the private sector. Examples of proactive approaches included the following:

- Provide training, education, and information for the private sector prior to disaster.
- Use of memorandum of agreement (MOA) with relevant private sector organizations that detail the nature of coordination and responsibilities of all parties.
- Establish trust with the private sector prior to a disaster to facilitate communication during a disaster.
- Create and expand "partnerships" with private-sector volunteers.
- Create a system of continuous monitoring of the community to increase awareness of new private-sector groups and organizations that should be involved.
- Include private sector representatives on government emergency preparedness committees to work together to develop policies and standardize emergency procedures and operations.

Typical responses of emergency managers on how to improve coordination with the private sector included the following:

- There are two new acronyms, COG and COOP. COG is continuity of government and COOP is continuity of operations. Both depend on the private sector being heavily involved in the preparedness and recovery process.
- Coordination with the private sector can help ensure everyone is on the same page. This will help reduce confusion and anxiety before, during, and after a disaster. One way to do this is to have community/governmental committees that meet regularly.
- Private–public partnerships already exist in the division and have vastly assisted us in all aspects of emergency management (before, during, and after). Private sector representatives volunteer to serve in various capacities from committee membership to advisory roles to offer oversight and advice to the Director of Civil Defense and the Vice Director of Civil Defense.
- Establishing relationships with the private sector prior to an event can help create trust and facilitate communication during an event. More communication and relationship building should begin before an event occurs.
- Our office maintains a robust coordination program to include regular meetings and contacts with our hotels, private sector businesses, energy suppliers,

utilities, nongovernment entities such as the American Red Cross and other private and government organizations. Disaster preparedness outreach and education for all sectors are vitally important to ensure a coordinated public response to a disaster. We can always improve this effort by continuously monitoring our community to ensure we are aware of new and emergent groups or organizations that we should be communicating or coordinating with.

Improving Coordination with the Media

In response to the question as to how might the media assist in emergency coordination before, during, and after disasters, most emergency managers felt that coordination with the media is essential to effective disaster management. Respondents noted the following ways to improve coordination with the media:

- Include media representatives and those journalists whose responsibility is to report on disaster in government sponsored emergency management coordination training sessions.
- Develop a closer working relationship between first responders and the media.
- Develop a closer working relationship between designated government agencies for disaster response and the media.
- Embed media representatives within the disaster management organizations and community level disaster drills and exercises.
- Develop a plan to increase the mutual effort on the part of media and emergency managers to provide accurate information in a consistent and timely manner before, during, and after disasters.
- Develop a plan to reduce turnover among disaster reporters to improve continuity of public reporting.

Some typical responses of emergency managers on improving coordination with the media included the following:

- Coordination with the media can be improved by researching and implementing some type of incentive (i.e., tax credits) to participate in emergency management communications programs such as the Emergency Alert System (EAS) and Amber Alert.
- The media is the best means of getting important information out to the public in a timely and accurate way. If a good working relationship is developed and nurtured, the media will do everything in its power to convey important information, be it preparedness information or actual "as it's happening" disaster information. The personnel in media, however, seem to constantly change. Therefore, we are continually working on establishing new relationships or nurturing existing ones.

- The major problem is the media themselves. If they would cooperate, coordination is no issue. However, they are profit oriented and will do anything to get a scoop. That attitude has a very negative effect on the ability to work within coordination guidelines.

- We have an excellent and caring media here in both print and television journalism. The most important issue is that as responsible journalists they are always willing to ask first, get educated, and then print or broadcast. The difficulty, however, is the high turnover rate in print and television reporters. This unfortunately leads to a need to regularly educate new staff on how the Civil Defense system operates in Hawaii.

- The problem with the media is that they look for sensationalism ... they are for profit and need the "big" breaking news. What is needed is more responsible reporting. This will help get information to people before, during, and after a natural disaster.

- Reporting accurately. The media needs to use the correct terminology when reporting the news. For instance, they come up with "Hurricane Alerts." There is no such thing. There are Hurricane Watches and Warnings. Maybe a closer working relationship between the first responders and the media would allow for better coordination.

Conclusion

The results of the survey of emergency managers in Hawaii included several extremely valuable recommendations that pertain to intergovernmental, private sector, and media coordination. These recommendations should be taken seriously and implemented throughout the country, adjusted somewhat for local conditions, issues, and problems. Hawaii, in some ways, can be considered as providing a model for reasonably effective disaster preparedness and response and should be further studied by high-level decision-makers from relevant organizations in the public, private, and nonprofit sectors that are responsible for homeland security.

Summary and Recommendation

Effective disaster preparedness and management require coordination and collaboration among public and private agencies and organizations on the local, state, national, and even international levels. The massive potential and actual loss of life and property due to natural and man-made disasters compel emergency planners and managers to improve upon existing disaster readiness and response plans and actions to minimize the devastating consequences. Glaring deficiencies of the emergency response systems were exposed in the wake of disasters such as the terrorist attack on the World Trade Center and the Pentagon on September 11 and the battering of Hurricane Katrina.

The technical, resource, political, and bureaucratic problems that surfaced seemed to be eclipsed by the woeful lack of coordination and collaboration among key elements in the emergency response systems. For example, the lack of inter-operable communication systems, the inadequate training and equipment, and the interagency rivalries, may well have been addressed prior to the disasters through intra- and interagency coordination and collaboration among rank and file. The unprecedented terrorist attack of 9/11 turned attention to homeland security threatened by man-made disasters, whereas Hurricane Katrina exposed the vulner-ability of an uncoordinated emergency command system overwhelmed by a natural disaster.

Subsequent analysis of recent disasters suggests that an "all risk/hazards" approach in the preparation and response to both man-made and natural disasters may help to mitigate the problems of coordination by building a strong, basic capacity for local emergency response. This would include a first-response system with personnel trained and equipped to handle a wide range of emergencies. Finally, a survey of emergency managers in Hawaii highlighted the need for intergovern-mental, private sector, and media coordination in preparing for and responding to a major man-made or natural disaster.

References

Bentley, E. and Waugh, W., Katrina and the necessity for emergency management standards (Ed.), *Journal of Emergency Management*, Vol. 3, No. 5, 2005, pp. 9–10.

Block, R., FEMA points to flaws, flubs in terror drill, *Wall Street Journal*, October 31, B1. See the report at Department of Homeland Security, Top Officials (TOPOFF) Exercise Series: TOPOFF2—After Action Summary Report for Public Release, December 19, 2003.

CBSNEWS.COM, Hijackers remain mysterious, September 11, 2002, www.cbsnews.com//stories/2002/09/11/september11/main 521523.html, 2002.

Central Pacific Hurricane Center (CPHC), The 1992 central pacific tropical cyclone season, http://www.prh.noaa.gov/cphc/summaries/1992.php#Iniki. Retrieved from the World Wide Web on March 13, 2006.

Cigler, B.A., Who's in charge: The paradox of emergency management, *PA Times*, Vol. 28, No. 5, 2006, pp. 7, 10.

EOSDIS, Synergy IV: Improving access to and application of EOA data, *Final Report*. Raytheon Company, Upper Marlboro, Maryland, 2005.

Farazmand, A., Crisis management or management crisis? *PA Times*, Vol. 28, No. 10, 2005, pp. 6, 10.

Federal Emergency Management Agency (FEMA), A nation prepared: Federal emergency management agency strategic plan. Fiscal years 2003–2008, U.S. Government Printing Office, Washington, DC, 2003.

Griffith, R.L. and Oshiro, R.C., The Queen's health system: Overview 99, The Queen's Medical Center, Honolulu, Hawaii, 1999.

Gulick, L., Notes on the theory of organization, *Papers on the Science of Administration.* L. Gulick and L. Urwick (Eds.), Institute of Public Administration, New York, 1937, p. 1.

Harris, J., State should keep hurricane fund intact for next disaster, http://starbulletin.com/2001/12/30/editorial/editorials.html. Honolulu Star Bulletin, 2001. Retrieved from the World Wide Web on March 18, 2006.

Hawaii Geographic Information Coordinating Council (HGICC), Geographic Information Systems for Hawaii State Government Agencies, *The Hawaii State-wide GIS Program,* 2006, www.hawaii.gov/dbedt/gis.

Hood, C., *The Art of the State: Culture, Rhetoric, and Public Management,* Oxford University Press, Oxford, 1998, p. 25.

Jansen, B., *Panel: Unfixable FEMA Should Close,* Portland Press, Herald, April 2006, p. 1.

Kamen, A., Hawaii Hurricane Devastates Kauai, 1992, http://www.washintonpost.com/wpsrv/weather/hurricane/poststories/iniki.htm.

Kettl, D., *The States and Homeland Security: Building the Missing Link,* Century Foundation, New York, 2003. www.tcf.org/publications/homeland_security/kehlpapers/kehl.pdf.

Kettl, D., Contingent coordination: Practical and theoretical problems for homeland security, *American Review of Public Administration,* Vol. 33, 2003, pp. 253–277.

Lewis, D., Political appointments, bureau chiefs, and federal management performance, 2005, www.wws.princeton.edu/researchpapers/09_05_dl.pdf, www.fema.gov/doc/library/tex_reader_fema_start_plan_fy03–08.doc.

Mangum, C., *Hawaii State Civil Defense Bulletin,* Asia-Pacific Homeland Security Summit, Vol. 3, November 20, 2003, p. 2.

Mouginis-Mark, P., *Disaster Management in the Pacific and Indian Ocean Regions,* Research Corporation University of Hawaii (RCUH), Honolulu, Hawaii, 2005.

PA Times, DHS announces changes for FEMA, *American Society of Public Administration,* Vol. 29, No. 3, March 2006, p. 1.

PA Times, Homeland security secretary announce new agenda for DHS, *American Society of Public Administration,* Vol. 28, No. 8, August 2005, p. 2.

Peach, D., What hurricane Andrew tells us about how to fix FEMA. http://www.theinformationist.com/index/trifecta/comments/fema_andrew_katrina_gao. United States General Accounting Office. March 18, 2006, p. 93.

Prizzia, R., Emergency management and disaster response in Hawaii: The role of medical centers and the media, *Journal of Emergency Management,* Vol. 2, No. 4, 2004, pp. 43–49.

Prizzia, R. and Helfand, G., The day after: Rebuilding mainland, USA, *When Terrorism Strikes Home: Defending the United States,* James Fagin (Ed.), Pearson Publishers, New York, 2006.

RAND Press Release, Rand study finds emergency responders believe they have inadequate protection, August 20, 2003. www.rand.org/hot/press.03/08.20.html. See Tom LaTourrette, D.J. Peterson, James T. Bartis, Brian A. Jackson, and Ari Houser, Protecting *Emergency Responders,* Vol. 2, Santa Monica, CA: RAND, Community Views of Safety and Health Risks and Personal Protection Needs, 2003.

Robinson, R., McEntire, D.A., and Weber, R.J., *Texas Homeland Defense Preparedness*, Century Foundation, New York, 2003, p. 28.

Rudman, R. and Metzl, J., Emergency responders: Drastically underfunded, dangerously unprepared. Washington: Council on Foreign Relation, Vol. 1, No. 6, 2003, http://www.cfr.org/pdf/Responders_TF.pdf.

Sensenig, D., Emergency management: Proactive or reactive? Both!, *PA Times*, Vol. 22, No. 3, March 1999, pp. 2–4.

Shea, R.F., FEMA Reengineering for Catastrophe Readiness and Response, Acting Director of Operations, FEMA, presentation at Emergency Management and Homeland Security/Defense Higher Education Conference, National Emergency Training Center, Emergency Management Institute, June 5–8, 2006.

Shirkhodai, R., Hazard clearinghouse: A decision support capability, Pacific Disaster Center, Kihei, Hawaii, 2003.

Simon, H., *Administrative Behavior: A Study of Decision-Making Processes in Administrative Organizations*, MacMillan, New York, 1947.

Sommer, A., The people of Kauai lived through a nightmare when the powerful storm struck, http://starbulletin.com/2002/09/08/news/story5.html, Honolulu Star-Bulletin, September 8, 2002.

Taylor, F.W., *Principles of Scientific Management*, Harper and Brothers, New York, 1911.

US Army Corps of Engineers, Hurricane Iniki Assessment, http://www3.csc.noaa.gov/hes_docs/postStorm/H_INIKI_ASSESSMENT_REVIEW_HES_UTILIZATION_INFO_DISSEM, 1993.

US Department of Health and Human Services, Accountability Report: Fiscal Year 2001. Washington DC: U.S. Government Printing Office, viii, http://www.hhs.gov/of/reports/account/acct01/pdf/intro.pdf.

Wells, J., Catastrophe Readiness and Response, (Paper Presentation) The Emergency Management Institute (EMI), 9th Annual By-Invitation Emergency Management & Homeland Security/Defence Higher Education Conference, National Emergency Training Center, Emmitsburg, Maryland, June 6–8, 2006.

CASE STUDIES AND LESSONS LEARNED: U.S. NATURAL AND ENVIRONMENTAL DISASTERS

Chapter 6

A Different Approach to Disaster Recovery: Alaskan Earthquake Disaster Recovery

Dwight Ink

CONTENTS

The Earthquake

On March 27, 1964, Alaska was devastated by the strongest earthquake ever recorded in this continent, measuring 9.2 on the Richter scale and lasting an unusual four minutes. The ground either rose or sank over 5 feet in an area exceeding 50,000 square miles where about 60 percent of the population lived. The base of its economy, fishing, vanished temporarily with the small boat harbors now either too shallow to accommodate the boats or too deep to be protected by the submerged breakwaters. Fishing boats were destroyed and canneries were knocked out. Highways were impassable, bridges had buckled, and the terminus of the railroad had fallen into the sound. Water and sewerage systems were inoperable. Thousands of homes and businesses were damaged or destroyed, and few had earthquake insurance. The ever-present Alaskan problem of inflation threatened to soar out of control under the pressures of rebuilding.

Earthquake recoveries present complications not encountered in the wake of hurricanes. Ground elevations change, property lines shift, and there can be considerable hidden structural damage that takes time to detect. Changed elevations, for example, exposed Alaskan communities to new tidal behavior whose impact on most waterfronts was hard to predict, raising serious questions as to whether several communities should be even rebuilt.

Alaska also had large areas underlain with Bootleggers Cove Clay. When saturated, it reacted to the motions of the earthquake very much like a layer of grease above which the overburden slid toward the ocean carrying homes and community waterfront facilities with it. Deep soil drilling equipment had to be slowly barged up the Pacific Ocean to carry out the massive tests required to determine where it was safe to build, a step that was difficult for Alaskans to watch as they impatiently waited for design and reconstruction to begin. Several towns now faced the difficult decision as to whether to relocate their entire community with the promise of federal assistance, or to remain where they were in seriously damaged conditions and more vulnerable to future earthquakes, without federal assistance for rebuilding.

In the midst of the sobering damage assessments that continued to flow in, it was very discouraging to learn that the Alaskan engineers did not believe that a sufficient amount of relocation, design, and construction of public facilities, especially that of harbors and water and sewerage systems, could be completed by the end of the short Alaskan construction season to avoid movement of roughly one-third of the Alaskan people to the lower 48 before winter.

Emergency Response

Despite the fact that there had been no warning, the initial emergency work of providing water, food, medicine, and shelter moved forward with remarkable speed. The Office of Emergency Planning (OEP) and other public agencies, private companies, and citizens went into action within the first several hours without waiting to be asked or worrying about who was supposed to do what under some central plan. The Red Cross and Salvation Army were among the excellent performers. One advantage was the fact that Alaska had a large military presence, and it performed extremely well.

But within hours, it became clear that the existing organizations of the federal, state, and local governments could not begin to cope with the complexity and magnitude of the physical and economic recovery Alaska faced. The state was in chaos, and the economy ruined. New organizations and operating approaches would have to be developed and employed very quickly if Alaska was to survive as a viable state.

Disaster Recovery

Federal Commission

Five days after the earthquake, President Johnson departed in dramatic fashion from the customary federal government approach to disaster recoveries by issuing Executive Order 11150 in which he appointed most of his cabinet as members of a temporary Federal Reconstruction and Development Planning Commission for Alaska.* This commission was to cooperate with the state in developing plans for both reconstruction and economic development. Not explicitly stated was Johnson's intent that this

---

* Members were the secretaries of defense, interior, agriculture, commerce, labor, HEW; the administrators of the Federal Aviation, Housing and Home Finance, and Small Business agencies; the chair of the Federal Power Administration; and the director of the Office of Emergency Planning (a predecessor of FEMA). The director of the bureau of the budget participated in the commission meetings. He and his management staff played a very important role. Nearly every other agency of the federal government eventually became involved, including the Department of State.

organization would provide strong leadership for the rapid reconstruction of the battered state. It was to be far more than a planning group.

Completely unprecedented in our history was Johnson's action in designating a powerful congressional ally, Senator Anderson, a democrat from New Mexico, to chair the commission. Anderson understood the executive branch because of his earlier experience as Secretary of Agriculture. He had experience with relief programs, and had conducted hearings on Alaska statehood as a member of the Senate's Interior and Insular Affairs Committee. This highly innovative action by the president demonstrated his deep concern about the disaster and set an example for innovative approaches to the recovery by all the elements of the federal government in a way that mere proclamations and exhortations never could.

State Commission

On April 3, Governor Egan issued executive order no. 27, establishing the State of Alaska Reconstruction and Development Planning Commission to partner with the federal commission. Mr. Joseph Fitzgerald was appointed the state coordinator. Fitzgerald traveled with me and participated in Commission staff meetings. His role as liaison with the governor and state agencies was invaluable.

Executive Director and Staff

Anderson provided very effective leadership for the federal commission, but a senator should not give operating direction to departments and agencies. Therefore, in an effort to avoid a constitutional issue, Johnson designated an experienced executive level V career person as executive director of the commission to lead the implementation of the commission policies and the presidential directives. That role fell to me. I was detailed from my position as assistant general manager of the Atomic Energy Commission where I had responsibilities somewhat similar to a COO, plus liaison with the White House and Congress. I am not sure this designation solved a possible constitutional question, and I would certainly not recommend this as a permanent arrangement. As a practical matter, however, this dual reporting did not create any problems. In fact, it strengthened my ability to act and to work with Congress.

As I was executive director of a commission comprised largely of Johnson's cabinet, to some extent I was also viewed by cabinet members as their staff person assigned by the president to help them carry out their recovery roles, a very useful perception. To nurture this view, our small commission staff exerted every effort to help the departments expedite their recovery activities, helping to make sure the departments received credit for their work. Anderson provided the public face of the federal role in the recovery, reducing to a minimum the time I needed to spend on public relations.* This unusual combined support from the president, a powerful senator, and the cabinet enabled me to quickly break bottlenecks and assume an occasional head-knocking role, even though my authority was not specified by law.

I was also helped by a little-known role of a presidential assistant, Lee White, who helped me understand how Johnson liked to operate. He also created an illusion that I had a close relationship with the president, which was not the case even though the fact that I could reach Johnson when needed was critical to my role. Having an inexperienced political intermediary would have been a fatal handicap in the case of Alaska where time was of essence. My staff members were detailed from federal agencies involved in the recovery except several highly qualified engineers who were detailed from congressional committees.† Two managers, three engineers, and two secretaries were the only full-time commission staff. Seventeen other members were part-time, serving largely as liaisons with their home agencies. They played an important role in making sure that their agencies were responding effectively, and would generally accompany me when I met with department and agency heads.

We were able to function with this extremely small staff because our role was not that of doing the work, but rather it was to mobilize, energize, and coordinate the agency men and women throughout the government who were the doers.

Alaskan Field Committee

The commission authorized me to establish an Alaska Field Committee tasked with helping to coordinate and expedite operations on the ground in Alaska. Chaired by the regional coordinator of the Department of the Interior, it was comprised of the senior official of each of the 18 federal agencies having field offices in Alaska. The state coordinator, Joseph FitzGerald, served as an ad hoc member.

Task Forces

Chairman Anderson immediately appointed an Alaskan Construction Consultant Committee with members drawn from the Associated General Contractors of America and the International Union of Operating Engineers. The American Institute of Architects and the Engineers Joint Council also provided advice on reconstruction and development plans. The commission established nine interagency task forces to make studies and help make sure that agencies worked together on issues that cut across departmental responsibilities. They reported to the executive director.

---

* Our open approach to the recovery activities also reduced the need for special press conferences and publications.
† They had originally been detailed from NASA and DOD to the Congress.

Nine interagency task forces were established to make special studies and prepare policy recommendations in areas in which several federal agencies had closely related responsibilities. They reported to the executive director.*

As there were no predetermined structures prescribed for the Alaskan recovery, we were able to develop whatever coordinating groups or structures best fit the particular conditions faced in Alaska. Despite starting from scratch, all of these organizations were in full operation two weeks after the earthquake, with the field committee planning actions that would soon mark the transition from the emergency work under way to the more complex recovery phase. Task forces had people busy in Alaska gathering data needed to plan reconstruction. No person or group had to wait to be asked or needed to worry about just how they fit into a detailed central plan.

It is worth mentioning that none of these recovery organizations had institutional authority. Their authority came from that which each member brought to the table from their home agency. We were careful to see that none became another layer in the processes. Rather they were to serve roles in information sharing, coordinating, and expediting.

Policy Role

Under the effective leadership of Senator Anderson, the commission moved quickly on policy issues. At its first meeting, for example, the commission decided that reconstruction would proceed in a way that would enhance future development rather than follow the past practice of rebuilding only what had been destroyed. This meant, for example, rebuilding highways and bridges to modern standards. It meant doubling the size of most small boat harbors. This policy paid off, but it complicated our ability to meet the already difficult schedules, and some projects required legislation before we could proceed. The commission also departed from past policies when it decided that federal assistance should not be provided to home and business owners to rebuild in areas that scientific evidence showed to be of high risk in the event of a future major earthquake. Not surprisingly, this policy generated considerable controversy.

Within two months of the earthquake the commission had approved a series of policies including tax rebates, increase in the federal share of federal–aid public facilities, debt adjustments, purchase of state bonds to help finance urban renewal projects, disaster loans, mortgage forbearance and refinancing, and cash

---

* The Transportation Task Force was chaired by the Undersecretary for Transportation in the Commerce Department, with members from the Department of Defense, the Federal Maritime Commission, the Alaska Railroad in the Department of Interior, the Federal Aviation Agency, and the OEP. The other task forces were Ports and Fishing, Natural Resource Development, Industrial Development, Financial Institutions, Economic Stabilization, Community Facilities, and Scientific and Engineering (located in Alaska).

payments. Those policies requiring legislation were incorporated in an omnibus bill forwarded to Congress on May 27. Temporarily blocked by the bitter 1964 Civil Rights debate and the 57 day Senate filibuster, we were fortunate in having Senator Anderson as our chair because of his ability to break through the filibuster and secure passage.

Recovery Operations

It was obvious that we had to develop new management approaches if we were to avoid thousands of families abandoning Alaska as freezing weather approached and the economy collapsed. Approaches customarily followed by less catastrophic disaster recoveries would not suffice. There were several strategies developed in Alaska that were especially critical to our prospects for success.

Streamlined Operations

Customary recovery approaches were believed to be too complex and slow moving for a successful recovery. There would be too much paperwork, too many clearances—often in sequence, and insufficient flexibility for innovation. There would be too many levels between the operating people in the field and the president to permit quick decisions and expedited actions. Rather than adding to the complexity of government through adding disaster procedures such as the National Response Plan, the Alaskan approach was to streamline, and at times suspend, existing processes. Simplification was the key.

The president and key congressional leaders permitted the recovery staff to suspend existing procedures that jeopardized those schedules needed to complete construction of critical public facilities before the construction season ended in the fall. This unprecedented degree of flexibility was used sparingly, but in some cases made all the difference in meeting important deadlines.

Similarly, instead of a large organization such as DHS that is separate from existing structures to lead recovery operations, in Alaska a tiny, yet very powerful, staff worked out of the White House to mobilize resources within the whole federal government to move the recovery forward. Because the leadership for this staff was a temporary cabinet level commission comprised of the participating departments, the DOD and the other departments were more willing to make their resources available quickly than the customary arrangement in which a department is asked to respond to a peer organization.

When the plans were in place and the most critical construction completed (in this case about six months), this temporary recovery machinery disappeared. Staff details ended, and they returned to serve full-time in their agency positions that they had never had to relinquish.

Unlike Katrina, the federal agency dealing with the Alaskan emergency needs of food, water, medicine, rescue, and shelter, the OEP, was autonomous and free to make decisions and take actions on its own.* In Alaska, the executive director had access to the president, a powerful senator, and the cabinet, giving him enormous strength in bringing the government together as a quick action team. At the same time, the operational coordinating personnel in the field reported directly to him as well as their agency leaders.

Expedited Schedules

The urgency of the initial emergency operations after a natural disaster or terrorist attack is obvious. Less apparent in most cases is the need for moving quickly with the recovery or rebuilding phase, yet it is of vital importance from the standpoint of human suffering as well as minimizing the heavy costs that result from slow recoveries. In Alaska, however, the short construction season meant that the recovery would fail unless it moved at a speed never seen in peacetime.

The simple organization and process streamlining mentioned above were critical to this departure from business as usual. In addition to these administrative actions, we tried to change some of the customary approaches to construction design and construction itself.

On my first day in Alaska, I found our construction people following a perfectly logical approach of reviewing past construction schedules and looking at where these timetables could be tightened. Unfortunately, on some of the most critical public utility projects, especially water and sewerage systems, these tightened schedules would not provide for the necessary relocation, design, and rebuilding before the construction season ended. This would require many communities to abandon the state, and we would have failed.

Improvising in the course of this discussion, I asked them to begin by setting a completion date before the construction season ended, and then work back to the present with intervening milestones that might look unreasonable and perhaps impossible. Instead of establishing tight, but reasonable, schedules, I asked them to establish schedules that permitted Alaskans to stay after cold weather stopped outside construction, regardless of how unrealistic they might be. In several instances where there appeared to be soil stability, this meant slashing normal schedules by 90 percent. I assumed that we would later have to compromise with reality and adjust some schedules, but I believed that this approach would result in more rapid construction than would a more "realistic" approach. It did.

---

* In addition to the fact that the OEP retained its full authority after the federal commission was established, the existence of the commission lent weight to the work of OEP and strengthened its ability to take action.

There were instances in which safety considerations limited how much schedule shortening could be done, especially where deep soil studies were required to assess ground movement in the event of future earthquakes. But most schedules were slashed sharply.

We pressed for change in every facet of reconstruction, and both the government and contractor people responded very well. The long daylight hours during Alaskan summers permitted double and triple shift operations, accounting for some of our ability to move rapidly. We streamlined the usual process of scoping the work and awarding the contracts. Construction moved almost concurrently with design where soil uncertainties were minimal.

The use of incentive fee contracts was pushed to new levels, including penalties for failure to meet cost or schedule targets. Lawyers cautioned against the litigation that the penalty clauses might generate, but we believed that potential litigation was a small price to pay for the incentive they provided to avoid slippages and cost overruns. I was relieved to find that no criticisms resulted from the high profits some contractors gained from early completion and cost savings.

Heavy reliance on incentive contracts required the engineering and management skill to thoroughly understand the work to be done, establish very specific objectives to be achieved, and provide close monitoring of the work.

Clear Leadership

President Johnson's action in declaring a disaster within hours and bringing into play the OEP and other federal agencies demonstrated strong leadership. He then got everyone's attention by his unprecedented action of establishing the cabinet level commission to be headed by a senator. Because Anderson was close to the president and had prior experience as a cabinet member, he had credibility and was a very effective chair.

This bold step of the president was followed by his designating an experienced career person as the executive director placed in charge of directing the recovery effort. Not being buried under several layers of political appointees with question- able qualifications, I had the tremendous advantage of access to and support from top administration officials, including the president. The fact that this was a temporary organization to last only a few months also greatly reduced possible concern that the White House might be intruding upon agency turf. The Alaskan recovery looked to political leaders for recovery policies, but unlike Katrina, it relied on experienced career personnel to lead operations.

Open Operations

The Alaskan recovery was exceptionally open to the public. Most operational decisions were made during open meetings, not in agency offices after the public sessions. These community meetings were generally held in high school gyms, most of which survived the earthquake quite well, where business leaders and the public were invited to participate. Everyone was entitled to speak, but time did not permit speeches or irrelevant comments. Several meetings lasted all night, causing some complaints about long meetings. However, this initial investment of time saved considerable time in the long run. It also had other advantages.

First, as one should expect, a number of the suggestions and complaints of homeowners and businessmen led us to significantly improve our reconstruction work. Second, providing people with an opportunity to voice their views and to see the reasoning behind the decisions substantially reduced opposition. And third, this participation gave many people a sense of ownership in the plans even if they did not agree with some of the details, and provided an incentive to put forth a greater effort toward success.

Intergovernmental Management

It was my practice to include both state and federal staff when I flew from one damaged community to another to develop plans and check on progress.* In the first round of community meetings, representatives of federal, state, and local governments gathered around a large table to develop initial plans, with citizens and business leaders in attendance and encouraged to participate. In each case, we agreed upon a preliminary group of especially critical projects, agreed upon an agency to provide leadership for each project, and a preliminary cost and time of completion estimate. These were not guesstimates that the participates had to take back to Juneau or Washington for possible modification before approval, but they were the plans on which work began; recognizing that in the next round of meetings, we would have to make adjustments based on intervening internal discussions.

This intergovernmental process saved an enormous amount of time over the customary practice of requiring multiple meetings and internal agency clearances before proceeding, followed by similar time-consuming procedures required for significant changes in the plans. This approach meant that each participant had to be well informed and equipped with sufficient authority to commit his or her agency, resulting in some degree of anxiety at the beginning. As time passed, many agencies became pleasantly surprised at how well their people in the field performed when they were given authority and good guidelines with respect to how to exercise that authority.

We did not refer to these plans as federal plans, state plans, or local government plans. Rather they were community plans in which all three levels of government were expected to function as a team. We developed a Seward plan, a Kodiak plan,

---

* Community observers likened this practice to the circuit riding of the nineteenth century circuit riding by country preachers.

several Anchorage plans, a Valdez plan that called for moving the whole town to a safer location, etc. The intergovernmental relations efforts that had been the focus of much of the federal government activity was replaced in our work with intergovernmental management that went far beyond good relationships.

Qualified Personnel

The urgency of the rebuilding and the need for innovation placed a high premium on highly qualified, experienced career leaders in each agency. It was also important that individuals who were not performing well be reassigned quickly. We had cases in which high-level managers were taken off their work within 24 hours of their inadequate performance coming to the attention of federal or state leaders. There was nothing we stressed more in our work with the agencies.

Today, there are more political appointees in the government, considerably more than other advanced countries use. This somewhat limits the operational leadership opportunities for the career service. Consequently, today it is not often that a career man or woman has the advantage some of us had of diversified assignments with major responsibilities, experience that helped us tremendously. Recovery from a catastrophic natural disaster or terrorist attack will usually involve scores of federal, state, and local agencies, requiring the in-depth knowledge of how the government works that experienced career managers possess.

Congressional Relations

The value of Senator Anderson in the Alaskan recovery cannot be overestimated. Not only did he give skillful leadership to the commission, he also gave me and our staff wonderful support. As President Johnson had foreseen, Anderson also provided great assistance to the president in arranging for quick legislative hearings and votes despite the bitter civil rights debate that dominated congressional attention at that time.

Also important in our executive–legislative relations was the congressional staff detailed to me. Originally detailed from NASA and DOD to the Hill, these were suburb engineers on whom I leaned very heavily. Most of the time, they were in Alaska inspecting the projects. However, even though they reported to me and functioned as though they were back in the executive branch, they were also expected to informally keep several key congressional committees informed of our work. This included setbacks as well as progress. In the hands of some people, this arrangement could be a problem. But in this case, it was of tremendous value to us. This independent flow of information, combined with the Anderson role, and our reliance on experienced career personnel combined to give Congress a high level of confidence in how we were managing the recovery. It reduced the amount of time I had to spend in formal congressional communications, and contributed to the tacit agreement of key members of Congress to our unusual freedom to suspend agency procedures that threatened successful reconstruction.

Oversight

The heavy emphasis we placed on streamlining agency processes and establishing tight schedules increased our vulnerability to waste and scandal. The priority given to use of highly qualified personnel, and the visibility of the rebuilding to the public, the media, and the Congress, greatly minimized this risk. But we also asked the agency oversight groups to follow our work carefully. Several days after my selection, I called the comptroller general to request the assignment of several GAO personnel to observe our operations. They had complete access to our records and were free to attend our staff meetings. We wanted to learn of any problems at the earliest stage so that we could take immediate corrective action. I looked upon these groups as allies in good management, and none of them engaged in the "gotcha" tactics that undermine the effectiveness of some oversight groups.* Fortunately, they also focused on the extent to which agencies achieved their cost and program goals rather than on the extent to which detailed procedures were followed.[†]

Interdependency

Our freedom to innovate across the board produced a synergism that relying on one or two elements of change would not have produced. This is illustrated by the fact that we would never have been granted so much flexibility had we not had an open approach, or had we not relied so heavily on career leadership, or ensured effective monitoring and oversight. Without that flexibility, we would have failed.

Outcomes

These organization and management strategies served us well in Alaska, exceeding our expectations. Of course, not everyone fully recovered, and a handful of people left the state. A few loans went bad and some businesses failed. No doubt the extreme amount of streamlining and cutting of schedules resulted in some inefficiencies. However, there was a broad consensus that the recovery was very successful overall.

---

* We did not have inspectors generals in those days, and the effectiveness of the existing agency oversight groups varied greatly. We tried to persuade several agencies to improve this area, but met with little success.
† Had GAO and other oversight groups placed adherence to procedures ahead of saving the state, we would have been graded as having failed.

The principal goals of President Johnson and the Alaskans, preventing abandonment by a substantial portion of the Alaskan residents and the collapse of the economy, were achieved. Soon helped by newly discovered oil, the economy moved forward. The devastated communities did rebuild. Both Anchorage and Valdez were declared All American Cities several years later.

Only five months after the earthquake, the *Anchorage Daily News* in an editorial titled, "Government at its Best," lauded the "remarkable" performance of the commission staff. It said

> In many cases the normal rules followed by federal agencies were sprung completely out of shape to fit the post-earthquake needs of Alaska. Tight time schedules established for construction work became even tighter under the staff's constant prodding and watchful eye . . . It was a rare day when a problem was posed without being accompanied by a solution." The editorial concluded with, "If more government officials functioned with the same type of positive outlook and attention to needs and details, that word 'bureaucrat' would soon fast disappear from popular dictionaries.

On October 5, President Johnson expressed his satisfaction, "The work done by the Alaskan Reconstruction Commission is in my view an outstanding illustration of cooperation among government agencies at all levels, and I want to especially acknowledge your contribution as Executive Director of the Commission . . ." Governor Egan said the commission "accomplished more than an outstanding job" in behalf of Alaska, and then stated that the "Federal, State, and local efforts were coordinated throughout the critical phase of the Rebuild Alaska program, in a way which, I am certain, has never been previously accomplished in the history of American disasters."

A year after the earthquake, in reference to all the public and private groups that had been involved in the recovery, the *Daily News* wrote, "The comeback from disaster was so dramatic there hardly seemed to be a gap between destruction and reconstruction. The recovery period was almost as dramatic and breathtaking as the earthquake."

The Alaskan recovery demonstrated how federal, state, and local governments can work together with business and nonprofit groups as community teams in overcoming the impact of a catastrophic disaster.

Recovery strategies used in Alaska were in a number of ways the opposite of that contemplated in our National Response Plan.* Rather than establishing a complicated special structure with many pages of processes to follow in rebuilding, the

---

* The NRP focuses heavily on the initial emergency response, and it is not entirely clear how far some of the provisions go in controlling agency recovery efforts that may extend over several years.

Alaskan approach was based on establishing a tiny, but powerful, central temporary entity that could plan and coordinate recovery actions quickly without red tape. It relied on leadership that could mobilize and energize the enormous resources of existing agencies throughout the government, and motivating them to innovate and drastically streamline their standard operating procedures. This arrangement has the capacity to adapt quickly to new and different challenges, because it does not predetermine structures and procedures to be followed in the recovery phase.

One caution is that the Alaskan approach depends heavily on presidential leadership, and on experienced political and career leaders who trust one another and can function as a team.

Chapter 7

Hurricane Hugo: Two States' Responses to the Disaster

Nancy S. Lind and Pam LaFeber

CONTENTS

Introduction

This chapter will examine the response to Hurricane Hugo that was led by the Charlotte, North Carolina, and Charleston, South Carolina, state governments. An identification of the various actors involved, the duties performed, and the outcome of such response efforts will be detailed in this chapter. The shared governance mode illustrated by both governments will also be discussed in addition to an analysis of the consequences of each community's disaster management priorities.

Hurricane Hugo: The Response in South Carolina

Hurricane Hugo struck South Carolina soon after midnight on September 22, 1989. Commonly, hurricanes weaken once they reach the land, but Hugo did not. This hurricane quickly ripped through Charleston and moved in a northwest direction toward its next victim. As the sun came up that morning, Hugo was gone, but not before leaving a path of death and destruction. The events leading to the hurricane's strike on September 22, 1989 are depicted in the following pages.

On Monday, September 18, the Charleston County Emergency Services Division notified the local police department that a hurricane watch had been declared (Greenberg et al. 1990: p. 26). Charleston officials then addressed the situation and acted under the assumption that Hugo would hit Charleston with maximum force. Unfortunately, this attitude was not enough to prepare the community for such a violent onslaught from the torrential weather system.

The Charleston Police Department set up a meeting with other law enforcement agencies on September 19. The main topics discussed at this meeting were evacuation scheduling and route management. Great emphasis was placed upon the policies and procedures for towing stalled vehicles, answering alarms, and investigating traffic accidents (ibid.: p. 27).

Under South Carolina law, only the government can order a mandatory evacuation (ibid.). Generally, this order is based upon a request from the local government. In all other instances evacuation is strictly voluntary. As Hugo rapidly approached the Carolinas, a voluntary evacuation had been recommended on September 20. Later that same day, utilizing the electronic media sources still available, Governor Carroll Campbell ordered a mandatory evacuation of the low-lying and coastal areas, as well as the barrier island (ibid.). He also requested the presence of the National Guard to help with the possible occurrence of social unrest. This early evacuation order caused an influx of traffic on all major routes. Fortunately, at least that part of the urgent problem had been addressed just two days earlier, and Charleston officials were prepared to keep traffic flowing to safer ground.

The broadcast and print media were of great assistance in communicating the evacuation routes and shelter location in this time of confusion. The media also provided up-to-date information to the public regarding where to find safe water and where to take relief supplies.

Emphasis was placed upon allocation of local personnel throughout the area. It was deemed important for personnel to be staged at predetermined safe locations during the storm to allow their rapid entry into the community as soon as the period of maximum danger had passed (ibid.: p. 30). The Charleston Police Department used four team headquarters including the main police building and two shopping malls. As the eye of Hugo briefly settled over the city, officers were sent out to rescue people in danger and investigate reports of looting.

A number of agencies from outside South Carolina sent personnel to augment Charleston's officers. Each of these additional officers was assigned with either a

Charleston officer or a National Guard unit to help them find their way around the unfamiliar territory (ibid.: p. 32). Although Charleston welcomed the extra help, if such manpower is not properly and gainfully utilized, its presence will be questioned and relief efforts will suffer. In the case at hand, this arrival of new personnel, coupled with the locality's lack of preparation, resulted in confusion and misallocation of resources. Thus, Charleston's great influx of manpower actually hindered its response efforts.

Once Hugo had passed, the problem of addressing the extended power failures materialized. The storm not only destroyed two vital steam-generating plants that provided the primary source of electrical power to the area, but main transmission lines from the other areas of the state were also down (ibid.). The pre-storm estimate of a few days inconvenience turned into a month or more for some. Especially for the individuals living in the low-lying areas, months went without electricity, telephones, or any contact with outside world (Schneider 1992: p. 139). As a result, the milling process in Charleston continued.

Turner and Killian (1972) define the milling process as a widespread search for meaning among the survivors. As the immediate disaster recedes, people are confronted with situations and problems that lie outside of bounds of normal, everyday existence (ibid.: p. 137). People do not know how to deal with such obstacles and begin to search for appropriate standards of behavior. Milling is the most pronounced when the existing procedures do not adequately address the situation at hand. Further exacerbation of the problem is when the lines of communication and coordination break down. This is exactly what happened in Charleston.

Another unanticipated problem that surfaced in the recovery stage was the management (or mismanagement) of incoming aid. Hundreds of volunteers flocked to the Charleston area and local officials had not prepared for such an invasion of assistance. Not only were there people arriving from outside of the area, but local inmates and prison staff were also available to help with relief efforts (Acorn 1990: p. 80). As a result of this influx, accountability was minimal. The absence of one main body of authority in Charleston also added to the problem by causing a lack of coordination.

The predominant explanation for this lack of coordination may be traced to the occurrences of the night before Hugo hit. The Emergency Preparedness Division located in South Carolina existed before Hurricane Hugo. However, the governor saw the necessity to hastily create another "central" disaster response unit. This dual system merely added to the local confusion. Residents were unsure of where to go for help and which agency to listen to for guidance. The standard operating procedures already structured in the Emergency Preparedness Division plans were adversely affected by the presence of another disaster response with no established rules. The emergence of an effective ad hoc communication and authority center is extremely difficult when given such a short warning period (Seigel 1985: p. 107).

As a result, the local-level government emergency management officials were largely ineffective because they were untrained and unprepared for the damages that did occur, but most importantly they did not know which procedures to follow (ibid. p. 139). This confusion did not stop at the local and state level. The federal level response reflected the same amount of incompetence.

FEMA's reporting, assessment, and inspection procedures were simply inappropriate for the severity of the disaster and extreme isolation of much of the population (ibid.). Hundreds of FEMA officials were sent to Charleston following Hugo. Unfortunately, these officials expected people to come to them and no provisions were made for people who were out of touch with the government for whatever reason. These individuals were largely forgotten during the weeks after Hugo (ibid.).

Charleston Mayor Joseph Riley was highly critical of the actions taken by the federal government. He stated, "The national government should assume full responsibility for a national disaster like Hugo" (ibid.). Senator Earnest Hollings went on to refer to FEMA as a "bunch of bureaucratic jackasses more concerned with regulations, forms, assessments, and inspections, than with helping those in need" (ibid.). Such statements reflected the general opinion of response efforts in South Carolina and labeled the disaster relief efforts a failure in Charleston.

South Carolina operated under the collaborative mode of shared governance, a general partnership between the levels of government. The federal government acts as the most dominant actor in this mode and bears the most of the financial and coordinating responsibilities. South Carolina and Charleston officials alike saw the federal government as the level that should be responsible for recovery efforts in the wake of Hurricane Hugo. To the dismay of both South Carolina and Charleston officials, and especially the residents of Charleston, the federal government was not operating from the same point of view.

According to FEMA's director, FEMA is to provide guidance, leadership, and when appropriate, direct financial aid to communities planning for, responding to, and recovering from major emergencies of all types (Guiffrida 1985: p. 2). FEMA is to serve as the federal coordinating agency in disaster management and response. FEMA is not to serve as the agency responsible for assuming all of the recovery activities. In this scenario, FEMA operated under the limited regulatory mode of shared governments. This mode places the responsibility of preparedness and response with the local government. This is exactly how FEMA conducts its assistance to communities. The basis of FEMA's coordinating facet reflects the notion that an ideal disaster response occurs when the local government is the first to address the situation, then the state level of government, and finally the federal government. In the occurrence of any disaster, the bulk of the responsibilities are to fall to the local government. FEMA exists as a secondary actor in disaster response.

An important note to stress here is that South Carolina had passed no laws that specifically address the use of nonstructural mitigations to deal with hurricane control (Comfort 1988: p. 95) Nonstructural mitigations refer to land use controls, zoning, and building codes. Government officials did not believe a hurricane would occur within the next ten years. The refusal to acknowledge the very real threat of a hurricane, coupled with an absence of hurricane legislation, left Charleston officials lacking adequate ways of addressing Hugo. Thus their attempts failed miserably.

Hurricane Hugo: The Response in North Carolina

Shortly after 6:00 a.m. on September 22, 1989, Hugo's wrath struck North Carolina. Technically, Hugo had been downgraded to a tropical storm before reaching Charlotte. However, the lessened severity of Hugo did not lessen Charlotte's preparation for its onslaught.

Charlotte, which is located in Mecklenburg County, reflected a successful preparation and timely response that was facilitated by a preexisting emergency management plan developed by the local Emergency Management Office (EMO). The joint city and county agency followed an all-hazard plan designed to cover any man-made or natural emergency, using generic components that addressed such areas as alert notification, emergency response, damage assessment, shelter needs, public information, and disaster recovery (Shook and Steger 1989: p. 10).

This plan was not specifically designed for a hurricane, but outlined within it are the measures to be taken when addressing storms and the problems that may accompany several storms such as heavy rains and flooding. The EMO director initiated standard emergency preparedness activities, including storm monitoring and alert-list telephone number verification on September 18, after confirming that Hugo would hit the South Carolina coast (ibid.).

By 2:00 a.m. on September 22, the EMO director had been notified of the severe weather by the warning branch of the EMO, the county police department. Once the reports had been confirmed by the local emergency operations center, response action began. Starting at 3:00 a.m., city and county police departments, city and volunteer firemen, emergency medical services personnel, and members of the EMO began their respective response duties. As Hugo quickly approached and conditions worsened, the county manager, assistant county manager, and assistant city manager were notified. In addition to such actors were representatives of the Charlotte–Mecklenburg Utility Department, Southern Bell Telephone, Duke Power, Charlotte–Douglass International Airport, the Red Cross, and 26 other city and county departments (ibid.).

Managing the disaster response were the assistant county manager and assistant city manager. These individuals are very important and may be held liable if known possible hazards were not included in their disaster management plans (Kemp 1984: p. 9). Before Hugo reached North Carolina, the managers met with other department representatives to discuss the extent of damage expected. The conclusion was reached that maintaining mobility was of paramount importance because any delay in the delivery of services would seriously affect recovery (ibid.: p. 32). The morning Hurricane Hugo struck, another meeting was held to outline the exact measures to be taken. Major thorough fares were to be cleaned first, followed by feeder roads and residential streets as soon as conditions allowed (ibid.). This plan was designed to keep paths open to hospital and other vital response centers.

As Hugo gained intensity, the number of 911 calls steadily increased. The city fire divisions responded to an unceasing stream of calls from 3:00 a.m. to 6:00 a.m. Later, the chief of the Charlotte Fire Department determined that 403 responses, triple the normal emergency load, had been made in the first 24 hours (ibid.).

Once Hugo had passed, a survey of the damage was done by the city and county managers to form concrete recovery decisions. Information provided by the law enforcement agencies, medical personnel crews, and the utilities helped to comprehensively examine the situation. In addition to these actors, an aerial survey conducted by a videographer and county building standards personnel enabled the emergency management team to quickly assess the destruction left in Hugo's path (ibid.).

The emergency management team chose not to activate the emergency broadcasting system because it would not be heard by most people. Instead, live daily news conferences were held to keep citizens abreast of the actions being taken by the local officials and the responsibilities that still fell to every individual. *The Charlotte Observer* maintained home delivery and proved to be the most effective media source because the reports that were carried electronically only reached a small audience by comparison.

One very important facet of this recovery operation in Charlotte was that EOC officials were present at all news conferences. This proved invaluable during the public information process, as both reports and citizens became accustomed to their presence and reports (ibid.: p. 13). Most importantly, however, this arrangement served as a check and balance in that all information released required approval by both city and county managers, which reduced the risk of inaccurate reports and increased the degree of accountability.

The first news conference held at 11:00 a.m. on Friday, September 22, announced the state of disaster declaration issued by the local Charlotte government (ibid.). The city and county received greater police powers and the clearance to request assistance from the North Carolina National Guard, including military policy (ibid.). Also made available were the North Carolina State Highway Patrol, the North Carolina Department of Transportation, and the North Carolina Forest Service. With nightfall approaching that first day, the threat of massive looting intensified. The increased police personnel (300–400 officers present during one shift) accompanied by the decree that even the threat of crime was cause enough for arrest saw the night pass without any major incident.

Twenty-four hours after Hugo hit land, public health and safety operations were in full force along with a telephone hotline accepting calls according to previously logged-in categories. Such categories included health concerns, financial assistance, and shelter relocation. The private sector participation greatly increased in the days following Hugo. Among important participants were the city and county budget officers. These individuals developed a financial report that would later serve as the request by the local government to declare the county a disaster area. Once this was accomplished, the area would become eligible for federal assistance.

It is important to stress here that in contrast to South Carolina, North Carolina passed critical legislation in 1974 with hurricane and flood mitigation elements (Comfort 1988: p. 90). The Coastal Management Act of 1974 outlined nonstructural mitigation elements which included land use controls, zoning, and building codes (ibid.: p. 88). Extremely important in this discussion is the fact that following Hurricanes Agnes and Eloise several states enacted legislation to address such disasters. North Carolina, a state not struck by either hurricane, passed its legislation in response to the federal Coastal Zone Management Act of 1972.

The 1982 study conducted by Rossi et al. concluded that a high possibility existed that North Carolina would experience a serious hurricane within the next ten years. This attitude is directly opposite of South Carolina's and may prove to be the reason why Charlotte's response to Hurricane Hugo was much more successful than that of Charleston.

The process in North Carolina worked form the bottom up, precisely as intended (Schneider 1992: p. 140). North Carolina illustrated the limited regulatory mode of shared governance. In this scenario, Charlotte was responsible for adhering to not only federal government regulations but also the state Coastal Area Management Act of 1974. Although the local disaster management plan did not specifically address hurricanes, officials manipulated the generalities to fit the situation at hand. The IEMS instructs the response to be handled exactly in this manner. FEMA's disaster management plan was also implemented as intended. Unfortunately, however smoothly the response and recovery procedures were performed, the community still needed substantial time to completely return to normal living conditions.

Conclusions

Disaster management is an area addressed by intergovernmental cooperation. Shared governance, in its most general form, embraces the notion that responsibilities can be shared among the layers of government (May, 1985: p. 41). The comparison of the response of the South Carolina and North Carolina government to Hurricane Hugo demonstrates that when a local government perceives a disaster as a potential threat, and places disaster management as a top priority, an effective response to such a disaster will usually result. Hence, FEMA's response will also be effective. In contrast, when a locality does not place any significance on disaster management, response efforts will suffer and FEMA's recovery model will not be viewed as successful.

References

Acorn, L.R. South Carolina inmates and staff pitch in for hurricane relief. *Corrections Today* 52: 80–82, 1990.

Comfort, L.K. *Managing Disaster: Strategies and Policy Perspectives.* Durham: Duke University Press, 1988.

Greenberg, R.M., Wiley, C., Youngblood, G., Whetsell, H., and Doyle, J.H. Law enforcement responds: Lessons of Hurricane Hugo. *The Police Chief* 57: 26–33, 1990.

Guiffrida, L. FEMA: Its mission, its partners. *Public Administration Review* 45: 2, 1985.

Kemp, R.L. A city manager's role in emergency management. *Public Management* 66: 9–12, 1984.

May Peter, J. Fema's Role in Emergency Management: Recent Experience. *Public Administration Review* 45: 40–48, 1985.

Schneider, S.K. Governmental response to disasters: The conflict between bureaucratic procedures and emergent norms. *Public Administration Review* 52: 135–145, 1992.

Seigel, G. Human resources development for emergency management. *Public Administration Review* 45: 107–117, 1985.

Shook, M. and Steger, D. How to handle a disaster: A study in teamwork. *Public Management* 71: 10–14, 1989.

Turner, R.H. and Killian, L. *Collective Behavior,* 2nd edition. Englewood Cliffs, New Jersey: Prentice-Hall, 1972.

Chapter 8

Hurricanes Katrina and Rita: The Critical Role of the Nonprofit Community in the San Antonio Disaster Response

Sandra A. Palomo-Gonzalez and Dianne Rahm

CONTENTS

Introduction

On Wednesday, August 31, 2005, the city of San Antonio opened an emergency operations center (EOC) after having been notified by Governor Perry that Texas was going to take Hurricane Katrina evacuees from Louisiana. With the activation of the EOC, the San Antonio Chapter of the Red Cross began the process of opening shelters to house the hurricane victims from New Orleans. The Salvation Army, the San Antonio Food Bank, Catholic Charities, United Way, Baptist Child & Family Services, and many other nonprofit organizations launched operations to assist the city with the Katrina crisis. On the 24th of September, less than a month after Katrina had pummeled New Orleans, Hurricane Rita devastated the Gulf Coast and San Antonio again received evacuees from this second storm. San Antonio assisted tens of thousands of evacuees from these back-to-back hurricanes that locally came to be called "Katrita."

What became increasingly clear as the disaster unfolded was that no unit of government had the capacity to adequately respond to the crisis. From the beginning of the disaster response, city, county, state, and federal government agencies in San Antonio relied heavily on the nonprofit sector. Part of this reliance was by design being codified in national, state, and local emergency response plans that designate nonprofits such as the American Red Cross or Salvation Army as key responders. The situation in San Antonio with the twin disasters, however, tested this relationship. Rather than building an independent capacity to respond, as time went on, the many government agencies involved grew increasingly dependent on the nonprofit sector. As the crisis moved from the immediate response phase into the long-term recovery phase, the nonprofit sector assumed the burden of both planning and service delivery.

The story of the San Antonio nonprofit sector's mobilization in response to these twin disasters is the subject of this chapter. Drawing on data gathered through participant observation, interviews with key nonprofit leaders, and an Internet survey of managers of nonprofit organizations in the greater San Antonio area, we explore the nature of the nonprofit community's disaster response. After providing the chronology of events as they unfolded, we discuss the role played by the nonprofit community in the disaster response. Drawing on personal interviews of key actors and results of a survey of nonprofit leaders, we discuss the perceptions of the San Antonio nonprofit community toward the disaster. We conclude with a discussion of the lessons learned and recommendations for future preparedness.

Methods

A brief discussion of the methods used to research this chapter is in order before beginning the larger discussion. There were four original data collection methods used. The first was via participant observer methodology. Both authors of this chapter served as volunteers for a local nonprofit organization directly engaged in the disaster response. Participation as volunteers allowed us to work in the shelters, attend Red Cross disaster services training, and to observe as we worked.

As observers (identifying ourselves as university faculty researching the disaster response) we attended a host of public meetings called by coordinating organizations associated with the disaster response. The first was an ongoing series of VOAD (Voluntary Organizations Active in Disaster) meetings. These meetings were public forums called by the VOAD leadership and attended by nonprofit community organizations involved with the disaster response and recovery operations. Government officials, including city, county, state, and federal, were frequently present to provide briefings to the VOAD members. The VOAD also provided ongoing information including updates of regulatory or operations changes and general briefings to VOAD members through an email listserv.

We also attended meetings of several faith-based coordinating groups involved in the relief effort. One of these, Community of Churches for Social Action, sought to bring together local African–American churches as part of the relief effort. Another group, which identified itself as the "faith-based" VOAD, held meetings of local, primarily Christian, churches to coordinate what came to be called the Faith-Based Family Sponsorship Program. We also participated in general discussions regarding the nonprofit community's response to Katrina and Rita hosted by a local umbrella organization called the Nonprofit Resource Center of Texas. We traveled to Houston and participated in a forum jointly sponsored by the Harris County Department of Education and United Way to discuss that city's emergency response and problems encountered. We participated in a day-long study and review session organized by the city of San Antonio, the San Antonio Office of Emergency Management, the University of Texas at San Antonio's Institute for the Protection of American Communities, and the Texas Homeland Security Alliance that focused on better understanding San Antonio's response to the hurricanes.

We conducted a series of personal interviews with leaders of the major non-profits involved with the San Antonio disaster response. These interviews allowed us to ask a series of questions regarding the specific involvement of each nonprofit in the response as well as to ascertain the primary barriers each observed during their efforts. Through the interviews we tried to probe into potential lessons learned by nonprofit organizations during this unprecedented occurrence.

With the collaboration of the Nonprofit Resource Center of Texas (NPRC), a local 501c(3) with the mission of education and training of nonprofit leaders, we conducted an Internet survey of organizations in the NPRC's database. The survey results provided information regarding the variety of local nonprofit organizations' involvement in the disaster response as well as the consequences to their ongoing operations in the long-term recovery phase.

Finally, the data collected by each of these above-mentioned methods was supplemented by archival resources including government documents (federal, state, and local), press releases or other published statements from nonprofit organizations and government agencies, and newspaper stories drawn from the local press.

Chronology of the Disaster

Hurricane Katrina, the eleventh named tropical storm of 2005, first made landfall in Florida on August 25 as a category 1 hurricane. It passed over the Florida peninsula and entered the warm waters of the Gulf of Mexico where it grew rapidly to a category 5 storm with sustained winds of 145 knot (167 miles per hour). By the time Katrina made its second U.S. landfall near New Orleans, Louisiana, it had decreased to a high-end category 3 storm with sustained winds of 100 knot (115 miles per hour) (Knabb et al. 2005). Katrina advanced up the eastern Louisiana coastline and inflicted destruction throughout the entire state of Mississippi and into Alabama. The storm almost totally destroyed all communications networks of landlines, cell towers, and electric power lines in the entire Gulf Coast region. Roads as far as 8 miles inland in Mississippi were submerged under 20 feet of water. The affected region was utterly devastated. Antebellum homes that had withstood Gulf Coast storms for 150 years were flattened (Kitfield 2005).

New Orleans survived the initial storm surge but the levee system that protected New Orleans from Lake Pontchartrain to the north failed. Although many had heeded the mandatory evacuation order issued by Mayor Nagin before Katrina made landfall, many tens of thousands did not (Treaster and Kleinfield 2005). Hundreds were stranded on rooftops without food or water where they waited to be rescued. Others wandered aimlessly or found refuge on Interstate 10, in areas above water. About 20,000 people, the bulk of the refugees, were holed up in or near the New Orleans Superdome (McFadden and Blumenthal 2005). The New Orleans Convention Center was also overwhelmed by those seeking shelter from the storm and the rising floodwaters (Wikipedia 2005a).

On August 31, Texas began accepting Katrina evacuees, especially those from the New Orleans Superdome. Houston's Reliant Astrodome rapidly filled and as of September 2 was unable to accept any more evacuees. With Houston filled to capacity, Governor Perry made arrangements for San Antonio and Dallas-Fort Worth to take an additional 25,000 evacuees each. By September 5, estimates suggest that about 140,000 evacuees were housed in shelters in Texas, adding to the approximately 90,000 who had driven in earlier and were residing in hotels or homes. With 230,000 evacuees in the state, Governor Perry declared a state of emergency in Texas and asked other states to begin taking evacuees (Wikipedia 2005a).

When Texas began taking evacuees on the 31st of August, the city of San Antonio called the San Antonio Chapter of the American Red Cross informing them they were opening an emergency operation center (EOC) and asked the Red Cross to open shelters. The immediate concern was that San Antonio would not have sufficient space to hold evacuees for what had by then become clear would be an extended stay. The Red Cross typically opens shelters for brief stays of no more than 48 hours. For such a stay, the Red Cross considers 20 square feet per person adequate. The Red Cross had established memorandums of understanding (MOUs) with enough facilities to house 68,000 people in the city if 20 square feet per person was occupied. Given the anticipated duration of the Katrina shelter operations, however, the Red Cross decided to provide 60 square feet per person. The new square footage requirement combined with the expectation of a large number of evacuees coming made it clear that there would not be enough space available in already identified facilities (Bennett, personal interview, October 14, 2005). The result was that the city decided to open several large shelters in vacant buildings at KellyUSA, the former Kelly Air Force Base, currently under city control. Buildings 171 and 1536 (two extremely large buildings capable of housing tens of thousands) were opened as emergency shelters to receive evacuees as were other shelter sites within the community including a vacant Montgomery Ward building at Windsor Park Mall and an old Levi Strauss factory building (Chapa 2005).

Rapidly, thousands of the Hurricane Katrina evacuees arrived in San Antonio. Some came in their own vehicles but many were brought in buses or by airplane (Chapa 2005). Countless evacuees had spent days in horrible conditions in New Orleans Superdome or Convention Center. Most had no homes to return to, given the extent of destruction caused by Katrina. They had lost everything.

Efforts began to assist the populations in the shelters and to move the thousands of evacuees from the shelters into hotels or more permanent housing. This process was slow and tedious. Hotels and more permanent housing had to be located, people without vehicles had to be transported, and evacuees leaving the shelter needed cash to buy food, clothing, and household items once they got to their destinations. Meanwhile the shelters had to provide emergency shelter, food, and health care for thousands on a daily basis.

More than 10,000 volunteers worked long hours at the shelters and in other activities to try to assist Katrina's victims. The Red Cross, the Salvation Army, the

San Antonio Food Bank, Baptist Child & Family Services, Southern Baptist Men, Catholic Charities, and a host of other nonprofit organizations assumed a primary role in case management, assistance in finding long-term housing and provision of services to meet other needs. The local Voluntary Organizations Active in Disaster (VOAD) sought to organize the relief efforts. A secondary faith-based VOAD formed to coordinate the efforts of local faith communities. The volunteers joined their efforts with the variety of government agencies that were participating in the relief efforts (FEMA, Bexar County, the city of San Antonio, San Antonio Housing Authority, the State of Texas, the Metropolitan Health System, and the independent school districts).

As the crisis moved into its second week, San Antonio requested assistance from a national incident management team. The U.S. Forest Service's Rocky Mountain Incident Management Team arrived to take over management of the shelters although FEMA, city, and county employees worked alongside of volunteers and the nonprofits to provide food, shelter, and health care for the evacuees. Nearly 90 government or nonprofit agencies set up operations in the shelters offering an array of services from meal assistance, to bus passes, housing, and religious counseling (Jesse 2005c).

Before the evacuees being housed in the shelters could be moved to hotels or other available housing, and before the community was fully able to respond to the needs of the Katrina evacuees in San Antonio, the Gulf Coast was hit by a second powerful hurricane. On September 24, 2005 only three weeks after Katrina, Hurricane Rita made landfall in between Sabine Pass, Texas and Johnson's Bayou, Louisiana as a category 3 storm with sustained winds of 120 miles per hour. Rita's storm surge resulted in the reflooding of parts of New Orleans. Houston escaped major damage but Governor Perry declared nine counties in Texas a disaster area (Wikipedia 2005b). Galveston county officials issued mandatory evacuation orders and Houston's mayor encouraged people to leave the city voluntarily. Many thousands followed the mayor's advice and headed for San Antonio.

McCreless Mall was used as a staging area where evacuees were registered, processed, and then directed to an appropriate shelter. Many of the Rita evacuees came to San Antonio in private vehicles, rather than arriving in buses or by plane. They were directed by electronic postings on interstates 35 and 37 as well as U.S. 87 to McCreless Mall (Chapa 2005). The governor's emergency management council that consists of 30 state agencies, the American Red Cross, and the Salvation Army was placed on level 1 alert. The state Division of Emergency Management moved food, water, and other supplies to the Dallas-Fort Worth area and to San Antonio in preparation for Rita evacuees (Zarazua 2005). More than 3 million people were evacuated from their homes as they fled Hurricane Rita (Sandalow 2005) making Rita the largest evacuation in Texas history. Traffic backed up on the evacuation routes for more than 100 miles. Four hundred eighty seven miles of interstates 45 and 10 to Dallas and San Antonio and U.S. highways 59, 69, and 96 were made one way. Nearly one third of all Texas state troopers were dispatched to control traffic (Driscoll 2005).

Rita complicated the shelter operation already under way for Katrina evacuees in San Antonio. To make room for Rita evacuees, officials sped up their efforts to move Katrina evacuees to hotels, more permanent housing, or other locations. A written notice issued on September 21, before Rita hit the Texas coast, informed the Katrina evacuees remaining at buildings 1536 or 171 at KellyUSA as well as the people in the Windsor Park Mall shelter that they either had to move to other housing in San Antonio or they could take advantage of a one-way plane or bus ticket to anywhere in the U.S. except New Orleans. Later in the day, the operations chief of the Rocky Mountain Incidence Management Team increased the choices to include moving into building 171 at KellyUSA (Heath and Davis 2005).

In the end, the Rita victims were sheltered in building 1536 and Katrina victims were either moved out of KellyUSA or to building 171 at KellyUSA. The initial idea was to keep the two groups separated because the Rita evacuees would not receive the same benefits as the Katrina evacuees unless the president declared Rita a national disaster (Wilson 2005b). This never happened. For the period of time that shelters were open to support large numbers of Hurricane Rita evacuees, the two populations separated in different facilities in San Antonio. Within a few days of the storm, over 2,500 Rita evacuees moved into shelter at building 1536 (Fikac and Castillo 2005). Loss of electricity and water in the wake of the storm kept numbers climbing in the shelter for a brief time.

With the flow of evacuees from Rita adding to the Katrina population, FEMA began looking into having a private contractor run the shelter operations. The shift to a private contractor allowed FEMA to pay for shelter operations directly rather than having the city of San Antonio provide cash for that effort and be later reimbursed by FEMA (Allen 2005). The shift to Shaw Group to run the shelters was accomplished via a no-bid contract with FEMA on October 21. The U.S. Forest Service's Rocky Mountain Incident Management Team returned to their regular duty as Shaw took over the operation (Jesse 2005b).

Unlike Katrina evacuees, most Rita evacuees were able to return home reasonably soon after the storm passed. Eventually both Rita and Katrina evacuees remaining in San Antonio's shelters were regrouped together in building 171 and building 1536 was closed. Shaw worked to move the remaining evacuees to more permanent housing and toward closure of the shelter. The last shelter in San Antonio, building 171 at KellyUSA, closed on December 31, 2005 having been in operation for four months.

Although shelters closed by the end of the year, hotels and other transitional housing units were still packed. By the end of 2005, San Antonio continued to house about 9000 evacuees in hotel rooms (Wilson 2005f) whereas many more had already been moved into transitional or more long-term housing.

The Nonprofit Community Response

Voluntary organizations were critical players in all aspects of the disaster response. The local chapter of the American Red Cross recruited thousands of volunteers, provided mass care, and offered individual assistance. Another first responder, the Salvation Army operated a warehouse for donated goods, food, and supplies. The San Antonio Food Bank provided food products to feed evacuees. Usually a secondary responder that moves in after FEMA and the Red Cross are gone, in this instance, Catholic Charities served as a first responder operating in the shelters. Another nonprofit, Baptist Child & Family Services, provided mass care for special needs evacuees. Faith-based organizations and local churches played a key role in the efforts as well. The Texas Baptist Men served hot meals to thousands of evacuees. Area churches raised in excess of $1 million to assist evacuees and provided countless volunteers. The faith-based VOAD established an evacuee adoption program whereby churches provide support for evacuee families for up to a year. The following sections examine the role that each of these groups played in the relief effort in greater depth.

American Red Cross

The American Red Cross has been chartered by the U.S. Congress to provide a system for disaster prevention and mass care during national and international relief situations. With 940 chapters across the nation, the agency responds to over 70,000 natural and man-made disasters annually. As a first responder, the Red Cross provides food, shelter, health, and mental health services to meet the immediate needs of disaster victims. The organization provides individual assistance to enable victims of disaster to purchase food, clothing, and essential items, and resume normal living activities (American Red Cross 2005). Nationwide, the Red Cross employs some 35,000 full or part-time staff and utilizes some 1 million volunteers (Bennett, personal interview, October 14, 2005).

Hurricane Katrina has been the single largest disaster response in the agency's history. The Red Cross estimates that it will spend over $2 billion on the effort. To date, nationally, the agency has provided financial assistance to some 1.2 million families and almost 3.5 million overnight stays to hurricane survivors in over 1100 shelters in 27 states and Washington, DC. In partnership with the Southern Baptist Convention, the Red Cross has provided over 27 million hot meals and 25 million snacks to hurricane survivors (American Red Cross 2006).

The San Antonio Chapter of the American Red Cross serves a 21 county area and has branches in surrounding communities. The local chapter provides health and safety training, disaster response services, support services to military members and their families, and education programs that facilitate their international work in partnership with the Red Crescent (San Antonio Red Cross 2005).

With its emphasis on disaster relief, the American Red Cross is one of the first on the scene to provide immediate care, but does not routinely remain at the site beyond 30 to 45 days. Hurricane Katrina evacuees were clearly going to be in shelters well beyond the usual stretch. As well, churches and school gymnasiums, the typical shelter sites for short term disasters were inadequate for what was to be a longer-term effort. The evacuees also arrived hungry and thirsty; many had not showered in days. They needed clothing, food, sleep, and medical attention (Bennett, personal interview, October 14, 2005). To compound matters, as evacuees arrived, there were few, if any, concrete details. Reports indicated that 5,000–10,000 evacuees were arriving, but those reports changed frequently (Hotchin and Idell Hamilton 2005). In other words, the Katrina relief efforts, especially because of the numbers of evacuees that arrived and the speed in which they came, clearly tested the local chapter's ability to respond.

As the evacuees arrived, the Red Cross in partnership with other nonprofits and assisted by thousands of volunteers began the massive undertaking of evacuee intake at the shelters. Evacuees received cots, food, water, and access to an initial source for medical information and referral under the assistance of a Red Cross volunteer nurse. Evacuees were then handed-off to a health systems provider for additional medical evaluation. The Red Cross continued to provide food, shelter, and clothing for evacuees as long as they were housed in the shelters (Bennett, personal interview, October 14, 2005).

In addition to mass care, the Red Cross provided evacuees with individual assistance, in this instance, debit cards. Funded by charitable donations, the assistance was intended to help Katrina victims with immediate needs such as food, shelter, and clothing. These funds were available to individuals so long as they could provide evidence that they had a pre-disaster address from an affected area. Individuals received debit cards valued at $365 per person and up to $1560 for a family of five. These funds were not meant to supplant, but rather supplement federal assistance (Bennett, personal interview, October 14, 2005; Simmons 2005). Evacuees receiving assistance were "treated as adults." That is, the Red Cross placed no controls on the money. Evacuees were free to use the debit cards as they saw fit. Additionally, because of the lack of congregate shelter space, the local chapter provided funds to enable some evacuees to find shelter in area hotels. As this was not an expense generally covered by the Red Cross, FEMA was expected to reimburse the agency for these expenses. The activity was not funded by donations (Bennett, personal interview, October 14, 2005).

Volunteers were an integral part of the operation. The Red Cross utilizes a disaster services human resource system (DSHRS) to recruit and train a corps of volunteers to assist with disaster relief. When disasters strike, these volunteers are deployed to affected sites across the country. As part of the training process, volunteers are utilized in disasters at the local level before they will be sent to off-site locations. The volunteers must commit to serve a minimum of 21 days. Because of the need to be available for three consecutive weeks on short notice, DSHRS volunteers are often retirees (Bennett, personal interview, October 14, 2005).

In preparation for Katrina's landfall, well before the evacuees arrived in San Antonio, the local chapter deployed 25 trained volunteers to the affected area. As evacuees later arrived in San Antonio, the chapter sought assistance from the national office to fill supervisory roles at local shelters. The national office was unable to fill the request for trained volunteers, however, because DSHRS volunteers had been deployed to hurricane impacted areas of the Gulf Coast states. In an effort to address the shortage, the agency relaxed the usual 21 day deployment requirement to a 7–10 day requirement. The local operation had no choice but to use volunteers with limited training and experience in supervisory roles (Bennett, personal interview, October 14, 2005).

The lack of trained leaders at local shelters contributed to confusion and frustration for evacuees and volunteers alike. In surveys of the local nonprofit community (discussed more fully later), one respondent noted that, "Red Cross volunteers were not usually well trained but put in leadership roles." Similarly, another nonprofit respondent explained that it was difficult to find a Red Cross worker at the shelter and that those "working with the Red Cross seemed to be unable to make any decisions without getting the go ahead from a higher up that they had no way of contacting."

The shortage of supervisory volunteers, moreover, was exacerbated by the outpouring of untrained, spontaneous volunteers seeking to assist at the shelters. The Red Cross alone had 12,000 volunteers present. Early on, the agency realized that it did not have the human resource capacity to handle the volume of phone calls from those interested in volunteering. The chapter thus made the decision to establish a volunteer intake center at the Joe Freeman Coliseum, a site located near the Red Cross San Antonio headquarters, but away from the shelters (Bennett, personal interview, October 14, 2005). As prospective volunteers arrived at the Coliseum, they completed an application. After a brief meeting with a Red Cross representative, volunteers were given an official name badge with the Red Cross logo. They were then instructed to show up at the shelter at a specific date and time. At least initially, the volunteer registration process was paper-driven. There were no computers at the intake site. Criminal background checks, which are regularly conducted as part of the registration process, were not conducted on these volunteers (Bennett, personal interview, October 14, 2005).

The Coliseum intake center, unfortunately, did not operate as smoothly as planned. In some cases, volunteers arrived at the shelter as scheduled, expecting to be on a roster with a preassigned role. However, it was clear that they were not expected. Often, volunteers were given a new name badge because the previously prepared name tag was not valid at the shelter. The volunteer check-in process at the shelters was largely a "low tech" operation. It was not until some weeks later that a database was fully operational and computers, albeit mismatched and without the same functionality, were placed at the volunteer registration table. At that time, as volunteers showed up at the shelters, their information could be retrieved, provided the names had been entered into the database correctly and that the Red Cross volunteer at the check-in table had computer experience.

Moreover, despite the huge number of spontaneous volunteers, shelters were sometimes understaffed, chiefly due to a mismatch between the needs of the shelter and the availability of volunteers. It was difficult to find volunteers able to make a long-term volunteer commitment. Shelters were often short of volunteers during the midnight to 6 a.m. shift, as well. Volunteers with specialized skills, such as nurses, were in high demand. Other problems arose. Some volunteers registered to assist but then failed to show up to work at a shelter (Idell Hamilton 2005a). At the peak of the Hurricane Rita relief effort, a shortage of Spanish-speaking volunteers became acute.

Problems with volunteer management aside, the fact remains that countless volunteers from the community helped the Red Cross in the shelters. These efforts cannot be discounted. Some volunteers staffed and stocked the store, a large area in the back of one of the shelters with donated clothing and goods. Others helped serve meals. Often volunteers just sat and listened to evacuees as they shared their stories. Some helped in the library, an area with donated books and magazines.

Salvation Army

The Salvation Army's role in disaster relief was affirmed by Congress under the Stafford Emergency and Disaster Assistance Act of 1988, the same act which created FEMA. Unlike the Red Cross, the Salvation Army provides short-term emergency services as well as long-term recovery assistance. A faith-based organization, its relief efforts consist of food service, emergency shelter, procurement and distribution of donated goods, cleanup and restoration services to rebuild affected areas; spiritual and emotional support for victims and providers; and financial assistance to victims. The Salvation Army also maintains the Salvation Army Team Emergency Radio Network or SATERN, a communication system that operates during emergency situations when traditional mechanisms, such as telephones, fail (Salvation Army 2005a). Like the Red Cross, the agency recruits and trains volunteers to assist during relief and recovery situations (Salvation Army 2005b). At the national level, the Salvation Army provided assistance to over 1 million Hurricanes Katrina, Rita, and Wilma survivors in 30 states (USA Southern Territory Salvation Army 2005).

In San Antonio, an area commander oversees the local Salvation Army's operations, which has five campuses and operates 13 programs including a child development center, senior citizens' residence, transitional living program, emergency shelter, a drug rehabilitation center, and three churches. With a disaster services office located on site, the Salvation Army has a long history of supporting disasters. Also, the Salvation Army has a record of collaborating with the city of San Antonio and with other governmental and nonprofit agencies in the area. Because the agency has been a fixture in the city for so long, the Salvation Army's access to elected officials during the twin hurricane response was facilitated. This access was critical to its key role in the relief efforts (Farr, personal interview, November 10, 2005).

To assist Katrina evacuees in the Gulf Coast area, the local chapter deployed a canteen to the Texas–Louisiana border to help migrating evacuees with food and assistance. Members of the top leadership were sent to the site as well. The Salvation Army then established a warehouse to collect and categorize donated goods as they arrived from all over the country. The items were shrink-wrapped and sent to Katrina-affected areas. As the evacuees began to arrive in San Antonio, however, the local Salvation Army shifted its focus and began to provide donated items for evacuees now located locally (Farr, personal interview, November 10, 2005).

The Salvation Army then set up a food pantry and distributed food, clothing, blankets, and hygiene items to evacuees. Additionally, the chapter provided counseling, referral services, rental assistance, and utility assistance to evacuees, so long as they had a FEMA number. At the evacuee's request, the Salvation Army provided pastoral care as well. Evacuees staying in hotels were eligible for Salvation Army assistance, so long as they had a FEMA number (Farr, personal interview, November 10, 2005).

Just as managing the unprecedented numbers of spontaneous volunteers that presented at the shelters challenged the capacity of the Red Cross, likewise, managing the outpouring of in-kind donated goods from the community proved to be a daunting task for the Salvation Army. At its peak, the donated clothing, shoes, toys, and toiletries covered hundreds of thousands of square feet of warehouse space (Conchas 2005). Volunteers were needed to help the Salvation Army sort the mountains of items that arrived daily (Idell Hamilton 2005b). At one point in the disaster response, an executive board comprised of city, county, and FEMA officials alongside representatives from the Red Cross and Salvation Army announced that they would no longer accept donated goods. There was simply no more room (Conchas 2005). In a visit to the shelter, the local Salvation Army Commissioner expressed gratitude for the public's generosity, and then stated as he pointed to the huge mountain of donated clothing in the background, "But people need to understand the huge burden this puts on our volunteers," (Idell Hamilton 2005b, p. 17A). He added that, if donors wanted to help, they should provide new clothing to help evacuees look presentable as they prepared to seek employment (Idell Hamilton 2005b). Indeed, although perhaps well-intended, donors often brought clothing in large garbage bags that was not presorted by size or gender; some items were badly stained or soiled.

San Antonio Food Bank

The San Antonio Food Bank (SAFB) also played a key role in the local relief efforts. Founded in 1980, the SAFB is a member of America's Second Harvest, the nation's largest charitable hunger-relief organization. With over 200 member food banks across the country, America's Second Harvest procures and distributes over 2 billion pounds of food and grocery items each year (America's Second Harvest 2005). The SAFB is the 18th largest member food bank in the nation and the oldest member food bank in Texas. The San Antonio Food Bank receives, stores, and delivers donated food and grocery products to 380 partner agencies in San Antonio, Bexar County and 15 surrounding counties. In collaboration with these partners, the SAFB distributes food to over 40,000 families every month (San Antonio Food Bank 2005).

The San Antonio Food Bank is well-equipped for disaster response. The national organization tracks and monitors disasters. At the state level, the food bank receives e-mail announcements from the State Office of Emergency Management. The agency has preexisting MOUs with the local chapters of the American Red Cross and the Salvation Army, as well. These MOUs stem from relationships fostered by America's Second Harvest at the national level. The SAFB executive director is also a member and former chair of the San Antonio VOAD. The executive directors from agencies including the Red Cross, Goodwill Industries, and the Food Bank maintain strong personal relationships with one another. They meet regularly at an area restaurant. These relationships proved important in helping forge a smooth and effective Katrina and Rita relief disaster response (Cooper, personal interview, November 8, 2005).

In preparation for Hurricane Katrina's landfall, the San Antonio Food Bank positioned its inventory with water, pop-top fruit cups, and snacks to send to the affected area. Truckloads of these items were then shipped to Louisiana and Mississippi. Soon, the local food bank felt the influx of calls from people who were evacuated from the affected area and were staying with friends, family, or in hotels. The SAFB referred these callers in need of assistance to the nearest food pantry to receive a food box (Cooper, personal interview, November 8, 2005).

Shortly thereafter, at a meeting with city officials, the food bank executive director recalled that he "panicked," when he learned that some 25,000 evacuees from New Orleans would soon arrive. The food bank feeds on average 40,000 households per month and turns its inventory over every two weeks. The logical response, the SAFB executive director added, would be to say no. The moral response, however, is "Yes, we'll do what we can do," (Cooper, personal interview, November 8, 2005).

The SAFB worked with the congregate feeders at the shelters. Donated food items were taken to the Salvation Army–run warehouse at one of the shelters. Products began to arrive from other food banks, food manufacturers, and wholesalers from around the country. Still, it was not enough. The food bank conducted food drives and purchased items to supplement its inventory. A three-day food drive in partnership with a local grocery chain yielded over 800,000 pounds of food from individual donors. In comparison, in all of 2004, SAFB received 690,000 pounds of donated food from individuals (Cooper, personal interview, November 8, 2005).

The relief efforts placed an enormous demand on the capacity of the local food bank. SAFB's caseloads were up 150 percent and 100 percent in September and October, respectively, over the previous year due to Katrina and Rita. At times, the agency did not have the staff, trucks, or space needed to meet the demand. As the executive director noted, the food bank rented trucks to transport product—a huge, unanticipated cost to the agency that the agency incurred on a "leap of faith." During a seven-day period, the executive director worked 7 a.m. to 11 p.m. daily. The agency's staff was taxed as well. After a week, the agency's management reflected on the health of the staff. They knew they had to let their employees get some rest. Volunteers provided some relief. Literally thousands of volunteers came out to sort, box, and get food items out to the shelters. In a typical month, volunteers at the SAFB log some 5000 hours. During a single week at the height of the Katrina related effort, volunteers put in some 2700 hours (Cooper, personal interview, November 8, 2005).

Like all agencies, the food bank strives to honor the wishes of its donors, a situation made more difficult by the relief efforts, especially, with perishable items. A large load of heads of lettuce earmarked for disaster relief arrived from California, for example. The shelters, though, did not have the resources to slice and prepare the lettuce. SAFB management had an obligation to honor the donor's wishes. At the same time, the lettuce would go to waste if not used and the agency had a moral obligation to feed the poor. Similarly, SAFB's regular inventory was not designated for disaster relief. To accommodate the needs of evacuees, the agency pulled from its inventory knowing that they would have to bring in additional product to replace the items used for the relief efforts. The lettuce was put in inventory, replacing items already sent from inventory to the shelters. No waste occurred.

Finally, some donors brought clothing to the agency's food drives. SAFB is not equipped to collect or distribute clothing. As a solution, the agency's executive director invited staff from the local chapter of Goodwill Industries to participate in the food drives and collect the clothing items (Cooper, personal interview, November 8, 2005).

Catholic Charities of San Antonio

Catholic Charities USA is one of the country's largest social service networks. Catholic Charities and its member institutions provide social services to those in need (Catholic Charities USA 2005). Catholic Charities of San Antonio is the official branch in the local archdiocese. In San Antonio, the agency provides an array of programs including adult education, refugee resettlement, immigration services, counseling and crisis intervention, adoption services, and a pregnancy program for adolescents (Archdiocese of San Antonio 2005)

Traditionally, Catholic Charities is a second responder involved in the recovery efforts after FEMA and the Red Cross complete their work. In this instance, however, Catholic Charities served as a first responder, providing services in the shelters. During the first week of the relief efforts, the staff at Catholic Charities worked alongside the city of San Antonio and the Family Services Association to assist with the massive undertaking of processing over 12,000 evacuees who arrived at Building 171 at KellyUSA. All of the agency's staff volunteered to assist with the effort and were on site from 6 a.m. until 2 p.m. the following day. The organization partnered with the United Way to recruit volunteers to provide additional assistance (Saldana, personal interview, November 1, 2005a). Moreover, because of the overwhelming needs at the shelters, every Catholic Charities employee was asked to give of their time to go and work with evacuees (McMorrough 2005).

Thereafter, Catholic Charities remained at the shelters and assisted with two other major functions—case management and transportation. Representatives located at the shelters provided case management alongside another agency, Family Services Association, and assisted with evacuee transportation. As the authorized FEMA-agency for transportation, Catholic Charities assisted over 1000 evacuees with long-distance transportation to help with family reunification. Catholic Charities also contracted with a shuttle company to provide local transportation for medical needs, such as doctor visits or for dialysis treatments. At the peak of the effort, the agency coordinated hundreds of these trips a day (Saldana, personal interview, November 1, 2005a).

Catholic Charities assumed additional responsibilities related to the relief efforts under the direction of the local archdiocese. That is, the San Antonio archdiocese named the president and CEO of Catholic Charities as the coordinator for all the diocesan relief (Saldana, personal interview, November 1, 2005a). Through a special collections initiative during the month of September, the Catholic archdiocese raised over $1 million from parishioners to assist evacuees with short- and long-term needs. With these funds, Catholic Charities provided vouchers for food, gas, and household items as well as bus passes for in-town transportation to evacuees (McMorrough 2005). Additionally, the agency partnered with other interfaith groups, including the Greater San Antonio Interfaith Disaster Recovery Alliance, to set up a warehouse to provide evacuees with donated items, including furniture, beds, and mattresses (Saldana, personal interview, November 1, 2005a). To help female evacuees secure employment, Catholic Charities awarded a $10,000 grant to a local nonprofit to provide attire for employment interviews and additional training after hire (Parker 2005d).

Although Catholic Charities served as a first responder, the agency did not relinquish its role as a second responder. In late December, Catholic Charities and Family Services Association continued to provide case management and were the only agencies still at the site (Saldana, personal communication, December 12, 2005b). In an interview with a local diocesan newspaper, the CEO of Catholic Charities, noted that the effort will be long term. As he explained, if some 3,000 to 5,000 evacuees remain in San Antonio, they will continue to have needs, such as job training and other resources for at least six months and perhaps up to a year (McMorrough 2005).

When asked what lessons were learned from the relief efforts, the CEO noted that he learned that the Catholic system is good, yet the Church needs resources and a plan of action to be able to react and make instant decisions during disasters (Saldana, personal interview, November 1, 2005a). That is, the Catholic Church's ability to respond during disasters has been hampered by the lack of a reserve pool of funding. Since last year, the diocese has discussed the establishment of a reserve fund, similar to what the Red Cross has in place, which would better position the Church to respond to the next disaster. The fund, which is still in the discussion phase, has not yet been approved (McMorrough 2005).

Baptist Child & Family Services

Like Catholic Charities, Baptist Child & Family Services (BCFS), played a key role in the relief efforts and one that was well outside its traditional role. An agency of the Baptist General Convention of Texas, BCFS serves individuals in Texas as well as three foreign countries. Its services include outreach programs, residential care for children in foster care and adults with mental disabilities, vocational training for adults with special needs, international humanitarian aid, and medical care for those in need (Baptist Child & Family Services, 2005).

Shortly before the evacuees arrived at KellyUSA, the BCFS president met with the Mass Care Coordinator for the Texas Governor's Office of Emergency Management (OEM) to discuss the state's plan for mandatory evacuation. Because BCFS operates a licensed assisted living facility for individuals with special needs in East Texas, OEM asked the president to develop a plan to assist with evacuating special needs populations. Not long after, on September 3rd, the president received a call from the OEM asking BCFS to provide care for Katrina evacuees with special needs. BCFS was then tasked with providing care for this special population, without a written plan in place (Dinnin, personal interview, November 1, 2005). The agency agreed to serve the special needs evacuees without knowing how many individuals they would serve or what types of special needs they would assist (Bird 2005b).

The effort strained the agency's human and financial resources. As BCFS began to prepare for the arrival of the evacuees, the management cancelled all scheduled time off for employees and advised employees that they would be "on call" every day of the week. If called, they should be prepared to work up to 12 hours per day (Bird 2005a). Without a written plan in place for special needs shelters in Bexar county, there were no MOUs in place nor were facilities identifed to house the evacuees. The BCFS president enlisted the help of the faith-based community. Four local baptist churches were identified as special needs shelters. In addition, the BCFS campus served as a shelter site. The churches, in turn, recruited volunteers to serve at the shelters (Dinnin, personal interview, November 1, 2005). As these sites filled, BCFS turned to the faith-based community once again. With the support of area churches, a grocery store turned warehouse, was converted into a sixth shelter (Bird 2005c). At a later date, the BCFS Executive Director went to Blossom Athletic Center and "claimed it" as a special needs shelter. At its peak, the BCFS-operation was the "largest nursing home" in San Antonio (Dinnin, personal interview, November 1, 2005). After Hurricane Rita made landfall, the Levi facility, which formerly housed Katrina evacuees, reopened as a shelter for Rita evacuees with special needs (Wilson 2005c).

During the Katrita event, BCFS provided care for over 1700 special needs evacuees. These clients included premature infants, amputees and the elderly, as well as individuals with chronic and acute illnesses, mental health needs, mental retardation, cancer, and incontinence (Dinnin, personal interview, November 1, 2005). Some evacuees were on dialysis or chemotherapy treatments; others were recovering from recent surgeries (Bird 2005c).

When asked what difficulties or barriers he encountered with the disaster response, BCFS President, Kevin Dinnin, reported that the lack of accurate information and lack of communication were major barriers to the efforts. He cited a well-publicized incident that involved the transfer of 310 special needs persons to a hospital in Waco, Texas. As the president explained, he was in a meeting when he received a conference call. During the call, which included several officials from the state, there were so many people on the line that he was not sure who was talking or who had the decision-making authority. The group decided that the special needs evacuees should be moved to an alternate location, the Veterans Affairs hospital in Waco, Texas, which would have 200 federal employees on hand to provide care. Later, when the BCFS president advised the evacuees that they would be moved, he personally assured them that they would be better served at the VA hospital. He added that if one of his family members had special needs, he would encourage them to go to the Waco site (Dinnin, personal interview, November 1, 2005).

Unfortunately, the VA hospital was not prepared to accept the evacuees when they arrived. The special needs evacuees were taken to a vacant Wal-Mart without adequate bedding, supplies, or bathrooms. Evacuee belongings, including medical records and prescriptions, which had been carefully packed, were tossed into a large pile, so they could be checked for contraband. Some items, including medication, were lost in the shuffle (Jesse and Wilson 2005).

The Faith-Based Community

As noted earlier, area churches provided facilities for shelters and provided volunteers to assist BCFS with mass care for special needs evacuees. This was just one example of the critical role that the local faith-based community played in the relief efforts. Most partnered with other churches and with area nonprofits to provide assistance to evacuees. Although some nonprofit leaders spoke of a moral obligation to assist with the relief efforts and other nonprofits are required to assist under a congressional mandate, most faith-based organizations and church members viewed their involvement in the relief efforts as a part of their ministry.

Church members were generous with their dollars and with in-kind contributions. A number of local churches held special collections to raise funds in support of evacuees. Oak Hills Church raised $195,000. United Methodist collected $63,000 and offered its education building to hold evacuees. Eagle's Nest Christian Fellowship and Second Baptist Church donated $61,000 and $10,000, respectively, to the American Red Cross (Parker 2005a). Collections conducted at Catholic churches in the archdiocese yielded over $1 million in support (Saldana, personal interview, November 1, 2005a). The Jewish community, likewise, offered to provide school uniforms and supplies to evacuees enrolling in a school in one of the local school districts. They supplied meals to evacuees at a special needs shelter and donated thousands of items of clothing, including over 2200 polo shirts (Parker 2005c). Another group, Communities of Churches for Social Action (CCSA), a coalition of over 20 churches from the local African–American community, raised in excess of $100,000 during worship services to assist Katrina evacuees. CCSA representatives met regularly to share information about the relief efforts and to assist evacuees remaining in the city over the long term (Watford, personal communication, December 20, 2005). Some CCSA members were vocal about the need to assist and minister to the evacuees who were predominantly African–American.

Area churches worked to provide in-kind donations, as well. The faith community called upon church members to assemble startup kits for evacuees. The kits include hygiene products, cleaning supplies, linens, cooking utensils, towels, diapers, and even stuffed animals (Parker 2005b). The kits were given to evacuees as they moved out of the shelters and into homes and apartments. A local church, St. Vincent de Paul, partnered with Catholic Charities to establish a warehouse to provide furniture and starter kits for evacuees (McMorrough 2005). Area churches provided chaplaincy services at the shelters for those seeking such assistance.

Some faith-based groups, including the Southern Baptist Convention and the Texas Baptist Men, were intimately involved in the relief effort. At the national level, the Southern Baptist Convention raised over $3 million to assist hurricane victims (Lewis 2005). The Red Cross and Southern Baptist Convention partnered to provide over 27 million hot meals to those in the affected area during the relief efforts, as well (American Red Cross 2006).

The Texas Baptist Men (TBM) is a nonprofit agency comprised of male members of Texas Baptist churches that are affiliated with the Southern Baptist Convention (Texas Baptist Men 2005a). As part of its ministry, the organization has provided disaster relief around the world since 1967. TBM trains and prepares volunteers to provide disaster assistance. The organization operates a fully equipped mobile feeding kitchen and coordinates with other units to supply disaster victims with hot meals and potable drinking water. In addition, members assist with emergency repairs, provide emergency child care, repair homes and churches, and offer chaplaincy or counseling services (Texas Baptist Men 2005b). In San Antonio, wearing their familiar bright yellow shirts, the TBM maintained a daily presence at the shelters as they prepared and served breakfast, lunch, and dinner for the evacuees. On some days, the group served as many as 15,000 meals to local evacuees (Wilson 2005a).

The Faith-Based VOAD

Another important group in the relief efforts was the faith-based VOAD. Throughout the Katrina and Rita relief efforts, the group met regularly to exchange information. An important outcome of the meetings was the establishment of the Faith-Based Family Sponsorship Program (FBFSP) conducted in partnership with the San Antonio Housing Authority (SAHA). Through the program, participating area churches sponsored evacuees living in SAHA units, for six months to a year. In so doing, the churches agreed to provide sponsored families with ongoing support, which included social services, household items, transportation assistance, employment assistance, counseling, and money to help the former evacuees become independent members of the community.

To participate, churches were required to submit an application and then send a representative to attend a two-hour orientation adapted from the Episcopal Migration Ministries and offered by the Diocese of West Texas. Over 100 individuals from 27 congregations received training through the program. As of December 2005, the faith-based VOAD continued to recruit churches for the FBFSP. In early 2006, the group planned to hold a strategic planning session to determine in what ways they will work to provide long-term recovery efforts. Indeed, as evacuees remain in the area, they will likely turn to the nearest resource, their local church and the faith-based community, for ongoing support.

Perceptions of Key Nonprofit Executive Directors Regarding the Disaster Response

When asked to identify the major successes of the relief efforts, most executive directors agreed that the city responded quickly to provide care for some 15,000 evacuees. One agency CEO noted that the community because of this disaster had gained the experience of responding, had learned who the major players are, and thus will be better prepared for future events (Dinnin, personal interview, November 1, 2005). Another interviewee suggested that a success of the event was the "unknown ability" of the community to deal with a catastrophic event (Bennett, personal interview, October 14, 2005). An additional success of the disaster response was the number and variety of organizations that partnered to assist in the effort. In some cases, these were systems that had not partnered in the past (Saldana, personal interview, November 1, 2005a). Government, nonprofit agencies, corporate partners, and the community came together (Cooper, personal interview, November 8, 2005). Moreover, the faith-based community, churches, and civic groups worked alongside each other (Bennett, 2005, personal interview, October 14, 2005). Some credited the mayor for the community-based effort. As one interviewee observed, "Early on, the mayor set a tone for inclusivity," (Farr, personal interview, November 10, 2005).

Clearly, another important success was the critical role that nonprofit organizations, secular and faith-based alike, played in the relief efforts. First responders, the Red Cross and Salvation Army, with the help of numerous other nonprofit partners and thousands of volunteers provided mass care and individual assistance for the Katrina and Rita evacuees. The San Antonio Food Bank provided food that enabled the Texas Baptist Men to feed the masses in the shelters. Some nonprofits provided services and assisted in ways that fell outside their traditional roles (Saldana, personal interview, November 1, 2005a). Catholic Charities or Baptist Child & Family Services are two prime examples. Faith-based organizations continue to be involved in the long-term recovery efforts.

Successes of the nonprofit community aside, clearly there is room for improvement in the relief effort. As one agency CEO stated, "I'd give this event a C+ or B−. Everyone did a good job without a lot of preparedness," (Dinnin, personal interview, November 1, 2005). When asked what barriers they encountered during the relief efforts, executive directors reported that insufficient communication and the lack of accurate information were major barriers to the success of the effort. Some voiced their frustration at the lack of a coordinated, centralized, and empowered point of contact to coordinate communication. A few noted that early on, in particular, information changed rapidly and frequently. As one executive director added, there were so many people involved, things happened so fast, and changes occurred as leadership transitioned at the shelters from the Red Cross to the Rocky Mountain Incident Team and then to Shaw (Saldana, personal interview, November 1, 2005a).

Plagued with misinformation, rumors were often rampant at the shelters. One persistent rumor involved the consolidation of shelters in 22 counties around the state, and subsequent arrival of some 12,000 additional evacuees in San Antonio. The information was first reported in an online edition of the *Beaumont Enterprise*. However, officials from the city, county, and local nonprofits did not know of the decision (Fikac and Castillo 2005). As one local newspaper reporter stated, "The uncertainty mirrors the confusion and strained communication between top officials and shelter managers, who privately bemoan not being kept better informed as the situation changes rapidly," (Wilson 2005d, p. 1A).

At the same time, the effort severely tested the financial, organizational, and human resource capacities of many agencies. Executive directors shared numerous accounts of the staff at their agencies working 24/7 to serve evacuees while continuing to serve their traditional clients. Likewise, the unprecedented numbers of unaffiliated volunteers that sought to serve in the shelters placed a huge demand on nonprofit professionals and emergency responders alike. Nonprofit managers, as well, often provided services on a leap of faith without knowing how or when they would be reimbursed.

Aware of these pressing financial concerns, the mayor established the San Antonio Hurricane Relief Fund. All donations to the fund were intended to benefit relief efforts in San Antonio (Jesse 2005a). More than 1000 donors contributed over $2.7 million to the fund. A committee conducted a survey of over 100 nonprofits involved in the relief process to determine which agencies should be funded. In November of 2005, the funds were awarded to the American Red Cross, Goodwill Industries, Salvation Army, San Antonio Food Bank, and the local United Way office (Wilson 2005g).

Perceptions of the Wider Nonprofit Community Regarding the Disaster Response

On, October 29, 2005, an Internet survey was sent to 575 managerial personnel listed in the Nonprofit Resource Center of Texas' Greater San Antonio Area List of nonprofit organizations. These individuals were identified in the list as highly placed members of nonprofit organizations including directors, managers, CEOs, board members, presidents, or equivalent titles. Two follow-up e-mail surveys were sent the following week. The survey process was closed on November 15 with 173 responses, yielding a total response rate of 30 percent.* The survey asked both closed- and open-ended questions regarding engagement in and perception of relief efforts associated with Hurricanes Katrina and Rita. The discussion below summarizes the results. Closed-ended questions are reported directly from the frequency analysis of response categories. Content analysis was used to distill the major categories expressed in the open-ended question responses. Those categories are reported and discussed below.

A variety of individuals from different organizational types responded to the survey. In responding to a question regarding the focus of the organization's activities, advocacy was listed by 18 percent of respondents, arts and culture by about 12 percent, community development/housing by about 12 percent, disaster relief by 8 percent, education and training by nearly 33 percent, elder care by 7 percent, environment by 2 percent, food and nutrition by nearly 10 percent, funding or grant provider or financial pass through organization by 3 percent, health care or mental health or substance abuse by about 18 percent, recreation by about 5 percent, religion or ministry by 12 percent, research by 2 percent, special needs by 10 percent, and youth services by 21 percent. Twenty-one percent of respondents listed their focus as other, specifying such foci as case management, animal welfare,

---

* In a few cases more than one person from the same organization responded to the survey. This occurred with six reporting organizations. For these cases, duplicate responses were eliminated from the data set.

information and referral, housing, telecommunications, civic society, or general social services.

The overwhelming majority of respondents (72 percent) identified themselves as associated with a secular organization whereas 28 percent said they were associated with a faith-based organization. Of those who responded, 69 percent said that they were independent organizations, 9 percent said they were a local chapter of a state or regional nonprofit organization, 15 percent indicated they were a state or local chapter of a national nonprofit organization, and 7 percent said they were a state or local chapter of an international nonprofit organization.

Respondents were asked to report the annual operating budget of their organizations. For those organizations reporting, the mean budget was slightly over $4 million, however, the median budget was reported as $1.3 million. The range was large with the smallest budget reported as zero and the largest as $80 million.* The age of organizations reporting varied from a foundation of 1887 to 2005. One fourth of the organizations reporting were established prior to 1955, one half before 1980, and three quarters before 1995. Respondents were asked to estimate the number of paid staff their organization employed. Nearly 8 percent said none and 17 percent reported between one and three. Thirty-one percent reported employing between 4 and 25 persons. Fourteen percent employed between 26 and 50, and 30 percent reported more than 50 employees. Respondents were asked to estimate in a typical month, how many volunteers their organization utilized. Nearly 8 percent said none, 34 percent said between 1 and 10, 15 percent reported between 11 and 25, 15 percent reported between 26 and 50 volunteers, while 28 percent reported more than 50.

A number of questions asked to the respondents were to reflect on the involvement they had with hurricane relief efforts and to discuss their perception of those efforts. Eighty-five percent of respondents indicated that they had been involved in either Hurricane Katrina or Hurricane Rita relief efforts either directly (by providing services) or indirectly (by providing assistance, support, or donations to those organizations directly involved). Sixty-nine percent said that staff members or volunteers from their organization traveled to and provided direct personal services at relief sites or shelters located in Texas. Another 7 percent indicated travel to and provision of direct personal services in Louisiana. None of the respondents reported activity in Alabama and only one respondent indicated traveling to Mississippi. Twenty-nine percent of those responding did not travel to any relief site or shelter nor did they provide any direct personal services.

For those who did engage in direct personal services, 67 percent worked in an emergency shelter, 37 percent served food and provided meals for evacuees, 25 percent provided emergency shelter for evacuees, 40 percent distributed clothing to evacuees, 35 percent provided intake assessment or case management for evacuees,

---

* This high figure was associated with a nonprofit health service provider.

18 percent provided education or training to evacuees, 17 percent provided chaplain/ministry services to evacuees, 27 percent provided medical, nursing, or mental health services to evacuees, 15 percent provided transportation for evacuees, 17 percent provided or arranged for long-term housing options for evacuees, 26 percent provided information services to evacuees including finding lost family members and locating needed services, 10 percent managed volunteers at a shelter, 9 percent staffed a phone bank, 25 percent recruited volunteers, 51 percent donated clothing or supplies, 29 percent donated food or water, 42 percent donated money, and 18 percent coordinated a fund drive or fund-raising event. Some more specialized activities that respondents said they were involved with included reading to children, providing shelter to evacuees' pets, providing furnishings and household goods, music or dance performances, providing sexual assault counseling, and providing chainsaw teams for East Texas.

Communication was an important issue in the crisis, so the survey asked respondents several questions regarding communication channels and the accuracy of information. When asked through what communication conduit did they hear about activities associated with the San Antonio-based Katrina and Rita relief efforts, 68 percent said e-mail, 54 percent indicated face-to-face personal conversation, 39 percent said group meetings, 14 percent said Internet blogs or Internet newsletters, 58 percent said from the newspaper, 27 percent said by phone, 31 percent said via radio, 48 percent indicated TV, and 13 percent said from a Web page. Other channels of communication included direct contact from evacuees needing services and referrals from emergency management staff.

During the crisis, nonprofit organizations relied on several authorities for information regarding the San Antonio-based Katrina and Rita relief efforts. Fifty-five percent of respondents said they relied on city of San Antonio government organizations (Mayor's Office, City Manager's Office, Department of Community Initiatives, city police, etc.), 24 percent relied on Bexar County government organizations (County Commissioner's Court, Bexar County Department of Housing and Human Services, county law enforcement, etc.), 23 percent relied on Texas state government organizations (Governor's Office, state police, etc.), 22 percent relied on U.S. federal government organizations (FEMA, military services, etc.), 65 percent on nonprofit organizations (Catholic Charities, Red Cross, Salvation Army, United Way, etc.), 19 percent relied on a local church, and 32 percent relied on random people spoken to during the crisis.

Reliability of information is critical during a crisis. The survey asked respondents to rate the quality (in terms of accuracy, timeliness, and relevance) of information received regarding the San Antonio-based Katrina and Rita relief efforts from several groups. Table 8.1 shows these ratings. Clearly the nonprofit community valued information most highly when communicated by another nonprofit organization or directly by face to face interaction.

Earlier in this chapter, we mentioned that 15 percent of respondents indicated they were not involved in relief efforts in any capacity. The survey asked these

Table 8.1   Internet Survey of Nonprofit Leaders Rankings of Quality of Information Received from a Variety of Sources

	Excellent	Good	Fair	Poor	No Information Received
City of San Antonio government organizations (in percent)	19	37	15	6	23
Bexar County government organizations	13	28	12	4	42
Texas state government organizations	7	30	23	8	32
U.S. federal government organizations	5	18	25	20	32
Nonprofit organizations	24	45	18	3	10
Local church	21	23	10	4	42
People I talked to[a]	18	43	21	3	15

Note: $N = 117$ directors, managers, CEOs, board members, presidents, or equivalent from the Nonprofit Resource Center of Texas' Greater San Antonio Area List of nonprofit organizations.

[a] Refers to the individuals whom the respondents spoke to at random during the crisis to obtain information.

Source: Authors' survey data.

respondents to explain why. It also asked respondents who felt that their organization was involved in a manner less than what they would have preferred to describe why. Capacity issues seemed to be a real barrier for many organizations. Thirty-eight percent of those responding to this question said the reason was that the primary activities their organization is involved with were not consistent with the needs of the relief efforts, 15 percent said they had to concentrate on serving their current clients, 28 percent said they had too few staff, and 22 percent said they had too limited funds. However, capacity issues were not alone in deterring some organizations from participation. Fifteen percent of respondents said that they were not asked to assist, 18 percent said they offered to provide assistance or greater levels of assistance but were turned away, and 20 percent said they wanted to provide assistance or greater levels of assistance but did not know how to coordinate or arrange for it. Other respondents explained their lack of engagement in the relief efforts by saying such things as "We made several calls but had no luck in contacting anyone."

Others complain of "mixed messages, mixed information, poor communication, and poor coordination between emergency sites." Some mentioned the fact that "the situation kept changing before we could respond appropriately." One respondent echoed the frustration of many, saying "The level of disorganization between government, nonprofits, and volunteers was a huge obstacle. It was primarily the dedication and diligence of the volunteers that helped the shelter effort to be as well organized as it was. The volunteers developed alternative methods of getting the job done. Communicating with FEMA et al. was not productive at all." Some respondents indicated that they "looked for funds to help us to help, but were told none were available unless we were the actual victim." Sadly, one respondent indicated that "too many of our church members do not like to be involved with 'those' kind of people."

When asked if there was a service that their organization did not offer but could have offered that might have been valuable to the relief efforts, nearly one quarter of respondents answered affirmatively. Services they felt they could have provided what included a "Listener's Corp" to listen to the evacuees stories, youth services, day services to people with mental retardation, coordination of health needs, bilingual and bicultural health information, early intervention chemical dependency counseling and treatment, assistance with intake and case management, provision of mental health workers, meeting the needs of pregnant teens, creating a better Web site presence to update information for the churches, dealing with domestic violence issues, and helping the homeless evacuees.

It is important to note that despite the frustration expressed by some respondents, when asked if their organization would be involved in the long-term Hurricane Katrina and Rita relief efforts, 41 percent said they would while another 25 percent were not sure. Only 35 percent of respondents said they would not.

Monetary support for the relief effort was one area that the survey probed. Seventy-five percent of respondents said they did not receive any corporate support for the relief efforts and 88 percent said they received no foundation support either.

A series of open-ended questions were asked in the survey. These questions sought to probe areas such as successes of the relief effort, barriers encountered in the relief effort, what might have been done better in the relief effort, what tools could the nonprofit community use to better prepare for another emergency response, concerns about the privatization of the shelters, and impacts of the relief effort on ongoing nonprofit community activities. Each of these is discussed below.

The respondents were asked to comment on the major successes of the San Antonio relief efforts. Four main areas of successes were identified: results, physical plant, leadership, and the spirit of cooperative volunteerism. The results of the relief effort were highlighted as a significant and substantial success. Respondents commented on the large number of people who were housed, clothed, and fed in a very short time. The results included not just the bare minimum of food, shelter, and clothing but an extensive list of additional services provided including special care for the infirm, health services, mental health counseling, spiritual support, services to assist the evacuees with finding lost relatives or friends, and information services to help evacuees find their way through the maize of necessary next steps.

The physical plant was listed as a success because San Antonio was able to rapidly provide large spaces to receive the massive influx of evacuees with little notice. The bulk of these spaces were located on military installations. The rapid mobilization of these assets and emergency equipping them with air conditioning necessary for south Texas life was seen as a triumph. The physical plant location, with a useable runway, was especially seen as excellent because it enabled evacuees to be airlifted directly to shelter. The buildings utilized were already equipped with loading docks that were readily put into use to receive and sort donated food, clothing, water, and other items.

Leadership, both that exercised by the city and that of the nonprofits was highlighted as a success. Respondents commented on the quick and decisive action by San Antonio Mayor Hardberger to accept any and all evacuees without hesitation and to provide resources to serve the evacuees without concern for payback or financing. Nonprofit leadership was also seen as a success as "nonprofit agencies stepped up and took charge where city, state, and federal agencies dropped the ball." School leadership was also cited as an important success, as the local schools rapidly opened enrollment for evacuee children to get them settled in new schools as soon as possible.

Finally, the spirit of cooperative volunteerism was emphasized as a huge success. Respondents commented on the smooth way that the large nonprofits (Red Cross, Salvation Army, and Food Bank) pulled together and worked as a team. There were many comments about the generous outpouring of money, donations, care, concern, and support from members of the San Antonio community. The heavy church involvement was emphasized as an important component of this spirit of cooperative volunteerism. The untiring efforts of the many nonprofits and thousands of volunteers working together to achieve a goal was seen by respondents as a stunning success.

Respondents were also asked to comment on any barriers they may have confronted as part of their relief efforts. The two, and somewhat interconnected, barriers reported were poor quality of information and inadequate coordination of relief activities. The poor quality of information was characterized by misinformation, lack of information, and conflicts in information. Respondents noted events such as calls through the media for specific items (such as large women's clothing) which when gathered and delivered to the drop-off point were rejected as unnecessary. Respondents noted the perfusion of rumors that spread rapidly through both the evacuee and assistance communities. Respondents also remarked that coordination of federal, state, and local information was challenging and frustrating. The poor quality of information was exacerbated by lack of information technology to adequately track evacuees, volunteers, donations, and unmet needs. Some respondents noted that even phone communication with large nonprofits, such as the

Red Cross, and government agencies, such as FEMA, were almost impossible largely because phones were not being answered.

Respondents commented that inadequate coordination of relief efforts was vexing. This was particularly the case in the large Red Cross–run shelters. Respondents reported that no one seemed to be in charge. This situation was made more difficult due to the rapidly changing circumstances in the shelters. What was true one minute would change the next minute. Protocols and procedures changed constantly, frustrating many volunteer workers. This resulted in a great deal of confusion that was made more troublesome by the Red Cross staffing at the shelters, comprised almost fully by volunteers not authorized to make decisions who did not seem to be in the information loop. Respondents reported that volunteers from their organizations were often turned away and were given conflicting instructions at different locations.

Respondents were asked to comment on what tools the nonprofit community could develop to better prepare for the next emergency response. Responses fell into two general categories. The most frequently stated need was for better technology to enable better communication and coordination. Respondents indicated the need for generally accessible information technology to match resources with needs such as a Web page, an Internet blog or newsletter, shared databases, or an e-mail group to match services with providers. The second category suggested the need for an umbrella agency to conduct ongoing planning exercises in the local community to establish and maintain a level of readiness among the nonprofits.

When asked what concerns they have, if any, regarding the privatization of the ongoing relief efforts, respondents were divided. About half of those responding had no concerns with a private company taking over the shelter operations under contract from FEMA. Those who did express concern generally focused on the issues of accountability, the potential for cronyism, and the belief that privatization would be more costly.

Finally, respondents were asked to assess the potential impact of the outpouring of support for the Katrina and Rita relief efforts on future fund-raising efforts. Fifty-one percent of those responding indicated that they thought it would hurt them, 20 percent thought it would not negatively impact their fund-raising efforts, 16 percent were not sure what the impact would be, and 7 percent thought it would help them in the long run.

Lessons Learned

The first lesson to take away from any analysis of the role of the nonprofits in the response to Hurricanes Katrina and Rita is the lesson of the centrality of nonprofit organizations to an adequate community response. The San Antonio nonprofit community was a vital part of the immediate hurricane disaster response and indispensable actor in the long-term recovery phase of the disaster response. Within the first few hours of the Red Cross shelter operation beginning, thousands of volunteers worked seamlessly with the city of San Antonio and Bexar County Emergency responders to erect what came to be a small city for the evacuees arriving from Louisiana. The outpouring of cooperative volunteerism provided a large and motivated workforce to meet the demanding staffing needs of shelter operation. Without utilizing the resources of the nonprofit community, especially the faith-based components, the long-term recovery effort would have stalled. Nonprofits took the lead in finding long-term and stable housing and living arrangements for evacuees. Nonprofits, with their separate areas of expertise, were able to bring many resources to the effort of dealing with the enormous number of displaced victims of the storms.

Although San Antonio was very well served by its nonprofit organizations and the army of volunteers brought into service during the Katrina and Rita response, some improvements could be made. There is a need for an ongoing umbrella organization for communication and coordination. This may be the VOAD in combination with the faith-based VOAD. The primary function of this organization is to provide for better preparedness coordination and updating of available resources. One of the central tasks of that effort is to match the capacity of the nonprofit community (resources and expertise) with needs that arise in a crisis. If there was an existent organization such as the VOAD already informed of the current capacity of nonprofit organizations to respond to disasters, when a disaster hit, it would be much easier to mobilize that community.

Much of the need for improvement in coordination and collaboration could be met with better use of information technology. For instance, the VOAD could establish a disaster-specific Web site that would allow better coordination and match resources with needs. This Web portal could act as a virtual volunteer coordination command center that could identify needs and deploy volunteers where needs exist.

Clearly, the relief effort helped to identify the major players in disaster relief. Agencies such as the Red Cross, Salvation Army, Catholic Charities, and the Food Bank held a key role in the relief effort. As the leadership in the aforementioned umbrella agency works to match the capacity of nonprofits with the needs that arise in a crisis, these groups will clearly be part of the conversation. As this study found, some agencies such as Catholic Charities and Baptist Child & Family Services provided services during the relief efforts that fell outside of their traditional roles. Local leaders should thus look beyond the immediate expertise of existing agencies when considering capacities. Some smaller and less well-connected agencies, including some that may have expertise in very specialized areas that could have benefitted the effort, were underutilized. When identifying nonprofits with resources and expertise to assist in relief and recovery situations, the umbrella agency should not overlook smaller agencies. Such nonprofits often have specific areas of expertise that may fill an important role.

Another important lesson learned is the need to recruit and train volunteers, in particular supervisory level volunteers, before disaster strikes. Locally trained volunteers who are ready to move in, begin work, and oversee unaffiliated volunteers lessen the dependence on volunteers from other locations. Also, they have a better understanding of the nuances of the local community. In San Antonio, a city with a large Hispanic population, bilingual volunteers who speak English and Spanish are needed.

Volunteer management aside, this study suggests that the public has a limited understanding of the capacity of nonprofits to accept and distribute donated items. Nonprofit leaders thus have a responsibility to educate the community about in-kind donations. One suggestion is that agencies post information on their Web sites or develop printed materials with information about in-kind donations. These should include a list of items that disaster victims need most as well as a list of frequently asked questions. Donors should be advised of the manner in which in-kind goods should arrive. Clothing should be in good condition and arrive sorted by gender and by size, for example. If an agency is limited in the goods it can accept, the informational materials should include the names of other agencies that are better equipped to accept these items. Equally important, all informational materials should include a statement to remind donors that cash contributions are always welcome and offer the greatest flexibility. It seems clear that agencies in this study place a premium on honoring donor restrictions. Nonprofits must be outspoken in their communication with the community about the importance they place on using gifts in accordance with the desires of the donor.

Conclusion

This chapter explores the role of San Antonio's nonprofit sector in the "Katrita" disaster response. The authors utilized multiple data collection methods for this analysis including interviews with key actors and an Internet survey of area nonprofit leaders along with information gathered from archival resources. Participation observation served as another important method of data collection. The authors attended meetings hosted by local organizations involved in the response including the faith-based community, volunteered in the disaster relief shelters and participated in disaster relief training to gather additional data for this chapter.

The data from these multiple sources form the basis for this story of the San Antonio nonprofit sectors' response to the twin disasters. Moreover, as the analysis clearly suggests, the nonprofit community played a central role in the disaster response. No governmental entity—be it city, county, state, or national—possessed the capacity to respond to the disaster. This situation persisted and deepened with time. That is, rather than building capacity to respond as time went on, the many government agencies involved grew increasingly dependent on the nonprofits. As the crisis moved from the immediate response phase into the long-term recovery phase, government actors focused on extraditing themselves as best they could from any ongoing role, relying more heavily on the nonprofit sector to assume the burden of both planning and service delivery.

At the same time, the relief efforts brought to the forefront some important concerns. Chief among these involves why similar efforts to assist the area's homeless and indigent populations have not kept pace. Some argue that assistance to evacuees occurred at the expense of those already in the community, a charge that is not without merit. In one incident, evacuees were allowed to bypass thousands of local families that had been on the waiting list for public housing (Wilson 2005e, h).

In the same way, there are concerns that the unprecedented outpouring of the community in response to the relief efforts may result in donor fatigue. Donors that "already gave" to assist Katrina and Rita evacuees may be less likely to open their wallets again at the expense of the needs of the local community. Indeed, the CEO of the local Red Cross chapter reported that fund-raising for the relief efforts exceeded its fund-raising for local disasters (Ayala 2005). At the time of preparing this chapter there was little evidence of donor fatigue, however. The local United Way campaign exceeded its $36 million fund-raising goal (Davis 2005). Other nonprofits reported that the relief efforts did not significantly impact their fund-raising goals. Smaller nonprofits without regular annual donors seemed to be those struggling with fund-raising, although there was no way to say with certainty if this was a result of the outpouring for the relief effort (Ayala 2005).

Two additional funding concerns warrant discussion. As some evacuees make San Antonio their permanent home, they will need long-term recovery assistance. The faith-based community with its family-sponsorship program will play an important role in assisting evacuees who remain in the area. Members of the faith-based VOAD continue to meet to determine in what ways they will assist those who remain in the community as well as how they will fund these efforts. Funding for the recovery effort is thus an ongoing concern.

Additionally, the Katrina and Rita relief efforts afforded the nonprofit community an opportunity to test its ability to respond to a disaster. Yet, this study highlights the need to have a plan in place to prepare for future disasters. Disaster preparedness requires funding and donor support. Nonprofits regularly appeal to donors for unrestricted contributions and for gifts to be used to meet a specific need. Agencies that anticipate future involvement in disaster relief might begin now to set aside some percentage of their unrestricted gifts to prepare for future disasters. An alternate solution is to set up a special fund for disaster preparedness, so that donors can designate their gifts for disaster mitigation. This is no easy fix. Nonprofit agencies are tasked with fund-raising to serve current clients while planning to address future disasters. Leaders in the charitable community must help donors understand the value of funding long-term relief efforts as well as the importance of funding for disaster relief planning. As time lapses, media coverage decreases and public support wanes. The time to educate donors is now.

In short, this study underscores the critical role of voluntary organizations in the Hurricane Katrina and Rita disaster relief and recovery efforts. At the same time, there is much work to be done as this analysis suggests. An umbrella organization to serve as a central point of coordination and to identify nonprofit capacities is vital to the success of future disaster relief efforts. Information technology could further enhance disaster response coordination. Nonprofit leaders should, likewise, act now to train a corps of local volunteers and to educate the public about cash and in-kind contributions. They must also help donors and the public alike to recognize the value of funding for disaster recovery and mitigation. These are no simple tasks. Nonprofits are charged with assisting in the long-term recovery effort while working to mitigate future disasters, without disrupting their current services to those in the local community. Finally, timing is key. Nonprofit leaders must not delay, but begin now to prepare to meet the next disaster.

References

Allen, E. 2005. FEMA May Pick Private Contractor to Run Shelters. *San Antonio Express News*, September 30. Accessed September 30, 2005 (http://www.maysanantonio.com/news/metro/stories/SA093005.9A.FEMA_shelters.1bf3ab43.html).

American Red Cross. 2005. Accessed December 9, 2005 (http://www.redcross.org/services/disaster/0,1082,0_319_,00.html).

American Red Cross. 2006. Facts at a Glance: American Red Cross Response to Hurricane Katrina & Rita. January 12. Accessed January 20, 2006 (http://www.redcross.org/news/ds/hurricanes/katrina_facts.html).

America's Second Harvest. 2005. About Us: Our Network. Accessed December 4, 2005 (http://www.secondharvest.org/about_us/our_network/).

Archdiocese of San Antonio. 2005. Social Services. Accessed December 5, 2005 (http://www.archdiosa.org/social.html).

Ayala, E. 2005. Despite Katrina and Rita, Charities Not Suffering Donor Fatigue. *San Antonio Express News* (6 November): 1K, 3K.

Baptist Child & Family Services. 2005. About BCFS. Accessed December 4, 2005 (http://www.bcfs.net/about_us.htm).

Bennett, M. 2005. Chief executive officer, American Red Cross, San Antonio Chapter. Personal interview conducted on October 14.

Bird, C.A. 2005a. BCFS Preparing to Care for Displaced Children's Home Residents and Special Need Victims of Hurricane Katrina. September 1. Accessed December 5, 2005 (http://www.bcfs.net/story_katrinaspecneedvics.htm).

—— 2005b. BCFS Caring for Special Need Victims of Hurricane Katrina. September 3. Accessed December 12, 2005 (http://www.bcfs.net/story_katrina3.htm).

—— 2005c. With Little Time to Waste, BCFS Turns Store Into Special Needs Shelter. September 6. Accessed December 5, 2005 (http://www.bcfs.net/story_katrinastoreopen.htm).

Catholic Charities USA. 2005. About Us. Accessed December 5, 2005 (http://www.catholiccharitiesusa.org/about/index.cfm).

Chapa, R. 2005. S.A. Mayor Confident of Evacuee Plan. *San Antonio Express News*, September 21. Accessed September 21, 2005 (http://www.maysanantonio.com/news/metro/stories/SA092105.17A.City_Prep.12b2a99a.html).

Conchas, E. 2005. Some Shelters Run Out of Room for Donations. *San Antonio Express News* (16 September): 17A.

Cooper, E. Executive Director, San Antonio Food Bank. Personal interview conducted on November 8, 2005.

Davis, V.T. 2005. United Way Campaign Surpasses $37 Million. *San Antonio Express News* (16 December): 3B.

Dinnin, K. 2005. President, Baptist Child & Family Services. Personal interview conducted on November 1, 2005.

Driscoll, P. 2005. The Good, the Bad, and the Ugly of Rita. *San Antonio Express News*, October 4. Accessed October 4, 2005 (http://www.maysanantonio.com/news/metro/stories/SA100405.01A.lessons_learned.d85a0e5.html).

Farr, H. 2005. Director of Administrative Services, Salvation Army. Personal interview conducted on November 10, 2005.

Fikac, P. and Castillo, M. 2005. Officials Deny Knowing About Plan to Shelter 12,000 More Evacuees in S.A. *San Antonio Express News,* September 30. Accessed September 30, 2005 (http://www.mysanantonio.com/news/metro/stories/MYSA093005.1A.beaumontevacuees.1c520d97.htm).

Heath, J. and Davis, V.T. 2005. S.A. Emptying Shelters? Evacuees Told to Pick Home, Another Site, Ticket Out. *San Antonio Express News* (21 September): 1.

Hotchin, S. and Idell Hamilton, T. 2005. KellyUSA Will Be Home to Thousands of Katrina Refugees. *San Antonio Express News,* September 2. Accessed December 20, 2005 (http://www.mysanantonio.com/news/metro/stories/MYSA090205.1A.katrina_refugees.185f9ecd.html).

Idell Hamilton, T. 2005a. Some Volunteers Prove to be No Shows. *San Antonio Express News* (7 September): 11A.

——— 2005b. Salvation Army Boss Says Long-Term Plan Needed. *San Antonio Express News* (16 September): 17A.

Jesse, L. 2005a. S.A. Leaders Create a Local Relief Fund. *San Antonio Express News* (8 September): 13A.

——— 2005b. No-bid Shelter Contracts to be Reopened. *San Antonio Express News,* October 17. Accessed October 17, 2005 (http://www.mysanantonio.com/news/metro/stories/MYSA101705.1A.shelter.contracts.865c259.htm).

——— 2005c. Top Authority Over Shelters Isn't Always Clear. *San Antonio Express News,* October 17. Accessed October 17, 2005 (http://www.mysanantonio.com/news/metro/stories/MYSA101705.1A.shelters.8a8aa24.htm).

Jesse, L. and Wilson, R. 2005. Folks with Special Needs Were Sent Into Misery. *San Antonio Express News* (1 October): 1A, 12A.

Kitfield, J. 2005. Poor Communications Slowed Military's Hurricane Response. *National Journal,* September 19. Accessed October 26, 2005 (http://www.govexec.com/dailyfed/0905/091905nj1.htm).

Knabb, R.D., Rhome, J.R., and Brown, D.P. 2005. Tropical Cyclone Report Hurricane Katrina 23–30 August 2005, National Hurricane Center, December 20. Accessed May 18, 2006 (http://www.nhc.noaa.gov/ms-word/TCR-AL122005_Katrina.doc).

Lewis, Nicole. 2005. More than $1.2 Billion Raised for Katrina Victims, *The Chronicle of Philanthropy*, September 29, pp. 14, 16.

McFadden, R.D. and Blumenthal, R. 2005, August 31. Bush Sees Long Recovery for New Orleans; 30,000 Troops in Largest U.S. Relief Effort. *The New York Times*. Retrieved May 18, 2006, from LexisNexis database.

McMorrough, J. 2005. Archdiocese Committed to Helping Evacuee Families. *Today's Catholic*, n.d. Accessed December 5, 2005 (http://www.archdiosa.org/banner_documents/Katrina/news_katrina.htm).

Parker, J.M. 2005a. Churches Open Doors, Wallets, Hearts. *San Antonio Express News* (11 September): 1B, 7B.

—— 2005b. Churches' Welcome Wagons Wanted. *San Antonio Express News* (16 September): 5B.

—— 2005c. S.A. Jewish Families Offer Homes. *San Antonio Express News* (20 September): 5B.

—— 2005d. Money to Help Evacuees Get Suited for the Workplace. *San Antonio Express News* (22 November): 3B.

Saldana, S. 2005a. President and Chief Executive Officer, Catholic Charities of the Archdiocese of San Antonio. Personal interview conducted on November 1, 2005.

—— 2005b. President and Chief Executive Officer, Catholic Charities of the Archdiocese of San Antonio. Personal communication, December 21, 2005.

Salvation Army. 2005a. Our Role in Disaster Services. Accessed December 30, 2005 (http://www.salvationarmyusa.org/usn/www_usn.nsf/vw-sublinks/8214F21A914E09CE80256-FE80071ECF1?openDocument).

—— 2005b. Profile of Response and Recovery Programs. Accessed December 30, 2005 (http://www.salvationarmyusa.org/usn/www_usn.nsf/vw-sublinks/85256DDC00727-4DF85256B8D000F0FC9?openDocument).

San Antonio Food Bank. 2005. San Antonio Food Bank Facts. Accessed December 4, 2005 (http://www.safoodbank.org/mainfacts.html).

San Antonio Red Cross. 2005. Accessed December 4, 2005 (http://www.saredcross.org/).

Sandalow, D.B. 2005. Testimony, Hearing on the Role of Science in Environmental Policymaking, Committee on Environment and Public Works, U.S. Senate, September 28, 2005.

Simmons, L.C. 2005. Red Cross Plans to Support Rita Victims. In the News, September 30, Accessed December 9, 2005 (http://www.redcross.org/article/0,1072,0_272_4674,00.html).

Texas Baptist Men. 2005a. About TBM. Accessed December 9, 2005 (http://www.bgct.org/TexasBaptists/Page.aspx?&pid=321&srcid=355).

—— 2005b. Disaster Relief. Accessed December 9, 2005 (http://www.bgct.org/TexasBaptists/Page.aspx?&pid=355&srcid=322).

Treaster, J.B. and Kleinfield, N.R., August 31, 2005. New Orleans is Inundated as 2 Levees Fail; Much of Gulf Coast Is Crippled; Toll Rises. *The New York Times*. Retrieved May 18, 2006, from LexisNexis database.

USA Southern Territory Salvation Army. 2005. Gulf Coast Hurricane Relief Fast Facts. Accessed December 30, 2005 (http://www.uss.salvationarmy.org/recovery.htm).

Watford, D. 2005. Executive Director, Communities of Churches for Social Action. Personal communication on December 20, 2005.

Wikipedia, 2005a. Hurricane Katrina. Accessed October 25, 2005 (http://en.wikipedia.org/wiki/Hurrican_Katrina).

—— 2005b. Hurricane Rita. Accessed October 25, 2005 (http://en.wikipedia.org/wiki/Hurrican_Rita).

Wilson, R. 2005a. They're Serving to Serve. *San Antonio Express News* (15 September): 10A.

—— 2005b. Katrina Victims Make Way. *San Antonio Express News*, September 22. Accessed September 22, 2005 (http://www.maysanantonio.com/news/metro/stories/MYSA09-2205.html).

—— 2005c. Special Needs Evacuees Get Care. *San Antonio Express News* (29 September): 3B.

—— 2005d. Who's Coming? Who Knows? *San Antonio Express News* (1 October): 1A, 12A.

—— 2005e. SAHA Lets Evacuees Cut in Line. *San Antonio Express News* (7 October): 1B, 5B.

—— 2005f. Transitional Housing Has Gaping Holes. *San Antonio Express News*, October 16. Accessed October 17, 2005 (http://www.maysanantonio.com/news/metro/stories/MYSA101605.21A.transitional.houseing.32bdd7f.html).

—— 2005g. S.A. Hurricane Fund Names Recipients. *San Antonio Express News*, November 15. Accessed December 20, 2005 (http://www.mysanantonio.com/business/stories/MYSA111605.01B.hurricane_funds.11b9443c.html).

—— 2005h. SAHA Delays Evacuee Housing. *San Antonio Express News* (21 November): 14A.

Zarazua, J. 2005. Mandatory Evacuation Declared in Galveston County. *San Antonio Express News*, September 21. Accessed September 21, 2005 (http://www.maysanantonio.com/news/metro/stories/MYSA092105.01A.texas_rita.12b28da7.html).

Chapter 9

Small Town Disaster Management: Lessons Learned from Katrina in Mississippi

Jack Pinkowski and George Bass

CONTENTS

Introduction

Long Beach, Mississippi, is a small town on the Mississippi coast of the Gulf of Mexico. It is also a resort town and bedroom community to other areas along the Gulf Coast where residents maintain employment. These include jobs in the vibrant casino industry in Gulfport and Biloxi, if the residents are not retired. As of July 2005, the population was approximately 17,283 residents according to the mid-decade estimate based on the 2000 census (U.S. Census, 2005a). Typical of many small jurisdictions, the town's ability to autonomously provide for disaster mitigation and response is limited by practical considerations of limited financial resources, a small tax base, and limited manpower. Disaster relief is generally funded to neighboring county seats or large population centers and the small towns have to rely on processing through the larger staging areas. More often than not, their needs are overlooked as there are just not enough resources to go around. The federal system of government requires state governments to call in the federal resources if the state wants to. In turn, the state authorities are in control of the allocation and apportionment of their own resources and those of the federal government if they are forthcoming. When funds and relief supplies are released, these usually pass on to the county administration as divisions of the state government whose responsibility includes providing relief to the local governments in their jurisdiction.

Many public officials in small towns serve in multiple capacities. In the case of Long Beach, one of them is the fire chief who is also the chief emergency services official in case of a major disaster. When Hurricane Katrina came ashore in the summer of 2005, the town and its fire chief were thrust into a situation over which they had very limited control. This is their story and lessons learned as told to me by Fire Chief George Bass. We hope that it will provide useful planning advice for other officials in similar jurisdictions. Small town administration can do some things on their own and can benefit from learning how their peers meet challenges and opportunities. Unfortunately, such accounts are generally lost in the reports of their bigger brothers.

Hurricane Katrina

Long Beach was incorporated as a town in August 10, 1905 and it was rightfully proud of its beautiful, expansive public beaches that came right up to Highway 90, west of Biloxi.

On August 29, 2005 the town administration had its priorities rearranged from a centennial celebration to survival. Hurricane Katrina roared ashore as a

Category 3* storm with wind speeds reported as high as 175 miles per hour. Long Beach was in the "sweet spot" on the "dirty side" of the storm, just 4 miles west of Gulfport (population 72,464) and 28 miles east of Waveland, Mississippi (population only 7,227), where the eye of the hurricane made its landfall. This is 30 miles east of New Orleans, which received most of the post-storm attention due to flooding of nearly 80 percent of the city following failure of the levees holding back the waters of Lake Pontchartrain. Katrina destroyed 90 percent of the buildings along the Gulf coast with hurricane-force winds that persisted in battering all structures along the coast for 16 hours, at least 100 miles per hour for seven hours, with a storm surge that exceeded 28 feet (9 m) in parts.† The fire chief of Long Beach personally recorded sustained winds of 145 miles per hour‡ with a handheld device during the storm.

The damage from the force of the hurricane winds was far more devastating on the Mississippi coast than in New Orleans, only 30 miles away. The storm surge west of Long Beach reached 32 feet. A distinguishing feature of the town is the railroad line that parallels the coast about one-half mile inland from the beach. The railroad engineers built a berm on which to lay their rail bed in the last century. This was intended to prevent dips and grades in the rail line as it traveled east and west loaded with cargo. But it served another purpose for the town during the storm as a hedge against the hurricane's storm surge. The railroad berm stopped the waves and flooding so well that most of the devastation was confined to the half-mile from the berm to the beach. The track is at 32–33 feet above sea level, just above the height of the storm surge. Beyond the railroad track, the town was well protected even from a Category 3 storm surge, which normally does not exceed 12 feet. However, in this case because the devastation was so confined relief from outside was limited. Nevertheless, the impact of water, wind, and waves seaward of the berm was quite extensive.

Financial Resources and Impact on the Tax Base

Long Beach did not have a great deal of financial resources to deal with the catastrophe. The median household income for all of Harrison County was $35,576 (SAIP, 2004). Mississippi is generally a poor state and has the lowest median income in the United States, $34,508 (U.S. Census, 2005b). Based with such financial realities, how does a small town deal with such devastation and protect life and property? Gulfport and Biloxi shared responsibility as the county

---

* The "official" strength of the storm has been revised by the National Weather Service through after-storm measurement analysis. Originally it was described before landfall as Category 5 and as Category 4 on the Saffir-Simpson Hurricane Scale when it came ashore.
† Storm surge greater than 18 feet generally relates to Category 5 storms.
‡ Wind speeds of from 131 to 155 miles per hour are categorized as Category 4 hurricanes.

seat and had much larger population. Gulfport is the second largest city in the state. Much of the immediate aid and recourses went to those communities. The fire chief in Long Beach was puzzled and frustrated by the knowledge that there were apparently idle National Guard troops in nearby Gulfport but county officials would not deploy them to Long Beach.

The Department of Homeland Security (DHS) and the Federal Emergency Management Agency (FEMA) had plans for reimbursing local governments for their immediate expenses but require detailed accounting and disbursement records. This requires accounting and procurement staff that small towns do not have in-depth and Long Beach had not prioritized in its emergency response and staffing plans. This was compounded by timing. The storm came through on the 29th of the month and bills came due on the first of the next month. But the town did not have access to either cash or its normal disbursement tools and personnel. Staff were sent to Birmingham, Alabama (300 miles distant) just so the government could print disbursement checks. They were then cashed on the spot in Birmingham and the cash couriered back to Long Beach for payroll and essential disbursements. This obviously involved some risk but there was little choice regarding safer options. The banks in town had moved all of their cash out in advance of the storm. Yet the contents of the banks' safe deposit boxes remained in place. They were found intact even though the vaults had been filled with water 4 feet deep. Although the town had a vault in city hall with some cash on hand, it had filled with water 3 feet deep.

Personnel Considerations

The first responders typically did not go home until they had been on the job for three days straight. The normal schedule for firemen is 48 hours on duty and 96 hours off. All three shifts were called in to work in advance of the hurricane's approach, about six hours before landfall. And they had to respond to a routine fire the evening before the hurricane came ashore that was not storm related. The shift practically became 24/7 for about six weeks. For the first four days of the disaster, the chief managed to get merely 30 minutes of total sleep time. Showers were another luxury both in terms of physical availability for all of the staff but more so in terms of time availability. This resulted in changing out of wet clothes into dry clothes four to five times in any 24 hour period, which required not only greater quantity of clothes but also the cleaning and drying equipment and personnel to handle them. There were 45 personnel to staff all fire services and an additional 50 personnel in the Long Beach police department. They had no contingency plan if city hall was destroyed. The fire department headquarters served as the command post just because most of the emergency services functions were operating out of there.

When employees are doing such jobs they are under a great deal of stress because of the magnitude of issues that they are dealing with. This is manifest in many behaviors including "flight and affiliation" behaviors where individuals either want to escape or are desperate to confirm the whereabouts of persons close to them, including extended families and neighbors (Mawson, 2005). In addition, they experience great angst because they do not know their own situations. Because they are out of touch with their own families, some of whom may have evacuated and may be temporarily at who-knows-where, the employees and their families are not aware of their own after-storm condition or emergency needs. In Long Beach several of the firefighters lost everything in the storm.

There is also the fear of discovering someone you know as a victim. This is especially likely in small towns. Therefore it would be very useful to create a network of grief counselors beforehand including the clergy to counsel rescuers in times of great strife and stress (Bown, 1995). Another recommendation in this regard comes from the practical reality of such situations. A list should be maintained as early as possible detailing where families and personnel will be staying, how they can be reached such as cell phone numbers and e-mail addresses, the next of kin for each, and if departing for parts unknown or with the expectation that they could be unreachable, a definite plan and schedule for how they will call in to learn the conditions and staffing needs back home. This also should include a preassigned contact person and method of contact, or bulletin board available anywhere, e.g., via the Internet. It should also anticipate that electricity and the Internet at town hall could be out and plan for alternative back-ups. "Telephone trees" work well in such situations where each staff person has a list of coworkers to contact, which is divided among the group and is redundant (Geno, 2007). This should not be limited to strictly contact via the telephone as lines may be down and there might be no power to recharge cell phones.

Schools were closed for three weeks and having students to care for all day added to the stress for displaced families. This also posed unanticipated constraints on recovery. In many cases, parents took their children out of town to schools elsewhere so that they could continue their education. That meant that when their jobs came back online, the workers were reluctant to return if it meant interrupting their child's education twice in one school year. Consequently, many chose to wait until the end of the school year to make themselves available. Others were not in the area and their exact whereabouts were not known for months, until the end of the school year. In the case of Long Beach, one elementary school building was destroyed and another one was used as a shelter. Retrofitting and cleaning a school building used as a shelter back to educational use further delays the return to normal and impacts the recovery. Before the schools are ready once again for students, they have to be cleaned. In some cases, this meant environmental cleanup services due to inadequate sanitation during the alternative use.

Asset Location and Planning

Some of the shelters were without any showering facilities. In Long Beach, the construction battalions of the U.S. Navy, the Seabees, from the Naval Construction

Battalion Center (NCBC) in Gulfport built portable outdoor showers for them (Wesselman, 2006). This leads to a recommendation that all communities consider building combination recreation—community centers with ample shower and sanitary facilities, hardened for storms, so that they could readily serve double duty in case of disasters. The capabilities of all branches of the military in engineering and temporary communities should be considered as part of emergency planning. They have experts in, e.g., making and storing water, cooking on a large scale, heavy equipment and heavy-equipment operators, tents and temporary living equipment and supplies as well as associated community sanitation and personnel hygiene expertise concerning temporary field operations. Many of these resources headquarters, especially concerning the National Guard, may be nearby and can be a significant source of aid for small communities. Prior planning should involve local citizens who are officers in the National Guard helping to create contingency plans. Incorporate their network into your network of storm and disaster preparedness contingency plans (McEntire, 2002).

Besides provisions for the staffs' basic needs, people need to be paid. Many of the government's families had emergency expense needs of their own. The payroll had to be met and checks cashed. This was compounded in Mississippi by the lack of availability of cash and governmental cash flow itself. There was little money coming into the town's coffers. And after the storm, even though recovery expenses would be greater, revenue would be much less due to the impact on taxable property. Ad valorem tax bills account for the majority of the town's own-source income and tax bills are usually sent out in November with a due date in March. Being in the middle of the year and before tax bills went out, there was little tax money from ad valorem taxes coming in. On top of that, 30–35 percent of the tax base was lost due to storm damage, which certainly will impact future tax collections and the willingness of citizens to pay taxes based on last year's assessed values. All of the built structures on street after street were wiped away or of little practical future value.

Part of the planning process for the future can be the use of portable GPS technology. By taking photographs 300 ft along the street, you would have a better idea of the structures that were in place before devastation as well as the possibility for survivors related to residential structures. This also will help the tax assessors determine the loss of value and facilitate the reconstitution of the tax digest based on lost structures.

Unintended Opportunities

The destruction affords opportunities for redevelopment but raises new concerns. One of them is the affordability of what will be built to replace what was destroyed or what must be razed due to inhabitability. Proposals for new condominiums on the beach will transform the look of the coast, the historic town, and the tax base. But associated with such changes are considerations for increased density, more intensive utility and public services, and greater risk to future devastation with more people and more property value at risk (Cho, 2005). It is likely that future property will be more expensive, taller, and have more exposure to potentially devastating winds in the future (Cordes et al., 1998).

How to cut expenses in light of future expected revenues became another thing to consider. Three personnel retired in the fire department after Hurricane Katrina, two to three from the police force. The federal government has an emergency loan bank available where the municipality could borrow 25 percent of its operating budget. State governments also have emergency revolving loan programs for not-for-profit fire and ambulance companies. Workshops on strategic budgeting initiatives should be considered as part of the recovery to maintain solvency, credit rating, and appropriate emergency plan expenses that are realistic and consistent with future revenues. Although loan banks may meet emergency needs, self-sufficiency and future budget planning must involve realistic governmental revenue projections instead of temporary funding that must be repaid.

Communications

Personal communications between individuals and between units providing services are always a problem, including the possibility that different groups of responders cannot talk to one another because of equipment compatibility issues (Bown, 1995; Pinkowski, 2001). In the case of Katrina in Long Beach, cell phones did not work, a combination of cell towers being blown down and back-up generators running out of fuel, which could not be resupplied due to the combination of the lack of a plan, availability of power to run pumps, and road and highways being blocked with storm debris. Chief Bass could not speak to colleagues in the next two towns nearest him because all communications that would normally be available were out. Cable television and Internet services were out for three weeks. Municipalities that had planned to communicate with citizens over the Internet via government Web sites found no one able to view the signal. After three days of continuous use, department radios began to go down and needed to be recharged. Satellite phones were rare and scarce. Probably one of the most requested items of procurement after widespread power outages caused by the recent string of hurricanes in Florida and the Gulf Coast is the request by municipalities for more satellite calling capability.

Cooperation and Planning with the Local Business Community

Maintaining services and acquiring essential commodities became a crisis. Fuel to run trucks, police cars, and generators became a critical need. Town emergency responders went to every retail store with an underground fuel storage tank and basically commandeered its fuel. In some cases, they made prior provisions with grocery store owners to leave the key to the storage tanks either with the department in advance or in a known, accessible location. Storeowners and bankers also need to plan ahead for doing business immediately after storms to provide commercial services by installing back-up generators (ABA, 2005). Tanker trucks delivering fuel need to be equipped with their own generators and fuel for those generators themselves to off-load the fuel. Suppliers also need to keep a record of what fuel is delivered where so that trucks go to empty tanks instead of already topped-up ones. Prior arrangements with distributors and manufactures of generators and other critically needed inventory would also benefit the public if prior arrangements could be made for priority resupply.

Grocery stores and hardware outlets are critical during this time and need to be reopened as soon as possible to allow people to rebuild, conserve, and protect their property, or just sustain the influx of out-of-town workers, who must clean up debris and start the recovery phases. Two grocery stores were operating within one month. But with bridges out to other communities whose normal outlets were no longer available, the demand became much greater than under non-storm conditions. This increased the demand on facilities that were open resulting from the shortage of outlets in the neighboring communities on top of the additional emergency response workers.

This brings to light an issue with sales-tax revenues and how it is redistributed from the states to areas where the sales are generated and the tax collected. The situation was not normal. Some communities had the ability to generate sales-tax revenue and others lost their sales-tax revenues stream. Another unpredictable revenue stream is the sales tax that is generated from temporary locations in disaster recovery such as temporary restaurants or fast-food establishments that reopen quickly. Where the sales are reported can make a determination as to the jurisdiction that gets credit for taxable sales. Conversely, the loss of a general hardware store cannot only inhibit recovery and rebuilding but it also represents a loss of the sales-tax revenue on normal sales. There are also in-fill and temporary businesses that need to be licensed. They collect sales tax at the point of sale and it should reflect such local activity instead of being aggregated in at a remote, headquarters location. These might include drug stories and providers of essential medical supplies, furniture stores with regional warehouses and multiple locations, carpet retailers, and other retailers who might temporarily occupy empty storefront locations.

If a community cannot facilitate its own business community quickly mobilizing and reopening, it is a risk of the transfer of its tax base to other nearby areas that reopen more quickly. It is essential that communities plan to document, license, and capture revenue that they would be eligible for during the disaster response phase. Otherwise it may go to an out-of-area destination because of the lack of documentation as to where sales are actually made. It also behooves local governments to have a plan to qualify such temporary businesses so as to protect citizens and transient workers from disreputable and unlicensed operators who prey on victims of disasters. Unfortunately, this licensing and regulation will also have additional costs and personnel needs associated with it. Local contractors might consider donating equipment for public works as the more rapidly the community reopens the sooner their own businesses get back to work.

Cooperation and Compacts with Sister Cities

The most workable plan for temporarily acquiring needed heavy equipment and trained operators is to prearrange compacts and mutual aid agreements with sister communities (Hughes, 2004; Michael et al., 1985; Tierney, 2005). This has the additional advantage that most of the time the operator's payroll will be covered in the immediate term by the lending jurisdiction. Long Beach was lucky in this regard; it had no prior sister cites or reciprocal pact arrangements. Fortunately, it had a National Aeronautics and Space Administration (NASA) facility nearby where many people had served temporary assignments and then moved on elsewhere in the country. Consequently, many people were well aware of the level of resources in southern Mississippi. One of them was now the city manager of Port Orange, Florida. He simply made a phone call to the fire chief asking him: "What do you need?" The question was well received and immediately answered: "food, boots, and 40–50 CamelBaks!"* The temperature during the day was in the low to mid 90s Fahrenheit with lows at night in the 80s. This was not untypical of the priorities of other first responders (Chudwin, 2005; ILEAS, 2006; Rescue, 2004).

Prior arrangements and cooperative agreements with other jurisdictions need to go beyond the standard fire department mutual aid agreements where units from adjoining municipalities respond and reciprocate in firefighting. The broader-based agreements should allow for different departments of various agencies to lend equipment or personnel when the need arises. This could include police and other law enforcement, search and rescue, engineering, emergency medical services (EMS), triage, bookkeeping and accounting personnel, and even tax assessors from other jurisdictions. Alternative routing mechanisms for e-mail is another useful tact that would greatly serve to assuage concern of family members as to the status of their loved ones. It also would serve employees who need to know when they can return to work or how they might arrange transportation or meet other essential needs.

Extra police are needed because of joy riders and curious people who are attracted to the devastation just to see the damage. At the same time, protecting citizens' rightful property is a sensitive issue because it can represent family memories and family treasures, which is merely storm debris to the curious outsiders. Law enforcement has simultaneously to deal with more than their usual assigned duties. They have to secure property, respond to numerous additional calls as a result of missing persons, and address injuries from storm-related health emergencies and

---

* CamelBaks are essentially backpacks with a drinking tube that can be worn with standard protective gear that are used for hydration when filled with water or ice.

accidents from residents who attempt their own cleanup or property conservation. Police also deal with missing, abandoned, or deserted pets without food or shelter (Heath et al., 2001). The best help for law enforcement in these situations is neighbors who know their neighbors. Often they can recognize and identify personal possessions and pets even if they do not know the owner's name. Still, neighbors are more likely to work together if they know each other beyond waving to each other as they pass by.

FEMA and state agencies should take a proactive stance in arranging these agreements and brokering volunteer aid. A network is needed to serve as a clearinghouse to match needs and available donors from among governmental and nongovernmental agencies. In the case of Hurricane Katrina, especially needed were more personnel, satellite phones, four-wheel drive vehicles, and boats with motors. Chief Bass said that "FEMA needs to make available more experts with familiarity with the Stafford book and staff to assist affected communities in processing claims for reimbursement." In the Katrina response, there was one FEMA representative for six coastal counties. This can result in unanticipated shortchanging in reimbursement. Due to technicalities of meeting the rules, Long Bay was reimbursed for only 16 hours per person per day instead of the 24 hours that personnel were actually on duty. And that reimbursement came nine months later. The local government has to carry those extra expenses in the meantime.

Utilities

Much is made in coastal and storm-prone areas regarding the efficiency and mobilization of private utility crews to restore electrical power (Geno, 2007). But also critically important are other utilities services whether provided by public entities or private concerns. Propane gas from retail sources and public utilities is another necessary supply-line component that must be incorporated in the long-range disaster response and recovery plan. When the water supply was cut off to the town, either due to the lack of power to operate the plant or its pumps, 35–40 percent of the people were cut off from basic sanitation. This included 85 percent of the commercial businesses. Long Beach still had 500 people in their shelter five days after the storm. These people needed to be fed and cared for regarding basic comforts in addition to emotional comfort.

Media Relations

Another very important lesson learned from the experience with Hurricane Katrina in Long Beach, Mississippi is how to manage the citizens' need to know what is going on and the media's right to know. The fire chief found that more and more of his personal time was involved with responding to media questions and interviews.

Citizens, responders, and stakeholders also required a good deal of communication and information sharing. Chief Bass found that hiring a full-time media spokesperson was a reimbursable expense under the FEMA guidelines and highly recommends this at an early stage for any local emergency services chief. It will provide professional information management and necessary communications for the entire community of stakeholders while it allows the executive to better perform his or her decision-making and coordinating functions. The reduction in interruptions and the redirection of effort detract from the effectiveness of emergency response as priority one. Turning the media relations function over to a specialist satisfies everyone's information requirements much better and greatly benefits the public, the media, and the disaster response. It would be most desirable to have someone identified as willing and capable of moving beforehand into this role that would become part of the disaster response leadership team.

Conclusion

All in all, Long Beach, Mississippi was pleased with their preplanning for Hurricane Katrina. They were confident that they had done a good job regarding the security of their headquarters building and operations center. But new concerns were raised after the devastation of the Category 3 hurricane that another storm in the same season, even a Category 1 or 2 storm could do even more complete devastation because the man-made barriers would have been wiped away. The buildings that were standing prior to the first storm's arrival as well as the existing landscaping and vegetation played a vital part in stopping the rising water and waves from moving inland. Most of those structures and obstacles were gone after Katrina.

The cost of building materials and supplies sky-rocketed after the storm. It would be a great contribution to effective prior planning to have made arrangements with manufacturers and distributors for fixed prices for storm survival and building materials needed during recovery. Thereby citizens and the government itself would not find that they were victims of supply and demand pricing. This would also contribute to quicker recovery and back-to-normal operations that would enable evacuees to return to their communities. Provision also must be made for alternative government services locations, such as a second building if the fire station headquarters were to be lost.

The police department would be well served if it were able to do standard background checks for people moving into the FEMA trailer parks for evacuees. Many people came there from out of the area and brought societal crimes with them such as prostitution and open drug-sales that made the environment of the whole camp unsavory. Police planning should include ways to track and identify known sex offenders in the temporary communities.

Prestaging of heavy equipment is one area that would have been very helpful. Equally important would be training and qualifications for heavy-equipment operators, e.g., backhoes and bulldozers. Hot sticks would also be useful to determine if downed power-lines are live.* Provisions for employees, their families, and pets should be part of the preplanning process. This should include recreation and health facilities (Posivach, 2005).

There is always room for improvement in disaster planning and response, but smaller communities will continue to face a major challenge regarding larger communities that control emergency resources distribution. Still, there are many practical ways that they can fend for themselves by simply forming partnerships and contingency plans with other communities and businesses in advance. You need to have a recovery plan in place before a disaster, not just an evacuation plan.

References

ABA, 2005. American Bankers Association. Should we buy a generator? *ABA Banking Journal, vol. 97* (12), pp. 16–20.

Bown, D. 1995. Oklahoma City, April 19, 1995: Managing when disaster hits. *Public Management, vol. 77* (December), pp. 6–9.

Cho, J. 2005. Smart infrastructures. *UN Chronicle, vol. 42* (1) (March/May), pp. 39, 42.

Chudwin, J. 2005. Front Line Reports from Hurricane Ground Zero with Chief Jeff Chudwin, Olympia Fields (IL) PD, TUESDAY, 09.13.05: P-1 Member special report from hurricane ground zero. Available https://www.policeone.com/writers/columnists/JeffChudwin/articles/118924/.

Cordes, J.J., et al. 1998. In harm's way: Does federal spending on beach enhancement and protection induce excessive development in coastal areas? *Land Economics, vol. 74* (1) (February), pp. 128–145.

Geno, T. 2007. How Entergys communication response to Hurricane Katrina boosted employee morale and sped service recovery. *Global Business and Organizational Excellence, vol. 26* (2) (January/February), p. 6.

Heath, S.E., Philip, H.K., Alan, M.B., and Larry, T.G. 2001. Human and pet-related risk factors for household evacuation failure during a natural disaster. *American Journal of Epidemiology, vol. 153* (7), p. 659.

Hughes, A.C. 2004. Homeland security: Interstate mutual aid. *Spectrum, vol. 77* (4) (Fall), pp. 16–17, 29.

ILEAS, 2006. Illinois Law Enforcement Alarm System. ILEAS Responds to Hurricane Katrina, February 2006. Available http://www.ileas.org/newsletters/february_2006.pdf.

Mawson, A.R. 2005. Understanding mass panic and other collective responses to threat and disaster. *Psychiatry, vol. 68* (2) (Summer), pp. 95–113.

McEntire, D.A. 2002. Coordinating multi-organisational responses to disaster: Lessons from the March 28, 2000, Fort Worth tornado. *Disaster Prevention and Management, vol. 11* (5), pp. 369–380.

Michael, S., Lurie, E., and Russell, N. 1985. Rapid response mutual aid groups: A new response to social crises and natural disasters. *Social Work, vol. 30* (May/June), pp. 245–252.

---

* Hot sticks are insulated poles for servicing high voltage lines.

Pinkowski, J. 2001. The potential for disaster: A case study of the Powell-Duffryn chemical fire and hazardous material spill. In Farazmand, Ali (Ed.), *Handbook of Crisis and Emergency Management.* New York: Marcel Dekker, pp. 433–449.

Posivach, E.S. 2005. Public safety Program Excellence Award in memory of William H.H., Sr. and Alice Hansell. *Public Management, vol. 87* (8) (September), p. 14.

Rescue Training Resource Guide 2004. Government Assistance to Volunteers. Available http://www.techrescue.org/smforum/index.php?topic=5509.msg5572.

SAIP 2004. U.S. Census Bureau, Small Area Income & Poverty Estimates, County Level Estimation, 2004. Available http://www.census.gov/cgi-bin/saipe/saipe.cgi.

Tierney, K. 2005. The 9/11 commission and disaster management: Little depth, less context, not much guidance. *Contemporary Sociology, vol. 34* (2) (March), pp. 115–120.

U.S. Census 2005a. U.S. Census Bureau, Population Estimates, Cities and Towns, All places, 2000–2005, SUB-EST2005-4. Available http://www.census.gov/popest/cities/SUB-EST2005-4.html.

U.S. Census 2005b. Three-Year-Average Median Household Income by State: 2003–2005. Available http://www.census.gov/hhes/www/income/income05/statemhi3.html.

Wesselman, R. 2006. Hurricane Katrina Responders Recognized. *Navy Newsstand,* 2/27/2006. Available: http://www.news.navy.mil/search/display.asp?story_id=22474.

Chapter 10

Emergency Contracting for Hurricane Katrina in New Orleans Gulf Area

Mary M. Dickens Johnson

CONTENTS

Acts of God have been occurring since the beginning of time. Since the development of modern nation states, there is the expectation on the part of the citizens that the government will care for the vulnerable and the victims, either through planning and preparation or remedies after the fact. The example of the New Orleans Category Four hurricane Katrina catastrophe illustrates what can happen with poor planning, preparation, and lack of institutional support to respond in a timely fashion.

According to a South Florida newspaper headline "Katrina fiascos cost us $2 billion: Audacious schemes, waste, bureaucratic mismanagement cited" (Lipton, 2006, p. A1). News reports after the disaster efforts were underway shed light on mismanagement and an inability to effectively help the victims of New Orleans and the Gulf area following the category 4 or 5 storm on August 25–29, 2005. Because the reports consistently blame bureaucratic mismanagement, one needs to examine the organizational context, leadership involved, and the rules that were followed that produced an inadequate organizational response.

Although there are organizations dedicated to these types of situations and provisions in the Federal Acquisition Regulations (FAR) to allow for emergency contracts, these were not effectively utilized during the time of hurricane notice or immediately after the fact. Part of the problem was the inexperience of this region in handling hurricanes and the learning that goes on after repeated experience. Another part of the problem was the institutional shortcomings of the organizations responsible for coordinating resources to remedy the situation in the affected area. This chapter will review relevant theories of leadership in organizations to pinpoint shortcomings in the bureaucratic response. Pertinent organizational theories describe the problems with the institutional response and possible remedies for future improvements. Furthermore, a review of the improvements that could possibly result from the learning that could occur after the hurricane experience in that region will be discussed. Special attention shall be paid to the institutional capacity of procurement actors in the governmental arena to remedy and provide goods and supplies in the immediate aftermath and reconstruction.

Governmental Institutions

The primary governmental institution responsible for supplying disaster regions with federal aid support in the provisions of goods and services is the Federal

Emergency Management Agency (FEMA). Under the reorganization of the Department of Homeland Security (DHS), FEMA was placed under the management of the DHS. The director of FEMA tends to attract public attention and credit or displeasure depending on the abilities to execute effective emergency response. The previous director, James Witt, appointed under the Clinton administration was extremely popular and known for responsible leadership and effective delivery. The director of FEMA under George W. Bush, Michael Brown, was assumed to be appointed to the position as a "political plum" because he lacked prior experience or qualifications to lead the agency.

In conditions of extreme disaster, such as this, the White House tends to play a role in guiding the activities and commitment of the FEMA and related support services. In the case of Katrina, George W. Bush was criticized as being remote and not returning phone calls promptly. In addition, other key personnel on staff were distant and nonresponsive. An important player in the Bush administration, Karl Rove, was out the week that the disaster occurred. It was not until approximately a week after the disaster that the White House became actively involved and engaged in policy decisions to put in place a recovery agenda.

Institutions under Similar Circumstances

A construction company field manager wrote in *Contract Management* that partnerships with preferred contractors who have experience in similar situations should be established so that work can begin almost immediately after disaster occurs. Chriss (2006) wrote that the reconstruction efforts of the Gulf Coast are not significantly different than those reconstruction efforts in the Middle East in the war zone. The most effective way to initiate and sustain reconstruction efforts by the government is to engage in partnerships with prequalified business partners with track records of experience and success in this area. For instance, a business entity, under a retainer for contract work, can prepare for disasters by "kitting" or preparing packaged bundles of supplies on hand for ready deployment. This technique remedies many of the last minute preparations and ensures rapid deployment.

Contracting Methods in Place to Ensure Rapid Deployment

The Federal Acquisition Regulations (FAR) Part 16.603 provides for letter contracts whereby the contracting officer can engage in a contract by one-page letter agreement if the price is considered fair and reasonable and the contract is "definitized" within 180 days of signing the contract or before 40 percent of the contract work is completed. To definitize a contract is to fill in and complete the necessary clauses, formatting requirements, and terms and conditions required by the FAR. This allows a contract to be enacted in short notice under conditions of duress.

Another contractual vehicle that may be employed is the usage of U.S. General Services Administration (GSA) schedules contracts. A list of the supplies that can be ordered through www.gsaadvantage.com may be found on the Web site and government purchasers with a purchasing card may order a wide range of products immediately from the Web site with direct deployment from the supplier within a week. The terms and conditions are established by GSA prior to posting on the Web site as well as the negotiated prices. It should be noted that state and local government purchasers are also allowed to utilize the GSA schedules for purchases. The products and services included in the schedules are vast and comprehensive and cover a multitude of supplies that could be engaged for remedy in case of disaster.

Why Was FEMA Ill-Prepared to Respond to Hurricane Katrina?

Given the methods described above to provide contractual support in case of disaster, one could ask: why was the response to the victims so slow? One organizational theory proposed by Scott (2001) is that the founding of the organization affects its behavior. In this case, the shift in organizational identify from an independent agency to being placed under DHS may have caused some problems with perceptions of organizational competency. Furthermore, the lack of experience of the director, as a political appointee without a track record in this area, may have also affected the commitment of the agency and its personnel to capably respond to the disaster.

Anecdotally, similar complaints about the slowness in response to Hurricane Andrew disaster in Florida some ten years ago should be noted (September 10, 2005. Retrieved from: www.PalmBeachPost.com on April 20, 2006). However, as a learning organization, the state and South Florida region in particular, evaluated the problem and began preparing remedies so that if another disaster were to occur, the response would be timelier. For instance, the state now has a system of satellite phones in place that allow communication should land and cell phone lines be rendered useless. In the case of Katrina, there were no satellite phones in place and communication was nil (Mohr, 2006). Distance communication in the Gulf area was achieved only through the tireless service of volunteer CB operators who saved hundreds of lives with their efforts (interview with anonymous CB operator, April 2006).

Furthermore, one could hypothesize that when the president appointed a non-qualified person as head of FEMA, there was a message sent about the leadership in relation to the "carriers of institutional values and relational structures" (Scott, 2001, p. 106) that cause the informal structures of professionalism and linkages to fall short. In organizational theory, it is presumed that the carriers of institutional values and relational structures will "link the organization with salient external actors, both individual and collective" (Scott, 2001, p. 106). Indeed, professionalism and commitment to the field of emergency management on the part of leadership could have led to a different record of performance and more effective deployment of support supplies and services.

In this sense, one could say that FEMA organization was not prepared as the primary national actor to lead a rapid and effective response to the area where the victims suffered from the aftereffects of Hurricane Katrina. A more committed and professional leadership could have initiated preparation efforts such as a supply of satellite phones to be deployed to the area to allow better communications. Or the kitting of necessary tools and supplies necessary to set up immediate response centers could have been put in place.

Furthermore, the more effective use of GSA schedules would allow a cost effective and timely delivery of products and services to provide for the hurricane victims. A staff of professional contract managers would have the knowledge of how to utilize GSA schedules and post orders and requests for quotation for bidder's response.

The Middle Range Theory Approach

Jreisat (2002) suggests that in comparative public administration, the most effective approach in offering pathways for those who wish to follow and imitate a successful public intervention is "the middle range theory" approach. This theoretical approach allows for application of a similar response under roughly similar circumstances or environment.

This theory applies to the reconstruction efforts experienced by contractors in Iraq or Afghanistan to be applied to the Katrina case. It allows for process improvements such as the kitting technique or partnership alliances to be transferred across national boundaries so that the technique can be applied to other situations as well. It also applies to the effectiveness of satellite phones when land lines are nil or when traditional cell phones lack towers to carry the frequency and are rendered useless.

A similar process improvement is to put in place a network of preferred and qualified contractors who are experienced and on contingency to enact the necessary disaster response and minimize chaos. If a group of skilled contractors were formed with procedures and controls in place to be deployed on short notice, the response could be quicker with less confusion. Furthermore, it should be noted that federal regulations require these contractors to subcontract to small and disadvantaged as well as local suppliers.

By building linkages and a flexible institutional structure that is ready to be deployed with contractors who are skilled and possess internal controls, the government would be situated in a position of readiness to deploy teams of skilled workers to assist in whatever disaster that may occur.

Preferred Providers

It should be noted that FEMA did utilize the services of experienced government contracting partners for this type of situation. Of the initial outlay of $60 billion awarded to FEMA, $100 million went to the Shaw Group to refurbish existing structures, $100 million went to Bechtel to provide temporary housing in Mississippi, $100 million went to Fluor Group to construct temporary housing, $100 million was awarded to CH2m Hill for temporary housing in Alabama, and Dewberry received $100 million for hazard mitigation, technical assistance, inspections, and management (Fineman, 2005).

FEMA also utilized government agencies to assist with the effort. Health and Human Services (HHS) received $155 million to provide care and establish 26 new health centers; the Department of Transportation (DOT) used $145 million to repair roads, bridges, and airports as well as trucks for delivery of goods; the Environmental Protection Agency (EPA) was employed for $134 million to assess damage to water systems and restore service; the Department of Labor (DOL) used more than $450,000 on unemployment insurance or temporary jobs for workers displaced by Katrina. In addition, the Department of Defense (DOD) spent $2.1 billion on military missions (Fineman, 2005).

The Army Corps of Engineers was awarded $400 million in funding for repairing civil engineering projects. Of this, $170 million was dedicated for operations and maintenance, i.e., repairs to damaged locks, channels, and waterways. In turn, $100 million was awarded to the Shaw Group for unwatering and roof repairs, and KBR (Halliburton firm) was owed $16 billion in previous contracts for levee fixes. Ashbritt was awarded four contracts for debris removal in Louisiana and Mississippi for $500 million, and Phillips and Jordan were one of the three firms awarded $500 million contracts for debris removal in Louisiana (Fineman, 2005).

Application of Structuralism Theory to Emergency Preparedness

If we consider the high performing organization as complex organization in a heterogeneous environment as stated above, then the most appropriate fit of organizational form to the environment of hurricane disaster recovery efforts would be an alliance of preferred provider contractors under the leadership of FEMA to the multitude of comprehensive measures needed to properly restore the affected area. In turn, these providers would be required to seek local and small or small disadvantaged firms to subcontract with. The complex and comprehensive requirements of disaster recovery efforts qualify for an environment of a heterogeneous nature. In this sense, we could strive to construct an organizational "class" of governmental preferred contractors who are "loosely coupled" with the local environment and the supply of subcontractors locally or available as contractor suppliers through the GSA schedules or other contract mechanism.

The FEMA organization, independent from DHS, could effectively establish leadership as the "channel" in the provider environment and the "class" of preferred providers could serve as the "net" in case of a needed response to a disaster or recovery to an affected war zone. With a multitude of decision makers in the implementation of recovery efforts, the living systems paradigm described by Ashmos and Huber (1987) could be implemented.

Furthermore, the forms of fit described by Drazin and Van de Ven (1985, p. 523) in the "task-contingency theory of work-unit design" model, with units of "specialization, standardization and discretion" will be able to produce a high performing organization capable of effective and immediate response. These "modes" reflect the complexity of the work difficulty and a method of organizing a thorough and comprehensive remediation that occurs in a timely fashion.

It is to be remembered that the ideal solution will produce recurring patterns that exhibit a form that fits within the societal context. As noted in the theoretical construct, the managerial archetypes will serve a useful purpose in disseminating the broad policies and guidelines. It is the decision makers within the class of preferred providers to effectively implement the recovery efforts under standards of professionalism and best business practices. It is the contractor suppliers who wish to establish the practice of kitting as a business best practice that can improve the process of supplying the affected situation with an immediate and effective response.

With continuous improvement, one can hope to see the coevolution of governmental management with business to produce an environment of cooperation and management that is dedicated and committed to an effective emergency response. An integrated system of actors, either loosely coupled or linked together in a form of organizational connectivity, could select a process that has tools and techniques capable of rapid and effective recovery in situations of disaster management.

Review of Leadership Theory

Decision Lapses

News reports consistently cite bureaucratic mismanagement (Lipton, 2006), and thereby a review of relevant leadership theory is provided below. According to Hammond et al. (2001, p. 144), "Making decisions is the most important job of any executive." Drucker (2001) lists six steps toward effective decisions. These include the appropriate category of the problem and its definition, as well as developing an appropriate response. It is important to distinguish a "right" answer before negotiations between concerned parties adapt the solution to serve vested interests. The decisions to provide individual payments, purchase trailers for temporary housing, and restore certain community centers share a concern for the victims and an effort to alleviate their misery. However, the action plan to implement the decision needs feedback mechanisms to evaluate and improve the response. In the case of Katrina, evaluations and audits occurred after the fact and not during the process. It appears that some of these steps were followed in the government administration's effort to remedy the disaster by the series of news analyses and reports that followed. Thereby, the bureaucratic failure must be analyzed from another perspective.

Creating the Organization That Works in the Environmental Conditions

Perhaps the solutions and programs implemented reflect an organizational problem. Weick and Sutcliffe (2001, p. 10) propose an alternative view in their "hallmarks of high reliability" organizational traits. It should be noted that the "high reliability organization (HRO)" (Weick and Sutcliffe, 2001, p. xiii) does not distinguish between situations of emergency and status quo because the group is forward thinking and persists in organizing for action according to its purpose. These organizational traits are (1) a preoccupation and careful reflection of every failure, (2) a reluctance to simplify and deliberate inclusion of observed important details, (3) concern with operations or front-line implementation effects, (4) dedicated resiliency or a commitment to provide solutions to operational details, and (5) "deference to expertise" (Weick and Sutcliffe, 2001, p. 16). Starting with the fifth trait, deferring to the experts, the characteristics of a HRO were not observed in the appointment of the administrator, Michael Brown. The individual was not trained or experienced in emergency management.

To take the analysis one step further, consider the "resource dependence perspective" by Pfeffer and Salancik (2003, p. xii) in their book entitled *The External Control of Organizations*. In this book, emphasis is made on the social and environmental influences of the organization. According to the authors, these effects are felt in the system of interdependencies that result in the rules, values, and leadership selection. As a consequence, the organization seeks to remain viable through linkages and alliances with other organizational bodies to politically advance the survival of the organizational unit. Immediately following the Katrina disaster, administrator Brown was unresponsive in initiating a response. President Bush knew of the impending disaster, but failed to put a plan in place to remediate the spiraling problem. Advisor Karl Rove was out of commission with an injury. Other important insider players dropped the ball at the initial onset. The alliances that sprang-up to remediate the disaster after the fact showed that FEMA had support from Congress to put into place a plan of recovery that would alleviate the damaging effects of the hurricane. It was after Congress passed the legislation that high-profile remediation companies were put into place and monitored by the host of organizations concerned, from the U.S. Army Corp of Engineers to the Department of Defense and all others in between. In this manner, an effort was made to turn to the professional remediation responders to implement a solution and remedy. However, the traits of the HRO were not adhered to through a lack of attention to the complexities and front-line reflections. Operational details were inadequately addressed and the necessary "preoccupation with failure" was not given adequate attention. Thereby, in the haste of solving the problems, wastage resulted as well as fraud. These were discovered later through audits by Congress, the Government Accountability Office (GAO), and the South Florida *Sun-Sentinel* newspaper. From leadership to project implementation, the operation suffered from many pockets of inexperienced bureaucratic administration. The environment attempted to respond, but lacked operational concern, attention, and reflection to avoid the massive waste of $2 billion out of $19 billion spent (Lipton, 2006).

Prospect Theory

This theory emerges from the value theory of the mid-1970s as described by Kahneman (2000). A decision theory is constructed incorporating utility theory and rational choice theories to illustrate the gambit of decision selection when monetary effects are involved with specific probabilities and the outcome is between two possible results. The model is comprised of ideas such as decision weights that are not linear, the relative values posing a referential condition, and the importance of framing. The importance of this theory is that the concept of rational agent is exposed as a flawed explanation in light of other factors affecting decisions, choices, and values.

March's Decision-Making Observations

Decision selection is based upon the participants' "perceptions of the preferences and identities" (March, 1994, p. 111). In addition, social institutions shape the preferences. Thirdly, the preferences that are outside the norm and observed as "divergences" (March, 1994, p. 112) are the choices that are reported. Thereby, one can assume that the role of organizational values, context, and norms of behavior is the core of decision-making behavior in organizations. March argues that decision makers are proactive in the selection of choices they pursue because of the future effects of developing habits or patterns of behavior. Furthermore, a note should be made about the development of identity. This can be developed in context and how it is measured is of utmost importance. For instance, if one considers himself or herself as a professional by means of education and specialized training, this would be an entirely different concept of identity of promotion by political appointment according to cronyism. In the case of the appointment by Michael Brown, a detachment from the operational side of things was exhibited because of concept of identity in relation to the president's team rather than the field perspective grounded in technical and professional knowledge of emergency management. As preferences by decision makers are exercised, there are some basic assumptions such as a consistent pattern of selection and the reliability of the decision over time.

Furthermore, inadequate attention is paid to the effects of these "preferences" on the status of the choices and the outcome they are meant to produce. Due to the social and hierarchical nature of the organization, the learned preferences that are taught and reinforced throughout the organization lead to a belief in the efficacy of ingrained behavior.

Garbage-Can Decision Processes in Emergency Situations

According to March (1994, p. 199), conditions of a temporal nature such as emergency environments or military engagements are aptly described as "organized anarchies." In these conditions, a multitude of actors are involved, and loose coupling occurs in the complexity of the moment. Under these conditions, success is difficult to define and there are ambiguous preferences to guide the key players. The participation by actors is irregular and unorganized. Participation fluctuates as many persons and organizations are involved. Each organization and its representative(s) bring with it the context of the organizational environment from which they originate. This environment results in conflicting views of proper solutions and means by which to accomplish the appropriate results. The bauble of interaction and communication occurs in a compressed time-frame and is appropriately described as a model of the garbage-can theory. Concerted and unified methods of action are difficult to reach consensus and agreement in the context of a need for rapid deployment. The widespread involvement of a multitude of actors from many levels and organizational frames makes a coordinated and orchestrated response next to impossible to achieve.

Consider the Military Model

In the introduction of the book entitled *High-Performance Government: Structure, Leadership, Incentives*, (Klitgaard and Light, 2005) suggests that the president should be given authority to lead a structural organization of agencies and their responsibilities. Evidently, an attempt was made to improve the efficiency and effectiveness of FEMA by placing it under the Department of Homeland Security. However, the decision was reversed after much spirited opposition on many fronts and FEMA returned to independent agency status. Robbert (2005) suggests that an effective way to promote leadership equipped to deal with management situations that require an organizational capacity to serve would be a model similar to the military. In particular, the organization would utilize the internship system to foster comradery and development of a professional corps as well as increased expenditures in education and learning seminars. That is not to mention an organization that would be hierarchically structured with a command and control orientation. Furthermore, the organization should be established so that it is highly mobile and able to respond to various demographic locations. Throughout the process, the observation and promotion of effective leaders within the group would be fostered to cultivate a culture of professionalism and commitment to operational capabilities as well as logistical abilities to achieve results.

It is this concern with professionalism in operational implementation, organizational leadership capable of carrying out productive outcomes in the context of incorporating feedback during the process, which is needed to create a backbone of professionalism and commitment to emergency management leadership.

Rational Models

According to Quattrone and Tversky (2003), a key component of the rational model is the assumption of invariance. That is, given a set of circumstances and alternatives, the person in a decision-making position will likely make the same choice without respect to background or training. This assumes that logical consideration will lead to a common consensus of maximum utility in a plan of action.

Drucker (2001) describes every decision-making activity as an inherently risk-taking proposition. However, a rational person would follow a sequence that involves a classification of the problem and its definition. Next, the rational man or woman would select among alternative courses the proper response given the conditions under which the circumstance exists. A plan of action would be designed to carry out the desired course, followed by evaluation and modification during implementation. A key element in the initial stages is defining the specifications, or what purpose the decisions are to accomplish within the context within which the action plan is to operate.

According to Hayashi (2001), an effective decision maker continually examines his conscience and reflects objectively and subjectively about the progress of a decision or its enactment. A certain amount of emotional involvement is necessary in the personal reflections of decisions and courses of action.

Decision Traps

The psychological dimensions of making a decision in the mind of an executive leader go beyond commonly considered errors in consideration according to Hammond et al. (2001). For instance, the blame cannot only rest with inadequate consideration of alternatives or lack of adequate alternatives and thorough evaluation. Causes for inadequate decision making can find their roots in aspects of anchoring, or giving extra consideration to initial alternatives, or forces of inertia that favor the preservation of existing circumstances. Alternatively, there is a tendency to repeat previous courses of action and reflect upon current models while lending a blind ear to alternative views. If one fails to adequately diagnose the problem in adequate detail, solutions are hindered. Moreover, a common fallacy to be avoided is the representation of an overly optimistic forecast that leads to criticism in the end.

Summary

If one were to pinpoint the source of organizational failure and bureaucratic mismanagement so frequently cited, it should be noted that the leadership appointment to head the agency was a source of many of the problems. However, leadership alone cannot account for the bureaucratic failings in the organizational context. Inadequate attention to professionalism and preparation resulted in an organizational capacity unable to enact operational responses that were effective and efficient in implementation. It is anticipated that the attention given to this case of emergency contracting management will produce learning that will enable organizations to construct a capable response in case future disasters of this type should occur. Moreover, best business practices in the field can result in the construction of an effective contingency response system and decision makers prepared to make a ready response in time of need. In some cases, the military model can contribute to an organizational structure capable of ready response.

A new commitment to professionalism by practitioners, government leaders, and contractors can help contribute to methods, processes, and effective implementation. Given the criticism aimed at FEMA commissioner Brown, it seems unlikely that future presidents would place someone in the post without the prerequisite experience or in-field service. The appointment of Florida veteran R. David Paulison by President Bush indicates a renewed commitment to experience and professionalism in the director position of FEMA (FEMA Head: I'll Watch Katrina Movie. retrieved from: http:www.cbsnews.com/stories/2006/ on July 31, 2006).

By utilizing the experience of contractors and agencies that have performed in similar circumstances, the construction of best practices and linkages can be built and applied to a variety of environments. With continual improvement, the best practices can be selected and applied with the most appropriate fit to the environment with maximum benefits and results in the context of middle range theory. At that time, the organization will be prepared to respond appropriately to disasters such as Katrina and better serve the populace affected by these challenging conditions requiring skilled professionalism in leadership and organizational capacity.

Bibliography

Books and articles:

Ashmos, D. and Huber, G.P. 1987. The systems paradigm in organization theory: Correcting the record and suggesting the future. *Academy of Management Review*, 12: 607–621.

Caplan, J. September 19, 2005. Katrina Brownout. *Time*.

Chan, A. and Garrick, J. 2002. Organization theory in turbulent times: The traces of Foucault's ethics. *Organization*, 9 (4): 683–702.

Chriss, R. January, 2006. Strategic Sourcing in an Emergency Contracting Environment. *Contract Management.*

Deetz, S. 2000. Putting the community into organizational science: Exploring the construction of knowledge claims. *Organization Science*, 11 (6): 732–739.

Drazin, R. and Van de Ven, A. 1985. Alternative forms of fit in contingency theory. *Administrative Science Quarterly*, 30: 514–531.

Drucker, P. 2001. The effective decision, in *Harvard Business Review on Decision Making.* Boston: Harvard Business School Publishing Corporation.

Eisenberg, D. September 26, 2005. Hurricane Katrina: How to Spend (Almost) $1 Billion a Day. *Time.*

Fineman, H. September 26, 2005. After Katrina: How Much Can We Afford? *Newsweek.* pp. 24–31.

Gharajedaghi, J. and Ackoff, R. 1984. Mechanism, organisms and social systems. *Strategic Management Journal*, 5: 289–300.

Hammond, J., Keeney, R., and Raiffa, H. 2001. The hidden traps in decision making, in *Harvard Business Review on Decision Making.* Boston: Harvard Business School Publishing Corporation.

Hayashi, A. 2001. When to trust your gut, in *Harvard Business Review on Decision Making.* Boston: Harvard Business School Publishing Corporation.

Jreisat, J. 2002. *Comparative Public Administration and Policy.* Boulder, Colorado: Westview Press.

Kanneman, D. and Tversky, A. 2000. *Choices, Values, and Frames.* New York: Russell Sage Foundation.

Katz, D. and Kahn, R. 1966. *The Social Psychology of Organizations.* New York: Wiley.

Klitgaard, R. and Light, P. 2005. *High Performance Government.* Santa Monica, California: Rand Corporation.

LaCayo, R. and Thomas, C. March 6, 2006. The Big Blank Canvas. *Time.*

Lindblom, C. 1959. The Science of "Muddling Through". Reprinted from *Public Administration Review*, taken from by Shafritz, J. and Hyde, A. 1997. *Classics of Public Administration, fourth edition.* St. Paul, Minnesota: Wadsworth, Thomson Learning.

Lipton, E. June 27, 2006. Katrina Fiascos Cost Us $2 Billion. *South Florida Sun-Sentinel* (Broward, Florida), p. A1.

March, J. 1994. *A Primer on Decision Making.* New York: The Free Press.

March, J. and Simon, H. 1958. *Organizations.* New York: Wiley.

Martin, J., Feldman, M., Hatch, M., and Sitkin, S. 1983. The uniqueness paradox in organizational stories. *Administrative Science Quarterly*, 28: 438–453.

Martinez, A. October 1, 2005. Bush Defends FEMA Deal with Carnival. *The Herald.* Miami, Florida.

McGregor, D. 1997. The human side of enterprise. *Classics of Public Administration, Fourth Edition.* Wadsworth: Thomsom Learning.

Miller, H. 2002. *Postmodern Public Policy.* Albany, New York: State University of New York Press.

Miller, J. 1978. *Living Systems.* New York: McGraw-Hill.

O'Matz, M., Kestin, S., and Burstein, J. October 9, 2005. FEMA is no match for fraud. *Sun-Sentinel.* Fort Lauderdale, Florida.

Pfeffer, J. and Salancik, G. 2003. *The External Control of Organizations*. Stanford, California: Stanford University Press.

Quattrone, G. and Tversky, A. 2003. Contrasting rational and psychological analyses of political choice in *Choices, Values and Frames*, edited by Kahneman, D. and Tversky, A., New York: Cambridge University Press.

Robbert, A. 2005. Developing leadership: Emulating the military model in *High Performance Government*, edited by Klitgaard, R. and Light, P. Santa Monica, California: Rand Corporation.

Scott, W.R. 2001. *Institutions and Organizations, Second Edition*. Thousand Oaks, California: Sage Publications.

Singh, J. and Lumsden, C. 1990. Theory and research in organizational ecology. *Annual Review of Sociology*: 16: 161–195.

Thomas, C. November 28, 2005. Hurricane Katrina: The Cleanup. *Time*.

Time magazine staff. (September 19, 2005). Four Places Where the System Broke Down. *Time*.

Weick, K. and Sutcliffe, K. 2001. *Managing the Unexpected*. San Francisco, California: Jossey-Bass, a Wiley company.

Weiss, R. 2000. Taking science out of organization science. *Organization Science*, 11 (6): 709–733.

Internet References

CBSNews staff (July 31, 2006). FEMA Head: I'll Watch Katrina Movie. Retrieved from: http://www.cbsnews.com/stories/2006/ Retrieved on July 31, 2006.

Hsu, S. 2006. Waste in Katrina Response is Cited: Housing Aid Called Inefficient in Audits. Retrieved from: washingtonpost.com on April 14, 2006.

Hurricane Andrew. 1993. Retrieved from: http://en.wikipedia.org/wiki/HurricaneAndrew on April 20, 2006.

Koffler, K. 2006. Bush blames bureaucracy for Katrina failures. Retrieved from: GOVEXEC. COM on March 21, 2006.

Lack of Hurricane Plan hurt Katrina-hit States (September 10, 2005). Retrieved from: PalmBeachPost.com on April 20, 2006.

Mandel, J. 2006. Better Training Needed for Emergency Purchases, Procurement Chief Says. Retrieved from: GOVEXEC.COM on April 7, 2006.

Mohr, H. 2006. Phone Troubles Hampered Katrina Emergency Crews. Retrieved from: www.aol.com news on March 8, 2006.

MSNBC Staff. 2006. After Six Months, There's No Shaking Katrina: Billions More Is Needed to Aid Rebuilding, and Years Are Needed to Ease Pain. Retrieved from: MSNBC.com on February 28, 2006.

Palmer, K. 2005. Post-disaster Contracting Rush Leads to Confusion. Retrieved from: GOVEXEC.COM on September 11, 2005.

Strohm, C. 2006. Ex-FEMA director: Restore agency's independence. Retrieved from: GOVEXEC.COM on March 6, 2006.

Swindell, B. 2006. Outlook Uncertain for Bill Creating Katrina Recovery Organization. Retrieved from: GOVEXEC.COM on January 30, 2006.

Chapter 11

Debris Disposal and Recycling for the Cedar and Paradise Wildfires in San Diego

Orelia DeBraal and Wayne T. Williams

CONTENTS

Summary and Overview

During October 2003, there were two massive wildfires in San Diego County, California that burned 400,000 acres and destroyed nearly 3,000 residences, 3,000 accessory buildings, and 4,000 vehicles (see Figure 11.1).

As a result of the ash and debris left by the wildfires, the county created the debris removal program to assist property owners. The program included two components: a bin program, where residents loaded bins located on or near the right of way; and a property clearing program, where the county contracted for debris clearing through a private company. In the first two months, the county managed the debris removal program by supplementing existing staff; then for eight months, a consulting firm (PBS&J) was retained to manage the program. The county also offered free removal of burned vehicles and stormwater consultations

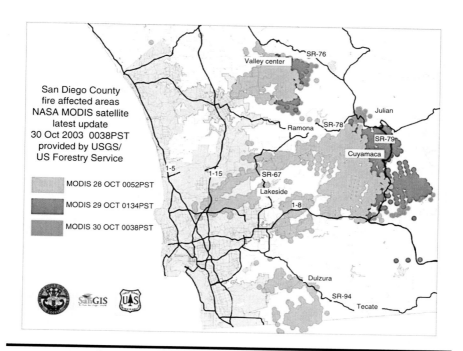

Figure 11.1   Fire affected areas, October 2003.

to prevent endangerments to local waterways. The county sponsored programs that assisted in the removal of 26,966 tons of fire debris from properties (Table 11.1).

County staff knew that recycling efforts would increase if inert recycling facilities were located in close proximity of the affected areas. As a result, two temporary mixed construction and demolition (C&D) recycling facilities were sited in Crest and Julian. These sites received over 42,000 tons of fire debris and had the ability to produce needed aggregate materials in the immediate area for rebuilding efforts.

Overall, more than 127,000 tons of debris from the unincorporated areas were generated as a result of the fire, and more than 79 percent of the tonnage was handled by private companies (Table 11.1). To assist with the cost of the cleanup, the privately owned landfills reduced the tipping fee to $20/ton and many of the existing inert recycling facilities reduced fees and offered free vouchers for concrete recycling. Analysis of the county fire response program data indicates that the county sponsored programs achieved a combined 43 percent recycling rate. Rates varied dramatically by program and by hauler. The PBS&J contracted bin placement program, where residents loaded their own bins, achieved a 45 percent recycling rate. In contrast, the property clearing program reached a 24 percent recycling rate (Table 11.1).

When combined with the independent recyclers, temporary C&D facilities, and recovery efforts at the bin sites, the county was able to preserve 185,000 cubic yards of landfill space.

Table 11.1   2003 Firestorm Recycling Rates (2003/2004)

	Tons Recycled	Tons Disposed	Total Tons	Recycling Rate (Percent)	Program (Percent)
County bin program	854	1,566	2,420	35	2
PBS&J managed bin program	3,622	4,420	8,042	45	6
Property clearing program	3,008	9,496	12,504	24	10
Burned vehicle removal	4,000		4,000	100	3
Total county programs	11,484	15,482	26,966	43	21
Private recycling and disposal	62,172	38,397	100,569	62	79
Total	73,656	53,879	127,535	58	

Data indicates that many debris materials are highly recyclable and the public is willing to separate materials for recycling. However, additional education and stringent monitoring of the clearing contractors are required to achieve a greater recycling rate. Local recycling companies showed strong interest to assist in the recovery of materials at lower rates than landfill tipping fees. Therefore, the potential for recycling to save time and program costs should be developed in further detail.

Structure of the Debris Removal and Recycling Program

There were seven primary goals for this program:

1. To assist residents with safe and timely removal of fire-related debris to protect human health and safety.
2. To develop an optimal operations strategy for managing and recycling disaster debris.
3. To meet 50 percent recycling rates as required under Assembly Bill (AB 939).
4. To save landfill space through recycling and reuse.
5. To protect local waterways from debris runoff.
6. To increase, through private investment, the number and type of private sector facilities that can process C&D debris.
7. To locate recycling processing centers in close proximity to the affected outlying areas.

The county implemented a two-phased fire debris removal program led by the Landfill Management Section with technical support from the Watershed Protection Program (which provided hotline and database staffing) and Solid Waste Planning and Recycling Section (which provided the first two months of hotline and recycling support). Two programs were implemented to help residents clear their properties: a bin program and a property clearing program. A free bin program, where residents loaded bins located on or near the right of way, was initiated first. A property clearing and abatement program, where the county contracted for debris clearing through a private company, began second. In the first two months, the county managed the debris removal program by supplementing existing staff; then for one year, PBS&J, a consulting firm, was retained to manage the program.

County staff implemented the debris removal and recycling program based on field visits and models from previous disasters in California. Reviews of the areas showed that the majority of materials by volume included vehicles, metals (vehicles, water heaters, etc.), masonry (chimneys, bricks, bird baths, etc.), charred structural wood, trees and brush, concrete (foundations, sidewalks), stucco, propane tanks, mixed debris (dirt, wood, masonry), and ash. Field staff noted that residents, volunteer groups, and SDG&E had separated materials into piles for recycling in

Figure 11.2   Destroyed property in Crest.

many locations. In some areas, residents segregated metals into ferrous and non-ferrous types (Figure 11.2).

County staff reviewed existing recycling efforts and models from other disasters to develop an operational approach that would maximize recycling and Federal Emergency Management Agency (FEMA) reimbursement. Under AB 939, the county is required to maintain a 50 percent recycling requirement. If 50 percent diversion from landfills is not met, the county could be liable for a fine of $10,000/day. All fire tonnage was tracked by jurisdiction and reported to the state quarterly. The Federal Emergency Management Agency (FEMA) also required a stringent tracking system and substantial documentation for tonnage. To meet this challenge, the county worked with transfer stations, haulers, and landfills to put in special codes at the gates to track fire debris. However, many C&D recycling facilities are not required to have scales, and it was difficult to implement tracking systems at those facilities.

A database was developed to track the amount and type of tonnage delivered to each facility using load monitors and tickets (Attachments 1 and 2). Haulers were required to use county approved tracking forms. Conversion factors were used for materials that were sent to facilities without scales.

The county hired several hauling companies for both programs through a competitive bid process. Companies were paid by the tons, based on each company's competitive bid. Because the unincorporated county is so large (3,572 square miles), bids were structured by the county based on material type and geographical zones to

County of San Diego
Fire Debris Load Ticket

No. 07501

Contractor Name	Date container placed in service

The County of San Diego has entered into a contract with your company directing you to pick up, transport and dispose fire-related debris within the Unincorporated County of San Diego. Such debris shall not consist of household refuse, liquid or hazardous waste. The County of San Diego is committed to maximizing recycling as part of this program. Please deliver to one of the authorized facilities listed for that material in the Fire Debris Facility Guide.

Site address	Property Owner	Zone

Type of Debris:

Clean Metal	Container # (if applicable)	Truck license number
Concrete, Asphalt, Concrete Block, Slump Stone and Rock		
Clean Wood	Container size	Container % full at site
Mixed Debris for Landfill		
Mixed Debris for Recycling		

Load Monitor 1 Name	Date	Load Monitor 2 Name	Date

Signature		Signature

Name of receiving facility	Date and time container arrives at receiving facility

Container % full at receiving facility	Material weight	Method of weight determination (Volume to Weight, Scale, etc.)

A copy of this Load Ticket and completed Facility Weight Ticket must be presented to the County for hauler payment.

White- Contractor to send to County   Canary- Contractor Copy   Pink- Load Monitor 1   Gold - Load Monitor 2

Notes

County of San Diego Public Works 11/28/03
Procedures for Debris Monitors

1. Wear County badge and orange safety vest if possible.
2. Leave Recycling Staff business cards for questions you can't answer.
3. To increase County knowledge of available volunteer groups, ask volunteer groups for a contact name and telephone contact.
4. Briefly train volunteers on site as soon as possible to separate materials into concrete, metals, and mixed debris. Train volunteers to fill out load ticket if monitor is not present when debris box is hauled.
5. To prevent extra work, inform volunteers not to overload the bin. The legal limit for debris boxes is ten tons. An overloaded box must have contents removed until it is within the legal limit. Metal bins may be full, but not stacked above the top of the bin. One cubic yd of concrete weighs a ton. For example, a 40 yd box may be a quarter full; a 30 yd bin can be a third full. If the materials are light, you can fill the bin. Use your judgment if heavy items are included.
6. Do not mix materials unless it is a mixed material bin.
7. If there is no sign denoting the material type of bin, improvise a sign for each bin.
8. Check on bins periodically if possible to ensure compliance with these standards.
9. Complete a pink slip while visiting site, whether bin has been delivered or not. pink slip back to Recycling Staff. After bin is loaded, confirm material has low contamination rates and complete load ticket. Either tape load ticket to the bin or hand it to the truck driver.
10. Please ensure that your vehicle's gas tank is filled at the beginning and end of the day. Return all vehicles to Seville Plaza, 5469 Kearny Villa Rd. and bring keys to Recycling Staff in Suite 305.
11. Fill out sheets throughout the day and turn into Recycling Staff at end of day.

To maximize recycling, have volunteers separate debris and place it in piles close to where the bins will be, but not in the public right-of-way. Separate into these categories:
1. Metal
2. Concrete, concrete with metal reinforcement and cinder blocks. (No foundations, sidewalks, driveways.

Mixed debris, including roofing, wallboard, etc..

Remember, wear proper safety gear, and be wary of any unknown items that you suspect may be hazardous. Call 1-877-713-2784 for safe hazardous materials disposal.

For pickup questions or if placing your materials on the edge of the road will cause a traffic hazard, call 1-888-846-0800.

For general questions of fire recovery, call the Fire Recovery Hotline at 1-866-402-6044.

Monitor Supervision

Morning Prep - before monitors arrive
1. Remove previous day's sheets from blue bins.
   a. Put all pink and yellow load tickets together with each monitor's assignment sheet. Give to Wayne.
2. Run off 4 copies of Monitor Bin Checklist. Put one by each bin.
3. Run off 1 copy of Monitor Phone List. Put on staging table.
4. Take Volunteer Sign In Sheet off bulletin board. Put on staging table with pen.
   a. Once complete, put back on bulletin board.
5. Get Assignment Sheet(s) and Maps.
   a. If Thomas Guide coordinates are not on it, start the first volunteer who arrives on that.
6. Get Large Map(s).
   a. If sites are not on it, have the next volunteer who arrives do that.
7. Set out extra supplies.
8. Get Volunteer Calendar. See how many (and who) are scheduled.
   a. Start dividing up the sites, based on how many volunteers, how many sites, proximity of sites to each other, and driving distance
9. Make 4 copies of Monitor Field Response sheets

Morning Prep - when monitors arrive
10. Have monitors sign in.
11. Have monitors choose a bin (same one they had yesterday if they drove)
    a. Have them label their bin with masking tape
    b. Have them take everything OUT of the bin, and check it off as they put it back.
12. Ask monitors if any have vehicles from their depts they can use today.
    a. If not, start lining up vehicles from Roads or wherever
13. Have monitors take a cell phone and put their names on the Phone List.
    a. Once that is complete, make 7 copies (1 for each of them, 1 ea for you, Mike & Wayne)
14. Assignment Sheet - if sites are not numbered (e.g. 1-16), number them
    a. Then make copies for monitors
15. Large map - once sites are on it, make copies for monitors
16. Site down with monitors to go over Assignment Sheet and Map
    a. Make assignments
17. Monitors who have done this before can then leave.
    a. Monitors who haven't, stay for further orientation

Monitor Supplies Checklist

Phone related
Cell phone
Phone adapter
Monitor/Staff Phone List

Routing
Assignment sheet
Large scale map page
Thomas Guide

Forms & Handouts
Fire Debris Monitor Log - Field
Vehicle abatement (8)
Right-of Entry Permit (8)
Fire Debris Cleanup Info (8)
How to Load (8)
Waste Hauler phones (1)
Contact Your Hauler (10)

Other supplies
Document protectors (8)
Duct tape
Pens (4)
Highlighter (optional)
Clip board
Dust masks
Car keys
County id badge
First aid kit (if not in trunk of car)

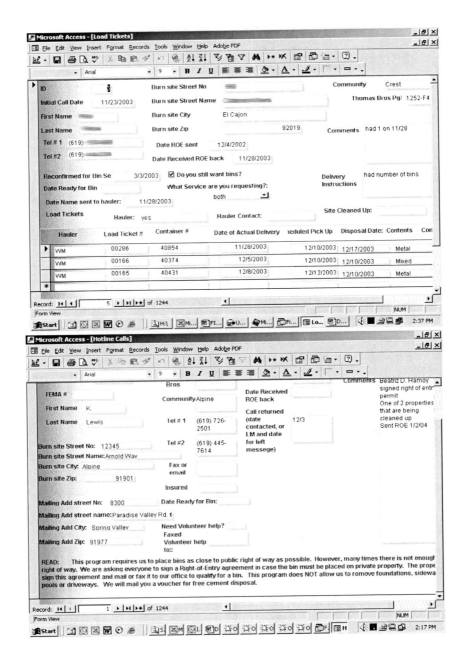

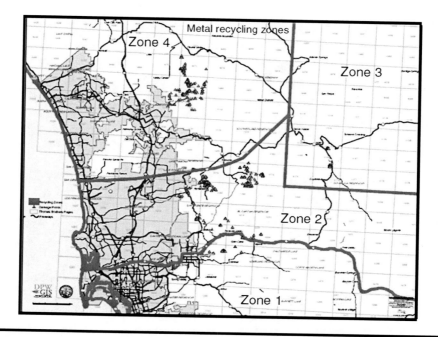

Figure 11.3   Hauler bid zones.

allow for different bids based on driving distances to the nearest end-use facility (Figure 11.3). If bids had been taken for bins placed anywhere in the county, the bids would have been very high to cover the bidders' risk of driving longer distances. Invoices were verified using weight tickets from the landfill or recycling facility. The county's fire debris hotline was used to provide information to the public concerning the programs and to coordinate cleanup times with the public.

The Department of Planning and Land Use used an existing contract for abandoned vehicle removal contract to recycle approximately 4,000 vehicles. This program is funded through a $1 fee, collected with the vehicle registration fee assessed on all vehicles registered in the county.

Hazardous Waste Handling

The county was concerned with residents and volunteers handling hazardous waste, including paint, car batteries, motor oil, pesticides, etc. Site inspections of the burned areas showed that there was little remaining household hazardous waste because of the intensity of the fires. To collect any remaining residential waste that could be hazardous to clean up volunteers and contractors, the Department of Environmental Health hosted three temporary household hazardous waste collection

Figure 11.4   Burned auto batteries and parts. (County of San Diego, Department of Public works.)

events in the affected communities of Julian, Alpine, and Valley Center. To assist residents in the Ramona and north county areas, the hours and days of operation at the Ramona permanent household hazardous waste collection facility were extended and appointments were not required for fire victims. In addition, fire victims were allowed to use the door-to-door collection program that was designed for disabled and elderly residents.

A total of 82,074 lb of material were collected at these events. It is estimated that 17 percent, 13,300 lb, of the material was from fire victims.

Overall Program Challenges
Challenge 1: Lack of a Plan for Managing Disaster Debris

The county's Emergency Response Plan did not contain information on disaster debris handling. Significant financial, staff, and time resources were required to implement the program. Staff required vehicles, radios, cell phones, field kits, and appropriate field clothing. Staff was pulled from all areas of the county (librarians, administrative assistants, etc.) and a significant amount of time was required to train and monitor the staff. If a jurisdiction has a preexisting plan in place, it is easier to obtain FEMA reimbursement.

Possible Solutions

Preplanning. The success of a disaster debris and recycling program depends on an operational strategy and negotiating hauling/facility contracts before the disaster occurs. "As-needed" service and supply contracts should be in place to expand current county service contracts. For example, the county's regular vehicle abatement program only had one towing company in place. The company, which had enough trucks to fulfill its regular contract, was overwhelmed and took several months to respond to residents.

The operational plan should include a recycling component and skeleton contracts, which can be directly awarded to both facilities and contractors if needed; a public relations plan for educating residents how to separate their debris; an overview of responsible agencies and how the program will be implemented. The plan should include fire debris tracking and recycling data in record keeping procedures to assist with FEMA reimbursement. Data systems should be designed before a disaster, and should include a mechanism to allow daily tracking of facility use.

Staffing. Recycling should be fully integrated into the task of debris management. A debris management/recycling coordinator position should be created to manage administrative and field operations, and Solid Waste Planning and Recycling Office should provide independent oversight to ensure that the planned recycling efforts are being implemented. Interdepartmental agreements should be secured to allow use of staff from "field-ready" departments such as building inspection, roads, and engineers. There should also be countywide coordination and regular meetings to realize resources and keep all staff aware of the county programs.

Challenge 2: Debris Impact on Local Landfills and Meeting State-Required Recycling Laws

Recycling of materials is a legal requirement to comply with California Integrated Waste Management Board (CIWMB) regulations under AB 939. If this is not established as a higher priority than present, the county could be liable for a fine of $10,000/day for not meeting a statewide 50 percent diversion requirement. The county is able to deduct disaster tonnages from its annual disposal tonnages if it is demonstrated that the county diverted a majority of the recyclable materials. In addition, recently released data from the 2003 Countywide Integrated Waste Management Plan Siting Element indicated that insufficient landfill capacity could exist as early as 2007, in terms of permitted daily disposal tonnages.

Possible Solutions

Scout Areas before Collection. Because the composition of debris is highly variable, areas should be scouted before collection to identify concentrations of materials that can be collected and delivered to source-separated recycling facilities.

Require Source Separation of Debris.   Residents, volunteer groups, and contractors should be required to separate debris into the following categories, metal, fire-related wood, source-separated inerts (if not from foundations, driveways, swimming pools). Mixed inerts can be a combination of concrete, asphalt, red clay brick, concrete block, with up to 10 percent sandy soils.

Management Must Require Recycling within the Removal Program.   To ensure that recycling requirements are met, managers must require that staff enforce recycling requirements with all contractors.

Load Check Oversight.   Many load checkers did not enforce recycling requirements and contractors were able to deliver recyclable loads to landfills. Therefore, a system must be developed to review the load checker's records each day.

Expand Recycling Availability.   Staff should work with local landfill, transfer stations, and any temporary drop-off sites to provide for recycling. The majority of the transfer stations and rural bin sites offered recycling drop-off sites for concrete, burned vegetation, and metals. Some metals were also recycled at Sycamore and Ramona landfills, but the two landfills did not separate concrete or other inerts from the waste stream.

Pursue Potential for FEMA Reimbursement for Mining the Isolated Fire Debris at Sycamore Landfill.   Many jurisdictions have sued FEMA for reimbursement due to lack of landfill space after a local disaster. Staff should pursue this and identify if existing funds could be used to match FEMA to purchase equipment to excavate and process materials buried at the Sycamore landfill (25 percent local jurisdiction: 75 percent FEMA).

Challenge 3: FEMA Reimbursement

It was difficult to determine what actions the county needed to take in this program to ensure reimbursement from FEMA. The direction received from FEMA was to proceed as "normal" and after the fact; FEMA would determine the eligibility of the program. The problem was that the county had never done this type of program before, so there was no normal and FEMA was unable to provide specific guidance to match the situation. For example, one FEMA requirement was that bins be provided only "curbside," and only as community bins for multiple residents (this is because FEMA covers debris in the road right of way but not on private property). This may work well in an urban setting where there are curb gutters and sidewalks, but was nearly impossible in the backcountry, where roads were winding and narrow, often with no shoulders, and where a resident's driveway can be half a mile long. Although the reason for this is that, in accordance with FEMA guidelines, "private property owners are responsible for their own debris removal," the fact is that immediately following a disaster everyone is anxious to clean up, and no one at that point has the means to do so on their own. Even those with insurance (which were few and far between) would not see money for debris removal for months.

In the end, FEMA only reimbursed the county for the costs of the bin program. The private property debris removal program was not approved for FEMA reimbursement even though the county's Department of Environmental Health conducted an ash characterization study that showed that there were state-regulated levels of hazardous constituents in the ash. The county's administrative appeals of this decision were denied, and no judicial appeal is allowed. As of January 2006, the county was working the State Office of Emergency Services to secure partial reimbursement of private property debris removal costs from the State.

Possible Solutions

Create a working relationship with FEMA to facilitate the exchange of useful information. Set up a protocol for bin placements and debris management in advance of next disaster. Have contacts and reports from other jurisdictions that have successfully obtained reimbursement from FEMA as case studies.

Bin Program

The county's bin program supplied empty roll-off bins, typically 30 or 40 cubic yards in size, to be used by citizens to quickly remove debris from their property. This program was provided at no cost to the fire victims. In the first two months, the county managed the bin program by supplementing existing staff; then for one year, a consulting firm, PBS&J, was retained to manage the program. Cleanup contractors were encouraged to place bins so that they could be used by the community as drop-off sites.

County Managed Bin Program

Through a competitive bid process, several waste hauling companies were hired by the county to provide bins to fire victims. When the bins were filled with fire debris, they were emptied at a landfill or recycling facility. Bids were requested based on geographical zones according to proximity to major disposal sites and roadways. Collection contracts included language indicating that the county required recycling and that haulers were expected to utilize recycling facilities in a particular order of preference. Five haulers were awarded the contracts: Waste Management, Ware Disposal, Pacific Waste, Dependable Disposal, and Tayman Industries. Haulers selected for contract awards were provided with training booklets for their field staff about program guidelines and facility requirements before starting work (Attachment 3). Companies were paid by the tons collected based on their competitive bid price.

The county coordinated heavily with volunteer groups in an attempt to coordinate bin placement with their activities. At first it was thought that these groups,

ATTACHMENT 3-FIRE DEBRIS RECYCLING GUIDE

County of San Diego

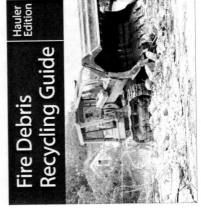

Hauler Edition

Fire Debris Recycling Guide

County of San Diego
Recycling
It's in our Nature

1.11.03

Listing in this directory is not an endorsement of one company over another. The County has identified these facilities as companies willing to accept mixed inerts or burned ferrous metals. If you are interested in providing this service, please contact the County's Recycling Program at (858) 874-4038.

♻ Printed on Recycled Content Paper

This guide contains facilities approved for delivery of source separated mixed inerts and metals from the County of San Diego Fire Debris Removal Contract.

It is the County of San Diego's intention to recycle fire debris to the maximum extent possible.

Homeowners will fill the first) delivered to the site with clean metal or inerts. Therefore, all haulers are expected to deliver loads to an authorized recycling facility.

In some cases mixed loads of source separated metals, wood, and inerts will be directed to a mixed recycling facility. These facilities will charge less than the landfill tipping fee of $22.35.

The County expects all drivers working under the Fire Debris Removal Contract to be trained in the County's recycling procedure and to have a copy of this guide in their trucks at all times.

County Recycling Procedure:

1. Load source separated metal and deliver to a metal recycling facility.

2. Load source separated inerts (concrete, concrete block, red clay brick, tile, masonry, asphalt, porcelain, rock and dirt with rebar and/or wire mesh) and deliver to an inert recycling facility identified in this guide or other facility approved by a field monitor.

3. Combine and load source separated metal, wood, inerts and deliver to a mixed debris recycling facility specified by the County of San Diego load monitor.

4. Load all remaining material and deliver to Sycamore or Ramona Landfill.

5. All facilities have been contacted and are ready to receive materials. Each facility will provide the driver with a weight ticket. This ticket must be submitted with invoice for payment.

6. The County of San Diego and/or its representative reserves the right to inspect all loads of fire debris at landfills and sites of origin. The County of San Diego will not pay for any load of material delivered to the landfill that is found to contain fire debris that is source separated or any mixed loads that would have been accepted at one of the facilities in this guide.

Clean loads can also be taken to any permitted recycling facility not listed in this guide when authorized by a field monitor.

If you have questions about delivery of materials to a facility, please contact the facility directly and/or the County's Recycling Program at (858) 874-4038.

Mixed Inert Recycling Facilities ● These facilities can also accept clean inert loads. For mixed load specifications, see comments.

Facility & Address	Telephone	Comments/Material Type	Delivery Hours	Price	Surcharges	Scales
Escondido Sand & Gravel 500 N. Tulip St., Escondido	(760) 432-4690	Accepts asphalt, concrete, concrete block, porcelain, and rock, with up to 5% dirt. Material can include oversize with rebar and wire mesh with surcharge.	Mon-Fri 7 am - 5 pm Sat 6 am - 3 pm	Bobtail $75 Roll-off $100 Semi $150	Double for rebar and/oversize, small amount of mesh OK	YES
Hester's Granite Company (J.Cloud, Inc.) 2094 Willow Glen Dr., El Cajon	(619) 593-9020	Accepts mixed inert loads containing more than 10% of dirt with asphalt, concrete, concrete block, tile, masonry, red clay brick, porcelain, and rock. Material can include oversize with rebar and wire mesh.	Mon-Fri 7 am - 4:30 pm Sat 6 am - 12:30 pm	Bobtail $80 Roll-off $110 Semi $200	Trash $25 - $100	YES
Julian Recycling 3578 Highway 78 (Turn left at Newman Rd), Julian	(760) 765-0062	Accepts asphalt, concrete, concrete block, red clay brick, tile, masonry, porcelain, and rock. No limit on dirt. Material can include oversize with rebar and wire mesh with surcharge.	Mon-Fri 7 am - 5 pm Sat 8 am - 3 pm	Bobtail $100 Roll-off $200 Semi $300		NO
LJS 1682 Mountain View Road (1/2 way between Crest and Harbison Canyon)	(619) 895-4844	Accepts asphalt, concrete, concrete block, red clay brick, tile, masonry, porcelain, and rock. No limit on dirt. Material can include oversize with rebar and wire mesh with surcharge.	Mon-Sat 7 am - 5 pm	Bobtail $50 Roll-off $60 Semi $75	Oversize, rebar, mesh Bobtail $30 Roll-off $30 Semi $50	NO
Re-Rock Inc. 504 Alta Road, East of Donovan Prison, at Alta Road and Kuebler Ranch	(619) 571-7175	Accepts asphalt, concrete, concrete block, red clay brick, tile, masonry, porcelain, and rock, with up to 50% dirt. Material can include oversize with rebar and wire mesh with surcharge. A ticket estimating the cubic yards of inerts will be given to the driver by this facility.	Mon-Fri 7 am - 4 pm Sat 7 am - 12 pm	Bobtail $50 Roll-off $75 Semi $125	Trash $50 - $100	NO

Metal Recycling Facilities

Facility & Address	Telephone	Comments/Material Type
California Metals 636 Front St, El Cajon	(619) 444-3111	Accepts non-ferrous metals and heavy steel.
Ecology Auto Parts 800 Energy Way, Chula Vista 1030 Airport Rd., Oceanside	(619) 661-1148 (760) 966-2866	Will pay for most metals and appliances.
Pacific Steel, Inc. 1700 Cleveland, National City	(619) 474-7081	Will pay for most metals and appliances.
Escondido Recycling Yard 1350 W. Mission Rd. Escondido	(619) 229-1004	Most metals and appliances.
Miller Metals 36 Front, El Cajon	(619) 444-2136	Accept non-ferrous metals and heavy steel, no appliances.
Pacific Coast Recycling 3055 Commercial, San Diego	(619) 238-6740	Most metals and appliances.
Julian Recycling 3578 Highway 78	(760) 765-0062	Most metals and appliances.

many of which were national religious organizations, could exclusively order the bins as they went through areas to assist with debris cleanup. It was quickly apparent, however, that these groups were limited in their resources and were only able to help certain communities. The county then extended the program to all residents. Free service was advertised at local victim assistance centers, and through local media.

To facilitate the free bin program, the county initiated and maintained a fully staffed, 8-hour-a-day fire debris hotline. The hotline provided information to the public and acted as a clearinghouse for all aspects of the county's fire debris removal efforts, including scheduling bin deliveries and pickups. The bins were requested by both individual property owners and by groups cleaning multiple properties. All bins were used by the surrounding community, which means that anyone could place structure burn debris in them, not just the person who requested the bin. The owners of the property on which the bins were placed were required to sign right-to-enter forms (Attachment 4) before receiving a bin. Residents requesting bins were also given information on proper bin loading and material handling safety (Attachment 4).

Staff worked with residents to identify an estimate of the quantity of material on site and schedule roll-off bins accordingly. Only structural fire and ash debris was allowed to be placed in the bins—no vegetation, concrete from foundations or walls, or asphalt from sidewalks or driveways, which was a requirement of FEMA. Residents were encouraged to separate large quantities of clean materials (metal,

Figure 11.5 Community drop-off site. (County of San Diego, Department of Public works.)

RIGHT-OF-ENTRY PERMIT
[Execution by Director, General Services]
[Gov't Code 25350.60, 53069; Admin. Code 73(b)]
Curbside Bin Placement Program for Debris Removal by Property Owner

_____ ("Owner"), hereby permits the County of San Diego, its officers, employees, and agents ("County"), to enter upon Owner's property commonly identified as _____(street)_____, _____(city/town)_____, County of San Diego, State of California ("Premises"), subject to all licenses, easements, encumbrances, and claims of title affecting the Premises upon the following terms and conditions:

1.   Grant of Right-of-Entry. Owner hereby grants County a right-of-entry ("Permit") over the Premises for the sole purpose of assisting Owner to remove and clear any or all fire-generated debris of whatever nature from the Premises, and/or placing a container thereon for the collection of such debris, subject to the terms and conditions set forth in this Permit. It is fully understood that this Permit does not create any obligation on the County to perform debris clearance.

2.   County Held Harmless. County shall not be liable for, and Owner shall hold harmless County and its officers, agents, employees and volunteers (collectively "County Parties"), against any and all claims, deductibles, self-insured retentions, demands, liability, judgments, awards, fines, mechanics' liens or other liens, labor disputes, losses, damages, expenses, charges or costs of any kind or character, including attorneys' fees and court costs (hereinafter collectively referred to as "Claims"), which arise out of or are in any way connected to County Parties' actions arising out of this Permit, and hereby release, discharge and waive any Claim and action, in law or equity, arising therefrom.

3.   No County Assumption of Liability for Remediation. In consideration of the assistance County is providing to Owner under this Permit, at no cost to Owner, County assumes no liability or responsibility, and Owner shall not seek to recover from County, the costs of any remediation of damages to the Premises incurred due to County's actions under this Permit.

4.   No Other Assistance. Owner will not receive any compensation for debris removal from any other source including Small Business Administration, National Resource Conservation Service, private insurance, individual and family grant programs or any other public assistance program for debris removal. Owner will report any insurance settlements paid to Owner or Owner's family for debris removal for the Premises that has been performed by the government.

5.   County's Agents. Any person, firm or corporation authorized to work upon the Premises by the County shall be deemed to be County's agent and shall be subject to all applicable terms hereof.

6. Authority. Owner represents and warrants that it has full power and authority to execute and fully perform its obligations under this Permit pursuant to its governing instruments, without the need for any further action, and that the person(s) executing this Permit on behalf of Owner are the duly designated agents of Owner and are authorized to do so, and that fee title to the Premises vests solely in Owner.

7. Entire Agreement. This Permit constitutes the entire agreement between the parties with respect to the subject matter hereof, and all prior or contemporaneous agreements, understandings and representations, oral or written, are superseded.

8. Modification. The provisions of this Permit may not be modified, except by a written instrument signed by both parties.

9. Partial Invalidity. If any provision of this Permit is determined by a court of competent jurisdiction to be invalid or unenforceable, the remainder of this Permit shall not be affected thereby. Each provision shall be valid and enforceable to the fullest extent permitted by law.

10. Successors & Assigns. This Permit shall be binding on and inure to the benefit of the parties and their successors and assigns, except as may otherwise be provided herein.

IN WITNESS WHEREOF, Owner and County have executed this Permit effective as of
_(Date:)_____.

COUNTY: OWNER:

COUNTY OF SAN DIEGO,   By: _____
a political subdivision of the
State of California   Site Address: _____

By: _____   _____
    John J. McTighe, Director,
    Department of General Services

Please return signed form to:
County of San Diego
Recycling Program-MS 0344
Attn: Fire Debris Removal
5469 Kearny Villa Rd., Suite 305
San Diego, CA 92123

The forms can also be faxed to 858-874-4058.

wood, concrete, dirt, etc.) from other burn debris, because those materials would be recycled. Residents were given six days to fill the bin.

The county had monitors checking the locations of the bins to ensure they were being placed on the properties for which right-to-enter forms had been received. The county placed load tickets on each bin that indicated what kind of load the driver was carrying and what type of facility the driver should take the load (Attachment 1). Load monitors also checked bins to ensure that non-fire-related debris and foundation/sidewalk/swimming pools were not placed in the bins. Carbon copies were returned to the load monitor allowing immediate load tracking capability.

Once the bins were filled, the hauling company picked them up. Recyclable materials were directed to inexpensive source-separated recycling facilities or to the pilot mixed inert recycling facilities. All remaining mixed debris and ash were sent to separate cells at Sycamore and Ramona landfills for possible future mining.

Figure 11.6 **Mixed load of fire debris. (County of San Diego, Department of Public works.)**

Figure 11.7   Clean load of metal. (County of San Diego, Department of Public Works.)

Figure 11.8   SDG&E utility pole recycling. (County of San Diego, Department of Public Works.)

PBS&J Managed Bin Program

In January 2004, a private consulting firm, PBS&J, was hired to manage the bin program and to start the property clearing protocol for getting bins to residents and created a more comprehensive monitoring system and online database for FEMA reimbursement.

The PBS&J monitoring program was more stringent than the county program in that sites were inspected prior to bin placement. Photographs of the right of way were taken with the suggested location of the bin placement from multiple directions. Each bin was issued a load ticket stating the location of disposal. Photographs were taken of the loaded bin and the material in the bin. The photographs were a valuable tool in obtaining FEMA reimbursement.

Outcome

Overall, the bin program was very successful in assisting in the timely cleanup of structure fire debris. Over 1,500 bins were provided, which facilitated the disposal or recycling of 10,590 tons of fire debris. The program had a 43 percent average recycling rate (Table 11.2).

Bin Program Challenges

Challenge 1: FEMA Reimbursement and Monitoring

FEMA requires evidence that the program is monitored to ensure that the bins only contain fire-related debris. Often, haulers did not communicate to their drivers that these tickets dictated the type of material and where the bin was to be taken for recycling/disposal.

Table 11.2   County of San Diego Bin Program Results (2003/2004)

	Tons			
	Recycled	Disposed	Total	Recycling Rate (Percent)
County bin program	854	1,566	2,420	35
PBS&J managed bin program	3,622	4,420	8,042	45
Total bin program	4,476	5,986	10,462	43

Note: For a complete list by facility and program see Appendix 11.1.

Possible Solution

Better training is needed for all contractors participating in the debris removal programs.

Challenge 2: Hauler Bids

Haulers bid varying prices per ton on hauling mixed inerts, metal, mixed debris, and trash. Although the money paid for the material by the recycling facility was intended to offset this difference, the end result was that the hauler could make more money per load by delivering the material to a landfill than a recycling facility (Appendix 11.3).

Possible Solution

Whether county staff or contracted vendors are utilized in disaster debris recovery operations, FEMA will require cost-effective operations as a condition for reimbursement. Resources devoted to monitoring of contracts, related to building renovation, building demolition, collection and hauling of debris, and delivery to processing facilities will more than pay for themselves to assure that the program is efficient and that FEMA does not disallow costs. It is important to ensure that trucks are full when they leave collection sites, that hauling prices are appropriate for the tonnage and type of material collected, and that claimed diversion rates are actually achieved. In addition, the city of Los Angeles was able to prove to FEMA that diversion activities should be reimbursed, even if they cost more than current disposal costs, based on FEMA's practice of honoring local policies and the Los Angeles policy of maximizing diversion in accordance with AB 939.

Research FEMA Requirements for Reimbursement. The county should negotiate with recycling and disposal facilities for the best rates for all materials. Haulers should be monitored closely to ensure they are using appropriate facilities. If hauler quotes are used, all quotes should be negotiated for the best price.

Challenge 3: Bin Misuse

As the bins were community bins (not for the exclusive use of a single property owner), and as they were left on-site for several days it was not possible to monitor the material placed into the bins resulting in several cases of non-allowed material being placed in the bins and several instances of the bins being filled beyond their weight capacity.

Possible Solution

Education. The county provided signs for the haulers to place on each bin that illustrated what types of materials would bring bins to weight capacity, and supplied the guidance to all volunteer community groups. In the future, more resources should be used to create large bin signs to educate residents on the materials that are allowed to go into the bin.

Large centralized collection areas for greater public use could be organized. Existing transfer stations, bin sites, private and public property (parks, roads, stations, etc.) could be used. This method was successfully used by Samaritan's Purse to clear a majority of the properties in Crest. Centralized drop-off sites also provide for easy monitoring to prevent illegal dumping and contamination of recycling bins.

Challenge 4: Bin Demand

Because of the high number of burned properties, there was a tremendous demand for bins both inside and outside the county program. There were a limited number of bins available in the region, which limited the number of bins available to the county's program. In many cases, residents wanted bins immediately, but then found that they did not have the means to fill them after quite some time. Because the backcountry had many large lots, it was difficult for people to move heavy items the distance to the bin. This further limited the availability of the bins. The unavailability of bins eventually led to the county supplementing the program, because the wait time for bins occasionally exceeded two weeks, which impeded the program.

Possible Solution

Work with haulers to see if additional bins would be available outside the region. Set up rules at the outset limiting the amount of time a bin will be provided (i.e., one week maximum). Consider using other sources than waste haulers for bins, including contractors with dump trucks and other equipment.

Property Clearing Program

The county property clearing program provided debris removal and disposal to private property owners. Cost to the property owner was based on the amount of insurance available for debris removal. Fully insured property owners were responsible for the entire cost of debris removal and disposal, while those underinsured were responsible for only a portion of the cost. Service was provided to uninsured property owners without cost.

The owners of the property to be cleaned were required to sign a right-to-enter form, which included homeowner's insurance information. County monitors checked on the cleanup work being provided by the contractors to insure only the correct materials were being removed from the property. The county contractors were required to separate metals for recycling from other burn debris. Only structure fire debris was cleaned from private properties—no vegetation, concrete from foundations or walls, or asphalt from sidewalks, driveways, patios, or swimming pools.

Several contractors, HVAC, A&D, and Whillock, were hired to do the work through a competitive bid process. Contractors were hired to clean properties to the foundation. Cleanup contracts included language indicating that the county required recycling, and that contractors were expected to utilize recycling facilities in a particular order of preference. Companies were paid by the tons collected based on their competitive bid price.

Outcome

Overall, the private property cleanup process was successful, with the county cleaning 333 parcels of structure fire debris. Almost 12,500 tons of fire debris were recycled or disposed. The program achieved 24 percent recycling rate (Table 11.3).

Property Clearing Challenges

Challenge 1: Getting Insurance Information

It took an inordinate amount of time to secure insurance information from a number of property owners. This information is important in determining if it is necessary to bill a property owner for a portion of, or the entire cleanup performed by the county. This lack of information inhibits the county's ability to have final closure to the program.

Table 11.3 Property Clearing Program: Percent Recycling and Facility Usage by Material Type for the County of San Diego Firestorm Response (2003/2004)

	Concrete		Metal		Trash		Total	
	Loads	Tons	Loads	Tons	Loads	Tons	Loads	Tons
Total loads/tons	136	1,610	441	1,398	970	9,496	1,547	12,504
Material type percent of total (percent)	13		11		76			
Total recycling rate (percent)	24							

Note: For a complete list by facility and program see Appendix 11.2.

Possible Solution

In the original right-to-enter forms, there needs to be more information concerning the time property owners have to provide insurance data and the consequences of not providing that information in a timely manner.

Challenge 2: Recycling

Contractors under the property clearing contract did not source separate. Although contract language required that property clearing contractors recycle, the program only reached a 24 percent recycling rate, with one of its contractors only recycling 15 percent of the tonnage handled (Appendix 11.2). In comparison, the free bin service, where residents loaded their own bins, the recycling rate was 43 percent (Appendix 11.1). The data indicates that the debris is highly recyclable and the public is willing to separate materials for recycling.

Possible Solution

More training, enforcement of separation at the site, and monitoring of trucks at the facilities were necessary to ensure they were attempting to meet the specifications and deliver the loads to the correct location. Strict monitoring of the property clearing contractors is required to achieve an optimal recycling rate. Noncompliance with recycling could result in nonpayment of contract invoices.

Recycling and Disposal Facility Use

Because the county does not own or operate any recycling or disposal facilities, the debris removal program used privately operated facilities for processing.

The general principles that guided the program's use of facilities were:

1. Develop several facilities located near the devastation to encourage competition, increase recycling rates, divert maximum tonnage from local landfills and minimize cost of tipping fees, standing time, and travel time.
2. Require monitoring and evaluation procedures, which ensure smooth mid-program changes when required, and provide information required by FEMA.
3. Encourage creation of permanent facilities that can process mixed C&D debris after the debris removal program has ended. The lack of this type of facility was cited in the county's AB 939 plan as a major barrier to achieving high recycling rates for this type of material.

At the outset of the fire debris removal program, all debris was delivered to transfer stations and landfills. The Regional Water Quality Control Board issued a waiver to allow for disposal of the ash in lined sections of local landfills. Emergency waivers were issued by the County of San Diego Local Enforcement Agency (LEA) for three landfills (Otay, Ramona, and Borrego Springs) to accept additional tonnage generated during the cleanup. In addition, the County of San Diego LEA issued two temporary emergency permits for C&D processing facilities (LTS in Crest and Julian Recycling). The City of San Diego LEA also issued a temporary C&D processing permit for the Sycamore landfill. The privately owned landfills reduced the tipping fee to $20/ton and many of the existing inert recycling facilities reduced fees to assist fire victims. Emergency waivers were also issued to five rural bin sites (Barrett Junction, Boulevard, Campo, Palomar Mountain, Ranchita) and five transfer stations (Julian, Viejas, Palomar Transfer, EDCO Station—La Mesa and Ramona MRF) to accept materials that exceeded the permitted daily totals.

The county worked with the Sycamore and Ramona landfills to recycle metal and the bin sites to accept wood and metal. In addition, two temporary emergency recycling facilities were added to the program. Not only did these actions increase the county's ability to recycle, but they also decreased hauling costs, because facilities were selected that were located in close geographical proximity to the various hard hit areas of the county, thereby decreasing the truck round trip travel time. Truck travel is estimated to cost $70/hour at public utility commission (PUC) rates, and is charged roundtrip.

Many privately owned recycling facilities exist within the County of San Diego that accept the types of materials generated by the program. These "source-separated" facilities generally have strict requirements for accepting materials to ensure that the quality of materials is appropriate for use in the manufacture of an end product or for reuse. Over the course of the program, recycling staff worked with six source-separated recycling facilities to relax their specifications. Each facility determined what would work for their site, and they charged a higher facility fee, however, the increased cost was much lower than the landfill tipping fee cost. This type of load was called "mixed inerts" and included a combination of concrete, asphalt, red clay brick, concrete block, with up to 10 percent sandy soils and 5 percent trash. These facilities provided more opportunities for decreasing program costs, standing time at facilities, and truck hauling time.

In contrast, facilities that recycle materials from mixed C&D loads did not exist in the County of San Diego. Therefore, all mixed loads that could not be source separated were directed to local landfills for disposal.

Facility Challenges

Challenge 1: Varying Rates for Haulers and Facilities

When bids were requested from haulers, there was a wide range in the bids from hauler to hauler, even though the haulers were using the same facility. This was

Table 11.4 PBS&J Managed Bin Program: Average Hauler Costs per Ton by Material Type for County of San Diego Firestorm Response (2004)

	Zone			
	1	2	3	4
Landfill (1/1/04–3/31/04)	$58.67	$66.25	$77.38	$70.00
Landfill (4/1/04)	$88.42	$96.00	$107.13	$99.75
Metal	$46.33	$50.50	$78.75	$51.67
Inerts	$51.33	$55.75	$75.00	$60.33
Dead run (no pickup)	$65.00	$65.00	$65.00	$65.00

Note: For individual hauler bids see Appendix 11.3.

mainly a result of separate agreements that each hauler had with each facility. In some cases, the cost for recycling was higher or equal to the cost of disposal (Tables 11.4 and 11.5). However, once landfill rates were restored in April 2004, most recycling rates were below the landfill costs.

Table 11.5 PBS&J Managed Property Clearing Program: Average Contractor Costs per Ton by Material Type for County of San Diego Firestorm Response (2004)

1/1/04–3/31/04	Zone			
	1	2	3	4
Landfill	$215.33	$218.67	$248.00	$233.67
Metal	$195.67	$199.00	$235.00	$217.33
Inerts	$61.00	$164.33	$187.33	$179.33
Effective 4/1/04				
Landfill	$207.75	$212.75	$256.75	$235.25
Metal	$209.92	$216.58	$253.25	$253.25
Inerts	$161.67	$171.67	$220.00	$220.00

Note: For individual contractor bids see Appendix 11.4.

Possible Solution

Consider Contracting Directly with Recycling Facilities. This approach would allow the county to get a better rate and diminish the desire for a hauler to take materials to the landfill/transfer station. It gives the county contractual leverage in pricing, materials specifications, and materials handling. In addition, this will allow the county to track the materials to ensure they were recycled allowing FEMA reimbursement.

Challenge 2: Determining Debris Sources

It was difficult to determine what debris was from the county sponsored program and what was from the private industry.

Possible Solution

Monitor Facilities. In any scenario, monitoring facilities is a crucial part of ensuring FEMA reimbursement. Site visits also ensure the quality of the data and that the material is being recycled. For example, under the system utilized in the 2003 firestorms, there was no method to track if the materials delivered to Transfer Stations were charged to the county as mixed debris or clean inerts. For more than a year there was a stockpile of about 4000 tons of clean inerts at one transfer station and no tracking method to determine how much of that was county hauled.

Challenge 3: Lack of Mixed Processing Facilities

San Diego County has an extensive network of source-separated material recycling facilities; however, there were no mixed processing centers.

Possible Solution

Work with companies to expand mixed debris processing capacity. In any disaster, mixed debris processing capacity will be required. There is a strong need for C&D processing capacity now. The county should work with local businesses to determine what their short- and long-term mixed debris processing plans are. Once prepared, in the event of a disaster, FEMA funds can be used to build additional temporary recycling infrastructure needs, to improve ongoing C&D recycling efforts that aid AB 939 compliance, to lower future C&D recycling costs (and therefore C&D costs in both the private and the public sectors), and to purchase equipment for county department maintenance activities that support recycling.

Temporary Mixed Recycling Facilities

With the advent of the fire, most of the aggregate recycling facilities lowered rates or allowed victims to deliver clean loads of concrete and asphalt for free. This assisted in recovering a significant amount of clean inerts for recycling. However, site visits to burned properties indicated that much of the aggregates were contaminated with a small amount of wood or metal material. The county worked with recyclers to allow small amounts of contamination in the loads and to document what the increased costs would be to the haulers. To educate haulers about the relaxed specifications, the county developed a "Fire Debris Recycling Guide" and disseminated the guide to all county contractors and franchised waste haulers (Attachment 1).

As part of the survey of recyclers, the county invited recycling companies to operate emergency C&D recycling facilities. Two new facilities were opened in Crest and Julian to efficiently handle fire-related materials. The prime materials targeted were inerts and metals. The recycling of these inert materials was also important to save landfill space, and to maintain county diversion rates required by the CIWMB. The establishment of the facilities was a part of the best faith effort needed to get credit for the fire-related tonnage saved when determining annual county diversion rate.

The primary objectives of these facilities were:

1. To save costs of transport.
2. To conserve the road infrastructure by reducing the mileage per trip from the ruins to distant recycling plants.
3. To reduce costs of materials when the rebuilding occurred by having stockpiles closer to the rebuilding sites.

Both sites were granted emergency permits that were lifted after one year of operation. Because so much recyclable metal remained at burned properties in Julian, metal recycling was added to the emergency permit. The Julian site received 3889 tons of concrete and 443 tons of metal. LTS received a total of 38,338 tons of debris. The results from the recycling facilities are included in Table 11.6.

Table 11.6 Total Tonnage Received by Julian and LTS Recycling Facilities: Independent and County Programs (2003/2004)

Facility	Tons				
	Concrete	Metal	Vegetative	Trash	Total
Julian Recycling	3,889	443			4,332
LTS	37,443	43	6	417	38,296
Total	41,332	873	6	417	42,628

Table 11.7   Types and Quantities of Material Recovered in Mixed Inert Loads at LTS

Concrete		Metal		Vegetative		Trash		Total
Percent	Tons	Percent	Tons	Percent	Tons	Percent	Tons	Tons
86	4260	5	239	0.07	5	8	417	4921
Total recycling rate (percent)	92							

It became clear shortly after opening the two facilities that the segregation of mixed materials was important. At LTS, a project was initiated through the recycling section of the Department of Public Works to segregate mixed loads of metal, wood, and mixed inerts. The mixed inerts pilot at LTS consisted of processing 703 loads. Of that total 45 loads (417 tons) were sent to the landfill. This equates to approximately 0.6 tons of waste per load. Assuming an average load weight of 7 tons, the following types and quantities of materials handled in the pilot can be extrapolated as follows (Table 11.7):

The total mixed program at LTS cost $16,092. Disposal costs were $10,017 (417 loads at $24/ton) and $6,074 in drop fees for the 25 yard roll-off bins. This equates to a program cost of $3.27/ton. When combined with the $18/ton tipping fee charged to the haulers, the facility cost was $21.27/ton for processing mixed inerts. This price was slightly higher than the temporarily reduced landfill tipping fee of $20/ton, however the location of the site saved significantly on transportation costs.

During the course of the program, the county worked with four additional private companies that stated a desire to operate emergency recycling facilities: Allied, J. Cloud, Escondido Sand and Gravel, and Ware Disposal. A description of efforts with these facilities follows:

- *Allied.* The Allied facilities (Sycamore and Ramona landfill) received the majority of the tonnage generated from the fires. Therefore, initial efforts were made to encourage the facilities to separate metal, wood, and inerts from the incoming materials. Both the Sycamore and Ramona landfills were granted emergency CDI recycling permits, however little material was recycled. Allied dedicated an excavator to pull large pieces of sheet metal from the incoming materials. However, at the peak times of processing they were only able to pull about 35 tons of metal per day from about 1000 tons of debris. Because the state law required that the debris be placed in a lined landfill, a separate cell was established to place the fire-related materials.

  Roll-offs for both wood and metals were also delivered to the county bin sites. This effort recovered a significant amount of material for recycling.

- *Escondido Sand and Gravel.* This company was willing to pilot receiving mixed inerts with up to 5 percent contamination. However, the county was unable to direct loads to the facility.
- *J. Cloud/Hestor Granite.* A meeting was conducted with J. Cloud to explore options. The company was interested, however, as the county program did not include the ability to direct loads, the facility did not receive the level of tonnage required to make a pilot project worthwhile.
- *Ware Disposal.* Discussions were held with Ware Disposal to have them process the debris in their C&D processing facility in Orange county. However, the company was unable to perform the hauling functions needed by the county and the contract was not utilized.

Temporary Facility Challenges

Challenge 1: Getting Emergency Permits for Facilities

It took time to get staff up to speed on current regulations and what documents were needed for the emergency permits.

Possible Solution

Have staff familiar with emergency facility permitting issues and have contacts with the LEA, the Department of Planning and Land Use, Air Pollution Control District, and any other pertinent agencies.

Challenge 2: Processing of Materials

The Julian Recycling Center has taken several years to process the tonnage from the fires because of equipment failure and staffing issues. As a result, the facility is working with the LEA to comply with the holding and processing regulations of the emergency permit.

Possible Solution

Have governmental assistance grants available for start-up facilities to improve infrastructure.

Program Recycling Rates

County contractors hauled a total of 3,190 loads and handled 22,969 tons of debris under the two fire response programs (Table 11.8). Of that total, 33 percent was

Table 11.8   All County Fire Debris Removal Programs: Percent Recycling by Material Type for San Diego County Firestorm Response (2003/2004)

	Concrete		Metal		Vegetative		Trash		Total	
	Loads	Tons	Loads	Tons	Loads	Tons	Loads	Tons	Loads	Tons
Total loads/tons	446	4,368	863	3,035	23	81	1,858	15,482	3,190	22,966
Material percent of total	19		13		0.4		67			
Total recycling rate (percent)	33									

Note: For a complete list by facility see Appendix 11.4. Does not include 4000 tons removed through vehicle abatement program.

recycled. Inerts comprised the largest fraction of the materials recovery totals (19 percent), however, because metal is significantly lower in density than inerts, more interesting was the amount of burned metal collected from the debris removal programs at 13 percent of the total or 3035 tons. When the 4000 tons collected through the vehicle abatement program are included, metal is 26 percent of the total material handled by all of the county programs (Table 11.9). The bin program stressed recycling more than the property clearing program, and recycling benefited when management had a recycling priority.

When a load analysis was conducted, 66 percent of all loads (by weight) were taken to the Sycamore and Ramona landfills (Appendix 11.1). Therefore, the potential for increasing the amount of recycling in future disasters is highly likely.

The two collection programs had very different recycling rates. The bin program, that required residents to separate materials for collection, averaged a 43 percent recycling rate (Table 11.10); whereas, the property clearing program only reached a 24 percent recycling rate (Table 11.11). The bin loading program recovered 2758 tons of inerts (26 percent) and 1637 tons of metal (16 percent) (Table 11.10). A small amount of burned wood and vegetation was recovered (81

Table 11.9   County of San Diego Debris Removal Program Recycling Rates by Material Type (2003/2004)

	Concrete	Metal	Vegetative	Trash	Total
Tons	4,368	7,035	81	15,482	26,966
Material type (percent)	16	26	0.3	57	

Note: Includes metal from the vehicle abatement program.

Table 11.10   Combined County and PBS&J Managed Bin Programs: Percent Recycling by Material Type for the County of San Diego Firestorm Response (2003/2004)

	Concrete		Metal		Vegetative		Trash		Total	
	Loads	Tons	Loads	Tons	Loads	Tons	Loads	Tons	Loads	Tons
Total loads/tons	310	2,758	422	1,637	23	81	888	5,986	1,643	10,462
Material percent of total	26		16		0.8		57			
Total recycling rate (percent)	43									

Note: For a complete list by facility see Appendix 11.1.

tons or 0.8 percent) at the Sycamore and Ramona landfills as well as at the mixed inerts pilot at LTS.

Contractors from the property clearing program primarily used the landfills; more than 76 percent of the loads were delivered to Sycamore and Ramona landfills (Appendix 11.2). Individual hauler recycling rates varied dramatically with HVAC recycling almost 72 percent of the materials collected versus A&D having a 15 percent recycling rate (Appendices 11.2.1 through 11.2.3).

The county staff managed bin program and the PBS&J managed bin program were compared (Tables 11.12 and 11.13). At the outset of the program, when the county staff managed the project, the program reached a 35 percent recycling rate. This program attempted to directly manage the designation of loads to recycling

Table 11.11   PBS&J Property Clearing Program: Percent Recycling and Facility Usage by Material Type for the County of San Diego Firestorm Response (2004)

	Concrete		Metal		Trash		Total	
	Loads	Tons	Loads	Tons	Loads	Tons	Loads	Tons
Total loads/tons	136	1,610	441	1,398	970	9,496	1,547	12,504
Material percent of total	13		11		76			
Total recycling rate (percent)	24							

Note: For a complete list by facility see Appendix 11.2.

Table 11.12   County of San Diego Managed Bin Program: Percent Recycling and Facility Usage by Material Type for the County of San Diego Firestorm Response (2003)

	Concrete		Metal		Vegetative		Trash		Total	
	Loads	Tons	Loads	Tons	Loads	Tons	Loads	Tons	Loads	Tons
Total loads/tons	42	317	110	524	2	13	200	1627	354	2481
Material percent of total	13		22		0.5		67			
Total recycling rate (percent)	35									

Note: For a complete list by facility see Appendix 11.1.1.

facilities through load tickets; however, throughout the two month period, the haulers ignored the load tickets and 68 percent of the loads were sent to Sycamore landfill (Appendix 11.1.1). The most significant form of recycling in this period was the recycling of metal by Waste Management at their transfer station in El Cajon.

During the PBS&J managed period, less than 31 percent of the loads were delivered to Sycamore and the recycling rate for the program reached 45 percent (Appendix 11.1.2). For this program a new contract was let with strict recycling requirements.

Table 11.13   PBS&J Managed Bin Hauling Program: Percent Recycling and Facility Usage by Material Type for the County of San Diego Firestorm Response (2003/2004)

	Concrete		Metal		Vegetative		Trash		Total	
	Loads	Tons	Loads	Tons	Loads	Tons	Loads	Tons	Loads	Tons
Total loads/tons	268	2441	312	1113	21	68	688	4420	1289	8042
Material percent of total	30		14		0.8		55			
Total recycling rate (percent)	45									

Note: For a complete list by hauler and facility see Appendix 11.1.2.

It should be noted that 314 loads or 1959 tons had no ticket associated with the load in the database. In many cases, the database indicated that the material was recycled. In most cases, this tonnage was allocated as landfilled mixed debris, therefore, the recycling rate could be up to 3 percent higher than reported.

Program Recycling Rates Challenges

Challenge 1: Program Recycling

It was difficult to guarantee that haulers and contractors recycled. The upper management of the hauling companies did not communicate with drivers and field workers about the load monitoring tickets and their purpose to direct loads of clean materials to recycling facilities.

Possible Solution

Use a Monetary Incentive to the Hauler for Use of a Recycling Facility. If the county chooses to receive bids to collect and haul the debris at a fixed cost per ton per load in the future (and it contracts directly with recycling facilities), it can consider including a monetary incentive for use of source-separated recycling facilities. Thus, contractors would have the incentive to haul loads, as quickly as possible and to ensure that the material is recycled to the highest extent possible. The county should require that loads be delivered to recycling facilities only, and give incentives if the load is delivered to a source-separated facility.

Provide numerous incentives for contractors to use recycling facilities. Throughout the debris removal program, haulers continually ignored county requirements to use recycling facilities. A point system in which contractors obtain points for using recycling facilities could be developed, or they should be fined using a noncompliance fee if the material is not delivered to the correct location.

Bin Sites

At the outset of the fire response, the county requested that Allied place roll-offs at the county rural bin sites to allow residents to bring source-separated wood and metal at no charge. The response to this program was overwhelming. The flow of materials to the bin site increased dramatically (Chart 11.1).

Of the total amount of debris sent to bin sites, 93 percent was recyclable materials (Table 11.14). This does not represent an accurate recycling rate because residents only delivered items that were free of charge. However, with more than 2800 tons collected at the bin sites, the potential for use of drop-off locations for future planning efforts is clear.

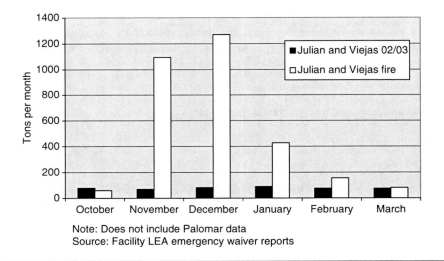

Note: Does not include Palomar data
Source: Facility LEA emergency waiver reports

Chart 11.1   Rural Bin Site Use before and during Firestorm.

Program Costs

The average cost per load was $1860 or $258/ton (Table 11.15). This cost includes $2.3 million for a management contract, but does not include county staff time.

More than 5400 tons (24 percent) of the entire tonnage collected were delivered to source-separated recycling operations for base, dirt, wood, and metal, this figure

Table 11.14   Rural Bin Sites: Percent Recycling and Facility Usage by Material Type During the County of San Diego Firestorm (2003/2004) (Tons)

Facility	Metal	Vegetative	Landfill Disposal	Total	Facility Percent of Total
Julian	1861	670	133	2664	87
Viejas	153	155	30	338	11
Palomar			59	59	2
Total	2014	825	222	3061	
Material type percent of total	66	27	7		
Total recycling rate (percent)	93				

Table 11.15   Debris Removal Program Costs for County of San Diego Firestorm Response

Program	Management	Contractor	Total	Cost/Load[c]	Cost/Ton[c]
Combined bin[a]	$1,109,309	$705,642	$1,814,951	$1,105	$173
Property clearing[b]	$1,225,999	$2,891,123	$4,117,122	$2,661	$329
Total debris removal	$2,335,308	$3,596,765	$5,932,073	$1,860	$258

[a] Haulers were paid for both county and PBS&J bin programs.
[b] Includes $81,000 for asbestos removal.
[c] Total loads = 3,190 and Total tons = 22,966.

does not include recycling or reuse at the landfills (Appendix 11.4). Tipping fees for these types of facilities range from $20/load for clean dirt to $22/ton for woody material. Base facilities charge approximately $10/ton and metal recycling facilities pay for burned metal on a per ton basis (Table 11.16). If haulers had been required to tip their loads at recycling centers significant money would have been saved.

Table 11.16   Average Costs by Source-Separated Recycling Facility

Facility	Average Cost per Ton	Material Type Recycled
Sycamore	$20	Disposal (reduced fee from $48/ton for fire debris)
Julian Recycling Center	$20	Clean and mixed inerts
LTS	$10–$18	Clean and mixed inerts
J. Cloud/Hestor Granite	$10–$12	
Hanson[a]	$10–$12	Clean inerts
Escondido Sand and Gravel	$10–$12	Clean inerts
Re-Rock	$7–$10	
Pacific Steel	Will pay for burned metal	Burned metal

[a] Hanson also gave vouchers to the county to give to residents for free recycling of concrete.

Program Costs Challenges

Challenge 1: Costs are Difficult to Compare

Because facility tipping fee costs were included in the per ton charge by the haulers, it is difficult to determine the actual costs and savings accrued by recycling.

Possible Solution

The county should have contractors bid on the program and then take an average. All haulers operating under the program agree to one cost. Any materials that can generate revenue, like metal, should be taken into consideration for the bids.

Independent Recycling Efforts

A survey of independent recycling companies was conducted as a part of this report to quantify the total amount of debris generated from the fires. Because many inert processors are not required to report by jurisdiction or did not have scales, measurement of tonnage was difficult. Of the facilities that were able to provide figures, it is estimated that private industry achieved a 62 percent recycling rate and handled over 100,000 tons of fire debris (Table 11.17).

Landfill Usage and Savings

The 2003 firestorms generated a significant amount of debris. The Ramona, Miramar, Sycamore, and Otay landfills received 58,993 tons of unincorporated fire-related debris from October 2003 to June 2004. The most tonnage was received from October to December 2003 (Table 11.18).

Landfill Savings

The county-operated fire debris removal and recycling program saved 11,484 tons (54,330 cubic yards) of landfill space (Table 11.19). When combined with the independent recyclers, temporary C&D facilities, and recovery efforts at the bin sites, the county was able to preserve 184,692 cubic yards (73,656 tons) of landfill space. It should be noted that the tonnage does not include concrete that was recycled at Hanson Aggregates and J. Cloud because the data were not available.

Table 11.17 Independent Recyclers: Estimate of Noncounty Program Related Fire Debris Recovery

Facility	Concrete	Metal	Vegetative	Landfill Disposal	Total Tons
LTS	36,199	241	5		38,338
Sycamore		689		27,179	27,868
Ramona		1		9,918	9,919
Romero	8,000				8,000
Ramona transfer station	8,000				8,000
Julian Recycling	3,824	173			3,997
Rural bin sites		2,014	825		2,839
Lakeside Land Company		2,200			2,200
Miramar			2	1,073	1,075
Otay				227	227
Total (tons)	56,023	5,318	832	38,397	100,570
Overall recycling rate (percent)	62				

Note: Figures were not available from J. Cloud and Hanson who handled a large portion of concrete and inert recycling.

Table 11.18 Unincorporated Fire Tonnage by Quarter

October–December 2003	36,435
January–March 2004	15,954
April–June 2004	6,534
Total	58,923

Note: Includes tonnage allocated to El Cajon because the unincorporated area of crest, which was hit particularly hard by the disaster, shares a zip code with El Cajon.

Table 11.19 Landfill Savings from County of San Diego and Independent Recycling for Firestorms 2003

	Concrete	Metal	Vegetation	Total
	(1 Cubic Yards = 0.6 Tons)	(1 Cubic Yards = 0.15 Tons)	(1 Cubic Yards = 0.54 Tons)	(Cubic Yards)
County debris removal programs	7,280	46,900	150	54,330
Independent recycling efforts	93,371	35,450	1,541	130,362
Total	100,651	82,350	1,691	184,692

Conclusion

Although more than 43 percent was recycled, in the county fire response, a higher recycling rate could have been attained by maximizing the use of the existing recycling infrastructure. The high recycling rate of the independent recyclers shows that fire debris is highly recyclable, the public is willing to separate debris for recycling, recycling facilities exist that can process the debris and maximizing recycling can decrease program costs. It is recommended that the county develop a plan to include recycling in the event of any future disaster.

Appendix 11.1 Combined County and PBS&J Managed Bin Programs: Percent Recycling and Facility Usage by Material Type for the County of San Diego Firestorm Response (2003/2004)

Facility	Concrete		Metal		Vegetative		Mixed		Total		Facility Percent of Total (Tons)
	Loads	Tons	Loads	Tons	Loads	Tons	Loads	Tons	Loads	Tons	
Sycamore	25	223	39	192	17	62	511	3,650	592	4,127	39
Ramona	20	191	11	60	3	15	185	1,230	219	1,496	14
LTS	131	1,185	51	182	1	1			183	1,368	13
No ticket	23	224	74	280	2	3	102	699	201	1,205	12
Waste Management			144	540			89	400	233	940	9
Julian Recycling	64	521	66	259					130	780	7
Pacific Steel			22	76					22	76	1
Escondido Recycling	10	65	2	6					12	71	1
Miramar	7	59							7	59	1
Pacific Coast			7	28					7	28	0.27
Misc. Metal Co.[a]	2	11	6	15					8	26	0.25
Misc. Concrete[b]	2	12							2	12	0.11

(continued)

Appendix 11.1 (continued) Combined County and PBS&J Managed Bin Programs: Percent Recycling and Facility Usage by Material Type for the County of San Diego Firestorm Response (2003/2004)

Facility	Concrete		Metal		Vegetative		Mixed		Total		Facility Percent of Total (Tons)
	Loads	Tons	Loads	Tons	Loads	Tons	Loads	Tons	Loads	Tons	
Eniss	1	12							1	12	0.11
Vista							1	7	1	7	0.06
Lakeside Land Company	25	256							25	256	
Total loads/tons	310	2,758	422	1,637	23	81	888	5,986	1,643	10,462	100
Material type percent	26		16		0.8		57		100.0		
Program recycling rate (percent)	43										

[a] Misc. Metal = Pacific Coast, Ecology Metal, CA Metals, Palomar.
[b] Misc. Concrete = Hestor's Granite, Madison Materials.

Appendix 11.1.1 County of San Diego Bin Program: Summary of Percent Recycling and Facility Usage by Material Type for the County of San Diego Firestorm Response (2003/2004)

Facility	Concrete		Metal		Vegetative		Mixed		Total		Facility Percent of Total (Tons)
	Loads	Tons	Loads	Tons	Loads	Tons	Loads	Tons	Loads	Tons	
Sycamore	1	14	1	61	2	13	200	1566	204	1653	68
Waste Management			98	404					98	404	17
Lakeside Land Company	10	88							10	88	4
Ramona	7	69							7	69	3
LTS	8	64							8	64	3
Miramar	7	59							7	59	2
Julian Recycling	5	0	4	32					9	32	1
Pacific Coast			7	28					7	28	1
Misc. Concrete Co.[a]	2	12							2	12	0.5
Misc. Metal Co.[b]	2	11							2	11	0.5
Total loads/tons	42	317	110	524	2	13	200	1566	354	2420	
Material type percent	13		22		1		65				
Program recycling rate (percent)	35										

[a] Misc. Concrete = Hestor's Granite, Madison Materials.
[b] Misc. Metal = Pacific Coast, Ecology Metal, CA Metals, Palomar, All-ways recycling.

Appendix 11.1.2 PBS&J Bin Program: Percent Recycling and Facility Usage by Material Type for the County of San Diego Firestorm Response (2004)

Facility	Concrete		Metal		Vegetative		Mixed		Total		Facility Percent of Total (Tons)
	Loads	Tons	Loads	Tons	Loads	Tons	Loads	Tons	Loads	Tons	
Sycamore	24	209	38	131	15	50	311	2084	388	2473	31
Ramona	13	122	11	60	3	15	185	1230	212	1427	18
LTS	123	1121	51	182	1	1			175	1304	16
Julian Recycling	59	521	62	227					121	748	9
Waste Management			46	137			89	400	135	536	7
Lakeside Land Company	15	168							15	168	2
Pacific Steel			22	76					22	76	1
Escondido Recycling	10	65	2	6					12	71	1
Eniss	1	12							1	12	0.15
Vista				15			1	7	1	7	0.08
Misc. Metal Co.[a]			6						6	15	0.19
No ticket	23	224	74	280	2	3	102	699	201	1205	15
Total loads/tons	268	2441	312	1113	21	68	688	4420	1289	8042	
Material type percent	30		14		1		55		100		
Program recycling rate (percent)	45										

[a] Misc. Metal = Pacific Coast, Ecology Metal, CA Metals, Palomar.

Appendix 11.2 PBS&J Property Clearing Program: Percent Recycling and Facility Usage by Material Type for the County of San Diego Firestorm Response (2004)

Facility	Concrete		Metal		Mixed		Total		Facility Percent of Total (Tons)
	Loads	Tons	Loads	Tons	Loads	Tons	Loads	Tons	
Sycamore	4	32	18	64	837	8,064	859	8,160	65
Ramona					125	1,384	125	1,384	11
No ticket	41	552	64	154	8	48	113	754	6
Pacific Coast	1	13	138	487			139	500	4
Eniss	39	494					39	494	4
Pacific Steel	2	18	91	366			93	384	3
Lee's Iron & Metal			111	272			111	272	2
C.W. McGrath	19	212					19	212	2
Escondido Recycling	11	112					11	112	1
Barona	5	96					5	96	1
LTS	9	59	1	8			10	67	1
Vista			17	42			17	42	0.33
Misc. Metal Co.[a]	5	23					5	23	0.18

(continued)

Appendix 11.2 (continued)   PBS&J Property Clearing Program: Percent Recycling and Facility Usage by Material Type for the County of San Diego Firestorm Response (2004)

Facility	Concrete		Metal		Mixed		Total		Facility Percent of Total (Tons)
	Loads	Tons	Loads	Tons	Loads	Tons	Loads	Tons	
Julian Recycling			1	5			1	5	0.04
Total loads/tons	136	1,610	441	1,398	970	9,496	1,547	12,504	
Material type percent of total	13		11		76				
Total recycling rate (percent)	24								

a Misc. Metal = Pacific Coast, Ecology Metal, CA Metals, Palomar.

Appendix 11.2.1 The HVAC Exchange: Percent Recycling and Facility Usage by Material Type for the County of San Diego Firestorm Response Property Clearing Program (2004)

Facility	Concrete		Metal		Mixed		Total		Facility Percent of Total (Tons)
	Loads	Tons	Loads	Tons	Loads	Tons	Loads	Tons	
Escondido Recycling	10	95					10	95	46
Sycamore			1	2	6	38	7	40	20
Pacific Coast			8	28			8	28	14
Misc. Metal Co.[a]	5	23					5	23	11
Ramona					2	14	2	14	7
No ticket					2	6	2	6	3
Total loads/tons	15	118	9	31	10	58	34	207	
Material type percent of total	57		15		28				
Total recycling rate (percent)	72								

[a] Misc. Metal = Pacific Coast, Ecology Metal, CA Metals, Palomar.

Appendix 11.2.2 A&D Fire Protection: Percent Recycling and Facility Usage by Material Type for the County of San Diego Firestorm Response Property Clearing Program (2004)

Facility	Concrete		Metal		Mixed		Total		Facility Percent of Total (Tons)
	Loads	Tons	Loads	Tons	Loads	Tons	Loads	Tons	
Sycamore	3	29			365	3322	368	3351	85
Lee's Iron & Metal			111	272			111	272	7
No ticket	4	50	44	82	1		49	131	3
Barona	5	96					5	96	2
Vista			17	42			17	42	1
Escondido Recycling	1	17					1	17	0.43
Ramona					1	13	1	13	0.33
Pacific Steel			5	6			5	6	0.16
Total loads/tons	13	191	177	402	367	3335	557	3928	
Material type percent of total	5		10		85				
Total recycling rate (percent)	15								

Appendix 11.2.3 Whilock Contracting: Percent Recycling and Facility Usage by Material Type for the County of San Diego Firestorm Response Property Clearing Program (2004)

Facility	Concrete		Metal		Mixed		Total		Facility Percent of Total (Tons)
	Loads	Tons	Loads	Tons	Loads	Tons	Loads	Tons	
Sycamore	1	3	17	62	466	4704	484	4769	57
Ramona					122	1357	122	1357	16
No ticket	37	503	20	72	5	42	62	617	7
Eniss	39	494					39	494	6
Pacific Coast	1	13	130	458			131	471	6
Pacific Steel	2	18	86	360			88	378	5
C.W. McGrath	19	212					19	212	3
LTS	9	59	1	8			10	67	1
Julian Recycling			1	5			1	5	0.06
Total loads/tons	108	1301	255	966	593	6103	956	8369	
Material type percent of total	16		12		73				
Total recycling rate (percent)	27								

Appendix 11.3 Hauler and Contractor Bids for Fire Debris Removal Program: Landfill Tip Fee Was Restored 4/1/04

	Zone			
Bin Program	*1*	*2*	*3*	*4*
Hauler 1				
Landfill (1/1/04–3/31/04)	61.00	64.00	67.00	67.00
Landfill (4/1/04)	90.75	93.75	96.75	96.75
Metal	39.00	42.00	45.00	45.00
Inerts	54.00	57.00	60.00	60.00
Dead run	65.00	65.00	65.00	65.00
Hauler 2				
Landfill (1/1/04–3/31/04)			106.50	
Landfill (4/1/04)			136.25	
Metal			100.00	
Inerts			100.00	
Dead run			65.00	
Hauler 3				
Landfill (1/1/04–3/31/04)	60.00	60.00	79.00	85.00
Landfill (4/1/04)	89.75	89.75	108.75	114.75
Metal	55.00	55.00	125.00	65.00
Inerts	45.00	45.00	85.00	65.00
Dead run	65.00	65.00	65.00	65.00
Hauler 4				
Landfill (1/1/04–3/31/04)	55.00	56.00	57.00	58.00
Landfill (4/1/04)	84.75	85.75	86.75	87.75
Metal	45.00	45.00	45.00	45.00
Inerts	55.00	56.00	55.00	56.00
Dead run	65.00	65.00	65.00	65.00

Appendix 11.3 (continued)   Hauler and Contractor Bids for Fire Debris Removal Program: Landfill Tip Fee Was Restored 4/1/04

Bin Program	Zone			
	1	*2*	*3*	*4*
Hauler 5				
Landfill (1/1/04–3/31/04)		85.00		
Landfill (4/1/04)		114.75		
Metal		60.00		
Inerts		65.00		
Dead run		65.00		
All Hauler Average				
Landfill (1/1/04–3/31/04)	58.67	66.25	77.38	70.00
Landfill (4/1/04)	88.42	96.00	107.13	99.75
Metal	46.33	50.50	78.75	51.67
Inerts	51.33	55.75	75.00	60.33
Dead run	65.00	65.00	65.00	65.00

Private Property Program	Zone			
	1	*2*	*3*	*4*
Contractor 1				
1/1/04–3/31/04				
Landfill	165.00	175.00	220.00	220.00
Metal	155.00	165.00	220.00	220.00
Inerts	165.00	175.00	220.00	220.00
Effective 4/1/04				
Landfill	194.75	204.75	249.75	249.75
Metal	155.00	165.00	220.00	220.00
Inerts	165.00	175.00	220.00	220.00

(continued)

Appendix 11.3 (continued) Hauler and Contractor Bids for Fire Debris Removal Program: Landfill Tip Fee Was Restored 4/1/04

Private Property Program	Zone			
	1	2	3	4
Contractor 2				
1/1/04–3/31/04				
Landfill	290.00	290.00	290.00	290.00
Metal	200.00	200.00	200.00	200.00
Inerts	150.00	150.00	150.00	150.00
Effective 4/1/04				
Landfill	319.75	319.75	319.75	319.75
Metal	155.00	165.00	220.00	220.00
Inerts	165.00	175.00	220.00	220.00
Contractor 3				
1/1/04–3/31/04				
Landfill	191.00	191.00	234.00	191.00
Metal	232.00	232.00	285.00	232.00
Inerts	168.00	168.00	192.00	168.00
Effective 4/1/04				
Landfill	220.75	220.75	263.75	220.75
Metal	155.00	165.00	220.00	220.00
Inerts	165.00	175.00	220.00	220.00
Contractor Average				
1/1/04–3/31/04				
Landfill	215.33	218.67	248.00	233.67
Metal	195.67	199.00	235.00	217.33
Inerts	161.00	164.33	187.33	179.33

(continued)

**Appendix 11.3 (continued) Hauler and
Contractor Bids for Fire Debris Removal
Program: Landfill Tip Fee Was Restored 4/1/04**

Private Property Program	Zone			
	1	2	3	4
Effective 4/1/04				
Landfill	207.75	212.75	256.75	235.25
Metal	209.92	216.58	253.25	253.25
Inerts	161.67	171.67	220.00	220.00
1 cubic yards metals = 0.15 tons				
1 cubic yards concrete = 0.6 tons				
1 cubic yards mixed recyclables = 0.54 tons				

Note: All values are in dollars.

Appendix 11.4 Bin and Property Clearing Debris Removal Programs: Percent Recycling by Material Type and Facility Usage for San Diego County Firestorm Response (2003)

Facility	Concrete		Metal		Vegetative		Mixed		Total		Facility Percent of Total (Tons)
	Loads	Tons	Loads	Tons	Loads	Tons	Loads	Tons	Loads	Tons	
Sycamore	29	255	57	256	17	62	1,348	11,714	1,451	12,287	53
Ramona	20	191	11	60	3	15	310	2,614	344	2,880	13
No ticket	64	776	138	433	2	3	110	747	314	1,959	9
LTS	140	1,244	52	190	1	1			193	1,434	6
Waste Management			144	540			89	400	233	940	4
Julian Recycling	64	521	67	264					131	785	3
Pacific Coast	1	13	145	515					146	528	2
Eniss	40	506							40	506	2
Pacific Steel	2	18	113	442					115	460	2
Lee's Iron & Metal			111	272					111	272	1
Lakeside Land Company	25	256							25	256	1
C.W. McGrath	19	212							19	212	1

Escondido Recycling	21	177	2	6					23	184	1
Barona	5	96							5	96	0.42
Miramar	7	59							7	59	0.26
Misc. Metal Co.[a]	7	34	6	15					13	49	0.21
Vista			17	42		1		7	18	48	0.21
Misc. Concrete[b]	2	12							2	12	0.05
Total loads/tons	446	4,368	863	3,035	23	81	1,858	15,482	3,190	22,966
Material type percent	19		13		0.4		67		100	
Program recycling rate (percent)	33									

Cubic Yards of Landfill Saved

1 cubic yards metals = 0.15 tons	46,900.73
1 cubic yards concrete = 0.6 tons	7,280.33
1 cubic yards mixed recyclables = 0.54 tons	161.98
Total	54,343.05

[a] Misc. Metal = Pacific Coast, Ecology Metal, CA Metals, Palomar.
[b] Misc. Concrete = Hestor's Granite, Madison Materials.

CASE STUDIES AND LESSONS LEARNED: INTERNATIONAL DISASTERS

Chapter 12

Disaster in the United States and Canada: The Case of the Red River

Donna R. Kemp

CONTENTS

Disaster management deals with the adoption and implementation of policies addressing the four phases of a disaster: planning and preparation, response, recovery, and mitigation.

North America incurs numerous disasters each year, many of which are likely to develop into prominent policy issues because they possess all four characteristics necessary to obtain immediate agenda status: objective dimensions of severity, range, and visibility; political aspects; symbolic aspects; and absence of private sector solutions (Schneider, 1995). As the dimensions of a crisis expand, ever wider government structures are needed, bringing into play local, state/provincial, national, and international resources.

The Border and Disaster Response

The distribution of the Canadian population and its exposure to natural and human-made risk is not uniform, but concentrated along the southern edge of Canada near the border with the United States. On both sides of the Canadian–U.S. border the population is concentrated in urban areas although there are vast tracks of land with very small populations. Overall, Canadians have less exposure to natural disasters than Americans and the size of their disasters is smaller. The United States has reached the point of spending $20–30 billion per disaster (Newton, 1997). While disasters in Canada have seldom surpassed C$1 billion. The trend has been a steady reduction in fatalities and a rapid increase in property losses (Mileti et al., 1995; Witt and Rubin, 1995).

Both Canada and the United States have disaster policies and processes at the national, provincial/state, and local levels to plan for and manage disasters. There are also agreements between the two countries and, in some cases, between individual provinces and states concerning disaster planning and response. Canada and the United States experience many of the same disasters, and face many of the same issues in disaster policy and practice. North America faces disasters that include fires, storms, floods, landslides, earthquakes, volcanoes, drought, and epidemics. This region is also vulnerable to intentional actions including terrorism. The Western Premiers' Conference in 2002 agreed that while the Canadian and U.S. national governments have primary responsibility for the border, state/provincial/territorial governments could coordinate their resources and those of local responders to act in emergencies.

A Bottom-Up System

In both countries the disaster system is established as a bottom-up process with the local governments being the first responders, calling upon the state/province if the disaster is too great for them to handle. Most disasters in the United States and Canada are handled at the local level and do not require assistance from a higher level of government.

The United States disaster response system is a bottom-up system in which first responders are local governments and voluntary agencies. First response is usually by local law enforcement, firefighters, ambulance services, public health, and civil defense. Local officials follow local emergency plans. Mayors, city councils, and county supervisors are responsible, and local government intergovernmental coordination is essential. Interagency and intergovernmental agreements are activated. As resources are exhausted at one level of government, the response process moves upward to the state level. The governor of a state may call a state emergency in individual counties, regions, or throughout the state. In the United States, each state is responsible to plan to address its own unique needs with some uniform conditions required by the federal government. The uniform requirements are developed through the government making planning funds available. Each state must have a single agency responsible for coordinating all state level activities between local and federal relief efforts. State and local officials are required to attend training sessions conducted by the federal government. In the United States, if resources are insufficient in the state, the governor may call for assistance from the national government. The request is made to the Federal Emergency Management Agency (FEMA). The agency then makes a recommendation to the President and the President may declare a national emergency in certain counties or states. FEMA is the main federal emergency agency, but they may coordinate many other federal agencies to assist. FEMA and other federal agencies will provide personnel, resources, and funding. Funding may be provided to the states, local governments, or individuals.

The Canadian disaster response system is also a bottom-up system. Most local emergencies are handled by local response organizations as first responders. Every province and territory also has an Emergency Management Organization, which manages any large-scale emergencies involving prevention, preparedness, response and recovery, and provides assistance and support to municipal or community response teams. The Government of Canada's departments and agencies support the provincial/territorial Emergency Management Organizations as requested or manage emergencies affecting areas of federal jurisdiction. Requests from the provinces to the Government of Canada are managed through the Office of Critical Infrastructure Protection and Emergency Preparedness (OCIPEP), which maintains close operational links with provincial and local emergency authorities, and maintains inventories of resources and experts in various fields. OCIPEP maintains the Government Emergency Operations Coordination Centre (GEOCC), which is located in Ottawa and operates full time. Canada has a Joint Emergency Preparedness Program (JEPP) that was established to encourage and support cooperation among the federal and provincial/territorial governments to meet emergencies of all types with a "reasonably uniform standard of emergency response" (OCIPEP, JEPP, n.d.). Through JEPP, the Government of Canada provides financial contributions to provinces and territories to assist in meeting the costs of projects focused on enhancing emergency response capability. A funding formula is used under Earmarked Funds to ensure that each province/territory has access to funds to develop a minimum emergency preparedness capability, which can also contribute to the national capability (JEPP, 2003).

One of the marked differences in the recovery approach in the United States and Canada is that in the United States individuals and businesses may receive disaster assistance funds directly from the federal government while in Canada federal disaster financial assistance is paid to provincial/territorial governments, and they reimburse individuals and communities in accordance with their disaster assistance programs. Federal disaster financial assistance becomes available only when the eligible provincial/territorial expenditures incurred for emergency response and recovery exceed an amount equal to $1 Canadian per capita of the provincial/territorial population (OCIPEP, Disaster Financial Assistance, n.d.).

In both the countries, nongovernmental organizations also assist in emergencies including the Red Cross, Blood Banks, the Salvation Army, and search and rescue. At the national level in Canada nongovernment emergency management organizations include the Canadian Centre for Emergency Preparedness, Canadian Red Cross, Canadian Traumatic Stress Network, Disaster Recovery Information Exchange, Institute for Catastrophic Loss Reduction, Radio Amateurs of Canada—Amateur Radio Emergency Service, Salvation Army, UNICEF Canada, World Relief Canada, and the Association of Public-Safety Communications Officials—Canadian Chapter.

Increasing focus is being paid in both countries to mitigation and to protection of critical infrastructures. The United Nation's Department of Humanitarian Affairs defines mitigation as "measures taken in advance of a disaster aimed at decreasing or eliminating its impact on society and environment" (1992, p. 41). Mitigation is the one way to affect what happens during a disaster before a disaster strikes. Proper mitigation should result in lower loss of life and injuries and less property damage. Unfortunately neither the United States nor Canada has put many resources into mitigation, and mitigation often occurs only after a disaster has struck. Although for both countries the term mitigation is relatively new, the United States had a program for mitigation before Canada.

Numerous major disasters in the United States in the late 1980s and the 1990s focused United States' interest on mitigation. When James Witt became director of FEMA in 1993, more focus was placed on reduction of damages. During his leadership a new Mitigation Directorate was formed. The program was initially formed from programs in the former State and Local Programs and Support Directorate and the Federal Insurance Administration.

> The amalgamation of disparate programs with a strong mitigation
> content was to be the hallmark of the new Directorate's evolution.
> To shift, however from the more common programmatic thrust of

governmental service delivery structures to a functional orientation more suited to the achievement of mitigation objectives would prove an immense undertaking. (Newton, 1997)

The first National Mitigation Conference was held in 1995, and in the same year FEMA published the document, "National Mitigation Strategy-Partnerships for Building Safer Communities" (FEMA, 1995). The mitigation policy placed an emphasis on partnerships and sharing. Despite a bottom-up approach to disaster management, the prevailing perception at state and local levels was that the federal government would absorb most of the costs of disasters (Platt, 1996). Taking this approach to mitigation requires altering public perception that the government would bail out those who sustained losses in a disaster. However, mitigation efforts are ongoing through such efforts as removing population from flood plains and reengineering buildings and freeways to withstand earthquakes.

The following case study shows how disasters are bringing about changes in policy and practice in Canada and the United States and in their cooperation along the border. The case of the Red River flood of 1997 looks at the past policies and practices of the United States and Canada in the Red River basin and how the 1997 flood has brought about policy change and attempts to prevent and mitigate future disasters.

The Red River Flood of 1997

During the spring of 1997, record floods devastated communities along the Red River of the North and Missouri River basins in North Dakota, western Minnesota, and Canada. The last great flood had occurred in 1852 (Rawson and Herndon, 1998). By the time the 1997 flood was over the flood was to cost $500,000,000 (Gross and Haddow, 2003).

The Red River is an unusual river because it flows for 400 miles from south to north across the United States–Canada border at the 49th parallel. The river is often called the Red River of the North. It is approximately 310 miles (500 km) long and is formed north of Lake Traverse in northeast South Dakota by the confluence of the Bois de Sioux and the Otter Tail rivers (Red River, 2001). It flows north between Minnesota and North Dakota and crosses the Canadian border into Manitoba, emptying into Lake Winnipeg. Its main tributary is the Assiniboine River. It drains the main spring wheat-growing area of the United States and Canada, the Red River Valley region.

The Red River basin includes the states of South Dakota, North Dakota, Minnesota, and the Canadian province of Manitoba. The Red River basin is the bottom of an ancient lake, Lake Agassiz, which has left the terrain very flat and prone to flooding. Snowmelt in the south can lead to flooding along the northern reaches of the river as the river meets ice jams in the north of unmelted ice. This can lead to floods that spread water across the region.

The Event

In 1997 a significant blizzard, "Hard Handed Hannah," left record snowfall levels at about 300 percent of normal (USGS, 1997). Flooding followed the traditional pattern beginning in the southern portion of the basin and moving north. The primary cause of flooding was a highly abnormal thaw during March and April of substantial winter snow and river ice. The region had a series of winter storms from September 1996 to April 1997 during which more than 200 percent of normal snowfall occurred in most of North Dakota, western Minnesota, and northeastern South Dakota (National Weather Service, 2004). The abnormal characteristics of the thaw included its timing, duration, and area extent, as well as the diurnal temperature changes during the periods of substantial snow and ice melt during March through April (National Weather Service, 2004). Although local governments were prepared for flooding, the magnitude of the flooding was not expected, and the flood waters over topped levees.

Forecasting lacked accuracy. The forecasting used a rating curve, which was based on the relationship between stream stages and flows. The flows were primarily based on historical data (USGS, 1997). The more extreme the flow, the less historical information was available and that meant the estimated flood stage forecast was less accurate. The forecasts also did not take into consideration important factors such as the impact the bridges would have on flooding. Local agencies prepared for lower flood levels than actually occurred, and initiated sandbagging of river dikes at levels, which were to be overtopped by the flood. The North Central River Forecast Center (NCRFC) issued two numbers for flood stage, one based on average temperatures and no subsequent precipitation and one based on average temperature with precipitation (Pielke, 1999). The typical river volume was around 5,000 cubic feet per second (cfs), and the highest recorded volume was 83,000 cfs during a 1979 flood. The rating curve used in the forecasts was extrapolated from the 83,000 cfs, but the volume of floodwater on the first day of the flood was already 136,000 cfs (USGS, 1997).

People mistakenly viewed these numbers as a range and were unaware of the uncertainties in the methodology used to generate the numbers, and large numbers of residents did not purchase flood insurance. Most homeowners knew about flood insurance, but only 20 percent of the residents purchased it (Philippi, 1999).

The U.S. Response

When the Red River flooded in 1997, North Dakota and East Grand Forks, Minnesota suffered extensive damage. Flood damage reached approximately $2 billion and the entire basin was disrupted for months. The population of Grand

Forks, North Dakota was 52,000 and the population of East Grand Forks was 9,000. In East Grand Forks only 27 houses were not damaged, and over 11,000 homes and businesses out of 15,000 were damaged in Grand Forks (Pielke, 1999). The Red River crested at 39.5 feet, 22.5 feet above flood stage at Fargo, North Dakota on April 17, breaking a 100-year-old record. It reached 54.2 feet on April 21 at Grand Forks, North Dakota, and East Grand Forks, Minnesota (*USA Today Weather*, 1997). The river level at East Grand Forks, Minnesota peaked at more than 6.6 m above flood stage, exceeding the 500-year statistical recurrence interval (National Weather Service, 2004). Record flooding also occurred in all major tributaries of the Red River during April.

Fargo, North Dakota experienced less damage because they had done scenario planning that had involved drawing up a map indicating the effects of various flood levels on the community. They had a color-coded schematic to show what parts of town would be affected based on different levels of flooding. A faulty river gauge predicted a higher flood stage for the town, and this actually benefited their preparation (Bonham, 1997). The river peaked at Fargo at more than 6.6 m above flood stage, a level reached only once in the past 100 years (National Weather Service, 2004).

Approximately 2000 customers in Grand Forks were without electrical service with some 700 living in major flood-damaged areas where the Division of Emergency Management and State Radio Communications (DEMSRC) believed service might never be restored. An additional 7400 customers were without natural gas service (DEMSRC, 1997, May 16). Thousands of acres of farmland were expected not to be planted that year because of flooding eroding croplands and riverbanks. Many roads were flooded or washed out and required repair.

When levees and dikes failed or were over topped, the river inundated 90 percent of Grand Forks and East Grand Forks covering almost 11 square miles of land (Families Get Limited Access, 1997). Local governments were quickly assisted by the states. In South Dakota, the disaster agency responsible was the South Dakota Office of Emergency Management. In North Dakota the DEMSRC was the disaster agency.

The state and local agencies were assisted by several federal agencies, including the Air Force, Coast Guard, Army Corps of Engineers, National Guard, EPA, Centers for Disease Control, and the U.S. Public Health Service. FEMA set up offices in the area in advance of the flood. Several military bases were in the area and were able to provide immediate assistance. The Environmental Protection Agency (EPA) conducted assessments in North Dakota, which indicated that 450 residential fuel oil tanks were damaged by flooding and had released fuel oil into basements, and some flooded homes and businesses were showing mold and fungal growth, which was posing a biological threat to residents and response workers. In Grand Forks, officials broadened a mandatory evacuation zone to cover 90 percent of the city's residents, and violators were subject to arrest. An estimated 30,000–40,000 people had to leave their homes (CNN, 1997, April 21). A fire broke out downtown and destroyed or severely damaged several buildings. Fire hydrants were submerged, and there was no water pressure, hampering efforts to put out the fire. Among the buildings destroyed was the *Grand Forks Herald*, the city's newspaper with the paper's archives, which dated back to 1879. The *Herald* continued to print paper by using a makeshift newsroom and printing on presses 300 miles away in St. Paul, Minnesota. Eventually, the city's water plant had to be shut down and water had to be trucked into Grand Forks. Levees and sandbagging continued for days, but eventually were overtopped.

In Minnesota, the governor declared an emergency on April 8 for 58 counties for severe flooding, winter storms, snowmelt, high winds, and rain and ice. The incident period was March 21 through May 24, 1997. The total cost of the disaster in Minnesota was $545 million. Severe flooding in the Red River and Minnesota River valleys resulted in six schools, one medical facility, and several other public facilities having to be replaced (Minnesota Homeland Security and Emergency Management, 2003).

The extent of the flood exceeded the level of planning in place. Many residents were concerned about what they believed were bad forecasts by the NCRFC and the National Weather Service (Pielke, 1999). President Clinton toured the damaged areas of North Dakota including Grand Forks. He declared 56 Minnesota counties, all 53 North Dakota counties, and all 66 South Dakota counties as disaster areas.

The U.S. Recovery

In Minnesota, the state emergency management agency, now the Minnesota Homeland Security and Emergency Management Agency (2003) worked with local governments and FEMA. In Minnesota, more than $92 million was spent to repair and replace buildings. The amount expended in protective measures exceeded any other disaster declaration in the state by $30 million. The federal government spent $173,293,739 and the state government spent $30 million. In addition, there was an estimated local cost of $26 million and an estimated insured loss of $90 million. More than 7,000 people applied for individual and family grants and 3,618 grants were approved for $7,561,713 (Minnesota Homeland Security and Emergency Management, 2003). By April 29, 1,862 disaster-housing checks totaling $2,428,942 were distributed in South Dakota (Disaster Relief, 1997).

In North Dakota, many agencies became involved in the recovery and a massive coordination effort was made. Douglas C. Friez, state director of the DEMSRC, made detailed situation reports on a regular basis to Governor Edward T. Schafer. These reports covered the nature of the disaster; deaths and injuries; damages; resources from the local, state, and federal levels; volunteer action; major actions; assistance needed; and outside help on scene.

The Red Cross, Salvation Army, Church World Service, and United Methodist emergency services all offered aid to the flood-stricken residents. As the waters receded, city employed crews in Grand Forks, North Dakota picked up material that could cause toxic problems such as paint cans, cleaning solvents, heating and diesel fuel, and kerosene. "You can't get it all," said Al Lange, the EPA coordinator on site. "But every bit helps. ... " (Disaster Relief, 1997). The EPA assisted state and local public health officials in assessing mold growth in homes, and had approximately ten teams using absorbent pads and vacuum trucks to cleanup spilled oil. The Salvation Army, in partnership with Northwest Airlines provided cleanup efforts in Grand Forks with 500 volunteers. Northwest Airlines also donated two flights to Grand Forks to transport volunteers. The Salvation Army operated five mobile feeding units in the Grand Forks area and warehouse and distribution centers in Grand Forks, Devils Lake, and Fargo. The Bates County Cattlemen's Association from Kansas city, Missouri held a massive barbecue dinner for Grand Forks, North Dakota and East Grand Forks, Minnesota residents at the Salvation Army's Grand Forks distribution center. The American Red Cross opened 7494 cases for assistance and closed 6440 with financial assistance and 386 with services. The Red Cross health services staff assessed 1260 people and their mental health staff visited 9240 people. The Civil Air Patrol logged 287 hours to assist with flood response and recovery. The University of North Dakota made available 310 dormitory beds to flood-displaced persons, and the disaster-housing program received 22 mobile homes and 102 travel trailers to reduce the number of people relying on public shelters (DEMSRC, 1997, May 16, p. 2).

On May 6, the governor of North Dakota issued an executive order extending until July 1 a suspension of statutes and administrative rules or orders to speed recovery. The suspension applied to six counties and dealt with contracting, bidding, public notices, and licensing. The secretary of state and the attorney general operated a one-stop shop in Grand Forks for transient merchant's and contractor's licenses.

Notifications of interest in applications for public assistance were made by 209 entities to the State/Federal Disaster Field Office. These notices were given by forty-two counties, one hundred and fifteen cities, twelve electrical cooperatives, four tribal governments, eight state agencies, nine park districts, six water districts, three universities, nine public school districts, and one private nonprofit organization. Eleven Disaster Recovery Centers were opened at northeast North Dakota locations, and more than 31,760 North Dakotans registered damages with the National Teleregistration Center (DEMSRC, 1997, May 16, pp. 3–4).

On May 23 the DEMSRC reported to the governor that there was a shortage of employees in Grand Forks. The North Dakota Department of Agriculture reported that field crews disposed of approximately 11 million pounds of animals that perished in the April blizzard and in the floods (DEMSRC, 1997, May 23).

The United Methodist Committee on Relief (UMCR) contracted with an architectural company to provide structural assessments of flood-damaged homes. A federal hazard mitigation team was conducting assessments of destroyed and significantly damaged structures and accelerated procedures were being considered by the state to acquire severely damaged property. After the flood, more than 3000 residences were demolished. Authorities did not allow buildings to be reconstructed in their former locations because of their close proximity to the river. Since the flood, the population of Grand Forks and East Grand Forks declined by 3000 (Pielke, 1999).

The secretary of Housing and Urban Development (HUD) visited Grand Forks in August and announced that North Dakota communities would receive $201.3 million in grants from HUD's Development Disaster Recovery Initiative with Grand Forks receiving $171.6 million of the funds. The last day to register for individual assistance was August 6 and a total of 36,494 people had reported personal property damages to the National Teleregistration Center, and 24,094 people had received more than $49.7 million in disaster-housing assistance (DEMSRC, 1997, August 7). The North Dakota Community Foundation approved $1.29 million in grants for Red River Valley agencies, organizations and governmental entities that suffered flood damage (DEMSRC, 1997, October 9).

As winter approached the North Dakota Department of Human Services Crisis Counseling Program found an increased level of anxiety among flood survivors. Families were experiencing more conflict and some children were avoiding school. "Flood survivors say they felt as if they are in limbo until civil leaders made decisions related to property acquisitions and floodplain management. They also have expressed concern about the potential for flooding next spring and their community's level of preparedness for such a possibility" (DEMSRC, 1997, October 9).

U.S. Mitigation

In the fall of 1997, North Dakota Emergency Management conducted a risk assessment of selected areas to assist local official in identifying and implementing mitigation measures for a possible flood in 1998 (DEMSCRC, 1997, October 9). The North Dakota State Water Commission, the Army Corps of Engineers and the FEMA's Geographic Information Systems (GIS) compiled a hazard mitigation database. The database included geographic reference points and elevations of structures in the Devils Lake basin. The State Water Commission compiled levee data for the Red River and transferred the information to GIS (DEMSRC, 1997, August 7).

As of 1999, above normal soil moisture content through North Dakota and seven years of flooding and additional precipitation had resulted in overland, river and flash flooding, and landslides and mudslides. The State Hazard Mitigation Team continued to receive applications for the Hazard Mitigation Grant Program including 61 applications in 1999 (DEMSRC, 1999, September 30). After flooding in North Dakota in 1999, disaster victims were reticent to apply for assistance because of their concern that their claims might limit assistance to victims of Hurricane Floyd. FEMA had to assure them that that would not be the case.

Ongoing mitigation efforts included creation of emergency outlets, installing interior drain tile systems and sump pumps, establishing multi-hazard mitigation plans for joint county projects, establishing a control structure on one of the lakes to prevent more water entering one of the contributories to the Red River, raising highway road beds, relocating of sewer lines and water lines, diking, land sloping, and relocation and removal of structures (DEMSRC, 1999, March 11).

In Minnesota, the Hazard Mitigation Grant Program funded 56 projects for a total of $29,282,125 for projects including acquisition, living snow fences, NOAA transmitters, infrastructure improvement, and power line rebuilds (Minnesota Homeland Security and Emergency Management, 2003).

The Canadian Response

In Manitoba, every local authority is responsible for developing an emergency preparedness, response, and recovery plan to protect lives, property, and the environment within their municipal boundary. The plan is based on a hazard and risk analysis used to identify resources that may be required to respond to an emergency. The plan must include contact numbers for emergency responders, identification of accommodations for people needing evacuation, a registration and inquiry capability, transportation routes for evacuation, a media strategy to inform the general public, technical communication capabilities, guidelines for emergency responders to apply in specific situations, and a recovery plan. The plan also identifies persons with special needs, the elderly or the very young, and those at risk that may need to be evacuated on a priority basis. The local authority is also encouraged to develop mutual aid agreements with neighboring municipalities for responding to emergencies, and to plan with local business, the Regional Health Authority, and voluntary organizations to prevent duplication and confusion in response. The local authority does not need to declare a state of emergency to implement its emergency plan, but a state of emergency is declared if there is a need for outstanding powers listed in Section 12 of the Emergency Measures Act.

If the capabilities of the local and mutual aid response are insufficient, then they can request the assistance of the province. The Manitoba Emergency Management Organization (MEMO) then coordinates and deploys resources to the community. They do not assume management of the emergency response unless that is the request of community officials. The province can supply provincial personnel, equipment, and other resources, declare a state of emergency, deploy an emergency preparedness advisor or, a provincial site coordinator to provide advice and assistance, activate the Manitoba Emergency Coordination Center, and convene the Central Task Team (CTT) (MEMO, 2003a). The CTT is chaired by the executive coordinator and is comprised of representatives from the departments involved in the emergency. It may include federal or other agency representatives. The CTT may be assembled before, during, or after a disaster to assess a potential emergency situation, review response plans and procedures, monitor operations, provide situation reports and make recommendations to the deputy minister, refer major problems for resolution to the Deputy Ministers' Committee, and implement the direction of the Deputy Ministers' Committee. The deputy minister of government services may convene and chair a Deputy Ministers' Committee to provide information and recommendations to the Minister of Government Services.

The minister may declare a provincial state of emergency under the Emergency Measures Act. If necessary, the province will arrange for federal resources. Provincial personnel deployed to the emergency have a parallel system to the community structure. The provincial site manager advises and assists the community site manager. The community site manager reports directly to the Community Emergency Operation Centre, while the provincial site manager reports to the Provincial Emergency Operation Centre. The Community Emergency Operation Centre has a direct link to the Provincial Operation Centre so the province can provide technical expertise and resources as requested by the community (MEMO, 2003a). In certain circumstances, the province may assume primary responsibility for management and coordination of the emergency response, for example, if no local government exists or if the emergency has rendered the local government not able to respond (MEMO, 2003a).

As the Red River flood moved north, the 750 residents of Emerson, Manitoba, a farming town along the United States–Canadian border, were ordered to evacuate, as Canadian military forces were brought in to fortify dikes along the river. Voluntary evacuations of persons from flood threatened areas can be recommended by local or provincial authorities without the implementation of emergency powers under a declared state of emergency, but the Minister of Conservation may order in writing the evacuation of diked areas or designated diking systems for which his department is responsible. The town of Emerson is one of those towns. At this phase, the emergency phase, provincial on-site response teams are dispatched to advise and assist local authorities in flood fights and evacuation.

The international border crossing at Emerson was closed. Manitoba's Premier Gary Filmon requested emergency federal aid. He was promised at least 400 soldiers and engineers from Canadian Forces.

The Canadians lost their first battle with the river at the small town of Ste. Agathe with 500 residents about 15 miles south of Winnipeg. The water surged past the dike surrounding the town, entering through a railway line, and covered the town in 6 feet of water. Some 18,000 people between the border and Winnipeg, the provincial capital, were evacuated with thousands more to be ordered out.

"Reg Alcock, a member of parliament, was spearheading the Canadian evacuation effort. He described the situation as being like a 30-mile-wide lake descending on the city of Winnipeg" (CNN, 1997, April 29). More than 25,000 Manitobans were evacuated from the Red River Valley (Disaster Relief, 1997). Thousands of people volunteered to remove appliances from homes, fill sandbags, answer phones for the Red Cross, and prepare food for the Salvation Army.

The river empties about 100 miles downstream into Lake Winnipeg. Winnipeg has a floodway, nicknamed "Duff's Ditch" after the Manitoba premier who had it built in the 1960s to protect the city of 660,000. The city has a 25-mile long dike along the southwest side and a 28.5-mile floodway that diverts the Red River around the city. Seventy teams monitored the dikes 24 hours a day, with each team consisting of two city employees and one or two citizens. By May 1.5 million sandbags had been filled and another 1.3 million empty bags were on standby. Three thousand families and businesses were placed on alert to evacuate (Disaster Relief, 1997). The river crested in Winnipeg May 4. By May 8 the flooding had ended, emptying into Lake Winnipeg. Winnipeg successfully repelled the flood as it did not overtop protective levees and dikes, but the city knows that a future flood could. Manitoba was saved by a change in wind direction at the time of the peak flood level.

The Canadian Recovery

The post-emergency phase of reentry/recovery occurred in southern Manitoba in rural areas and small towns where evacuations or flooding occurred. Activities such as cleanup, restoration of utilities, flood damage estimation, and claims for compensation were carried out. Manitoba received an interim advance payment of C$25 million from the federal government to cover some of the initial costs under an agreement between the Province of Manitoba and the Government of Canada (Canada–Manitoba Agreement, 1997). The Manitoba Premier, Manitoba Government Services Minister, and the Federal Ministers of Foreign Affairs, National Defense, Natural Resources, and the Secretary of State for Western Diversification signed the agreement. The agreement was in addition to Manitoba's Financial Assistance Policy and Canada's Disaster Financial Assistance Arrangements. The province could use the funds to provide compensation to local governments and individuals. The settlement limit for individual homeowners and property owners was raised from $30,000 to $100,000 to match limits in other provinces (Canada–Manitoba Agreement, 1997). Eligible farmers were to be compensated at levels similar to those under the Crop Insurance Program. Two years after the flood, over 50 percent of flood proofing projects for individual homes and businesses in the Red River Valley had been completed. Construction of the Ste. Agathe ring dike was underway and the Roseau River community dike was near completion, but some other ring dikes had reached bottlenecks (Provincial Government, 1999).

The 1997 flood was the largest of the twentieth century with an estimated unregulated discharge downstream of the Assiniboine River of 4535 m^3/s. The 1852 flood had a similar recorded discharge rate of 4620 m^3/s, but a 1826 flood had a recorded discharge rate of 6300 m^3/s, which was nearly 40 percent greater than the 1997 flood. The chance of a flood occurring at that magnitude is about once in 667 years (Haque, 2000). The scale and loss in 1997 of life, property and disruption was due, as it is in many other flood-prone regions, a reflection of more people settling in disaster-prone areas. In this case Canada has a much larger population area that can be affected by the Red River, but the smaller communities on the U.S. side of the border are in a riskier geographic position.

Canadian Mitigation

After the 1997 flood, Manitoba amended the Manitoba Emergency Plan and established an annual review, as well as updating of all the municipal emergency plans. As part of the Manitoba Emergency Plan, Emergency Action Guidelines were established to clearly define the areas of responsibility of MEMO, provincial departments, and communities (Provincial, 1999). Dike break guidelines were established for letting essential services personnel remain in ring dike communities during a flood to protect infrastructure, and trigger mechanisms were established for community evacuations. These guidelines have been developed because flooding occurs on a regular basis throughout much of Manitoba because of severe weather and ice conditions during spring thaws. A set of action guidelines and trigger points for various dike structures determine when evacuation will occur. For example, for a dike greater than 10 feet, all nonessential personnel within less than half a mile of the dike, depending on the nature of the topography, will be ordered to evacuate when the water level is 4 feet below the top of the dike or when access to a clear road is threatened (MEMO, Emergency Plan, Flood Emergency Guidelines, 2003b).

The lead provincial agency for floods is the Water Resources Branch of the Department of Conservation. Beginning in February each year, the Flood Forecasting Committee evaluates the possibility of spring flooding and preliminary flood forecasts are made. Key departments are alerted and the Interagency Emergency Preparedness Committee meets to monitor the flood threat. The provisional emergency management organization's advisors increase their visits to municipalities in flood-prone areas and grain stocks are moved from those areas. In the warning/alert phase stores, equipment and human resources are checked. Fodder and equipment as well as livestock may be evacuated. Provincial staff advises and assists local authorities.

A case management delivery system was established to improve client services in the Disaster Financial Assistance Program, and an automated claims information and evaluation management system was established. Technical areas were developed to deal with special issues such as financial anomalies, foundation damage, and mold contamination (Provincial Government, 1999).

Cross-Border Cooperation

The governments of the United States and Canada directed the International Joint Commission to review the disaster and to report on the causes and effects of the floods and to recommend ways to reduce and prevent future harm. The International Joint Commission prevents and resolves disputes between the United States and Canada under the 1909 Boundary Waters Treaty and is an independent and objective advisor to the two countries.

The review led to the creation of the International Red River Basin Task Force. The task force made over 40 recommendations in a report "Living with the Red," including response policies, emergency operations, intergovernmental cooperation, forecasting, communications, the use of armed forces, relief, education, pollution, and contamination (Rawson and Herndon, 1998).

There were numerous discussions immediately following the flood about the need for better information and data and the need for different types of data, especially geo-spatial (GIS) data and improved tools for flood fights. The IJC recognized the need for data management and began development of the Red River Basin Disaster Information System (RRBDIN). The RRBDIN was to be an internet-based decision-making support tool for flood-related emergency management in the river basin, and to make data available to those responsible for solving flooding problems, fostering international cooperation including the Global Disaster Information Network, and strengthening interorganizational relations (RRBDIN, n.d.). Out of this work came the establishment of the Red River Basin Decision Information Network by the U.S. Army Corps of Engineers. The network is an Internet-based decision-making support tool for flood-related emergency management in the Red River basin. It provides access to multiple sources of data and information via the Internet, and it is designed to be useful to local decision makers during an emergency (About the Basin, 2003). Numerous tasks were completed in the first phase including the initial development of the web site, defining the data needs of users, and conceptually developing tools for local decision makers. The initial project phase was completed in 2000 and identified a number of challenges including nonuniform standards and formats for geo-spatial data between states, Canada and the United States; the inaccessibility of geo-spatial data within Canada; the general lack of geo-spatial data; and technological limitations for the implementation of internet-based tools (RRBDIN, n.d.). The name was changed to the Red River Basin Decision Information Network and included staff from the St. Paul District of the U.S. Army Corp of Engineers, and numerous cooperating agencies and organizations comprising a project review team and project design team. The organization emphasizes a bottom-up approach to ensure local support.

Canada and the United States also jointly sponsored the International Flood Mitigation Initiative (IFMI) that focused on basinwide mitigation, public education, and research on the effects of mitigation. Participants included representatives of the states of Minnesota and North Dakota and the province of Manitoba including legislators; provincial and state executives responsible for public health, the environment, water, and natural resources, federal emergency management, environment and water agencies; political government officials; disaster relief agencies; environmental organizations; university leaders; charitable foundation representatives; and international water management agencies. The initiative created five goals: develop a basinwide approach for forecasting, cooperation and communication; forge public–private community partnerships to ensure best practices; support strategies that protect human life and property; support mitigation strategies that enhance ecological, economic recreational opportunities and historical preservation; and establish methods for oversight and coordination of funding strategies (Gross and Haddow, 2003).

A legislators forum was established under which some 30 legislators meet on an annual basis to address mitigation issues. In addition a greenway initiative, the Greenway on the Red, works to establish a continuous greenway along the entire river corridor to mitigate future flood damage and enhance conservation and wildlife habitat, recreational opportunities, and economic development. A media partnership, River Watch provides easy to understand information to the public during a flood emergency, as well as ongoing public education related to mitigation efforts.

Both Canada and the United States have taken major steps to work together to prevent such major damage from occurring again on either side of the border. Nearly two and a half years after the flood most of the 40 recommendations of the International Joint Commission were implemented or underway as well as 58 recommendations of the Manitoba Water Commission (Provincial Government, 1999).

In 2001, the final report, Flood Protection Studies for Winnipeg, was released. The studies were commissioned by the governments of Canada, Manitoba, and the city of Winnipeg, following the 2000 International Joint Commission report on the Red River flood of 1997. It was conducted by the Winnipeg consulting engineers and project management company, KGS group. The study involved the federal minister, Ron Duhamel, under the Canada–Manitoba Infrastructure Agreement; the Premier of Manitoba, Gary Doer; and the mayor of Winnipeg, Glen Murray. The three government partners announced the following steps:

- Launching a series of consultations in several Red River Valley communities, headed by Terry Dugrid, chair of the Clean Environment Commission, to gather public feedback on the two main flood protection options studied in the report.
- Establishing an all-party committee of the legislature to advise the government on choosing the appropriate flood protection project.
- Committing to a first stage of relatively smaller but necessary projects that will improve protection for Winnipeg. These projects can proceed independently of the major projects (Action on Winnipeg, 2001).

The report placed the financial risk of exposure from flooding damage, not including potential business losses, at $50–$70 million per year without one of the proposed flood protection projects. The Winnipeg floodway was predicted to have a 37 percent risk of being overwhelmed in 50 years (Final Winnipeg Flood Protection Report Release, 2001).

The two major options explored were an expanded Winnipeg floodway at a project cost of C$660 million or a large dam structure near Ste. Agathe at a projected cost of C$543 million. The International Joint Commission Report on the 1997 Red River flood projected the floodway cost as higher and the Ste. Agathe project as less expensive than the Winnipeg Flood Protection Report (C$768 million for the floodway and C$475 million for the dam) (Final Winnipeg Flood Protection Report Release, 2001).

The existing Red River floodway was estimated to have prevented at least $9 billion in flood damage over its 35-year history (Red River Floodway, 2003). The floodway project would more than double the water volume diverted through the floodway and would provide increased flood protection during the construction phase. The Ste. Agathe option would involve creating dam devices on three rivers and would also require major earthen dams at the West Dike, and require two large diversion channels. It would probably provide the most protection for the most people, but would provide no protection until completion (Final Winnipeg Flood Protect Report Release, 2001). The Ste. Agathe option would have benefited some rural areas and small towns as well as Winnipeg. The project chosen was the floodway expansion. The floodway's capacity is expected to accommodate a 1-in-700-year flood. The advantages and disadvantages of the project were

- It would not have adverse upstream flooding effects for the Red River Valley south of Ste. Agathe—southern Manitoba, Minnesota, and North Dakota.
- It would have no major legal and interjurisdictional hurdles regarding cross-border or First Nations artificial flooding.
- It would perform better than the Ste. Agathe option if its capacity was exceeded.
- It would provide more protection for fewer people than the Ste. Agathe option—with notable exceptions including improved protection immediately south of the floodway inlet in the case of a 1997-level flood.
- It would have large potential for annual summer flood control in Winnipeg.
- It would have more recreational potential.
- It would reduce the probability by a factor of three-to-one or higher than state-of-nature flooding south of the city.
- It would likely be less intrusive environmentally.
- It would provide increased flood protection every year of Construction as it is being built (Final Winnipeg Flood Protection Report, 2001).

In April 2003, the Canadian Prime Minister Jean Chrétien and Manitoba Premier Gary Doer announced that their governments would each contribute C$80 million towards the expansion of the Manitoba Red River floodway. That is the largest provincial–federal infrastructure investment partnership since the original construction of the floodway (Prime Minister Chrétien, 2003). The project was made the top infrastructure priority in Manitoba. When completed the floodway expansion will also fulfill the recommendations of the International Joint Commission. The project was also seen to be consistent with Canada's new focus on mitigation under the National Disaster Mitigation Strategy.

Since the 1997 flood, the Governments of Canada and Manitoba have jointly invested C$130 million in flood protection including C$100 to protect rural residents (Prime Minister Chrétien, 2003). Thus, they did not ignore the fact that the other option would have had more benefits to rural Manitoba. The city of Winnipeg was also improving and upgrading flood protection infrastructure to complement the floodway expansion as part of the overall flood protection strategy of the region. Canada and the United States are moving to reduce the risks of natural disasters. Yet " . . . predicting the magnitude and areal extent of future Red River flooding is strongly dependent on forecasts of the timing of the March–April thaw. Unfortunately, . . . reliable predictions . . . are presently not possible" (National Weather Service, 2004).

Erlingsson (2002) has proposed that there be an international standard for mitigating natural disasters. The objective of this standard would be to decrease the risk of disaster and increase the availability of money for mitigation and encourage lower interest rates. Local, regional, and national governments would use the standard in physical planning and for preparing for disaster prevention, mitigation, response, and recovery. The standard would be hierarchical, so that disaster prevention plans for a region could only be certified if all the communities in the region had certified plans. The purpose would be to break the cycle of disasters largely with a market economic approach by stimulating private investments at lower interest rates if the investors felt their risks had been decreased. Funding for the creation and implementation of a disaster prevention plan could be of interest to the World Bank and other aid programs. The standard would require an international certification and at a minimum would cover

- Definitions
- Natural hazard, vulnerability, and risk assessments (from satellites to interviews)
- Data formats and analyses methods
- Prevention, mitigation, preparation, and reaction planning
- Certification

Canada and the United States will never be able to prevent all disasters, but certainly mitigation can reduce the impacts when a disaster occurs. Canada and the United States are part of a global community and because of their proximity what happens on what side of the border impacts the ability to respond on the opposite side of the border. Planning and funding from the regional and national levels is of increasing importance for both countries.

References

About the basin: Project background, 2003. Red River Basin Decision Information Network. Available at: http://www.rrbdin.org/thebasin.htm.

Action on Winnipeg Flood Protection Project announced by Premier, November 15, 2001. Legislative Electronic Publications. Available at: http://www.gov.mb.ca/chc/press/top/2001/11/2001–11–15–03.html.

Bonham, K., 1997. Lower crest prediction raises sprits in Fargo. *Grand Forks Herald*, April 11, p. 1. Canada–Manitoba agreement signed on Red River flood disaster assistance (1997, May 1). Legislative Electronic Publications. Available at: http://www.gov.mb.ca/chc/press/top/1997/05/1997-05-01-01.html.

CNN, 1997, April 21. Red River's misery flows north into Canada: Grand Forks still waiting for river's crest. CNN Interactive Weather. Available at: http://www.cnn.com/WEATHER/9704/21/flooding.pm/.

CNN, 1997, April 29. Canada loses first town to Red River flooding: Winnipeg area braces for river's arrival. CNN Interactive Weather. Available at: http://www.cnn.com/WEATHER/9704/29/canada.floods/.

Disaster Relief, 1997. Red River Basin Decision Information Network. Available at: http://www.rrbdin.org/thebasin.htm.

Division of Emergency Management and State Radio Communications (DEMSRC), 1997, May 16. Situation Report No. 41, Incident No. 97-015.

Division of Emergency Management and State Radio Communications (DEMSRC), 1997, May 23. Situation Report No. 43, Incident No. 97-015.

Division of Emergency Management and State Radio Communications (DEMSRC), 1997, August 7. Situation Report No. 59, Incident No. 97-015.

Division of Emergency Management and State Radio Communications (DEMSRC), 1997, October 9. Situation Report No. 68, Incident No. 97-015.

Division of Emergency Management and State Radio Communications (DEMSRC), 1999, February 1. Situation Report No. 1, Incident No. 99-009.

Division of Emergency Management and State Radio Communications (DEMSRC), 1999, September 30. Situation Report No. 35, Incident No. 99-009.

Erlingsson, U., 2002. An international standard for mitigating natural disasters? Available at: http://www.erlingsson.com/disasters/standard.html.

Families get limited access to homes in Grand Forks, 1997, April 18. Available at: http://www.disasterrelief.org/Disaster/970428flood/index-txt.html.

Federal Emergency Management Agency (FEMA), 1995. *National Mitigation Strategy-Partnerships for Building Safer Communities*. Washington, DC: Mitigation Directorate.

Final Winnipeg Flood Protection Report Release, 2001, November 15. Legislative Electronic Publications. Available at: http://www.gov.mb.ca/chc/press/top/2001/11/2001-11-15-01.html.

Gross, D. and Haddow, G., 2003. *International Flood Mitigation Initiative for the Red River*. Available at: http://www.unisdr.org/focus/.

Haque, C.E., 2000. Risk assessment, emergency preparedness and response to hazards: The case of the 1997 Red River Valley flood, Canada. *Natural Hazards*, 21: 225–245.

Joint Emergency Preparedness Program (JEPP), 2003. Manitoba EMO—JEPP—Introduction. Available at: http://www.gov.mb.ca/gs/memo/jeppintro.html.

Manitoba Emergency Measures Organization (MEMO), 2003a. *Manitoba Emergency Plan.* Available at: http://www.gov.mb.ca/gs/memo/mepfwd.html.

Manitoba Emergency Measures Organization (MEMO), 2003b. *Manitoba Emergency Plan. Flood Emergency: Emergency Action Guidelines.* Available at: http://www.gov.mb.ca/gs/memo/mepa1.html.

Mileti, D.S. et al., 1995. Towards an integration of natural hazards and sustainability. *The Environmental Professional*, 17 (2): 117–126.

Minnesota Homeland Security and Emergency Management, 2003, August 28. Past Disaster Information. Red River Flood Minnesota. FEMA-1175-DR-MN (1997). Available at: http://www.hsem.state.mn.us/Hsem_Subcategory_Home.asp?scatid=56&catid=1.

National Weather Service, Climate Prediction Center, 2004, June 17. Regional Climate Highlights, North America, Flooding of the Red River Valley and Tributaries during April 1997. Available at: http://www.cpc.ncep.noaa.gov/products/assessments/assess-97/river.html.

Newton, J., 1997. Federal legislation for disaster mitigation: A comparative assessment between Canada and the United States. *Natural Hazards*, 16: 219–241.

Office of Critical Infrastructure Protection and Emergency Preparedness (OCIPEP), n.d. Disaster Financial Assistance: Frequently Asked Questions. Available at: http://www.ocipep.gc.ca/fap/dfaa/faqs_e.asp.

Office of Critical Infrastructure Protection and Emergency Preparedness (OCIPEP), n.d. Joint Emergency Preparedness Program (JEPP). Public Safety and Emergency Preparedness Canada. Available at: http://www.ocipep.gc.ca/fap/joint_emerg/en_jeppl_e.asp.

Philippi, N., 1999. Major deficiencies remain in flood control policies. *Issues in Science and Technology*, 16 (4): 34.

Pielke, R.A. Jr., 1999. Who decides? Forecasts and responsibilities in the 1997 Red River flood. *Applied Behavioral Science Review*, 7 (2): 83.

Platt, R., 1996. Hazard mitigation: Cornerstone or grains of sand? *Disaster Research* 202, Boulder, CO (Item 1).

Prime Minister Chretien and Premier Doer announce $160 million for the Red River Floodway expansion, 2003, April 3. Legislative Electronic Publications. Available at: http://www.gov.mb.ca/chc/press/top/2003/04/2003-04-03-02.html.

Provincial Government to Review Flood Proofing, 1999, December 3. Manitoba Government News Release. Legislative Electronic Publications. Available at: http://www.gov.mb.ca/chc/press/top/1999/12/1999-12-03-09.html.

Rawson, B. and Herndon, D., 1998. Getting ready for the next Red River flood. *Focus: International Joint Commission*, 23 (2): 1.

Red River Basin Decision Information Network (RRBDIN) (n.d.). About the basin: Project background. Available at: http://www.rrbdin.org/TheBasin.htm.

Red River floodway: Past, present and future, 2003, April 4. Legislative Electronic Publications. Available at: http://www.gov.mb.ca/chc/press/top/2003/04/2003-04-04-02.html.

Red River, Rivers, United States and Canada, 2001. *The Columbia Encyclopedia.* New York: Columbia University Press.

Schneider, S.K., 1995. *Flirting with Disaster: Public Management in Crisis Situations.* Armonk, New York: M.E. Sharpe.

United Nations Department of Humanitarian Affairs, 1992. Internationally agreed glossary of basic terms related to disaster management. Geneva: DNA/93/36.

United States Geological Survey Service (USGS), 1997. *1997 Floods in the Red River of the North and Missouri Basins in North Dakota and Western Minnesota.* Washington, DC: USGS.

USA Today Weather, 1997. 1997 Red River flood index. Available at: http://www.usatoday.com/weather/wsflood1.htm.

Witt, J.L. and Rubin, R.E., 1995. *Administration Policy Paper—Natural Disaster Insurance and Related Issues.* Washington, DC: Federal Emergency Management Agency and Department of the Treasury.

Chapter 13

Variability of Natural Hazard Risk in the European Alps: Evidence from Damage Potential Exposed to Snow Avalanches

Sven Fuchs and Margreth Keiler

CONTENTS

Introduction

The historical shift of a traditionally agricultural society to a service industry- and leisure-oriented society led to socioeconomic development in mountain environments and foreland regions. This shift is reflected by an increasing use of those areas for settlement, industry, and recreation. On the other hand, areas suitable for land development are relatively scarce in the Inner Alpine valleys, e.g., in Austria, only about 20 percent of the whole area is appropriate for development activities [1]. Moreover, those areas are located line-shaped along the valley bottoms. Consequently, a conflict between human requirements on the one hand and naturally determined conditions on the other hand results. Due to an increasing concentration of tangible and intangible assets and to an increasing number of persons exposed to natural processes, which in the case of harm to human life or property are considered as natural hazards, there is an emerging need for the consideration of risk in land-use development.

Dealing with natural hazard processes has a long tradition in European Alpine countries. Early attempts in dealing with natural hazards include the establishment of official authorities in the second half of the nineteenth century, e.g., in Switzerland in the late 1870s [2] and in Austria in 1884 [3]. For more than half a century, technical mitigation measures were developed and implemented. These active measures, which represent the human reaction to hazard processes, appeared to be the appropriate way to cope with this challenge. There was little impetus toward an integrative dealing with natural hazards before the 1950s and 1960s, when extreme avalanche events occurred over wide areas of the Alps. Extraordinary governmental expenditures involved with the technical coping strategies resulting from those extreme events made traditional reactive measures increasingly obsolete. Consequently, ideas of complementary passive protection measures emerged, such as hazard mapping and land-use restrictions.*

---

* To identify hazard zones, defined design events are used to estimate the range and pressure distribution of the hazard processes. The methodologies applied therefore differ slightly between the Alpine countries, but the principle for drawing up hazard maps is similar, the listing describes the delimitation for snow avalanches in Switzerland [4] and Austria [5]. Inside areas marked with red color, the construction of new buildings is legally forbidden. In blue and yellow areas, particular regulations have to be considered with respect to the expected avalanche pressure, such as the reinforcement of walls at the hillside of a building.

■ In Switzerland, red color indicates areas where pressure from avalanches with recurrence intervals T between 30 and 300 years exceeds a lower limit that ranges from 3 kPa for $T = 30$ years to 30 kPa at $T = 300$ years. The entire area affected by (dense flow) avalanches with $T < 30$ years is also marked in red. Blue indicates areas where pressure from avalanches with recurrence intervals T between 30 and 300 years falls below 30 kPa. Areas affected by powder avalanches with reoccurrence intervals $T < 30$ years and a pressure <3 kPa are also marked in blue.

Only recently, the responsible authorities in most of the European mountain countries developed theoretical models of integrated risk management, which follow mainly the engineering approach to express risk as a product of hazard and values at risk [5–7] (see Equation 13.1). The development of these models is strongly connected to the considerable amount of damage in the Alps due to natural hazards in recent years [8].

$$R = p_{Si} \cdot A_{Oj} \cdot p_{Oj,\,Si} \cdot v_{Oj,\,Si} \tag{13.1}$$

where

R	is risk
p_{Si}	is probability of scenario i
A_{Oj}	is value at risk of object j
$p_{Oj,\,Si}$	is probability of exposure of object j to scenario i
$v_{Oj,\,Si}$	is vulnerability of object j, dependent on scenario i

According to Equation 13.1 it becomes apparent that all parameters have a linear influence on the results of risk analyses. The procedure of hazard assessment is methodologically reliable in determining the hazard potential and the related probability of occurrence (p_{Si}) by studying, modeling, and assessing individual processes and defined design events [9,10]. So far, little attention has been given to the damage potential (A_{Oj}) affected by hazard processes, particularly concerning spatial patterns and temporal shifts. Until now, studies related to the probability of exposure of an object ($p_{Oj,\,Si}$) to a defined scenario and the appropriate vulnerability of the object ($v_{Oj,\,Si}$) have predominantly been carried out as proposals to determine the risk of property and human life with the focus on a specific location and a specific point in time [6,9,11,12].

However, risk changes over time. Due to climate change processes and the associated impact on the Alps [13], magnitude and frequency of the natural process will most probably slightly increase for those processes where water is the driving agent [14]. In contrast, recent studies with respect to snow avalanches suggested that the natural avalanche activity seems to be constant in the European Alps during the last decades [15]. This led to the conclusion that the change in risk—presumably

---

The run-out areas of powder avalanches with reoccurrence intervals $T > 30$ years and a pressure <3 kPa are marked in yellow, as well as theoretically not excludable but extremely rare avalanches with a reoccurrence interval $T > 300$ years.

■ In Austria, red color indicates areas where pressure from avalanches with recurrence intervals $T = 150$ years exceeds a limit ≥ 10 kPa.

Yellow indicates areas where pressure from avalanches with recurrence intervals $T = 150$ years is >1 kPa and <10 kPa.

indicated by remarkable damage in the 1990s—has to be attributed to changes in the damage potential affected [16].

Socioeconomic developments in the human-made environment led to asset concentration and a shift in urban and suburban population in the Alps. Thus, the temporal variability of damage potential is an important key variable in the consideration of risk. Recently, conceptual studies related to the temporal variability of damage potential exposed to snow avalanches have been carried out, focusing both, the long-term and the short-term temporal evolution of indicators [17–19]. Furthermore, owing to the requirement of economic efficiency of public expenditures on mitigation measures, there is a need for a precautionary, sustainable dealing with natural hazard phenomena, taking into account particularly the values at risk [20–22].

On the basis of these studies, the multi-temporal development of values at risk is presented with respect to snow avalanches in Alpine settlements. This multi-temporal approach aims to demonstrate the different superimposed temporal scales in the development of damage potential complementing each another.

Temporal Development of Values at Risk

Case studies have been carried out in Davos (Switzerland) and Galtür (Austria) [17,18]. Both villages represent typical mountain resorts dependent on winter tourism, thus, the results mirror recent developments of society in Alpine destinations. Methodologically, the areas affected by avalanches were deduced using the incident cadastre of former events, the legally valid hazard maps, and the avalanche model AVAL1-D. This model is a one-dimensional avalanche dynamics program that predicts run-out distances, flow velocities, and impact pressure of both flowing and powder snow avalanches (a detailed description is given in Ref. [23]).

The values at risk were obtained analyzing the zoning plan with respect to location and perimeter of every building. Additional information, such as building type, year of construction, and replacement value, as well as the number of residents were provided by the official authorities and joint using Geographic Information Systems (GIS). The number of endangered tourists was derived from tourism statistics of the municipalities.

A general shift in damage potential resulted from the development of mountain areas from traditionally agricultural societies to tourism centers within the twentieth century. This development could be evaluated using decadal study periods, and provided a general idea about the development of assets in endangered areas. This approach mainly focused on the development of values in areas endangered by avalanches, such as the number and value of buildings, or the number of persons inhabiting those buildings.

A second development of damage potential, especially focusing on mobile values and intangible assets, is based on a seasonal and diurnal assessment of variations in damage potential. This approach had also been applied for an application related to the number of tourists staying temporally at a specific endangered location.

Long-Term Development of Values at Risk

Regarding the long-term development in numbers and values of endangered buildings, a significant increase could be proven in both study sites for the period between 1950 and 2000 [17].

In Davos, the total number of buildings has almost tripled, from 161 in 1950 to 462 in 2000 (Figure 13.1). This increase was due to the shift from 51 to 256 in the category of residential buildings, while in the other categories the number of buildings was approximately unchanging. A significant increase in number dated back in the 1960s and 1970s before the legally hazard map came into force [16]. The total value of buildings increased by a factor of almost four. In 1950, the total sum of buildings was EUR 240 million and in 2000, the total sum was EUR 930 million. In 1950, the proportion of residential buildings was less than 15 percent, compared to the total amount of endangered buildings. Until 2000, this ratio changed to almost 50 percent. Regarding the category of hotels and guest houses as well as the category of special risks, nearly no increase in value could be observed. However, those categories showed a higher average value per building than residential buildings. The number of endangered permanent residential population increased slightly. In 1950, a population of 1098 persons was exposed to avalanche hazards, until 2000 this value increased to 1137 persons.

This is a relatively moderate increase of 3.6 percent, compared to the increase in tangible assets. If the classification into different building functions is carried out, this increase turned out to be larger. In residential buildings, 673 persons were concerned in 1950 and 1116 in 2000, which is an increase of two-thirds.

In Galtür, the total number of buildings inside avalanche-prone areas rose by a factor of 2.5 (Figure 13.1), from 41 in 1950 to 108 in 2000. This increase is due to the relative development in the category of hotels and guest houses, and—obviously less important—in the category of agricultural buildings. The number of buildings in all other categories stayed nearly constant. The decrease in the number of residential buildings since 1980 resulted from a modification of buildings formerly used for habitation to accommodation facilities subsequently used for tourism. The total value of buildings rose by a factor of almost six. In 1950, the total value of buildings amounted to EUR 12 million and in 2000 to EUR 64 million. Since the 1960s, the category of hotels and guest houses held the highest proportion of the total amount of endangered values per decade and per category. In 1950, the proportion of hotels and guest houses was about 30 percent, compared to the total value of buildings. In 2000, this ratio changed to approximately 75 percent. In contrast, the number and value of residential buildings showed nearly no change between 1950 and 2000. Generally, the number of buildings in the community of Galtür has risen

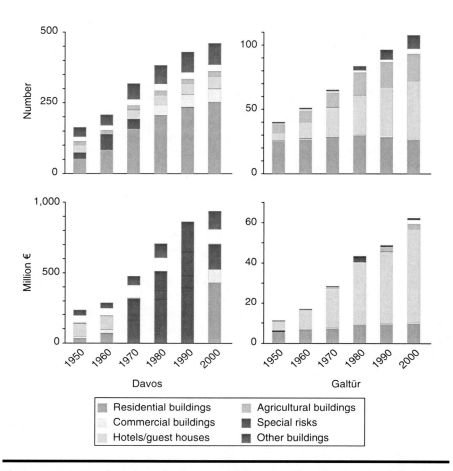

Figure 13.1 **Development of values at risk in Davos (CH) and Galtür (A) related to the respective avalanche-prone areas, subdivided in decades and building categories. (From Fuchs, S., Keiler, M., Zischg, A., and Bründl, M., *Nat. Hazards Earth Sys. Sci.*, 5(6), 898, 2005.)**

above average in comparison to the numbers of the federal state of Tyrol. In 2000, a quarter of the total value of all buildings in the municipality was found to be located in the avalanche-prone areas. The proportional increase in the value of buildings was significantly higher than the proportional increase in the number of buildings. Buildings inside avalanche-prone areas showed a lower average value as buildings outside those areas. The number of endangered persons increased substantially between 1950 and 2000. In Galtür, in 1950, approximately 850 persons were located inside exposed areas, consisting of 460 residents and 390 tourists. Until the year 2000, this value increased to 4700 persons, of which 770 were residents and 3930 were tourists. The increase in residential population was about 60 percent, while the increase in temporal population was a factor of ten.

Short-Term Development of Values at Risk

Parallel to the long-term increases described in "Long-Term Development of Values at Risk," remarkable short-term variations of persons at risk were detectable. Those variations could be determined on seasonal, weekly, and hourly resolution.

Results of the community of Davos have shown, that subdividing the utilization of hotels and guest houses into months, peaks arose during holiday periods such as Christmas and the end of February.

According to the analysis of the avalanche bulletin of the Swiss Federal Institute of Snow and Avalanche Research SLF, these periods coincided closely with periods when there was an above-average occurrence of days with high avalanche danger, resulting from typical meteorological situations with a stationary cyclone above Northern Europe and an anticyclone above the Atlantic Ocean (Figure 13.2). As a result, considerable amounts of snowfall occur in the Alps, and temporal risk peaks within the time frame of weeks arise.

In the community of Galtür, similar developments have been quantified for the number of endangered persons. Over the whole study period, the total number of endangered persons fluctuated by a factor of almost six. Based on a fluctuation approach outlined in Ref. [18], strong variations could be observed during the

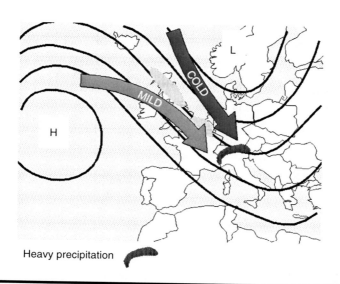

Heavy precipitation

Figure 13.2 Typical meteorological situation in Europe, leading to heavy precipitation in the Alps.

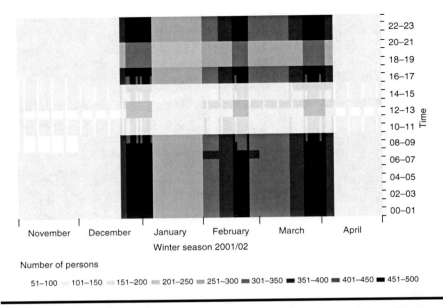

Figure 13.3 Monthly, weekly, and diurnal fluctuations of the number of exposed persons in the study area of Galtür (A). (From Keiler, M., Zischg, A., Fuchs, S., Hama, M., and Stötter, J., *Nat. Hazards Earth Sys. Sci.*, 5(1), 55, 2005. With permission.)

winter season as well as in daytime (Figure 13.3). The seasonal fluctuation was characterized by a strongly increasing number of tourists at Christmas time and the Easter travel season. The end of the winter season was highlighted by a sharp decrease in the number of persons to nearly the amount of the permanent population. Considering the diurnal fluctuation, the weekly structure could be easily followed. From the beginning of the winter season, these patterns were overlapped by general movements of the tourists during daytime. The number of persons varied by a factor of 1.4 between minimum and maximum in the off-season, and by a factor of 3.4 in the period of the main season. These changes could occur extremely rapid within one or two hours.

Multi-temporal Approach for an Effective Risk Reduction

As presented in the previous sections, the development of values at risk due to socioeconomic transformation in the European Alps varies remarkably on different temporal levels. Long-term changes and short-term fluctuations have to be considered when evaluating risk resulting from natural hazards.

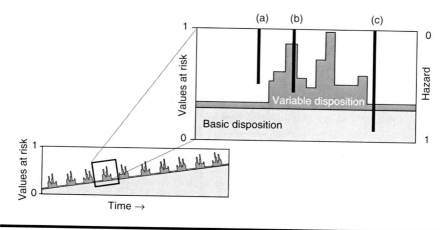

Figure 13.4 Schematic description of the concept of basic (long-term) and variable (short-term) damage potential and the relation to triggering events.

Long-term changes in values at risk could be considered as basic disposition (Figure 13.4). To reduce the risk resulting from this basic disposition, permanent constructive mitigation measures could be constructed and land-use regulations implemented. As a consequence, the basic risk could be reduced due to a spatial reduction of the process area. As pointed out in Ref. [24] for the study area of Davos, the risk due to snow avalanches decreased fundamentally since the 1950s, even if the values at risk increased in the municipality. This development could be mainly attributed to the construction of permanent mitigation measures, and is strongly related to immobile values. Similar results were obtained for the study area Galtür [25]. However, extraordinary losses could be estimated if rare events with severe effects occur, because the delimitation of the respective process areas is based on defined design events. This problem emerged during the avalanche winter 1999 in Switzerland [26] and Austria.

Short-term fluctuations in damage potential supplement this continuing development of damage potential within a specific range. Thus, they have to be considered as variable disposition. To mitigate those fluctuations, temporal measures could be applied, such as evacuations or temporary road closures.

Furthermore, because socioeconomic development differs within Alpine regions, studies on the long-term behavior of values at risk contribute to the ongoing discussion of passive and active developing regions and suburbanization [16]. However, if a potentially dangerous natural event occurs, it depends on the actual amount of values at risk (basic and variable disposition) within the process area whether or not damage will be triggered.

Long-term as well as short-term variations in damage potential should be implemented into risk management approaches. In Figure 13.4, the significance for a consideration of variable as well as basic damage potential is presented. As shown in example (a) the event will not hit any values at risk, and thus, the level of risk reduction is sufficient. In example (b), due to high amounts of variable values at risk, damage will occur. As a result, temporal mitigation strategies could reduce the variable damage potential until a critical level. In example (c), basic and variable values at risk are affected by a process. Thus, temporal measures are no more sufficient enough for an effective risk reduction. These examples clearly indicate the strong need for an incorporation of dynamic assessments of damage potential in community risk management strategies.

Such risk management strategies should include an objective risk assessment that is based on both, hazard analysis and an analysis of damage potential. Risk assessment has to be followed by a risk evaluation procedure. In this evaluation process, the level of accepted risk and the level of (residual) risk to be accepted should be defined by a participative process. Using these results, the risk management strategy could be defined, aiming at both a risk minimization and an economic efficient use of public expenditures. Thus, a combination of mitigation strategies, such as passive and active measures, could be chosen to meet these prerequisites. Thereby, temporal variations of the risk have to be considered seriously.

Discussion

Information on the general development of damage potential and seasonal, weekly, or diurnal peaks should be implemented in the risk management procedure, because the range of the results is remarkably high, and the values at risk have a key influence on the risk equation. Even if the results with respect to avalanche risk suggest—due to the long-term increase in damage potential—a similar shift in risk, in general, the risk decreased fundamentally as a result of the construction of mitigation measures and the introduction of land-use restrictions in endangered areas.

However, short-term fluctuations in damage potential might lead to a temporal increase in risk, resulting from a modified recreational behavior within the society. Until now, there is a particular lack in information related to short-term fluctuations of values at risk. In contrast to the immobile damage potential (buildings and infrastructure, etc.), persons and mobile values can either leave or be removed out of hazard-prone areas in case of dangerous situations. For developing efficient and effective evacuation and emergency plans, information on the numbers of persons and mobile values as well as their location and movements in the area is needed. In consequence, permanent mitigation structures could be complemented by temporal measures to achieve an efficient and effective risk reduction.

Information on the temporal variability of values at risk both from a long-term as well as from a short-term point of view provided in combination with process knowledge is the basis for dynamic risk visualization. Such information may help to recognize high-risk situations more easily and enables a situation-oriented and risk-based decision making [19,27,28]. Apart from the damage potential, risk analyses are based on the concept of recurrence intervals of hazard processes. If those defined design events would be exceeded, the remarkable increase of values at risk would result in a significant shift in monetary losses (and presumably fatalities). First results on risk associated with torrent hazards suggest an increase in the probabilities of the design events in the Alpine region, however, these results still need some additional analyses to be verified, and are subject to ongoing research.

To conclude, risk analyses concerning natural hazards should be carried out with respect to a dynamic change of input parameters. This is essential for efficient disaster risk reduction and contributes to the concept of resilience as part of proactive adaptation. Regarding snow avalanches in the European Alps, the most important input parameter is the temporal variability of damage potential, because the natural avalanche activity did not vary substantially during the past decades. Thus, future research is needed to quantify the impact of modifications in damage potential on (1) the result of risk analyses, (2) the assessment of risk in the cycle of integrated risk management, (3) the adjustment of coping strategies, and (4) the perception of risk by all parties involved, including policy makers.

The latter is the most crucial issue in Europe, because until now, dealing with natural hazards is based on mono-disciplinary approaches. In Austria, the forest law of 1975 restricts all hazards planning to forestry engineers [5], in France, experts responsible for these issues are predominantly geologists [29], while in Italy, the requirement for those specialists is a PhD in agriculture or a master's degree in forestry or geology [30]. However, because risk resulting from natural hazards is a subject matter affecting life and economy within the whole society, multiple stakeholders' interests have to be considered when mitigation measures and coping strategies are developed and decisions are made. Thus, there is a particular need to involve (1) economists with respect to an efficient and effective use of public expenditures, (2) social scientists with respect to both society's risk perception and an enhanced risk communication, (3) geographers and land-use planners as well as (4) all other disciplines representing any other party involved.

References

1. BEV, Regionalinformation der Grundstücksdatenbank des Bundesamtes für Eich- und Vermessungswesen, 2004, www.bev.at (access 15.01.2006).
2. Frutiger, H., History and actual state of legalization of avalanche zoning in Switzerland, *Journal of Glaciology* 26, 313, 1980.
3. Bergthaler, J., Grundsätze bei der Erarbeitung von Gefahrenzonenplänen in Wildbächen der Nördlichen Kalkalpen und der Grauwackenzonen, *Österreichische Wasserwirtschaft* 27, 160, 1975.
4. BFF and SLF: *Richtlinien zur Berücksichtigung der Lawinengefahr bei raumwirksamen Tätigkeiten*, Davos and Bern, Bundesamt für Forstwesen und Eidgenössisches Institut für Schnee- und Lawinenforschung, 1984.

5. Republik Österreich, *Forstgesetz 1975*, Bundesgesetzblatt Nr. 440/1975, in der Fassung BGBl. I Nr. 83/2004, http://recht.lebensministerium.at/file-manager/download/6119/, 2003 (access 20.01.2006), and additional executive order, *Verordnung über Gefahren-zonenpläne*, BGBl. Nr. 436/1976, http://recht.lebensministerium.at/filemanager/download/6128/, 1976 (access 20.01.2006).

6. Borter, P., Risikoanalyse bei gravitativen Naturgefahren—Methode. *Umwelt-Materialien* 107/I, BUWAL, Bern, 1999.

7. Repubblica Italiana, G.U. n. 134/1998: DD. LL. 11 giugno 1998, n. 180. Misure urgenti per la prevenzione del rischio idrogeologico ed a favore delle zone colpite da disastri franosi nella regione Campania. *Gazzetta Ufficiale della Repubblica Italiana*, 134, 1998.

8. MunichRe, *Topics geo—Annual Review Natural Catastrophes 2005*, Münchener Rück, München, 2006.

9. Heinimann, H. et al., Methoden zur Analyse und Bewertung von Naturgefahren. *Umwelt-Materialien* 85, BUWAL, Bern, 1998.

10. Kienholz, H. and Krummenacher, B., *Symbolbaukasten zur Kartierung der Phänomene*, BWG and BUWAL, Bern, 1995.

11. Wilhelm, C., Wirtschaftlichkeit im Lawinenschutz. *Mitteilungen SLF*, 54, Davos, 1997.

12. Barbolini, M. et al., Empirical estimate of vulnerability relations for use in snow avalanche risk assessment, In: Brebbia, C., Ed., *Risk Analysis IV*, Southampton, 2004, p. 533.

13. Wanner, H. et al., *Klimawandel im Schweizer Alpenraum*, vdf-Hochschulverlag, Zürich, 2000.

14. Bader, S. and Kunz, P., *Klimarisiken—Herausforderung für die Schweiz*, vdf-Hochschulverlag, Zürich, 1998.

15. Laternser, M. and Schneebeli, M., Temporal trend and spatial distribution of avalanche activity during the last 50 years in Switzerland, *Natural Hazards* 27, 201, 2002.

16. Fuchs, S. and Bründl, M., Damage potential and losses resulting from snow avalanches in settlements in the Canton of Grisons, Switzerland, *Natural Hazards* 34, 53, 2005.

17. Fuchs, S. et al., The long-term development of avalanche risk in settlements considering the temporal variability of damage potential, *Natural Hazards and Earth System Sciences* 5, 893, 2005.

18. Keiler, M. et al., Avalanche related damage potential—changes of persons and mobile values since the mid-twentieth century, case study Galtür, *Natural Hazards and Earth System Sciences* 5, 49, 2005.

19. Zischg, A. et al., Temporal variability of damage potential on roads as a conceptual contribution towards a short-term avalanche risk simulation, *Natural Hazards and Earth System Sciences* 5, 235, 2005.

20. Benson, C. and Clay, E., *Understanding the Economic and Financial Impacts of Natural Disasters*, The World Bank, Washington, 2004.

21. Dilley, M. et al., *Natural Disasters Hotspots, a Global Risk Analysis*, The World Bank, Washington, 2005.

22. Johnson, L. et al., Planning for the unexpected: Land-use development and risk. Planning Advisory Service Report 531, American Planning Association, Washington, 2005.

23. Christen, M. et al., AVAL-1D: An avalanche dynamics program for the practice, Proceedings of the INTERPRAEVENT 2002 in the Pacific Rim—Matsumoto, October 14–18, 2, 715, 2002.
24. Fuchs, S. et al., Development of avalanche risk between 1950 and 2000 in the municipality of Davos, Switzerland. *Natural Hazards and Earth System Sciences* 4, 263, 2004.
25. Keiler, M. et al., Avalanche risk assessment—a multi-temporal approach, results from Galtür, Austria, *Natural Hazards and Earth System Sciences* 6, 2006, pp. 637–651.
26. SLF, Ed., *Der Lawinenwinter* 1999, SLF, Davos, 2000.
27. Zischg, A. et al., Uncertainties and fuzziness in analysing risk related to natural hazards: a case study in the Ortles Alps, South Tyrol, Italy, In: Brebbia, C., Ed., *Risk Analysis IV*, Southampton, 2004, p. 523.
28. Schwab, J. et al., Eds., Landslide hazards and planning, Planning Advisory Service Report 533/534, American Planners Association, Washington, 2005.
29. Stötter, J. et al., *Konzeptvorschlag zum Umgang mit Naturgefahren in der Gefahrenzonenplanung*, Innsbrucker Geographische Gesellschaft, Ed., Jahresbericht 1997/98, Innsbruck, 1999, p. 30.
30. Autonome Provinz Trentino-Südtirol, *Beiblatt Nummer 5 zum Amtsblatt der Autonomen Region Trentino-Südtirol vom 28. April 1998* 18–I/II, Trient, 1998.

Chapter 14

Disaster Management Structure in Turkey: Away from a Reactive and Paternalistic Approach?

N. Emel Ganapati

CONTENTS

I am indebted to Dr. Oktay Ergunay for his comments on the manuscript.

Introduction

The disaster management structure in Turkey underwent significant reorganization in the aftermath of the August 17, 1999 earthquake, one of the most damaging earthquakes in the country's recent history. This chapter traces the evolution of the current disaster management structure in Turkey, and outlines the changes that have happened since the earthquake. Within the context of these changes, it clarifies the organizational responsibilities with respect to the four phases of disasters (i.e., disaster preparedness, emergency response and rescue, disaster recovery, and disaster mitigation), the scholarly literature on which is scant. Despite the changes, there are several shortcomings in the present disaster management structure.

Before the August 17, 1999 earthquake, the disaster management structure in Turkey was paternalistic, wherein the state was responsible for almost all phases of disasters. The provincial and district governments, which are arms of the central government, were responsible for disaster preparedness, and emergency response and rescue. The Ministry of Public Works and Settlement (MPWS) was in charge of disaster recovery, and designed mitigation policies that were implemented by the provincial and local governments within their own jurisdictions. The state also stepped in as a father figure to look after the disaster victims. It promised to replace or repair the lost or damaged property of homeowners by constructing permanent housing units or by distributing monetary aid. Within this structure, the households, private sector, and nongovernmental organizations (NGOs) had no or little legal role to play.

Since the August 17, 1999 earthquake, the state has shifted some of its logistic, administrative and financial burden to the NGOs, private firms, and homeowners. NGOs such as voluntary search and rescue teams are now allowed to collaborate with the state in its preparedness and emergency response activities. Private firms are in charge of inspecting construction and reporting to the local governments for issuance of necessary permits in selected provinces. Homeowners in all urban areas in Turkey are mandated to carry an earthquake insurance to be eligible for housing aid from the state in the aftermath of an earthquake.

Although all these changes introduced in the aftermath of the August 17, 1999 earthquake were proactive in nature, with more emphasis placed on disaster preparedness and mitigation, the current disaster management system in Turkey has several major shortcomings. There is no single central government agency, for instance, with the legal responsibility to coordinate disaster preparedness in the country. Partly related to this, there is no national level comprehensive disaster preparedness plan that outlines the structure of coordination between different levels of government, NGOs, and the private sector during emergencies. There is more than one agency at the central government level with coordinative functions during emergency response and rescue phase of disasters. Some of these agencies have overlapping functions. The agency in charge of coordinating disaster mitigation activities in the country lacks human and administrative resources to undertake its responsibilities in an effective manner. Furthermore, local governments and disaster victims that are more familiar with local conditions are excluded from disaster recovery processes, which are still heavily controlled by the central government.

The rest of the chapter is divided into four sections. The second section provides a profile of natural disasters in Turkey with an emphasis on earthquakes. Earthquakes have been the major bane for the country, and have influenced the evolution of the Turkish disaster management structure. The third section traces the historical evolution of such structure in Turkey and explains how this structure has moved gradually from a reactive one to a proactive one, especially in the aftermath of the August 17, 1999 earthquake. The fourth section outlines the current disaster management structure in Turkey based on a review of laws and regulations that relate to disasters. The fifth section concludes with the major features and key steps that could be undertaken to overcome shortcomings of the current disaster management structure.

Profile of Natural Disasters in Turkey

Turkey is threatened by a variety of disasters—earthquakes, floods, landslides, rockfalls, and avalanches. Generally, an event is declared as a disaster by the Council of Ministers upon the recommendation of different agencies. Such agencies include the MPWS in cases of earthquakes, landslides, and avalanche; the Ministry of Energy and Natural Resources (that houses the State Water Works) in cases of floods; and local governments and village administrations (subject to approval of the district head and the governor) in cases of fires. The disaster petition of an incident is usually bottom-up (e.g., from district to province and from province to the central government) (JICA 2004: 42).*

The central government decides whether or not to intervene in a particular disaster based on criteria outlined in the Decree on Basic Principles Related to Disasters Affecting the Life of the General Public (Official Gazette No. 13007). According to this decree, one criterion for disaster is based on the scale of collapse or heavy damage based on the size of settlements (Table 14.1). Although the main

---

* Central government in Turkey is composed of two branches: central administrative organs in the capital (e.g., the Office of the President, Office of the Prime Minister, Council of Ministers, Ministries, and organizations attached to the ministries) and the provincial administration throughout the country. Provincial administration is composed of provinces and districts (headed by provincial and district governors), which take and implement decisions on behalf of the central government within their jurisdictions. In Turkey, there are 81 provinces, 850 districts, 36,527 villages, and 42,000 smaller settlement units (called *mezra*) attached to the villages (JICA 2004: 19). Local governments carry out local public services. They are not part of the central government structure.

Table 14.1 Main Disaster Criteria in Turkey

Settlement Type	Number of Buildings Heavily Damaged or Collapsed
Villages/rural areas	At least 10 buildings
Settlements with a population of less than 5,000	At least 20 buildings
Settlements with a population between 5,000 and 10,000	At least 25 buildings
Settlements with a population between 10,000 and 30,000	At least 30 buildings
Settlements with a population between 30,000 and 50,000	At least 40 buildings
Settlements with a population of more than 50,000	At least 50 buildings

Source: Adapted from the Decree on Basic Principles Related to Disasters Affecting the Life of the General Public [Afetlerin Genel Hayata Etkinligine Iliskin Temel Kurallar Hakkinda Yonetmelik] (effective by 21 September 1968), in *Kanunlar Yonetmelikler ve Kararnameler.* Afet Isleri Genel Mudurlugu, Ankara, 2000.

criterion for a disaster is the number of severely damaged homes, the decree allows for other aspects to be taken into account, such as the human death toll, injuries, damage to public facilities, access to the location, and the weather conditions. The decree also stipulates that disasters can be declared in rural areas if there is animal loss or damage to one-third of agricultural crops.

Among the different types of disasters, earthquakes have posed the biggest problem in terms of death toll, number of people affected, and the financial damage in the country. Turkey is located on the Alpide earthquake belt, one of the three prominent earthquake belts in the world, which stretches from Indonesia through the Himalayas, the Mediterranean, and into the Atlantic.* According to the 1996 seismic hazard zone map of the MPWS, 71 percent of Turkey's population lives in the first- and second-degree seismic hazard zones. As Table 14.2 illustrates, most industries and dams are also located in high-degree seismic zones (76 and 69 percent, respectively). The EM-DAT International Disaster Database reveals that major earthquakes alone have led to 97 percent of disaster-related deaths and

---

* The other two earthquake belts in the world are the circum-Pacific seismic belt (also known as the Ring of Fire) and the Mid-Atlantic Ridge.

Table 14.2   Distribution of Seismic Hazard Risk in Turkey

Seismic Hazard Zone	Surface Area (percent)	Population (percent)	Industry (percent)	Dams (percent)
First-degree zone	42	45	51	46
Second-degree zone	24	26	25	23
Third-degree zone	18	14	11	14
Fourth-degree zone	12	13	11	11
Fifth-degree zone	4	2	2	6
Total	100	100	100	100

Note: Earthquake risk zones are calculated based on the expected peak ground acceleration (PGA) values.

Source: Adapted from JICA (Japan International Cooperation Agency), *Country Strategy Paper for Natural Disasters in Turkey,* JICA, Ankara, 2004, p. 25—based on data from the General Directorate of Disaster Affairs.

88 percent of disaster-related damages between 1903 and 2006 in Turkey.* During this period, 1,247 people lost their lives, and 96,825 people have been affected on average per major earthquake. Tables 14.3 and 14.4 show the total impact of disasters in Turkey and averages per disaster event.

As Table 14.5 depicts, the deadliest earthquake in Turkey since 1903 was the December 27, 1939 Erzincan earthquake that claimed 32,968 lives. It was followed by the August 17, 1999 Golcuk (Kocaeli, Marmara) earthquake with an official death toll of 17,480 (PMO-CMC 2000: 4). Unofficial estimates of the August 17, 1999 earthquake, however, put the death toll between 40,000 and 50,000. This earthquake also damaged 213,843 housing units, the most number of housing units damaged by any earthquake in Turkey.

The August 17, 1999 earthquake struck early in the morning at 3.02 a.m. and measured 7.4 on the Richter scale. Although it lasted for 45 seconds, it had more

---

* EM-DAT International Disaster Database is an initiative of the Office of U.S. Foreign Disaster Assistance (OFDA, the U.S. Agency for International Development) and the Centre for Research on the Epidemiology of Disasters (CRED). For an event to qualify as a disaster for entry into the database, it should meet at least one of the following criteria: (i) ten or more people were reported to be killed; (ii) hundred people were reported to be affected; (iii) there was a call for international assistance; or (iv) there was a declaration of "state of emergency" (EM-DAT International Disaster Database [http://www.em-dat.net/guidelin.htm]. Accessed 28 August 2006.).

Table 14.3   Natural Disasters in Turkey (1903–2006)

Disaster Type	Number of Events	Persons Killed	Persons Injured	Persons Rendered Homeless	Persons Affected Otherwise	Total Persons Affected	Damage (US$, in Thousands)
Earthquake	71	88,538	92,866	1,160,850	5,620,850	6,874,596	16,096,600
Epidemic[a]	7	589	N/A	N/A	204,625	204,625	N/A
Extreme temperature	6	98	N/A	N/A	8,000	8,000	N/A
Flood	31	1,260	211	99,000	1,586,520	1,685,731	2,193,500
Slides	8	591	208	185	1,905	2,298	N/A
Wild fires	4	13	N/A	350	500	850	N/A
Windstorm	9	100	139	N/A	13,500	13,639	2,200
Total	136	91,189	93,424	1,260,385	7,435,900	8,789,739	182,922,300

[a] The EM-DAT: OFDA/CRED International Disaster Database uses the following diseases for epidemic: measles, meningitis (polio), malaria, and diarrhea/enteric (cholera).

Source: Adapted from EM-DAT International Disaster Database [http://www.em-dat.net/disasters/country.php]. Accessed 20 August 2006.

Table 14.4   Natural Disasters in Turkey—Averages Per Event (1903–2006)

Disaster Type	Average Killed Per Event	Average Injured Per Event	Average Homeless Per Event	Average Affected Per Event	Average Total Affected Per Event	Average Damage Per Event (US$, in Thousands)
Earthquake	1,247	1,308	16,350	79,167	96,825	226,713
Epidemic	84	N/A	N/A	29,232	29,232	N/A
Extreme temperature	16	N/A	N/A	1,333	1,333	N/A
Flood	41	7	3,194	51,178	54,378	70,758
Slides	74	26	23	238	287	N/A
Wild fires	3	N/A	88	125	213	N/A
Windstorm	11	15	N/A	1,500	1,515	244

Source: Adapted from EM-DAT International Disaster Database [http://www.em-dat.net/disasters/country.php]. Accessed 20 August 2006.

Table 14.5   Top Ten Earthquakes in Turkey Based on Death Toll (1903–2006)

Place (Province)	Date	Magnitude	Death Toll	Number of Housing Units Damaged
Erzincan	December 27, 1939	7.9	32,968	116,720
Golcuk (Kocaeli)	August 17, 1999	7.4	17,480	213,843
Ladik (Samsun)	November 27, 1943	7.2	4,000	40,000
Gerede-Cerkes (Bolu)	February 1, 1944	7.2	3,959	20,865
Muradiye (Van)	November 24, 1976	7.5	3,840	9,232
Erbaa (Tokat)	December 20, 1942	7.0	3,000	32,000
Turkish–Iran Border	May 7, 1930	7.2	2,514	N/A
Varto (Mus)	August 19, 1966	6.9	2,396	20,007
Lice (Diyarbakir)	September 6, 1975	6.6	2,385	8,149
Erzurum-Kars	October 30, 1983	6.9	1,155	3,241

Source: Adapted from PMO-CMC (Prime Minister's Office-Crisis Management Center) [T.C. Basbakanlik Kriz Yonetim Merkezi], *Depremler 1999*, PMO-CMC, Ankara, 2000, p. 4, 8; Bogazici University Kandilli Observatory and Earthquake Research Institute [Bogazici Universitesi Kandilli Rasathanesi Ulusal Deprem Izleme Merkezi, Available at: [http://www.koeri.boun.edu.tr/sismo/default.htm]. Accessed 20 August 2006.

than 1000 aftershocks, some of which reached 5.6 on the Richter scale (World Bank 1999: 8). The earthquake brought widespread building damages and deaths in eight provinces: Bolu, Bursa, Eskisehir, Istanbul, Kocaeli, Sakarya, Yalova, and Zonguldak. These provinces are distributed across Marmara, Black Sea, and Central Anatolia regions in Turkey. They cover 6.85 percent of the total surface area, and they housed approximately 24 percent of the total population in the country before the earthquake (SIS 2000). As the eight provinces affected by the earthquake accounted for 34.8 percent of gross domestic product (GDP) in Turkey in 1998 (SIS 2000), the impact of the earthquake on the country's economy was extensive. According to the World Bank (1999: 2), economic losses from the earthquake were between US$10.8 and US$16.1 billion.

The August 17, 1999 earthquake revealed the severe shortcomings in disaster preparedness and mitigation in Turkey. It highlighted that there was a lack of coordination in undertaking emergency response and rescue activities for large-scale disasters, lack of search and rescue teams to respond to large-scale disasters, and lack of mitigation measures and their enforcement in the country, among others. With the revelation of such shortcomings, the disaster management structure in the country has been revised to a great extent in the aftermath of this earthquake, as it will be detailed in the following two sections.

Evolution of the Disaster Management Structure in Turkey

The Republic of Turkey inherited its disaster management structure from the Ottoman Empire. Historical records suggest that the highly centralized Ottoman state responded to natural hazards on a case-by-case basis and in a top-down manner in the aftermath of disasters. In cases of major disasters, imperial orders were issued by the Ottoman sultans on disaster relief and housing reconstruction, including occasionally on disaster mitigation. For instance, Sultan Beyazit II issued an imperial order for the reconstruction of Istanbul after a major earthquake took place on September 14, 1509, which killed 13,000 people and razed 1,047 buildings and 109 mosques in the city (TBMM 1999). The order conscripted 50,000 workers for the reconstruction, mainly between the ages of 14 and 60 years. It banned construction on reclaimed land. It encouraged construction of wooden houses (*ahsap karkas-bagdadi*) that could stand earthquakes. Moreover, the imperial order suggested that each family affected by the quake was to be given 20 gold coins for reconstructing their homes. Within six months of the earthquake, 2000 homes were reconstructed and several mosques were repaired in Istanbul (TBMM 1999). Such a direct paternalistic intervention of the state continued even after the Republic of Turkey replaced the Ottoman Empire.

Four periods could be identified in the evolution of the disaster management structure from a reactive one to a proactive one since the establishment of the Republic in 1923: period I (1923–1942), period II (1943–1952), period III (1953 to August 1999), and period IV (since August 1999).*

During period I (1923–1942), there was a reactive approach to disasters, in which the government responded to disasters on a case-specific basis and only after the fact. In other words, the focus of disaster management was on response and

---

* Other studies use different periods. For instance, TBMM (1999) uses three periods: Pre-1944, 1944–1958, and 1958 to present. JICA (2004) also uses the same time periods as TBMM, but it divides 1958 to present into two more, namely 1958–1999 and post-1999. Thus, JICA uses four periods, each of which is termed as (i) post-event response, (ii) feeble countermeasures, (iii) ministry responsible for disasters and construction, and (iv) awakening, respectively.

recovery as opposed to preparedness and mitigation. Following the Erzincan earthquake in 1939, the government passed its first law on disasters on January 17, 1940. Called "Law on Assistance to Those Who Suffered from Damages in Erzincan and in Areas Affected by Erzincan Earthquake" (Law No. 3773), this law provided disaster victims with tax relief, financial aid, land, and construction materials. However, it did not include any measures on preparedness or mitigation in case of a future disaster event. It is possible to argue that some planning laws of this period, such as the 1933 Municipality Construction and Road Law (Law No. 2290), had an indirect impact on mitigation. Although Law No. 2290 did not include any clause on disaster mitigation per se, it made it mandatory for local governments to prepare settlement plans and detailed issues related to inspection of construction.

During period II (1943–1952), the first proactive disaster laws of the Republic were introduced. The first such law was passed in 1943 in the aftermath of a number of floods that had taken place between 1935 and 1943. It was called "Precautions for Prevention of Floods and Underground Waters" (Law No. 4373).* The law on floods was followed in 1944 by another proactive law on earthquakes called "Law on Precautions to be Taken Before and After Earthquakes" (Law No. 4623). Similar to the law on floods, the law on earthquakes was introduced following a series of earthquakes that had claimed more than 10,000 lives and destroyed close to 100,000 buildings together.[†]

Law No. 4623 was indeed the first comprehensive law on earthquake preparedness and mitigation in the country.[‡] When this law was passed in Turkey, there were only two other countries that had similar disaster laws. These were Japan (with its 1924 Urban Building Law, which introduced provisions related to seismic safety of buildings) and Italy (with its 1909 Royal Decree No. 193 [R.D. 193/1909], which specified construction details and building dimensions).[§] The state of California had also introduced its 1933 Field Act, which required that all public school buildings be earthquake resistant (TBMM 1999).[¶]

---

* A directorate for hydraulic works was established in the same year.
[†] These earthquakes included those in Erbaa-Tokat (1942), Hendek-Adapazari (1943), Ladik-Samsun (1943), and Gerede-Cerkes-Bolu (1944).
[‡] According to a JICA report (2004: 38), the importance of this law gradually diminished in the 1950s due to other pressures on Turkey, such as rapid population growth, urbanization, agricultural modernization, and industrialization.
[§] In Japan, the law was introduced in the aftermath of 1923 Great Kanto earthquake which claimed about 140,000 lives. In Italy, the decree was introduced in the aftermath of 1908 Messina Straits earthquake which claimed about 80,000 lives.
[¶] TBMM (1999) suggests that three countries had similar disaster laws before Law No. 4623 was passed in Turkey. These countries are listed as Japan (1924), the United States (1933), and Italy (1940). However, the United States as a whole did not have such law at the time; rather, disaster legislation was limited to California alone.

During period III (1953 to August 1999), there was emergence of an organizational structure for disaster management in Turkey. The first governmental unit related to disasters, the Earthquake Bureau, was established in 1953 under the auspices of the Department of Construction and Settlement Works (the Ministry of Public Works) to mitigate earthquake risks in the country. It was then restructured and renamed several times. Another disaster management organization which emerged in the 1950s, was the General Directorate of Civil Defense under the (Ministry of Home Affairs). The directorate and its local branches were established in 1958 with Law on Civil Defense (Law No. 7126), and they were given the tasks of disaster response and preparedness.

The organizational structuring was accompanied by further refinement of the institutional structure. During this period, the most important institutional development was the introduction of an umbrella law on disasters in 1959, namely Law on Measures and Assistance to be Put into Effect Regarding Disasters Affecting the Life of the General Public (Law No. 7269, also referred to as the Disaster Law). This law put together different laws on disasters and formed the legal basis for different phases of disaster management. Although the law has been modified several times since then, it is still in effect.*

Another significant law of the 1950s was the Settlement Law (Law No. 6785), which overrode the 1933 Municipality Construction and Road Law of the earlier period. The Settlement Law was put into effect in 1959, and had an impact on mitigation practices in the country. It paid special attention to the importance of inspection of construction and identification of areas prone to hazards in determining settlement areas (METU 1998: 1–3, 1–4). The Settlement Law was later replaced by the Development Law (Law No. 3194) in 1985.†

During period IV (August 1999 till present), several organizational and institutional reforms have been introduced towards a less paternalistic and more proactive approach in disaster management structure. Before the August 17, 1999 earthquake, the state—especially the central government—was fully in charge of disaster management in Turkey. The provincial and district governments, arms of the central

---

* The law was modified, for instance, in 1960 (Law No. 74), 1968 (Law No. 1051), 1981 (Law No. 2479), 1985 (Law No. 3177), 2001 (Official Gazette No. 24600), and 2001 (Law No. 4684).

† In addition to these laws, a number of other disaster-related laws and regulations were introduced during this period. They include the following: (1) a decree specifying the criteria for declaring disasters in 1968 (Official Gazette No. 13007); (2) a decree detailing the procedures for spending from the Disaster Fund in 1970 (Official Gazette No. 13517); (3) a law establishing a separate earthquake fund in 1972 (Law No. 157); (4) a decree outlining the emergency assistance organizational structure in 1988 (Law No. 88/12777); (5) a law outlining the procedures of distribution of financial aid to areas affected by disasters in 1995 (Law No. 4123); (6) a decree detailing the design principles for earthquake resistant buildings in 1997 (Official Gazette No. 23098); and (7) instructions explaining the procedures to be followed by municipalities affected by disaster in 1999 (Law No. 4123).

government, were mainly in charge of disaster preparedness and emergency response and rescue periods. The central government had a free hand in disaster recovery. It also designed mitigation policies, which were implemented by the provincial governments and local governments within their jurisdictions. The private sector had no legal role to play in this disaster management structure. The roles that could be played by NGOs were also not acknowledged, except for the Turkish Red Crescent Society called Kizilay (Turkish counterpart of Red Cross), which is a nongovernmental agency that has the legal duty of providing support function to government agencies in cases of disasters (as described later).

The state was also like a paternal figure whose responsibility was to look after the disaster victims. In line with his role, it constructed permanent housing and business units for disaster victims whose units were completely destroyed or were heavily damaged. It distributed funds to disaster victims for retrofitting slight- and medium-damaged housing and business units. According to a JICA report (2004: 98), the state gave assurances to the people that "the all-powerful state will eventually replace all lost property, rebuild every shop, and rehabilitate effected [*sic*] economic investments through low-interest loans, debts annulments and free credits." Homeowners or small businesses had no incentive to purchase disaster insurance because the state guaranteed the eventual replacement of their lost property.*

Since the August 17, 1999 earthquake, the Turkish state has moved away from this traditional paternalistic approach to disaster management. It has reallocated the responsibility of construction inspection from local governments to private Building

---

* It is possible to argue that the paternalistic nature of the disaster management structure was a reflection of historical trends of the Turkish state. The Turkish state has traditionally been strong. The roots of this tradition indeed date back to the Ottoman Empire (Heper 1985). The Ottoman Empire emerged in the thirteenth century as a federation of small tribes, with minimal power in the center. Ottoman sultans, however, centralized power starting from the fifteenth century through unique institutions they developed (particularly with respect to land management and recruitment of the ruling class). Even after the replacement of the Empire with the modern Republic of Turkey in 1923, the Turkish state remained a strong one. Ataturk, the founder of the Republic, gave the Turkish state a very important task: to guide the new republic in its modernization (i.e., westernization) process from above. His thinking was reflected in his principle of etatism (statism). Etatism referred, in the broader sense, to a strategy of state intervention in all aspects of life. It implied that the state must take charge and impose radical measures, if necessary, for the greater public good. The historically strong Turkish state has also been paternalistic since the Ottoman Empire. The Ottoman sultans regarded the masses "as 'God's property' and adopted a benevolent attitude towards them" (Karpat 1973: 21). They were considered as paternal figures for the masses, personally responsible for their welfare (Mardin 1969: 260). The notion of a paternal state continued to persist among the masses even after the break up of the empire, as expressed in such current folk expressions as Devlet Baba (Father State) or memleket cocuklari (children of the nation). The Turkish state replaced the Sultan as a paternal figure. Its role was considered be to "provide for, look after, and protect the common men, to be accessible, to dispense and maintain an orderly society" (Dodd 1979: 70).

Inspection Firms (BIFs) (Law on Building Inspection, No. 4708, 2000; Decree on Procedures and Principles for Construction Inspection, No. 24491, 2000). It has acknowledged that NGOs, especially voluntary search and rescue teams, could play important roles in preparing for disasters and saving lives during the emergency response and rescue period (Ministry of Home Affairs' Directive on Conditions of Participation of Volunteers in Civil Defense Service, 2000).

In addition, partly due to the realization that reconstruction of permanent housing and business units in the aftermath of major disasters is quite costly to the government, the state stepped back from direct dole outs to disaster victims. Rather, it introduced a mandatory earthquake insurance scheme (Decree with the Power of Law on the Mandatory Earthquake Insurance, No. 587, 1999; Decree on Working Procedures and Principles of Natural Disasters Insurance Administration, No. 246000, 2001). This scheme requires that homeowners—except those located in rural areas—insure their property against earthquake disasters by paying mandatory annual premiums to the newly established Natural Disasters Insurance Administration (under the Treasury) so that they could be entitled to receive permanent housing or subsidies for housing repair from the government.

All these measures introduced in the aftermath of the August 17, 1999 earthquake indicated a move away from the traditional paternalistic nature of Turkish disaster management structure. The measures were also proactive in nature. Several other proactive laws were introduced during this period as well. For instance, the response capacity of the Ministry of Home Affairs, which houses the government's search and rescue teams, has been enhanced with the establishment of provincial directorates of civil defense in selected provinces (Decree with the Power of Law on Directorates of Civil Defense for Search and Rescue Attached to the Ministry of Home Affairs, No. 586 and 596, 2000). Local governments, whose involvement was legally limited to mitigating disasters before the August 17, 1999 earthquake, have been given supportive tasks with respect to disaster preparedness as well as emergency response and rescue phases of disasters (Law on Municipalities, No: 5272, 2004). A new governmental unit called the General Directory of Emergency Management (attached to the Prime Minister's Office) has been established to undertake disaster mitigation measures (Decree with the Power of Law on Acceptance of the Decree on Organization of the Prime Minister's Office with Amendment, No. 583, 1999). An independent earthquake council has been established to identify priority research areas for disaster mitigation and to scientifically assess earthquake predictions (Mandate on the Establishment of the Independent National Earthquake Council, No. 2000/9, 2000). Furthermore, professional competence standards of engineers and architects involved in construction have been enhanced (Decree with the Power of Law on Changes Related to Laws Concerning Engineering and Architecture and Turkish Union of Chambers of Engineers and Architects, No. 601, 2000). In spite of these proactive measures which were introduced during period IV, however, there are several shortcomings in the current disaster management structure, as detailed below.

Current Disaster Management Structure in Turkey

There is little clarity with respect to the current organizational structure of disaster management in Turkey. As shown in Table 14.6, the structure is based on a number of different laws and regulations related to disasters. Several governmental units at the central, provincial, district, and local levels are involved in different aspects of disaster management. These units include disaster-related departments of certain ministries, the Prime Minister's Office, provincial and district governments, local governments, the Turkish Red Crescent Society, and the Turkish armed forces. There is no single national office with the authority and resources to coordinate disaster management activities of all these units. Instead, a number of governmental units at the central level have coordinative functions—sometimes with overlapping responsibilities—in different phases of disasters.

In general, disaster management in Turkey is quite hierarchical and centralized, with much of the onus going to the central rather than to local governments. Table 14.7 summarizes the responsibilities of all governmental units (at the central, district, and local levels), NGOs, and private firms (e.g., BIFs) in disaster management based on laws and regulations that are still in effect. The roles of different units are further detailed below according to four phases of disasters (disaster preparedness, emergency response and rescue, disaster recovery, and disaster mitigation).

Disaster Preparedness

The key organizational units involved in disaster preparedness phase in Turkey include provincial and district level governments. Both are mandated by law to have rescue and aid committees (RACs) headed by governors (*Valis*) in the provinces and by district heads (*Kaymakams*) in the districts. These committees have the duty of preparing for and responding to emergencies. They include heads of various provincial or district departments, and representatives from the armed forces and the Turkish Red Crescent Society. RACs prepare Emergency Assistance Plans for their jurisdictions. In this, the plans prepared by provincial and district governments are reviewed by the RACs at the provincial level and approved by the governors. To respond to disasters in an effective manner, RACs are legally required to undertake preparedness training and drills for personnel in units that are involved in the emergency response and rescue phase.*

---

* In addition, the Ministry of Public Works and Settlement houses the European Disaster Training Centre called Avrupa Dogal Afetler Egitim Merkezi (AFEM), which provides disaster training for government personnel. AFEM is a nonprofit organization established in 1988. The agency receives funding from the European Open Partial Agreement (OPA) budget, Turkish Government, and international organizations. It offers courses on disaster preparedness and management and undertakes activities to educate the public. According to a JICA report (2004: 43), AFEM is currently inactive because of changing policies of the Ministry on public education programs.

Table 14.6 Selected Current Laws and Regulations Related to Disaster Management in Turkey

Law/Regulation and Attendant Regulations (English)	Official Gazette/ Effective Date	Law/Regulation Implementing Body	Organizational Focus	Details
Decree on Basic Principles Related to Disasters Affecting the Life of the General Public	Official Gazette No. 13007, dated September 21, 1968	Ministry of Public Works and Settlement (MPWS)	Ministry of Public Works and Settlement	It outlines basic criteria to be used in declaring disasters, such as the number of buildings damaged, death toll, number of injured, and damage to agricultural crops.
Decree on Design Principles for Buildings in Disaster Regions	Official Gazette No. 23098, dated March 6, 2006	Ministry of Public Works and Settlement	Ministry of Public Works and Settlement	It specifies principles for designing earthquake resistant buildings as well as for retrofitting.
Decree on Working Procedures and Principles of Natural Disasters Insurance Administration	Official Gazette No. 24600, dated December 1, 2001	Treasury	Natural Disasters Insurance Administration (under the auspices of the Treasury)	It outlines the responsibilities of the Natural Disasters Insurance Administration as well its working procedures and principles.
Decree with Power of Law on Acceptance of Decree on Organization of	Official Gazette No. 23884, dated November 22, 1999	Council of Ministers	General Directorate of Emergency Management (GDEM) (under the auspices of	It establishes the General Directorate of Emergency Management and describes its responsibilities.

Law	Official Gazette		Responsible Agency	Description
Prime Minister's Office, with Amendment (No. 583 and 600)			the Prime Minister's Office)	
Decree with the Power of Law on Organization and Duties of the Ministry of Public Works and Settlement (No. 180)	Official Gazette No. 18251, dated December 14, 1983	Council of Ministers	Ministry of Public Works and Settlement	It describes overall responsibilities of the ministry and its organizational structure. It also details the specific tasks of organizational units of the ministry.
Decree with Power of Law on the Obligatory Earthquake Insurance (No. 587)	Official Gazette No. 23919, dated December 27, 1999	Council of Ministers	Natural Disasters Insurance Administration (under the auspices of the Treasury)	It establishes the responsibilities of the Natural Disasters Insurance Administration and details how it is governed. It also describes the earthquake insurance requirement.
Development Law (No. 3194)	Official Gazette No. 18749, dated May 9, 1985	Council of Ministers	Ministry of Public Works and Settlement, State Planning Organization, Provincial Governments, Local Governments	It outlines principles of preparation and implementation of plans for settlements, building construction, and building permits by local and provincial governments. It also outlines role of Ministry of Public Works and Settlement regarding settlement plans, and that of State Planning Organization regarding regional plans.

(continued)

Table 14.6 (continued) Selected Current Laws and Regulations Related to Disaster Management in Turkey

Law/Regulation and Attendant Regulations (English/Turkish)	Official Gazette/ Effective Date	Law/Regulation Implementing Body	Organizational Focus	Details
Law on Building Inspection (No. 4708)	Official Gazette No. 24461, dated July 13, 2001	Council of Ministers	Ministry of Public Works and Settlement, Provincial Governments, Local Governments, Building Inspection Firms (BIFs)	It details the responsibilities of Building Inspection Firms and Inspection Committees. It also has sections on oversight of BIFs.
Law on Civil Defense (No. 7126)	Official Gazette No. 9931, dated June 13, 1958	Grand National Assembly	General Directorate of Civil Defense (under the auspices of the Ministry of Home Affairs)	It establishes the General Directorate of Civil Defense under the Ministry and describes the responsibilities of the directorate and its local branches. It also addresses the issues of training on civil defense.
Law on Measures and Assistance to be Put into Effect Regarding Disasters Affecting the Life of the General Public (No. 7269)	Official Gazette No. 10213, dated May 25, 1959	Grand National Assembly	Council of Ministers, Ministry of Public Works and Settlement, Provincial and District Governments	It details extraordinary powers given to provincial governors and district heads and responsibilities of other key players in cases of disasters. It also includes statements on relocation of settlements.

Law on Municipalities (No. 5272)	Official Gazette No. 25680, dated December 24, 2004	Council of Ministers	Local Governments	It establishes the responsibilities of municipalities and describes their organizational structure. It also details their budget arrangements.
Law on Organization and Duties of the Ministry of Home Affairs (No. 3152)	Official Gazette No. 18675, dated February 23, 1985	Council of Ministers	Ministry of Home Affairs	It describes overall responsibilities of the ministry and its organizational structure. It also details the specific tasks of organizational units of the ministry, including the General Directorate of Civil Defense.
Mandate on Establishment of the Independent National Earthquake Council (No. 2000/9)	March 21, 2000	Scientific and Technical Research Council of Turkey (TUBITAK)	National Earthquake Council	It establishes the National Earthquake Council and describes its composition and responsibilities.

Table 14.7 Organizational Responsibilities for Different Phases of Disasters

Level of Government	Agency	Prepared Phase	Response Phase	Recovery Phase	Mitigation Phase
Central government/Prime Minister's Office	General Directorate of Emergency Management		C		C
	Central Disaster Coordination Council		C		
	Crisis Management Center		C		
Central government/Others	Ministry of Public Works and Settlement (various directorates)	P	C	P	P
	Ministry of Home Affairs (General Directorate of Civil Defence)	S	S	S	
	Treasury (Natural Disaster Insurance Administration)			P	
	Provincial/district governments[a]	P	P		P

Local governments		S	S	S	
Others	Turkish Red Crescent Society (NGO with special status)	S	S	S	
	Armed forces	S	S		
	National Earthquake Council (Independent)				S
	Building Inspection Firms (Private)				S
	Civil Defense Volunteers (nongovernmental organizations [NGOs])	S	S		

Note: Tables 14.7–14.11 are not necessarily comprehensive in depicting the role of all agencies involved in preparing for and responding to disasters. They illustrate how the responsibilities can be summarized based on existing disaster-related laws and regulations rather than on practices per se. Also, the tables do not include "state of emergency" situations that are declared by the Council of Ministers.

[a] Provincial/district governments are under "central government" because they are the arms of the central government.

P: primary responsibility; S: support responsibility; C: coordinating responsibility.

Three other organizations traditionally play important roles in disaster preparedness. These are the General Directorate of Civil Defense under the auspices of the Ministry of Home Affairs, the Turkish Red Crescent Society, and the Turkish armed forces. The provincial and district level branches of the General Directorate of Civil Defense prepare "Civil Defense Plans" in collaboration with RACs. Implementation of these plans is overseen by the directorate's central office in Ankara. The directorate and its branches undertake civil defense training and drills for disaster preparedness. In addition, they have the legal responsibility of educating the public about disasters.* Turkish Red Crescent Society is an NGO with a special status due to its role in disasters.† It formulates Disaster Preparedness and Intervention Plans at the national, regional, and local levels in preparation of emergencies. It has several facilities that support its emergency operations. These include a tent production facility and storage facilities for logistic support (a central storage in Ankara and satellite storages in seven other provinces). Turkish armed forces develop their own plans called Military Emergency Assistance Plans in coordination with the provincial and district governments. These plans are revised every year and approved by the Land Forces Command. The armed forces also have logistic support coordination centers to ensure timely response to emergencies.

Until the August 17, 1999 earthquake, local governments and NGOs other than the Turkish Red Crescent Society had no legal role to play in disaster preparedness. Since the earthquake, new laws and regulations have been introduced to include their participation. Local governments are now responsible for making disaster and state of emergency plans, and that they can have programs to educate the public on disasters (Law on Municipalities, No. 5272, 2004). Volunteer search and rescue teams can take part in training and drills undertaken by the General Directorate of Civil Defense (Directive on Conditions of Participation of Volunteers in Civil Defense Service by the Ministry of Home Affairs, 2000). Table 14.8 summarizes the key aspects of the organizational structure for disaster preparedness phase in Turkey.

As the above description shows, provincial and district government units and their RACs play an important role in disaster preparedness phase. Their role raises two major concerns. First, provincial governors and district heads are not elected officials in Turkey. Rather, they are appointed by the central government and considered as civil servants. They have a high turnover rate, and, in most cases,

---

* As per 1985 Law on Organization and Duties of the Ministry of Home Affairs (No. 3152).
† Although the Turkish Red Crescent Society is an NGO, it has a special status compared to other associations, mainly due to its role in disasters. It was established in 1868 under the name of "Society for Helping Sick and Wounded Ottoman Soldiers." Its activities prior to 1924 focused on victims of war and immigrants. The organization was renamed as the Turkish Red Crescent Union after the establishment of the Turkish Republic in 1923, and it joined the International Confederation of Red Cross in 1930. In 1947, it assumed the present name. The society has 650 branches in the country (JICA 2004: 66).

Table 14.8   Organizational Structure for Disaster Preparedness Phase in Turkey

Level of Government	Responsibility	Agency
Central government/ Other	Primary	Ministry of Public Works and Settlement (General Directorate of Disaster Affairs) ■ Ensures that Emergency Assistance Plans are up to date ■ Educates the public and government personnel on disasters
	Supportive	Ministry of Home Affairs (General Directorate of Civil Defense) ■ Provincial and district branches prepare "Civil Defense Plans" in coordination with Rescue and Aid Committees (RACs) at the provincial and district levels ■ General Directorate of Civil Defense in Ankara oversees implementation of Civil Defense Plans, undertakes civil defense training and drills, educates the public about disasters
	Primary	Provincial and District Governments ■ Form Rescue and Aid Committees and prepare Emergency Assistance Plans ■ Undertake training and drills
Local governments	Supportive	Municipalities ■ Prepare "Disaster Plans"
Others	Supportive	Turkish Red Crescent Society ■ Prepares "Disaster Preparedness and Intervention Plans" at the national, regional, and local levels ■ Has logistic support centers and production facilities

(*continued*)

302 ■ Disaster Management Handbook

Table 14.8 (continued) Organizational Structure for Disaster Preparedness Phase in Turkey

Level of Government	Responsibility	Agency
	Supportive	Armed forces ■ Prepare "Military Assistance Plans" (approved by Land Forces Command) in coordination with the "Rescue and Aid Committees" ■ Have logistic support centers
	Supportive	Civil Defense Volunteers ■ Can take part in the General Directorate of Civil Defense training and drills at the district and provincial levels

they are unfamiliar with the local conditions as opposed to popularly elected mayors (JICA 2004: 98). The participation of mayors or of other local government representatives in RACs is not required by law. Second, the responsibility of ensuring the currency of emergency assistance plans prepared by provincial and district RACs lies with the General Directorate of Disaster Affairs within the MPWS. This constitutes a problem since provincial and district governments are affiliated with another ministry, the Ministry of Home Affairs.

There are several other problems with respect to disaster preparedness in Turkey. For instance, while the responsibilities for disaster preparedness are fragmented, there is no single governmental unit at the central level, which is legally in charge of coordinating disaster preparedness activities in the country. Although some argue that the General Directorate of Emergency Management (GDEM) under the auspices of the Prime Minister's Office (established in the aftermath of the August 17, 1999 earthquake) is responsible for coordination of disaster preparedness at the central level, existing laws and regulations do not assign such task to the agency. The agency's coordinative functions are legally limited to emergency response and disaster mitigation phases.

Another problem with respect to disaster preparedness is that while there are several emergency plans prepared by different agencies at the local, district, and provincial levels involved in disaster preparedness phase, there is no national level disaster preparedness plan. A national plan, similar to those in the United States (National Response Plan) or Japan (Basic Disaster Management Plan), is necessary to provide operational direction and enable effective interaction among governmental units at the central, provincial, district, and local levels; private sector; and the NGOs during large-scale emergencies.

Emergency Response and Rescue

The key organizational units involved in emergency response and rescue phase of disasters in the country include provincial and district level governments, whose RACs implement the Emergency Assistance Plans in this period. To undertake their tasks, provincial RACs are divided into nine subcommittees with different responsibilities (communications, accessibility/transportation, search and debris removal, first aid and medical services, damage assessment and temporary shelter, security, purchase–rental distribution, agricultural services, and electricity–water sewer). In implementing the Emergency Assistance Plans, governors and district heads—the heads of RACs—are required to rely on public resources initially and request additional assistance, if required, from nearby provinces, armed forces, or private companies/individuals.*

To cope with the emergencies, both provincial governors and district heads are granted extraordinary powers that could be exercised within 15 days of the disaster, as detailed in the 1988 Decree on Emergency Assistance Organization and Planning Related to Disasters (No. 88/12,777). These powers include the following: (1) to mobilize and assign tasks to men between the age of 18 and 65 (except military officers and judges); (ii) to confiscate public and private land, buildings, vehicles (including live animals), equipment, or any other needs of the public (e.g., food, medicine, clothes); and (iii) to utilize necessary equipment for emergency communication and mobilization of emergency assistance, such as phones, radios, and TV stations.

Governors and district heads are mandated to implement a state of emergency, if it is as declared by the Council of Ministers in the case of a disaster. The council is headed by the prime minister, and it could declare the state of emergency only after consulting with the National Security Council and getting Parliament's approval.†
A state of emergency could be declared under any one of four circumstances, which

---

* Military officials need to follow the orders of governors and district heads without waiting for consent of their commanders in cases of emergencies.
† Until recently, National Security Council was a constitutionally mandated body chaired by the President of Turkey. It was composed of civilian (e.g., ministers) and military officials. The Council gave the generals a chance to present their views on a wide range of issues and to influence the policies of the civilian government. As part of the reforms undertaken by Turkey to join the European Union, the Council ceased to be an executive body, and became a purely advisory one. Political representation on the Council was increased, and its governance (i.e., the secretariat) was handed over to the civilian administration.

includes natural disasters (the others being dangerous epidemics, economic crisis, and violence against the democratic order and fundamental rights). The duration of an emergency period could be up to six months and could be extended in blocks of four months. During a state of emergency, the council could issue decrees with the force of law on matters related to the state of emergency without prior authorization from the Parliament.* Governors enjoy more or less similar authority under a state of emergency except that they could request and have command over armed forces, which are authorized to use force (e.g., use of weapons).

In addition to the provincial and district governments, the General Directorate of Civil Defense, Turkish Red Crescent Society, and the Turkish armed forces also play important roles in emergency response and rescue period. In emergencies, the General Directorate of Civil Defense undertakes search and rescue, and provides first aid, food, and temporary shelter in accordance with their Civil Defense Plans. It also tracks disaster-related deaths and missing persons, controls traffic, provides security and prevents looting in disaster areas. In addition to its central office in Ankara and provincial/district level branches throughout the country, the agency has 11 Directorates of Civil Defense and Rescue and Emergency in selected provinces (established in the aftermath of the August 17, 1999 earthquake) to undertake search and rescue activities in disaster-stricken areas.

Turkish Red Crescent Society provides first aid and health services, and distributes tents and other immediate basic needs (e.g., food, blankets) to disaster victims in accordance with its disaster preparedness and intervention plans. The armed forces implement Military Emergency Assistance Plans and undertakes functions similar to the General Directorate of Civil Defense and Turkish Red Crescent Society in the immediate aftermath of disasters. These functions include carrying out search and rescue activities and providing services related to security, health, temporary shelters, transportation, communication, and basic needs of disaster victims. The armed forces has 17 Regional Disaster Commands, and they house Natural Disasters Search/Rescue Battalions (established in the aftermath of the August 17, 1999 earthquake) to respond to emergencies. Battalions are subordinate

---

* In a state of emergency, coordination is undertaken at the top level by the State of Emergency Council under the Prime Minister's Office. If an emergency is declared due to a natural disaster, the State of Emergency Council is headed by the prime minister. It includes such members as the Ministers of Public Works and Resettlement, Health, Forestry and Agriculture, Industry and Commerce, and Energy and Natural Resources as well as the General Director of the Turkish Red Crescent Society and the Secretary of the National Security Council. At the regional level, coordination is achieved by the Regional State of Emergency Council, which is headed by the regional governor and includes provincial governors, garrison commander, and other public officials. The regional governor has the authority to request help from government agencies and establish State of Emergency Bureaus in the provinces. See the 1983 Law on State of Emergency (No. 2935) and the 1984 Decree on State of Emergency Council (No. 84/7778) for details on state of emergency situations.

to Special Forces Command, and they are composed of a battalion headquarter and three search/rescue units.*

A number of ministries, government agencies, and the Prime Minister's Office are also mandated by law to be involved in different capacities during the emergency response and rescue period. For instance, Ministry of Foreign Affairs coordinates foreign aid and aid workers. Ministry of Health undertakes first aid and health services, and it takes measures for preventing the spread of communicable diseases. Prime Minister's Office allows for import of required materials, secures gasoline in the disaster-stricken area, and undertakes measures to inform the relevant authorities as quick as possible about the disaster. In addition to these organizations, local governments implement their "disaster" and "state of emergency plans."

There is more than one unit at the central level that is in charge of overall coordination of disaster response and rescue phase of disasters. These are the General Directorate of Disaster Affairs within the MPWS, the GDEM within the Prime Minister's Office, and the Central Disaster Coordination Council. Two other units, the Crisis Management Center and State of Emergency Coordination Council within the Prime Minister's Office, may also be involved in coordination efforts depending on the context.

General Directorate of Disaster Affairs coordinates emergency assistance in cases of disasters. It also provides emergency financial aid to provincial and district governments in the disaster-stricken region. GDEM (established in the aftermath of the August 17, 1999 earthquake) is in charge of top-level coordination during response and rescue phase of disasters. In the aftermath of disasters, GDEM coordinates the following: (1) utilization of motor vehicles (air, land, and sea); (2) utilization of search and rescue equipment; and (3) receiving of and distribution of disaster aid materials. Besides, it could introduce incentives for individuals and organizations that make donations in the aftermath of disasters.

The Central Disaster Coordination Council is an ad hoc and temporary agency. It normally meets in the aftermath of disasters that affect multiple provinces. It is headed by the undersecretary of the MPWS.† Its members include undersecretaries from the ministries of national defense, foreign affairs, home affairs, finance, national education, health, transportation, agriculture and rural affairs, industry and trade, forestry, and environment.‡ In addition, the council includes the General Director of Turkish Red Crescent Society and a high-level representative from the Turkish General Staff. The council is legally mandated to provide coordination

---

* Each unit has one search dog section and six search and rescue teams that are composed of professional soldiers (e.g., officers, specialists) from the army, navy, air force, and gendarmerie (with six personnel each). The units can deploy within three hours and operate without resupply up to 15 days.

† General Directorate of Disaster Affairs functions as the secretariat for Central Disaster Coordination Center.

‡ Each of these ministries has its own disaster affair units related to its tasks as well.

among the governors and other government agencies as well as to coordinate domestic and foreign aid. It also formulates short- and long-term measures to be undertaken in disaster areas, keeps the Prime Minister's Office updated, and executes its orders.* If a state of emergency is declared by the Council of Ministers, however, top-level coordination at the central level is handled by the Prime Minister's State of Emergency Coordination Council and State of Emergency Sub-Commissions rather than by the Central Disaster Coordination Council.

The Prime Minister could also establish a Crisis Management Center, another ad hoc and temporary agency, within his or her office with regional crisis centers if he or she declares a crisis management situation. In such situations, relevant governmental units also set up their own crisis centers in their headquarters. The Crisis Management Center comprises of a Crisis Coordination Council, a Crisis Assessment and Monitoring Council, and a Secretariat. The Center is opened depending on the need for a comprehensive approach to the disaster. It could stay active during the disaster recovery period. For instance, a Crisis Management Center was formed in the aftermath of the August 17, 1999 earthquake and stayed active until late stages of the recovery efforts. Table 14.9 provides a summary of the organizational structure for disaster response phase in Turkey.

Clearly, one of the major issues with respect to emergency response and rescue phase in Turkey is that there are several central government agencies with coordinative functions. The ineffectiveness of this system became apparent in the aftermath of the August 17, 1999 earthquake. Although thousands of international and domestic voluntary organizations were willing to provide help in the aftermath of the earthquake, they could not provide emergency response and rescue activities in an effective manner, partly due to lack of coordination at the central level. Some foreign search and rescue teams, for instance, were not directed to the earthquake zone in a timely and organized manner. They had to wait at the airports or ports due to bureaucratic confusion.

There have been attempts to improve coordination during emergency response and rescue period since the earthquake, such as the establishment of the GDEM. However, these attempts were not aimed at ensuring clear-cut responsibilities in coordinating emergency response and rescue. Because the responsibilities of this directorate units are overlapping with other agencies such as the General Directorate of Disaster Affairs within the MPWS, the creation of GDEM added to the confusion as to which agency will do what in case of a disaster and to agencies stepping on each other's toes.

Another main area that requires improvement with respect to emergency response and rescue phase is support for participation of communities in responding to (and preparing for) disasters. As the disaster literature suggests, a high percentage of earthquake victims were saved and received medical help through their families,

---

* Prime Minister's Office steps in to resolve issues that cannot be done so by the Central Disaster Coordination Center.

Table 14.9   Organizational Structure of Disaster Response Phase in Turkey

Level of Government	Responsibility	Agency
Central government/ Prime Minister's Office	Coordinative	General Directorate of Emergency Management ■ Provides coordination with respect to utilization of motor vehicles and search and rescue equipment ■ Provides coordination with respect to receiving and distributing aid materials
	Coordinative	Central Disaster Coordination Council ■ An ad hoc and temporary structure that meets in the aftermath of disasters ■ Provides coordination among the provincial governors and other governmental agencies ■ Coordinates domestic and foreign aid ■ Formulates short- and long-term measures to be undertaken in the aftermath of disasters ■ Informs the Prime Minister's Office and executes its orders
	Coordinative	Crisis Management Center ■ An ad hoc and temporary structure that is established in the aftermath of disasters if a "Crisis Management" situation is declared by the prime minister ■ Could stay active during disaster recovery
Central government/ Other	Coordinative	Ministry of Public Works and Settlement (General Directorate of Disaster Affairs) ■ Coordinates emergency assistance ■ Provides emergency financial aid to provincial and district governments
	Supportive	Ministry of Home Affairs (General Directorate of Civil Defense) ■ Implements "Civil Defense Plans" ■ Undertakes search and rescue, distributes relief aid and temporary shelter ■ Tracks disaster-related deaths and missing persons ■ Controls traffic, provides security, prevents looting

(*continued*)

Table 14.9 (continued) Organizational Structure of Disaster Response Phase in Turkey

Level of Government	Responsibility	Agency
	Supportive	Ministry of Home Affairs (General Directorate of Civil Defense) ■ Implements "Civil Defense Plans" ■ Undertakes search and rescue, distributes relief aid and temporary shelter ■ Tracks disaster-related deaths and missing persons ■ Controls traffic, provides security, prevents looting
	Primary	Provincial and District Governments ■ Implement "Emergency Assistance Plans" to respond to disasters ■ Rely on public resources initially and request assistance if required ■ Governors and district heads with extraordinary powers in the aftermath of disasters
Local governments	Supportive	Municipalities ■ Implement "Disaster Plans"
Others	Supportive	Turkish Red Crescent Society ■ Implements its "Disaster Preparedness and Intervention Plans" ■ Provides first aid and health services ■ Distributes relief aid and temporary shelter
	Supportive	Turkish armed forces ■ Implements its "Military Emergency Assistance Plans" ■ Undertakes search and rescue ■ Provides services related to security, health, communications, and transportation ■ Distributes relief aid and temporary shelter
	Supportive	Civil Defense Volunteers (NGOs) ■ Undertake search and rescue

friends, and neighbors during the emergency response and rescue period of the August 17, 1999 earthquake. Since the earthquake, several communities have established voluntary search and rescue teams to provide help to their own communities and beyond in cases of emergencies. Although the central government (i.e., the Ministry of Home Affairs) now acknowledges the roles that could be played by such volunteer search and rescue teams in responding to disasters, it needs to provide more logistic and financial support to these teams. Because most of the search and rescue teams have been supported through international donors (i.e., Dutch Interchurch Aid and the Swiss Agency for Development and Cooperation) in the aftermath of the August 17, 1999 earthquake, some would not be sustainable in the long run without such support from the government.

Disaster Recovery

The key organization involved in disaster recovery phase of disasters is the MPWS. Responsibility for tasks related to disaster recovery is assigned to different units of the ministry. The General Directorate of Disaster Affairs is given the task of damage assessment as well as reconstruction and rehabilitation of damaged housing, work places, and infrastructural facilities. The directorate also disburses emergency assistance funding to disaster victims, such as aid for housing repairs and reconstruction, and rental aid. In addition, the directorate is the primary unit in charge of temporary housing. It has regional centers for production and storage of prefabricated buildings to accommodate disaster victims.

The General Directorate of Construction Affairs within the MPWS is the primary unit in charge of preparation of plans and construction of permanent housing areas and their infrastructure. The unit may also be involved in the preparation of regional and urban plans in areas affected by disasters. General Directorate of Highways, another unit of the ministry, is involved in the rehabilitation of existing roads and construction of new roads to permanent housing areas in the aftermath of disasters. General Directorate of the Bank of Provinces, a development and investment bank affiliated with the ministry, provides financing for reconstruction and rehabilitation of the infrastructure (e.g., water distribution networks, water treatment plants, sewerage systems, and waste water treatment plans).*

In the aftermath of disasters, settlements or parts of settlements could be relocated, if necessary.† Relocation decisions are taken by a committee composed of representatives from the MPWS and from the ministries of home affairs, finance, health, agriculture, education, and industry. Legally, local governments and residents

---

* In addition to undertaking its banking operations, the Bank's major function is to provide financial and technical assistance to local authorities in Turkey.
† Relocation of settlements could take place before a disaster occurs as well (for mitigation purposes).

are not required to be involved in the relocation decision. These decisions are typically imposed from above. If the area where the settlement is being relocated to is within the same administrative boundary, then the committee's decision is approved by the MPWS and the Ministry of Home Affairs. If it is not, the decision needs to be approved by the Council of Ministers. The responsibility for implementation of relocation decisions is given to the MPWS. For relocation purposes, the MPWS has the authority to confiscate property on behalf of the Treasury by using eminent domain. The ministry can also acquire land or buildings that belong to the Treasury or to the local governments.

In addition to the MPWS and its units, other central government units are involved in disaster recovery period. The Ministry of Education is responsible for the repairs of damaged schools, and it could allocate schools as temporary shelters, if required. Ministry of Transportation repairs rail tracks, airports, and ports. Ministry of Industry and Commerce provides financial aid for repairing public and private industrial establishments. Ministry of Energy and Natural Resources restores electricity in the aftermath of disasters. If foreign aid is involved, governmental units other than MPWS may be involved in the design and construction of permanent housing areas. For instance, in the aftermath of the August 17, 1999 earthquake, Project Implementation Unit (under the auspices of the Prime Minister's Office) was given the responsibility for constructing permanent housing areas that were financed by the World Bank.

Although there is a multiplicity of coordinative agencies during the response and rescue phase, there is no single agency mandated to undertake the overall coordination during disaster recovery phase. The Central Disaster Coordination Council or the Crisis Management Center, however, may undertake the responsibility to coordinate if formed and active during this period. Table 14.10 outlines the organizational structure during disaster recovery phase in Turkey.

Major weaknesses related to the disaster recovery phase in Turkey are twofold. The first is the lack of a coordinative agency as mentioned before. The second is the exclusion of local governments and communities from disaster recovery processes. Although the central government (especially the MPWS) has a large role to play in this phase of disasters, local governments that are familiar with local conditions have almost no legal role with respect to reconstruction activities (e.g., reconstruction of permanent housing and business units or relocation of settlements). Furthermore, there is no provision in current disaster or development laws that mandate participation of disaster victims in disaster recovery phase.

Development Law (Law No. 3194) indeed mandates that local governments with a population of 10,000 or more need to prepare, approve, and implement local-level settlement plans within their jurisdictions in Turkey. The MPWS is normally not involved in local-level plans but it is involved in large-scale plans, such as territorial and regional plans (e.g., 1/25,000 and 1/100,000 scale). However, Article 8 of the Development Law allows the Ministry to intervene in the preparation and revision of plans that relate to disasters affecting the life of general public.

Table 14.10   Organizational Structure of Disaster Recovery Phase in Turkey

Level of Government	Responsibility	Agency
Central government/ Other	Primary	Ministry of Public Works and Settlement ■ Damages assessment ■ Reconstructs and rehabilitates damaged housing, work places, and infrastructure ■ Disburses aid to disaster victims ■ Responsible from temporary and permanent housing ■ Prepares regional plans (and sometimes urban plans) for areas disaster-stricken areas ■ Approves decisions of relocation committee for settlements (in collaboration with the Ministry of Home Affairs) if the settlement is being located to an area within the same administrative boundaries ■ Confiscates property on behalf of the Treasury
	Supportive	Ministry of Home Affairs ■ Approves decisions of relocation committee for settlements (in collaboration with the Ministry of Public Works and Settlement) if the settlement is being located to an area within the same administrative boundaries
	Primary	Treasury (Natural Disaster Insurance Administration) ■ Collects mandatory earthquake insurance from homeowners under its the Turkish Catastrophe Insurance Pool before disasters ■ Pays for building damages caused by earthquakes or other disasters triggered by earthquakes (including for construction of permanent housing) for households with insurance coverage
Local governments	Supportive	Municipalities ■ Could prepare urban plans if there is no intervention by the central government

In the aftermath of the August 17, 1999 earthquake, the Ministry used the authority granted by this article. It announced within six days of the earthquake that it would prepare local-level plans as well as the plans for permanent housing areas in provinces that had high death toll and property damage from the earthquake. The Ministry's move essentially implied that local governments and earthquake victims were divorced from the disaster recovery processes. Disaster laws and regulations in the country need to address this issue and enable local governments and earthquake victims to participate in disaster recovery processes because they are nearest to the disaster location and know the local conditions the best.

Disaster Mitigation

Ministry of Public Works and Settlement is the main organization that designs mitigation policies in Turkey. Within the Ministry, the General Directorate of Disaster Affairs determines high-risk areas prone to disasters (e.g., areas subject to liquefaction, landslides, avalanches, floods, etc.) and undertakes necessary precautions for mitigating risks, as noted in the 1983 Decree on Organization and Duties of the Ministry of Reconstruction and Public Works (No. 180).* The directorate also prepares earthquake hazard maps for the country. Another directorate within the ministry, namely General Directorate of Technical Research and Implementation, undertakes research on disasters and reduction of disaster losses. In addition, this directorate prepares the building code and standards for construction in disaster-prone areas, including the standards for emergency shelters.

Although mitigation policies are developed by the MPWS, key organizations involved in the implementation of these policies are local, district, and provincial governments. Enforcement of building codes and other standards related to urban development and planning—including regulations on earthquake resistant design—within municipal boundaries is the responsibility of local governments that are governed by popularly elected mayors. Local governments are also mandated to take measures in high-risk areas (e.g., restricting of construction in high-risk areas which are not suitable for construction). Implementation of building codes and standards outside the municipal boundaries, however, is left to provincial and district governments. These authorities also have the power to demolish buildings in areas determined by the MPWS to be high risk.[†]

---

* Areas subject to floods, however, are determined by the State Water Works.
[†] According to JICA (2004: 106), there is an overlapping authority with respect to enforcement of codes. Although development law states that seismic regulations are enforced by local and provincial governments, the 1988 "Regulation for Buildings to be Constructed in Disaster Areas" states that the enforcement will be undertaken by the Minister of Public Works and Settlement.

In the aftermath of the August 17, 1999 earthquake, private BIFs were introduced as key players in the implementation of mitigation policies, mainly because of the central government's belief that the local governments had faltered in inspecting construction practices. BIF services are now mandatory for all new buildings (except public ones) in 19 pilot provinces.* The fees for these services are regulated by the government. BIFs are entitled to inspect all construction projects and report to local or provincial governments—depending on the jurisdiction—for issuance of construction and occupancy permits. The firms are directly responsible for the structural defects of the buildings (e.g., liable for payment of compensation for the damages) for fifteen years and for non-structural defects for two years. However, they are not responsible for the damages that occur due to changes made by the owner in the original approved design.

BIFs are regulated by the central government through a Building Inspection Commission. This commission follows the activities of BIFs and maintains their performance records. It also resolves disputes involving different BIFs.

In addition to BIFs, three other important players were introduced in the aftermath of the August 17, 1999 earthquake with respect to disaster mitigation. The first is the GDEM (under the Prime Minister's Office), which oversees disaster mitigation measures undertaken by government agencies at the central level. The second is an independent organization called the National Earthquake Council, which consists of scientists (e.g., earth scientists, structural and earthquake engineers, environmental engineers, architects, urban planners, and psychologists). One of the council's major tasks is to identify priority research areas with respect to disaster mitigation in the country.[†] The council, however, does not have any enforcement powers. The council presented its first proposal of earthquake mitigation strategies in its 2002 report called "National Earthquake Mitigation Strategy." Due to recent changes made by the government in the Scientific and Technical Research Council of Turkey, however, the council could not conduct its duties as expected, and it has effectively ceased to exist (JICA 2004: 48).

The third important post-August 17, 1999 player is the National Disasters Insurance Administration (under the Treasury). The administration manages the Turkish Catastrophe Insurance Pool, which collects the mandatory earthquake insurance from homeowners. It is directed by an Executive Board consisting of seven members from the public and private sectors (e.g., insurance and finance organizations) and academia. Most operations of the agency are outsourced to different companies and agencies. For example, the agency's operational

---

[*] The pilot provinces were Adana, Ankara, Antalya, Aydin, Balikesir, Bolu, Bursa, Çanakkale, Denizli, Düzce, Eskişehir, Gaziantep, Hatay, İstanbul, İzmir, Kocaeli, Sakarya, Tekirdağ, and Yalova.

[†] Some of its other tasks include undertaking scientific assessment of earthquake predictions; providing consultancy services to public authorities and developing policy and strategies; and dealing with ethical matters concerning earthquake predictions.

management is currently contracted out to Garanti Sigorta A.Ş., a leading insurance company in the country. Policy distribution and marketing are undertaken by 24 insurance companies and their agencies.*

Earthquake insurance collected by the Natural Disasters Insurance Administration is mandatory for all units in residential buildings located within municipal boundaries of local governments in Turkey. Public buildings, industrial and commercial buildings, and buildings in rural areas outside the municipal boundaries are exempt from the mandatory earthquake insurance. Those homeowners who are required to carry the mandatory earthquake insurance and fail to do so are not eligible to receive compensation from the government for housing repair or reconstruction in the event of an earthquake. The coverage of the mandatory earthquake insurance is determined according to the size of the unit and the predetermined cost of construction per square meter. The maximum insurance coverage is currently 100,000 YTL (approximately US$67,500 as of August 2006). If the value of a dwelling exceeds this amount, policy holders can buy additional coverage from insurance companies. The insurance typically covers damages to the building caused by earthquakes, including fire, explosion, and landslide damages triggered by earthquakes. It does not compensate for bodily injury or damages to household assets. Table 14.11 provides a summary of the organizational structure for disaster mitigation phase in Turkey.

There are several main issues that still need to be addressed with respect to disaster mitigation in Turkey. First is that the newly established GDEM lacks necessary human and financial resources to undertake its coordinative tasks on disaster mitigation (JICA 2004). As noted by the JICA report (2004: 11), "passing laws and regulations and establishing government agencies for natural disaster reduction are by themselves not sufficient to bring about the desired results. These agencies must be accorded the necessary financial means for fulfilling their mandates." Second is that BIFs inspect construction and report to the local and provincial governments only in selected pilot provinces. There is a need to expand the services of these firms to other provinces in the country, as the firms fill in a significant gap in local and provincial governments—which often lack qualified building inspection personnel. Third is that the policies of mandatory earthquake insurance scheme in Turkey are limited to damage from earthquakes alone (as opposed covering other disasters as well, such as floods, landslides, or avalanches). In addition, the scheme does not provide funding or incentives for mitigation purposes—unlike the mandatory insurance scheme in New Zealand, which sets aside resources for mitigation research and education of the public. Fourth is lack of community involvement in disaster mitigation. As suggested by Maskrey (1989) in his seminal study, successful mitigation strategies take into consideration the

---

* NDIA [http://www.dask.gov.tr]. Accessed 26 August 2006. Also, see the 2001 Decree on Working Procedures and Principles of Natural Disasters Insurance Administration (No. 246000) for more details on the National Disasters Insurance Administration.

Table 14.11   Organizational Structure of Disaster Mitigation Phase in Turkey

Level of Government	Responsibility	Agency
Central government/ Prime Minister's Office	Coordinative	General Directorate of Emergency Management ■ Oversees disaster mitigation measures
Central government/ Other	Primary	Ministry of Public Works and Settlement ■ Designs mitigation policies ■ Determines high-risk areas prone to disasters ■ Undertakes precautions in areas prone to disasters ■ Undertakes research on reduction of disaster losses ■ Prepares earthquake hazard maps ■ Prepares the building code for construction and construction standards in areas prone to disasters
	Primary	Provincial and district governments ■ Implement mitigation policies (e.g., enforce building codes and other standards, and take measures in high-risk areas) outside the municipal boundaries
Local governments	Primary	Municipalities ■ Implement mitigation policies within their jurisdiction
Other	Supportive	National Earthquake Council (Independent) ■ Identifies priority research on mitigation
	Supportive	Building Inspection Firms (Private) ■ Inspect construction ■ Report to local and provincial governments for issuance of construction and occupancy permits ■ Supervised by a two-tier system at the provincial/district and central levels

particularities of local realities and involve local people and their organizations. Current laws and regulations do not only exclude communities from the disaster recovery processes but also from taking control of disaster mitigation in the country.

Conclusion

This chapter detailed the disaster management structure in Turkey based on laws and regulations. As the organizational structure for disaster management evolved with the different laws and regulations on disasters, it is murky and difficult to conceptualize. There are several governmental units at the central, provincial, district, and local levels that are involved in different phases of disasters. The disaster management in Turkey, however, has traditionally been paternalistic, with much responsibility vested with the state.

The current disaster management structure in the country has been moving away from its paternalistic approach since the August 17, 1999 earthquake, one of the major disasters in the history of the Republic of Turkey. The state and its actors, especially the central government, still exert strong influence over different phases of disasters. The provincial and district governments, which are arms of the central governments, have the primary responsibility for both disaster preparedness and emergency response and rescue phases of disasters. The MPWS controls the disaster recovery process. It also determines disaster mitigation policies, which are implemented both by provincial and local governments. The state, however, has reallocated some of its preparedness and responsibilities to voluntary search and rescue teams, its construction inspection responsibilities to private BIFs, and its financial burden of replacing or repairing damaged housing units in urban areas to homeowners since the earthquake. All these actors now play an increasing role in preparing for and responding to disasters in the country.

In the post-August 17, 1999 context, the disaster management structure continues to be revised in Turkey. The MPWS, for instance, has replaced its 1997 decree on principles for earthquake resistant buildings with another decree issued on March 6, 2006. The new decree addresses the important issue of retrofitting buildings for earthquakes, which had been ignored in the earlier decree. The Ministry has also proposed a new law (dated February 9, 2006) to replace the existing disaster law (No. 7269), which has been in effect since 1959 in Turkey. The proposed law, which is expected to be discussed by the Parliament next year, however, does not introduce radical changes in the disaster management structure in Turkey. It has been criticized to a great extent by the Union of Chambers of Turkish Engineers and Architects, mainly because it does not introduce proactive measures which would place more emphasis on preparedness and mitigation in the country (TMMOB 2006).

Several key steps could be undertaken to overcome the shortcomings of the current disaster management structure in Turkey. These reforms include the following: (1) introduction of a national level comprehensive plan that would outline the structure of coordination between different actors (e.g., the central government and its arms, local governments, NGOs, and the private sector) during major national disasters; (2) assigning of the legal responsibility to coordinate disaster preparedness and recovery activities in the country to one agency at the central level; (3) removing the confusion regarding which agency at the central level is in charge of emergency response and rescue; (4) inclusion of local governments and disaster victims, who are familiar with the local conditions, in disaster recovery phase (and inclusion of disaster victims in mitigation initiatives); and (5) providing the newly established GDEM with enough human and financial resources so that it could undertake its coordinative functions with respect to mitigation in an effective manner.

Bibliography

Bogazici University Kandilli Observatory and Earthquake Research Institute [Bogazici Universitesi Kandilli Rasathanesi Ulusal Deprem Izleme Merkezi], [http://www.koeri.boun.edu.tr/sismo/default.htm]. Accessed 20 August 2006.

Decree on Basic Principles Related to Disasters Affecting the Life of the General Public [Afetlerin Genel Hayata Etkinligine Iliskin Temel Kurallar Hakkinda Yonetmelik] (effective by 21 September 1968), in *Kanunlar Yonetmelikler ve Kararnameler*. Afet Isleri Genel Mudurlugu, Ankara, 2000.

Decree on Design Principles for Buildings in Disaster Regions (Official Gazette No. 26100) [Afet Bolgelerinde Yapilacak Yapilar Hakkinda Yonetmelik] (effective by 6 March 2006). *Resmi Gazete* [http://rega.basbakanlik.gov.tr]. Accessed 28 August 2006.

Decree on Emergency Assistance Organization and Planning Related to Disasters (No. 88/12777) [Afetlere Iliskin Acil Yardim Teskilati ve Planlama Esaslarina Dair Yonetmelik] (effective by 8 May 1988), in *Kanunlar Yonetmelikler ve Kararnameler*, Afet Isleri Genel Mudurlugu, Ankara, 2000.

Decree on Organization and Duties of the Ministry of Reconstruction and Public Works (No. 180) [Bayindirlik ve Iskan Bakanliginin Teskilat ve Gorevleri Hakkinda Kanun Hukmunde Kararname] (effective by 14 December 1983), in *Kanunlar Yonetmelikler ve Kararnameler*, Afet Isleri Genel Mudurlugu, Ankara, 2000.

Decree on Procedures and Principles for Construction Inspection (Official Gazette No. 24491) [Yapi Denetimi Uygulama Usul ve Esaslari Yonetmeligi] (effective by 12 August 2001), *Resmi Gazete* [http://rega.basbakanlik.gov.tr]. Accessed 28 August 2006.

Decree on State of Emergency Council (No. 84/7778) [Olaganustu Hal Kurulu ve Burolarinin Kurulus ve Gorevleri ile Yukumluluklerinin Karsiliginin Tesbit ve Odenmesi Hakkinda Yonetmelik] (effective by 8 March 1984), in *Kanunlar Yonetmelikler ve Kararnameler*, Afet Isleri Genel Mudurlugu, Ankara, 2000.

Decree on Working Procedures and Principles of Natural Disasters Insurance Administration (No. 246000) [Doğal Afet Sigortalari Kurumu Yönetim Kurulu Çalişma Usul ve Esaslari Hakkinda Yönetmelik] (effective by 1 December 2001), Dogal Afet Sigortalari

Kurumu [http://www.dask.gov.tr/daskhakkinda/yonetmelik.htm]. Accessed 28 August 2006.

Decree with the Power of Law on Acceptance of the Decree on Organization of the Prime Minister's Office with Amendment (No. 583) [Basbakanlik Teskilati Hakkinda Kanun Hukmunde Kararnamenin Degistirilerek Kabulu Hakkinda Kanunda Degisiklik Yapilmasina Dair Kanun Hukmunde Kararname] (effective by 22 November 1999), in *Kanunlar Yonetmelikler ve Kararnameler,* Afet Isleri Genel Mudurlugu, Ankara, 2000.

Decree with the Power of Law on Changes Related to Laws Concerning Engineering and Architecture and Turkish Union of Chambers of Engineers and Architects (No. 601) [Muhendislik ve Mimarlik Hakkinda Kanun ile Turk Muhendis ve Mimar Odalari Birligi Kanununda Degisiklik Yapilmasina Dair Kanun Hukmunde Kararname] (effective by 22 November 2000), *Resmi Gazete* [http://rega.basbakanlik.gov.tr]. Accessed 28 August 2006.

Decree with the Power of Law on the Mandatory Earthquake Insurance (No. 587) [Zorunlu Deprem Sigortasi Hakkinda Kanun Hukmunde Kararname] (effective by 27 December 1999), Dogal Afet Sigortalari Kurumu [http://www.dask.gov.tr/daskhakkinda/mevzuat.htm]. Accessed 28 August 2006.

Development Law (No. 3194) [Imar Kanunu] (effective by 9 May 1985), Basbakanlik [http://mevzuat.basbakanlik.gov.tr/mevzuat/metinx.asp?mevzuatkod=1.5.3194]. Accessed 28 August 2006.

Directive on Conditions of Participation of Volunteers in Civil Defense Service [Gonullulerin Sivil Savunma Hizmetlerine Katilma Esaslari Yonergesi] (effective by 2000), Sivil Savunma Genel Mudurlugu [http://www.ssgm.gov.tr/mevzuat/mevzuat.html]. Accessed 28 August 2006.

Draft Disasters Law [Afet Kanunu Tasarisi Tasagi] (dated 9 February 2006), Ministry of Public Works and Settlement [http://www.bayindirlik.gov.tr/turkce/haberduyuru detay.php?ID=66]. Accessed 25 August 2006.

Dodd, C.H., *Democracy and Development in Turkey,* Eothen Press, London, UK, 1979.

EM-DAT International Disaster Database [http://www.em-dat.net/disasters/country.php]. Accessed 20 August 2006.

Heper, M., *The State Tradition in Turkey,* Eothen Press, Walkington, UK, 1985.

JICA (Japan International Cooperation Agency), *Country Strategy Paper for Natural Disasters in Turkey,* JICA, Ankara, 2004.

Karpat, K., *An Inquiry into the Social Foundations of Nationalism in the Ottoman State: From Social Estates to Classes, From Millets to Nations,* Research Monograph No. 39, Princeton University, Princeton, 1973.

Law on Building Inspection (No. 4708) [Yapi Denetimi Hakkinda Kanun] (effective by 13 July 2001), *Resmi Gazete* [http://rega.basbakanlik.gov.tr], Accessed 28 August 2006.

Law on Civil Defense (No. 7126) [Sivil Savunma Kanunu] (effective by 13 June 1958), Sivil Savunma Genel Mudurlugu [http://www.ssgm.gov.tr/mevzuat/mevzuat.html]. Accessed on 28 August 2006.

Law on Measures and Assistance to be Put into Effect Regarding Disasters Affecting the Life of the General Public (No. 7269) [Umumi Hayata Muessir Afetler Dolayisiyle Alinacak Tedbirlerle Yapilacak Yardimlara Dair Kanun] (effective by 25 May 1959), in *Kanunlar Yonetmelikler ve Kararnameler,* Afet Isleri Genel Mudurlugu, Ankara, 2000.

Law on Municipalities (No. 5272) [Belediye Kanunu] (effective by 24 December 2004), *Resmi Gazete* [http://rega.basbakanlik.gov.tr]. Accessed 28 August 2006.

Law on Organization and Duties of the Ministry of Home Affairs (No. 3152) [Icisleri Bakanligi Teskilat ve Gorevleri Hakkinda Kanun] (effective by 23 February 1985), Sivil Savunma Genel Mudurlugu [http://www.ssgm.gov.tr/mevzuat/mevzuat.html]. Accessed 28 August 2006.

Law on State of Emergency (No. 2935) [Olaganustu Hal Kanunu] (effective by 27 October 1983), in *Kanunlar Yonetmelikler ve Kararnameler*, Afet Isleri Genel Mudurlugu (T.C. Bayindirlik ve Iskan Bakanligi), Ankara, 2000.

Mandate on the Establishment of the Independent National Earthquake Council (No. 2000/9) [Bagimsiz Milli Deprem Komisyonun Kurulusu ile Ilgili Genelge] (effective by 21 March 2000), National Earthquake Council [http://udk.tubitak.gov.tr/genelge]. Accessed 28 August 2006.

Mardin, S., Power, Civil Society and Culture in the Ottoman Empire, *Comparative Studies in Society and History*, 11 (3), 258–281, 1969.

Maskrey, A., *Disaster Mitigation: Community Based Approach*, Oxfam Press, Oxford, 1989.

MPWS (Ministry of Public Works and Settlement) [Bayindirlik ve Iskan Bakanligi], *Seismic Hazard Zone Map of Turkey (Turkiye Deprem Bolgeleri Haritasi)*, MPWS, Ankara, 1996.

METU (Middle East Technical University) [Orta Dogu Teknik Universitesi], *On Rapor: 3194 Sayili Imar Kanunu ve Yonetmeliklerinin Yeni Bir Yapi Kontrol Sistemi ve Afetlere Karsi Dayanikliligi Saglayacak Onlemleri Icermek Uzere Revizyonu Arastirmasi Musavirlik Hizmeleri*, O.D.T.U. Deprem Muhendisligi Arastirma Merkezi, Ankara, 1998.

PMO-CMC (Prime Minister's Office-Crisis Management Center) [T.C. Basbakanlik Kriz Yonetim Merkezi], *Depremler 1999*, PMO-CMC, Ankara, 2000.

SIS (State Institute of Statistics) [Devlet Istatistik Enstitusu], *Statistical Yearbook of Turkey 1999*, SIS, Ankara, 2000.

TBMM (Parliament of Turkey) [Turkiye Buyuk Millet Meclisi] (issued in 1999), *Deprem Raporu*, Belgenet [http://www.belgenet.com/rapor/depremrapor.html]. Accessed 13 February 2005.

TMMOB (Union of Chambers of Turkish Engineers and Architects) (issued on 16 August 2006), Press Release [http://www.tmmob.org.tr/modules.php?op=modload&name=News&file=article&sid=1408&mode=thread&order=0&thold=0]. Accessed 25 August 2006.

World Bank, *Turkey: Marmara Earthquake Assessment*, World Bank, Washington, DC, 1999.

Chapter 15

HIV/AIDS in Africa: Botswana's Response to the Pandemic

Keshav C. Sharma and Thabo Lucas Seleke

CONTENTS

322 ■ *Disaster Management Handbook*

Introduction

Africa is highly affected by the HIV/AIDS pandemic. According to the Joint United Nations Programme on Aids (UNAIDS) report 2006, sub-Saharan Africa is home to nearly 24.7 million of the world's 42 million people living with HIV/AIDS. This represents 67 percent of sub-Saharan Africa's population, with the southern African region being the epicenter of the HIV/AIDS pandemic representing 32 percent of people living with HIV/AIDS and 34 percent of AIDS deaths globally. Nearly 2.4 million of the world's global infected children with HIV and AIDS come from the African soil with 380,000 deaths (UNAIDS, 2006).

This pandemic has not only deprived Africa and the southern African region of its productive labor force, but has shattered families and turned children into orphans. Gaye (2002) observed that Africa is an orphan continent with 95 percent of orphans. This explosive rate of spread of HIV/AIDS across Africa, regionally and nationally has created one of the greatest crises of modern times. The number of people dying from AIDS varies greatly in African countries. HIV data gathered in South Africa's extensive antenatal clinic surveillance system suggests that HIV prevalence has not declined and shows a continuing rising trend. Similarly Swaziland and Mozambique have shown a remarkable increase in adult HIV prevalence rate and death rate. In Somalia and Senegal the HIV prevalence is under 1 percent of the adult population, whereas in Zambia around 20 percent of adults are infected with HIV (UNAIDS, 2006).

HIV and AIDS in Botswana: Magnitude of the Problem and Preparedness

HIV/AIDS is the biggest challenge faced by Botswana. In his address to the UN General Assembly in June 2001, President Festus Mogae summed up the situation by saying

> We are threatened with extinction. People are dying in chilling high numbers. It is a crisis of the first magnitude.

The first case of HIV/AIDS in Botswana was diagnosed in 1985 and the country is considered to have the highest number of individuals living with HIV/AIDS in the world with an estimated 38.7 percent people in total (UNAIDS, 2006). This constitutes a high percentage of the total 1.7 million people in the country. After more than 20 years against HIV/AIDS, Botswana is still in a state of paralysis with the AIDS virus continuing as the deadliest enemy the country has ever faced. HIV/AIDS has to date claimed so many lives in Botswana including young and the old. It is estimated that there are 80,000 orphans due to HIV/AIDS in Botswana. There have been projections that by 2010, more than 50 percent of the country's children will be AIDS orphans and the average life expectancy will have fallen from 47 to 27 years (www.soschildrenvillage.org.uk/aids-africa).

Botswana being one of the most affected countries, has tried to confront the problem with high degree of commitment. President Mogae in 2000 declared HIV/AIDS a national emergency and therefore, developed a national strategic framework to turn the tide of the HIV/AIDS epidemic in Botswana. In 2001, the Government of Botswana (GOB) also introduced an ambitious treatment aptly named Masa (New Dawn), a symbol of hope for those living with the virus.

The Masa program provides free antiretroviral (ARV) drugs and counseling nationwide. During the same period, Botswana introduced prevention of mother to child transmission (PMTCT) program throughout the country. It was launched in 1999 and piloted in Francistown and Gaborone with the support of UNICEF. Masa program manifests itself in public–private partnership developed between the GOB and African Comprehensive HIV/AIDS Program (ACHAP) and Merck and the Bill and Melinda Gates Foundation. Drug companies and NGOs are donating funds to the country's comprehensive prevention and treatment efforts. Botswana has received grants for its universal ARV drug program totaling more than $100 million over five years from Bill and Melinda Gates Foundation and drug maker Meck and has committed $50 million over years to help Botswana strengthen its health infrastructure. In addition, the Harvard AIDS institute has built $4.5 million AIDS research laboratory and is training health care workers to address the epidemic. Botswana has also received $20 million in the fiscal year 2004, $40 million in 2005, and $343 million in 2006 from the U.S. President's Emergency Plan for AIDS Relief (PEPFAR) and is expected to receive $70 million for the year 2007, by Embassy of United States of America (Botswana Guardian, 2006). This money is meant to combat HIV/AIDS and is geared towards prevention, treatment, and care programs. Similarly the country has received substantial amount of funding from Global Fund (although 65 million was withdrawn from this fund recently due to the alleged mismanagement of the fund and failure to comply with the set conditions by the donors). In its 2007–2008 budget, P700 billion was allocated to Ministry of Health to help curb the pandemic (GOB, 2007).

Botswana's Policy for Fighting the HIV/AIDS Pandemic

Policies and strategic plans on HIV/AIDS are the foundations for any meaningful and sustained response to the epidemic. Policies serve as a guideline and provide operating framework for prevention, treatment, care, support, and reduction in the impact of the epidemic. These direct the strategic plans and the allocation of funds to activities aimed at achieving the stated objectives of the management of the HIV/AIDS. It is against this background that the Botswana government signed the declaration on HIV/AIDS at the United Nations General Assembly in June 2000. The declaration resolved that by 2003, countries including Botswana should have developed multi-sectoral national strategic plans and financing that directly address the HIV/AIDS epidemic. Such plans must be developed jointly with key stakeholders and may include the government, the NGOs, the private sector, donors, and other partners.

The first national policy on HIV/AIDS in Botswana was developed in 1992 and was revised in 1998 to keep pace with developments. However, the country's response to the HIV/AIDS epidemic can be traced as far back as 1987 and has developed in three stages (GOB, 1997a). The early stage (1987–1989) focused mainly on public awareness of HIV/AIDS, as well as clinical protocols for the management of infected people. The second stage (1989–1997) and the first medium term plan (MTP) also focused on public health perspective, educational, and communication campaign programs aimed at sensitizing the nation about the scourge. During this stage in 1993, Botswana government adopted the Botswana National Policy on AIDS. The third stage started in 1997. It was during this period that the response to HIV/AIDS was broken down into different facets and included the public health perspective, educational campaigns, prevention, and comprehensive care including the provision of the ARV treatment and community support activities such as home-based care (HBC). It also focused on multi-sectoral approach to fighting the pandemic and put in place structural frameworks and mechanisms to the fight the "black death" disease.

In 2000, the Botswana National AIDS Coordinating Agency (NACA) was formed with the primary objective of mobilizing and coordinating multi-sectoral response to HIV/AIDS. This agency works under the National AIDS Council (NAC) that is chaired by the president and has wide representation from other relevant stakeholders such as civil society, public sector organizations, and the private sector. At the same time the country developed National Strategic Framework for HIV/AIDS in 2003 representing a fundamental shift in the development and execution of the national response.

Public–private partnership has been a cornerstone of HIV/AIDS policy in Botswana. Almost $100 million will be provided over five years (beginning in 2002) through this partnership for treatment, care, support, and prevention activities led by ACHAP. Additionally as already mentioned earlier, the Gates Foundation has promised $50 million over a five year period and Harvard University has given $1 million in the establishment of a new laboratory and to train health care workers. The country has also at the same time received substantial amounts of money from PEPFAR and Global Fund in the fight against HIV/AIDS, tuberculosis, and malaria. Because policy framework in the fight against HIV/AIDS in Botswana is donor driven as shown above, international organizations have played a significant role in designing many programs and decision-making institutions in the country.

Realizing the need for spreading education and information, and strengthening the preventive measures against the spread of the epidemic, the government has tried to popularize the slogan ABC: A to abstain, B to be faithful, and C to condomize. The message that is being conveyed is that the people in the first instance must try to abstain from indulging in premarital and extramarital sex; they should be faithful and stick to one partner; and if at all they indulge in sex, they must use condoms to guard against infection. In pleading for not having sex before marriage, the youth is also being told not to be ashamed of virginity. Recently the Youth Health Organizations (YOHO) have also raised the slogan: Do-it-yourself (DIY or masturbation).

Administrative Machinery for Fighting HIV/AIDS in Botswana

Botswana has developed a two tier system in terms of mainstreaming and fighting HIV/AIDS, at the levels of central government and districts. It has also at the same time developed institutional framework for the successful implementation of government's HIV/AIDS policies. This is in line with the World Bank Multi Country HIV/AIDS program (MAP) that was launched in September 2000. The overall development objective of MAP is to dramatically increase access to HIV/AIDS prevention, care, and treatment programs, increase support to community organizations and the private sector.

In 2000, Botswana established NACA as already stated. This organization was primarily established to ensure coordination and harmonization of the inputs from various government ministries, civil society organizations, and the private sector. It was also mandated to monitor decentralization of HIV/AIDS policies and their implementation at the district levels and ensure integration of HIV/AIDS policies into district development plans coordinated by the Ministry of Local Government. In carrying out all its activities and functions it directly reports to NAC which is chaired by the state president. NAC has a wide representation from other stakeholders such as the private sector, public sector, NGOs, civil society, and the legislature. Its primary role is to serve as the highest organ to monitor and coordinate the implementation of the national AIDS policy and programs that are developed by NACA and other relevant stakeholders (GOB, 2003).

Realizing the need and significance of decentralization, the government has organized administrative machinery at the district levels in the country. District multi-sectoral HIV/AIDS committees (DMSAC) in collaboration with the district development committees (DDCs) are the pivotal organs at the district levels for giving leadership to and coordinating all HIV/AIDS-related activities. DMSAC, like the DDC, is an interdepartmental and multi-sectoral body consisting of representatives of different governmental, nongovernmental, and civil society organizations operating at the district level. It includes members from organizations such as district councils, District Commissioner's Office, tribal administration, land boards, community-based organizations (CBO), and government departments operating at district level (GOB, 2005). DMSAC functions as the voice of the people at the local level and manages inputs facilitating the development of multi-sectoral HIV/AIDS action plans. DMSAC is housed under the Ministry of Local Government and is served by district AIDS coordinators, who are chairpersons of DAMSAC. District aid coordinators are expected to play a key role in the development, facilitation, and monitoring of the district response and work in close cooperation with all relevant stakeholders to ensure the effective contribution of the district to the overall national response. They are primarily the eyes and the ears of central government at the district level. The Ministry of Local Government works in collaboration with NACA to ensure that annual multi-sectoral planning is undertaken. It also facilitates the provision of technical assistance for the planning and management of local response.

Nongovernmental organizations, CBOs, civil society, and the private sector are also active partners at the national and local levels. For strengthening its effectiveness, the private sector has formed Botswana Business Coalition on AIDS (BBCA). This was established in 1994, using the best practice models from Global Business Coalition on AIDS (GBCA). This coalition coordinates HIV/AIDS interventions in the workplace in different private sector organizations. Private sector organizations have come up with workplace interventions in educating and sensitizing their employees about the disease, in accessing existing government HIV/AIDS services, in assisting the government and partners in reaching more people, and in increasing uptake levels for their services. The private sector is also addressing the issues of stigma and discrimination of employees infected with the virus. As AIDS is destroying workforce, productivity is declining and absenteeism is increasing, the private sector has to complement and supplement the government effort.

In Botswana, Debswana mining company (a partnership between the GOB and DeBeers Mining Company) was the first to provide ARVs to its employees. Other companies such as Bamangwato Concession Limited (BCL) followed suit. This arrangement has also been made easier by the public–private partnership drive. Medical aid companies have now come in as players in providing disease management service and they are doing this within the framework of National Treatment Protocol, National Health Policy, and National Development Plan. The medical aid companies provide ARV drugs to ease the congestion at the public hospitals.

Civil society organizations have demonstrated their partnership by forming organizations such as Botswana Network of AIDS Service Organizations (BONASO), Botswana Network on Ethics, Law and HIV/AIDS (BONELA), Botswana Christian AIDS Intervention Programme (BOCAIP), to promote their coordinated input and play an advocacy role. They help in facilitating community interactions, distributing resources such as condoms, changing social attitudes, and representing public interest in policy matters. They play a role in contributing to devising of innovative strategies, complimenting government's efforts in social mobilization, confronting difficult issues such as those related to sexuality, stigma, discrimination, human rights, and access to treatment. These organizations also work with CBOs, which have closer relations with the locals.

Challenges Faced by Botswana in Fighting the HIV/AIDS Pandemic

Although Botswana has developed a clear policy, has established administrative machinery at the national and local levels of governance, and has allocated significant amount of resources, it is faced with enormous challenges in its fight against the HIV/AIDS pandemic. Faced with the unprecedented challenge that threatens the fabric of Botswana's society, President Mogae upon assuming presidency made HIV/AIDS a presidential lead project and in 2001 declared the scourge a national crisis. Following this commitment, the country resolved to have an AIDS free nation by 2016 (Vision 2016). As committed political leadership is an essential prerequisite for the success of such programs requiring widespread social mobilization, administrative effort and resources, such clear commitment of political leadership became an asset in the case of Botswana. This was not so conspicuous in the country during the early years of the spread of the epidemic. Independent observers such as Kjertsi (2005) have pointed out that to mitigate the effects of HIV/AIDS and reversing the epidemic's further spread it should be made a top political agenda. Jones (2005) has also argued that "... strong, proactive leadership, coordinated multi-sectoral governance responses are regarded as critical factors in mitigating the impact of HIV/AIDS." Boone and Batsell (2001) have noted that in spite of increasing evidence of the detrimental impact of the epidemic, there is often a political vacuum and it is not handled with the sense of urgency that it requires. This can be said about Botswana's preparedness for the fight against the epidemic in the late 1980s and 1990s. During that period Botswana was also unfortunate in that in the mid-1980s and early 1990s international agencies had withdrawn aid from Botswana, because the country was perceived to have moved to the high middle income group and they felt they could deploy their resources elsewhere. Botswana was then left to fund almost all of its HIV/AIDS control programs, thus creating an additional drain on the national resources.

The failures of Botswana in terms of its fight against the HIV/AIDS in the late 1980s and continuing increase in the numbers of people affected, were compounded by the inability of government to successfully coopt the religious and traditional leaders (Chiefs) in the fight against HIV/AIDS. This weakened the political leadership and public support. In some cases the chiefs wanted to put up their own posters in their Kgotla to educate the community on HIV/AIDS but they needed permission from NACA, for which they had to remain waiting indefinitely, in some cases for more than two years (Allen and Heald, 2004). The traditional leaders in the past continued to view HIV/AIDS as an external problem, affecting the people living in the towns. In their view, the victims were coming to their villages only to die and to be buried. The local political leaders such as councilors, MPs, members of the Village Development Committees did not take much interest in the problem. It was a taboo to engage in any open discussion relating to the disease so much so that even the family members were being disowned when they were identified as affected. This kind of situation needed a vigorous and positive leadership at national and local levels to put up a serious fight against the epidemic. For the past few years increased involvement and commitment of political leadership at national and local levels is noticeable.

Botswana has recognized the need and significance of partnership and participation of relevant stakeholders such as the government, private sector, NGOs, and donor agencies in the fight against the pandemic. The agencies contributing to the government effort include ACHAP, Bill Gates Foundation and the Merck Company Foundation, Botswana and U.S. Government Agreement (BOTUSA) project, Global Fund, Bristol Myers Squibb Foundation, PEPFAR, and the Harvard School of Public Health, BONELA, Botswana Network of AIDS Services,(BONASO), Botswana Council of Non-Governmental Organizations (BOCONGO), and BBCA. Their involvement is multifaceted and is geared towards funding of HIV/AIDS interventions such as treatment campaigns, prevention, care, and support programs. The public–private partnership has made a significant contribution towards the fight against the pandemic. The introduction of the ambitious Masa program, which provides free ARVs and counseling throughout the country, has brought hope and new lease of life to many in Botswana. Although at the initial stage of inception the target was to enroll about 19,000 of the 110,000 (according to 2001 estimates) infected people who could benefit, this was not achieved, as only few people were coming forward to be tested and enrolled on antiretroviral treatment (ART). By 2004, only 24,000 people had been enrolled on Masa, of whom 24,0000 were receiving ARV drugs. By June 2005, the number of people receiving treatment shot up to 43,000 representing half of the 75,000 in need. This coverage exceeded 95 percent by the end of 2006 when around 84,000 were receiving treatment. This increase in numbers has been treated as a significant achievement (GOB, 2006). The promising results obtained from Masa program also extend to other interventions such as educational campaigns, provision of free condoms, the introduction of support and care programs such as the HBC, voluntary/routine testing, and counseling and PMTCT on AIDS.

There is a serious problem of access to ARV drugs. As revealed by BONELA (2007) and *Sunday Standard* (2007), "The Parliamentary Health Committee touring health facilities throughout the country in 2005 was told how patients have to travel long distances for medical attention because clinics in their areas had run out of medicine and drugs". Indications are also rife that government dispensaries may be turning away patients while much needed supplies are rotting on shelves at the central medical stores. The revelations by the *Sunday Standard* are indeed shocking and pose a challenge that needs effective logistics especially in the area of drug procurement. Another major challenge the country is facing in this context is the recent revelations about the theft of the ARV drugs from the government hospitals, clinics, and central medical stores. It is reported that of late there has been continued pilferage of drugs, in particular ARVs, throughout the Botswana government owned hospitals (Botswana Guardian, 2007). These drugs are believed to be having a market among private as well as government doctors, many of these alleged to be of foreign origin. This has compelled the country to put in stringent security measures such as installation of close circuit televisions to prevent drug theft. It is also shocking to note that recently the central medical stores had to destroy P20 million ($3.5 million) worth of expired medicine with an additional P12 million ($2 million) worth of medical supplies still to be tested, while pharmacists at government dispensaries throughout the country were turning back patients because there was a shortage of medical supplies (*Sunday Standard*, 2007).

The current technologies that are used throughout the country, e.g., CD4 and viral load counting machines are too bulky, too expensive and require high-level expertise. This is a serious constraint to be reckoned with (Darkoh, 2004). These observations made by Darkoh are further cemented by Seleke's research (2007), which reveals that the viral load and CD4 count machines in the two areas of his study, Francistown and Selibe Phikwe, only function for close to six months in a year and they have to be taken for repairs for the subsequent months which normally take close to five months. This is primarily so because of the heavy workloads that these machines have to endure. As a result, the lists of people waiting to be tested continue to grow and one could say that in some instances citizens actually die before they can even be enrolled in ART.

Stigma and discriminatory attitudes of people towards those living with HIV/AIDS are a serious challenge in the fight against the pandemic. Discrimination of people with HIV/AIDS within workplace is also noticeable, in spite of the government policy to the contrary. Allen and Heald (2004) and Letamo (2005) revealed high prevalence of stigmatization among people infected by the virus in Botswana. Right from the beginning, the epidemic of HIV/AIDS has been accompanied by fear, ignorance, and denial, leading to stigmatization and discrimination against people living with HIV/AIDS. (USAID, 2002). This fear has further prevented people from participating in voluntary counseling and testing, for programs to prevent mother-to-child transmission and from preventing mothers to take their children to be tested. The stigmatization of the HIV/AIDS and spread of the virus has somehow also been incorrectly associated with women, who have in some cases been accused of increasing the spread of HIV/AIDS (*Daily News*, 2006). Such assertions cannot only be seen as plagued by denial and the reality of HIV/AIDS spread, but also as insult to females. Women in Botswana continue to be victims of rape, sexual violence, and intimate partner's violence, which have aggravated the spread of the epidemic. More aggressive measures are needed to give increased protection to women.

Provision of ARV drugs to large numbers of people is posing a serious challenge in further spread of the disease in that some people in Botswana are now beginning to view ARVs as safety nets. There is an apprehension that the people receiving ARV drugs are indulging in unprotected sex thinking incorrectly that ARV drugs are giving them adequate protection. Some not yet affected are beginning to indulge in risky behavior with the understanding that they can resort to the use of ARV drugs if infected. Education and understanding continue to remain a big need. The country needs to focus its energy and funding towards prevention and educational programs. As of now public health education revolves primarily around ABC (abstain, be faithful, and condomize). This method of campaign does not appear to have been very successful (Allen and Heald, 2004).

There is also a health workforce crisis in Botswana. There are simply not enough doctors, nurses, pharmacy technicians, pharmacists to provide effective preventive health and clinical care. This shortage of trained health workers has put the country under desperate situation so much so that recently the Honorable Minister of Health, Professor Sheila Tlou, made a plea to the medical doctors, specialists, and pharmacists to consider marrying Botswana women and they will be guaranteed citizenship (*MidWeek Sun*, 2007).

Although Botswana has been fortunate in receiving high level of donor support in terms of resources and this assistance has added to the large pool of resources allocated by the government, this high degree of dependence on donor support raises serious questions related to the prudent management of donor funds and sustainability. If donors can pull out due to lack of confidence in the management of indigenous organizations or Botswana's case for foreign assistance becomes weaker due to its enhanced economic performance or availability of diamond generated resources, the management of all HIV/AIDS-related efforts is not going to be easy. At present Botswana's HIV/AIDS-related programs are donor driven and 72 percent of spending on HIV/AIDS comes from external sources that are multilateral and bilateral (Economist 2002). Of the $113 million spent in HIV/AIDS in 2001, $96 million came from external donors. Sustainability of ambitious programs such as free ARVs and PMTCT throughout the country is going to be very difficult. Funding for Masa is going to dry in 2009 and alternative sources of funding will have to be located.

Split jurisdiction of ministries and departments, such as the Ministry of Health, Ministry of Local Government, and NACA creates problems of coordination and harmonization. Integration of efforts of NGOs and CBOs with those of different government agencies poses additional problem. Despite the existence of strong political commitment, NAC and NACA which have been established to oversee the implementation of the strategy and action plan, there lies a great challenge in mainstreaming and coordination of HIV/AIDS activities in Botswana. NACA, although placed under the head of state, appears to be struggling in enforcing its authority for command, coordination, and control over several organizations operating at the central as well as local government levels.

Coordination of the efforts of several governmental and NGOs at the local levels is even more difficult. The Ministry of Local Government coordinates the district response through DMSAC, but harmonization of input of different ministries and stakeholders creates insurmountable problems. The Ministry of Health, which is responsible for giving leadership in health-related matters, has its administrative machinery (such as Public Health Specialist) at the local levels working closely with the local level organizations such as the District Councils, Town Councils and City Councils and the office of the District Commissioners. The cordiality of relationship and team spirit between the staff belonging to this ministry and those in the councils and the District Commissioners offices remains a problem due to the vertical loyalties of the specialist staff and their accountability. Although placed in the District Councils, they are not accountable to the council bosses. Not only that, a significant number of health workers belonging to the council (such as doctors, nurses, pharmacists) are answerable to these specialist staff of the Ministry of Health, instead of the normal council hierarchy. As ARV coordinators are a part of the council staff but receive their pay from NACA, the arrangements pose problems of accountability and control between NACA and the councils.

Management of donor funds also poses challenges. Government has been accused by major HIV/AIDS network organizations such as BOCAIP, BONASO, BONELA, and BONEPWA that it does not have a proper funds management system in place. This became evident when Global Fund withdrew P54 million (S$9.5 million), out of the funds allocated to fight AIDS, tuberculosis, and malaria. The Global Fund alleged that NACA had failed to meet the conditionalities and it failed to submit the country report which could enable the Global Fund to ascertain as to how the funds allocated in the first installment were utilized. NACA, in turn shifted the blame to the HIV/AIDS network organizations and asserted that it was these organizations which had to take the responsibility for meeting the conditionalities (Mmegi, 2007). A lot of questions have been raised in the country since then as to what action has been taken by the Ministry of Finance and Development Planning and NACA to address the problem, and why did these problems surface in the first place resulting in such a serious consequence as withdrawal of funds by the donor.

As HIV/AIDS funds are not centralized, bottlenecks arise in their management. Some funds bypass the state revenue fund and are not incorporated in the national budget. There is therefore, a need to find mechanisms and ways to address this problem and to check misuse and abuse. There is a need to guard against white collar crime because it is alleged that HIV/AIDS has been used by many bogus individuals and NGOs for their selfish ends. This became evident when in 2002, the founder of Total Community Mobilization (TCM) (an NGO started with the support of GOB and BOTUSA to engage in door-to-door educational campaigns informing and educating individuals and communities about the pandemic) Amdi Peterson, the cofounder of TCM was arrested on charges of tax fraud and embezzlement worth millions of dollars for a number of transactions in his foundation (www.gov.bw/cgi-bi/news.cgi). Amdi Peterson is alleged to have an empire with clandestine operations worldwide. TCM is no longer in existence in Botswana but the damage done leaves some lessons.

As the hospitals, clinics, and medical care facilities in the country are over-stretched; HBC program has been established. HBC was not something that was started by the state. It was started in communities where groups of people would get together to supplement the government effort. Sometimes these groups were formed at the Kgotla which is the traditional village centre. It is unfortunate that men play a very insignificant and passive role in the HBC program, despite the fact that they are decision makers at the family level. It is essentially the compassion on the part of women that sustains the HBC program.

The HIV/AIDS pandemic has shattered families and turned children into orphans. AIDS is responsible for leaving vast numbers of children across the country without one or both parents. It is estimated that there are 78,000 orphans in Botswana due to HIV/AIDS and that there are about 120,000 children who lost their parents due to AIDS by the end of 2005 (www.botsblog.com). The death of parents is creating a major problem of orphans and vulnerable children (OVC). The traditional family structures are being drastically altered due to AIDS deaths or illness often resulting in "child headed household." The devastating impact of AIDS at the household level compelled Botswana government to intervene and develop the National Orphan Program in 1999 to respond to the immediate needs of orphaned children. Within that policy framework, the government runs a food basket scheme, where a basket of food is provided to orphaned household once a month. Although, Botswana adopted such a policy, as its implementation was slow, it resulted in a big damage to the social fabric of the country. Cases have also been reported of abuse of the food basket program where false claims have been submitted to benefit those who are not supposed to.

Conclusion

HIV/AIDS has since its detection in the early 1980s become one of the greatest challenges facing sub-Saharan Africa. It has posed a significant threat to the region's socioeconomic development. Sub-Saharan Africa remains the worst affected globally with southern Africa being the "epicenter." Despite early signals after HIV/AIDS was detected in Botswana, the government failed to undertake aggressive measures for fighting the pandemic until late 1990s. In 2000, President Festus G Mogae adopted a battle outcry "Ntwa e bolotse" (The war has started). This could be defined as the turning point in Botswana's drive to fight the HIV/AIDS scourge.

Despite the government effort, allocation of resources, support of international donors and the public–private partnership, the war against the HIV/AIDS is far from over. The war against the pandemic is faced with major obstacles and setbacks. People are still dying in Botswana in chilling high numbers and some die even before they are enrolled on ART. Majority of people in need of treatment are not receiving it, especially in remote areas.

Because of its political stability and economic success, Botswana was able to attract and develop partnerships with foreign donors companies, pharmaceutical agencies and foundations to fight the HIV/AIDS scourge. The Masa program, the first of its kind in Africa, gave a hope and new lease of life to many Batswana. Under this program free ARV drugs were made available to its citizens countrywide. It was later followed by the PMTCT program.

The policies and administrative measures adopted by the government indicate political commitment of the country's leadership in the fight against the pandemic. It is hoped that such a commitment which was late to surface, will continue with the new leadership waiting in the wings. The degree of success achieved in the execution of all the interventions has been made possible by the existence of policy frameworks and the administrative machinery both at the central and local government levels. Success of the efforts can also be attributed to the realization that it is the community level where the outcome of the battle against HIV/AIDS will be decided and recognition that the local capacity for prevention, care, and support efforts need to be recognized affirmed and strengthened.

Organizations responsible for coordination, control, monitoring, and enforcing accountability such as NACA and MFDP at the national level and DAMSAC at the local levels need to be made more effective. The multi-sectoral approach undertaken by the government in the fight against HIV/AIDS needs to be strengthened in such a way that it does not create conflict and confusion among the various government ministries and local government machinery. To avoid such conflicts, local government administration machinery needs to be given increased autonomy.

Botswana has been fortunate in being endowed with resources and the liberal donor support, however, heavy reliance on donor funding could create problems for sustainability and pose a threat to its autonomy for decision making. Stigma associated with the HIV/AIDS scourge will have to be confronted so that the victims could have access to the relief measures and do not suffer from the psychological and social tensions.

Because Botswana has aspired to be producing an HIV-free generation by 2016 (GOB, 1997b) more emphasis needs to be placed on measures related to prevention and education. Unless a significant impact is made on the sexual behavior and cultural patterns of living, the war against the pandemic will be difficult to win. In the male dominated society, the male attitudes and behavior have a bearing on the continued spread of the pandemic. It is primarily the men who appear to be having multiple sexual partners, tend to determine the mode and timing of sex. Because of the unequal power balance in gender relations, dismal poverty and economic status of women, and their dependence on men even for survival (survival sex phenomena), women have lower bargaining power because men have the power to determine when, where, and how sex takes place. They are the ones who in some cases tend to exploit the women being weaker sex. They are the ones who quite often under the influence of alcohol indulge in careless sexual conduct without protection. Vigorous education campaigns need to be strengthened further realizing that the ABC campaigns are not working effectively.

References

Allen, T., 2004, Why don't HIV/AIDS policies work? *Journal of International Development*, 16, 1129–1140.

Allen, T. and Heald, S., 2004, HIV/AIDS policy in Africa: What has worked in Uganda and what has failed in Botswana? *Journal of International Development*, 16, 1141–1154.

Boone, C. and Batsell, J., 2001, Politics and aids in Africa, *Africa Today*, 48 (2), 3–33.

Botswana Daily News, 2006, Gaborone, 31 January, 13 November.

Botswana Daily News, 2007, Gaborone, 28 May.

Botswana Gazette, 2007, Gaborone, 14 March.

Botswana Guardian, 2006, Gaborone, 1 December.

Botswana Guardian, 2007, Gaborone, 22 April.

Darkoh, 2004, Feature, *State of Aids Care*, 10 (10), 379.

Government of Botswana (GOB), 1997a, *Botswana HIV and AIDS Second Medium Term Plan: 1997–2002*, Gaborone: Lentswe La Lesedi Publishers.

Government of Botswana (GOB), 1997b, *Long Term Vision for Botswana: Towards Prosperity For All*, Gaborone: Government Printer.

Government of Botswana (GOB), 2001, *Botswana National Strategic Framework for HIV/ AIDS 2003–2009*, Gaborone: Pyramid Publishing.

Government of Botswana (GOB), 2005, *DMSAC Planning Toolkit*, Gaborone: Government Printer.

Government of Botswana (GOB), 2006, Status of the HIV/AIDS National Response, October–December 2005 Report (NACA).

Government of Botswana (GOB), 2007, *Budget Speech of the Minister of Finance and Development Planning for 2007–2008*, Gaborone: Government Printer.

Jones, R., 2003, African state in crises, *Journal of Democracy*, 14 (3), 159–170.

Kjersti, K., 2005, Governance and HIV/AIDS in South Africa and Uganda. Thesis submitted in partial fulfillment of Masters Degree, University of Bergen, Bergen: Department of Comparative Politics.

Letamo, G., 2005, Prevalence of factors associated with HIV/AIDS related stigma and discriminatory attitudes in Botswana, *Journal of Health Population and Nutrition*, 21, 347–357.

Mmegi, 2007, Newspaper, Gaborone, 3, 8, and 9 March.

Seleke, T., 2007, HIV and local government in Botswana: Challenges and responses, Gaborone (Ongoing research project supported by the University of Botswana).

Sunday Standard, 2007, Gaborone, 6 May.

USAID, 2002, *What Happened in Uganda? Declining HIV Prevalence, Behavior Change and the National Response*, Washington, DC: U.S. Agency for International Development.

Web Sites

http://www.afraf.oxfordjournals.org

http://www.bonela.org/press/31_ Jan_2007.html

http://www.botsblog.com

http://www.avert.org/aidsbotswana.htm

http://www.debeersgroup.com/debeersweb
http://www.economist.com/display
http://www.gov.bw/cgi-bin/news.cgi (BOPA Daily News Archive)
http://kaisernetwork.org/daily
http://www.pbs.org/newshour/bb/health
http://www.unaids.org (2004)
http://www.unaids.org (2006)

Abbreviations

ABC	Abstain, be faithful, and condomize
ACHAP	African Comprehensive HIV/AIDS Partnerships
AIDS	Acquired immunodeficiency syndrome
ART	Antiretroviral therapy
ARV	Antiretroviral treatment
BBCA	Botswana business coalition on HIV/AIDS
BOCAIP	Botswana Christian Aids Intervention Program
BCL	Bamangwato Concession Limited
BONASO	Botswana Network of Aids Services Organizations
BONELA	Botswana Network on Ethics Law and HIV/AIDS
CBO	Community-Based Organization
DDC	District development committee
DIY	Do-it-yourself
DMSAC	District Multi-Sectoral HIV/AIDS Action Committee
GBCA	Global Business Coalition on Aids
GOB	Government of Botswana
HBC	Home-based care
HIV	Human immunodeficiency virus
MAP	Multi Country HIV/AIDS Program
MTP	Medium term plan
NAC	National Aids Council
NACA	National Aids Coordinating Agency
NGO	Nongovernmental organization
OVC	Orphans and vulnerable children
PEPFAR	President's Emergency Plan for Aids Relief
PMTCT	Prevention of mother to child transmission
TCM	Total Community Mobilization
UNAIDS	Joint United Nations Programme on Aids
YOHO	Youth Health Organization

Chapter 16

Toward Disaster Resilient Communities: A New Approach for South Asia and Africa

Uma Medury

CONTENTS

Introduction

Disasters pose a serious threat to nations, disrupt economic activities, destroy the social structure, and endanger the communities. Once considered as inevitable happenings or occurrences, which are beyond human control, disasters now are being looked at as the outcome of interaction between hazards and vulnerability. These are no longer perceived as sudden eruptions that can be handled by emergency response and rescue services, but as those incidents that can be prevented or the impact of which can be significantly reduced through appropriate risk reduction strategies. Disasters presently are considered an integral part of the development process in contrast to random or isolated acts. These, despite the negative effects, also have at times been a catalyst for social transformation with the community as the focal point.

Disasters may not be prevented, but through specifically designed measures, its impact on people and property can be lessened. The fatalistic attitude on the part of the community is giving way to the acceptance of danger or threats of impending disaster. The approach toward this state of mind is giving significance to building and strengthening the capacities, skills, and knowledge of the people who are likely to face the wrath of the disasters. The concept of resilience or resistance or sustainability of communities is occupying the center stage in the debate on management of disasters.

In this chapter, an attempt is made to provide a conceptual framework of disaster resilience and establish the interrelationship between resilience, resistance, and sustainability. It examines few important disaster resilience strategies with special reference to India, Africa, and other South Asian countries. The gender perspective pertaining to this approach is also analyzed. Creation of disaster resilient communities requires a multipronged strategy and needs to take cognizance of certain problem areas, which are identified in this chapter.

Disaster Management: A Paradigmatic Shift

Risk reduction, as a key strategy is being directed toward achievement of sustainable development and protection of people and livelihoods. In a traditional sense, disasters have always been associated with rescue and relief, which is top-down in nature. Once a disaster occurs, it is the responsibility of the state institutions to provide immediate assistance supplemented by other nongovernmental organizations, philanthropic and community-based institutions, and international organizations. The general notion has always been that the affected communities are helpless and passive receivers of aid instead of partners or active players in the entire process. But now, there is a sea change in these trends as reflected in Table 16.1.

There is a paradigmatic shift from the traditional relief and disaster preparedness toward a developmental approach that is multidimensional, incorporating a combination of strategies aiming at the institutional and community levels. The earlier emergency management approach has given way to disaster risk management. It is increasingly realized that one needs to be aware of the risks involved with disasters

Table 16.1   Disaster Management: A Paradigmatic Shift

From	To
Helplessness of the victims	Awareness of the ability to cope
International response	National reliance
Outside response	Community self-reliance
Emergency agency responsibility	Everyone's responsibility
Individual aid	Restoration of social system
Victims as receivers	Victims as actors
Good dole out	Training and institution building
Donor focused	Victim focused

Source: Asian Disaster Preparedness Centre, United Nations Economic and Social Commission for Asia and Pacific, International Federation of Red Cross and Red Crescent Societies, and European Commission Humanitarian Aid Office, Third Disaster Management Practitioners' Workshop for Southeast Asia Proceedings, Bangkok, 2004. With permission.

and should be able to handle them. According to Sonny (1999), this strategy focuses on the underlying conditions of risk generated by unsustainable development, which lead to disaster occurrence. Its objective is to increase capacity to manage and reduce risks and hence the occurrence and magnitude of disasters. A disaster risk is the probability of injury, loss of life and damage to property, disruption of services and activities, and negative environmental effects.

There is a gradual emergence of an "alternative approach" in managing disasters. In this effort, strengthening the resilience of communities by understanding and addressing their vulnerabilities and capacities is gaining ground. The limited success of the top-down approach in managing disasters brought to the fore the need for people-centered and bottom-up approaches aiming at local communities and their resources, and the need to evolve local-specific risk reduction strategies.

A beginning toward an integrated disaster management strategy was made in May 1994, with the Yokohama Strategy emanating from the International Decade for Natural Disaster Risk Reduction. The Yokohoma strategy emphasized that disaster prevention, mitigation, and preparedness are better than disaster response in achieving the goals and objectives of vulnerability reduction. The Yokohama Strategy for Disaster Reduction centered on the objective of saving human lives and protecting property. It focused on

- Development of a global culture of prevention
- Adoption of a policy of self-reliance in each vulnerable country and community

- Education and training in disaster prevention, preparedness, and mitigation
- Development and strengthening of human resources and material capabilities and capacities of research and development institutions
- Involvement and active participation of the people
- Priority to programs that promote community-based approaches to vulnerability reduction
- Effective national legislation and administrative action
- Integration of private sector on disaster reduction efforts
- Involvement of nongovernmental organizations
- Strengthening the capacity of the United Nations system in disaster reduction

The International Strategy of Disaster Reduction (ISDR) pronounced in 2000 is intended to enable all societies to become resilient to the effects of natural hazards and related technological and environmental disasters to reduce human, economic, and social losses. The ISDR considered that appropriate disaster reduction strategies and initiatives at the national and international level, as well as the implementation of Agenda 21, can strengthen the likelihood of reducing or mitigating the human, economic, and social losses caused by disasters and thereby facilitate sustained growth and development. It called for participation of communities as an essential element for successful disaster reduction policy and practice. Vulnerable communities, especially in developing countries, demonstrate extraordinary capacities to prevent such losses. The Strategy emphasized the need to create disaster resilient societies and prevent human, economic, and social losses through public participation at all levels of implementation of the strategy.

The World Conference on Disaster Reduction held in January 2005 at Hyogo, Japan, identified the specific gaps arising out of the Yokohama Strategy (Hyogo Framework for Action 2005–2015). These are

- Governance: organizational, legal, and policy frameworks
- Risk identification, assessment, monitoring, and early warning
- Knowledge management and education
- Reducing underlying risk factors
- Preparedness for effective response and recovery

The conference adopted the framework for action for 2005–2015 as Building the Resilience of Nations and Communities to Disasters. It promoted a strategic and systematic approach to reducing vulnerabilities and risks to hazards. The Conference identified strategies, important among which are

- Effective integration of disaster risk considerations into sustainable development policies, planning, and programming at all levels, with a special emphasis on disaster prevention, mitigation, preparedness, and vulnerability reduction.

- Development and strengthening of institutions, mechanisms, and capacities at all levels, in particular at the community level, which can systematically contribute to building resilience to hazards.
- Systematic incorporation of risk reduction approaches into the design and implementation of emergency preparedness, response, and recovery programs in the reconstruction of affected communities.
- Inclusion of gender perspective into all disaster risk-management policies, plans, and decision-making processes.

The community hence is occupying a central role in disaster risk-management. In the dual roles of being a key actor as well as beneficiary in the process, the strategy of developing disaster resilient communities (DRC) is becoming prominent.

Disaster Resilient Communities: A Conceptual Framework

The efforts focused on two key components, namely, communities and resilience, and paved the way for achievement of a broader goal of quality of life of any community. The term community, in simple terms, implies a group of people sharing common ideas, ideals, resources, aspirations, etc. The characteristics of community are

- Geographically demarcated area
- Social systems with inherited customs
- Feeling of belongingness
- Personal, social, and group membership identity (Barnen, 1996)

As disasters are the outcome of interplay between hazards and vulnerabilities, it makes it all the more important to address the latter. The question as to who are the most vulnerable to disasters may not find an answer in clear terms. But generally those who are exposed to all or any type of vulnerabilities become the target of the threat. Some of the critical causes of vulnerability can be

- Lack of access to resources (material/economic vulnerability)
- Disintegration of social patterns (social vulnerability)
- Degradation of the environment and inability to protect it (ecological vulnerability)
- Lack of strong national and local institutional structures (organizational vulnerability)
- Lack of access to information and knowledge (educational vulnerability)

- Lack of public awareness (attitudinal and motivational vulnerability)
- Limited access to political power and representation (political vulnerability)
- Certain beliefs and customs (cultural vulnerability)
- Weak buildings or weak individuals (physical vulnerability) (Aysan, 1993)

These vulnerabilities aggravate the condition of the communities. The need to strengthen the communities arises from the reality that they are the first responders to any crisis before any other assistance from outside comes forth. Resilience is the capacity to cope with unanticipated dangers after they have become manifest and learning to bound back (Wildavsky, 1991). But communities, in general, are knowledgeable and aware of the hazards and disasters they are exposed to. This makes them conscious of the threats and instills in them a sense of coming together and facing the situation.

Human beings in general are endowed with the resilient capacity to absorb the stresses arising from their surroundings. The degree to which one is able to cope with adversity varies. In disaster situations, the portrayal by media reflects the helplessness of the communities and their dependence on external aid. It is beyond doubt that initial assistance is required, but gradually the communities come together, pool in their resources, and initiate efforts to rebuild their lives. People do have the innate capability to survive, hence they attempt to reconcile with the situation and bounce back to normalcy. The capacity of individuals to withstand disasters is determined by the internal strengths and weaknesses of a given society.

The United Nations International Strategy for Disaster Reduction (ISDR) (2004) defines resilience as "the capacity of a system, community or society potentially exposed to hazards to adapt, by resisting or changing in order to reach and to which the social system is capable of organizing itself to increase this capacity for learning from past disasters for better future protection and to improve risk reduction measures." The significance of disaster resilience arises from the realization on the part of communities that

- They are exposed to serious threats.
- Disasters or hazards have an uncertain nature that makes it difficult to prevent.
- They have to take necessary actions to strengthen the capacity to absorb the shocks and develop a mindset to recover as quickly as possible.

The acceptance of significance of vulnerabilities is leading to strengthening of resilience. This depends on the extent of shocks any socioeconomic system can absorb, and the degree to which the system reacts to this through self-organizing and capacity building. The Resilience Alliance, a multidisciplinary research group that explores solutions to coping with change and uncertainty in complex socio-ecological system, identifies the following characteristics of resilience:

- Amount of change the system can undergo and still retain the same controls on function and structure
- Degree to which the system is capable of self-organization
- Ability to build and increase the capacity for learning and adoption (www. resalliance.org)

There is a transition from vulnerabilities to capacity assessment and building particularly of the community. Table 16.2 brings out these features.

Another approach toward disaster resilience brings in the concept of disaster resistance. Geis (2000) prefers the term resistance over resilience, because the former suggests that a community can be built to resist or withstand a hazard to prevent far-reaching disaster proportions, an idea which he argues is more marketable than the latter, which refers to the ability of a community to adapt or recover quickly from a disaster. He considers that building disaster resistance is part of a wider goal of achieving a "sustainable quality of life community" which is the most human/ socially, environmentally, and economically viable community possible, one that first optimizes the safety, health, and well-being of the community and its residents. Disaster resistant communities are those which are aware of the hazards and disasters they are exposed to, and are in a way prepared to face and have the necessary skills to protect themselves against these hazards and disasters.

Table 16.2   Transition from Traditional Approach to Community Based Disaster Management

Features	Traditional	Community Based
Locus of concern	Institution	Community
Participation	Token	Dominant to control
Decision making	Top-down	Bottom-up
Main actors	Programme staff	Community residents
Resources	Programme based	Internal resources
Main methods used	Extension services	Community organizing
Impact on local capacity	Dependency creating	Empowering

Source: Asian Disaster Preparedness Centre, United Nations Economic and Social Commission for Asia and Pacific, International Federation of Red Cross and Red Crescent Societies, and European Commission Humanitarian Aid Office, Third Disaster Management Practitioners' Workshop for Southeast Asia Proceedings, Bangkok, 2004. With permission.

Yet another move toward building disaster resilient communities is also making them sustainable communities. Sustainability has a key role in hazard prevention, and mitigation and integration of this principle in evolving local community resilience would be a strategic measure. According to Beatley (1998), "Sustainable communities minimize exposure of people and property to natural disasters; sustainable communities are disaster-resilient communities." Sustainable communities . . . where people and property are kept out the way of natural hazards, where the inherently mitigating qualities of natural environmental systems are maintained, and where development is maintained, and where development is designed to be resilient in the face of natural forces (Godschalk et al., 1998).

Communities according to Beatley (op. cit.) are sustainable when they can survive and prosper in the face of major natural events. Avoidance is the preferable approach, but sustainable communities recognize that some exposure is inevitable. The sustainable communities

■ Are aware of the interconnectedness of social, economic, and environmental goals
■ Are resilient communities that seek to understand and live with the physical and environmental forces present at its location
■ Strive to balance risk against other social and economic goals
■ Recognize fundamental ecological limits and seek to protect and enhance the integrity of ecosystems
■ Promote a closer connection with and understanding of the natural environment

Be it disaster resilient, resistant, or sustainable communities, the key facets that need to be taken cognizance of include prioritizing sustainable development goals; communities owing responsibility for determining and choosing the developmental priorities; fostering local resilience and responsibility; and strengthening community's social, economic, cultural, and environmental resilience. Resilience can pay results only if communities are willing to accept the responsibility.

Geis (op. cit.) suggests the following principles as core guide in attempting to create a DRC:

■ Need for a holistic and integrated approach.
■ Redevelopment of existing communities in consideration of the natural and built environment.
■ Process of creating DRCs must be within the context of an overall larger and integrated process of creating sustainable quality life communities.
■ Local government's role should be recognized as it is at this level that the planning of development process occur.
■ A DRC must be built up from the grassroots levels, respecting the unique qualities of each community.
■ Disaster risk-management function should be enhanced by providing the best support for developing risk reduction measures.

- Additional benefit of a DRC—environment, social, and economic opportunities can motivate and empower communities and actually implement it.
- Living in communities as safe as possible from natural hazards should not be considered a luxury or bonus, but a basic necessity, as basic as a human right.
- Process of creating a DRC is the single most important tool available for reducing the exponentially increasing costs related to natural hazards.
- Core focus of a DRC is to minimize human, property, and environmental losses and social and economic disruption.

As the resilience of communities is directly linked with vulnerability reduction, several approaches in this direction are being put forth. McEntire et al. (2002) proposed a paradigm called comprehensive vulnerability management, which they define as "holistic and integrated activities directed toward the reduction of emergencies and disasters by diminishing risk and susceptibility and building resistance and resilience." This approach is considered inclusive, and holistic that

- Involves a concerted effort to identify and reduce all types of disaster vulnerabilities
- Addresses all types of triggering agents, natural or otherwise
- Incorporates comprehensive emergency management
- Requires participation of a wide range of actors

Strengthening Community Resilience: Major Strategies

There is a clear move from superimposed efforts to handle an emergency arising out of disasters toward the people at risk. The strategies through which people at risk manage, respond, and find alternatives to crisis and stress are gaining prominence. The need to instill the principles of self-resilience and self-help into the vulnerable communities is gaining ground. In the Central American Island of Honduras in 1998, a hurricane with sustained winds of 180 miles an hour resulted in severe flooding of nearby areas. Thousands of areas of land were swept away and thousand miles of roads and more than a hundred bridges were left impassable. Relief and assistance came from all quarters. As the government began sorting out the offers of aid, drawing up project proposals, people accustomed to being self-resilient began to put their communities back together. It was expressed that, "we want the government to lend us bull dozers to clear the streets, we will do the rest. We don't have money to rent machines like that, but we do have lots of strong arms and a willing spirit" (National Geographic, 1999).

There are several such initiatives that are being taken in India and other South Asian countries to support the resilience of communities to prepare, mitigate, respond, and recover from the disaster impact—in such a manner that leaves communities less at risk than before.

In the state of Andhra Pradesh in southern India, the efforts made by the rural community in the drought-affected village Zaheerabad in Medak district reveals how, with the right help, communities can build their resilience. In this region, low rainfall and deforestation have left the soils arid and eroded. Also, most of the crops were wheat, rice and cotton, which are prone to pests and require expensive fertilizers and pesticides.

A local nongovernmental organization, Deccan Development Society (DDS), employs various strategies to help increase local resilience. These are

- Forming women's collectives and encouraging collective farming by women
- Initiating programs to restore arid land back into a productive asset
- Promoting afforestation and mini-watershed management
- Creating community gene and grain fund

The DDS works with local communities to enable them cultivate idle land and reintroduce customary farming practices. Local food grains, which are drought-resistant and less dependent on expensive and external inputs, are grown. The grain, which is grown, is stored in each village land and is the community grain fund (CGF). Each community identifies the poorest households who buy the grain at the subsidized rates. The money earned becomes a revolving fund. Three principles distinguish DDS's strategy from the government-managed public distribution system: local production, local storage, and local consumption.

To further boost the capacity of farming families to withstand drought, DDS has promoted the innovative idea of a seed bank to rescue traditional crop varieties that thrive in arid conditions. Seeds of different varieties were collected from villages and the community gene fund has grown into a movement across the region. As the changes brought about in these villages are based on knowledge, skills, and resources largely internal to the community, rather than being dependent on large investments of external money or technology, this is a path that other communities in semi arid regions follow to create a more resilient future (International Federation of Red Cross and Red Crescent Societies, 2004).

Reducing the Vulnerabilities of the Communities at Risk

Vulnerability in a way implies that there is a deficit of capacities among the people who are at risk. What is required is to identify the different types of vulnerabilities at various levels. Efforts are being made by several organizations including the national governments to analyze the strengths, capacities, and vulnerabilities.

Livelihoods are the most to be affected by disasters. Agriculture being the primary livelihood in many countries, this gets disturbed and there is always lack or underdevelopment of secondary or tertiary sectors such as agro-based industries, processing units, etc. The traditional and crafts industries also receive a setback. Strategies to strengthen the livelihoods and provide sustainability are occupying a prominent place in disaster management.

In the aftermath of the Gujarat earthquake in 2001, in the village Patanka, which had 250 families, the damage was extensive wherein 170 houses collapsed and the rest were badly damaged. The village leader had taken the initiative of approaching a Delhi-based disaster management organization Sustainable Environment and Ecological Development Society (SEEDS) and solicited its support for rebuilding their lives. The SEEDS team helped the villagers procure building material; the villagers obtained their own stones, bricks, wood, roof-tiles, masons, and labor. The architects and engineers from SEEDS taught the masons, laborers, and villagers about the earthquake technology. A pool of trained masons was created. This enabled people understand the advantage of do-it-yourself, low-cost, earthquake-resistant construction (Sharma and Palakudiyil, 2003).

Communities are a resource because

- They are knowledgeable about disasters happening in their own environment and are sometimes able to forecast them.
- They are rich in experience of coping, both in preparedness and in emergency. Their coping methods, practiced over time and derived from their own experience, suit the local environment best. The richness and diversity of ordinary people's coping strategies is certainly a resource to be recognized (Malalgoda, 1999).

The renewed emphasis on identifying and building strengths, rather than just examining deficits, represents a paradigm shift in how to address issues of concern to communities living with risk. This does not mean that only the more able members of the community get recognized. Rather, the assumption is that even the worst-off may have some potential, so the focus of interventions must be on removing constraints in realizing this potential.

In the development field, the Sustainable Livelihoods (SL) approach first promoted by Chambers and Conway (1992) has become an important organizing framework for the efforts of a wide range of multilateral agencies, donors, NGOs, and government bodies. SL is concerned with the potentials, competence, capacities, and strengths rather than weaknesses and needs of the communities. It recognizes a range of strengthens or assets called capitals to sustain a livelihood. These include:

Natural capital: This includes water, land, rivers, forests, and minerals necessary for the survival of both rural and urban population.

Financial capital: Access to financial capital such as income, savings, remittance, and credit is a critical resilience factor.

Human capital: Human capital in the form of knowledge, skills, health, and physical ability determines an individual's level of resilience more than any other asset.

Social capital: In the sustainable livelihoods context, it is taken to mean the forms of mutual social assistance upon which people draw. These include networks such as clan or caste; membership of more formalized groups such as women's associations etc.

Physical capital: It comprises the basic infrastructure, goods, and services needed to support sustainable livelihoods including secure shelter and buildings, clean water supply, sanitation, and access to information and communications (International Federation of Red Cross and Red Crescent Societies, 2004).

In India, there are attempts to reduce the vulnerability of communities through strengthening the employment and livelihood strategies. Micro-finance is increasingly being used to create safety nets and enable families manage disaster risks. It helps communities mobilize money and invest in preventive activities like building of drainage system, dykes and dams, etc. The Self-Employed Women's Association (SEWA), along with International Fund for Agricultural Development (IFAD), the World Food Programme (WFP), Government of India, and Government of Gujarat, has launched a seven-year livelihood security project called *Jeevika*. It organizes women into groups called *swashrayee mandals* and provides them loans, and also inculcates a culture of savings among the rural poor that helps them during crises. The assistance is given to enhance community risk-coping strategies, in the form of operating grain or fodder banks and other disaster preparedness activities.

Building Local Capacities

Local communities need to and at several places have evolved their own, indigenous activities to cope or live with disasters. For example, many rural communities in Africa are vulnerable to food shortages because of drought, but they are able to prevent full-blown famine by employing a variety of coping mechanisms that allow them to ride out the hungry season until the next harvest. In Northern Ghana, hundreds of young men travel south in the dry season to look for work in the cocoa-producing regions of Ashanti or the Ivory Coast. In the Zambesia province of Mozambique, the main coping strategy of vulnerable groups to deal with food shortage and drought is to change the diet and reduce food intake. They change the diet from staple crop to fruits, wild fruits, locally grown vegetables, etc. (www.proventionconsortium/org).

Disaster Resilient Communities: A Gender Perspective

Disasters impact men and women in a different way. The basic needs and services of women vary. Women in general, especially in developing countries, are in a disadvantaged position with minimal access to literacy, employment, decision-making, control over economic resources, etc. Women's physical, psychological, social, and economic vulnerabilities are ignored. The consequences of disasters are looked at mostly from the purely physical point of view whereas social realities are generally not taken cognizance of and gender concerns get marginalized.

A gender sensitive approach, which for quite some time has been lacking in disaster management planning, is now gradually being adopted. This recognizes the need for fulfillment of practical needs of men and women in disaster situations and appreciates the role of women in risk and emergency management. The role of women is pertinent and needs to be given due importance as they immensely display courage, appropriate leadership skills, traditional coping knowledge as well as high resilience in crisis. Women assume responsibilities in disaster situations, in providing care to the affected family members, and arrange for food, water, and fuel. They generally discharge multifaceted functions.

In Bangladesh, where frequent flooding is a regular feature in most parts of the country, women take on the role of preparing and storing food items, which can be the source of energy and nutrition for the family for days when the floods come. As studies have shown, in Faridpur, women prepare a mixture of puffed rice and dried coconuts for this purpose, secured in appropriate packaging and safe from floodwaters. This is a food item that has long durability and gives sufficient energy when consumed in small quantities. Women in this area also ensure that their meager belongings such as clothing and bedding are stored in such a way that they can be easily removed when floodwaters rise (Malalgoda, 2004).

In the dry zone of Sri Lanka, people face scarcity of food and water during the long dry periods. Women, as regular managers of the food and water, take care of the needs of the family and resort to various mechanisms to survive the difficult conditions. Families, who generally take three meals of rice a day, change the composition of the meals to reduce the rice consumption; millet, corn, and other cheaper and less favorable food grains are introduced to substitute rice. As drought advances, the number of meals taken for a day is reduced, to preserve the available food grains. *Rice seettu* (5–10 families get together to contribute a given quantity of rice to a common pot every week or month. The collection is accessed by each family on a rotating basis.) organized by women in the drought-affected villages is a common practice to avoid the risk of starvation of the family. In Andaraweawa, it was noted that women also get into *seettu*, where small amounts of cash are contributed. Generally, under normal circumstances, when it is their turn to collect the lump sum of money, women are in the habit of purchasing special items such as furniture, crockery for the house, or long awaited items of jewelry, with this money. However in Andaraweawa, many women went into *seettu* to collect money to purchase large plastic barrels to collect and preserve water to meet their family's water requirements during the long dry periods (ibid.).

In Jhang, Punjab, Pakistan, in the aftermath of floods when affected people return to their destroyed houses, male members usually start rehabilitation work on agricultural land and in caring for livestock. Women share responsibilities with them in the handling of animals and in the rebuilding of houses, which involves preparing mud and doing construction work (Hameed, 2001).

Banaskantha, situated in the North of Gujarat in the western part of India is a drought-prone and arid area where the unpredictability of rainfall results in long drought spells. Lack of water is the main problem threatening the livelihoods of the people in this area. The main occupation is agriculture, and livestock are an essential part of the farming system, providing the main source of transport, power for agriculture, food during scarcity, and a source of cash income. The community falls back on livestock as a resource when the rains fail and crop cultivation is adversely affected. In the long drought spells when families are forced to migrate in search of food and water, they also take their animals with them. The responsibility for ensuring fodder for livestock lies mainly with women. Having assessed the threats and disruptions to their livelihoods from drought, women have formed themselves into a cooperative to ensure fodder security for animals during the dry spells, with support from the Self-Employed Women's Association (SEWA) and distributing fodder to ensure fodder security for all the families with livestock, and it is managed by the women in the village. As a result of this initiative they are not dependent on relief during the drought periods, and have also increased their capacity to support their own livelihoods (Bhatt, 1997).

In India, after the tsunami, many grassroots women's groups have initiated activities toward strengthening community resilience. These women themselves have been the survivors of disasters and could therefore train and teach other disaster-hit communities on how to shape resilience and recovery processes and how to condition the government, NGO, and donor-led programs to the advantage of disaster-affected families and communities. For example, grassroots leaders from an NGO, *Sanghamithra Service Society*, in the coastal region of the southern state of Andhra Pradesh formed emergency response teams. The men were initially hesitant to let women join these teams. But the women argued that it was necessary for them to protect lives and homes during disasters, as men would often be away on account of fishing chores. Once trained, the emergency teams of men and women themselves have been involved in training people in other villages. The federations of savings groups have been formed in six districts of Tamil Nadu, another southern state, which helped organize affected women, fish vendors, and seashell gatherers to help them restore and diversify their livelihoods. In the western state of Maharashtra, with the help of NGOs, in some earthquake-affected villages, women's self-help groups had undertaken new sanitation practices that include waste management, garbage disposal, drinking water, and toilets for houses (www.sspindia.org).

The M.S. Swaminathan Research Foundation (MSSRF) has been working in Tamil Nadu and Pondicherry since 1992 focusing on biodiversity and information and communication technology for development. During and post-tsunami, the foundation started its activities in different coastal villages of Tamil Nadu and Pondicherry by establishing Village Knowledge Centers that are equipped with several electronic and telecommunication devices that provide information and knowledge to villagers on various issues such as fish movement, height of waves, weather forecasts, etc. These are generally managed by members of self-help groups (SHGs). Women play an active role in managing these centers. The foundation is planning to expand these centers to other coastal villages to create awareness about managing disasters by empowering the communities (http://www.disasterwatch.net/tsunami_il.htm).

The local communities also utilize traditional wisdom and knowledge in handling disasters. They do bring in a lot of insight into disasters based on the age-old beliefs and traditions, which many a time proves useful. For example, in cyclone-prone areas, the continuous blowing of wind from the eastern direction, a strange rather thundering sound from the sea for quite some period is said to indicate the striking of a cyclone. In case of floods, people infer the onset of disaster based on the color of clouds, their formation, and their movement. In Nepal also, during the monsoon period, observing the water levels in the river is done by all, but particularly by women. Accustomed to spending most of their day, in and around the village, engaged in cultivation, collecting water and fuel wood, they have extensive knowledge and powers of observation to know the slight changes in the movement and the levels of water. Such observations help them to make decisions such as when to leave their huts and move to safety. Guided by their own judgment, they move to nearby safe places with cattle when the water levels rise beyond the safety levels. Once the water levels recede, they come back to continue with their livelihood (Malalgoda, 2004).

Creation of Disaster Resilient Communities: Key Concerns

The complexion and nature of disasters are changing. We have to go beyond the assessment of needs and vulnerabilities to put the community resilient enough to face the challenges. This requires a multipronged strategy on the part of national governments, nongovernmental organizations, international agencies, and other key stakeholders. This requires

- Promoting acceptance or realization on the part of the community that it is not just the nature, which is the cause of disasters. To a large extent, they are the outcome of the interaction between the physical environment and individuals.
- Developing a long-term approach toward risk management that encompasses preparedness, mitigation, response, and rehabilitation.
- Fostering interdependence, collaboration among several sections of the community and other stakeholders.
- Analyzing the root causes of vulnerability that the community is exposed to and attempt to tackle them.
- Integrating sustainable development to risk management. The communities need to play a proactive role in assessing the environmental resources and disasters they are likely to face and combine appropriate mitigation strategies in sustainable development.
- Mobilizing social capital, as investment in this arena would go a long way in mitigating the negative social consequences of disasters. This is important, as the community itself is the first responder in disasters.
- Taking cognizance of strengths of local livelihoods and capacities, community perspectives and priorities, and attempt to build social consensus.
- Bringing change in the cultural perceptions about risks, hazards, and disasters.

Disaster resilience as a strategy, beyond doubt, enhances the community's ability to bear the brunt of disasters and overcome the extreme repercussions with minimal outside assistance. This depends on investment in several critical areas—social, economic, political, cultural, environmental, and so on. There are certain problem areas also in the creation of resilience or resistance or sustainability. Some of these include

- Paucity of resources including technical know-how of incorporating or integrating disaster resilience mechanisms in disaster/risk management plans.
- Lack of political leadership and commitment. The creation of disaster resilience requires a proactive approach and futuristic vision as the results or impact of this cannot be immediately realized. This is a long-drawn process and requires sustained efforts on all fronts.
- Prevalence of public apathy resulting in inertia and absence of pressure from the people. In spite of awareness about the possible threats, a fatalistic view still remains with certain segments of society, which could act as an impediment toward building resilience.
- Inability on the part of the community to initiate measures toward disaster risk reduction. This coupled with lack of institutional efforts at government and corporate levels slowdown the process. Certain steps require external interventions and hence the community is not fully empowered to address the causes of vulnerability.
- Absence of clear-cut indicators to gauge the areas requiring disaster resilience. The identification of focal points or spheres where investments are required becomes at times a critical task.

Concluding Observations

The complexion of disaster management is undergoing transformation. Risk reduction as a significant disaster management strategy is gaining significance. This encompasses several components such as institutionalizing and strengthening national systems and capacities, improving governance mechanisms at the local level, addressing and reducing the vulnerabilities of the communities at risk as well as identifying and building the capacities of people. The ultimate goal to improve the quality of life of people can be realized when communities are enabled to accept uncertainty through reducing vulnerability by self-resilience. The communities are the repository of resources, ideas, zeal, and enthusiasm. These need to be channelized in avenues that would in the long run benefit the community. A little help initially from the national, state, local governments, nongovernmental organizations, and international organizations would boost the morale of the community and instill trust to ensure continuity of the activities. Disaster resilience is an ongoing process, and a sustainable strategy is to be evolved which is people-centered and sharpens their skills to cope with the risks of disasters. In the current scenario, people are being considered as a resource, and this should be seen as a positive change paradigm in the field of disaster management. M.S. Swaminathan, the

Chairman of the National Commission on Farmers (NCF), India envisages setting up of Village Knowledge Centers across the country under the Jamsetji Tata National Virtual Academy, and from each village, a man and a woman will be trained and elected as a fellow of the academy. The commission will train the communities in disaster preparedness and management (*The Hindu,* 2005).

Any country, developing or developed, is susceptible to disasters, natural or man-made. In tune with the global efforts in taking a series of measures toward risk reduction, with special reference to building community resilience, this has to be a part of the efforts promoting sustainability. Resilience is one such strategy, whereupon its significance is to be demonstrated, and information widely disseminated so that success stories could be replicated in tune with the local milieu.

References

Asian Disaster Preparedness Centre, United Nations Economic and Social Commission for Asia and Pacific, International Federation of Red Cross and Red Crescent Societies and European Commission Humanitarian Aid Office, 2004, Third Disaster Management Practitioners' Workshop for Southeast Asia Proceedings, Bangkok.

Aysan Y.F., 1993, Vulnerability Assessment, in P.A. Merriman and C.W.A. Browitt (Eds.), *Natural Disasters: Protecting Vulnerable Communities,* Thomas Telford, London.

Barnen R., 1996, *Social Work and Administration—Methods and Techniques,* Sweden, Radda Barnen.

Beatley T., 1998, The vision of sustainable communities, in Raymond Burby (Ed), *Cooperating with Nature, National Academy Press,* Joseph Henry Press, Washington DC.

Bhatt M., 1997, Maintaining families in drought India: The Fodder Security System of the Banaskantha Women, in Priyanthi Fernando and Vijitha Fernando (Eds.), *South Asian Women: Facing Disasters, Securing Life,* Duryog Nivaran, Sri Lanka.

Chambers R. and Conway G.R., 1992, *Sustainable Livelihoods: Practical Concepts for the 21st Century,* IDS Discussion Paper No. 296, Institute for Development Studies, University of Sussex.

Dan H. and Kovacks P., 2004, Background Paper on Disaster Resilient Cities (www.dmrg.org/resources).

David M. et al., 2002, A comparison of disaster paradigms: The search for a holistic policy guide, *Public Administration Review,* 62 (3).

Emergency Management Institute, FEMA, *Building Disaster Resilient and Sustainable Communities.* (www.training.fema.gov)

Geis, D.E., 2000, By Design: The Disaster Resistant and Quality of Life Community, *Natural Hazards Review,* 1 (3).

Godschalk et al., 1998, Integrating hazard mitigation and local land use planning, in Raymond Burby (Ed.), *Cooperating with Nature, National Academy Press,* Joseph Henry Press, Washington DC.

Hameed K., 2001, cited in Malalgoda M.A., 2004.

Hyogo Framework for Action 2005–2015; Building the Resilience of Nations and Communities to Disasters (www.unisdr.org).

International Federation of Red Cross and Red Crescent Societies, 2004, World Disasters Report.

Malalgoda A.M., 1999, *Defeating Disasters: Ideas for Action*, Duryog Nirvaran, Sri Lanka.

Malalgoda A.M., 2004, Women: The risk managers in natural disasters (www.ssri.hawaii.edu research/GDW website/pages/background.html).

McEntire, David et al., 2002, A Comparison of Disaster Paradigms: The Search for a Holistic Policy Guide, *Public Administration Review*, 62 (3): 267–281.

Williams A.R., *National Geographic*, November 1999, After the deluge, 196 (5).

Swaminathan M.S., Beyond tsunami: An agenda for action, *The Hindu*, 30 March 2005.

Sharma A. and Palakudiyil T., 2003, The Lessons of Gujarat in Tom Palakudiyil and Mary Todd (Eds.), *Facing up to the Storm How Local Communities Can Cope with Disaster: Lessons from Orissa and Gujarat*, Christian Aid, New Delhi.

Sonny J., 1999, Fundamentals of disaster risk management: How are Southeast Asian countries addressing this? In *Risk, Development and Disasters: Southern Perspectives*, University of Cape Town, Department of Environment and Geographical Sciences.

United Nations, 2004, International Strategy for Disaster Reduction, Geneva.

Wildavsky A., 1991, Searching for Safety, New Jersey, Transaction Publishers.

www.unisdr.org/world_camp/2005/case study 4-Microfinance, The Experience of SEWA.

Zenaida D.G., Community risk management—A living legacy (www.hyogouncrd.or.sp/publication/proceedings/2004 symposium).

FIRST RESPONSE AND EMERGENCY MANAGEMENT

Chapter 17

National Incident Management System: Bringing Order to Chaos

Bruce J. Moeller

CONTENTS

Introduction

In the first half of the first decade of the new millennium, the United States was struck by two of its worst disasters—one man-made and one natural. The events of September 11, 2001, terrorized a nation and brought the issues of terrorism and homeland security to the forefront in citizen's mind. Hurricane Katrina striking New Orleans in 2005 changed our focus back to the threats from natural disasters. Together, these two events provide a fitting context for a discussion on how to bring order to the chaos that ultimately arrives with each disaster.

A disaster is, by almost any definition, events whose demands far outstrip the ability of society to effectively respond. It almost always results in large loss of life and property, or otherwise disrupts society. As such, a certain degree of chaos almost always accompanies its arrival. Hurricane Katrina was one of the most significant chaotic incidents in recent times (Schneider, 2005). Prevention of, preparedness for, responding to, recovering from, and mitigation of potential disasters—whatever they may be—are necessary for any type of incident, man-made or natural. This concept is described as an all-hazards approach to emergency management. U.S. Homeland Security Presidential Directive #5, issued by President Bush shortly after the September 11 attacks, establishes a National Incident Management System (NIMS) to address multi-jurisdictional and multi-organizational challenges that arose from the response to New York City's World Trade Center (Perry, 2003; Walsh et al., 2005).

Communities that experienced significant disasters have learned all too painfully that emergency management, to be effective, must provide a rapid and effective response. Unfortunately, learning from previous disasters is often limited to the specific lessons of that earlier event. It is often found that "policies and programs have been instituted and implemented in the aftermath of a disaster, based almost solely on that disaster experience, and with little investment in capacity building to deal with the next disaster" (Waugh, 2000). This is most often seen in the development of new programs, or passing of legislation, that has immediately followed major events (Rubin, 2004). Because of these same issues, some critics believe that current efforts to develop a national response system for dealing with all types of disasters will likely fall short (Buck et al., 2006). Only time will tell if those predictions will come true. However, it is clear that failure by senior managers and leaders to understand the purpose, basic structure, and obstacles to NIMS will almost surely cause their efforts to fail. Accordingly, although this chapter will provide a basic overview of NIMS and issues regarding its successful implementation, the chapter is not intended to prepare individuals to operate under the National Response Plan. Rather, readers should first undertake formal NIMS training and then use the following information as a roadmap to avoid common errors in its implementation.

Community leaders and emergency managers know they must be prepared to provide an emergency response within a coherent system, one that is well-coordinated horizontally and vertically across government agencies. This horizontal and vertical integration requires a structure that meets two essential criteria. First, the system must be flexible. Flexibility in emergency response is required because of the unknown causes and contingencies that must be addressed when managing a major disaster. Often, it is the lack of experience in dealing with emerging problems that leads to the disaster itself. With time and experience, emergency responders become more proficient and better prepared—making the disaster less so—simply because they have learned from prior events. The corollary to this premise is that first-time incidents challenge emergency managers and policy makers. Experience is a valuable tool when dealing with unknown contingencies.

The second criterion for an effective system is that it must be scalable. The response to an event will always start small, perhaps a single police vehicle or fire engine, regardless of its magnitude. From that point, the event will expand rapidly such as during September 11. In some circumstances there is a delayed acceleration, as when the levies failed hours after the initial landfall of Hurricane Katrina. As the situation becomes clearer, and more resources are brought to bear, the emergency management system must be able to expand and contract as circumstances dictate. The lessons learned from prior disasters help provide a context and understanding of the challenges that emergency managers, political leaders, and ultimately the public must endure in future events.

History

The major lessons learned, and experience gained, from emergency response is largely rooted in the American fire service. When "routine emergencies" occur every day in our communities, law enforcement, ambulance, or the fire service respond. These routine emergencies are called such because the emergency responders are well equipped to handle them—resources are sufficient to manage the event. However, when the incident is of a proportion where demand outstrips resources, a disaster has occurred. Historically, these events have most often been handled by the fire service. Wildland fires, hazardous materials accidents, tornados, or airline crashes have forced the fire service, civil defense practitioners, and other emergency responders to develop more coherent plans. These events require the management of a large number of resources that are necessary to effectively respond. Today's incident management systems are rooted in the wildfire experiences of the 1970s.

FIRESCOPE and Fire Ground Command

The fire service's first major efforts to develop incident management systems were directed at managing large-scale wildland fire in the western United States. The FIRESCOPE (Firefighting Resources of California Organized for Potential Emergencies) project began in the early 1970s and its focus was on larger rural events.

The need for firefighters from across California, from many different agencies, required significant coordination and support as events often lasted multiple weeks. Wildland firefighters had to be deployed, staged, fed, housed, and supplied. Accounting of personnel, equipment, and other resources was a sizable undertaking.

However, the system did not lend itself well to smaller events of greater frequency that often occur in urban settings. This resulted in several efforts, the most noteworthy being the Fire Ground Command (FGC) system developed by the Phoenix Fire Department. FGC focused on managing basic house fires and other incidents often responded to by urban and suburban fire departments. These events differed from wildland fire fighting in that the number of personnel required to manage the incident was often number less than 20 individuals. These events lasted only hours instead of days and weeks. And most important, the incident was typically handled by a single agency. Although many characteristics were similar, FGC was not designed for all types of events.

Incident Command System

It soon became evident that several issues were unaddressed by the FIRESCOPE and FGC systems. In essence, competing systems, using different nomenclature and approaches, were used for different types of incidents. However, lack of practice and daily integration into operations made users resistant to use the appropriate system when needed, and less proficient when they did. The result was the development of a hybrid system that took advantage of the strengths in FIRESCOPE and FGC. What soon developed was a common nomenclature that was built to be used for daily incidents both large and small, and the infrequent catastrophic events (National Fire Service Incident Management System Consortium, 2000).

An obstacle and mistake often made by inexperienced emergency managers is to attempt to implement a centralized decision-making organization to manage a highly uncertain environment. In fact, although overall policy must be established from a centrally established command center, individuals who are close to the action must make many of the incremental decisions. Those closest to the problem are better suited to identify and react to unexpected contingencies that are inherent in disaster response (Bigley and Roberts, 2001; Roberts et al., 1994).

Today, incident command systems are used much more extensively than just in the fire service. The application of incident command system's has been applied to the recovery operation of the space shuttle Columbia (Donahue, 2004) and the management of a public health outbreak involving the poultry industry (Moynihan, 2005). One of the greatest values in incident command systems is their hierarchical nature—providing an overall structure from which both flexibility and scalability can be achieved. Hierarchy is essential and has been shown to provide better performance in dynamic decision-making environments (Artman, 1999). In recent years, the application of incident command concepts has been applied to fire services in the United Kingdom. These include a clear line of command, manageable span of control, sectorization of the incident scene, decision support systems, and collaboration between agencies (Smitherman, 2005).

Overview of NIMS

After the September 11 attacks, President Bush issued Presidential Homeland Security Directive #5. The federal government undertook a revision of its National Response Plan, created the Department of Homeland Security, and called for the development of a National Incident Management System that would encompass all types of incidents—an all hazards approach—while integrating emergency responders across all levels of government, nonprofit, and private sectors. These far-reaching efforts resulted in the development of the National Incident Management System document first released in March 2004 (U.S. Department of Homeland Security, 2004).

The NIMS is comprised of six major components that work together to establish a structure for local, state, federal, and private sector organizations to use in the response to major domestic incidents. The following summaries of these components outline their overall purpose under NIMS.

Command and management provides the backbone of emergency incident response, the Incident Command System (ICS) that all emergency providers are expected to be familiar with. This component also addresses methods to provide multiagency coordination, both for operations and public information. Public information is an essential dimension of emergency management.

Preparedness encompasses the planning, training, and exercising for emergency response. Many elements of emergency response will not be effective unless they are utilized or exercised routinely. Simply having a written plan will not make for an effective emergency response system. Systems must be used in daily activities, exercised frequently, or developed in a continuing fashion. In addition, the preparedness component considers the needs for personnel and equipment certifications so that effective mutual aid can be accomplished. Although a framework for personnel and equipment qualifications has been developed, there is no final or agreed upon approach for all such areas. Although it is typical for a single entity to have specific meaning assigned to a title or term, no single state or local government can be expected to deal with all types of disasters. Therefore, a common language is essential to allow for a well-coordinated mutual aid response.

Resource management defines standardized mechanisms and requirements to inventory, mobilize, dispatch, track, and then recover assets over the course of an incident.

Communications and information management includes both incident management communications, such as voice and data, and the information management processes necessary for the communication to occur.

Supporting technologies is closely related to the above. Here we are dealing with specific hardware and software systems to make information flow timely and meaningful. Beyond typical limitations, the real trick is these systems must accommodate multiple organizations across geography, jurisdiction, and role.

Ongoing management and maintenance provide a process by which NIMS must ensure both routine review and refinement in its processes. Earlier comments emphasized the value of experience in managing uncertainty. Assuring NIMS utility will require critical analysis of its failures.

The Incident Command System

The major backbone for managing an emergency incident rests with the incident management system. This is not to minimize the need for proper preplanning or training. However, when a large event happens, each responder must know their role under ICS and how they contribute to the overall goals.

Researchers have identified four essential dimensions for affective incident command. These are (1) an effective accountability system, (2) meaningful situational assessment, (3) appropriate resource allocation, and (4) effective communication system (Jiang et al., 2004). ICS allows for each of these dimensions to be met, assuming the incident commander (IC) effectively uses the proper elements of the incident command system. ICS defines basic operating characteristics, the management components, and the overall structure that emergency response organizations must utilize throughout the life cycle of an incident. The ICS is the cornerstone of NIMS.

In its most typical form, ICSs utilize the concept of a singular command—one individual is in charge. However, the realities of attempting to coordinate multiple entities from multiple jurisdictions required an alternate command structure as well—that of a unified command. In unified command, all other components of the command structure remain intact, and everybody still reports to only a single individual, except for the IC. In unified command strategic decisions, those at the highest level are made by a unified group with representatives from each entity and jurisdiction. It is the role of the IC to be both part of that group and then implement the strategic decisions made under unified command. In practice, unified command is only used in larger incidents where multiple groups, not of the same jurisdiction or organization, are required to successfully manage the event.

The traditional concept of government response to an emergency incident has assumed a single organization would respond and deliver services based on that event. This traditional concept has been replaced to reflect a reality of public services increasingly being provided by multiple organizations rather than a single entity (Moynihan, 2005). This response scenario involving collaborative networks integrated both vertically and horizontally, requires the incident management system to accommodate competing interests. Under NIMS, these competing interests are managed by a single operational chain of command being led by a single IC taking policy direction from the unified group.

Two essential leadership qualities are a problem-solving orientation and adaptability to rapidly changing circumstances (Donahue, 2004). For the IC, these are necessary traits. Managers, as contrasted with leaders, are often risk adverse. In times of uncertainty, the need for calculated risk-taking and an aggressiveness to attack emerging problems permit the IC to stay ahead of rapidly changing conditions. However, the IC does not manage the incident alone. Many others are involved in developing the strategic priorities and then implementing the incident action plan.

In large-scale incidents, there are four major sections under the IC, each with a specific role. The acronym FLOP is a useful memory aid for Finance/Administration, Logistics, Operations, and Planning. In daily use of ICS, only the operations section is often put in place. In fact, the incident commander often functions both as IC and the operations chief (remember this is a scalable system). The use of a planning, logistics, or finance section only occurs in larger, more complex, or extended operations.

The finance section provides accountability. This is an item often ignored or overlooked in the initial stages of an incident, but the attention of policy makers often shifts to budget impact and accountability for operations when the initial crisis subsides. The finance section, or one of its subordinate units, tracks personnel time dedicated to various functions, expenditures for supplies, and works with the logistics section to obtain necessary resources.

The logistics section provides for the long-term needs and resources often overlooked in major events. Logistics must anticipate long-term requirements for continued operation and assure resources are provided. As with the other sections, various predefined specialty units consisting of communications, food unit, or facilities unit may be needed depending on the long-term operational plan. For example, who is going to feed and provide temporary sleeping accommodations for emergency responders?

The operations section is the most utilized area of incident management. Its organization depends on the specific type of event and the priorities established by the incident action plan. This section may be organized by jurisdictional areas, geographic boundaries, functional needs, or any combination of these.

The planning section's role is often overlooked not only in local incidents, where its usefulness is less critical, but also in larger or long-term events where a lack of planning can be critical. The planning section should be comprised of experienced personnel who have the skills to provide meaningful and timely analysis and then project conditions that may exist in the near future. Additionally, many incidents require the planning section to be staffed with subject-matter technical experts whose specific qualifications are determined by the incident at hand.

Experienced IC's know that success is determined by more than simply "filling in the boxes" on an incident command organizational chart. There are numerous challenges in successfully implementing the ICS. These challenges of incident management need to be considered and addressed to assure successful handling of a disaster.

Challenges of Incident Management

Implementation of effective incident management is not without its challenges. After the terrorist attacks of September 11, three key issues were identified as particularly troublesome. First, emergency responders were able to rely only on voice communications. At least initially, other types of communication were either ineffective or not utilized. Second, there was limited situational awareness. This inability to successfully integrate multiple data sources into the formation of an effective representation of the crisis limited the ability of emergency responders to effectively call for and utilize resources. Finally, long-standing problems between police, fire, and other emergency responders were magnified by the lack of interoperability among their respective communication systems (Bahora et al., 2003). These challenges, and recommended actions to minimize the impact, are detailed below.

Situational Awareness

The ability to achieve and maintain situational awareness is one of the most significant challenges in managing large-scale emergency events. Situational awareness has been described as having a perception of the incident in its current environment, comprehension of its meaning, and a projection of the incident into the near future (Endsley, 2000; McQuaid, 2003).

The loss of situational awareness has been shown to lead to disastrous results. Accordingly, much more effort must be paid to establishing and maintaining situational awareness to successfully manage a large incident. A common problem for incident commanders is the tendency to focus on single components of an incident, disregarding other attributes. This tunnel vision inhibits a true comprehension of the incident and its future impact. Because of that limitation, the ability to forecast near-term events is restricted. To overcome this problem, the IC must perform rapid information sampling. This process requires a continuous assessment of information flowing into the command center, seeking critical clues and essential elements from the overall flow of information rather than focusing on one or two seemingly critical components. This permits the IC to more accurately assess all current conditions and anticipate future ones (McQuaid, 2003).

Sonnenwald and Pierce (2000) found that interwoven situational awareness between the individual, group, and among groups facilitates emergency response. This is accomplished by ensuring frequent communications occur between all participants. The ability of incident managers, especially among those from different organizations, to establish trust with each other is essential to successful incident management. As emergency events occur without warning, and because of the increasing need of multiple agencies to work together, this positive impact can be obtained by interagency planning and tabletop exercises. The benefits will then be seen when incident managers are put together under live emergency conditions.

However, these efforts may be hampered by "contested collaboration," a term used to describe competition between groups that leads to dysfunctional actions. Such contested competition is often seen between elite military units during noncombat times. The goal is to ensure these adverse behaviors do not continue once emergency operations are underway. Trust is also enhanced when leaders share norms and a vision of successful incident mitigation. The establishment of shared norms/vision requires a rapid and accurate flow of information from the field, wide dissemination of this information (in raw form) to all team members, and communication among incident managers regarding the meaning of the information received. Such communication often occurs, and is enhanced, when the process is less formal and not constrained by typical hierarchical processes. This leads to a common sense of urgency regarding the incident and its resolution (Moynihan, 2005).

Communications

A specific unit under logistics that has received much attention after recent disasters is the communications unit. Many senior managers and policy makers often hear the term "interoperability" when discussing radio communications. Much of this discussion has focused on the radio system itself—the hardware. Yet this is only a part of the issue. Manufacturers have engineered systems to patch multiple radio systems together, though admittedly with some limitations. The larger question is the ability of multiple responders to communicate clearly in an interoperable environment. Some critics stated that a single radio system during September 11 may have dramatically changed outcomes. This assertion ignores the fact that 3000 emergency responders cannot all work on a single radio channel. The ability to organize communications rationally among large numbers of emergency responders, and assure that the right person talks to the right person, is essential. The failure to bring a coherent structure to radio communications will result in chaos. Policies and procedures are needed, and must be exercised, which assign certain functions or organizational units to different radio channels (or talkgroups in a trunked radio system). Communications among these groups must allow for communications between the unit leaders and the overall IC. Predetermination of which channels are used for what purpose will reduce initial confusion in the incident.

Resources

The ability to deliver all needed resources to the correct location at the correct time, under emergency conditions, highlights the challenges that await emergency managers. Experience has shown that resources are scarce initially. However in some incidents, such as in hurricanes, the arrival of water and ice may occur days to weeks after the local region is beginning to recover or when demand is already met by other sources. In this later example, a problem develops where supplies are wasted and sit idle.

366 ■ Disaster Management Handbook

The planning section must be skilled at predicting needed resources and the burn rate at which expendable supplies are consumed. Operational managers must anticipate how many personnel and equipment will be needed in the future and assure those needs are communicated. Resources arriving to a disaster scene most often will be placed into a staging area where they are checked in before being deployed or used. Therefore, the tracking of resources is essential.

In the aftermath of Hurricane Katrina's landfall on New Orleans, those remaining in the city fled to the convention center upon advice of city officials. In anticipation of food, water, and ice that never arrived, FEMA lost track of their supplies once they left their initial staging area. In 2006, FEMA made significant efforts to track resources during future disasters. Each truck leaving a FEMA staging area is now equipped with GPS tracking equipment so that disaster managers can track those resources as they move into disaster areas.

Tracking of resources provides for the financial accountability that will be required long after the initial press coverage of an event has waned. Personnel accountability assures the safety of emergency responders and allows managers to know what resources are already on-hand and available for potential redeployment. Tracking of expendable supplies allows for reimbursement and provides information to the planning section so future demands can be anticipated. Although not necessarily a high-profile function, the failure to properly track resources—as was seen during Hurricane Katrina—can have significant impacts on the ability to meet urgent needs of those impacted by an event.

Conclusion

Effective response to disasters requires strong leadership. But leadership cannot occur in a vacuum. The basic structure that NIMS hopes to achieve allows for emergency responders to understand their role, to whom they report, the overall objectives of their tasks, and how this all fits together. Therefore, leadership requires setting a clear mission and communicating that mission clearly to all emergency responders.

Local leaders, especially elected officials, need to assure that incident commanders have the necessary resources needed to accomplish the mission. This requires that typical justification for resources and cost accounting be relaxed. Flexibility is required as uncertainty exists in disasters. Further, scalability and the ability to respond quickly require that some resources may be ordered in anticipation of future requirements, and then are never needed. Such circumstances are unavoidable and must be tolerated during extreme circumstances.

Most importantly, both elected officials and senior managers must prepare to manage potential disasters. This requires training and the building of capacity. The establishment of robust communications systems and the design of information systems to achieve and maintain situational awareness will require capital. Emergency responders must then plan and practice their response. Certain elements must be institutionalized so that everyday practices will prove useful in extreme events. Only then can communities hope to avoid the chaos inherent in disaster management.

References

Artman, H. 1999. Situational awareness and cooperation within and between hierarchical units in dynamic decision making. *Ergonomics, 42*(11), 1404–1417.

Bahora, A., Collins, T., Davis, S., Goknur, S., Kearns, J., Lieu, T., et al. 2003. *Integrated Peer-to-Peer Applications for Advanced Emergency Response Systems. Part 1: Concept of Operations.* Paper presented at the Proceedings of the 2003 Systems and Information Engineering Design Symposium.

Bigley, G., and Roberts, K. 2001. The incident command system: High reliability organizing for complex and volatile task environments. *Academy of Management Journal, 44*(6), 1281–1299.

Buck, D., Trainor, J., and Aguirre, B. 2006. A critical evaluation of the incident command system and NIMS. *Journal of Homeland Security and Emergency Management, 3*(3), Article 1.

Donahue, A. 2004. *What Can the Department of Homeland Security Learn about Incident Management from the Space Shuttle Columbia Recovery Operation?* Paper presented at the Public Policy Analysis and Management 26th Annual Research Conference, Atlanta, Georgia.

Endsley, M. 2000. Theoretical underpinnings of situation analysis: A critical review. In M. Endsley and D. Garland (Eds.), *Situation Awareness Analysis and Measurement.* Mahwah, NJ: Lawrence Erlbaum Associates.

Jiang, X., Hong, J., Takayama, L., and Landay, J. 2004. *Ubiquitous Computing for Firefighters: Field Studies and Program Types of Large Displays for Incident Command.* Paper presented at the CHI 2004, Vienna, Austria.

McQuaid, M. 2003. The impact of time based text visualization on situational awareness. Unpublished Doctoral dissertation, University of Arizona, Phoenix.

Moynihan, D. 2005. *Leveraging Collaborative Networks in Infrequent Emergency Situations*: IBM.

National Fire Service Incident Management System Consortium. 2000. *Model Procedures Guide for Structural Firefighting* (2nd ed.). Norman, OK: Fire Protection Publications.

Perry, R. 2003. Incident management systems and disaster management. *Disaster Prevention and Management, 12*(5), 405–412.

Roberts, K., Stout, S., and Halpern, J. 1994. Decision dynamics in two high reliability military organizations. *Management Science, 40*(5), 614–624.

Rubin, C. 2004. Major terrorist events in the US and their outcomes: Initial analysis and observations. *Journal of Homeland Security and Emergency Management, 1*(1), Article 2.

Schneider, S. 2005. Administrative breakdowns in the governmental response to Hurricane Katrina. *Public Administration Review, 65*(5), 515–516.

Smitherman, M. 2005, microphone off. *British Styles of Incident Safety: Command Decision making and Team Knowledge.* Paper presented at the Fire Department Integrated Risk Analysis and Management, Fairfax, Virginia.

Sonnenwald, D. and Pierce, L. 2000. Information behavior in dynamic group work contexts: Interwoven situational awareness, dense social networks and contested collaboration in command and control. *Information Processing and Management, 36,* 461–479.

U.S. Department of Homeland Security. 2004. *National Incident Management System.* Washington, DC: Government Printing Office.

Walsh, D., Christen, H., Miller, G., Callsen, J., Christian, Cilluffo, F., and Maniscalco, P. 2005. *National Incident Management System: Principles and Practice.* Boston: Jones and Bartlett Publishers.

Waugh, W. 2000. *Living with Hazards, Dealing with Disasters.* New York: M.E. Sharpe.

Chapter 18

Hospital Emergency Preparedness

Nicholas V. Cagliuso Sr., Eliot J. Lazar,
Andrew N. Lazar, and Laurence J. Berger

CONTENTS

Introduction to Hospital Emergency Preparedness

Any grasp of hospital emergency preparedness begins with an understanding of the fundamental goal of healthcare institutions, i.e., to maximize the provision of safe, efficient, and high quality care to all patients. Arguably, the hospital is the cornerstone of the healthcare system, and it is the hospital that receives the injured, infected, bleeding, and broken during a major incident [1]. Consequently, the hospital must prepare via an all-hazards approach that acknowledges the full range of natural, technological, and deliberate incidents it may face, both as a service provider and a victim.

Unfortunately, and quite vividly, Hurricanes Katrina, Wilma, and Rita; the Northeast Blackout of 2003; and the events of 9/11 have served as sundry examples of how challenged the nation's healthcare system is in managing disasters. Although many in the field argue that institutions are doing the best they can, rigorous assessments that examine the overall quality of preparedness of the U.S. healthcare system do not exist. Nor are there agreed-upon metrics that hospital leadership can utilize to benchmark their activities.

This chapter is an introduction to emergency preparedness for U.S. healthcare organizations. With over 5700 hospitals in the United States in 2005 [2], each with varying service areas, financial structures, and management arrangements, and each providing a spectrum of care ranging from primary to quaternary services, the need for this vital sector of the nation's economy to prepare has never been stronger.

But none of this is new. The events of 9/11 served to crystallize a decade-long evolution in the role of hospitals in emergency preparedness and disaster management [3]. To that end, healthcare institutions must now learn to function as coordinated components of a regional response to crises that are more far-reaching;

these new roles are accompanied by a host of issues, including, but certainly not limited to, education, communication, and institutional response [3]. Additionally, healthcare institutions must view themselves as potential targets as well as responders. In many respects, the health system is now viewed as a foundation of national security [1] that must provide care anytime, anywhere, without fail, and in an ever-expanding way, such as in the case of its roles expanding into the concept of "first receivers." Similarly, over the last several decades, hospitals have been viewed as sites of community refuge, facilities that will be the last to lose power, food, or water, and patients now converge on hospitals during crises, even in the absence of illness or injury. Whether hospital leadership agrees with this changing role for their organizations during times of disaster is questionable, but they increasingly recognize their institution's responsibility in ensuring they are capable of fulfilling it.

The resilience of hospitals can be cultivated through improvements in information acquisition and dissemination, resource management, mobility management, incident command, and staff versatility [4]. Healthcare leaders must realize that the day-to-day operations, although trying and stressful, often involve the ability to impart deliberate and methodical processes to function. Even pressing decisions are often data driven and can usually wait until more comprehensive information is available. Conversely, during emergencies, healthcare leaders must impart judgment based on the best available data, which is often incomplete, incorrect, or both; remain cognizant of the time sensitive nature of the issue at hand and for the most effective outcomes; and ensure that a well-defined command structure is initiated and remains intact throughout the duration of the incident.

Factors Shaping Hospital Preparedness

As a service oriented business, U.S. hospitals spend more dollars per capita than any other country in the world, yet there is a perception that the U.S. healthcare industry is antiquated and inefficient, unable or unwilling to respond to business prerogatives or properly use modern management methods and information technology. With these perceptions comes increased scrutiny to provide improved care, which combined with close operating margins often places initiatives that do not directly impact the hospitals' bottom line, such as emergency preparedness, to suffer. Following is a brief treatment of the factors that shape hospital emergency preparedness.

No Direct Improvements to Bottom Line

Hospitals' main goals during any emergency are twofold: to sustain the provision of day-to-day services and to respond to increased needs created by the emergency event. Yet, preparedness initiatives are perceived to be at direct odds with the fundamental notion of productivity and efficiency that drives healthcare today.

Daily operating expenses such as those that support regulatory and accreditation requirements often stretch hospitals' already strained resources. Further, the constant restructuring of the U.S. healthcare system continues to alter the sizes and complexities of healthcare institutions and may be increasing their susceptibility of untoward events [4].

Accreditation

The Joint Commission (JC) is the primary credentialing group for hospitals and its standards related to emergency management in hospitals [5] outlines emergency management requirements for hospitals. Although accreditation programs can improve overall quality, they may also increase costs without necessarily increasing revenues, such as in the case of emergency management. This forces emergency preparedness activities to compete for resources and makes their implementation even less likely. For reasons of prudent stewardship, and because of the requirements of accreditation and licensure, hospitals must prepare for disasters [4].

The Uninsured/Bad Debt

The majority of hospitals in the United States lose money serving Medicare and Medicaid patients, and nearly a third of healthcare institutions lose money overall [2]. Combine that with the fact that about 45 million Americans lack health insurance and hospitals must then provide about $25 billion in uncompensated care [2]. Coupling both of those facts with our desire to provide the best care possible while maintaining a constant state of preparedness makes it difficult to focus on preparedness efforts that are often perceived as costly, unnecessary, or both, as they provide either no or low additions to the bottom line.

Staffing

The current state of healthcare with its widespread staffing shortages, namely in the field of nursing, negatively impacts preparedness efforts. The supply of caregivers is not meeting the demand for even basic healthcare services, so the notion of surge capacity, particularly in terms of nursing resources, is not necessarily feasible. And within that fact lies decreasing rates of experienced staff and increasing turnover, making the seasoned professionals that we have come to rely upon as our first line of care, particularly during crises, nonexistent.

Hospital Overcrowding

U.S. hospitals and emergency departments in particular, continue to experience increased demand for their services, pushing many to breaking points as outlined by the Institute of Medicines' report on the future of emergency care [6]. The report notes that the current emergency medical system is overburdened, under funded, and highly fragmented, and calls for a significant blend of resources to strengthen the U.S. emergency medical system's capabilities. To that end, if first receivers, that is, the frontline clinicians and administrators in U.S. emergency departments, are overwhelmed and faced with demands that exceed capacity on an "average" day, then the ability to sustain their core services, particularly during times of crisis when surges in demand is forecast to be significant, becomes even more difficult, and may lead to less-than-optimal patient outcomes. To help remedy the financial impacts of hospital overcrowding, suggestions have been made that the federal government reimburse hospital emergency departments that care for uninsured patients [6].

An outgrowth of these facts leads to the notion of emergency department diversion of ambulances to other hospitals, which results in a "burden shifting" approach that merely moves demand from one already crowded emergency department to another in an attempt to balance cases at the individual hospital level. Although this may appear justifiable from an individual institution's context, in light of the idea that hospitals are part of a larger, collaborative regional response to crises, doing so all but negates this activity as a viable alternative. Calls to increase the number of clinical specialists involved in the provision of emergency care and improvements in regional collaboration to help increase capacity over larger geographies are but a few steps in transforming the U.S. emergency medical system, but these issues continue to plague hospitals as a vexing challenge without a clear solution in sight.

Unrealistic Expectations

The public, media, elected officials, and hospitals themselves have come to expect that every patient and every incident, whether large or small, internal or external, be handled appropriately, in every instance, "or else." And though it is true that healthcare organizations strive to provide the highest quality care to the greatest numbers of people, the expectation that doing so must take place without compromise is unrealistic. Yet for as impractical as it may be, failing to meet these expectations can result in poor public perception and damaging impacts on reputation, community and patient and politician trust, negative media coverage, and decreasing patient satisfaction. Consequently, emergency preparedness efforts that seek an organization-wide level of readiness can aid hospitals in ensuring that they are able to meet their core functions regardless of the incident at hand and help curtail the perceptions that they are without imperfection.

The Hospital as Victim

Although much has been written about healthcare's long history of providing care to countless numbers, little until recently has been documented on the notion of how to prepare for times when the hospital itself needs care, that is, when it is a victim of a disaster. As many hospital emergency efforts concentrate on the hospital as a disaster responder—with a fully operational facility—able to treat mass casualties from a well-defined scene [7–9], many are ill prepared to cope if they become victims of the resulting incident [7,10,11]. Not surprisingly, well-thought out, comprehensive preparedness programs that include all staff and acknowledge an all-hazards approach remain the best means for hospitals to survive untoward events that place them in need of care.

The Hospital as Target

Hospitals are frequently listed alongside malls, schools, and entertainment venues as potential targets of choice by terrorists. Given the important function hospitals play in local and regional crises, and the relative ease of access to them, hospitals are realizing their vulnerabilities to attack and are increasingly focusing on hazard vulnerability analyses and target hardening initiatives, as well as other topics traditionally foreign to the typical healthcare administrator, to ensure bringing these activities into the routine lexicon of preparedness efforts in healthcare.

Importance of Stakeholder Buy-In

The fact that most disasters are low probability, high-consequence events forces much of the allocation of resources to other initiatives that provide what are often deemed more important; that is, those that directly affect patient care and as a result, the hospital's bottom line. It is not difficult to see why the buy-in of key hospital stakeholders necessary for successful hospital emergency preparedness initiatives is seemingly unobtainable. Many are unwilling to invest resources to activities that have no direct positive impact on the bottom line, and in some cases, these activities drain resources, for example, when clinical staff is sent offsite to attend preparedness training. Nonetheless, steps of this sort often prove imprudent, as the cost to recover will always outweigh the cost to prepare.

As many disasters extend beyond the physical boundaries of individual healthcare institutions and yield widespread effects on people, infrastructure, and consequently the economy, a trenchant case is made for the need to place emergency preparedness on the daily agendas of healthcare personnel at all levels.

The Role of Hospital Leadership

As discussed above, there has been relatively little study of the roles of hospital leaders as incident commanders during crises. Moreover, although instructional material aimed at executives on Incident Command Systems (ICS) is widely available, few examinations of the role of hospital leaders—e.g., chief executive officers, chief operating officers, chief medical officers, and chief nursing officers—in preparation for, response to, and recovery from disasters, exist to assess their competencies in leading their organizations through times of crisis.

As the magnitude of the disaster increases, taken within the context of the already constrained environment hospitals operate in, their ability to respond to increased service demands becomes severely limited. Each hospital's susceptibility to any number of hazards combined with the incidental variations and impacts of all disaster events and the inadequacies of real-time knowledge, pose relentless problems of foreknowledge for hospital emergency managers [4]. A key then to enhanced hospital emergency preparedness is to recognize the uncertainties that limit health-care leaders' foreknowledge, and derive a clearer framework for building capacities for resilient decision making from them [4].

Partnerships and Collaboration

Although all disasters may be local, or at least commence in that fashion, disaster research provides vivid examples of the concentric circles that emanate from the epicenter of a disaster site. And given the reality that resources are quickly overcome, the value of collaboration of all types within the hospital, between hospitals, and with outside partners (e.g., public health, police, fire, and emergency medical services) can take many forms. These include mutual aid agreements within which signatories agree to share resources during times of crisis, as well as disaster credentialing approaches, which allow practitioners from other facilities to function in their professional capacity at another site. Most are written vaguely enough that there is significant leeway in the volume of goods or services that can be shared, acknowledging that sites will of course be expected to take care of themselves first, and with any surplus, assist mutual aid partners.

In no case should these agreements include punitive actions for no-participation. Rather, their value comes in going beyond the traditional handshake agreements that often exist. Along these lines, the notion of transcending geographic, political, and corporate boundaries, albeit a sensitive set of topics, are frequently needed during disasters.

The seriousness with which a hospital plans for crisis depends in part on how likely its leaders believe it will face one [4] coupled with the realization that disasters cut across functional and jurisdictional boundaries, and therefore, require multi-organizational cooperation in response [12].

Mutual aid agreements and disaster credentialing policies afford the opportunity for hospitals to share resources that include staff, supplies, pharmaceuticals, and plans with other entities in the community [13]. A number of comprehensive templates exist to assist hospitals in developing these documents [14,15].

All Disasters are Local and Collaboration is Key, but the Limitations are Real

Competition is an ever-present issue in business, and the field of healthcare is no exception to that fact. Although many view competition's ability to ensure the provision of the highest quality services, one can also argue that competition, as it leads to "turfing," can force the notion of collaborative planning efforts into virtual silos. As healthcare institutions compete for rankings, market share, and case mix indexes on a daily basis, planning for, responding to, and recovering from disasters implore healthcare leaders to look to the benefits and efficiencies of collaboration with competitors to ensure care for the greatest number of patients and longevity of their institutions during times of crisis.

Labor issues are another challenge, the degree of which can depend on the represented labor makeup of the institution. Institutions have come to learn that no matter how much better off staff, patients, and the institution itself will become through sound preparedness activities, it is impossible to mandate training or competencies if they are not within the employee's scope of duties, particularly if they are a union or represented employees.

This section has served to provide an outline of the challenges healthcare leaders face in emergency preparedness. The following section provides some solutions, but it cannot be overemphasized that without relationships, that is the buy-in of key stakeholders, any attempts at achieving success is a moot point.

What Can Be Done?

More than any other requirement that will ensure improved preparedness in hospitals is the buy-in and support of key stakeholders. These individuals, or more broadly groups, departments, divisions, and the like, are the deciding factor in achieving success. This buy-in may occur in the allocation of resources dedicated to emergency preparedness activities, in the latitude given to hospital emergency managers in formulating new policies, procedures, and programs and ultimately, the ability for direct accountability to senior clinical, operational, and financial management. Having regular access to these leaders will ensure that the requisite levels of attention and support are in place and that preparedness goals and objectives are achieved within reasonable time frames. Furthermore, those charged with hospital emergency preparedness must retain a degree of authority in the organization that supports decision making, coupled of course with a thorough knowledge of the incident command system and current trends in healthcare preparedness.

The Hazard Vulnerability Analysis

In today's resource-constrained healthcare environment, it is not realistic to plan for every conceivable hazard or eventuality that might befall the institution [16]. Although disasters are not predictable with any great accuracy, many consequences of disasters can be anticipated as part of a comprehensive emergency management plan that includes a hazard and vulnerability analysis (HVA) [16]. In its most basic form an HVA is a tool employed by emergency managers to screen for risk and plan for the strategic use of limited resources [16]. Hospitals by their very nature are particularly vulnerable to disruption as the mere interruption of its services can be harmful [4]. Healthcare institutions' complex combinations of equipment, and hazardous materials, along with ever-changing visitors and patients of varied conditions of physical and mental health, make these sites more susceptible than other kinds of facilities to untoward events [17].

Hospital Incident Command System

The Incident Command System (ICS) was created for use at emergency scenes and has become a model tool for command, control, and coordination of an effective emergency response [18]. Through the application of leadership and business principles to emergency response, the efficiency and effectiveness of resources dedicated to the incident are improved. Specific to hospitals and healthcare organizations, the Hospital Incident Command System (HICS), provides a manageable scope of supervision for all personnel, similar to the ICS principles. Through HICS, a predictable chain of command is established, which although structured, is flexible and adaptable to meet the incident at hand as it evolves, changes scopes, and eventually devolves to a state of "normalcy." Through this chain of command, hospital leaders can ensure accountability during times of crisis through the use of clearly defined roles and responsibilities, most often communicated through the institution's emergency management plan and job action sheets. The boundaries to decision making that HICS imparts are often the key elements in an incident's success. By having each person reporting to one individual, the flow of communication, which is often the most frequent element of an emergency incident to fail, is streamlined between both the sender and receiver.

Although the ICS organizational arrangement was developed exclusively for fire response, the initial version has been adapted for application to a broad spectrum of emergencies of varying type, size, and complexity that include natural disasters, hazardous materials incidents, mass gatherings, and terrorist incidents [19]. Recent widespread incorporation of incident command procedures includes its inclusion into the national incident management system (NIMS), established by Homeland Security Presidential Directive (HSPD)-5, making it a national standard. In 2005, the adoption of ICS became a qualification for entities that receive federal preparedness assistance, namely in terms of funding [20,21]. To that end, the Federal Emergency Management Agency (FEMA) offers basic and advanced NIMS and ICS courses online, free of charge [22].

Concerns about hospitals' capacity to deal with multifaceted emergencies are multiplied as the number of possible hazards mount due to various factors including extreme weather conditions, the increasing urban concentration of population, the use of new types of hazardous materials in industrial production, new possibilities for civil unrest, and the emergence of new infectious agents, coupled with threats of radiological, chemical, and biological weapons [23]. Given these concerns, paired with the reality that incident command is rather simple to teach, incident command is extremely pragmatic and with frequent drills and exercises can become enjoyable as it provides people with a defined role and reporting structure during crises, makes it difficult to justify resisting its implementation. Moreover, for as much as people dislike being told what to do, those who want to assist during an emergency event can become elated when assigned a specific, concrete task under the auspices of an ICS arrangement. Some of the most functional staffers are those that are informed of their role (e.g., logistics section chief), are trained in the role, (e.g., completion of a hospital emergency incident command system course), and are aware of their reporting relationship (e.g., to the incident commander). Summarily, hospital emergency preparedness goes hand-in-hand with the order that ICS establishes, and it works.

Communications

A significant component of any hospital emergency preparedness program is the ability to share information among leadership, incident command staff, administrators, clinicians, patients, visitors, and external agencies. Yet, communications are often the weakest component of an emergency incident in terms of failure of the physical infrastructure and failure of sound procedures for keeping the appropriate people informed. Emergency management plans should include updated lists of key hospital personnel, with multiple means for contact (e.g., home, mobile, satellite, pager). Technology can help accomplish this as a number of software programs exist that will compile this information, provide a predefined message, and automatically contact large numbers of people and record the results (e.g., spoke with, left message, line busy).

Although technology can inform key personnel at large, face-to-face communication, as practicable, can be a valuable means to instill a sense of leadership and confidence during all phases of an emergency.

Administrator-on-Call

Many hospitals designate an administrator-on-call (AOC) to function as an off-hours administrative representative who is responsible for the overall administrative operation of the hospital at night, on weekends, and on holidays. In addition to serving as liaison between medical and nursing staffs and patients and their families, the AOC responds to all emergencies and implements the site's emergency preparedness plan, serving as the interim incident commander pending the arrival of senior administrative staff. AOCs can prove invaluable as hospitals work to achieve seamless levels of preparedness around the clock.

Mass Vaccinations and Prophylaxis

Recent strategies to protect the public include the development of points of distribution or PODs, where prophylactic medications or vaccinations can be quickly distributed to large numbers of people during a public health emergency. PODs are often located in schools, community centers, and other large public spaces and are staffed by a variety of clinical, administrative, and support workers, both in paid and volunteer capacities. From the hospital perspective, the mass vaccination and prophylaxis of healthcare employees is paramount and will require that organizations undertake an organized approach to ensure that the greatest numbers of their staff receive the appropriate protective measures and then provide treatment to the population at large. In both cases, those for healthcare employees and those of the general pubic, PODs should be managed under an ICS structure to ensure greatest efficiencies.

Stockpiling and Critical Supply Logistics

The ability for a healthcare institution to remain self-sufficient to provide and sustain core services without the support of external assistance for at least 96 hours from the inception of an incident, with a goal of seven days, remains a vexing problem for healthcare leaders.

The efficiencies realized through the use of just-in-time inventory management are directly counter to the concept of preparedness. Although these processes seek to minimize costs and waste by delivering products as needed, thin supply chains can result in shortages of many material resources such as pharmaceuticals, blood products, oxygen masks, disposables, and ventilators when demand rises sharply. Near-empty warehouses are indicative of an efficient inventory management system but they also lead hospitals to increased levels of vulnerability if their supply chains are cut off. A simple rule of thumb is if a resource is not accessible by foot, it does not exist.

Surge Capacity/Surge Demand

Although many cite 9/11 as the turning point in hospital preparedness, as noted elsewhere [3,24], there were seminal efforts prior to 9/11 resulting in fundamental changes to the healthcare industry's approach to surge capacity. More than 20 years earlier, crises in emergency department overcrowding provided insight into the necessity for flexing the number of hospital beds, providing rapid discharge of inpatients, delaying scheduled surgeries, diverting ambulances based on triage criteria, and altering practice paradigms to allow "auxiliary" nursing staff to provide necessary emergency care [24]. Although a number of definitions exist, Hick et al. [18] define surge capacity as "the ability of the healthcare system to manage patients who require specialized evaluation or interventions."

The goal of surge capacity planning relates back to basic economic principles, namely, resource allocation. To that end, emergency managers develop a series of prepositioned processes to ensure the delivery of appropriate care with appropriate resources in a graded, phased response [24]. Key elements of hospital surge capacity include core system capacities, equipment and supplies, space, and staff. Core system capacities are those goods, services, or activities that are necessary to fulfill the core mission of the organization and may include diagnostic and treatment capabilities, a well-trained staff, and emergency preparedness.

Managing Volunteers/Credentialing

Well-intentioned volunteers are the hallmark of American society during disasters, but without a coordinated method of managing these resources, unnecessary confusion can ensue. The American College of Emergency Physicians recommends that all hospitals have a detailed process in place to allow for the emergency privileging of additional physician staff who arrive at a facility to support response efforts to a declared hospital disaster [13], noting that "disaster credentialing" should be completed before an event and mirror the credentials of providers of their "home hospitals." However, hospitals providing these credentials must also be prepared to provide professional liability coverage for physicians who provide care during a disaster in their institution and be primed to address issues of compensation for injured workers [13,25,26]. Identification and credentialing are topics that mutual aid agreements can cover so that as they arrive at the scene or hospital, the site security and incident command personnel can quickly determine who can enter and the roles they may perform. The federal Health Resources and Services Administration is spearheading an initiative known as the Emergency System for the Advance Registration of Volunteer Health Professionals (ESAR-VHP) to make available uniform credentialing and identification procedures.

Exercises

The success of implementing a hospital disaster plan is directly proportionate to the realism with which it conducts training, drills, and exercises, specifically in hazard-specific scenarios. Moreover, reflecting on experiences during real events where the plan was put into effect can provide invaluable information on both areas of success and improvement. JCA [6] notes that the quality of emergency preparedness exercises, rather than their frequency will build familiarity and competency with an organization's protocols and policies and challenge its capacity and capability to identify strengths and weaknesses.

Performance Metrics in Hospital Emergency Preparedness

A basic premise of the use of performance measures is that they are simply tools, and by their very nature do not lead to substantive improvements unless they are well designed, used appropriately, and applied within an entity that is capable of accepting change. That said, organizational culture plays a significant role in the success of quality improvement in healthcare and is even more important in attempting to apply these tools to the relatively new field of hospital emergency preparedness.

Recent emphasis on hospital emergency preparedness demonstrates that now is a critical juncture for stakeholders, who range from board members, staff, clinicians, and patients, who often use published performance measures to become better informed about the services they both provide and as consumers themselves, receive. Moreover, institutions are inextricably linked to findings of quality improvement initiatives as consumers will look to these measures when deciding where they will obtain care.

Performance metrics researchers will continue to examine the links between performance measures and improved outcomes, and it is there that hospital emergency preparedness lacks its greatest asset, that is, the ability to demonstrate that improved, or at least increased, preparedness is worthwhile in terms of improved clinical outcomes. But therein lies the problem. Can an institution control for the myriad factors that go into mitigating events that adversely affect the hospital, and if so, can they be linked to preparedness efforts? Surely this question has arisen in more traditional clinical aspects of healthcare, and more specifically public health, but to date, no such work exists that applies these tools to hospital emergency preparedness. Although certainly a gap, this also speaks of the tremendous opportunity to realize via formal, evidenced-based means, the value that preparedness efforts have not only on the institution's bottom line, reputation and recognition, and viability, but also on the outcome of patients. It is there that performance metrics in hospital emergency preparedness remain a work in progress.

Will healthcare evolve to this point where emergency preparedness activities fall under a regulatory body or will a pay for performance system be developed to provide incentives for improved preparedness functions? Given the Joint Commissions revised standards on hospital emergency management [5], one can make considerable assumptions that further change regarding the requirement for hospitals to demonstrate preparedness with the accompanying incentives and disincentives may be forthcoming.

Healthcare Employee Personal Preparedness

It is not difficult to understand that when torn between caring for loved ones and reporting to work, most would do the former. Many hospital staff members' willingness to report to work will be influenced by concerns for their family, themselves, and the confidence they have in their own ability to provide care during times of crisis. Further, the ability to physically report to their hospital may be impacted by transportation issues and personal obligations such as caring for children, elders, and pets. Institutions must realize that employees prepared on an individual, personal basis are better able to help themselves and others, and therefore serve their institutions and the greater good. Personal preparedness resources that range from checklists for food, water, medications, and financial records, as well as recommendations for pediatric and geriatric preparedness items are popular resources that will assist healthcare leaders ensure that the notion of preparedness is rooted at home.

Summary

Healthcare institutions are part of a greater whole, with their own unique operating environment, areas they excel in, and, of course, limitations. While recent emphasis on the increased importance in hospital emergency preparedness roles becomes more evident, hospitals must, to ensure their long-term viability, function as coordinated components of a healthcare-system-wide endeavor and lead local, state, regional, federal, and industry emergency preparedness activities. Box 18.1 offers some examples of these efforts.

As investment in hospital emergency preparedness activities has been light [27] and concerns about how to plan for crises that directly impact hospitals exist [4], employing evidence-based, peer-reviewed approaches to hospital emergency preparedness activities are imperative if the field desires to provide substantive contributions that healthcare community at large accepts.

Although hospitals can never totally prepare for a disaster since specific conditions to be faced cannot be known reliably ahead of time, new lessons and insights are gained each time they conduct a training session, complete an exercise, or experience an actual event, taking from each that there are always ways to do things

---

Box 18.1   Solutions Applied: A Selection of New York-Presbyterian Healthcare System's Emergency Preparedness Initiatives

As one of the nation's largest, not-for-profit, nonsectarian, nongovernmental healthcare systems that comprises 42 acute care, long-term care, specialty, and rehabilitation sites in the states of New York, New Jersey, Connecticut, and Texas, New York-Presbyterian Healthcare System (NYPHS) has a vested interest in ensuring that its facilities are well prepared to address any emergency. Based in New York City, the most densely populated, ethnically diverse metropolitan area in the world, NYPHS continues to demonstrate its ability to provide unsurpassed clinical, operational, and administrative leadership and coordination to its members through proactive preparedness programs. These include

- Bimonthly, Systemwide Emergency Preparedness Meetings Open to All NYPHS Member Institutions
- Secured Intranet Web Sites:
  - Emergency Preparedness
  - Emergency Medicine Directors
  - NYC Department of Mental Health and Hygiene/Federal Office of the Assistant Secretary for preparedness and response (OASPR) Emergency Preparedness Grant
  - NYC Department of Mental Health and Hygiene Hospital Preparedness Task Force for Patients with Burns
- Development of the Senior Healthcare Leader Emergency Preparedness Competencies Self-Assessment Tool with VHA Health Foundation
- NYPHS-Wide Hospital Emergency Response Information System (HERIS)
- Sponsor of Acute and Long-Term Care Site Hazard Vulnerability Analyses
- Participation and Close Collaboration with Local, State, Federal, and Industry Partners.

---

better. The next disaster rarely provides a preview of its exact location, type, magnitude, or duration, but a continuous, honest appraisal of the question, "Are we prepared?" must become commonplace in daily hospital operations and agendas for all involved if these key components of our communities are to remain viable.

References

1. Chaffee, M.W. and Oster, N.S., The role of hospitals in disaster, in *Disaster Medicine*, Ciottone, G. (Ed.), pp. 34–42, Elsevier, Pennsylvania, 2006.
2. American Hospital Association, Hospital Statistics, 2005 Edition. Available at: www.hospitalconnect.com/aha/resource_center/fastfacts.html.

3. Berman, M.A. and Lazar, E.J., Hospital emergency preparedness—Lessons learned since Northridge, *N. Engl. J. Med.*, 2003 Apr 3; 348(14):1307–8.
4. Sternberg, E., Planning for resilience in hospital internal disaster, *Prehosp. Disaster Med.*, 2003; 18(4):291–300.
5. Joint Commission on Accreditation of Healthcare Organizations, Standard on Emergency Management, June, 2007.
6. Hospital Based Emergency Care: At the breaking point, Institute of Medicine of the National Academies, July 2006. Available at: http://www.iom.edu/?id=35018.
7. Chavez, C.W. and Binder, B., A hospital as victim and responder: The Sepulveda VA Medical Center and the Northridge Earthquake, *J. Emerg. Med.*, 1996; 14(4):445–454.
8. Waeckerle, J.F., Disaster planning and response, *N. Engl. J. Med.*, 1991; 324:815–821.
9. Aghababian, R., Lewis, C.P., Gan, L., and Curley, F.J., Disasters within hospitals, *Ann. Emerg. Med.*, 1994; 23:771–777.
10. Martchenke, J. and Pointer, J.E., Hospital disaster operations during the 1989 Loma Prieta earthquake, *Prehospital Disaster Med.*, 1994; 9:146–152.
11. Norcross, E.D., Elliott, B.M., Adams, D.B., and Crawford, F.A., Impact of a major hurricane on surgical services in a university hospital, *Am. Surg.*, 1993; 59:28–33.
12. Auf der Heide, E., *Disaster Response: Principles of Preparation and Coordination*, pp. 34–35, CV Mosby, St. Louis, Missouri, 1989.
13. Geiling, J. and Fosher, K., Mutual aid, in *Disaster Medicine*, Ciottone, G. (Ed.), pp. 182–192, Elsevier, Pennsylvania, 2006.
14. American Hospital Association, Model hospital mutual aid memorandum of understanding. Available at: http://www.kyha.com/documents/modelmou.pdf.
15. New Hampshire Hospital Association and Vermont Hospital Association, Draft model language for hospital mutual aid agreements. Available at: http://www.mhalink.org/public/disaster/files/prep-2003-13-2.pdf.
16. Chang, J.C., Gluckman, W., and Weinstein, E.S., Health care facility hazard and vulnerability analysis, in *Disaster Medicine*, Ciottone, G. (Ed.), pp. 117–123, Elsevier, Pennsylvania, 2006.
17. Pan American Health Organization: Principles of Disaster Mitigation in Health Facilities 2000: Washington, DC: Pan American Health Organization, pp. 14–17.
18. Sutingco, N., The incident command system, in *Disaster Medicine*, Ciottone, G. (Ed.), pp. 208–214, Elsevier, Pennsylvania, 2006.
19. FEMA EMI: Basic incident command system independent study, US Government Printing Office, Washington, 2000.
20. Federal Emergency Management Agency, National Incident Management System. Available at: http://training.fema.gov/EMIWeb/IS/is700.asp.
21. Homeland Security Presidential Directive/HSPD-5. Available at: www.whitehouse.gov/news/releases/2003/02/20030228-9.html.
22. Federal Emergency Management Agency, National Incident Management System, Incident Command System Resource Center. Available at: http://training.fema.gov/EMIWeb/IS/ICSResource/index.htm.
23. Arnold, J.L., Disaster medicine in the 21st century: Future hazards, vulnerabilities and risk, *Prehosp. Disaster Med.*, 2002; 17(1):3–11.
24. Casani, J.A.P. and Romansky, A.J., Surge capacity, in *Disaster Medicine*, Ciottone, G. (Ed.), pp. 193–202, Elsevier, Pennsylvania, 2006.

25. American College of Emergency Physicians, Hospital disaster planning, *Ann. Emerg. Med.*, 2003; 42(4):607–608.
26. 2003 American College of Emergency Physicians' board of Directors, Hospital Disaster Privileging, Policy No. 400326, Approved February 2003. Available at: http://www.acep.org.
27. Treat, K.N., Williams, J.M., Furbee, P.M., et al., Hospital preparedness for weapons of mass destruction incidents: An initial assessment, *Ann. Emerg. Med.*, 2001; 38:562–565.

Chapter 19

Media Relations and External Communications during a Disaster

Mordecai Lee

CONTENTS

In many respects, strategies and policies for disaster public relations by government can be separated into two categories, those that came before and those that came after the three seminal mega-disasters that occurred during the first half-decade of the twenty-first century: 9/11, the 2004 tsunami in south Asia, and Hurricane

Katrina in 2005. Although 9/11 was, of course, a matter of homeland security, it should also be considered a disaster and, therefore, is applicable to this discussion as well. These three cataclysmic events not only have greatly influenced how practitioners and faculty view public administration in general, but also have significant bearing on their implications for external communications in a crisis.

Parallel to the before and after perspectives on crisis communications as a result of those three disasters, there has also been a great divide in communications technologies, the two sides of the divide being pre-digital and digital technology. Roughly, the decade between 1995 and 2005 (overlapping with these three global disasters) reflected a transformation in government-to-citizen (G2C) communications, including the emergence of the Internet, handhelds, laptops, wi-fi, cell phones, and so many other new forms of instant communications. However, for all that these three über-disasters and technological developments have transformed our view of crisis communications, the advice from practitioners and specialists about government public relations during a disaster has remained remarkably stable. This suggests that the normative and applied literature, seeking to give guidance to practitioners, has provided real-world principles and guidelines that are not only tried-and-true, but also on the mark irrespective of the march of time or the evolution of technology.

Disaster Communications versus Normal Communications: What's Different?

Crisis management is more than hurry-up public administration. Rather, it is a condition when many of the regular rules of operation no longer apply. Therefore, although some of the literature about normal government public relations may be helpful and relevant [1], there is much about a crisis that involves exceptional circumstances and, therefore, exceptional actions. Conventional expectations disappear at times of crisis. External relations during a crisis is fundamentally different from other, more routine, time frames *. Furthermore, successful communications is indispensable to resolving the substantive impacts of the disaster itself. According to Garnett's review of the international literature, "effective crisis communication is crucial to handling crises successfully" [3].

There are two key factors that differentiate crisis communications from normal public relations in the public sector. First, public relations programs by government agencies (or other organizations, for that matter) cover a panoply of activities, audiences, and forms of communication [4]. However, in times of crisis, all these forms of external communication are compressed to a single medium: instant communication, such as news media relations, and other instantaneous means

---

* For example, during a lingering disaster, there is a temptation to view it as a gradual resumption of normalcy. This understandable inclination needs to be avoided. For a case study of a lingering crisis, see [2].

of communications that were previously nontraditional, such as Web sites, official blogs, and e-mails. There is no time to prepare magazine articles, publish brochures, send pamphlets through the mail, conduct briefings for neighborhood groups, maintain a lecture bureau, or write reports. Therefore, in a time of crisis the public manager and the entire staff of the agency need to change mentality to instant information only. In other words, dealing with the news media (along with digital channels of communication) is the only useful and usable outlet. Media relations becomes the only game in town. It is the sole medium for transmitting information. The media rely heavily on official and governmental sources for their ongoing coverage [5].

Second, at the beginning of an emergency, external communication is sometimes the only or fastest way to communicate internally, whether within an organization or throughout a network of agencies. At those moments, external communications is functioning as an exoskeleton of public administration, replacing the traditional internal flow of information that is not in the public realm. According to Radvanovsky, one of the key roles of the public information officer during a crisis includes communicating to an internal audience [6]. Crisis managers should not hesitate to use the news media to convey important information to colleagues, allies, and team members *. In sum, at the peak of a disaster, it is accurate to state that crisis communications *is* public administration. It cannot be considered secondary to other activities or as an ancillary project. Rather, it is so integral to disaster management that it, at times, becomes the essence of coping with a crisis.

These highly unusual aspects of governmental external communications in a crisis jibe well with the crisis mentality of the news media itself. Given the emergency, reporters have an insatiable desire for information. This is, of course, radically different from the normal routines of media coverage, when reporters and their editors have little interest in government news, which they (often rightly) consider boring and self-serving. The changed stance of the news media welcomes nearly unlimited amounts of official information and does not discriminate between information useful to the victims, aimed at residents in the nearby geographical area, or intended for unaffected news consumers worldwide. They want any information they can get and they want it now. Without in any way viewing a disaster as an opportunity for media manipulation, the public administrator has an ally in the news media. Both sides of the normally adversarial relationship need to (and usually do) set aside their usual inhibitions and self-imposed limitations.

Crisis communications is a prevalent theme regarding the practice of public relations in the private sector. To some degree, that business-oriented perspective can be helpful to public sector practitioners too [8–12]. Lessons regarding nonprofit sector emergency communications can be helpful as well [13]. A pan-sectoral theme that recurs in the literature generally zeroes in on different aspects of organizational effectiveness at dealing with disaster communications. Reporters are seeking

---

* For a more general discussion of inter-organizational communications during a crisis, see [7].

a spokesperson who is well informed, truthful, volunteers information, helpful, willing to act as a fact-finder, and has unlimited access to the highest level of officials in the agency. But the most important element of crisis communications is the golden rule.

Golden Rule: One Voice Providing a Niagara of Information

The golden rule of disaster public relations is to have a sole spokesperson who releases as much information as soon as possible all the time *. The goal is to give the public "accurate, coordinated, timely and easy to understand" information [15]. The focus on releasing a Niagara of information should trump all other considerations, such as whether it makes the agency look good or bad in the short run or whether the timing of the release is convenient or inconvenient. *Get it out, get it all out, and get it out as fast as possible.* Then, do it all over again with the latest updated information. Disaster communications is the governmental analog to contemporary cable-news networks, with a new rolling deadline every half hour, or even more frequently if the situation calls for it.

The lesson of having a public face for crisis communications during 9/11 paralleled the unlessons of Hurricane Katrina. Only one spokesperson should be designated to release all information and make all official announcements. When New York Mayor Giuliani emerged as the sole spokesperson after 9/11, he was providing updates that were not restricted to the municipal level of government which he headed. (In New York, city and county governments are merged.) He also became briefly the de facto spokesperson for all other relevant activities of regional, state, and federal governments. He was "it" for all major matters [16]. This is not to imply that other officials were not also functioning occasionally as spokespersons in the post-9/11 period. But they were subsidiary and supportive of Giuliani's role. The opposite happened in the aftermath of Hurricane Katrina. Within the federal government, there was confusion whether the public affairs staff from the Federal Emergency Management Agency or their (theoretically) superiors from the departmental public affairs office were in charge. Further, the federal government and Louisiana's state government had their own spokespersons, sometimes releasing contradictory information or directives. This multiple spokesperson approach conveyed not only the appearance of lack of cooperation, but also the reality underlying that perception. It *was* disorganized [17]. Thus, symbolism is very important in crisis communication (as well as during noncrises) because symbols convey realities, whether intended or not. The goal is to project the image of the "fearless leader" [18].

---

* For a discussion of the work of local government spokespersons during non-crisis periods, see [14].

The difference regarding spokespersons during these two disasters was not the only key feature regarding success or failure in crisis communications. The disasters of 9/11 and Katrina also were mirror images of lessons about what was being released. New York City Mayor Giuliani tried to convey that he was informing the audience of everything that he knew at that time. A few hours later, if he had to amend what he had previously said, there was little complaint about his earlier mistake or, worse, an accusation of deliberately misleading the media and the public. Rather, he said what was known and then restated it when more was known. Conversely, the multiple spokespersons of Katrina seemed at times to be ill informed, misinformed, or withholding information. This was a recipe for a communications disaster overlaying a natural disaster, as indeed occurred in the days, weeks, and even months of the aftermath of Katrina.

Permanent Principles: Media Savvy, Credibility, Access, and Monitoring

A longitudinal study of the literature by and for public sector practitioners regarding crisis communications reveals several fixed principles [19–24]. Although society and technology have changed considerably over the years, these principles recur on such a consistent basis that they can be identified as constants of governmental communication. These maxims are media savvy, credibility, access, and monitoring.

First, all forms of crisis communications need to be sensitive to the professional and technical needs of the news media. Therefore, the government must "understand the often Byzantine nature of the modern press corps" [25]. The fastest way for a government agency to assure that coverage shifts to a negative tone is to be ignorant of the modus operandi and expectations of working reporters. For example, notifications of an upcoming announcement need to be disseminated to everyone. The technical prerequisites for television versus radio coverage are inherently different and both need to be accommodated. Print copies and digital versions of major information releases need to be made available as quickly as possible. Similarly, the physical location of a media center needs to be announced and that site needs to provide the essential prerequisites to allow reporters to do their jobs. Also, this is not the time to try to track down news leaks, to ignore leak-based questions from the media, or to say "no comment" [26].

Second, all government news during a disaster needs to be credible and trustworthy [27]. The spokesperson "must speak, and be seen to speak, clearly and authoritatively" for the agency [28]. A single attempt to mislead the media (and, by extension, the public), withhold information or deliberate release of incorrect information is enough to transform the atmosphere of the newsroom from welcoming to accusatory. Unfortunately, the principle of credibility contradicts the "Goulding rule." Phil Goulding had been the spokesman for the Pentagon during the Viet-nam war and other assorted crises. He developed the rule that "first reports are always wrong" [29]. The essential accuracy of his rule was still valid at the beginning of the next millennium. In 2000, a conference at the University of Virginia concluded that "A major challenge of covering a critical incident, especially in the first minutes and hours, is to avoid repeating inaccurate or exaggerated reports—an easy policy to state but often a difficult one to follow, given the pressure for speed and the insatiable demand for new details" [30].

Certainly, Goulding's rule can be misperceived as a justification for not releasing information until everything can be fully confirmed. But, that would be a misapplication of his key insight. Rather, during disasters governments should release information about important developments as fast as possible, but with the explicitly stated caveat that the first report was sketchy and that the spokesperson is in the midst of fleshing out, confirming, or disproving such initial reports. There is a major difference between telling a partial story because that's all you know and not telling what you know because it hasn't yet been confirmed. Therefore, concluded Graber, "The principal challenge facing public affairs officials during crises is to obtain and release accurate information without causing unwarranted panic or complicating recovery efforts" [31]. It's not easy to find the right balance, but nonetheless releasing information should almost always be the path chosen.

Third, whoever becomes the "face" of the government during a disaster has to be more than merely a mouthpiece or martinet. She or he needs to be present at the highest operational levels of the government's crisis headquarters and must be viewed by the top decision makers as an integral part of the command staff [32]. This obtains two key benefits. First, the spokesperson is well informed and can provide information to the fullest extent that it is available. Second, the spokesperson can contribute to major policy decisions that are made behind the scenes and at the highest levels. He or she might advise for or against doing something that is being considered because of how that decision might play out once it is in the public realm. Spokespersons tend to be sensitive to certain factors that other decision makers might otherwise not bring into consideration. Savvy public administrators know to keep their communications adviser nearby at all times and in the room when decisions are being made [33].

Finally, notwithstanding the frenetic pace of disaster management, it is crucial to monitor media reports of one's own announcements. This function was pioneered by Commerce Secretary Herbert Hoover when he was the on-site coordinator of the federal response to the Mississippi River floods in 1927. He instructed his staff back in Washington to monitor newspaper coverage of his work and to wire summaries of those clippings to him. Two or three times a week he would personally review the summaries [34]. By knowing the tone of coverage, Hoover was able to instantly adapt what he was doing and saying in reaction to problems in the federal response that the media was covering. This gave him an instant feedback loop that increased his sensitivity to potential issues he should address. The same principle holds true nearly a century later. Notwithstanding the revolution in communications technology, it is vital that the headquarters continuously monitor what the media covers and how it covers those subjects. This helps improve disaster communications for several reasons. For example, the spokesperson may realize that there is an unintentional gap between what was intended to be communicated and what the media is saying. So, perhaps using a different vocabulary, explaining intent, and other techniques can then instantly correct such problems.

Conversely, the headquarters staff can learn from media coverage. Journalists become the de facto eyes and ears of the government, essentially an intelligence service of the latest developments. Two much-recounted communications failures occurred during Hurricane Katrina in 2005. The head of the federal response team claimed he did not know for several crucial days that evacuees were being sheltered in New Orleans' Superdome stadium, even though it was being reported on television [35]. Also, key officials did not know for 24 hours that the levees had been breached [36].

It might be a slight misnomer to term this monitoring function as feedback. More correctly, given the fluidity of events during a disaster, it should be considered a feed-forward loop. From that perspective, monitoring helps affect upcoming crisis communications activities and decisions, not just as a documentation of what has already occurred. Feed-forward monitoring is a way to engage in instant midcourse corrections of crisis communication strategies.

Planning and Preparedness

Knowing these ingredients of successful government public relations in a crisis, what needs to be done before that disaster occurs? Is it possible to plan for the unknown? To some, perhaps the very concept of planning for a crisis may appear to be an oxymoron. Yet, time after time, it has been demonstrated that it is possible for governments to engage in crisis communications planning. Perhaps the most helpful perspective is an axiom that has been attributed to President Eisenhower, planner of D-Day in World War II: "plans are useless, but planning is indispensable" [37]. That saying captures both the benefits and limits of disaster planning. Yes, some aspects of a crisis cannot be foreseen and, therefore, are unplannable. However, other elements of crisis communication are relatively consistent and recurring, making it useful to have gone through a planning process.

A report on bioterrorism in 2001 emphasized the connection between planning and operational success: "Establishing credibility with the public and with the news media before an event occurs is the best way to avoid inaccurate, panicky, irresponsible reporting when the crisis comes. The process of developing a plan should be conducted as openly as possible and a special effort should be made not only to inform the public and media as a plan takes shape, but also to include media representatives in realistic training exercises" [38]. For example, the federal Center for Disease Control was unprepared for the media aspects of the anthrax crisis of 2001 [39]. In other words, planning can be a key contributor to having credibility and obtaining media cooperation when disasters eventually occur. It *is* possible to prepare for media relations in a disaster.

Several practitioner sources have developed checklists and guidelines for the elements that should be considered for inclusion in a crisis communications plan [40–42]. For example, they include the need to involve all possible partners in developing the plan, having the support of the top officials of the agencies involved, engaging in practice and mock simulations to test the operational relevance of the plans, preparing standby media centers, and designating on a rotating basis a go-team of staffers who are on duty 24 hours a day. These generic templates can be easily adapted to the particularistic needs of government agencies at different levels of government and with different areas of responsibility. Also, just as emergency service and first responder departments often sign mutual aid agreements with their nearby counterparts, so public information offices can develop emergency mutual aid agreements with colleagues in other localities. This helps provide an instant method of expanding staff capabilities with supplemental and temporary expertise of other trained and trusted government communications professionals [43].

In part, disaster communication planning is an activity that is undertaken by information specialists as they try to foresee operational problems that might occur during an unforeseeable crisis. However, it is important that planning not be ghettoized to the public information office or to the emergency management office. Senior level officials need to have a basic awareness of such plans and, crucially, agree with them. For example, it is one thing for a crisis communication plan to be disseminated to a newly appointed departmental head. But it is quite another for that new director to explicitly agree, for example, that he or she will not be the spokesperson and face of the agency during a crisis.

This raises the basic issue of generalist public administrators having a core understanding of the role of external communications in government management, whether in times of disaster or not. Training programs in public administration, especially MPA, program used to include components about public relations, but that subject gradually got squeezed out of the core curriculum [44]. However, in the post-9/11 world, the recognition of the importance of communications training has somewhat increased in public administration and it is slowly being reestablished as an important competency that should be part of an overall training program. Raphael and Nesbary focused on the crisis communications aspects of the 2003 fatal explosion of the space shuttle Columbia as a demonstration of the importance of restoring communications to the standard public administration curriculum [45]. Government's reaction to disasters will undoubtedly improve when senior agency officials have the background and training in communications to understand what needs to be done at a time of crisis.

Disaster communications planning does not need to be limited to in-house activities. The public-at-large can be involved as well. For example, helpful planning and standby information can be widely disseminated so that individuals can feel that they are prepared and well informed. Techniques can include, for example, refrigerator magnets with URLs and hotlines to use in times of emergency, checklists of items to have on hand in family disaster kits, and lists of important information that should be duplicated and stored off-site for use by family members if separated. For example, in 2004, the Sunday issue of a widely circulated daily newspaper in Wisconsin included an insert entitled "Public health emergencies: Your prepared-ness guide" [46]. The ten-page booklet contained helpful information for citizens to both be prepared for a disaster and what to do when a disaster occurs.

Finally, Garnett and Kouzmin identify another important stage in disaster communications, namely the learning and feedback phase [47]. This can sometimes be dismissed as an activity that is mostly part of the blame game that politicians love to engage in [48] or that academics are attracted to, often analyzing post hoc events in terms that are largely irrelevant to the real world of the practitioner. Although both these concerns have some validity, it is important for the disaster communi-cations planner to understand that the learning and feedback phase is an integral part of the planning process. In fact, the learning and feedback phase needs to be conceived as the first step in the planning process. Only by learning from past mistakes can future plans improve on previous organizational behaviors and increase the effectiveness of disaster communications.

The Future of Crisis Communications: Focusing on Reaching the Public

The preoccupation with communicating through the news media during disasters is both understandable and worthwhile. However, it is important to remember that it is possible to reach the public-at-large through the intermediary of the mass media *and* directly [49]. For example, as we approach the beginning of the second decade of the twenty-first century, a large percentage of the population will have personal-ized access to the internet through land-line connections, broadband cable, and wi-fi. Similarly, access is not only through personal computers, but also through cell phones, handhelds, laptops, ThinkPads, and all manner of small personal appli-ances. It is imperative that disaster communications convey information through traditional dissemination means as well as by using the latest technological advances in communications that are in public use. Gradually, greater and greater portions of the audience will not be obtaining information by watching television. Instead, they'll be getting the same information by watching a live video-streaming of a press conference, accessing emergency Web sites, and receiving e-mail notifications.

Therefore, part of disaster communications needs to attend to this growing audience that is reachable directly [50]. It is absolutely necessary to be sure that press conferences and other in-person events are video streamed on the Web, that the front of the podium used for announcements lists a URL for further informa-tion, that the central emergency information site is immediately and continuously updated with the latest announcements and information, and that all hotlinks to related sites are working properly. As technology improves, the twentieth-century concept of the news media and of broadcasting might largely atrophy, and even become an anachronism. Even the shift from over-the-air broadcasting to cable narrowcasting (such as niche cable channels) may have only been a transitional stage. It could well be that the traditional intermediary role of the news media will significantly decline as society shifts from broadcasting to webcasting as the central means of G2C communication. When the tipping point of that trend eventually occurs, the traditional approach to crisis communication will have been upended. Instead of the primary focus on reaching the public through the news media and a secondary focus on reaching them directly, direct communication with the citizenry will become the main venue for disseminating information, and the indirect method of communication through the news media will become minor, even negligible.

When that revolution occurs, probably by the second quarter of the twenty-first century, then the principles of crisis communication will continue unaffected, but the methods and technologies for implementing those principles will be vastly different.

References

1. Lee, M., Globalization and media coverage of public administration, in *Handbook of Globalization, Governance, and Public Administration*, Farazmand, A. and Pinkowski, J., Eds., Taylor & Francis, Boca Raton, Florida, 2007, chap. 8.
2. DeVries, D.S. and Fitzpatrick, K.R., Defining the characteristics of a lingering crisis: Lessons from the National Zoo, *Public Relations Review*, 32:2, 160–167, 2006.
3. Garnett, J.L., Epilog: Directions and agendas for administrative communication, in *Handbook of Administrative Communication*, Garnett, J.L. and Kouzmin, A., Eds., Marcel Dekker, New York, 1997, chap. 33, p. 759.
4. Lee, M., Public information in government organizations: A review and curriculum outline of external relations in public administration, *Public Administration and Management: An Interactive Journal*, 5, 183, 2000. Retrieved July 6, 2007: http://www.pamij.com/5_4/5_4_4_pubinfo.pdf.
5. Hutcheson, J. et al., U.S. national identity, political elites, and a patriotic press following September 11, *Political Communication*, 21, 46, 2004.
6. Radvanovsky, R., *Critical Infrastructure: Homeland Security and Emergency Preparedness*, Taylor & Francis, Boca Raton, Florida, 2006, p. 105.
7. Garnett, J. and Kouzmin, A., Communicating during crises: From bullhorn to mass media to high technology to organizational networking, in *Essays in Economic Globalization, Transnational Policies and Vulnerability*, Kouzmin, A. and Hayne, A., Eds., 10s Press, Amsterdam, 1999, pp. 194–195.
8. Mitroff, I.M., *Why Some Companies Emerge Stronger and Better from a Crisis: 7 Essential Lessons for Surviving Disaster*, American Management Association, New York, 2005.
9. Arpan, L.M. and Roskos-Ewoldsen, D.R., Stealing thunder: Analysis of the effects of proactive disclosure of crisis information, *Public Relations Review*, 31, 425, 2005.
10. Pinsdorf, M.K., *All Crises Are Global: Managing to Escape Chaos*, Fordham University Press, New York, 2004.

11. Englehardt, K.J., Sallot, L.M., and Springston, J.K., Compassion without blame: Testing the accident decision flow chart with the crash of ValuJet flight 592, *Journal of Public Relations Research*, 16, 127, 2004.
12. Heath, R.L. and Vasquez, G., Eds., *Handbook of Public Relations*, Sage, Thousand Oaks, California, 2001, chaps. 12, 40–43.
13. Thompson, R.L., Contingency and emergency public affairs, in *The Nonprofit Handbook: Management*, 3rd ed., Connors, T.D., Ed., John Wiley, New York, 2001, chap. 13.
14. Lee, M. The agency spokesperson: Connecting public administration and the media, *Public Administration Quarterly*, 25, 101, 2001.
15. Radvanovsky, R., *Critical Infrastructure: Homeland Security and Emergency Preparedness*, Taylor & Francis, Boca Raton, Florida, 2006, p. 75.
16. Mortlock, M., Hurricanes and learning organization obsolescence, *The Public Manager*, 34:3, 10, 2005.
17. United States Government Accountability Office, *Preliminary Observations on Hurricane Response*, GAO-06-365R, February 1, 2006; and United States Department of Homeland Security, Office of Inspector General, *A Performance Review of FEMA's Disaster Management Activities in Response to Hurricane Katrina*, OIG-06-32, March 2006, 56–62. Retrieved July 2, 2006: http://www.dhs.gov/interweb/assetlibrary/OIG_06-32_Mar06.pdf.
18. Brown, L., *Your Public Best: The Complete Guide to Making Successful Public Appearances in the Meeting Room, on the Platform, and on TV*, 2nd ed., Newmarket Press, New York, 2002, p. 165.
19. Martin, R.A. and Boynton, L.A., From liftoff to landing: NASA's crisis communications and resulting media coverage following the *Challenger* and *Columbia* tragedies, *Public Relations Review*, 31, 253, 2005; Kaufmann, J., Lost in space: A critique of NASA's crisis communications in the Columbia disaster, *Public Relations Review*, 31, 263, 2005; and Kersten, A. and Sidky, M., Re-aligning rationality: Crisis management and prisoner abuses in Iraq, *Public Relations Review*, 31, 471, 2005. (These three articles are case studies of media relations by government agencies in times of disaster or crisis.)
20. Berry, S., We have a problem... Call the press! *Public Management*, 81:4, 4, 1999.
21. Kellar, E.K., Communicating with elected officials, in *Effective Communication: A Local Government Guide*, Wheeler, K.M., Ed., International City/County Management Association, Washington, DC, 1994, p. 63.
22. Helm, L.M., Meeting the problems of crises; Agnes: The politics of a flood; and Sunshine mine: Handling the media in a disaster, in *Informing the Public: A Public Affairs Handbook*, Helm, L.M., Hiebert, R.E., Naver, M.R., and Rabin, K., Eds., Longman, New York, 1981, chaps. 22–24.
23. Spitzer, C.E., Information and policy, in *The Voice of Government*, Hiebert, R.E. and Spitzer, C.E., Eds., John Wiley & Sons, New York, 1968, p. 58.
24. Ratzan, S.C. and Meltzer, W., State of the art in crisis communication: Past lessons and principles of practice, in *Global Public Health Communication: Challenges, Perspectives, and Strategies*, Haider, M., Ed., Jones and Bartlett, Sudbury, Massachusetts, 2005, pp. 321–347.
25. Burns, N., Talking to the world about American foreign policy, *Harvard International Journal of Press/Politics*, 1:4, 10, 1996.

26. Craig, M. et al., Crisis communication in public arenas, *Public Relations Review*, 32:2, 172, 2006.
27. Federal Communicators Network, *Communicators Guide: For Federal, State, Regional, and Local Communicators*, rev. ed., University of Florida IFAS/Extension, Gainesville, Florida, 2001, p. 27.
28. Burns, N., Talking to the world about American foreign policy, *Harvard International Journal of Press/Politics*, 1:4, 10, 1996.
29. Goulding, P.G., *Confirm or Deny: Informing the People on National Security*, Harper & Row, New York, 1970, p. 103.
30. Critical Incident Analysis Group, University of Virginia Health System, *Threats to Symbols of American Democracy: The Media's Changing Role [Part 5]*, 19. Retrieved July 6, 2007: http://www.healthsystem.virginia.edu/internet/ciag/publications/report_threats_to_symbols_c2000.pdf.
31. Graber, D.A., *The Power of Communication: Managing Information in Public Organizations*, CQ Press, Washington, DC, 2003, pp. 244–245.
32. Radvanovsky, R., *Critical Infrastructure: Homeland Security and Emergency Preparedness*, Taylor & Francis, Boca Raton, Florida, 2006, p. 104.
33. Trattner, J.H., Working with the media, in *Learning the Ropes: Insights for Political Appointees*, Abramson, M.A. and Lawrence, P.R., Eds., Rowman & Littlefield, Lanham, Maryland, 2005, p. 98.
34. Barry, J.M., *Rising Tide: The Great Mississippi Flood of 1927 and How It Changed America*, Simon & Schuster, New York, 1997, pp. 273, 288–289.
35. Kranish, M., "Bush vows probe of 'what went wrong,'" *Boston Globe*, September 7, 2005.
36. United States Department of Homeland Security, Office of Inspector General, *A Performance Review of FEMA's Disaster Management Activities in Response to Hurricane Katrina*, OIG-06-32, March 2006, 33. Retrieved July 5, 2006: http://www.dhs.gov/interweb/assetlibrary/OIG_06-32_Mar06.pdf.
37. Andrews, R., Ed., *The New Penguin Dictionary of Modern Quotations*, Penguin Books, London, 2003, p. 162.
38. Critical Incident Analysis Group, University of Virginia Health System, Preliminary Report: Public Responsibility and Mass Destruction: The Bioterrorism Threat, 4. Retrieved July 6, 2007: http://www.healthsystem.virginia.edu/internet/ciag/publications/report_bioterrorism_threat_c2001.pdf.
39. Winett, L.B. and Lawrence, R.G., The rest of the story: Public health, the news, and the 2001 anthrax attacks, *Harvard International Journal of Press/Politics*, 10:3, 3, 2005.
40. Federal Communicators Network, *Communicators Guide: For Federal, State, Regional, and Local Communicators*, rev. ed., University of Florida IFAS/Extension, Gainesville, Florida, 2001, p. 26.
41. Bjornlund, L.D., *Media Relations for Local Governments: Communicating for Results*, International City/County Management Association, Washington, DC, 1996, chap. 7.
42. Wise, K., Pre-crisis relationships, in *Global Public Health Communication: Challenges, Perspectives, and Strategies*, Haider, M., Ed., Jones and Bartlett, Sudbury, Massachusetts, 2005, pp. 155–164.
43. Alsop, R., PIO emergency mutual aid, in *Delivering the Message: A Resource Guide for Public Information Officials*, 2nd ed., Krey, D., Ed., California Association of Public Information Officials, Sacramento, California, 2000, p. 71.

44. Lee, M., Public relations in public administration: A disappearing act in public administration education, *Public Relations Review* 24, 509, 1998.

45. Raphael, D.M. and Nesbary, D., Getting the message across: Rationale for a strategic communications course in the public administration curriculum, *Journal of Public Affairs Education*, 11, 133, 2005.

46. Division of Public Health, Wisconsin Department of Health and Family Services, *Public Health Emergencies: Your Preparedness Guide*, 2004. Accessed July 1, 2007: http://dhfs. wisconsin.gov/preparedness/pdf_files/PublicHealthGuide.pdf.

47. Garnett, J. and Kouzmin, A., Communicating during crises: From bullhorn to mass media to high technology to organizational networking, in *Essays in Economic Globalization, Transnational Policies and Vulnerability*, Kouzmin, A. and Hayne, A., Eds., IOS Press, Amsterdam, 1999, pp. 188–189.

48. See, for example, A Failure of Initiative: The Final Report of the Select Bipartisan Committee to Investigate the Preparation for and Response to Hurricane Katrina. Retrieved July 2, 2007: http://a257.g.akamaitech.net/7/257/2422/15feb20061230/ www.gpoaccess.gov/katrinareport/mainreport.pdf.

49. Taylor, M. and Perry, D.C., Diffusion of traditional and new media tactics in crisis communication, *Public Relations Review*, 31, 209, 2005.

50. Haider, M. and Aravindakshan, N.P., Content analysis of Anthrax in the media, in *Global Public Health Communication: Challenges, Perspectives, and Strategies*, Haider, M., Ed., Jones and Bartlett, Sudbury, Massachusetts, 2005, Chap. 24, p. 403.

Chapter 20

Responding to Natural Disasters: An Increased Military Response and Its Impact on Public Policy Administration

DeMond S. Miller, Matthew Pavelchak,
Randolph Burnside, and Jason D. Rivera

CONTENTS

Introduction

The social effects of Hurricane Katrina have raised many concerns about the adequacy of federal response to natural disasters and the role of the military. During the immediate aftermath of the hurricane, branches of the military executed one of the largest search and rescue operations in the United States' history, which was repeated after Hurricane Rita shortly thereafter. The U.S. Coast Guard deployed hundreds of air and boat crews to rescue over 24,273 people and assisted with the evacuation of an additional 9,462 patients and medical personnel from hospitals and nursing homes; in total 33,735* lives were saved or medically evacuated.

This chapter explores the implications of relying on the military to administer recovery efforts after major natural disasters. Specifically, we argue that an increased military response to disasters will shape the recovery experience for survivors, reshape the role of the military, enhance presidential power, and fundamentally recast the administration of public policy. With concerns about the adequacy of a federal response to natural disasters, questions about what role the military lawfully plays in recovery efforts is paramount. The executive branch of government has alluded to the possibility of military deployment as the first stage of response to disasters, as defined in the broadest context, in the future. Military deployment on American soil is not without precedent, although the legalities can be confusing. This chapter makes a clear distinction between the natural disaster response and the terrorist disaster response. With the creation of new legislation, which expanded the role of state and federal military units, the military had a more prominent role in disaster relief and its implications.

The Military's Response to Disaster Before and After September 11

Since the terrorist attacks of September 11, 2001, there have been extensive changes made to help the federal government effectively respond to major disasters and

---

* Katrina: 24,135 lives saved and 9,409 evacuated; Rita: 138 lives saved and 53 evacuated. (See Hurricane Katrina: What Government is Doing. [September 24, 2006]. US Department of Homeland Security. www.dhs.gov/xprepresp/programs/gc_1157649340100.shtm. Retrieved December 10, 2006.)

terrorist attacks. The Department of Homeland Security was created through the incorporation of 22 federal agencies, and its mission is to prevent and respond to terrorist attacks and natural disasters (The Department of Homeland Security, 2004a). During this restructuring, the Federal Emergency Management Agency (FEMA) lost its cabinet level status and was placed under the authority of the Secretary of Homeland Security (FEMA, 2006). Additionally, President George W. Bush ordered the creation of the National Response Plan and the National Incident Management System (Bush, 2003). These strategies were designed to create an "all hazards manual" for the federal response to all "Incidents of National Significance." However, these strategies, along with the new label of "Incidents of National Significance," were designed mainly for terrorist attacks (Styles, 2005). Many people that these measures have reduced the federal government's ability to respond effectively to natural disasters.

Hurricane Katrina: A Failed Response

Hurricane Katrina has raised many questions about federal government agencies' abilities to respond to significant threats (whether natural or terroristic in nature) that are spread over a wide geographic area. Due to the sheer size of the disaster area created by Hurricane Katrina, which extended over four states* and affected 117 counties, the area was identified by FEMA as eligible for individual and public assistance. The disaster has called into question the federal government's capacity as the leader in providing the necessary manpower and resources needed to effect immediate change in relief efforts. As reports from more areas of death, looting, and violence spread, local officials became overwhelmed and survivors became desperate for aid. Continued media reports of the lack of responsiveness, cohesiveness, or substantive progress in aiding the effected areas forced President Bush to recall the director of FEMA, Michael Brown, from duty and appoint Coast Guard Admiral Thad Allen to administer the disaster relief (Chertoff, 2005). In a presidential address to the nation on September 15, 2005, from Jackson Square in New Orleans, President Bush spoke of the federal failures.

> The system at every level of government was not well coordinated, and was overwhelmed in the first few days. It is clear now that a challenge on this scale requires greater federal authority and a broader role for the armed forces—the institution of our government most capable of massive logistical operations at a moment's notice.   (Bush, 2005, p. 4)

---

* Initially Florida, then Louisiana, Mississippi, and Alabama.

By acknowledging the military's capabilities in reference to performing the needed functions in reference to the recovery efforts, the president laid the foundation for a publicly acceptable military involvement strategy in disaster relief.

After the failures of the Hurricane Katrina recovery effort, the House of Representatives appointed a special committee to investigate the possible reasons for the failure. Their final report was a scathing criticism of the government at the local, state, and federal levels. The report comments, "It remains difficult to understand how government could respond so ineffectively to a disaster that was anticipated for years, and for which specific dire warnings had been issued for days. The crisis was not only predictable, it was predicted. If this is what happens after we have advance warning, we shudder to imagine the consequences when we do not" (U.S. House of Representatives, 2006, p. xi).

The Military's Role in Disasters

The National Guard units stationed in every state and territory of the United States draw their lineage back to the state militias at the founding of the nation and answer to the governors of their state. In some instances, National Guard forces can be called into federal action, at which time they draw their orders from the Pentagon leaders and the President. Governors normally call on National Guard troops to aid in disaster relief caused by minor storms. In the case of a large storm, agreements exist among states that allow for the lending of National Guard troops from other states to aid in the relief of the effected region. In fact, during Hurricane Katrina; all 50 states provided some form of personnel assistance (House of Representatives, 2006).

Federal troops can also be used in the response to large disasters, as outlined in the National Response Plan (Department of Homeland Security, 2004b). The use of federal troops is not uncommon. In fact, federal troops have been used domestically 175 times in the last 200 years (Carafano, 2005), of which many examples exist of responses to natural disasters. During the Loma Prieta Earthquake of 1989, the Department of Defense (DOD) provided aid in many forms. Marines landed on the coast of California and cleared debris from roads and ports. In all, 35 ships provided support to the region, delivering supplies and launching rescue aircraft (DOD, 1993). In 1992, Hurricane Andrew crippled Florida, and the DOD was again called on for disaster relief. Surprised by the vast devastation, President George H.W. Bush ordered the DOD to provide any assistance needed. A week later, the DOD had 16,000 troops on the ground, which was later increased to 20,000 troops to supplement Florida National Guard troops operating in the region. The DOD was responsible for delivering mobile tents, water, field kitchens, and the restoration of the transportation infrastructure (McDonnell, 1993). In 2004, Hurricane Charley struck Florida. Under the control of FEMA, the DOD provided military bases as staging areas and logistical support and conducted rescue missions into disaster areas (Department of Homeland Security, 2004b).

Under current laws, the DOD is subordinate to the lead federal agency during an "Incident of National Significance," a term conflating both natural disasters and terrorist attacks. In the case of a natural disaster, FEMA is the lead federal agency with the option to request assistance from the DOD for specific tasks, as outlined by the National Response Plan. The Department of Homeland Security and The Secretary of Defense must approve these requests, and Northern Command executes all military orders (Bowman et al., 2005). Although the use of federal troops may seem like an apparent option in disaster relief strategies, there have been laws enacted over the course of American history that limit the ability of the government to use the army on domestic soil. Passed in 1878, the Posse Comitatus Act prevents the use of federal troops to perform law enforcement activities; however, this law does not pertain to National Guard units operating under the control of a governor, but it does cover federalized National Guard troops (Brinkerhoff, 2002). The Posse Comitatus Act does not prevent federal troops from performing most tasks needed in a natural disaster, such as the evacuation of stranded victims and the distribution of food.

The Necessity and Impact of an Increased Military Role

In light of the colossal failures of response to Hurricane Katrina, there has been a push by the executive branch to give the military a greater role in future disaster relief. One of the recommendations put forth by the White House's analysis of relief efforts states that: "The Department of Defense should prepare for disasters when it may be appropriate due to the extraordinary circumstances for the Department of Defense to lead the federal response" (The Whitehouse, 2006, p. 94). The response to Hurricane Katrina demonstrated how unprepared the federal government was for a large-scale disaster. Following Hurricane Katrina, vast amounts of aid were needed in the form of communications infrastructure, food, and security. Meeting these needs required diverse and expensive equipment, such as fleets of helicopters, large trucks capable of operating in adverse conditions, and ships to support coastal efforts.

Since President Carter's creation of FEMA in 1976, the agency has been responsible for managing relief operations after storms such as large hurricanes (FEMA, 2006). The fact of the matter, however, is that in this role FEMA does not own many of the resources needed for effective and efficient relief strategies. Although FEMA stockpiles food, water, ice, and tarps, the agency lacks the ability to effectively evaluate where they are most needed and sometimes lacks the ability to mobilize its resources. It does not make sense economically to maintain a special fleet of helicopters for domestic disaster food drops at the same time as maintaining another fleet of military helicopters that could accomplish the same missions. It makes more economic sense for the military to participate in, if not be totally responsible for, disaster recovery efforts due to the resources they already have, which would cut down on the government spending needed to duplicate resources.

In its role of defending America, the DOD has developed an effective and complex logistics system for supplying troops in the field, which could lend itself well to disaster relief. As part of its ongoing operations, the DOD's officials will always have more experience handling complex missions than FEMA officials will. In the case of large disasters, increased militarization seems necessary to help FEMA cope with the scope of devastation.

A Militarized Disaster Response and Its Impacts on Civilians

Militarization of disaster relief is a new phenomenon that seems to be eminent for handling mass disasters in the United States given the recent changes to the Insurrection Act by Congress. Although the military has played an important role in supporting disaster rescue and recovery efforts, it has never spearheaded the overall effort. Hence, it is important to analyze the role that the DOD played in the response to Hurricanes Katrina and Rita to try and gain some understanding about what we can expect in the future.

Hurricane Katrina prompted the largest deployment of federal troops in the United States since the Civil War (House of Representatives, 2006). As events unfolded, FEMA asked the DOD to assume its failing logistics distribution responsibilities. The DOD agreed and was responsible for the logistics of delivering food to the affected areas. They assumed this responsibility only after the storm hit and FEMA was overwhelmed. Because the DOD has at its disposal a host of helicopters and high-wheeled vehicles, this mission went well under DOD supervision (House of Representatives, 2006).

After the storm passed, the devastation made it hard to communicate in the region; FEMA had little to no situational awareness of conditions in large areas of the disaster zone. In its assigned roles and with the use of helicopters and large vehicles, federal troops had a much better situational awareness on the ground. However, in its assigned role, the DOD needed specific orders from FEMA to undertake missions in the region. Because FEMA lacked the information to request the services needed for specific locations, the DOD began writing its own requests for aid. These requests were written as if FEMA was requesting DOD assistance. They were then sent to FEMA officials to be signed and submitted. In this way, the DOD began to take the lead as other agencies faltered (House of Representatives, 2006).

Due to the DOD's performance during Hurricane Katrina, they were given a much more pronounced role in administering aid during Hurricane Rita. In this situation, although FEMA still remained in control of the relief efforts, the DOD's assets were requested and deployed before the storm hit. The DOD was able to bring in several large ships right behind the storm and to pre-position other assets just outside the hurricane's path (Bush, 2005).

In the future, the first line of emergency preparedness will lie with state and local officials and their respective National Guards. However, given the recent changes to the Insurrection Act, federal troops can be used to enforce laws and will be essential in assisting police agencies with maintaining order. Although state and local officials have a greater sensitivity for the weaknesses and strengths of their communities and are therefore critical to relief efforts, the recent changes have made it very clear that the President will play a much larger role in state level disaster management. Hence, in the case of a hurricane or other natural disaster that can be predicted, involving the DOD from the start will not be optional and will likely improve conditions for people affected by the disaster.

In the execution of its main mission of protecting the nation, the DOD maintains large stockpiles of ready-to-eat meals, generators, and other emergency supplies, and is uniquely qualified to handle the logistical challenges of delivering these supplies. Providing the DOD with a greater role and more autonomy before the storm hits will undoubtedly allow the DOD to provide greater assistance in a timelier manner. This in turn would translate into improved conditions for victims in the days following a storm through more efficient evacuations, better distribution of food and water, and greater access to field hospitals. The increased role the DOD is expected to fulfill can be directly traced to the new role of the President in the disaster management sphere. The President's new powers will give him the flexibility to use the DOD in a much broader context as indicated by the changes made to the Insurrection Act.

The Tenth Amendment, Posse Comitatus, and the Future of Military Intervention

The text of the Tenth Amendment of the U.S. Constitution, which states that "The powers not delegated to the United States by the Constitution, nor prohibited by it to the States, are reserved for the States respectively, or to the people," seems to indicate that disasters should be managed by individual states. Over time, states have used this clause, known as the *States Rights Clause*, to justify not following laws that were passed by Congress. In many instances, cases have gone to the Supreme Court and states have won major victories over the federal government. One example is *Garcia v. San Antonio Metropolitan Transit Authority (1985)*, the Supreme Court declared that Congress could not enact legislation that would unduly burden the states. Hence, the pattern of the Supreme Court has been one that indicates a firm belief in preventing willful violations of the Tenth Amendment by the federal government at the expense of the states.

The significance that the events of September 11 and Hurricane Katrina have had in affecting major changes to the federal government's role in managing disasters cannot be understated. Before these two catastrophic events, the Tenth Amendment, The Posse Comitatus Act of 1878, and the Insurrection Act of 1807 worked against the use of the military in a law enforcement capacity by the federal government against

U.S. citizens. The goal of these acts was to limit the power of the President as much as possible by relying on state and local governments to take action in the event of a crisis (Trebilcock, 2000; 10 U.S.C. 331; 18 U.S.C. 1385). As discussed earlier, the Supreme Court played an important role in insuring that states' rights were protected with regard to federal intervention under some circumstances.

So what has happened to change the balance of power on this subject? First, President Bush and his administration were subjected to a barrage of negative publicity based on its handling of Hurricane Katrina. Hurricane Katrina has been categorized as one of the greatest natural disasters ever experienced by the United States and one of the worst managed. Hence, the inadequacy of the federal government's response to Hurricane Katrina exemplified the lack of coordination by the federal government in response to crisis in a post September 11 environment. To create a more effective federal government response, on September 30, 2006, Congress made substantial changes to the Insurrection Act of 1808 as a part of the 2007 Defense Authorization Bill. In effect, the changes gave the President more power to use troops as a means of law enforcement at the state and local levels. To be more precise, the President may

> employ the armed forces, including the National Guard in Federal service to ... Restore public order and enforce the laws of the United States, when as a result of a natural disaster, epidemic, or serious public health emergency, terrorist attack or incident, or other condition in any state or possession of the United States, the president determines that—(i) domestic violence has occurred to such an extent that the constituted authorities of the state or possession of the United States are incapable of maintaining public order.   (Public Law 109-364 H.R. 5122 Section 1076)

The changes made in 2006 to the Insurrection Act make the Posse Comitatus Act of 1878 irrelevant, because the Posse Comitatus Act states that "except in cases and under circumstances expressly authorized by the constitution or act of Congress (18 U.S.C 1835)" put in its full context the changes made to the Insurrection Act were made by Congress; hence the recent changes supersede the Posse Comitatus Act of 1878. This change is important because it now provides the President with a number of powers he did not legally possess before the changes. First the law is that it gives the President the sole power of determining when a state is incapable of maintaining public order. Secondly, the law not only gives him the power to intervene, but it also gives him the power to use troops in a law enforcement capacity. Lastly, the law broadens the President's powers by adding an array of incidents or actions (e.g., insurrection, large-scale domestic violence events, or conspiracy) that can be used as the rationale for the federal government's intervention in emergency situations.

The events surrounding September 11 and Hurricane Katrina provided the impetus needed to expand the President's role in emergency management at the state and local levels. In effect, it has placed the state leadership in a precarious situation because they can no longer act with impunity. Hence, the changes made to the Insurrection Act have now made the federal government (i.e., the President) a key player in how emergency situations will be handled in the future.

The Impact of an Expanded Role on the Military

Because the DOD has taken on a greater role in future large-scale disasters, it is important to understand the implications this will have on the military's other responsibilities. If the military is asked to lead future disaster relief operations, these missions will be overseen by Northern Command, which was created in 2002 for the purpose of engaging in homeland defense (Tierney, 2005). According to the Commander of Northern Command, Admiral Timothy J. Keating, and the Assistant Secretary of Defense for Homeland Defense, Paul McHale, the DOD had been considering training and equipping active duty forces for disaster response before Hurricane Katrina (House of Representatives, 2006).

Such a military force devoted to responding to natural disasters is not without precedent. In 1994, Russian President Boris Yeltsin created the Ministry for Emergency Situations (EMERCOM) (Thomas, 1995). EMERCOM has 23,000 troops that are only armed for self-defense and specialize in swift response to natural disasters. They have received many awards for their quick responses to disasters and logistical prowess. Since its creation, EMERCOM forces have performed over 200,000 missions, which include delivering food to New Orleans *via* military aircraft following Hurricane Katrina (Pravda News Service, 2005).

It is also important to assess how increased domestic demands on the military might affect the ability of the military to perform in the field internationally. The DOD has repeatedly asserted that the ongoing conflicts in Iraq and Afghanistan have not weakened the strength or battle readiness of the troops. When questioned after Katrina, the DOD and National Guard officials stated that the ongoing wars did not weaken their ability to respond to the disaster; however, some evidence does exist to contradict this statement. As units are deployed to Iraq, they take with them their combat equipment. Along the way, much of this equipment is broken or destroyed. Additionally, when troops return home, they often leave their working equipment behind for the next units to use. In the case of several units responding to Katrina, they lacked adequate radios during the relief effort because their radios were in Iraq (Bowman et al., 2005). More frequent use of military assets at home and abroad could further stretch limited supplies of equipment.

The DOD has seemed uneasy with the idea of taking too much responsibility for natural disaster mitigation. In the Quadrennial Defense Review Report (DOD, 2006) issued in February 2006, the DOD explained that the capabilities it maintains during a terrorist attack can be used for natural disasters in the short term. The report goes on to explain that over time, they look to other agencies to build a capacity to execute their responsibilities with only supplementary aid from the military. Despite this, the report states that the DOD will charge Northern Command with increasing pre-incident deployment of forces and equipment for disasters. The DOD also expresses its wish to have Congress lift pre-disaster spending limits (DOD, 2006). These developments seem to indicate that the DOD is preparing to take a greater role in disaster relief in the future than they ever have before.

The Future of an Increased Militarized Disaster Response and Public Administration

The public administration issues associated with an increased military role cannot be overlooked. As presented earlier, overlapping responsibilities and resources from various governmental agencies are associated with disaster response. The difficulties associated with their coordination pose a threat to civilian life, public order, and national security. Response in the aftermath of disasters requires effective coordination among the participating agencies or organizations due to the multitude of civil servants, bureaus, divisions, and appointed officials who make decisions affecting all other participants (Breyer et al., 2006, p. 75). Decisions made by one agency or department head have the potential to affect hundreds of thousands of federal employees, and result in the expenditure of billions of federal dollars (Platt, 1999). Additionally, administrating response efforts on a broad scale among several different agencies is further complicated by each agency's own specific culture, which is derived from its own history, mission, leadership, headquarters location, and political connections (Platt, 1999, p. 278). Platt further explained that due to each federal agency's "... ever-changing complexity, comprising [of] subagencies, offices, programs, divisions, branches, and units ... Each major agency and its components operates within a unique web of executive, congressional, and judicial authority ... Each undergoes frequent reorganization, engaging its staff in endless competition for budget, space, and personnel ..." (1999, p. 278), which may detract from more public service oriented behaviors. Moreover, in some circumstances agencies have difficulties coordinating their internal policies, which detrimentally affects their ability to coordinate policies with other agencies (Breyer et al., 2006). For disaster responses to be effective, agency goals must be clear, final, consensual, measurable, and consistent (Kirschenbaum, 2004; Robbins, 1983), which according to Kirschenbaum (2004) rarely occurs. Kirschenbaum (2004) explains that only in a military-type chain of command or in highly formalistic bureaucratic organizations can such a level of conciseness be achieved.

Political agendas inherent in every agency (Breyer et al., 2006) seem to adversely affect the ability of these organizations to effectively provide the services needed in the aftermath of disasters. An agency's agenda, or rather its leadership, must adhere to a mission and a set of goals that reflect the best interests of its clients, which, in the case of disaster relief and response, is the general public.

As a human service provider, disaster agencies must answer to their clients, the potential victims of disasters. The reason for this is fairly simple – it is the public who legitimizes and financially subsidizes these organizations. We, the public, are in fact its major stakeholders—its clients.   (Kirschenbaum, 2004, p. 74)

Because the stakeholders and clients of disaster response agencies are the public, agency leadership should not be held by political appointees who have the tendency to follow the specific political agenda of their patrons; they should be held by elected officials who are more concerned with the welfare of constituents, even if their only motive is to be reelected (Breyer et al., 2006). The militarization of disaster response attempts to accomplish this by placing the President fundamentally in charge of relief efforts because he is the commander and chief. In 1971, the Ash Council believed that placing the President in charge of an agency or any host of agencies would be more visible to the public and therefore more easily held accountable for the organization's performance (Ash Council of 1971, as cited in Breyer et al., 2006, pp. 180–181). Additionally, *Myers v. United States* has shown that the President is a more appropriate voice of the people on a national level than most other elected officials in some circumstances.

The President is a representative of the people just as the members of the Senate and of the House are, and it may be, at some times, on some subjects, that the President elected by all the people is rather more representative of them all than are the members of either body of the Legislature whose constituencies are local and not countrywide . . . (*Myers v. United States*, 1926, as cited in Breyer et al., 2006, p. 85)

By placing the responsibility of disaster response in the hands of the President, who in turn coordinates the relief efforts using the military, a more streamlined approach to saving lives and property can be accomplished through the adherence to a unified command structure—a structure effectively employed in the military. The combination of both a leader receptive to the national public's interests and an organizational structure that promotes immediate action when leadership decisions are made will eliminate the amount of time wasted during the interim between the declaration of disaster and the first actions taken by relief personnel. Moreover, through the use of the military, response personnel will have a mission, interagency jurisdiction, political insulation, and the authority needed to be time-effective in the aftermath of disasters (Breyer et al., 2006).

Although militarization will most likely aid in the efficacy of disaster response, there are inherent effects their actions will have on public administration at all levels of government. On the local and state levels, the President's ability to respond to disasters militarily, with or without the requisition of action on the part of state authorities, will cut down the bureaucratic authority and structure of those local governmental units. Mayors and governors will have to adhere to the military chain of command during times of emergency, effectively placing the emergency area under direct control of the White House. Moreover, during the time that the President decides to enact a state of emergency, local and state governments will have to adhere to a more authoritative style of government not usually seen in democratic regimes; however, this flirtation with a militaristic-style of government will be temporary.

At the federal level, Congress will have to setup procedures and stipulations related to the oversight of military efforts during times of emergency. Congressional checks—such as regulating the length of time the military can police its own citizenry, determining what extent and powers the military can exercise during an emergency situation, and deciding what information can be deemed classified to the general public or Congressional authorities in the name of national security during a domestic emergency crisis—will be needed to ensure against abusive use of the military against its own citizens. Additionally, clarification is needed of the meaning behind the statement " . . . to restore public order and enforce the laws of the United States . . . " found in Section 1042 of the Defense Authorization Bill of 2007 (2006) so that presidential interpretation is not abused. Although the creation of oversight committees and investigation boards will add to the bureaucratic processes that already plague the governmental system, they will unquestionably be needed to avoid what the Posse Comitatus Act, the Insurrection Act of 1807, and the Tenth Amendment to the Constitution have all attempted to protect against in the past.

Conclusion

Hurricane Katrina was a natural disaster unrivaled in size, but in an age when global terrorism is a constant threat, many citizens were taken aback by the poor relief efforts following its landfall. As FEMA became overwhelmed, the military began to assume many of the relief tasks and proved rather successful in doing so. However, because the military was not involved in many key tasks until it was critical they do so, the relief effort as a whole was very disappointing. In looking toward the future, it is inevitable that there will be many more disasters such as Hurricane Katrina. Therefore, it is a vital function of the federal government to meet the needs of the communities and states affected when they are overwhelmed by disasters of this magnitude.

One way to improve the effectiveness of the federal response would be to assign greater roles to the military. However, if as a nation we choose to charge the military with a broader disaster relief role, we must make sure that it does not adversely affect the military's other missions. In addition to adversely affecting the military in the international arena, a great deal of administrative attention must be given to the issue as well. With the ability to police the nation's population in severe emergency situations, the office of the President will enter into a new era marked by more executive power and authority. Congressional oversight of the military, especially in circumstances dictating military use on American soil, will be needed to guard against possible excessive use, or worse, permanent military governing authority.

References

Bowman, S., Kapp, L., and Belasco, A. 2005, September. CRS report for Congress: Hurricane Katrina: DOD disaster response. Retrieved November 10, 2005, from http://www.fas.org/sgp/crs/natsec/RL33095.pdf.

Breyer, S.G., Stewart, R.B., Sunstein, C.R., and Vermeule, A. 2006. *Administrative Law and Regulatory Policy: Problems, Text, and Cases.* New York: Aspen Publishers.

Brinkerhoff, J. 2002, February. The Posse Comitatus Act and homeland security. Retrieved November 10, 2005, from http://www.homelandsecurity.org/journal/Articles/ brinkerhoffpossecomitatus.htm.

Bush, G.W. 2003, February. Homeland security presidential directive/ HSPD-5. Retrieved December 18, 2005, from http://www.whitehouse.gov/news/releases/2003/02/print/ 20030228-9.html.

Bush, G.W. 2005, September 15. President discusses hurricane relief in address to the nation. Retrieved January 9, 2006, from http://www.whitehouse.gov/news/releases/ 2005/09/print/20050915-8.html.

Carafano, J.J. 2005. Critics of the hurricane response miss the mark in focusing on Posse Comitatus. Retrieved October 3, 2005, from http://www.heritage.org/Research/ HomelandDefense/em983.cfm.

Chertoff, M. 2005, September. Statement by homeland security secretary Michael Chertoff. Retrieved January 11, 2006, from http://www.dhs.gov/dhspublic/display? theme = 43&content = 4795&print = true.

Defense Authorization Bill. 2006. S. 2766 – FY07 Defense Authorization Bill. Reported by the Committee on Armed Services on May 4, 2006. Retrieved January 8, 2007, from http://rpc.senate.gov/_files/L41DefAuthS2766.pdf.

Department of Homeland Security. 2004a, August. Department of homeland security responds to Hurricane Charley. Retrieved March 15, 2006, from http://www.dhs. gov/dhspublic/display?theme = 43&content = 3944&print = true.

Department of Homeland Security. 2004b, December. National response plan. Retrieved October 23, 2005, from http://www.dhs.gov/interweb/assetlibrary/NRP_FullText.pdf.

Department of Defense (DOD). 1933, April. Department of defense response: Loma Prieta earthquake. Retrieved March 15, 2006, from http://www.usace.army.mil/usace-docs/ eng-pamphlets/ep870-1-44/c-2.pdf.

Department of Defense (DOD). 2006, February. Quadrennial defense review report. Retrieved February 6, 2006, from http://www.comw.org/qdr/qdr2006.pdf.

Federal Emergency Management Agency (FEMA). 2006, March. FEMA history. Retrieved January 10, 2006, from http://www.fema.gov/about/history.shtm.

House of Representatives. 2006, February. A failure of initiative: Final report of the select bipartisan committee to investigate the preparation for and response to Hurricane Katrina. Retrieved February 15, 2006, from http://katrina.house.gov/full_katrina_ report.htm.

Kirschenbaum, A. 2004. *Chaos Organization and Disaster Management*. New York: Marcel Dekker, Inc.

McDonnell, J. 1993, January. Hurricane Andrew: Historic report: U.S. Army corps of engineers. Retrieved March 15, 2006, from www.hq.usace.army.mil/history/Hurricane_files/ Hurricane%20 Katrina%20Bibliography.doc. *Myers v. United States*. (1926). 272 U.S. 52, 123.

Myers v. United States. 272 U.S. 52, 123 (1926).

Platt, R.H. 1999. *Disasters and Democracy: The Politics of Extreme Natural Events*. Washington, DC: Island Press.

Pravda News Service. 2005, December. Russian rescue service rated one of the best in the world. Retrieved December 29, 2005, from http://english.pravda.ru/printed.html? news_id = 16685.

Robbins, S.P. 1983. *Organization Theory: The Structure and Design of Organizations*. Englewood Cliffs, NJ: Prentice-Hall.

Styles, R. 2005, June. Why revolutionary change is needed in emergency management. Retrieved January 10, 2006, from http://www.emforum.org/vforum/lc050914.htm.

Thomas, T.L. 1995. EMERCOM: Russia's emergency response team. Retrieved November 11, 2005, from http://www.fas.org/nuke/guide/russia/agency/rusert.hm.

Tierney, K. 2005, June. Recent developments in U.S. homeland security policies and their implications for management of extreme events. First Conference on Urban Disaster Reduction. Kobe, Japan. January 18–20, 2005. Retrieved October 30, 2005, from http://www.training.fema.gov/EMIWeb/edu/highpapers.asp.

Trebilcock, C.T. 2000. The Myth of Posse Comitatus. Retrieved December 12, 2006, from http://www.homelandsecurity.org/journal/articles/Trebilcock.htm.

U.S. House of Representatives. 2006. A Failure of Initiative, Retrieved March 16, 2007, from http://www.gpoaccess.gov/katrinareport/mainreport.pdf.

The Whitehouse 2006, February. The federal response to Hurricane Katrina: Lessons learned. Retrieved March 1, 2006, from http://www.whitehouse.gov/reports/katrina-lessons-learned/.

Chapter 21

Military Involvement in Disaster Response

Jay Levinson

CONTENTS

Introduction

Disaster response has few full-time personnel. Those who are employed are generally at the planning level. There are numerous job functions (municipal fire, police, and medical) that require around-the-clock shifts; however, staffing is geared for routine problems and not disasters. A primary exception is the aviation industry, and then particularly in airports, where international regulations require firefighters on duty during all takeoffs and landings.

When disasters do occur, immediate responders tend to be the general public, quickly followed by security and health crews (fire, police, and ambulance). Later, specialized teams (social workers and housing officials) are often brought in. The immediate responders are employed on a daily basis to cover the routine needs of communities (house fires, traffic accidents, and sports crowds). Staffing is not based upon the requirements of a large disaster.

A complicating factor in bringing in auxiliary personnel is that local potential responders may also be victims themselves. Hence, additional personnel must often be brought in from elsewhere.

One approach to finding auxiliary forces is through mutual aid agreements with neighboring communities. These understandings have the benefit of using trained personnel who can arrive quickly, but they have the negative effect of diminishing emergency response capabilities in the neighboring areas. Obviously, the bigger the disaster (hence the greater the need for assistance), the larger the "fan out" will be in looking for assisting forces.

Another option to finding responders is by calling in the military. This has a historic background, and both positive and negative ramifications.

A Historical Overview of Civil Defense

There is a historical progression in disaster planning. A key date is June 1917, when German aircraft started a month-long campaign of almost daily aerial attacks on London. This was repeated, of course, during World War II, when London and other English cities were subjected to repeated aerial bombing. As a result, much response planning has had its roots in the civil defense programs developed before and during World War II, and subsequently during the Cold War (Dynes, 1994). These plans essentially disregarded civilian and nonmilitary needs (such as public transportation). The plans were part of an overall military strategy, and they were based upon the notion that a rigid hierarchical command system is needed to handle disasters, just as the military functions in war scenarios.* This is implicit in the U.S. Federal Civil Defense Act of 1950.

The civilian population was seen at best as a bothersome appendage to military concerns. The central concept was to defend against the armed enemy. Worry about

---

* It can be inferred from Dynes (1994) that turning over disaster response planning to police and fire services, both hierarchical organizations, is a remnant of the military focus and mindset. He also postulates that many civilian disaster plans are based upon the assumption that a "strong hand" (i.e., military-style orders and commands, though in a civilian context) is needed in disaster response.

natural disasters was far from the planners' minds. After all, in an earthquake or flood (or even an industrial accident) there is no enemy to be bombed in retaliation. Some academics felt that something was missing in the military mindset thinking. Mileti (1999) suggests that modern disaster research began during this same period of military-oriented planning. It is important to note that civilian disaster planning was not yet pragmatic; it was still restricted to research.

Through the decades following World War II the emergence of the Cold War sustained the military role in civil defense planning. It was hard to move from the notion of civil defense to the modern concept of civil protection, while the military threat of the Cold War was still considered real.

In the United States, as late as the 1990s, it was still necessary to have military-oriented civil defense programming in place before disaster funding could be released. A blatant example was the requirement to maintain fallout shelters, to be used in the event of a nuclear attack by a foreign government. With the fall of the Soviet Union and the disappearance of the Cold War, fallout shelters were generally regarded as a relic of the past, but attitudes do not change quickly. Only in relatively recent years has planning been shifted to civil protection, stressing non-military accidents and natural events, and their response (albeit still often cast in a military mindset). One example of change has been a movement in the United Kingdom to replace provisions of the Civil Defence Act 1948 with legislation stressing civil protection (ICDDS, 2000). The British Institute for Civil Defence and Disaster Studies now emphasizes civil protection; as their name suggests, their organizational beginnings were in the pre-World War II atmosphere of aerial bombings and acts of war (Jackson, 1988).

Many of the remnants of civil defense have not been totally obliterated and can still be discerned. In some areas, "modern" disaster shelters are still planned on the model of the 1950s fallout shelters.

In Israel, where military thinking in civilian offices is particularly pronounced, there is a different expression of military perspective. The Israel Ministry of Interior disaster planning office is still staffed by retired military careerists. Not only do they bring their military frame-of-mind with them, but also receive relatively little training to handle civilian problems (except for on-the-job training most often provided by other military retirees). Although an Israeli exercise regarding an incident involving a train was a key event during the early 1990s in civil protection, the scenario went along the lines of military thinking and not according to a course-of-business civilian accident.

This same military approach was true in many parts of the United States for the career span of World War II veteran soldiers (in many cases well into the 1970s), and to a much lesser degree the working years of Vietnam veterans. This entire approach stressing the war perspective and shelters left little place for response to major civilian accidents or natural disasters (of which there were quite many).

Gerber, writing in 1952, summed up emphasis in the military-oriented civil defense approach, "The Civil Defense set-up affords opportunity to develop an organization prepared to meet any emergency, not just those resulting from enemy attack or sabotage." The approach was naïve and simplistic, when viewed in retrospect. The needs of the civilian population during peace time cannot be met by wartime planning.

Perhaps placing disaster response with the military was, to a certain degree, flight from reality for many planners. It meant transferring responsibility away from the civilian sector to the military, where the general rule was secrecy, whether justified or not. Thus, planning was removed from public scrutiny, if not awareness.

Each generation has its own concepts of what it wants for itself and for its future. The generation of today has, for the most part, rejected compulsory military conscription and armed confrontation. The Cold War has been declared over and a military threat in Europe is considered a remote theoretical possibility. If there is a threat today, it is held out to be terrorism, which politicians metaphorically call a war. Military intervention in civilian life is simply deemed inappropriate.

Nor is the military capable of true disaster response. They have soldiers, not planners. The military response is for now, without insight for tomorrow.

Hierarchy

The idea of hierarchy is a concept well cherished in the military. In civilian planning it has its problems. It assumes that upper echelons know what is best, and they impart their wisdom downward in the system (Dynes, 1994). In reality, upper management in civil administration has little real-disaster experience (except, perhaps, for a prior incident that might have happened sometime during their tenure); but, senior echelons do have management skills. Disaster-specific knowledge, both theoretical and practical, is more often found at the lower, technical levels of bureaucracy, where workers tend not to have broad-based management skills.

Military Models

Due to the close historical relationship of military civil defense and civilian disaster response, armies have applied lessons learnt in operational problems found in the army to disaster response. Yet, there are vast differences between civilian accidents and military events. One cannot compare a civilian air crash with passengers from numerous countries, to a military flight with a known passenger list and in virtually all cases medical records already on file for identification purposes. One cannot compare the convergence of bereaved families gathering at an airport to military widows and their families, who sit at home until a soldier brings them the bitter news.

The military also operates on coordination by legal mandate; the army is structured by rules and statutes, which clearly define responsibilities. There is structure in the civilian community, but it is much more fluid, without the harshness of commands. International cooperation in particular operates on the basis of good will, not command and control.

One must also remember that wartime thinking is based upon different priorities, different capabilities, and different legal structure—even in the civilian sector. The affected population is different in times of war, because it is plausible to conjecture that most able-bodied men are in uniform or on their way to report for military service. These factors definitely effect the decision-making process and highlight once again the inappropriateness of forcing military models on civilian applications.

As discussed, the roots of government planning are in the military experience. However, the roots of private business sector disaster planning are in security programs (whether for plant security, compliance with government regulations, or insurance company dictates). In recent years in the private business sector this planning has taken a new identity upon itself as business recovery. This is not a new subject, but it is only lately that it has been formalized.

Military Capabilities

There are many different circumlocutions for the word "army." Sometimes the soldier-image is hidden by the names, National Guard or Home Front. Despite all that has been said, under certain circumstances, the military can play a positive role in a disaster response, particularly when the incident is large scale or when specialized logistics are required. The appropriate role is not in command or planning. It is in manpower and logistics.

In a disaster, the biggest strength of an army is generally logistical support—the ability to mobilize a large number of vehicles (land, sea, and air) and to deliver specialized materials. In one case in Israel (December 12, 2000) a bus tumbled off the road down steep hills and into a valley. The army provided nighttime lighting and ropes to assist civilian responders descend the incline, retrieve the injured, and bring them to the road. The weakness of military support is that armies tend to be cumbersome, requiring extensive lead-time unless specialized units, always on call, are utilized.

Brute manpower is appropriate when prior training is not involved. One example is dividing an area into sections and searching for survivors of a disaster. Providing soldiers with disaster awareness training can only give better understanding when a catastrophe arises. Operational training, however, is a totally different matter. A cardinal rule in disaster response is to field personnel in positions requiring skills as close as possible to their normal jobs. That is very possible with fire (fire and rescue), ambulance (evacuation of injured), and police (traffic control, area security, and public order). Only technical units in the military (e.g., communications, logistical support) have skills with a direct disaster response application. To field other units, training requires assigning units with potential disaster response responsibilities, providing training and drills, then periodic refresher courses, not to speak of updates in policy and technology. One wonders if such a comprehensive program would not be at the cost of the real training that soldiers require military functions.

The military does have strength in information (i.e., intelligence) collection. During a disaster updated information about the current situation of the disaster is often required. Some of that information comes from military sources such as aircraft (Perry et al., 1993), and has to be integrated with information received from civilian sources. The military, however, has to make the mental switch from enemy targets to civilian needs, which again requires prior training. Another information gathering application is the search for airplane survivors either in the sea or in nonpopulated areas.

Potential Problems

A standing army in nonconflict situations is heavily administrative with either symbolic operational manpower or with a minimum of soldiers required to hold defensive positions in case of attack until reservists can be drafted and sent to the front. Thus, reality is that particularly following a sudden disaster an army is at its lowest strength when assistance is most needed—in the immediate few hours after a disaster. In times of disaster using the army is further complicated by the fact that soldiers can, themselves, be victims or missing persons.

It is often forgotten that many military supplies are inappropriate for the civilian population.

- Although an army might be able to supply a large number of blankets and tents to disaster victims, storerooms have neither children's clothes nor medicines for serious diseases that would preclude army service.
- In many cases, armies have been used to provide food in the first stages of a disaster response; army food is oriented towards MRE's (meals ready to eat), but it has limitations in that it does not include special diet foods (e.g., salt or sugar free) common in the civilian sector.
- Career military doctors do treat the wounded and can administer first aid, but they do not routinely handle medical problems associated neither with the young or elderly, nor with the handicapped, all of whom are not in military service.
- There are also legal questions involving protection against suit when a military doctor renders treatment (a) to a civilian, or (b) for a problem outside his true field of expertise.

Thus, if military logistics are used, this must be in support of a civilian-generated assistance program and not a military program initiated for civilians.

Civilian vs. Military Control

It is a mistake to put the army in control of a civilian situation, unless the basic civilian infrastructure has been totally destroyed, and lawlessness can be thwarted only by the imposition of martial law. Even when this is not the case, martial law has been prematurely declared in numerous incidents. Its net effect can be more negative than positive.

The imposition of military rule might well have the short-term benefit of restoring order by brute force. That, however, is not disaster response. It is an extreme solution to a law enforcement problem.

In a democratic society one obeys the law because of values, and not because of mere fear of arrest. When there is theft following disaster, the army cannot restore values. At best it can only instill fear.

Expectations from the Military

Armies are meant to work independently using only their own resources. That is a key element in battle strategy, where outside assistance is impossible; hence, it is a general underlying principle in military thinking. Soldiers do not have a clue neither about the other players and their functions in a disaster situation, nor are they trained to work with "outsiders" (nonmilitary personnel). On the other hand, civilian agencies can ask for outside help or not, depending upon circumstances. Because civilian agencies routinely work with coordination (even to the extent that the cooperation is so routine that it is taken for granted), they do not necessarily see their agency as the dominant organization that must take control (although it is common to see post-incident reports claiming that the writer's agency "did all the work").

The very method of thinking in an army is different from a civilian situation. As Averch and Dluhy (1997) point out, a military commander knows that in war the first casualty is peace-time planning. An innovative approach is often what is required. In the civilian sector, however, pre-incident disaster plans are expected to set the parameters for response. Even if innovation is in order, the bureaucracy expects compliance and will instinctively reject deviation.

It is also a mistake to utilize individual soldiers from the military, except in special situations. Armies are not individual soldiers; they are designed to be viable units, and they are taught to function as units. These units must be mobilized, equipped, and positioned to do what they are trained to do. If artillery units are taken to rescue people from the wreckage of a crashed aircraft or from damaged buildings, they will be performing a highly technical task without training.

It is similarly a mistake to think that the army is needed for command and control. That is a military solution with poor application to the civilian sector.

Even in smaller disasters one should realize that there is a danger of speaking in civilian terms, but thinking in military terms. Some people speak of civilian "emergency management," yet at the same time they really think in terms of military "command and control."

Example: Israel—Hizbullah War

In this conflict the Home Front Command of the Israel Defense Forces (IDF) played a key role in disaster-related issues, but not in disaster response.

The Home Front Command was in charge of telling the civilian sector when to enter air-raid shelters and operating sirens. After missiles fell in a community the army and police dealt with rendering fallen katyusha pieces (enemy weapons) safe, but only the civilian sector dealt with classic disaster response (food distribution, medical, fire, traffic patterns for emergency vehicles, victim identification, etc.). As the existence of the state of Israel was not at stake, a national state of emergency giving command to the army was never declared.

On the Lebanese side of the fighting, where damage to cities was much more extensive than in Israel, disaster response also remained totally within the civilian sector. The military was deemed inappropriate. Surprisingly, there was no network of air-raid shelters in Lebanon. The civil defense organization provided fire and medical response, transferring the wounded to hospitals for treatment and the dead for identification.

Conclusion

Calling in the military to assist in a large civilian disaster should not be a natural reflex. It should be a calculated decision weighing both pros and cons. One of the basic issues to be considered is if the military has received proper training to handle the civilian tasks involved.

Moving from assistance to control constitutes a very serious difference in the role of the army. Issuing a call for assistance is very different from relinquishing command control. That latter step should be taken only after all civilian options have been considered.

References

Averch, H. and Dluhy, M.J., Crisis decision making and management, in Peacock, W.G., Morrow, B.H., Gladwin, H., Eds., *Hurricane Andrew: Ethnicity, Gender, and the Sociology of Disasters*, International Hurrican Center, Miami, 1997.

Dynes, R.R., Community emergency planning: False assumptions and inappropriate analogies, *International Journal of Mass Emergencies and Disasters*, 12(2), pp. 141–158, 1994.

Gerber, S.R., Identification in mass disasters by analysis and correlation of medical findings, *Proceedings of the American Academy of Forensic Sciences*, 2(1), pp. 82–98, 1952.

Institute of Civil Defense and Disaster Studies (ICDDS), NCCP proposals for a new civil protection act, *Alert*, January–March 2000, p. 4.

Jackson, A.A., *The Institute of Civil Defence 1938–1955: A Short History of Its First Seventeen Years*, Institute of Civil Defence, London, 1988.

Mileti, D.S., *Disasters by Design: A Reassessment of Natural Hazards in the United States*, John Henry Press, Washington, DC, 1999.

Perry, W.L., Schrader, J.Y., and Wilson, B.M., *A Viable Resolution Approach to Modeling Command and Control in Disaster Relief Operations*, Rand Corporation, Santa Monica, California, 1993.

HUMAN, PERSONAL, AND INTERPERSONAL ISSUES

V

Chapter 22

Disaster Management and Populations with Special Needs

Susan J. Penner and Christine Wachsmuth

CONTENTS

... the test of a civilization is in the way that it cares for its helpless members.

Pearl Buck, 1954

Given the complex logistical problems involved in disaster management, it is not surprising that populations with special needs are often overlooked and underserved. The recent tragedies in managing the Hurricane Katrina disaster is one example (CDC, March 10, 2006). The 1994 Northridge and the 1989 Loma Prieta earthquakes affecting California communities provide additional examples of disaster planning, response, recovery, and mitigation challenges for special needs populations (California Department of Rehabilitation, April 1997). Even with increased attention to this issue, in a recent report, planning for people with special needs and vulnerable populations received the lowest percent of "sufficient" responses compared to all other areas of disaster planning at both the state and urban levels of government (U.S. Department of Homeland Security, June 16, 2006).

In a recent disaster preparedness study of level I and II trauma centers in the United States, it was identified that the majority of hospitals participating [89–93 percent] had written plans for special patient care needs involving psychosocial support for patients, staff, and visitors. However, only about half of the studied trauma centers had similar plans for people who are disabled, elderly, or immuno-compromised (NFTC, September 2006).

Disability advocates and the U.S. Department of Homeland Security are among the growing number of concerned residents and public officials calling for greater input and attention to special needs populations in disaster management planning (National Council on Disability, April 15, 2005; U.S. Department of Homeland Security, June 16, 2006).

Disaster Definitions

Before discussing disaster management issues for special needs populations, some relevant terms are defined for reference throughout this chapter. The term "disaster" is defined as a serious disruption of a community, causing threats or losses that exceed the ability of the affected community to cope without the support of outside resources. By contrast, an emergency is defined as a deterioration in the ability of a community, group, or individual to cope, which may require community or outside assistance. A hazard is a natural or human initiated event that adversely affects human activity, safety, or property. These are adapted from the definitions developed by disaster relief offices of the United Nations (UNDP/UNDRO, 1992).

For example, a gallon of gasoline spilled in a parking lot presents a hazard that could result in an emergency, risking the safety and property of one or more individuals at risk of fire or inhalation of fumes. Damage to an oil refinery causing a fire storm might escalate from an emergency to a disaster when the community requires help from other communities, the state, or federal agencies. The focus of this chapter is on disasters, although some community wide emergencies may require a level of response similar to a disaster.

Disasters may be caused by natural events, such as earthquakes, wildfires, hurricanes, and floods, or may result from accidental or deliberate human causes, such as terrorist attacks, release of radiation, or accidental hazardous chemical spills. Disasters may also result from a pandemic outbreak of communicable disease and relate to natural, social, and geopolitical factors such as the worldwide impact of the 1918 Spanish influenza pandemic (CDC, March 2, 2006). Large-scale casualty incidents such as an airline crash, building collapse, or a transit wreck, with many severely injured victims, can also be defined as a disaster when the event overwhelms a community's ability to provide rescue and medical treatment response.

Typical concerns posed by disasters include large numbers of ill and injured people overwhelming the existing health care system, disruption of basic services such as transportation, communication, and electrical power; public confusion and panic; the need for mass evacuation and housing relocation; and adequate provision of food, water, and shelter under emergency conditions. Depending on the scope of the disaster incident the emergency health care system and first responder services of police, fire, and emergency medical systems (EMS) may also be quickly stretched to their capacity and capability requiring residents to rely on their own resources and support systems.

Special Needs Definitions

This chapter's definition of a special needs population is based on the definition used by PrepareNow.org (n.d.). Special needs populations include groups whose needs are not fully addressed by disaster service planners and providers who assume that traditional services are sufficient. As a result, people with special needs frequently may feel they cannot safely or comfortably access and use the resources provided in disaster preparedness, response, recovery, and mitigation. Examples of special needs populations include persons with physical or mental disabilities, limited or no ability to speak English (or the prevailing language), social or cultural isolation, medical or chemical dependence, the homeless and the frail elderly. Other functional impairments may also represent disabilities (U.S. Department of Justice, September 30, 2004). When the term "special needs" is used in this chapter, it refers to needs of the population of persons with functional limitations who require unique attention from disaster planners and those professionals who operationalize emergency response plans for their communities.

This chapter does not discuss the special needs of children, as it is assumed that for legal and social reasons, children will be supervised by parents, disaster workers, or other responsible adults. Other special needs populations excluded from this discussion include institutionalized persons, such as persons who are hospitalized, imprisoned, or otherwise confined to residential facilities such as nursing homes and rehabilitation centers. It is assumed that these institutions are responsible for disaster management planning and are more easily identified for disaster services than populations with special needs living in the community. However, there may be populations who "fall through the cracks," such as persons considered homeless and living on the streets, those using homeless shelters, living in single room occupancy hotels, and residents of board and care homes.

The term "vulnerable population," often used interchangeably with "special needs population" is not used in this chapter. It is assumed that a disaster may cause otherwise healthy persons to convert to disability status related to injuries or separation from medical support (Kailes, 2005). Anyone at risk of safety or property loss in a disaster situation is vulnerable to the hazards posed by the event, but might not pose special needs for services such as evacuation and shelter.

The two special needs populations this chapter focuses on to the greatest extent are adults with disabilities and the frail elderly. The frail elderly are often designated as seniors with health problems that limit the person's independence and increase the need for assistance in activities of daily living such as maintaining a household, food preparation, and personal care (Fernandez et al., 2002).

Disaster management specialists should anticipate that both the disabled and the frail elderly populations are growing over the foreseeable future. Although estimates differ, it is thought today that approximately one in five Americans have some type of disability and about one in ten have a severe disability (U.S. Department of Commerce, December 1997). Approximately 7.2 million Americans received home health services (indicating their medical classification as homebound with an illness or disability) in 2000, with about 1.4 million (most of whom were Medicare elderly or disabled beneficiaries) receiving home health services at any one time (Feldman et al., 2005).

With Baby Boomers beginning to reach age 65 in 2011, age-related disabilities are likely to increase in greater numbers. The numbers of persons over age 85, who are more likely to be disabled, frail, and with limited support systems, are also expected to increase more rapidly. Today, an estimated half of all Americans over age 65 (approximately 18.4 million) are estimated to have some kind of disability (U.S. Census Bureau, August 9, 2006). Frail elderly and persons affected with disabilities are expected to live longer, and to increasingly reside in the community rather than in institutions.

Special needs populations often experience serious economic and social problems that limit their resources for personal emergency preparedness. Fernandez et al. (2002) point out that the frail elderly often expend all their reserves on basic survival. Many persons with disabilities live in a similar day-to-day survival mode with few or no reserves for adequate emergency preparedness, poverty or near-poverty incomes, and limited personal support systems. A survey of Katrina survivors found that the biggest reason (55 percent) they did not evacuate was they did not have a car, with 22 percent of the respondents reporting they were physically unable to leave, and apparently without personal emergency evacuation plans (The Washington Post–Kaiser Family Foundation-Harvard University, September 2005). Disaster preparedness agencies should realize that many persons in special needs populations will not have the recommended 3–7 day supplies of food, water, medications, and other essentials (American Red Cross, n.d.).

This chapter presents strategies for community-based approaches to address special needs across all four stages of disaster management: mitigation, preparedness, response, and recovery. Agencies responsible for disaster management need to collaborate and coordinate efforts with agencies serving populations of persons with disabilities, the elderly, and others who will present special needs in a disaster. Problems identified in recent disasters that affect special populations, and that are targeted for this discussion of community-based strategies include:

- Difficulties identifying and providing outreach
- Inadequate evacuation and shelter support
- Inaccessible or unaffordable housing restoration or replacement (California Department of Rehabilitation, April 1997; U.S. Department of Homeland Security, June 16, 2006).

Identification and Outreach

Increasingly, persons with special needs who have disabilities or health problems reside in their homes and in the community. Unlike institutionalized populations in locations such as hospitals, nursing homes, and assisted living facilities, persons living alone or with elderly relatives in the community may be difficult to target throughout the stages of disaster management.

Mitigation

Disaster mitigation is a preliminary stage of community or regional disaster management, in which natural and human-related hazards are identified as potential threats. Estimates are made for the potential risk of disaster posed by each of these hazards, and assessments made of the vulnerability to human safety or property loss should a disaster occur. Mitigation activities may be implemented to eliminate or reduce the hazard, associated risk, and vulnerability of life and property (FEMA, April 14, 2006; Washington State EMD, March, 2003).

When documenting, assessing, and implementing activities for disaster mitigation, it is important to determine whether there are any special hazards or risks to special needs populations. Census data might help pinpoint concentrations of elderly, and collaboration between disaster management and community-based agencies could better identify concentrated populations of persons with disabilities (such as the blind or mentally ill) who would be at greater risk should a hazard lead to a disaster situation. Another strategy is to identify and mitigate potential residential hazards for persons with special needs. Housing authorities might partner with disaster management and volunteer agencies to appropriately retrofit or secure housing and items such as hot water heater tanks to improve safety and prevent property loss. Local gas, electric, and utility companies frequently make customer service employees available to seniors, people with disabilities, and homebound individuals to suggest disaster mitigation strategies for the home (for example, gas and water turn-off valve instruction and hot water heater immobilization).

Preparedness

Advocates and representatives from special needs populations must be included in local, state, and federal disaster planning boards, to keep concerns visible and ensure they are addressed throughout the disaster preparedness process (California Department of Rehabilitation, April 1997; JCAHO, September 2005; U.S. Department of Justice, September 30, 2004). Community coalitions such as Collaborating Agencies Responding to Disasters (CARD) working in the California counties of Alameda and San Francisco serve in advocating for persons with disabilities, coordinating advocacy efforts and enhancing resources to support these clients should a disaster occur (Fernandez et al., 2002).

Preparedness efforts include identifying individuals living in the community who are members of special needs populations. Lists of clients with their special needs and their location could be maintained in agency databases, as recommended by the San Francisco Collaborating Agencies Responding to Disaster (San Francisco CARD, n.d.). Agencies such as Area Agencies on Aging, Meals on Wheels, home health care, public health departments, and other agencies serving special needs populations could work with local CARD groups to develop client databases.

Service agency providers should assess clients for disaster preparedness, share preparedness information and provide educational workshops for clients and caregivers, and help organize "buddy" systems to locate clients and provide support during a disaster. Home care agencies, meals-on-wheels programs, and social support agencies should consider including a disaster preparedness assessment during initial client intake evaluation process. Public health departments and local offices of emergency services can provide assistance to families, individuals, home health care workers, primary health care providers including physicians about disaster planning resources available in the community to assist people with special needs. The American Red Cross (2006) provides extensive disaster preparedness materials for home and family preparation both in print and online. Disaster preparedness training may also be available through local American Red Cross chapters.

Many government, community, and health care organizations have developed disaster preparedness checklists for home and family that are easily accessible from the Internet (see Box 22.1: Disaster Management "Toolkit" for Special Needs Populations). The city of San Francisco has developed disaster preparedness materials in the predominant languages of the city's population (English, Spanish, and Chinese) and all are available to the public on the city's web page. Many of the materials in the "Toolkit" can be downloaded and customized for a specific client group or service population.

Response

Special needs populations should be aware and informed of resources such as transportation and shelters that will be made available once a disaster has occurred (California Department of Rehabilitation, April 1997). Emergency warning systems should be designed and adapted for visual, hearing, and cognitive impairments, and should be redundant and communicated via multiple media (Fernandez et al., 2002).

Buddy systems, client registries, and other identification and location strategies should be implemented to assist disaster service workers in their efforts at search and rescue, and are facilitated by interagency collaboration. For example, in San Francisco the Department of Public Health Emergency Medical Service Agency sponsors and maintains a registry program for seniors and persons with disabilities, to be shared with fire department first responders following a disaster (San Francisco EMSA, 2006).

Recovery

Following the disaster, special needs populations require timely and accurate information. This information may range from how to obtain essentials such as food, water, shelter, and medical care; whether it is safe to return to the affected community; transportation availability; and housing vouchers. A community's medical, mental health, and other support services may be disrupted, possibly for extended periods of time following a disaster (Rudowitz et al., August 29, 2006), so updates and alternative resource information is important. As with warning systems, multiple media and accommodations for visual, hearing, and other limitations should be provided to ensure that special needs populations obtain information and support.

Box 22.1   Disaster Management "Toolkit" for Special Needs Populations

■ ABA Committee on Homeland Security and Emergency Management (April 6, 2005). A checklist for state and local government attorneys to prepare for possible disasters. American Bar Association—State and Local Government Law Section. Chicago, Illinois. http://www.abanet. org/statelocal/checklist406.pdf.

■ American Red Cross Family Disaster Plan and Personal Survival Guide. Six page downloadable form and checklist of key resources and information necessary for home and personal disaster preparedness. Accessed December 13, 2006 from http://www.hhhi.net/Survival_ guide.pdf.

■ Are You Prepared? Seniors and disabled disaster preparedness web page available online in English, Spanish, and Chinese. Accessed December 13, 2006 from http://www.72 hours.org/seniors.html.

■ Home Safety Tip inventory for the elderly. Accessed December 13, 2006 from http://www.hhhi.net/safety.htm.

■ Joint Commission on Accreditation of Healthcare Organizations (JCAHO). (September 2005). *Standing Together: An Emergency Planning Guide for America's Communities.* Oakbrook Terrace, Illinois: Joint Commission. http://www.jointcommission.org/NR/rdonlyres/FE29E7D3-22AA-4DEB-94B2-5E8D507F92D1/0/planning_guide.pdf.

■ New York State Office of Advocate for Persons with Disabilities (OAPD). (n.d.). *Accessibility Checklist for Existing Facilities.* Albany, New York. http://www.ghi.com/pdf/adachecklist.pdf.

■ Pacific Gas and Electric Company Safety in the Home. (2006). Natural Disasters and Emergency Preparedness. Accessed December 13, 2006 from http://www.pge.com/safety/.

■ PrepareNow.org (2003). Online preparedness library providing assistance for organizations whose client base includes people including planning tools for individuals. The information in this library makes it possible for organizations with limited staff and funding to make preparedness information available to a broader audience. http://www.preparenow.org/prepare.html.

■ San Francisco Emergency Medical Services Agency (EMSA) (2006). Disaster registry for seniors and persons with disabilities disaster vulnerability checklist. San Francisco, California: San Francisco Department of Public Health. http://www.sanfranciscoems.org/form/vcl.pdf.

■ San Francisco Emergency Medical Services Agency (EMSA). (2006). Registration form disaster registry for seniors and persons with disabilities. San Francisco, California: San Francisco Department of Public Health. http://www.sanfranciscoems.org/form/conseng.pdf.

Evacuation and Shelter
Mitigation

Disaster management officials, working with representatives of special needs populations, should assess the community and potential hazards to estimate the extent of risk posed to transportation systems, as well as determining shelter requirements should evacuation occur.

Registries of agency clients would assist in identifying populations with special needs, such as persons requiring dialysis, oxygen, or other medical equipment or care. The existence of accessible transportation, such as buses equipped with wheelchair lifts, should be inventoried. Shelters that meet accessibility guidelines established by the Americans with Disabilities Act (ADA) of 1990 should be identified and the need for more ADA accessible shelters assessed (OAPD, n.d.).

Interagency coordination requires planning, so that agencies serving special needs populations such as the elderly and persons with disabilities can work together in responding to a disaster. Representatives of special needs populations and agencies serving these populations must be identified so they are included in disaster planning and training at all levels of government. Another issue is to clarify regulations such as privacy guidelines established by the Health Insurance Portability and Accountability Act (HIPAA) so service agencies are able to plan to appropriately share client data (U.S. Department of Homeland Security, June 16, 2006).

Preparedness

It is essential to plan how individuals with special needs will be transported to shelters or other emergency facilities. Community disaster plans must include arrangements for people with hearing, vision, mobility, and other impairments, full-time caregiver needs, service animals, and the need for oxygen or other special equipment such as wheelchairs. Transportation vehicles must be accessible and capable of accommodating wheelchairs and personal attendants (JCAHO, 2005; U.S. Department of Justice, September 30, 2004). A unique challenge facing communities during disaster evacuations is tracking locations of displaced populations. Persons with disabilities who may be referred to distant locations for services, will require special assistance and follow-up during and after their emergency transport (CDC, March 10, 2006; Congressional Briefing, November 10, 2005).

Planning considerations of particular importance for special needs clients include tracking of people displaced by the disaster including exact location, and the use of multiple sources to notify family and friends of displaced people (such as using local media and dedicated disaster victim "home pages"). Other strategies include helping clients prepare lists of emergency family contact numbers, setting up mechanisms for the retrieval of critical medical information, health history and drug prescriptions, and replacement of critical aids such as glasses, hearing aids, canes, and walkers.

Once safely evacuated from the disaster area, a second issue is the availability of shelters to meet the special needs of persons with disabilities. Although many of these evacuees may be immediately relocated in the homes of their social supports or in institutional settings, some evacuees with special needs will need, at least temporarily, to use public emergency shelters. Both Section 504 of the Rehabilitation Act of 1973 and Title II of the ADA of 1990, which concern state and local government responsibilities, require that services are accessible to people with disabilities (OAPD, n.d.).

A survey inspection of existing facilities for ADA compliance is one strategy to prepare for sheltering special needs populations (OAPD, n.d.). The survey should include inspection of parking lots, stairs, doorways, and bathrooms for accessibility. Policies prohibiting "pets" may require revision to allow service animals such as guide dogs for the blind (U.S. Department of Justice, September 30, 2004). If barriers to access exist, it may be possible to work with the facility managers to remove the barriers. If some shelters cannot meet ADA guidelines, then other ADA compliant housing will need to be identified for use should a disaster occur. Advance consideration should be given for the use of hotels, schools, community health centers, and gyms which were constructed or renovated to meet current ADA standards. A community inventory of these resources and advance communication with owners and managers may open the door to new levels of involvement in community disaster preparedness.

Shelter staff must, however, be aware of civil rights issues in relief work with special needs populations. In most cases, persons with disabilities should not be sent away from shelters to other shelters designated for them, as in situations in which a person with special needs self-refers or does not want to be transported to a designated ADA compliant shelter. Persons with disabilities should not be segregated within a shelter, but should be provided the same services and allowed to use the same shelters as anyone else in the community (U.S. Department of Justice, September 30, 2004).

Volunteers and staff must understand the special needs of persons with disabilities and the frail elderly, and be able to manage assistive devices, access needs, and other related resources. Specific training on the operation of assistive devices and availability of local, regional, and state resources should be provided, particularly to staff who will assume leadership in a disaster (California Department of Rehabilitation, April 1997). The American Red Cross recently developed a training course for its staff and volunteers to better serve the needs of persons with disabilities in a disaster (Lawson, September 29, 2006).

Response

The benefits of relief worker training and interagency coordination become evident when special needs populations require relocation and sheltering when a disaster occurs. Kailes (June, 2006) emphasizes the need for adequate, accessible transportation, ensuring that all shelter workers understand that caring for people with special needs is one of their responsibilities, and coordinating agencies serving special needs populations with disaster services during a disaster. Timely and regular broadcasts, preferably using multiple media (including radio, TV, Internet, and newspapers), must also be available to inform and update special needs populations and their caregivers regarding the availability and location of transportation and shelter (California Department of Rehabilitation, April 1997).

Recovery

Housing vouchers, medical equipment, prescription drug replacements, social services, and accessible transportation are examples of resources that may be required by special needs populations as they transition from temporary shelter to restored or replacement housing. Information must be available to special needs survivors so they can locate and access postdisaster recovery assistance without unnecessary delay or difficulty.

Housing Restoration or Replacement
Mitigation

Specific risks posed by hazards to existing housing in a geographic area should be identified for all special needs populations. For example, earthquake zones may require homes to be bolted to foundations and homes in floodplains may require elevation by construction. Individuals with special needs may require additional financial and planning assistance to secure their home or property. Referral agencies for accessible transitional housing, resources for housing restoration, and potential locations of permanence replacement housing must also be identified.

Preparedness

Planning must take place for referral to accessible transitional housing, and for the restoration or replacement of permanent housing (California Department of Rehabilitation, April 1997). Representatives of special needs populations, including the elderly and persons with disabilities, must be included as advocates in this planning process (Kailes, June 2006). Planning should include how housing vouchers or other housing assistance will be made available and publicized to persons with special needs who may be widely scattered and who may lack their usual social networks following evacuation and sheltering.

Response

Depending on the extent of threats to safety, special needs populations may remain in their homes during a disaster, or be evacuated and sheltered. As soon as it is possible to inspect the affected residential areas, homes may be declared "yellow-tagged" as temporarily uninhabitable, or "red-tagged" as permanently uninhabitable (California Department of Rehabilitation, April 1997). Local disaster response agencies should anticipate the number of "FEMA trailers" that are either wheelchair accessible or ADA compliant which might be needed in the event that housing in the disaster zone is uninhabitable for extended periods of time.

Recovery

Special needs populations often have limited financial resources, so that following a disaster the cost of home repair or increased rent can pose a significant problem. It is essential to restore or replace housing so that it is affordable and accessible. Repairs to housing should be expedited, with an emphasis on safety and relatively simple modifications for access, such as installing ramps (California Department of Rehabilitation, April 1997). If homes have been declared uninhabitable, affordable, and accessible replacement housing should be expedited.

A disaster may also disrupt the social networks, medical and pharmaceutical services, durable medical equipment industries, and other assistance that persons with special needs rely on for day-to-day functioning and survival (CDC, March 10, 2006; Rudowitz et al., August 29, 2006). Relocation of persons with special needs requires that attention is given to necessary, affordable, and accessible support services (Congressional Briefing, November 10, 2005). Considerations include portability of insurance benefits, maintenance of prescription medications, expedited replacement of medical equipment (including eyeglasses, ambulation aids [walkers and canes], mobility equipment [motorized chairs and electric wheelchairs] and proximity to social networks so travel is not an added burden). A key issue is that people with special needs are able to maintain functional independence to the greatest extent possible, despite the disaster event (Kailes, June 2006).

Recommendations and Community Examples

Four major problems encountered in disaster management for special needs populations have been discussed:

1. Difficulties identifying and providing outreach
2. Inadequate evacuation and shelter support

3. Inaccessible or unaffordable housing restoration or replacement
4. Problems associated with including this population in their own disaster planning and training (California Department of Rehabilitation, April 1997; U.S. Department of Homeland Security, June 16, 2006).

This section summarizes recommendations to address these problems, with some examples illustrating how communities can make disaster management work for their special needs populations. A "toolkit" for special populations disaster management resources is provided in Box 22.1.

Disaster Registries and Information

In 2006, the San Francisco Emergency Medical Services Agency created and implemented a Disaster Registry Program for senior citizens and persons with disabilities (San Francisco EMSA, 2006). This system provides advance information on the location and special needs of homebound individuals who may require wheelchair accessibility or other support considerations in a disaster. This information is provided with the individual's consent so that privacy and confidentiality concerns are addressed. The EMS agency, under the jurisdiction of the Department of Public Health, is responsible for outreach to ensure that the program reaches all persons eligible for the Registry and maintains the Registry for accuracy.

Text Message Emergency Alerts

Another initiative sponsored by the city and county of San Francisco in 2006 is the AlertSF Notification System (n.d.). Local residents as well as persons visiting San Francisco can register online and free-of-charge to receive weather or other alerts, as well as disaster information such as the location of shelters AlertSF will send tsunami alerts, severe weather/flooding notifications, and postdisaster information to the registered wireless devices or e-mail accounts 24/7. Future anticipated information alerts include traffic delays, power outages, and road closures. Users can also enter addresses and ZIP codes of concern and obtain emergency information specific to those locations (Vega, October 18, 2006). Although this does not replace the need for public broadcasting alerts and emergency information in other media such as radio broadcasts, it is an enhancement that has potential value, usefulness, and around-the-clock accessibility for many persons in special needs populations.

Interagency Coordination

Collaborating Agencies Responding to Disasters groups are active both in Oakland and San Francisco, California. Activities include interagency coordination, disaster preparedness workshops, materials such as agency checklists for preparedness for their operations and their clients, and focus on clients with special needs in a disaster. In addition, CARD organizations network with local emergency management services, the American Red Cross, the faith community, and other entities such as public utility providers to share information and enhance disaster planning (CARD, n.d.; San Francisco CARD, n.d.; San Francisco Congregational Disaster Preparedness Conference, May 17, 2006). This kind of interagency coordination can help in providing input for addressing the needs of special populations in a disaster, and aid in the development of disaster registries, accessible shelters, and other emergency assistance.

Conclusion

As Kailes (June 2006) observes, "If planning does not embrace the value that all should survive, they will not." Kailes (2005) also argues that people with special needs should not be considered a "special interest group" in disaster management, but are people who live in our communities and are integrated into society. Disaster management with attention to special needs populations should improve disaster management for everyone.

References

ABA Committee on Homeland Security and Emergency Management, April 6, 2005, A checklist for state and local government attorneys to prepare for possible disasters. American Bar Association—State and Local Government Law Section. Chicago, Illinois. http://www.abanet.org/statelocal/checklist406.pdf.

AlertSF™ Notification System, n.d., 24/7 text-based emergency information to your wireless device. Accessed October 19, 2006 at: http://www.alertsf.org.

American National Red Cross (2006). Prepare.org website. Washington, DC: The American National Red Cross. http://www.prepare.org/.

American Red Cross, n.d., Disaster preparedness for people with disabilities. Publication A5091. Accessed April 6, 2006 at: http://www.redcross.org/services/disaster/0,1082,0_603_,00.html.

Buck P.S., 1954. *My Several Worlds*. Pocket Books, Simon & Schuster, New York.

California Department of Rehabilitation, April 1997, Disaster preparedness for persons with disabilities: improving California's response. A report by the California Department of Rehabilitation, April 1997. California Governor's Office of Emergency Services. http://www.oes.ca.gov/Operational/OESHome.nsf/97859617169196278825 6b350061870e/66952778A6D2FA7C88256-CEF006A8967?OpenDocument.

Centers for Disease Control and Prevention (CDC), March 10, 2006, Rapid assessment of health needs and resettlement plans among Hurricane Katrina evacuees—San Antonio,

Texas, September 2005. *MMWR Weekly*, 55(9):242–244. http://www.cdc.gov/mmwr/preview/mmwrhtml/mm5509a6.htm?s_cid = mm5509a6_e.

Centers for Disease Control and Prevention (CDC), March 2, 2006, Emergency Preparedness and response. http://www.bt.cdc.gov/.

Collaborating Agencies Responding to Disasters (CARD), n.d., Oakland, CA: Collaborating Agencies Responding to Disasters. Accessed October 2, 2006 at: http://www.firstvictims.org/.

Congressional Briefing, November 10, 2005, Emergency Management and People with Disabilities: Before, During and After. Congressional Briefing November 10, 2005, hosted by The National Council on Disability, the National Council on Independent Living, the National Organization on Disability, the National Spinal Cord Injury Association and the Paralyzed Veterans of America. Washington, DC. http://www.ncd.gov/newsroom/publications/2005/pdf/transcript_emergencymgt.pdf.

Feldman, P.H., Nadash, P., and Gursen, M.D. (2005). Chapter 9: Long-term care. In A.R. Kovner and J.R. Knickman (Eds.) *Health Care Delivery in the United States*, 8th ed., New York: Springer, pp. 274–325.

FEMA, April 14, 2006, *Understanding Your Risks: Identifying Hazards And Estimating Losses. FEMA 386-2*. Washington, DC: Department of Homeland Security, Federal Emergency Management Agency. http://www.fema.gov/txt/plan/mitplanning/howto2.txt.

Fernandez, L.S., Byard, D., Lin, C.C., Benson, S., and Barbera, J.A., April–June 2002, Frail elderly as disaster victims: Emergency management strategies. *Prehospital and Disaster Medicine*, 17(2): 67–74. http://pdm.medicine.wisc.edu.

Joint Commission on Accreditation of Healthcare Organizations (JCAHO), September 2005, *Standing Together: An Emergency Planning Guide for America's Communities*. Oakbrook Terrace, Illinois: Joint Commission. http://www.jointcommission.org/NR/rdonlyres/FE29E7D3-22AA-4DEB-94B2-5E8D507F92D1/0/planning_guide.pdf.

Kailes, J. (2005). Disaster Services and "Special Needs:" Term of Art or Meaningless Term? Kailes-Publications, California. http://www.jik.com/resource.html.

Kailes, J., June 2006, Serving and Protecting All by Applying Lessons Learned—Including People with Disabilities and Seniors in Disaster Services, Center for Disability Issues and the Health Professions at Western University of Health Sciences, Pomona, California, and California Foundation for Independent Living Centers. http://www.cfilc.org/site/c.ghKRI0PDIoE/b.1545243/k.97B8/Disaster_Preparedness_Serving__ProtectingbrPeople_with_Disabilities.htm.

Lawson, K., September 29, 2006, *New Red Cross Training Course Aims to Better Serve People with Disabilities Following a Disaster*. Washington, DC: The American National Red Cross. http://www.redcross.org/article/0,1072,0_312_5678,00.html.

National Council on Disability, April 15, 2005, *Saving Lives: Including People with Disabilities in Emergency Planning*. Washington, DC. http://www.ncd.gov/newsroom/publications/2005/pdf/saving_lives.pdf.

National Foundation for Trauma Care (NFTC), September 2006, *US Trauma Center Preparedness for a Terrorist Attack in the Community*. Accessed December 13, 2006 at: http://www.traumafoundation.org/public/publications.php.

New York State Office of Advocate for Persons with Disabilities (OAPD), n.d., *Accessibility Checklist for Existing Facilities*. Albany, New York. Accessed May 26, 2006 at: http://www.ghi.com/pdf/adachecklist.pdf.

PrepareNow.org, 2006, *Definition of Vulnerable Populations*. San Francisco Bay Area: PrepareNow Partners. Accessed September 26, 2006 at: http://www.preparenow.org/pop. html.

Rudowitz, R., Rowland, D., and Shartzer, A., August 29, 2006, Health Care In New Orleans Before And After Hurricane Katrina. Health Affairs—Web Exclusive DOI 10.1377/ hlthaff.25.w393-406. http://www.healthaffairs.org/WebExclusives.php.

San Francisco CARD, n.d., Agency Disaster Plan. San Francisco, CA: San Francisco Collaborating Agencies Responding to Disaster. Accessed October 2, 2006 at: www. sfcard.org.

San Francisco Congregational Disaster Preparedness Conference, May 17, 2006, Sponsored by American Red Cross Bay Area Chapter, Jewish Community Relations Council, San Francisco Foundation Faith's Initiative, San Francisco CARD, San Francisco Interfaith Council, San Francisco Office of Emergency Services and Homeland Security and the Walter & Elise Haas Fund, San Francisco, California.

San Francisco Emergency Medical Services Agency (EMSA), 2006, San Francisco Disaster Registry Program Information. San Francisco, California: San Francisco Department of Public Health. http://www.sanfranciscoems.org/drpform.php.

San Francisco Emergency Medical Services Agency (EMSA), 2006, Disaster registry for seniors and persons with disabilities disaster vulnerability checklist. San Francisco, California: San Francisco Department of Public Health. http://www.sanfranciscoems. org/form/vcl.pdf.

San Francisco Emergency Medical Services Agency (EMSA), 2006, Registration form disaster registry for seniors and persons with disabilities. San Francisco, California: San Francisco Department of Public Health. http://www.sanfranciscoems.org/form/conseng.pdf.

The Salvation Army, 2006, The Salvation Army National Headquarters, Alexandria, Virginia. http://www.salvationarmyusa.org.

The Washington Post/Kaiser Family Foundation/Harvard University, September 2005, Survey of Hurricane Katrina Evacuees. Publication #7401. http://www.kff.org/newsmedia/ upload/7401.pdf.

U.S. Census Bureau, August 9, 2006, Newsroom: Facts for Features Special Edition 300 million. CB06-FFSE.06. Washington, DC: US Census Bureau. http://www. census.gov/Press-Release/www/releases/archives/facts_for_features_special_editions/ 007276.html.

U.S. Department of Commerce, Economics and Statistics Administration, Bureau of the Census, December 1997, Disabilities Affect One-Fifth of All Americans: Proportion Could Increase in Coming Decades. CENBR/97-5. Washington, DC: Department of Commerce. www.census.gov/prod/3/97pubs/cenbr975.pdf

U.S. Department of Homeland Security, June 16, 2006, In cooperation with the U.S. Department of Transportation. Nationwide Plan Review Phase 2 Report. Washington, DC. http://www.dhs.gov/interweb/assetlibrary/Prep_NationwidePlanReview.pdf.

U.S. Department of Justice, Civil Rights Division, Disability Rights Section, September 30, 2004, An ADA guide for local governments: Making community emergency preparedness and response programs accessible to people with disabilities. http://www.usdoj. gov/crt/ada/emergencyprep.htm.

United Nations Development Programme/Office of the United Nations Disaster Relief Co-ordinator (UNDP/UNDRO) Disaster Management Training Programme, 1992,

An Overview of Disaster Management, 2nd ed. United Nations. www.undmtp.org/english/Overview/overview.pdf.

Vega, C.M., October 18, 2006, San Francisco—Text messaging plan for emergency alerts. San Francisco Chronicle, p. B-3. http://www.sfgate.com/cgi-bin/article.cgi?file=/c/a/2006/10/18/BAGVBLR8351.DTL.

Washington State EMD, March 2003, *Comprehensive Emergency Management Planning Guide*, 2nd ed. Camp Murray, Washington: Washington State Military Department Emergency Management Division, Analysis and Plans Section. http://emd.wa.gov/3-pet/pal/plan-guide/plan-guide.pdf.

Chapter 23

Disaster Psychology: A Dual Perspective

Grant Coultman-Smith

CONTENTS

Introduction

It is a well-known fact that individuals react differently to stress and traumatic incidents. This being the case, in this treatise I briefly examine the psychological effects of traumatic stress on people as individuals and how it affects their personal recovery and the overall recovery of their family. I will also examine the effects of such traumatic incidents, both positive and negative, on Emergency Service Personnel and the overall benefit of discipline both within the emergency services and the general populace as a tool to mitigate the immediate effects of trauma. Throughout the chapter, I rely on recognized and authoritative texts and my extensive personal experience in facing and attending traumatic and critical incidents.

It is recognized that, during a traumatic incident, individuals will act with surprising courage and level-headedness especially when given some form of leadership and an attainable goal. Once the incident is over and there exists the opportunity for reflection on the sheer magnitude of the event and the realization of the closeness of death, that the psychological effects of involvement either as a victim or an emergency service professional take hold. For the majority, such effects can be easily remedied with post-incident counseling (both formal and informal) leaving no long-term effects, but in the case of a minority, the effects are far more long reaching and deep-seated. The symptoms of which, unless recognized and treated, can become extremely serious indeed.

Theory

Psychological Effects of a Traumatic Incident

As a person begins to realize the enormity of the occurrence and tries to come to terms with the horror, death of friends and family, destruction of homes, and the fact of their survival, they tend to go through recognizable set reaction stages from realization to recovery. Although this is not always the case, in the main the following appears to be the format.

Denial and Shock

During the early stages, after a loss or traumatic incident there will often be a sense of denial of the existence of the event and an inability to believe that the event has occurred. This is a visible manifestation of shock.

Distress, Despair, Hopelessness, and Sadness

A feeling that no matter what is done that there is no control whatsoever over one's destiny so one may as well just let it all happen, as it is no good trying to prevent a reoccurrence. "I may as well just give up." "This one didn't get me but the next one will."

Sleep Loss and Change of Habit

Some will experience difficulty in sleeping and behavioral changes such as an increased alcohol intake, changed eating habits, heavy smoking, and loss of appetite.

Alienation, Withdrawal, and Isolation

On occasion even the most outgoing people will become withdrawn from the rest of the community and even their closest family, which can lead to alienation and develop into a sense of isolation.

Remorse and Guilt

A belief that "It's my fault." A feeling that if one had not been there it would not have happened and family members would still be alive. "If only we'd gone yesterday...."

Panic

This can develop as a feeling that one is no longer in control of one's destiny and faces an uncertain future. A feeling of being trapped and the certainty of one's death combined with the inability to think of what to do to survive.

Unable to Plan or Make Decisions

The emotional pressures brought on by a traumatic event can cause difficulty in one's ability to plan for the future and to make decisions in critical situations, especially those affecting the future of self and family. "What's the point?"

Anger, Hostility, and Resentment

Usually directed at authority as a target of blame but can be directed to those close and sympathetic to the victim, "What would you know, it didn't happen to you, you don't understand." Used to avoid closeness or when embarrassed over sympathy.

Idealization

This is a desire to grasp the past rather than face the uncertainties of the future. "Remember how good it was before ... " or "It'll never be that good again ... "

Acceptance

Eventually this will progress steadily toward acceptance of the scope of the incident and the ability to plan for the future thus placing the incident in its proper perspective. This develops a renewed strength, energy, hope, and confidence in the future, in the vast majority of victims.

This process may take days, weeks, or in extreme cases, years before the victim actually accepts the loss and is able to place the incident where it belongs in its correct perspective and therefore then be free to get on with life as before (Carter 1991; Erikson 1976; Hodgkinson and Stewart 1991).

Personal Experience (the Reality)

I have experienced, at close range, the reactions of civilian victims of traumatic and critical incidents. This experience was heightened having been thrust, somewhat unwillingly, into the role of rescue worker during Cyclone Tracy, Darwin, Australia, Christmas Eve, 1974. This commitment was both during and immediately after the emergency had passed and relief, cleanup, and recovery operations were beginning. At this time, I was a member of the Australian Army. In this regard, although I suffered no personal loss, I was probably both victim and emergency worker concurrently.

Being both a professional soldier and a Vietnam veteran was a distinct advantage. I was acclimatized to extreme trauma and seeing death. I was able to switch off and simply act. A compatriot of mine, also an Army NCO, Darwin resident and Vietnam veteran related the following: "It was an advantage being an Army NCO as I was conditioned to assess and act upon high risk situations both quickly and decisively." Not so those whose safety became our responsibility. Both of us, found shelter from the storm at the Naval female barracks. Although being military personnel, they were female Naval Ratings billeted in the building of which the top floor had blown away. Had it not been for a female Naval Lieutenant utter panic would have reigned. Being suddenly exposed to the prospect of a sudden and violent death, the majority of the girls, on the exposed floor, simply froze with fear and had to be either verbally abused or manhandled, by us, to move them to a place of safety. Their discipline came to the fore and they readily accepted direction. Once they knew that they were relatively safe they calmed down and quickly became rational and were then able to perform tasks given by their superior officer. I have not spoken to the WRANS since so cannot gauge the long-term effects, if any, of their exposure to such a traumatic experience.

The following morning, Christmas day, I found that, in the main, the populace appeared to be somewhat shell-shocked but calm and readily accepted evacuation of the women and children. There was also very little looting. This was with the exception of some members of the ethnic Greek community who tried to push their way onto the evacuation aircraft, including the males and seemed to be the only looters, with the exception of several prisoners who escaped when Fanny Bay Jail blew down. I have no wish to vilify the Australian Greek Community as a whole. It is simply a fact that defies explanation. It was as if a portion of an ethnic group simply panicked and threw all feeling of community and socially accepted behavior out the window. Other than this apparent aberration, there was no major break-down of law. Control was quickly regained by the police and armed military personnel. (The official death toll was 49, making it the worst single disaster in Australian history. This figure did not take into account the hundreds of hippies living in tents on the beaches, who were blown away or simply disappeared. Obviously, for political reasons the casualties found after the official figure were not included in the tally. It is my personal opinion, supported by rumour and innuendo, that the true figure was closer to 500. This cannot be substantiated and therefore remains an "urban legend.")

During the cleanup operation, where Army personnel were demolishing unstable houses and clearing the rubble, the legendary Australian stoicism came to the fore. Homeowners supplied the troops with cold beer as they watched their unstable properties being levelled. In one instance, a mistake had been made and a perfectly sound house was levelled by the crew I commanded. The owner, bless him, turned up and instead of going troppo (berserk) as one would expect, he simply went away and returned with his utility full of cold beer for the boys. He just shrugged and said, "Stiff, I guess it was time for a new one anyway." It was noted by many that there must have been some divine intervention, as all of the pubs (hotels/bars) survived.

Albeit brief, insulated and attitude influenced, my experience appears to be in severe contrast to much of the currently accepted victim reaction to exposure to such a traumatic event. Speaking to victims some time later, mainly military personnel and their families living in Darwin, the only symptoms they appeared to suffer were:

Denial and shock. After the initial onset of the cyclone although this appeared to last an extremely short time. Those who survived the cyclone, in the main, grasped the enormity of the situation and willingly followed the direction of the authorities regarding evacuation and casualty treatment.

Panic. Initial panic did set in but was immediately submerged in the need for immediate survival. Where the responsibility of leadership was adopted, panic ceased and people calmly went about necessary tasks under the calming influence of their leaders.

Idealization. Occurred sometime after the event during the rebuilding stage. Those who decided to remain and rebuild initially had an unrealistic image of life before the cyclone that soon dissipated when the reality of the enormity of the reconstruction task set in.

Acceptance. In this case, acceptance seemed to appear before idealization and in many cases even supplanted any feeling of panic. This is evidence that Australian stoicism in the face of disaster is not a myth but a very real attribute, especially in the "bush," in which Darwin had always been proud to be included.

Anger, hostility, and resentment. This did not occur until the rebuilding phase. There had been ample warning but due to many previous warnings coming to naught, was mainly ignored by the general populace. Anger was aimed at the authorities due to delays in the relief and rebuilding program, not as a personal attitude toward family and community members as a whole.

The personal recovery cycle, in this case, appears to be rather disjointed and out of sequence. This is probably due to the fact that a large number of the populace were Defence Force personnel or Defence Department employees. The former being subject to varying levels of discipline, the latter automatically following the example of their military counterparts.

This is not to say that no long-term psychological effects amongst these groups were experienced although it has been my personal experience that amongst those of which I am acquainted, no long-term effects appear to have manifested themselves. Yet again, they experienced only destruction and loss of property not any major physical injury or loss of a family member. Had this occurred, no doubt the effects would have been somewhat different.

Occasionally, I am haunted by the image of a person being sliced in half by a piece of wrought iron roofing, witnessed, by me during the storm. This and a slight but controllable fear of heavy winds appear to be the only ill effects I suffered both as a victim and an emergency worker. The image at times does tend to merge with those from Vietnam and thus becomes part of an overall experience of trauma. During the cyclone, I recall fear and possibly frustration over the fact that, as opposed to combat, this was a situation over which I had no control whatsoever.

Discipline. I believe that the presence of discipline and training can assist in the way people deal with a traumatic event. Those who are or have been exposed to discipline or have experienced command tend to use the pressure of an emergency situation as motivation. They act with purpose and can actively assess a situation and naturally provide leadership and a focus for those without such attributes and experience. In an emergency situation, it can be equated to the shepherd and the sheep. Without a shepherd, the sheep simply mill about in confusion. The shepherd gives direction. This is a mantle that in my experience is automatically adopted by those with military and especially command experience. This experience is not confined to the Armed Forces alone. All the emergency services are moulded around the military model and during training provide the grounding necessary for members to accept the responsibility of leadership in an emergency situation. In fact, the civilian population automatically look to emergency service members, especially police, to provide that leadership. The value of discipline in a critical incident cannot be underestimated. This factor is not mentioned in any of the authoritative texts. For reasons unknown, it has either been overlooked or rejected in the interests of "political correctness." Sadly, discipline is no longer considered an attribute in modern western society.

Reaction of Emergency Service Personnel to Trauma

It is said that whatever does not kill you serves to make you strong. If this were the case, Emergency Service Workers would be superheroes. It may sound stupid and vehemently denied by some, but that is exactly the public perception. We do not feel. We are expected to do our job no matter what the circumstances. We are expected to sift through the mangled bodies of adults and children without hesitation or thought for our own personal safety. We do not show weakness. We only display strength and fortitude. We are the buffer between the people and disaster. The thin blue line. God help us if we fail or make a mistake. Human frailty is a luxury we can ill afford.

If the above appears to be overly dramatic and unrealistic, think about it for a moment and you will agree with its thrust. This perception of the emergency service professional is a huge responsibility for anyone to bear. It is the mere fact that he or she is a professional that this attitude can inflict the exact same belief in his or her invulnerability and can engender and proliferate this exact attitude amongst emergency personnel. This in itself makes the possibility of being vulnerable a frightening possibility and one to be denied. To seek counseling after a traumatic incident has been, in the past and is still, seen by some, as a sign of weakness amongst one's peers. Even where counseling is now compulsory (members of the police force after a shooting incident), the attitude is, "Told them nothing, I wouldn't have gone if I didn't have to." It is our very strength and professionalism that is our greatest enemy in the fight against stress-related illness and yet is the very attitude we need to retain our sanity. In fact, we thrive on it (Lunn 2000; Moran 1995; Patterson 2001).

The following is a combination of my own personal experience of the effects of stress and trauma and those encountered in coworkers in my capacity as a soldier, Police Sergeant and first-line supervisor supported by the studies and papers referred to in this chapter.

Psychological Benefits of Emergency Work

Recently awareness has increased of the effects, both immediate and residual, of post-traumatic stress experienced by emergency workers resulting from exposure to extreme situations. This awareness and recognition is definitely a positive step in the treatment of such stress. Despite the inherent risks of emergency work, many people welcome the opportunity to participate in it (Moran 1995).

Surprisingly there is little systematic information available on the personality characteristics of emergency workers other than that revealed in anecdotal reports or reflected in organizational "culture." In the past, a high level of stoicism was the expected primary characteristic, but recently it has been suggested that this may be a narrow and inappropriate opinion. The following are regarded as positive characteristics although not all emergency workers will demonstrate all discussed.

Altruism

It is often expected that at least part of the reason that emergency workers participate in their role is a desire to help others. This is commonly the case with volunteer workers but can also be noted amongst professionals. Despite arguments that no behavior is truly altruistic, that we only do what we do to gain pleasure, there does exist pure altruism. It is true that emergency workers gain a feeling of personal pleasure and achievement at being able to help others does not mean that altruism is a selfish act (Moran 1995).

Adventure, Excitement Seeking

As a combat veteran, I joined the Victoria Police Force as I believed it gave me that feeling of risk I needed to feel alive. It also relieved me from the humdrum of a 9 a.m.–5 p.m. existence and gave me the opportunity to use my organizational and command skills in emergency situations. The main reason that emergency service workers love "the job" so much is the fact that no one knows what they will have to face around the corner. That feeling of uncertainty and risk can engender excitement and a feeling of anticipation (Moran 1995).

Humor

Humor is a recognized coping mechanism and emergency workers are recognized as having a good, if not decidedly sick, sense of humor. It is my belief that: "Life is too serious to take seriously. You must be crazy to stay sane. If you stop laughing you start screaming." This humorous outlook, especially at the scenes of critical and emergency situations can be seen, by outsiders, as unfeeling and heartless but in fact demonstrate a high awareness of the seriousness of the situation (Moran and Massam 1997).

Where children are involved as victims, however, there is no humor. Where children are concerned, all I have ever seen are tears (A firefighter friend [fellow Vietnam veteran] and me attended the suicide of a 16-year-old girl, having both attended six similar incidents in the previous month. We both had teenage daughters and once the incident had been dealt with, simply looked at each other then embraced in tears. We had had enough! Neither of us could see any humor in this situation). Although excessive or hysterical humor can be a cause for grave concern, humor is a beneficial coping mechanism that prevents emergency workers being overwhelmed by tragedy and able to do their job effectively (Moran 1995; Moran and Massam 1997).

Positive Reactions after a Major Incident

Positive reactions after a major incident are common but less frequently discussed than negative reactions in a formal context. These are often bypassed or ignored because now the focus is on the symptoms manifested post-trauma. Debriefing also focuses on the negative aspects and therefore it is felt to be inappropriate to mention anything positive. The overriding consideration and the inanimate need for "political correctness" being to focus on the negative aside, many people do feel good after the successful handling of a major incident and it is appropriate to acknowledge this and them. These positive feelings are as follows:

Exhilaration. Emergency workers often report coming off duty almost on a "high" of exhilaration. They may be fatigued but need time to wind down. There is a strong physiological component to this reaction, which reflects increased sympathetic nervous system activity, for example increased adrenalin levels and racing heart. There is also a psychological component and the high level of alertness and activity is often in itself pleasurably exciting (Hodgkinson and Stewart 1991).

Sense of achievement. One of the most powerful positive feelings that emergency workers report is the sense of achievement or feeling good about being of assistance (altruism). In one study, over 90 percent of a large sample reported this (Moran 1995). It has also been my experience, that this is indeed the case and definitely contributes to the reduction of adverse reaction to stress. In fact, it is extremely important to engender the feeling of achievement no matter what the results of the situation are. Despite everything, a feeling of achievement amongst the emergency workers is essential, not only for their psychological well-being, but also to gain positive practical lessons from the incident.

Love of life and colleagues. The concept of mateship is an integral part of Australia's self-image and is exemplified in situations of extreme stress with people working together, the strong helping the weak, against an external force and facing overwhelming odds. It is the trust and bond between soldiers in the same section (squad) who watch each other's back. It is also the feeling between emergency workers after a major incident. It is the bond of success gained, risks shared, and survival. It manifests itself in an increased love of life and a strong sense of "family" and a recognition that "only those who have faced death can really appreciate life." It is the knowledge that no matter what, your life is in good hands (Patterson 2001).

This feeling of "oneness" has recently been the subject of derision and fear in the case of the Victoria Police, referred to as "police culture" and something to be eradicated. God help us all if this feeling of brotherhood should disappear. For once gone from the police force, the other emergency services will follow. It is something to be nurtured, not destroyed. The sanity of the emergency worker is at stake if he or she does not have the closeness of family within which to be supported and nurtured.

Sense of control. Arguably, one of the greatest stressors in the human experience is lack of control over one's destiny. In the Emergency Service environment, the sense of control is somewhat enhanced, especially when the effects of an incident are minimized or contained. Many emergency workers have experienced this increased sense of control as a positive feeling. In the context of my role as an emergency service professional and a supervisor, the feeling of control is one I relish and goes hand-in-glove with the feeling of achievement and a job well done (Moran 1995).

There is no direct evidence that the aforementioned psychological benefits lead to enhanced physical well-being in the context of the emergency worker. However, in health psychology generally there is a growing body of anecdotal evidence that psychological factors such as positive attitude, mood, brotherhood, and sense of control are directly associated with improved psychological well-being.

Despite the aforementioned positive aspects of working in a stressful environment, as a team, the potential for post-traumatic stress following an emergency incident cannot be dismissed. Those positive aspects, must be recognized as offsetting the more traumatic effects but cannot be seen as long-term prevention strategies. They can, however, be utilized to better understand and recognize the onset of post-traumatic stress symptoms in emergency workers and therefore facilitate earlier treatment and relief thereof. It must also be emphasized, through ongoing training, that to attend counseling is not an admission of frailty or insanity but simply another form of debriefing and another tool to enable the emergency worker to better deal with the natural pressures of "the job" and therefore become both more effective and more professional (Moran 1995).

It must be recognized that although I have concentrated on the positive aspects of stress in the emergency services, that members do suffer from post-traumatic incident stress disorders which left unrecognized can cause the "pile-up" effect and seriously affect their family, friends, workmates, and efficiency. Some never recover but most respond to careful counseling either by psychological professionals or mainly, their colleagues (Mitchell and Bray 1990).

Individuals react differently to stress and various stressors. It must also be recognized that individuals often react differently to post-incident trauma counseling. A formal structure can adversely affect emergency workers as it can be seen to be imposing a requirement to speak only of negativity while refusing to recognize the positive aspects of the incident. Dwelling upon the negative feelings can often be counterproductive and cause some individuals to believe that they are being blamed for the event rather than congratulated for a job well done. Often the individual is not given the benefit of the doubt and assumptions are made that only intervention experts can solve problems with trauma, therefore failing to recognize that individuals both have the right and the ability to utilize their own personal coping mechanisms (Violanti 2001). Acceptance of individual differences in reactions to traumatic stress may assist in the formulation of training and post-incident debriefing procedures. This will also raise acceptance of the procedure amongst emergency workers (Moran 1998; Patterson 2001).

Although debriefing has been generally reported as helpful, there appears to be no correlation to the overall rate of recovery. In fact, there would appear to be a trend toward a lower recovery rate amongst those who have attended formal debriefing sessions. Furthermore, it was generally found that there was no relationship between the reported degree of helpfulness of debriefing and the actual onset (or lack thereof) of symptoms of post-trauma and other detrimental psychological effects (Kenardy 1998; Orner et al. 2003).

Conclusion

It can therefore be deduced that exposure to stress, risk, and danger is a two-edged sword. On the one hand, it enhances awareness and feelings of achievement, control, and a zest for life not normally experienced. On the other hand, overexposure can lead to a buildup of personality stressors that unless released can lead to long-term psychological damage or even permanent psychological damage affecting work, family, and personal relationships. In addition, the value of discipline cannot be discounted. Victims, who are members of a disciplined organization, fare far better than those from the general population, as do their families.

Personally, I am a great believer in the informal debriefing, where the team gets together, has a few drinks, a few laughs, share their experiences, and winds down. I have found this to be extremely effective, but recognize that this can be ably supported by counseling from professionals in the field. Used in conjunction I have no doubt that the onset of stress-related illness both among the emergency services and victims of trauma would noticeably decrease. I equate it to the difference between myself, as a professional soldier and a National Serviceman (Conscript/Draftee) both having returned from Vietnam. On one hand, we professionals could submerge ourselves in our peers, over a few drinks, share our experiences, and even cry on each other's shoulders. Sharing the experience does tend to diminish the trauma. There being no formal counseling structure, we simply debriefed ourselves and we are still doing it. On the other hand, the National Serviceman (Draftee), was thrust back into society and simply told to get on with it, without the benefit of the support of his peers. He had no one to talk to. There was no form of counseling available. Of the Vietnam veterans who have either gone "Troppo" or committed suicide, the ratio is approximately 3:1 in favor (or otherwise) of the National Serviceman (Draftee) (This is anecdotal evidence as no official study of the specific criteria has been conducted and is in direct contrast to the findings of a survey of British Gulf War [first] veterans, in 1994, who found there was no marked difference between those that had been debriefed and those who had not (Kenardy 1998)). Sadly, the advent of "political correctness" in Australian society has made the practice of drinking with one's peers, socially unacceptable.

It is therefore essential that there be a network combining peer support and professional counseling readily available for both civilian victims and emergency workers exposed to extreme trauma. Yet the beneficial effects of stress must be recognized and utilized as a yardstick to assess the onset of stress-related effects amongst victims and professionals alike. It must also be recognized that the value of the unofficial debrief with one's peers, in my belief, supported by experience, cannot be undervalued. I believe that it is possibly of far greater value than formal intervention, in the coping with stress and trauma within the Emergency Services "family." I believe that the "formal" post-incident debriefing be available but on a voluntary basis only (It is recognized that in the case of a police incident [shooting etc.] that a formal structure must be adhered to in the interests of transparency and the conservation of evidence). Far more emphasis must be placed on the undeniable benefits of peer support and the unofficial debriefing.

References

Carter, N.W., 1991. *Disaster Management.* Asian Development Bank, Manilla, Phillipines, pp. 303–305.
Erikson, K.T., 1976. *In the Wake of the Flood, an Account of a Dam Burst in Buffalo Creek, West Virginia, USA on 26th February 1972.* Simon & Shuster, Canada.

Hodgkinson, P.E. and Stewart, M., 1991. *Coping with Catastrophe*. Routledge, Chapman & Hall, New York, pp. 174–205.

Kenardy, J., 1998. Psychological (stress) debriefing: Where are we now? *The Australasian Journal of Disaster and Trauma Studies*, 1998, p. 1.

Lunn, J., 2000. Critical incident staffing: prevention is better than cure. *Australian Journal of Emergency Management Winter*, 2000, pp. 48–52.

Mitchell, J. and Bray, G., 1990. *Emergency Service Stress*. Englewood Cliffs, New Jersey: Prentice Hall, pp. 19–21, 88–94.

Moran, C., 1995. *Psychological Benefits of Disaster and Emergency Work*. Victoria Police (Australia) Bulletin, 1/95.

Moran, C. and Massam, M., 1997. An evaluation of humor in emergency work. *The Australasian Journal of Disaster and Trauma Studies*, 1997, p .3.

Moran, C., 1998. Individual differences and debriefing effectiveness. *The Australasian Journal of Disaster and Trauma Studies*, 1998, p. 1.

Orner, R.J., King, S., Avery, A., Bretherton, R., Stolz, P., and Ormerod, J., 2003. Coping and adjustment strategies used by emergency services staff after traumatic incidents: Implications for psychological debriefing, reconstructed early intervention and psychological first aid. *The Australasian Journal of Disaster and Trauma Studies*, 2003, p. 1.

Patterson, G.T., 2001. Reconceptualizing traumatic incidents experienced by law enforcement personnel. *The Australasian Journal of Disaster and Trauma Studies*, 2001, p. 2.

Violanti, J.M., 2001. Post traumatic stress disorder intervention in law enforcement: Differing perspectives. *The Australasian Journal of Disaster and Trauma Studies*, 2001, p. 2.

Chapter 24

Managing the Spontaneous Volunteer

Brian J. Gallant

CONTENTS

Introduction

When disaster strikes a community, whether it is man-made or natural, specific emergency management and many not-for-profit agencies routinely respond according to a preestablished plan. Each of these designated organizations has a specific role to play in ensuring an effective response to and recovery from the tragedy's devastation.

However, there is one element within the present system that continues to create a daunting challenge: the spontaneous, unaffiliated volunteers.

In times of disaster, regardless of the location, people's natural tendency is to offer assistance. Most of us are taught as youngsters to help our neighbors, relatives, etc., in times of need. Often, people flock to the scene of a disaster and want to help in whatever capacity as may be needed.

The spontaneous, unaffiliated volunteers, who are often our neighbors, friends, and ordinary citizens, frequently arrive at a disaster scene "ready to help." But because they are not connected with any part of the existing emergency management response system, group, or organization, their offers of help are regularly underutilized and can even be challenging to most professional responders. The irony is very clear: people have a willingness to volunteer, but the system's is lacking the capability to use them effectively. This can create a "disaster" within the disaster. This can cause traffic problems, issues for law enforcement agencies and other emergency agencies responding to and dealing with the incident, as well as a host of other probable and possible troubles.

How the volunteer helpers are dealt with can make or break that portion of the disaster response. The use of volunteers is not always encouraged or warranted; however, if volunteers are needed, there is a definite place for them, provided they are managed properly. The fact that volunteers are not always encouraged to participate in an emergency needs some explanation. Let me try to do that.

There are some emergencies, such as those involving criminal activities, hazardous materials, or situations where responders need very specific training. In these instances, it would not be wise to use volunteers in certain roles. There certainly is a great deal of liability involved, not to mention the potential to have the volunteers become victims themselves.

The Professionals

In large-scale events, the police, fire, municipal administration, emergency medical, highway department, and the emergency management officials within the community are initially going to be overwhelmed dealing with their typical response duties, as well as those related to the emergency. These typical duties can include the following:

- Evacuation
- Sheltering

- Traffic control
- Fire response
- Lack of power
- Law enforcement issues
- Hazardous material response
- Wires down
- Dealing with limbs and trees blocking roads
- Medical response to injured and ill residents, and transients and guests
- Declaration of disaster
- Day-to-day administrative functions

The professionals, during a disaster, will be inundated with calls from the public requesting information, reporting situations that require attention (some more serious than others), etc. Some callers may also call to see if "they need help?" Other individuals may just feel like helping and show up at or near the scene or respond to the Police Department, Fire Station, or Sheriff's Office. Initially, the dispatchers may not have enough time or information to provide to these callers, and as a result a large number of people want to help and have no direction, guidance, or leadership and can cause more problems by acting without authority, training, and leadership.

Managing the Volunteers

The management of spontaneous volunteers in times of emergency is often a difficult task. Some of the following information may be helpful to those individuals who are responsible for directing these volunteers. Please remember that volunteering is a valuable part of every strong community. Volunteers come from all walks of life and very often provide much needed services. Every person has the potential to contribute strength and resources in times of emergency situations.

Ideally, all volunteers should be affiliated with some recognized and reputable organization and be trained for specific disaster response activities. However, the spontaneous nature of people volunteering is inevitable; therefore it has to be anticipated, planned for, and managed.

Four Emergency Phases Can Include Volunteer Involvement

There are some valuable and appropriate roles for spontaneous volunteers in mitigation, preparedness, response, and recovery, as well as in other areas of community needs. The response phase provides an opportunity to direct volunteers toward longer-term affiliation and community involvement.

Volunteers are a valuable resource to the community, especially, when they are trained, assigned properly, and supervised within established emergency management systems (like the Incident Command System [ICS]). Much like the donations management, that we will discuss later, an essential piece of every emergency management plan is the clear designation of responsibility for the on-site coordination of unaffiliated volunteers. A volunteer coordinator (or a team) is usually the way to ensure the effective utilization of these resources. This way, the volunteers are initially dealing with a designated person (or a team) and they may feel more comfortable.

Everyone Has a Little Responsibility

The enlistment, management, and support of volunteers are largely a responsibility of local government and the not-for-profit agencies, with some form of support from the state government. Specialized planning, information sharing, and an organization structure are extremely necessary to coordinate efforts and capitalize on the benefits of volunteer involvement and response.

Volunteers will be successful contributors in disasters or emergencies when they are flexible, self-sufficient, conscious of the various risks they might be exposed to, and prepared to be coordinated by local emergency management officials. Volunteers must accept the obligation to "do no harm."

Priorities

The main concern of all volunteer activity in disaster situations is assistance to others. When the spontaneous response by community folk is well managed, it definitely affects the volunteers themselves and also adds to the confidence level of both individuals and the entire community.

Most communities include some individuals or organizations that know how to activate, organize, and involve volunteers effectively. Emergency management directors should try to identify and use all available resources to assist with the integration of spontaneous volunteers.

Common Terminology

When working with volunteers involved in emergency management, it is always helpful to use consistent terminology. Emergency management professionals, although it may be difficult, should avoid the use of acronyms and abbreviations that the volunteers may not initially understand. Often, terms, abbreviations, and acronyms that are used in disasters may have another meaning to personnel not involved in the emergency services. Take for example CERT, which not only stands for community emergency response team, but may also be construed as certificate, and has connotations in the computer realm, as well. Spontaneous volunteers are not part of a recognized voluntary agency and most have no formal training in emergency response. They are motivated by an unexpected desire to help others in times of trouble. They also come with a variety of skills. There is a place for most of these people, but let us not turn them off by using terminology that confuses them to the point that they no longer want to assist.

Plan of Attack

It is wise to have a plan of attack prearranged to deal with the onslaught of volunteers and folks that want to help. Some thoughts should include the following:

- Location to direct volunteers for reporting
- Preprinted applications (see below)
- Supplies to deal with the application process (pens, paper, clipboards, etc.)
- If outdoors, a shelter (tent) to keep folks out of the elements
- Water

A recent event following Hurricane Katrina put a local sheriff's office in this position. Hundreds of people from at least three states showed up in an effort to help out with evacuees who were due to arrive from Louisiana and Mississippi. The question became, "Now what do we do with these folks?" The sheriff did not want to discourage people from helping, but there was nothing in place to deal with the large numbers of people—all showing up to help at the same time.

Within 30 minutes, we had a system in place to take applications. The applications were printed forms to gather much needed information, such as

- Name and address
- Any specialized training (nurse, teacher, physician, social worker, etc.)
- References
- Schooling
- Employment

Some of this eliminates the questions/concerns

- What can I do?
- I don't want to do that.

By having an application, the volunteer can tell us what he or she does or does not want to help with. It is never a good thing to have a volunteer assigned to a task they do not want to perform.

Additionally, we had the entire group fill out CORI (Criminal Offender Registry Information) forms. We felt it was extremely important to determine if any of the volunteers had criminal records, or, worse, had outstanding warrants. Most of the group filled out the forms with no problem. However, a few actually said, "Thanks, but I don't think I will pass a CORI check." They sat for a few minutes and then left quietly, so as not to draw attention to themselves. Others, with criminal records, filled out the forms and had to be told that we could not use their services (obviously, this is done discreetly). Some individuals who had minor criminal records were interviewed and at the discretion of a Sheriff's office official, it was decided to allow the person to stay or not. None of our folks had outstanding warrants.

We felt the CORI form and background check was important, as we thought there was a potential for the volunteers to be exposed to children and others, so we did not want someone with a violent past or sexual misconduct dealing with any of the evacuees. Once the background checks were conducted, a photo identification card was issued to each volunteer. This would alleviate some of the daily checks that would be normally required.

Volunteer Welcome Center

A plan should be developed to determine a site (and alternate sites) for the volunteers to report, be processed, and referred to organizations or groups who may need their services.

A "go kit" is recommended to be ready at all times. The kit should include various office supplies, forms, lists, maps, equipment, etc. Some of the items might include

- Registration form
- Safety orientation training briefing checklist
- Volunteer instructions
- Disaster volunteer referral
- Sign in/out sheets

A volunteer application is included at the end of this document for use as needed. Please feel free to revise it for your organization's needs.

Tasks

Volunteers might be asked to assist with the following tasks, and I am sure there are several more:

- Administrative duties, such as telephone calls, filing, and documentation efforts
- Warehousing of supplies (disaster supplies)

- Delivery of goods to shut-ins and others
- Meal preparations or feeding
- Light search techniques (missing or lost individuals)
- Babysitting (at shelters, etc.)
- Medical triage/minor first aid duties
- Dead and dying
- Heavy lifting

Please keep in mind that not everyone is comfortable with all of the tasks that may be involved in the disaster operation. Remember, also, they are volunteers, and we cannot force anyone to do a particular job. If a volunteer balks at performing a task that is assigned, reassign him or her to another job and get someone to replace him or her.

Supervision

As a person in charge of the volunteers, you need to direct and keep them focused and involved. It is extremely important to thank every volunteer every day. This is not too much to expect from the leadership, especially for people who do not have to be there—and remember they are volunteers—they are not getting paid. If they need to leave early or cannot stay late, do not yell or complain, instead, thank them for their efforts and attempt to get another volunteer who can help with the extra work or after hour's project. Do not forget the thank you.

Some of the other issues that came up for us included the following:

- Food, water, breaks, sunblock
- Safety briefings daily (reminders to folks)
- Scheduling of volunteers for their work shift
- Tracking of personnel: Sign in/out daily
- Documentation issues, who was present, what did they do, man-hours
- Lessons learned
- To let people know what is happening (keep them informed)
- Not to let them overstep their level of training or their roles and responsibilities
- Communication with volunteers should be within that group. Volunteers should not be dealing with the incident command staff of the overall incident
- Not to let the volunteers get "too involved" dealing with the victims. They can become overwhelmed and get taken advantage of

Some Guidance

Do not ever let a volunteer position interfere with a full-time job or one's family life. Tell the volunteers that and also tell them "If you can be here, great." Oftentimes, volunteers see the need for their assistance and they become caught up in the moment. Many times they do not eat properly, as "they are too busy" helping. In addition goes for medication. Also, their normal commitments to their family and work seem to be put on the back burner, because "they need me to be here." Volunteers should be told that they are appreciated; however, their family and jobs should be number one priorities. I recently recall a couple volunteering numerous hours—great workers and extremely dedicated to their volunteerism. Some months later I learned that they were so wrapped up in volunteering, that they had forgotten family birthdays and her parents' anniversary. It needs to be stressed that as volunteers—they come first. It is much better to be able to tend to the needs of yourself, family, neighbors, and then the community.

Donations

In times of disaster, people come out of the woodwork to donate to the cause. Experience shows that, while most people have a good heart, others may be "donating" their junk in the form of clothing, furniture, appliances, etc. It may seem like a good deed, and it probably is, however, if your organization is not equipped (storage, repair, delivery, pickup, etc.) to deal with these items, do not even start to accept the items. My suggestion is to refer the donors to agencies or organizations that are better equipped to handle these items. This can become overwhelming in a short period of time. In a recent incident, several church groups organized (although did not communicate with the organization handling the response activities) clothing drives. Seventeen truckloads of clothing were attempted to be delivered. There were only 282 people involved with the disaster. All of the church groups that donated had to be referred to other agencies. Clothing needs to be clean, sorted by age, sex, size, season, etc. (lots of work, requiring lots of storage, and people to help).

Be careful of any and all food donations. It is great if you are equipped to handle food products, but accepting them can be a huge headache if you are not prepared. There are regulations that deal with storage, refrigeration, etc. Imagine accepting a truckload of food and having no place to refrigerate it. What's worse is having a large amount of food placed into a warehouse and not having the proper equipment to keep out mice and other critters. Expiration dates are also important items. The last thing your group needs is to have people getting sick from food or supplies that you have control over.

Buddy System

No volunteer should ever be allowed to work alone. Safety of the volunteers is the number one priority in each and every incident. We always try to stress the buddy system. It does not mean that we have volunteers holding hands. It does mean we need to work as a team. The buddy system does a lot of things for us:

■ Two heads are better than one, usually.
■ If someone needs help, the buddy, hopefully, will be able to call for assistance.
■ Makes lifting easier.
■ It gives people a chance to communicate with someone.

Stress

Last but not least, I want to mention that dealing with a disaster or any type of emergency is stressful. This goes for the professional, but more so for the volunteer. Someone should be assigned to monitor the group of volunteers to ensure that they are

■ Not getting too involved
■ Taking care of their personal needs
■ Not becoming overwhelmed

Given the limited resources available at the federal, state, and local levels, the successful combination of citizen involvement in actual emergency management surroundings is essential to prepare for, respond to, recover from, and mitigate the effects of disasters in each of our communities. However, success will require reaching higher levels of cooperation and commitment to partnership among the volunteer sector, professional first-responder agencies (such as police, fire, and emergency management), as well as all levels of government. While this possibly will be a challenging goal, the priority and long-term value of this work cannot be overlooked.

Volunteer Application

Personal Information:

Name: _____

Address: _____

Phone numbers: _____

E-mail address: _____

Employment information (title, place of employment): _____

_____

Emergency contact information (name, phone numbers): _____

_____

Describe any restrictions on your activities (physical, medical, mental): _____

_____

Date of last tetanus shot: _____

General Availability:

	Sunday	Monday	Tuesday	Wednesday	Thursday	Friday	Saturday
AM							
PM							

Do you have personal transportation:_____
Are you willing/able to do manual labor: ☐ Yes ☐ No

Skills and Qualifications:

Fluency in language(s) other than English:_____
Licenses/professional certification: _____
_____

Professional background: _____
_____

Education background: _____
_____

Computer skills:_____
_____

Prior or current volunteer experience: _____
_____

Prior disaster relief experience: _____
_____

Other skills:

☐ Administrative/secretarial
☐ Accounting/finance/bookkeeping
☐ Civil servant
☐ Child care
☐ Customer service
☐ Food service
☐ Health services (doctor, nurse, EMT)
☐ Transportation (professional truck/bus driver)

☐ Human resources (interviewing, recruiting)
☐ Mental health counselor/ social worker
☐ Management
☐ Technical
☐ Trade:_____
☐ Other:_____

Volunteer Agreement:

1. The information provided is complete and true. If information given on this application is incomplete or untrue, I understand my assignment may be terminated.

2. I understand that my own insurance will be used as coverage for illnesses and injuries and that I am ultimately responsible for any costs incurred in my volunteer efforts.
3. I agree to respect the rights, property and confidentiality of emergency workers, agencies involved, and individuals affected by disaster.
4. I agree to adhere to the rules/instructions of my job assignment(s) so as not to jeopardize emergency operations or procedures.

Signature: _____

Date: _____

Chapter 25

First Responders and Workforce Protection

Paula J. Havice-Cover

CONTENTS

The author has been involved in disaster mental health on several levels. On the local community level, she has served as a first responder, planner, and consultant to the public health department as well as on a community-based team, Mental Health Responders to Critical Incidents (MHRCI). On the state level, she has been involved in disaster response planning for mental health/substance abuse services for the state of Colorado and a member of the Colorado Disaster Medical Assistance Team (DMAT) with a position on the team as mental health/psychological intervention and public information officer (PIO). On the national level, she is an active member of the National Medical Response Team (NMRT) that responds to weapons of mass destruction as a decontamination unit, and other "all hazards" responses. The Colorado DMAT and NMRT teams are both divisions of Federal Emergency Management Agency (FEMA) and the Department of Homeland Security. In addition, she was deployed to the state of Florida for hurricane recovery efforts from four storms that produced massive damage and three deployments to Hurricane Katrina.

First Responders and Workforce Protection

During deployment for the Hurricane Katrina response in Houston, Texas at the Astrodome and Reliant City (as it came to be known), the Federal Response Team was composed of 58 professional and paraprofessional disaster medical responders. Their job was to field triage evacuees for medical and psychological emergent issues before they were sent into the shelters or transported to an emergent facility. Prime consideration must be given in disaster response to the first responders. If they are not functional, the entire operation is in jeopardy.

Mental Health Care for First Responders

Every individual dealing with traumatic events, whether as caregiver, rescuer, or functioning in various other capacities, has the very real possibility of simply exceeding their storage capacity for exposure to traumatic events. This results in stress and the need to reprocess and repackage to allow for additional mental storage capacity. Traditional mental health has focused on diagnostics and therapy and a heavy emphasis on couch time. So it is natural for mental health councilors to deal with these issues when someone had gone off of the deep end and was deemed to be having a nervous breakdown. However, the function of mental health councilors in a disaster usually looks very different from a Sigmund Freud type of interaction like "Tell me about your mother, or how does that make you feel?" Contemporary mental health in the disaster context functions in a much different way.

One facet of the job concerning first responders is as mental health providers; another is as a workforce protection resource. Mental health providers on scene can be the conduit to understanding why the staff (or management) is not behaving. Once you understand why your staff is always late for work or why there is conflict between groups or burnout and short tempers, it opens the door to the next step, which is creative problem-solving.

To share a story that happened in the Hurricane Katrina response in Houston at the Astrodome and Reliant City, there were two shifts of first responder medical personnel doing triage on over 900 evacuees per day. Shifts were assigned, either a day shift that worked 10 a.m. to 10 p.m., or a night shift that worked 10 p.m. to 10 a.m. An "us and them" mentality began to develop between the shifts. Day shift staffs said, "we do all the work, see all of the patients, set up all the tents and restock all of the supplies in the heat and rarely get a break. Night shift doesn't do anything, except watch movies and take turns sleeping in between meals." The night shift staff said, "we are n't seeing as many evacuees, so there's not much to restock, sure, we've seen a few movies, and sometimes we get a chance to rest but we are staffing this mission and ready to respond when we are needed. Besides we get the middle of the night busloads of evacuees where they are really unpleasant. You guys (day shift) at least get to see patients and work on your tan. And sleep at night."

This became an issue of near hostile exchanges between the shifts. An analysis of human behavior said, "Houston we've got a problem." Was it a diagnosable, pathological get to therapy kind of issue? For a moment it may have seemed that way but the mental health cure required analyzing why there was conflict between the groups. And was it causing significant work-related problems. There very well may have been unequal workloads, unequal environmental factors, and a general feeling from both sides that it was not fair. But the perception on both sides that the other shift had it better was the crux of the problem. So how do we find a way to restore balance? We could have ordered the two shifts to stop talking about it and sent anyone home who complained but we needed to maintain a healthy first responder work force for the reasons that we were all assigned to the disaster response in the first place. We tried listening.

The workload was evaluated and a more equitable distribution was negotiated between the shifts. We could not really do anything about patient loads. The busses carrying evacuees arrived when they arrived and most came during the day. We considered offering to let people switch with someone on the other shift because both think that the other shift had it better, but this was a risky venture. What if people wanted to go to the other shift and no one wanted to trade with them? As predicted, most of them chose to stay with the shift they were already on. One staff member out of a staff of 65 switched from nights to days. The essential thing is that when people are given a choice, it is perceived as being the better option. People polarize toward their choice. As a result, the conflict resolved and the two shifts began feeling sorry for the other shift. They began to have compassion for the other shift, and the conflict was resolved.

Middle management first responders have one of the toughest assignments in a disaster response. They have to answer to upper management about why their staff is doing or not doing a specific task. They have to explain to their staff what needs to be done and who is going to do it. There is always potential for confusion. Are they bad managers because they have issues like the one just mentioned? Not necessarily, the fact is they are busy managing staffing and training needs for the event. Embedding mental health providers with the first responder teams may help to avoid such conflicts before they develop.

A review of Maslow's hierarchy of needs shows that physiological needs are the basic first order of business that needs to be taken care of. First responders need water, food, and rest. Mental health staff is sometimes tasked with making sure this is addressed. A schedule should be posted so that staff knows what hours they are expected to work that includes required breaks. Resist the urge to allow someone to work past his or her scheduled time, this includes management. Go home at the end of your shift.

Second on Maslow's list of needs is a need for safety. When your first responders feel unsafe, they are anxious about their safety and work performance declines. Or as it sadly turned out in New Orleans they abandon their posts when they do not feel safe. They need to feel as if their employers are concerned about their safety enough to issue adequate gear such as personal protective equipment. Inform them of the risks of being first responders. Management can also support the safety of their first responders by requiring their workforce to have a family safety plan. Several first responders deployed to New Orleans were worried about things at home, which can only be compounded by standing orders such as "no phone calls during your shift." Workers are still human. They may have young children at home and they may just get reassurance that their families were taking good care of themselves. The stress of family life does not have to add to and compound the natural stress from this line of work that is magnified by witnessing traumatic events.

In short, first responders can benefit from mental health providers as a resource that can help with people issues. Mental health providers based on their professional training can also help manage the situation by analyzing human behaviors and help to creatively solve issues with a win/win situation if at all possible.

Consideration for the Mental Health Care of Volunteers

Most of the people coming to Houston from New Orleans came in busses and private vehicles. They were medically and psychologically stable enough to proceed to the shelters, which speaks to the miraculous resiliency of the people. About two percent of the daily arrivals of evacuees were in need of urgent care (18–20 of the 900+). The remaining 98 percent were shuttled to shelters such as the Astrodome for temporary living quarters and a place to seek refuge from the unspeakable conditions that they may have escaped from.

The federal response team was allowed to see the facilities at the shelters to know the types of services that were offered to the evacuees that they would be seeing. There were thousands upon thousands of cots with blankets and toiletries, a medical clinic, a CVS drug store to fill prescriptions, a play area for preschoolers, organized activities for school aged children, a constant supply of hot and cold food and snacks, and TV in the balconies. And there was a constant drone of announcements from an overhead public address (PA) system reminiscent of a George Orwell novel. The city of Houston opened their doors to their fellow Gulf Coast neighbors in ways that the rest of the nation could use as a textbook example.

Volunteers were in abundance and were a valuable resource, but volunteers can become a liability. At the Reliant Center complex, they eventually had to turn away volunteers and at one point there were two volunteers for every evacuee. Early in the response in Houston, there were 16,000 volunteers on duty. Every three hours another busload of 50 volunteers arrived to help and some chose to do what to them seemed like a logical decision despite safety concerns. In their zeal to help, some interfered with medical triage by running out to meet the busses before the law enforcement agencies had declared the vehicle safe, or approached arriving helicopters in very dangerous proximity. By and large, there just was not enough for them to do. Accepting volunteers without adequate training can open the door to their own physical and mental illnesses. There is an underutilized alternative in using the survivors themselves.

Consideration for the Mental Health Care of Survivors

Although the idea of accommodating several thousand houseguests for an undetermined amount of time may be commendable, the analytical side would lead one to try to make sense of the psychological issues that could arise. Upon arrival, the evacuees were searched for weapons and other contraband, then field-screened for urgent medical or psychological concerns. Upon passing these tests they were given food, water, clothing, and toiletries while they registered with FEMA and the Red Cross. A band was placed on the arms of all evacuees who were registered that would allow them access to services and shelters. They were shuttled to shelters where they chose cots and settled in. That was the point that many of the evacuees began to sink into despair.

There was nothing to do in so far as planned activities or the idle time. Many wandered the streets and some just sat on their cots. The crime rate increased dramatically. The able-bodied evacuees could be utilized as volunteers. They can help in the work force to manage the newly created city. Everything we know about learned helplessness, victim vs. survivor mentality, resiliency and strength-based interventions, entitlement behavior and enabling should be considered and lead to the conclusion that the survivors and evacuees could be put to use to help. This would avoid the resulting feeling that they are helped to the point of giving up on the idea of doing things for themselves. Someone builds the cots they sleep on, cooks the meals and brings those in need food and drinks, picks up the trash, entertains the children. Why cannot some of them be volunteer evacuees? It may help them avoid thinking only about the hopelessness of their own situation.

Although the lifestyle of being waited on hand and foot and doing nothing for yourself may sound appealing to some, most of the people wish they could have something useful to do or a job to make some money during this time of forced displacement. Can we incorporate a self-run shelter into our disaster plans? Could evacuees who have food service experience prepare meals for their fellow evacuees? Are there any evacuees who can set up cots or pass out blankets or unload trucks? How about displaced medical personnel running the clinics at the shelters? What types of creative funding can provide for a day labor type of wage for those who wish to work? When life is spinning out of control for people in a disaster situation it makes sense to give them the dignity of being able to have some control over their destiny. Of course there are those who cannot or will not wish to participate in their own relief efforts, but for those who can and are willing to, we should make it happen.

Conclusion

This brief chapter does not propose to have all of the answers regarding this dilemma. But hopefully it opens the door to beginning to explore a scenario where people are able to help themselves. Can we give them tools to help them help themselves early on in the recovery process before the "new" wears off of the disaster? Our generosity and willingness to help makes this a great nation. At what point do we allow and encourage people to take the reins and aid in their own recovery? Are those who escaped with their lives going to be added to the victims or can they be more mentally healthy as survivors? A victim struggles to maintain a state of normalcy. A survivor knows normal no longer exists and carries on despite hardship and trauma.

Chapter 26

Disaster Rehabilitation: Towards a New Perspective

Alka Dhameja

CONTENTS

Introduction

Disaster rehabilitation is an integral part of disaster management. Disasters, as we all know, are catastrophic events that can seriously degrade a country's long-term potential for sustained development. They can also cause governments to considerably modify their socioeconomic priorities and programs. Disasters also create psychological stress leading to many dysfunctional consequences. In the process, they do highlight high-risk areas where necessary actions must be taken before another disaster strikes. Managing disasters thus is an uphill task. Disasters are very costly in terms of both human life and resources and require a long gestation period of rehabilitation. Disaster management should therefore involve systematic policy making and effective use of resources to make a potent dent in disaster relief, rehabilitation, and long-term recovery.

In common parlance, disaster rehabilitation involves methodical steps for necessitating changes in the disaster-affected site, with a view of ensuring long-term recovery. Disaster rehabilitation may be considered a transitional phase between immediate relief and recovery. It refers to actions taken in the aftermath of a disaster to enable basic services to resume functioning, assist victims' self-help efforts to repair physical damages, revive economic activities, and provide support for the psychological and social well-being of the survivors.

To understand the intricacies of disaster rehabilitation process, its place in the disaster management cycle needs to be comprehended. The cycle comprises five major stages:

1. Disaster preparedness and mitigation, which rests on the principle that prevention is better than cure. It involves all the steps necessary for creation of disaster-resilient structures and communities.
2. Disaster response, which includes immediate disaster search and rescue operations.
3. Disaster relief, which involves provision of food, clothing, and shelter for the affected.
4. Disaster rehabilitation and reconstruction that takes into view the efforts to restore all essential facilities to pre-disaster status.
5. Disaster recovery, which focuses on measures that will pave the way for long-term recovery of social, economic, and physical structures, as well as processes in such a way that future disasters are unable to impact severely and irreversibly.

All the five stages are well-integrated into the disaster management cycle. These stages could be examined separately, but it needs to be kept in mind that they essentially complement and supplement each other in an attempt to rectify the disaster-related problems. Disaster rehabilitation is thus preceded by disaster response and relief, and followed by disaster reconstruction and recovery. Disaster preparedness and mitigation, however, are continual processes that are part of each and every stage of disaster management cycle.

It is often not possible to suggest any time frame for disaster rehabilitation, reconstruction, and recovery, as these processes are completely intertwined. Reconstruction represents long-term development assistance that could help the affected people to rebuild their lives and meet their present and future needs. Rehabilitation and reconstruction should together lead to long-term recovery, but this may not happen unless certain measures are closely adhered to. A comprehensive rehabilitation and reconstruction plan, or what can be called long-term recovery plan should take into consideration both physical and nonphysical requirements of the affected areas, or else it may result in large and unwieldy investments in infrastructure. The plan then may not be able to provide for the necessary inputs to help the victims in becoming socially ready, economically self-sufficient and psychologically fit.

Rehabilitation and reconstruction programs need to base themselves on a few guiding principles. The broad priorities in a disaster rehabilitation plan could be:

1. Provision of emergency relief to be operationalized by the way of mobilizing human and material resources, ensuring food security, constructing temporary structures and making available all basic needs.
2. Relocation of all the displaced people, restoration of basic and alternative means of livelihood along with community-based infrastructure and institutions.
3. Initiation of long-term development interventions, which would lead to sustainable community-based strategies for disaster reduction (Medury and Dhameja, 2005).

Disaster rehabilitation planning needs to be broadly based on these three priorities. However, it can produce results only if it entails sub-plans pertaining to the different facets of rehabilitation.

Dimensions of Disaster Rehabilitation

There are three types of rehabilitation, namely physical, social, and psychological. Physical rehabilitation is a very important facet of rehabilitation. It includes reconstruction of physical infrastructure such as houses, buildings, railways, roads, communication network, water supply, electricity, and so on. It comprises short-term and long-term strategies towards watershed management, canal irrigation, social forestry, crop stabilization, alternative cropping techniques, job creation, employment generation and environmental protection. It involves rehabilitation for farmers, artisans, small businessmen, and those engaged in animal husbandry. The physical rehabilitation and reconstruction package must also incorporate adequate provision for subsidies, farm implements, acquisition of land for relocation sites, adherence of land use planning, flood plain zoning, retrofitting or strengthening of undamaged houses, and construction of model houses.

Social rehabilitation is also an important part of disaster rehabilitation. The vulnerable groups such as the elderly, orphans, single women, and young children would need special social support to survive the impact of disasters.

Thus, construction of infrastructure such as community centers, day-care centers, anganwadis or homes for women, balwadis or crèches and old age homes is a vital part of social rehabilitation. The rehabilitation plan must have components that do not lose sight of the fact that the victims have to undergo the entire process of re-socialization and adjustments in a completely unfamiliar social milieu.

Another crucial dimension of disaster rehabilitation is psychological rehabilitation. Dealing with victim's psychology is a very sensitive issue and must be dealt with caution and concern. The psychological trauma of losing relatives and friends, and the scars of the shock of disaster event can take much longer to heal than the stakeholders in disaster management often presume. The fear of changing the means of livelihood could lead to occupational disruption and subsequently high degree of occupational redundancy in the victims.

Thus, counseling for stress management should form a continuous part of a disaster rehabilitation plan. Efforts should be made to focus more on psycho-therapeutic health programs, debriefing, and trauma care. While implementing the disaster rehabilitation program, tradition, values, norms, beliefs, and practices of disaster-affected people need to be kept in mind. It is, therefore, essential that social welfare and psychological support measures be considered immediately after a disaster event so that they could be made a vital part of a rehabilitation program.

The economic, social, and psychological requirements of the affected population would vary from one disaster-affected site to the other. Even within the same site, the satisfaction of one need or requirement may not result in the satisfaction of the other needs. For example, rehabilitation in terms of provision of houses for the displaced may not take away the psychological trauma of having lost the dear ones. This makes it necessary to design and implement the rehabilitation program to cope with specific aspects of the victim's lives at all the stages of disaster rehabilitation.

It is essential that a systematic rehabilitation plan treats the affected communities as heterogeneous. Gender analysis should be introduced at the level of rehabilitation planning itself. A gender-sensitive approach helps to identify differing vulnerabilities, capacities, and coping strategies of men and women to crisis situations. It has to be seen that no affected group is left out of the rehabilitation operations to avoid social tensions and enable the inclusion of different categories of the affected population in specific sub-plans.

Community participation at all levels of disaster rehabilitation can go a long way in making rehabilitation effective. The participation of the community should go hand-in-hand with the assessment of unmet needs and response capacity. No disaster rehabilitation plan can achieve its objectives, unless the disaster-affected community participates in the formulation, implementation, and evaluation of its various components.

In the tsunami-aftermath in southern India in 2005, joint efforts of community–nongovernmental organizations (NGOs) such as Tsunami Farmers Self-help Groups in Tamil Nadu and Pondicherry Multipurpose Social Service Society have been quite pertinent. The experience of these initiatives must find a place in the disaster rehabilitation plan. The long-term counter disaster rehabilitation plan must give due weightage to on building the resilience of victims. A number of Community Based Disaster Management (CBDM) Projects and Disaster Task Force initiatives are coming up. These need to be encouraged and the lessons learnt through them must be assimilated in the larger rehabilitation plan.

The role and responsibilities of all the stakeholders (planners, governmental agencies, NGOs, international agencies, self-help groups, and community) need to be clearly demarcated in the rehabilitation plan. The measures pertaining to rehabilitation cannot be sustained if they are not institutionalized. Local authorities have to be in active conversation over priorities must focus on providing a frame-work for rehabilitation strategies. Efforts have to be made to establish and sustain the institutions that are involved in disaster rehabilitation such as microcredit societies, environmental forums, grain banks, fodder banks, seed banks, mahila mandals, pani panchayats, and so on. There is also a need to fix accountability on each organization involved in disaster rehabilitation. The duties of the army, paramilitary, home guards, civil defence, police, fire services, public sector, and media need to be streamlined to avoid haphazard coordination, multiliplicty of tasks, duplicity of organizations, red tapism, delay, and wastage.

The media can play an important role in strengthening disaster rehabilitation and building strong communities. As an important channel of communication, media transmit facts from disaster site to general public. Accurate, timely and consistent information dissemination by the media could be a useful contributor to disaster rehabilitation exercise. The media should try to highlight the stories of hope and courage in disaster aftermath, instead of merely focusing on human misery and distress. The information, communication and technology revolution has opened up new vistas for use of communication in disaster rehabilitation. Options such as HAM radios, wireless, and Incident Command System can be supplemented with new technologies of Internet, Intranet, Extranet, and Webblogs.

Damage assessment is a precondition for effective disaster rehabilitation. Unless we are clear about the nature, extent, and intensity of damage in the aftermath of a disaster, we can never plan out, implement, or evaluate the disaster rehabilitation plans and strategies. Perception, assessment, and mitigation of risks are some of the dimensions of damage assessment. It can be done through systematic sample surveys, Earth Observation Program, Geographical Information Systems, aerial photography, and remote sensing. Possible uses of aerial photography include hazard mapping, vulnerability analysis, and reconstruction planning. Feasibility study is also an important step towards damage assessment and rehabilitation of infrastructure.

The rehabilitation plan must be clear, transparent, structured, objective, access-ible, accountable, and responsive. It has to be adaptive in nature so that it can change as per the demands of a new situation. Flexibility norms in terms of structure, processes, and finances need to be ingrained in the plan. The key issues pertain to assessment of damage, fixation of responsibility, prioritization of requirements, execution of major mitigation strategies, and most importantly monitoring, evaluation, and general review of the development process.

One of the most crucial components of the rehabilitation plan is financial infrastructure that needs to be strengthened. In India, the government, both at the central as well as state levels, has specific schemes for providing funds for disaster management activities. Though much of the funds go towards immediate disaster relief work, a small amount is also earmarked for disaster rehabilitation. Calamity Relief Fund is one such arrangement at the central level. Other measures include National Calamity Contingency Fund and Prime Minister's National Relief Fund. Various insurance schemes such as Swarnajayanti Gram Swarozgar Yojna, National Agricultural Insurance, Seed Crop Insurance, Kisan Credit Card, etc., are also slowly becoming popular.

The rehabilitation plan should also have adequate provision for building disaster-resistant structures as a guiding principle. Nearly 55 per cent of India is earthquake-prone. The traditional housing techniques based on the use of timber and bamboo have been successful in India. The structural system for quake resistance needs to be tensile and material used should be flexible. These houses should have tie-bands just above the level of the floor, at the level of the doors and windows, and another at the roof. Flexible steel rods or wood panels can be used at the corners to enhance elasticity. Doors and windows should be few, small, and systematically placed away from corners. As far as flood-resistant housing is concerned, structures need to be erected on a higher elevation on best bearing soil and raised mounds, using concrete cement and waterproofing. Cyclone-resistant structures have to be sturdy, wind resistant, and concrete in texture.

Building authorities and research institutes in India such as National Building Construction Corporation (NBCC), Building Materials and Technology Promotion Council (BMTPC), Housing and Urban Development Corporation (HUDCO) have laid down certain guidelines for housing in disaster-prone areas. The rehabilitation plan must pay attention to these aspects. It must see that properties of symmetry, ductility, deformability, rectangularity and simplicity are strictly followed in building disaster-resistant houses. An effective control mechanism for adherence to the disaster-resistant design rules has to be established.

The oughts and shoulds in disaster rehabilitation planning are innumerable. They often make for a good reading. In reality, however, India does not even have anything that can be remotely referred to as a disaster rehabilitation plan at the central, state, and local levels. Therefore, solutions have to be searched within the framework of an altogether new paradigm. The conventional approach of treating disasters as isolated one-time events has not borne fruit. We may go about harping on the composition of rehabilitation plans, but unless we change our approach and start viewing the problem of disaster rehabilitation differently, we may slip further away from tackling the issue.

The solution to the problems of rehabilitation and reconstruction lies in the establishment of interlinkages between disasters and development. The relationship between disasters and development is not that of straight cause and effect. There are many complex interconnections governing the interface. Rehabilitation plan should encompass issues related to the negative impact of disasters on socioeconomic system and also the ways and means through which these challenges could be converted into developmental opportunities. We certainly need a new paradigm for looking at the whole issue of disaster rehabilitation.

Towards a New Perspective

Ensuring effective disaster rehabilitation is not an easy task. Many convoluted issues need to be addressed. A simplistic solution would be to prepare a picture perfect disaster rehabilitation plan and implement it through controlled monitoring and evaluation. This may lead to goal-achievement on a short-term basis. A larger or macro-view would, however, focus on long-term analysis of a disaster situation by positioning it in a disaster–development matrix.

Although disasters are calamitous events, lessons learnt and incorporated into long-term development planning may serve to reduce future vulnerability. The destruction of unsafe infrastructure and buildings can provide an opportunity for rebuilding with better standards or relocation to a better place if the present site is found specifically vulnerable. Particularly damaging disasters will also focus on relief aid and rehabilitation investment, thereby providing developmental opportunities that have been previously unavailable. Damaged buildings may highlight structural weaknesses, which could be rectified and may serve to improve building and planning regulations.

Thus, disasters and development affect one another in a significant manner. In the present context, disasters can no longer be viewed as random occurrences caused by the nature's wrath. The distinction between natural and man-made disasters is getting blurred with time. The frequency and intensity of disasters has recorded an all-time high, as the harmonious balance between human beings and nature is being disturbed to almost irreparable proportions.

Faulty urbanization, population explosion, civil strife, and unbalanced industrial growth have led to severe environmental degradation. Global warming, deforestation, desertification, soil erosion, and salinization reflect the denuded face of earth's environment. The degradation of environment and its mismanagement may aggravate the frequency, severity, and predictability of disasters. The relationship between disaster management and environmental protection thus needs to be examined against the backdrop of the disaster–development matrix.

It has been observed that the frequency and intensity of disasters can be attributed to flawed environmental policies. The global environmental situation appears to be grim. The beaches of a third of the 200 islands of the Maldives are being swept away. A quarter of all species of plants and land animals could be driven to extinction. Sea ice in the Arctic Ocean has decreased by 10 per cent.

Coastal areas in the United States, China, Bangladesh, and India are also threatened (Saxena, 2006).

Globally, the Earth's climate is warmer today than it has been at any time in the past 140 years. An acutely alarming analysis of data collected from the Greenland glacier suggests that earth is moving towards a speedy end. Greenland's glaciers are melting twice as fast as previously, pointing towards a scary reality. The Earth's oceans are rising at such a high speed that by 2050 cyclones, tsunamis, and submerging islands would become the headline news everywhere (ibid.).

The relationship between environmental degradation and disasters needs to be clearly surveyed. There are many International Environmental Treaties such as Kyoto Protocol, United Nations Framework Convention on Climate Change, Basel Convention on Transboundary Movement of Hazardous Wastes, Convention on Biological Diversity, Convention on Climate Change, Convention to Combat Desertification, Convention on International Trade in Endangered Species (CITES), Convention on the Law of the Sea (LOS), and Montreal Protocol on Substances that Deplete the Ozone Layer. These treaties and conventions have set guidelines for environmental protection. The rehabilitation plan should keep the underlying features of these treaties into view and integrate environmental protection measures wherever required. A sustainable environment-friendly rehabilitation plan is thus the need of the hour.

Sustainable Livelihood Framework: The Key to Disaster Rehabilitation

To promote environmental protection and create long-term vulnerability reduction conditions, a "sustainable livelihood framework" is required urgently. The livelihood approach advocates an increase in economic opportunities of work without degrading the natural environment. It seeks to understand the many factors that influence people's choices of conventional and alternative livelihood strategies. Creation of livelihood options is a crucial step towards disaster rehabilitation.

Sustainable development involves more than growth. It requires a change in the content of growth to make it more equitable in its impact. The main objective of sustainable development is to prevent acts of nature from becoming disasters. The main focus of sustainable development is to mitigate the conflict between development and environment to safeguard the resources for the present and future generations. While at first glance, this may seem unrelated to disaster prevention, the truth is that they are intricately entwined (Dhameja, 2001).

Sustainable living patterns have always been an integral part of rural India. There has been a long tradition of living in harmony with nature. Traditional practices of water conservation such as "Kuhls" of Himachal Pradesh, "Kundis" and "Rapats" of Rajasthan and "Palliyals" of Kerala have held people in good stead against low-intensity droughts. "Sumers" and "Chaukhats" of Rajasthan are inimitable earthquake-resistant structures from India's heritage and past. People have followed traditional practices of coping with disasters, but are now increasingly becoming dependent on external agencies to withstand the disaster aftermath. These traditional practices are being abandoned to make way for new technologies. At a time when we need a thoughtful blend of the old and the new, we are slowly loosing our traditional wisdom to a haphazard approach to modern development.

The success stories in India are few yet noteworthy. The endeavors such as greening of Arvari River in Alwar (Rajasthan), rejuvenation of Sukhha Lake in Chandigarh, and Build Your Own Check Dam in Saurashtra have been initiated by community groups and NGOs. These need to be woven coherently to build a strong knowledge base for disaster rehabilitation. Of late, the Narmada Bachao Andolan in India has been drawing attention to the travails of project-affected people (PAPs). It has been trying to highlight the reckless development and rehabilitation policies by focusing on issues such as noncompliance with rules, violation of human rights, and hardship of the poor.

It has been observed is that unlike the environmentalists, those who equate development with huge shopping malls, big dams, vehicular explosion, and global merchandise are never called "ideologues." They are never faulted for the negative consequences of development process that ignores the norms of equity, environmental protection, and social justice (Iyer, 2006). However, we will not go into the debate of mega projects over here. In fact, the issue to ponder over here is that if in normal times, development projects can cause so much displacement and inadequate rehabilitation of the affected people, can we expect a comprehensive rehabilitation policy for natural disasters? What happens to those, who are already vulnerable, in disaster aftermath?

A systematic rehabilitation plan should make way for a right mix of traditional practices, sustainable ways of living, and modern technological development. A sustainable livelihood program needs to analyze the existing socioeconomic conditions prevailing in the area before the occurrence of a disaster, examine the occupational pattern in the affected area, survey the prevailing infrastructure facilities, adjudge the awareness levels of the people, and gauge the mind-set of the affected. It needs to recognize the premise that the community's relationship with the environment is a basic unit for rehabilitation planning and implementation activities.

Self-reliance should be promoted and administrative interventions should follow a rights-based approach. It is essential to ensure that the people are not treated as mere beneficiaries, but they also participate in the development process. This kind of approach could be beneficial in creating sustainable livelihood conditions and the disaster rehabilitation plan should keep this in view.

There is also a need to strengthen the legal, organizational, and procedural facets of disaster management. The sustainable disaster network (SDN) could be a way out. It is a global network of organizations whose mission is to encourage policies that allow individuals to pursue their goals in consonance with the environment. The SDN focuses on the institutional framework within which the people pursue their goals and make an optimum use of resources in a bid to protect the environment.

The United Nations (UN) is committed to promote sustainable development and mitigate disaster losses. The World Bank and the regional development banks have also begun to engage with issues surrounding the relationship between disaster risk reduction and economic development. The World Bank's Board of Executive Directors has endorsed a viable Environment Strategy on July 17, 2001.

The strategy has four interrelated objectives:

■ Improving people's quality-of-life, enhancing the prospects for quality of social and economic growth.
■ Protecting the quality of the regional and global environmental commons, rational and planned growth of agricultural, industrial, and tertiary sectors of the economy.
■ Creating employment opportunities, programs for the youth, women, and physically handicapped.
■ Promoting alternative cropping patterns, irrigation, and water harvesting techniques, social and farm forestry, as well as skilled labor.

The connection between population growth, poverty, and development is strong and complex. When assessed in terms of growth of the gross domestic product (GDP), India is still far behind. Food insecurity, lack of means of livelihood, and insufficient capacity to access resources characterize the lives of the poor even in nondisaster situations. Conditions of poverty often contribute to greater vulnerability of some sections of a population to an environmental disaster.

An effective rehabilitation plan has to be sustainable and must therefore give credence to creation of sustainable livelihood opportunities and alternative technologies. The United Nations Development Programme (UNDP) has a vision on human development, which treats development not merely in terms of mere rise or fall of national incomes, but envisages a space where people can develop to their full potential and lead productive and creative lives, in accordance with their needs and interests. This idea of human development has to be translated into action to uphold the values of equity and justice in the disaster rehabilitation exercise.

The new perspective that is gaining relevance pertains to convergence of relief, rehabilitation, and development. The basic premise for linking of relief and rehabilitation with development (LRRD) holds the key to future strategies towards disaster rehabilitation. The development policy often ignores the risks of disasters and the need to protect vulnerable households by helping them to develop appropriate coping strategies. If relief and development were to be linked, these deficiencies could be reduced. It has been pointed out that better development can moderate the need for emergency relief; better relief can contribute to development; and better rehabilitation can ease the intermediary process between relief and development.

The linkage between development, relief, and rehabilitation operations consti-tutes a complex network of relationships, which have to be examined within the specific policy framework or strategic planning. The components of the LRRD and their design should be considered in the light of the contextual realities of the country or region concerned. A comprehensive long-term recovery plan should keep into view the interlinkages between all the stages of disaster management, as well as the connection between disaster rehabilitation, reconstruction, and the larger devel-opmental planning.

Adequate backward and forward linkages between disasters and development can, therefore, reduce the vulnerability to disasters. If we analyze the vulnerability of coastal communities to natural hazards within the parameters of the World Bank's 1991 Environment Strategy and the disaster–development matrix, we can say that by promoting certain development measures, the disaster impact can be made less severe in the coastal areas. These include

- Establishing a regional early warning system
- Applying construction setbacks, greenbelts, and other no-build areas in each region
- Promoting early resettlement with provision for safe housing, debris clearance, potable water, sanitation and drainage services
- Providing for access to sustainable livelihood options
- Enhancing the ability of the natural system to act as a bioshield to protect people
- Restoring wetlands, mangroves, spawning areas, sea grass beds and coral reefs
- Seeking alternative construction design that is cost-effective, appropriate, and consistent

The Road Ahead

A futuristic perspective would have to look into the contours of disaster–development interface and come up with a systematic disaster rehabilitation strategy. Certain developments in the recent past could be regarded as the much needed steps in the right direction. A rehabilitation–reconstruction–tracking matrix is being produced. Its objective is to provide salient information on the overall recovery effort. The matrix aims at bringing together information from tsunami-affected countries with regard to the nature of work in the area, functions of stakeholders, monitoring and evaluation of impact, and availability of resources. The matrix is being designed to give information at three levels of resolution-regional overview, sector level status by a region or a country, and project level status by a country. It is expected to provide a comprehensive view of rehabilitation and long-time recovery.

The advancement in science and technology could be used with advantage for speedy long-term recovery. The international developments in terms of various environmental treaties, international consortiums, sustainable data forums, and declarations focus on the use of technology, information exchange, coordination mechanism, and environmental protection. These are ProVention Consortium, Fribourg Forum, Hemispheric Conference, and South Asian Livelihood Options Project. The International Decade for Natural Disaster Reduction (IDNDR 1990–2000) has helped raise the profile of discussions surrounding the social and economic causes of disaster, and has acknowledged the mitigation of losses through technological and engineering solutions.

Yokohama strategy in May 1994 has endorsed these objectives, and further underlined the need to strengthen the link between disaster reduction and sustainable development. The focus has been on prevention, preparedness, and mitigation, with an aim to increase public awareness, necessitate people's participation, strengthen infrastructure, create disaster-resilient communities, and ensure accountability of the stakeholders in disaster management.

The International Strategy for Disaster Risk Reduction (2000) has been carrying the good work ahead. The Strategy aims at increasing public awareness on the risks of natural, technological, and environmental hazards; obtaining commitment by public authorities to reduce risks to people, their livelihoods, social and economic infrastructure and environmental resources; engaging public participation at all levels of implementation through increased partnership and expanded risk reduction networks at all levels; and reducing the economic and social losses of disasters.

The World Conference on Disaster Reduction (2005) held in Kobe, Hyogo, Japan has adopted a framework for action (2005–2015) on "building the resilience of nations and communities to disasters." It is a positive step, as the Conference has provided a unique opportunity to promote a strategic and systematic approach to reducing risks and vulnerabilities to hazards.

The World Health Organization (WHO) Meet in Bangkok, in December 2005, has identified the gaps in addressing response, preparedness, and recovery for health needs of the affected. One of the major objectives of the Meet has been to develop benchmarks and corresponding course of action (*The Hindu*, December 28, 2005). The focus of attention has shifted to health-related facets of disaster management. New and old techniques of health surveys such as Nutrition Centred Health Assessment and Epidemiological Surveillance are being amalgamated for effective health surveillance.

Disaster management is acquiring a global connotation. Besides the United Nations and the World Bank, many international organizations such as Caritas India, Lutheran World Service, Asian Development Bank, Intermediate Technology Development Group (ITDG), Danish International Development Agency, Swedish International Development Agency, Cooperative for Assistance and Relief Everywhere (CARE), Sustainable Environment and Ecological Development (SEEDS), International Federation of Red Cross and Red Crescent Societies, Oxfam, etc., are doing substantial work in the area of disaster relief, rehabilitation, and recovery.

In India, National Institute of Oceanography in Goa has developed a Real-Time Reporting and Internet Accessible Coastal Sea-level Monitoring System. The Sea-level Network in Indian Ocean has been upgraded. Deep-Ocean Assessment and Reporting of Tsunamis (DART II) is under development. A Siesmographic Network and Tsunami Warning Centres Network has been proposed (Prabhudesai and Joseph, 2006). The Bureau of Indian Standards (BIS) has also initiated several pre-disaster mitigation projects to reduce the impact of natural disasters on life and property as well as bring down social vulnerabilities.

The Bureau has undertaken standardization efforts in the area of earthquake engineering. New earthquake-resistance techniques have been developed. One of them is the Base Isolation Technology. It aims at reducing the forces transmitted to the building from the ground by placing the building atop a mechanical system of isolators, sliders, and dampers. Such technologies along with Diagonal Bracing, Disaster Resistant Pier System, Welded Wire Fabric Reinforcement could help in disaster-resistant construction and favorable resource utilization for disaster rehabilitation.

The National Advisory Council, which works as a think tank for the central government in India, has proposed a National Rehabilitation Commission to ensure rehabilitation for all those affected by mega projects, including dams, mines, highways, and natural disasters. The Disaster Management Act (2005) has been passed in India. The act aims at speedy handling of natural and man-made disasters. It has led to the setting up of a National Disaster Management Authority at the central level. There is also a provision for a State Disaster Management Authority at the state level. The authority has the responsibility to lay down policies and guidelines for disaster management to enable timely and effective response to disasters. The National Centre for Disaster Management has been reconstituted as the National Institute of Disaster Management. How far and how much of disaster management goals would these new developments be able to achieve is a question only time can answer.

Disaster management has been incorporated in the training curricula of All India Services with effect from 2005. There is a separate faculty in the area of disaster management in 29 State Level Administrative Training Institutes. The Central Board for Secondary Education (CBSE) in New Delhi has introduced disaster management as a subject in standards VIII and IX at school level. The National Council for Educational Research and Training (NCERT) books in India include lessons on disaster management for school children.

The All India Council for Technical Education has been advised to incorporate engineering aspects of disaster management in engineering courses. This education and training impetus needs to be sustained through informed people's participation. A simple philosophy for coping with disasters is infact, one of government and people working together in a coordinated way, by means of a coherent disaster management system.

A completely fresh perspective of linking disasters with development can draw from these developments in the area of science and information technology, legal and administrative framework, as well as education and research. Development has to be environment-friendly and sustainable. It should give due regard to the goals of equality, human rights, and social justice. Disaster planning has to, therefore, be a crucial component of overall development planning of a country.

The road ahead is full of complexities, as well as promise. In consonance with the new perspective, disasters can be viewed as developmental opportunities. Howsoever paradoxical it may sound, but it is true that whereas faulty development policies may lead to disasters, many disaster events also open up new possibilities of development. An often quoted phrase needs to be reiterated over here; "development should be such that guards against disasters, development in itself should not lead to disasters." We may conclude by saying that we still have miles to go. It is indeed a long and arduous tread ahead.

References

Dhameja, A., 2001, Droughts and foods: A case for 'dying wisdom,' in Sahni, P. et al. (Eds.), *Disaster Mitigation: Experiences and Reflections*, Prentice-Hall, New Delhi.

Iyer, R.R., 2006, Narmada project: The points at issue, *The Hindu*, April 13.

Medury, U. and Dhameja, A., 2005, Rehabilitation of cyclone affected people, in Singh, A. (Ed.), *Administrative Reforms, Towards Sustainable Practices*, Sage, New Delhi.

Prabhudesai, R.G. and Joseph, A., 2006, Cellular-based sea level gauge, *Frontline*, January 13.

Saxena, S., 2006, Global Warming, *Sunday Pioneer*, April 9.

The Hindu, December 28, 2005.

Bibliography

Aysan, Y. and Davius, I., 1993, Rehabilitation and reconstruction, module prepared for Department of Humanitarian Affairs (DHA), UNDP as Disaster Management Training Programme (DMTP), 1st Edition.

Carter, W.N., 1991, *Disaster Management: A Disaster Manager's Handbook*, Asian Development Bank, Manila.

Dhameja, A., 2003, Disaster risk reduction through disaster-resistant construction techniques, in Sahni, P. and Aryabandhu, M.M. (Eds.), *Disaster Risk Reduction in South Asia*, Prentice-Hall, New Delhi.

Dhameja, A., 2006, Rehabilitation and Reconstruction, IGNOU Masters Programme Material, MPA-O18, Unit 15.

Gupta, H.K., 2003, *Disaster Management*, University Press, Hyderabad.

HUDCO Initiatives, 1998, *Disasters and Development*.

Indira Gandhi National Open University (IGNOU), 2003, Certificate Programme in Disaster Management (CDM-2), Disaster Management: Methods and Techniques.

IGNOU Postgraduate Programme in Disaster Management (PGDDM), 2006, Course MPA-007 on Rehabilitation, Reconstruction, Reconstruction and Recovery.

Jayanth, V., 2005, The anatomy of a disaster, *The Hindu*, December 26.

Krishnakumar, R., 2006, A question of accountability, *Frontline*, January 13.

Nair, R., 2005, Building for the future, *The Hindu*, December 26.

Parsai, G., 2005, When nature strikes back, *The Hindu*, December 25.

Santhanam, R., 2006, We are now in the reconstruction phase, Interview with the State Relief Commissioner, Tamil Nadu, *Frontline*, January 13.

Sridhar, V., 2006, Partners in rebuilding, *Frontline*, January 13.

Stephenson, R.S. and DuFrane, C., 2002, Disasters and development: Understanding and exploiting disaster–development linkages, *Fred C. Cunny Memorial Continuing Education Series*, 17 (3), July–September.

Stephenson, R.S., 2002, Disasters and Development Module for Disaster Management Training Programme (DMTP).

The Hindu, December 13, 2005.

United Nations Development Programme, 1991, *Disaster Management Manual*, December 13.

Website

www.adb.org/Document/Events2005/RehabilitationandReconstruction.

Chapter 27

The Half-Full Glass: How a Community Can Successfully Come Back Better and Stronger Post-Disaster?

David W. Sears and J. Norman Reid

CONTENTS

Introduction

No community would ever volunteer to be struck by the next hurricane, the next big earthquake, the next toxic chemical release, the next deadly tornado, the next terrorist attack, the next tsunami, or the next volcanic eruption. Nonetheless, to paraphrase the bumper sticker: "Disasters Happen." And somewhere in the United States, very soon, some community will be struck.

And although, of course, this disaster will be a tragedy, possibly with much loss of life and property, it will also be an opportunity. This chapter focuses upon that opportunity. We spell out the process that the post-disaster community can use to take maximum advantage of the possibilities for coming back stronger than ever. We take a look at the most recent major case study: community redevelopment in Louisiana post-Katrina/Rita. Finally, we compare our general principles and guidance with the Katrina/Rita experience.

Before we go any further, we need to clarify a couple of terms. Throughout this chapter we will be talking about "redevelopment." In contrast, much of the material dealing with how to move forward in a post-disaster community focuses on "recovery." As we understand it, the goal of recovery is to recover what was lost. Or, in other words, successful recovery will bring the community back to exactly where it was before the disaster.

The goal of redevelopment, however, is to create a different community—one that is better and stronger, and one that is more effective in providing a good quality of life for those who live there. This is why we emphasize that the post-disaster redevelopment process is an opportunity for the community.

This chapter is divided into six major sections. First, we explain what we mean by community redevelopment. Next, we describe a set of ten core community redevelopment principles. Third, we talk about how these core principles apply in the special case of a post-disaster community. Fourth, we turn to our major case study to discuss the community redevelopment process in post-Katrina/Rita Louisiana. Fifth, we rate the post-Katrina/Rita community redevelopment process in terms of our core community redevelopment principles. Finally, drawing upon the earlier sections, we present some guidance for the participants in the community redevelopment process that will follow the next major disaster.

Community Redevelopment

Successful community redevelopment is built on a set of core principles. We see no difference between the terms "community development" and "community redevelopment," though we will primarily use the latter term.

A long-established field of community development exists. The aim of this field is to provide guidance to communities wishing to improve their situations. Often the community in question is one that is "distressed"—in terms of a high poverty rate, a high outmigration rate, a disintegration of physical infrastructure (both in the public sector (e.g., roads) and in the private sector (e.g., housing quality)), an assortment of social problems (e.g., poor health status, high rates of drug addiction, high crime rates), declining economic opportunities (e.g., low rates of new business formation, high unemployment rates), or a deterioration of key institutions (e.g., low performance schools, low quality or over-priced retail establishments).

However, even communities that most of us would call "well functioning" can, of course, be improved. Thus, the principles and practice of community development can be usefully applied to any community, regardless of its level of distress.

Community redevelopment is the process that a community goes through to improve its situation when it has been hit by a significant challenge. That challenge might be a single disaster event (e.g., hurricane, earthquake, terrorist attack). In other communities, that challenge might be a nondisaster single event (e.g., the state or federal government will flood the community by construction of a new dam or a major employer will shut down its local facility). In many other communities, however, the challenge requiring redevelopment might be the cumulative effect of many years of economic, social, or physical difficulties.

The main point here is that communities struck by disaster differ from many other communities in need of redevelopment primarily in the urgency and breadth of their situation, not in terms of its basic character. Therefore, a community engaged in post-disaster redevelopment has much to learn from the core principles of community redevelopment.

For purposes of our discussion here, a "community" is a compact geographic space occupied by people and institutions with some common attributes. Typical examples of communities include an urban neighborhood, a small suburban town, or a rural village or town. Often the community will have imprecisely defined boundaries (e.g., is the new shopping center on the edge of town in our community or not?) rather than precisely defined ones (e.g., the northern boundary of the community is 45th Street).

Core Community Redevelopment Principles

Community redevelopment, like most human endeavors, is as much art as science. Nonetheless, experience shows that following the principles enumerated here will increase the community's odds for success (see Table 27.1). None of these principles is mandatory, but they are all strongly encouraged. And a community that ignores the bulk of these principles does so at its peril.

Principle 1: Community Assessment

Before the community tries to figure out where it wants to go and how to get there, it would be wise to know where it is now. That's what we call community

Table 27.1 Core Community Redevelopment Principles

Principle Number	Core Community Redevelopment Principle
1	Community assessment
2	Strategic planning
3	Plan implementation
4	Evaluation and feedback
5	Citizen participation
6	Leadership development
7	Accountability
8	Partnerships
9	Learning community
10	Positive attitude

assessment. At the simplest level, a community assessment could be carried out by having a few community leaders sit around someone's dining room table or conference table for a few hours to simply spell out on a big piece of paper the group's composite description of the community. Such an approach is better than nothing, but it's not the recommended scenario.

Generally, a more systematic and comprehensive approach to community assessment will produce more useful results. A common approach to assessment is to document the community's strengths, weaknesses, opportunities, and threats (the SWOT approach). Getting input from a broader array of community members, not just leaders, is strongly recommended (for more on this, see Principle 5).

A stronger assessment will involve gathering some available data (e.g., current community population (actual or estimate) from a state university data center, or last year's high school dropout rate from the local school board). Getting original data is time-consuming and may be expensive, but it may be worthwhile to do so for one or two critical items (if health care access is a major issue, for instance, the community may want to collect data on where residents received health care services over the past two years).

Sometimes an outside group (e.g., a panel of experts, a consulting firm) may be called in to help carry out a community assessment. But the community itself needs to play a very central role in the assessment; this will assure that the assessment touches upon all the key resources and issues seen by the community, and in addition this will lead to stronger community buy-in on the assessment results. In short, the community assessment will enable the community to know, quite objectively, pertinent recent trends and the current status of the community in terms of a number of important economic, social, and environmental arenas.

Principle 2: Strategic Planning

Community assessment provides the jumping-off point for strategic planning. The purpose of strategic planning is for community members to discuss, and then agree upon, where the community should be in ten years or twenty years (some would even encourage dreaming) and to put down on paper a plan for getting there. Some of the common terms used when describing strategic planning include visioning, goals, objectives, tasks, and actions. Not everyone uses these terms identically.

The main point is that community members participating in a planning process will first describe a better future community; this initial step is often called "visioning." A community's vision can often be stated in a single sentence that expresses its view of itself and its aspirations for the future. For instance: "Cedarville is a town we are proud to call home, with a vibrant economy and a safe and healthy environment for all."

Once that visioning is completed, the community will need to figure out how to get there from here. "Here" is described in the already completed community assessment. The road map to getting "there" can be spelled out in some combination of goals, objectives, tasks, and actions. The strategic plan should spell out exactly (1) what work is to be done, (2) who (the persons or organizations) is to do that work, (3) when it is to be done (usually in terms of a completion date), and (4) what resources (dollars, volunteer hours, others) are to be used to do the work.

Typically the strategic plan will be on the outer edges of what reasonable people would call realistic. Thus, the community's strategic plan should lay out a set of actions that are plausible, but would require some very hard work to achieve the stated goals and objectives.

For instance, consider a community that is developing a strategic plan with a major emphasis on substantially improving K-12 school quality. That strategy may include rehabilitation of deteriorating school buildings, upgraded training for all teachers, mentoring for first year teachers, recruitment bonuses for high-performing principals willing to move to underperforming schools, and increased teacher salaries. Using just teachers' salaries as an example, the community might find that raising those salaries by 5 percent over the next five years may be slightly helpful in improving school quality, but would not (for most communities) be much of a stretch. On the other hand, doubling K-12 teacher salaries over the next five years might be enormously important for upgrading school quality but would (for most communities) be outside the realm of possibility. So, the community might want to choose an intermediate approach, one that is ambitious but not impossible, such as perhaps increasing teacher salaries by 40 percent over the next five years.

In strategic planning, the temptation may be to chop the plan into several discrete pieces, and let the most interested parties handle each piece independently. (For instance, let the hospital administrator and a couple of high-profile doctors take charge of the health sector.) Although, on the surface, this division of labor looks rational, it will often not produce the best plan. It is useful to get an outside perspective on any sector, so, for example, having a high school teacher or a real estate specialist on the health care team may lead to some new and exciting ideas that the experts might not see.

Once independent committees have worked on key sectors, the community should not miss the opportunity to look for synergies across two or more sectors. For example, the work plans for the workforce training strategy and the business development strategy will both be stronger if the two are linked together—assuring that workers will be trained to perform real jobs that are emerging in new or expanding businesses.

Principle 3: Plan Implementation

Plan implementation is the process of taking the community's plan and making it a reality. Those who will implement the strategic plan must fully adhere to the plan's direction, but do not need to be bound meticulously to every detail. No matter how careful and thorough the planning process, not every contingency can be anticipated.

New information, new challenges, and new opportunities will arise during plan implementation; therefore, it is reasonable to expect that the best plan implementation will diverge in some respects from the written plan. But, in general, the strategic plan should be taken very seriously and should guide what actually happens on the ground to achieve the community's vision. When necessary, the plan should be amended to reflect changed conditions or objectives.

Action is imperative. An excellent community strategic plan that just sits on the shelf is of no value. In fact, an excellent strategic plan that is not implemented is of negative value, because that inaction will convert the community enthusiasm generated during the strategic planning process into cynicism.

Successful plan implementation will depend heavily upon strong citizen participation (see Principle 5), strong accountability (see Principle 7), and effective partnerships (see Principle 8).

Principle 4: Evaluation and Feedback

A community will want to learn from its mistakes—and from its successes. To engage in such learning requires, first, gathering data on what the community did and what was accomplished. In addition, this data must be analyzed to determine what made the difference in producing the observed results. In short, the community needs to obtain feedback on what happened.

For instance, if a community implemented a plan that emphasized improving K-12 school quality, then the community should gather information on the real world impact of its efforts. Gathering such data in a way that is truly meaningful in determining the impact of plan implementation is often very challenging. For instance, actions such as the rehabilitation of school buildings and upgraded teacher-training may take awhile to make a difference; therefore, it might be necessary to wait several years to measure any differences in school quality. Continuing with this example, the community also faces the dilemma of what measures of school quality to use: High school graduation rate? Average test scores on the statewide 8th grade reading exam? Literacy rate for 18 year olds?

The point of feedback, of course, is not just to answer interesting questions. To be of value, the community must use the feedback to inform its further work in building a better community. Many of us are familiar with the term "feedback loop"; in this context it means that the obtained feedback must be used as critical information in a loop to rethink the earlier community assessment and strategic plan. If the community determines that, five years after increasing the salaries of middle school teachers by 40 percent, the local school moved from the 20th percentile on the statewide 8th grade reading exam to the 40th percentile, this finding alters the community assessment of school quality, and it provides useful input for modifying the strategic plan.

This feedback could raise a number of critical questions during a revisit of the strategic plan. For instance, achieving such a substantial improvement in education means that, when it focuses its resources on a critical issue, this community can do wonders, so what else can it do? Achieving the 40th percentile is a strong improvement, but the school is still below average, so is this accomplishment "good enough"? What else could the community do to improve school quality even further?

Often the community will find that it wants some outside expertise to design and manage its feedback process. Typical sources of such expertise are colleges, regional planning commissions, university extension agents, and consultants. Outside experts will be able to bring some useful experience and techniques to the community. But, a few key persons from the community must play a critical part in designing the feedback process. And, once the feedback process is up and running, the community must be involved. Otherwise, the feedback results are likely to be ignored by community members.

Principle 5: Citizen Participation

Every community has a small group of people who are the "leaders." They seem to be involved in every action or event that makes a difference. If there's a new firm that's coming to town, these leaders are involved. If the recreation center is being renovated, these leaders are involved. If the local community college is adding a new curriculum in health technology, these leaders are involved. And so on.

However, the community is more than these leaders. And, these leaders do not have a monopoly on the knowledge and insights needed to build a better community. And they are certainly not the only ones affected by the redevelopment process.

Therefore, our Principle 5 requires that a broad range of citizens participate in the process of building a stronger community.

Ideally, these participants should represent all key segments of the community. Included in the community development process should be persons from all racial and ethnic groups, from all income brackets, from all age ranges (teenagers, young adults, the middle-aged, and senior citizens), newcomers and old timers. This broad citizen participation must go well beyond just "token" representation of various groups. In fact, specific projects can be targeted to particular groups as a way of engaging their participation. But caution is needed here, to avoid extreme compartmentalization (e.g., when the teachers deal only with the schools and the downtown merchants deal only with Main Street issues).

The appearance of 150 citizens broadly representative of the community at a single community listening session, although important, is not enough. Citizen participation means that a number of citizens, well beyond the usual leadership core, are also actively participating in some of the key community development processes, including community assessment and strategic planning.

The community will benefit from such broad participation in two ways. First, active involvement of many community members will broaden the scope of community buy-in on the process and the product. Thus, for example, a community strategic plan built by the active involvement of 50 persons will have much broader support across the community than another community's plan that was constructed by only five or six community leaders. In larger communities, task forces or committees focusing on separate issues, areas, or neighborhoods may be a useful way to organize citizen participation.

Second, the leaders, as bright, knowledgeable, and dedicated as they might be, don't know everything. The broader set of active citizens will bring to the table new and different sets of knowledge and perspectives. Thanks to the richness of this broad citizen input, the community's work will be that much stronger.

Principle 6: Leadership Development

Closely related to citizen participation is leadership development. Starting with the typical community where most important decisions are made by a handful of leaders, the community redevelopment process provides a great opportunity to broaden the local leadership cadre. In fact, leadership development is so important to successful community redevelopment that it might be considered as a critical redevelopment project in itself.

By and large, leadership development should occur through on-the-job training. When many citizens become active participants in community assessment and strategic planning a few of them will demonstrate (to themselves and to others) their strong leadership capability. The rest of the community, both the traditional leaders and the general citizenship, should encourage the growth of these new leaders.

Such emerging leadership skills can be further nurtured via some formal leadership training, mentoring, or professional coaching. Many communities will find that providing such assistance to their newly emerging leaders is a very good investment.

Principle 7: Accountability

Accountability is really just a subset of plan implementation (Principle 3), but it is so important that it merits special attention.

It is important that the community's strategic plan is followed. The community needs to have an accountability system in place to assure that work is being carried out as specified in the plan (or that any changes are based on a clear and reasonable rationale). Thus, in its accountability system, the community should compare what was intended to happen, as spelled out in its plan, with what is actually happening. These comparisons should be made frequently (perhaps monthly).

The process used for tracking progress should be simple enough that it is easy for both citizens and community leaders to see in a single short report (perhaps two-to-five pages long) what was planned and what has been accomplished to date. This report should focus on the big picture, omitting details.

Without such an accountability system in place, the community is in danger of misusing its resources. In the long term, the larger potential tragedy is that the community's goals and objectives will not be achieved, and the better community envisioned in the strategic plan will not be built.

Principle 8: Partnerships

No matter how resourceful and determined the community is, the mission of building a stronger community will always be substantially enhanced by working with partners. The community must take the lead: that is mandatory. But the community is strongly encouraged to call upon partner institutions for assistance in designing and implementing its strategic plan.

Examples of partner institutions that could be useful to the community on one or more aspects of its community redevelopment process include the state department of commerce or economic development, the state association of mayors, the state rural development council, a local university or community college, professional organizations of planners, foundations, and regional planning agencies.

Partners can bring a variety of useful resources to the community, including dollars and in-kind resources, such as office space, supplies, and services. But perhaps even more useful, truly engaged partners can offer the community expertise, technical assistance, volunteers, and often the partner institution can bring a fresh perspective to the table.

For partnering to work, the community must provide the leadership. Otherwise, most likely, partners will not be willing to participate. Or, perhaps a partner will show up to develop a strategy that reflects the partner's hopes and dreams for the community rather than the community's goals, thus wasting both resources and the opportunity for a more useful outcome. In short, although partners are critical, the community cannot just sit back and wait for the partners to come knocking on the door to tell the community what to do or to tell the community what they (the partners) will do.

Principle 9: Learning Community

A community will be stronger, and will more successfully design and implement a strategic plan, when it builds upon a broad foundation of knowledge. This is true because no one person knows it all. And no one institution knows it all. The concept of learning community starts from this premise.

There are two sources of the knowledge critical for community success. First, community members and institutions should be encouraged to share knowledge with each other. For instance, a dozen Main Street shopkeepers can come together once a month to share their knowledge on how to retain their customers in the face of new competition down the road. For instance, the teachers in a successful elementary school can share their knowledge and experience with teachers in an underperforming school.

A second source of knowledge for the community will be from outside the community. The Internet is, of course, a robust source of outside ideas; but it is sometimes a difficult source of knowledge to digest and use because much of the information provided may be wrong or it may be inapplicable to a particular community.

A traditional source of knowledge and ideas is the outside expert. If the community, for example, wants to redesign a downtown or neighborhood square with a mix of commercial and residential and public uses, why not turn to a nationally recognized architect or planner who has developed successful similar projects in other communities? Or if the community wants to recruit health care professionals to better serve the community's uninsured population, why not bring in a public health expert who has worked on this issue in similar communities?

Another useful source of knowledge can be peer communities. Whatever the community's situation, there are other communities that have faced something similar. Those communities are often willing to share their experiences: what worked, what did not, what to think about, dangers to watch out for. A community can even learn much from the mistakes of comparable communities that were largely unsuccessful in meeting their challenges.

In some instances, the community may want to work with a team of outside experts or peers, rather than talking only one-on-one with individuals. Any of these conversations with outsiders can take place via e-mail or telephone. However, often the most productive interactions will take place in traditional face-to-face meetings.

Regardless of the quantity and quality of knowledge obtained from outside experts and peers, the community should not blindly follow the advice and insights from these sources. A community is similar to many other communities, but is identical to none. Outsiders will have interesting observations about the community, and sometimes an astute understanding. But community members must live with the results, and they, not the outsiders, must determine how the outside advice will be used.

Principle 10: Positive Attitude

If most community members bring a positive attitude to the community redevelopment process, then this bodes well for success. A few upbeat community members can often be very influential in setting a positive tone at the outset.

On the other hand, there will be naysayers and defeatists in almost any community. Their attitude will be that we have tried that before and it never worked; or that this community is so far down it will never be up again. If this is the dominant attitude, then the community will begin its community redevelopment process with two strikes against it.

A fuzzy gray line separates a positive yet realistic attitude from a Pollyannaish unrealistic attitude. So the community not only needs to keep both feet firmly planted in reality (it's not likely, for example, that a community with a low skilled labor force will be chosen as the site for the next Toyota plant), but has to also look hard at its assets (boarded-up storefronts may be architectural gems from an earlier era that could be rehabilitated into a lively street).

Final Note on Principles

We do not believe the above ten principles are universally mandatory. But we do present them as solid guidance established over years of trial-and-error in thousands of communities across the country. In short, the principles presented here represent community redevelopment best practices.

Redevelopment in Post-Disaster Communities

Every community faces challenges. The village of Adams has a crumbling municipal building and a deteriorating water system. The Burnwood neighborhood has high rates of drug abuse and violent crime. Many of the high school teachers in the small town of Cherryton do not meet state standards. The unemployment rate in the Deanside neighborhood is 25 percent overall and over 50 percent for men aged 18–34. And so on.

But a small rural town, a suburban community, or an urban neighborhood recently hit by a disaster will face some special challenges. In this section, we revisit each of the ten core principles spelled out above. In this revisitation, we point out the ways in which the community redevelopment process in post-disaster communities will need to be handled differently than in other (nondisaster) communities.

Principle 1: Community Assessment

A post-disaster community will need to assess its conditions. It is likely to want to put a lot of emphasis on its physical infrastructure: the roads, schools, factories, stores, offices, homes that were destroyed or severely damaged. The community needs to go beyond an assessment of that infrastructure, however.

First, the shredding of social networks (friends, families, neighbors, and coworkers who are displaced, injured, and killed) and public/private services (schools, criminal justice system, bars and restaurants, and other meeting places) can be losses just as great and important to document as the infrastructure destruction. Second, the community's post-disaster situation should be seen not just as a problem, but also as an opportunity; therefore, the assessment should inventory assets as well as problems.

One asset seen often immediately following the disaster is a greater sense of common purpose and destiny; this results from the common challenge all residents have faced and the typical "coming together" of community members to assist those most in need. This common bond is there for a few days or weeks but it usually fades over time. To most fully capitalize upon this strong initial heightened sense of community, the community may want to move quickly to begin its assessment and get moving on its community redevelopment process.

On the other hand, a disaster-struck community may need at first to focus 100 percent of its energy on the very tough shorter-term issues: how to save lives, tend to the wounded, avoid further injury and disease, restore power and water, and so on. Embarking on the community redevelopment process may have to wait. In fact, if undertaken too early, long-term community redevelopment may be so overshadowed by the need to carry out immediate post-disaster clean-up and survival actions that it will fail.

The immediate post-disaster community may be one where many residents had to go elsewhere to live because their homes or their jobs were destroyed. This will make the community assessment process more challenging, for it may not be clear which residents and jobs will ever return (and if so when). But, of course, successful community redevelopment can help convince wavering former residents and former employers that the post-disaster community will become a good one that is becoming even stronger by taking advantage of its opportunities.

Principle 2: Strategic Planning

Strategic planning in the post-disaster setting may be especially challenging: the post-disaster community may focus so heavily upon the calamity of the recent tragedy that it may be difficult to get people to think positively about what a stronger future community would look like.

In some cases, such as a tornado, the disaster will have hit unevenly, wiping out certain houses or blocks or sectors, while leaving others largely untouched. The temptation might be to focus the strategic plan only on those areas hardest hit, and to pay little or no attention to the other areas. But the post-disaster community would be wise to use this as an opportunity to develop a strategic plan for the entire community. For instance, if 100 homes were destroyed or severely damaged in a neighborhood or village of 400 homes, the strategic plan might be the place to think about ways to upgrade the substandard homes among the standing 300, rather than thinking only about how to replace the destroyed 100. Or, if one of the four schools in the community was destroyed in the disaster, the strategic plan might be a great opportunity to look beyond that single school and to take a broader look at the school system's ability to serve the community's children.

Because all the sectors of the community are interconnected, even if only one or two sectors were damaged or destroyed in the disaster, a comprehensive strategic plan will often be appropriate in the post-disaster community. Therefore, even if the disaster destroyed a number of homes, but no businesses, the community would benefit from conducting a full strategic plan, covering the business community as well as the housing sector. For instance, it is possible that the replacement homes could be sited and built in such a way that the community will become more attractive for both residents and tourists, thereby opening up new business opportunities. Or, on the flip side, poor planning for replacement housing could reduce the customer base for local businesses, leading some to go out of business or relocate out of town.

In terms of community assessment and strategic planning, let us be crystal clear: community redevelopment is absolutely essential for the long-term success of a disaster-struck community. Our cautions above relate only to getting the timing right, to get the maximum benefit from community redevelopment.

Principle 3: Plan Implementation

We see no unique aspects of plan implementation for post-disaster communities. Those communities should follow the same plan implementation guidelines recommended for any community. However, implementing the strategic plan can be much more difficult in disaster-impacted communities. Resources may be severely stretched; for instance, cash may be less available as the tax base declines and human resources may be hard to find if many people have left the area. In addition, following a disaster, there is often a greater urgency than during normal times to move forward quickly with plan implementation.

Principle 4: Evaluation and Feedback

We see no unique aspects of evaluation and feedback for post-disaster communities. We believe those communities should use the same evaluation and feedback guidelines recommended for other communities.

Principle 5: Citizen Participation

As pointed out earlier, in the immediate post-disaster community, some residents may be living outside the community because their homes were destroyed or their jobs disappeared. This will make the recommended broad-based citizen participation more difficult to pull off.

Some (perhaps many or even all) of the displaced residents and jobs will return at some point, so they will have a stake in the shape of the redeveloped community. Those displaced will represent a unique (and particularly vulnerable) segment of the community, so a strong effort should be made to get them involved in the community redevelopment process.

Getting those displaced by the disaster involved in the redevelopment process will be anything but straightforward. Logistical issues include knowing who are the displaced, where they are now, how to contact them, how to encourage them to participate, how to design a process that permits those hundreds of miles away to participate.

Even among the citizens who were not displaced, the impact of the disaster will be felt unevenly. The community will therefore want to make a special effort to encourage and enable participation in the community redevelopment process by those hardest hit by the disaster (who may find it especially difficult physically or psychologically to participate). At the other end of the spectrum, citizens least affected by the disaster may also need special encouragement to work on a process that they may see as helping "others."

Principle 6: Leadership Development

For post-disaster communities, although the same leadership development guidelines recommended for any community apply, fewer people may be available to take leadership roles, or they may be less willing to take on those roles, because they are busy putting their lives, homes, and businesses back in order.

Principle 7: Accountability

We see no unique aspects of accountability for post-disaster communities. We believe those communities should use the same accountability guidelines recommended for other communities. Of course, in most post-disaster communities, there will be more public, private, and nonprofit dollars in play than in other redeveloping communities. Therefore, the need for good attention to accountability is especially strong in these communities.

Principle 8: Partnerships

A post-disaster community will find that there are some special programs and some dedicated agencies that are available to work with the community on its redevelopment process. Typically federal agencies, such as FEMA, and state agencies, such as departments of housing, commerce, or community affairs, will have programs targeted to post-disaster communities. The private sector can be important in generating reinvestment in the community and should be made welcome early in the process. The community is likely to find other institutions as well that have assistance geared toward the post-disaster situation. In many instances, however, this assistance (e.g., from the American Red Cross) is aimed at crisis intervention and is not intended to support community redevelopment.

The post-disaster period is a time to capitalize on any regional or national climate of sympathy that may exist, and enlist available resources actively and as quickly as possible. It must be remembered that public attention to the disaster may quickly fade after the initial period of response, even though community redevelopment needs may continue for months or years.

The community needs to keep clearly in mind that even though some special funding or technical assistance programs may be offered to post-disaster communities, these resources should represent the beginning, not the end, of the available partnership opportunities. Potential partner institutions with experience working with non-disaster-impacted communities will often be able to bring extremely useful resources to the table.

Principle 9: Learning Community

The community should not fall into the trap of assuming that the only pertinent knowledge and experience will come from experts on disaster-struck communities or from other post-disaster communities. The post-disaster community will have many characteristics in common with a large number of communities, most of them not hit by disaster. And experts on community redevelopment in general, without any specific experience on post-disaster community redevelopment, may offer extremely useful insights.

Principle 10: Positive Attitude

A post-disaster community may find it especially difficult to build and maintain a positive attitude across the community. Many community members may be extremely disheartened about the situation. It is important for them to accept the frustrations and setbacks that will inevitably occur, but not to be complacent or satisfied with ineffective plans or outcomes. At the same time, special attention needs to be devoted to assuring that animosity is not created and that citizens are not demotivated.

Nonetheless, the post-disaster community should attempt to follow the same positive attitude guidelines recommended for any community.

Community Redevelopment in Post-Katrina/ Rita Louisiana

In this portion of the chapter, we will describe the post-hurricane community redevelopment process carried out in southern Louisiana through a collaborative local–state–federal effort. Two major hurricanes struck the Gulf Coast in August and September 2005. Hurricane Katrina, the most devastating disaster in American history, struck on August 29, 2005, passing through the New Orleans region and devastating a number of parishes (i.e., counties) in the southern and eastern parts of the state. On September 24, 2005, Hurricane Rita struck the southwestern part of the state, causing severe damage in coastal parishes from Louisiana's western border as far east as Jefferson Parish, adjacent to New Orleans. Because the damage from these two hurricanes called for similar responses and occurred at approximately the same time and in overlapping areas, FEMA, the state, and the localities responded to them with a combined effort. (Note: Both hurricanes had impacts beyond Louisiana, but for purposes of this chapter, we focus attention exclusively on Louisiana.)

Hurricane Katrina was the most costly and one of the deadliest hurricanes in U.S. history. It was the sixth strongest Atlantic hurricane ever recorded. Katrina's eye struck near New Orleans. Katrina's large size devastated the Gulf coast over 100 miles from its center. In Louisiana, storm surge breached a number of levees in the New Orleans region, flooding over 80 percent of the city and many neighboring areas. Katrina is estimated to have created $81.2 billion in damages. According to the Louisiana Department of Health and Hospitals, it resulted in 1464 deaths in Louisiana alone [1] and the displacement of hundreds of thousands of citizens, many if not most of whom had not been able to return home a year later. In addition to damaging businesses, housing, roads, bridges, water and sewage treatment plants, hospitals, and other infrastructure, the storm had severe effects on the coastal environment, causing substantial beach erosion and completely devastating some coastal areas, including barrier islands. Katrina's impacts were heaviest in south-eastern Louisiana, especially in those parishes designated as "multi-sector" (see Figure 27.1). Multi-sector parishes are those in which several elements of the community, including the economy, environment, housing, and physical infrastructure, were heavily damaged or destroyed.

Media coverage of Hurricane Katrina has principally centered on New Orleans, deservedly so, for it suffered severe damage in many of its neighborhoods from the storm surge and breaches in several levees. But the damage was equally if not more

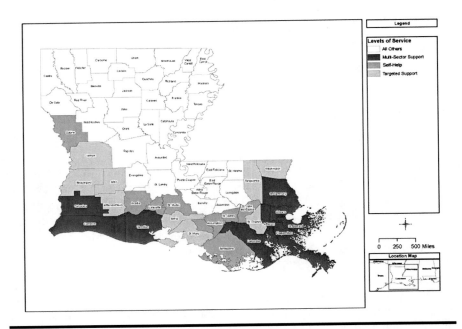

Figure 27.1   Long-term community recovery planning service levels: Louisiana, 2006.

severe—on a per capita basis—in other parishes. Neighboring St. Bernard Parish, just east of New Orleans, was totally inundated by the storm surge and all structures in the parish were heavily damaged or destroyed. To the west of Orleans parish (New Orleans), suburban Jefferson Parish was not affected by levee failures, but many drainage canals overflowed when the pumping stations were shut down because of emergency conditions and wind damage to roofs left homes and businesses vulnerable to rain damage. Some 27,000 homes in Jefferson Parish were damaged in this way, and nearly 100,000 of the parish's residents had been unable to return home as of early 2006 [2].

Hurricane Rita, the fourth-most intense Atlantic hurricane on record, was an even stronger storm than Katrina. The storm struck near the Louisiana–Texas border, carrying storm surge that caused extensive damage along the southwestern Louisiana coast and completely destroying some coastal communities. Its effects were felt all across southern Louisiana, as far east as New Orleans, where an already-compromised levee protecting the lower 9th Ward was overwhelmed. Though it killed only seven persons outright, many others died during evacuation and from indirect effects of the storm.

Like Hurricane Katrina, Rita caused considerable damage to the economy, infrastructure, and coastal environment of the impacted parishes. Rita's most severe effects were felt in rural parishes in the southwestern part of the state (see Figure 27.1), notably in Cameron Parish, where the communities of Holly Beach, Hackberry, and Cameron were totally destroyed, and Calcasieu Parish, where the communities of Lake Charles, Sulphur, Westlake, and Vinton suffered heavy damage [3].

Key Players in the Community Redevelopment Process: FEMA, Louisiana Recovery Authority, and Localities

When ten homes are destroyed by a tornado, the community itself will typically organize the community redevelopment process. When the scale is enormously bigger, however, federal or state government leadership may be called for. Thus, in Louisiana, FEMA and the Louisiana Recovery Authority (LRA) played a large role in the community redevelopment process for many hard-hit parishes.

For FEMA in Louisiana, the starting point was the long-term community recovery (LTCR) process, conducted by a team known as Emergency Support Function (ESF) 14. Immediately following a major hurricane or other major disaster, FEMA puts in place several ESFs, each focused on a specific functional area, such as transportation, food, housing, and public health/medical services. All ESFs, with the exception of ESF14, are aimed at providing an immediate response to the disaster.

ESF14 is new; it was organized in 2005 just before Hurricanes Katrina and Rita, and was put in place in September 2005 for the first time.

ESF14's mission, as stated in its draft standard operating procedures (SOP) [4], is "to coordinate federal assistance and to support State, local and tribal governments in advancing long-term community recovery from the impact of extraordinary disasters." The main functions of ESF14 are

- Assessing the impacts of the disaster on the community
- Coordinating FEMA's transition from immediate response to redevelopment actions
- Working with state and local governments and other organizations to develop long-term redevelopment plans
- Identifying federal programs to fund specific projects listed in the community redevelopment plans
- Coordinating and streamlining program application processes
- Monitoring program delivery across all pertinent organizations to assure effective plan implementation

It is important to note that although we generally speak of "redevelopment" in this chapter, FEMA uses the term "recovery" to describe its efforts. This is not an accident. FEMA's statutory basis emphasizes helping communities recover to their pre-disaster condition, and much of FEMA's funding—especially its Public Assistance (PA) program—is restricted to this purpose. Nonetheless, ESF14 recognizes the value of development that extends beyond recovery, and although its main focus is indeed on recovery, it may legitimately be described as a redevelopment program. In the case of post-Katrina/Rita Louisiana, however, as will be spelled out below, FEMA did little to push the envelope beyond recovery to move into the realm of community "redevelopment."

ESF14 is invoked at the request of the state governor. In 2005, the governors of Alabama, Louisiana, and Mississippi requested ESF14 to be established in their states. Texas, which was also hit by Hurricane Rita, did not request ESF14 assistance.

ESF14 represents a collaboration of federal and state agencies in support of local communities. Federal agencies include primary agencies and supporting agencies. The primary agencies, which are participants in response to all disasters, are the departments of agriculture, commerce (i.e., Economic Development Administration), homeland security (i.e., FEMA), housing and urban development, treasury and the small business administration. Supporting agencies, which are sometimes involved, depending on the nature and location of the disaster, include the departments of commerce (i.e., NOAA), defense (i.e., Army Corps of Engineers), energy, health and human services, transportation, Environmental Protection Agency and the American Red Cross.

Local responses are organized initially from one of the ten regional FEMA offices. As soon as practicable, a regional response coordination center (RRCC) is established in the regional office to coordinate the initial response to the event. Shortly thereafter, a joint federal office (JFO) "stands up" within each affected state, where a staff is assembled to conduct response and recovery actions. The JFO is headed by a federal coordinating official (FCO), who is paired with a state coordinating official (SCO). As FEMA's assistance is provided in response to the state's request, the state will also create a parallel policy-setting agency. In Louisiana, the Louisiana Recovery Authority (LRA) was formed by the governor by executive order; the LRA was later established in law by Louisiana's legislature. (Note: The LRA was the state parallel to the entire FEMA effort, covering all aspects of the immediate post-hurricane response as well as longer-term redevelopment.)

All 64 of Louisiana's parishes (counties) were included in the presidential disaster declaration. However, an assessment by ESF14 identified only 24 parishes as seriously impacted by the two hurricanes. Later, another—East Baton Rouge Parish—was included in the list because of the large number of evacuees it absorbed, swelling its population and causing heavy demands on its capacity to provide public services. ESF14 and the LRA focused their community redevelopment work on these 25 parishes.

Figure 27.1 shows the initial 24 parishes identified as eligible for FEMA and LRA planning assistance in Louisiana. They are shown as shaded in the map. Parishes shaded in dark grey given multi-sector planning assistance, that is, their plans were relatively comprehensive. Light grey shaded parishes received "targeted" assistance to one or a few sectors that were particularly impacted by the storms. Medium grey parishes were designated as "self-help" parishes and were provided with limited technical assistance, a planning workshop, and copies of FEMA's Self-Help Guide.

Details of the Community Redevelopment Process in Louisiana

The long-term community recovery (ESF14) process began by conducting an assessment to identify those parishes in need of planning assistance, as mentioned above. The assessment was accomplished by using an assessment tool [5] devised by FEMA.

The tool consists of two stages. In stage one, which takes only a few hours, the assessor quickly rates the overall extent of the damage to the community. If the stage-one assessment indicates substantial damage has occurred, then FEMA will provide its long-term community recovery assistance.

Once FEMA decides that the community is eligible for such recovery assistance, then stage two of the assessment tool kicks in. In stage two, the assessment is aimed at determining the damage sustained, and the community's capacity to respond, in each of three sectors: the economy, housing, and infrastructure. All communities that suffered substantial damage are classified, at a minimum, as self-help; stage-two analysis determines whether the damage was sufficient to warrant designation as either targeted or multi-sector assistance communities.

In January 2006, parish level planning teams were formed in 19 of the 25 eligible parishes. The remaining six parishes were less severely impacted and deemed capable of conducting their own planning. Each was provided with one FEMA employee to assist them, along with a Self-Help Guide [6] to use during the planning process. Three of these six self-help parishes accepted this assistance and went on to develop "parish recovery plans."

The Self-Help Guide is a 110 page document that describes the long-term community recovery process and identifies 12 action steps for communities to undertake to complete that process. Written in language that makes it accessible to community leaders, it is a good starting point for a community, though it omits or provides inadequate coverage of some of the key community redevelopment principles presented earlier.

For each of the 19 most devastated Louisiana parishes, FEMA provided a full-time professional staff to work on community redevelopment. The staff sizes varied across the 19 parishes from about 4 or 5 to 20 or more. The staff FEMA provided included employees from FEMA and other federal agencies (e.g., HUD, USDA), as well as contractors. The FEMA team for each parish represented an array of expertise useful for successful community redevelopment. Community planning, budgeting, engineering, and business development skills were included on most teams, as well as coastal and environmental specialists in areas with coastal damage.

In essence, the role of this team of outside experts was to facilitate, guide, and support a community-driven redevelopment process. The key functions of this outside team included

1. Collecting key data
2. Conducting an initial community needs assessment
3. Gathering input from local leaders and others in the community
4. Assessing community capacity
5. Developing a community redevelopment plan, including vision, goals, programs, and projects
6. Preparing a printed or Web-based version of the plan
7. Handing-off the plan to local governments and other stakeholders for implementation

These team functions are consistent in many respects with the community redevelopment principles laid out earlier. The teams were directed by FEMA to work on a fast track to generate the community redevelopment plans.

Projects and other redevelopment activities were identified and defined in consultation with local officials and other key community stakeholders, often numbering in the hundreds. Each team member specialized in one or more of the issue areas and contacted relevant community representatives to discuss their needs and possible projects to address them. Based on these interviews, team members wrote up descriptions of potential projects and entered them into a Web-based planning tool, described below.

In addition to consultation with stakeholders, a Louisiana Planning Day was held on January 21, 2006 (Figure 27.2). The Planning Day consisted of open houses in each of the parishes, as well as in other cities in Louisiana and in other states with large populations of evacuees. Attendees were presented with wall charts listing possible values, issue areas, and critical choice options and were given dots to attach to the charts indicating their preferences. In addition, they were invited to attach notes, explaining their views, to the charts. The results of this expression of preferences were captured in a database and were closely followed in developing each parish's statements of values and priorities, as well as proposed projects.

Following the development of parish plans, they were entered into the Parish Recovery Planning Tool, a Web-based system that describes each project, its estimated cost and time for completion, and possible sources of funding (http://www.louisianaspeaks-parishplans.org/). The plans were then subjected to intensive scrutiny by several teams of reviewers who applied a Recovery Valuation Tool [7] to determine which projects were most critical to parish redevelopment. The first two rounds of reviews were conducted by several teams of outside reviewers with special expertise in the subjects of the plans (e.g., housing or small business development) and who had received special training to help assure consistency in rating the individual projects. Then, the completed plans were given additional scrutiny by a

Figure 27.2   Louisiana Planning Day, Jefferson Parish.

single statewide team that attempted to assure cross-parish consistency. At the same time, the final review made tough choices so that only the most critical recovery projects received a score of "high."

These project rankings are shown on the plan Web site and are intended to help parishes to begin their efforts with the most critical redevelopment actions. During the recovery valuation process, nearly two-thirds of the original projects were deleted from the plans, to keep the parishes highly focused on actions needed to lay the groundwork for successful community redevelopment. Many of the proposed lower ranking "redevelopment" projects were reclassified as "community interest" projects but retained in the plans.

The communities were not involved during this FEMA-prescribed review and reclassification process. FEMA's rationale for excluding the communities included a lack of time, the tendency of communities to include projects that had been high on their priority lists before the hurricanes, and the low levels of leadership capacity available at the parish level. In general, the criteria used by FEMA in deleting projects from the parish plans were designed to focus attention on the highest priority recovery projects, to avoid dilution of the overall effort by attempting too many things at a time, and in some cases to eliminate duplicative projects already covered in the plan of a neighboring parish. (Each of the deleted projects was retained in the Web database and the files developed during the planning process were turned over to the parishes to support possible work on them in the future.)

Overall, then, the planning process was overwhelmingly top down, and heavily controlled by FEMA. Although the LRA was represented in each parish by two National Guard members, their role tended to focus on logistics rather than direct engagement in planning activities. Given ESF14's large role in selecting and even rewriting the final projects, it is hard to conclude that the planning process was community driven.

The primary products of the planning process were redevelopment plans for each of the parishes, which will help focus their actions on projects of key import-ance in reestablishing their communities as places in which to live and work. In addition, however, this first implementation of ESF14 provided an opportunity for FEMA to develop important tools for use in the planning process: the Play Book, Recovery Valuation tool, the Parish Recovery Planning (Web-based) Tool, and the Self-Help Guide for use by communities in carrying out a redevelopment planning process. Although all four of these tools need revision based on the Louisiana experience, and to better conform with the core community redevelopment principles, they are now available for use by other communities in response to future disasters.

Of the 19 parishes served by FEMA teams, in 15 the community redevelopment planning work was substantially completed by late March 2006. The FEMA teams for those 15 parishes were demobilized at that time. FEMA teams continued to operate until May 2006 in the four most severely devastated parishes.

A number of projects included in the parish plans showed great innovation in meeting the challenges posed by the hurricanes' destruction. In New Orleans, for example, the plan proposes to invest $94 million to create business incubators in several industries, including a BioInnovation Center in the heart of the medical district and the Louisiana Artworks Incubator to encourage the growth of small arts businesses and low-to-moderate income artists. The incubators would help replace approximately 150,000 small business job losses. Vermillion Parish, a coastal parish heavily damaged by Hurricane Rita, plans to devote $47 million to relocate schools in some areas and protect others serving a unique cultural commu-nity with a levee. Jefferson Parish, adjacent to New Orleans and struck by both hurricanes, plans to invest $100,000 to implement a smart growth process that will inventory important natural resources and incorporate them into area comprehensive plans.

How the Post-Katrina/Rita Community Redevelopment Process Rates

How well did the post-Katrina/Rita community redevelopment process in Louisiana match the community redevelopment principles we presented earlier in this chapter? In this section, we examine this question. (Note: We are writing this chapter approximately one year after the two hurricanes struck.)

We need to acknowledge here that none of the key institutions involved in the post-Katrina/Rita work in southern Louisiana claimed to be engaged in community redevelopment. So, in that sense, our analysis below is holding the federal, state, local, and private sector and citizen participants to a standard to which they never explicitly aspired. On the other hand, as we have pointed out earlier, a major disaster presents a significant opportunity for redevelopment of the community, rather than just recovery. Thus, we feel it is useful, if perhaps not completely "fair," to rate the post-disaster effort in Louisiana against our community redevelopment template.

Rating on Principle 1: Community Assessment

FEMA played the central role in the community assessment that was the basis of the strategic plans. ESF14 identified needs in nine key functional areas. Those areas—environmental management, housing and community redevelopment, economic and workforce development, education, flood protection and coastal restoration, human services, public health and health care, public safety, transportation and infrastructure—although not comprehensive, covered a broad spectrum of redevelopment needs. The FEMA assessment, however, was heavily focused on needs, without much attention to the community's assets and opportunities. Even within the realm of needs, the assessment looked separately at each of the nine identified sectors, but with little focus on cross-sector relationships and synergies.

In addition, the assessments omitted other key areas that would be expected to be included in a comprehensive community development strategic plan such as cross-sector and cross-institutional partnerships, leadership development, and civic engagement. Also, topics such as the court system and solid waste disposal were not covered. In addition, little attention was given to assessing the community's institutional capacity to implement the plans. FEMA originally intended to document each parish's governmental organization strength as a surrogate for a capacity assessment. However, given the volume of other work required, this organizational documentation was abandoned late in the assessment process.

Rating on Principle 2: Strategic Planning

The community redevelopment plans developed by the FEMA teams differed from comprehensive strategic plans in several important respects. In the first place, the plans were not comprehensive, as discussed above. Neither were they strategic, though they were intended to be. Rather, the plans tended to be sector-oriented lists of projects usually nominated by sector-specific stakeholders.

So these plans seldom included cross-sector project proposals (e.g., proposing that the new health care center be located in a new courthouse or town hall) and seldom brought together multiple institutions (e.g., proposing a new community education center to be developed jointly by the community college, the local high school, the state department of labor, and the parish public library). And because the starting point was needs, the plans centered on addressing needs, rather than on exploiting opportunities. Within these fairly severe limitations, the plans laid out some of the highest priority redevelopment projects the parishes should undertake.

Rating on Principle 3: Plan Implementation

FEMA's involvement in the planning process was limited, for the most part, to the development of the plans. Once completed, the plans were turned over to the parishes and the LRA for implementation. FEMA provided support to the LRA for workshops in each parish that provided information about grantsmanship and maintaining the parish project data on the Web-based planning tool.

In addition, as ESF14 demobilized, a new unit was formed within FEMA, the Recovery Support Branch. This branch provided continuing planning assistance, as well as help in identifying possible funding sources. However, the branch's work was limited to the four hardest-hit parishes—Cameron, Orleans (New Orleans city), Plaquemines, and St. Bernard.

In short, plan implementation was put almost entirely in the hands of the parishes. This was in stark contrast to the earlier assessment and strategic planning, where the federal and state governments played very large roles. There is not necessarily a right or wrong approach here. But the danger is that some parishes may feel abandoned when a huge federal and state presence suddenly vanishes when it is time for implementation.

Rating on Principle 4: Evaluation and Feedback

FEMA conducted an "after-action review" shortly after ESF14 demobilized. This resulted in a number of valuable recommendations for modifications, which were incorporated into program guidance and especially into the curriculum for a July 2006 workshop to train those who will be responsible for FEMA's response to the next big disaster. FEMA has expressed its commitment to continuous improvement of its guidance: its standard operating procedures (SOP), concept of operations (CONOPS) [8], and a field operating guide that is being developed. Future revisions need to incorporate more fully the community redevelopment principles. Less clear is the extent of evaluation and feedback at the state and local levels.

Rating on Principle 5: Citizen Participation

Citizen participation was a key objective of the ESF14 process, but success in its implementation was varied. In many parishes, especially the more rural ones, frequent public meetings were held to identify important redevelopment issues and review drafts of the recovery plans. All parishes, as well as sites in other cities within Louisiana and in other states where large populations of displaced Louisianans were living, participated in Louisiana Planning Day on January 21, 2006. As discussed elsewhere, citizens were invited to attend open houses and vote on their most important values for redevelopment, the issues they regarded as most important, and their views on difficult choices that needed to be made. The information obtained from these votes provided important input for early drafts of the plans.

Two other forms of citizen participation were important as well. First, a wide array of stakeholders was consulted about both redevelopment needs and strategies, and their opinions were given great weight in the plans. And second, the Parish Recovery Planning Tool was created in part to make the plans public via the Web. That Web-based planning tool describes each project in the parishes' plans and allows parish leaders to update the descriptions to report progress in obtaining funding for the projects. The site can be viewed at http://www.louisianaspeaks-parishplans.org/.

In spite of some impressive outreach efforts, caution is called for in assessing the success of citizen participation. The FEMA and LRA designers of the planning process deserve high marks for creating a highly visible Louisiana Planning Day, for enabling displaced citizens to participate, and for obtaining citizen votes on values and issues.

Nevertheless, the exclusion of citizens from the pruning process—where the majority of the projects included in the community's strategic plan were deleted—was a grave affront to any notion of real citizen participation. Public processes should be citizen driven. In this case, with FEMA calling the shots about timing and deadlines, the process was not truly citizen driven, resulting in less local ownership. In consequence, it is not clear that enough interest and buy-in was obtained to assure strong and broad citizen support for the longer and harder plan implementation process. It is too early to know.

Rating on Principle 6: Leadership Development

Leadership capacity was an issue in all parishes, including Orleans (New Orleans) and Jefferson, the two largest parishes. Although the urban parishes would normally have sufficient capacity on hand, their ability to bring professional staff focus on redevelopment was significantly reduced because of a lack of housing for displaced workers and a major loss of the local tax revenue base, plus the need for available staff to work on short-term post-disaster issues along with the normal operation of public services. In the more rural parishes, a serious lack of professional staff capacity existed before the hurricanes. FEMA's ESF14 began a survey of parish capacity to implement the plans, but no objective tool for assessing this capacity exists, and FEMA did not want to risk offending parish leaders by accurate but blunt subjective assessments. For these reasons, as well as a lack of time and resources, the assessment was abandoned.

Nonetheless, some efforts were made to build staff and citizen capacity in both project management, using the Web-based planning tool, and grantsmanship. The LRA, with FEMA's assistance, conducted workshops in 18 parishes focusing on both topics. In addition, FEMA's Recovery Support Branch continued, beyond March 2006, to assist the four most severely affected parishes with technical support, and it was able to negotiate a grant from the Greater New Orleans Foundation for detailed grantsmanship training for St. Bernard Parish. In general, these efforts focused on working with the existing leadership, and appear to have done little to bring new leaders—especially from often-disenfranchised groups—into the community redevelopment process.

In addition, and notably, Louisiana, which had no state level planning capacity before the hurricanes, decided on the basis of the FEMA–LRA locality plan development experience to develop statewide planning functions that extended beyond post-disaster planning.

Rating on Principle 7: Accountability

The principal mechanism for public accountability in plan implementation is the Web-based planning tool, which displays descriptions of each project in the redevelopment plans and enables citizens to track progress in their implementation. This tool was enthusiastically accepted by the LRA, which has agreed to maintain the system in the future and extend its use to all parishes as a part of the state's new planning functions. As plan implementation has barely begun, it is of course way too early to assess the success of the accountability mechanisms.

Rating on Principle 8: Partnerships

ESF14 made considerable efforts to build supportive partnerships for the parish plans. The primary agencies and some supporting agencies each had representatives stationed in Baton Rouge alongside FEMA staff to review planned projects and to identify those they might be in a position to help fund. Funding possibilities are shown in the Web-based planning tool. Fewer and weaker partnerships existed with foundations and private sector players during the planning process. Although some universities conducted studies in one issue area or another, their studies tended to be either proprietary or were not integrated into the ESF14 plans for one reason or another. On the other hand, generally strong relationships existed with the multi-parish planning and development districts, which were closely engaged in most areas. In sum, the community redevelopment process used in Louisiana encouraged some level of partnership, but certainly not all potential partner institutions were brought fully on board.

Rating on Principle 9: Learning Community

Both FEMA, through its ESF14 support, and other partners made efforts to assist communities to become learning communities. One of the most successful of these was a series of charettes in three parishes conducted by Andres Duany of Duany Plater-Zyberk & Company. (A charette is a one-time highly intense community planning process, typically bringing together citizens representing an array of interests. Although charettes can be broad ranging, the focus is usually on land use, buildings, and other physical infrastructure.) These charettes, each conducted over a period of several days, enabled citizens to confront their tendency toward rebuilding their communities as they had been before the storms and to become more open to seeing the redevelopment process as an opportunity to rebuild a different, better community. The charettes were sponsored by the LRA and were attended by representatives from some of the other parishes.

ESF14 staff themselves represented a variety of expertise in subjects related to redevelopment. In their interactions with stakeholders, they too introduced new concepts about rebuilding in new and better ways.

It is not always clear in advance what expertise a particular community will find useful, and when during the process that expertise will be needed. In some Louisiana parishes, for instance, engineers and similar technical experts were provided throughout the strategic planning process when they were only necessary near the end of the process for help in determining the feasibility and costs of some specific infrastructure projects.

On the other hand, some Louisiana parishes, especially the hardest-hit rural ones, might have benefited greatly from a longer outside expert presence. Apparently, early on FEMA promised to provide many parishes with an outside planning expert for one to two years, but this assistance was severely truncated.

Thus, when ESF14 responds to future major disasters, careful consideration must be given to what experts will be sent, and on what schedule, to impacted communities.

Rating on Principle 10: Positive Attitude

For the most part, local officials maintained a very positive attitude during and after the planning process and citizens were remarkably committed to restoring their communities, despite their personal hardships and in full knowledge that it will take years to achieve their objectives. It is too early to know whether this generally positive attitude can be maintained over the difficult implementation road of the next few years.

Final Words: Guidance for the Next Big One

Looking back at the community redevelopment process in post-Katrina/Rita Louisiana can serve as a useful jumping-off point for thinking about better ways to go about the community redevelopment process after the next major disaster strikes. As successful community redevelopment requires the participation of several key institutions, all can and should listen carefully to the lessons from Louisiana. These listeners should, of course, include FEMA and other federal players. But responsibility for community redevelopment goes well beyond the federal government. Therefore, other key players should also be listening. These other players include state planning and economic development agencies, other state agencies, local governments, and a variety of nonprofits.

In the previous section, we assessed the Louisiana experience to date in terms of the ten core community redevelopment principles. That assessment is a piece of the lessons learned from Louisiana, but we intend to go somewhat further here.

A full evaluation of the success of Louisiana's community redevelopment process will have to wait for several years, at the least, so it is too soon to fully assess its success in pointing development in the most helpful direction. The plans themselves were constructed for a three to five year horizon. Many of the projects, once an often-lengthy funding process has been negotiated, will take two years or more to complete. Thus, a "final" assessment of the community redevelopment process in Louisiana might appropriately be conducted in about 2015, ten years after the Katrina/Rita disaster.

Although each parish now has a clear plan for the funding it needs to secure, this process is proceeding slowly. A review of the Web-based planning tool will show that although some funds have already been committed to projects, few have been fully funded as of mid-2006. One of the key programs, the Department of Housing and Urban Development's (HUD) Community Development Block Grants (CDBG), was entirely committed by the state to its Road Home program for housing, leaving no funds available as nonfederal match for federal programs addressing other issues.

Nobody said that post-disaster community redevelopment would be easy. It's not. The involved parties in southern Louisiana should get lots of points for trying hard in a very difficult situation. In Louisiana as elsewhere, successful post-disaster community redevelopment involves some artful juggling by many parties. We conclude by describing some of the most critical balancing acts that must be effectively handled by the key community redevelopment players.

Balancing Act 1: Outside Expertise versus Community Engagement

The provision of outside expertise is extremely useful, if not in fact mandatory, for the community struck by a major disaster. Even a well-endowed suburban community is unlikely to have all of the specialized expertise appropriate for planning and implementing community redevelopment following a disaster. Communities that were struggling economically and socially before disaster struck will be even more in need of such expertise. Outside experts can bring experience from similar communities, knowing some of the ideas and projects that have worked well elsewhere, and some that may sound reasonable but have not worked very well in other places. FEMA and the state government (e.g., the LRA in Louisiana) are providing an extremely valuable resource by offering this outside expertise.

All outside experts are not, of course, the same. Each will bring to the community his or her own background, skills, and perspectives. A team of experts will usually be preferable to a single expert, no matter how astute that person may be. Bringing experts to town serially, however, may be frustrating for the community, as each newly arrived outside expert will ask a series of questions and want a briefing on many of the same issues raised by the previous expert. The community may begin to tire of the need to bring each new outsider up to speed. The expert who sticks around for a few weeks is in a stronger position to gradually earn the community's trust.

A real danger is that the "outside" institutions (in Louisiana: FEMA, ESF14, and the LRA) will swoop into town with a cadre of experts and excitement, collect reams of data, facilitate the generation of lots of ideas (the community's strategic plan), and then pack their bags and ride out of town, never to be seen again. At one level, this may be appropriate behavior (e.g., this might be deemed consistent with the ESF14 mission). But, at another level, the community will often feel that the outsiders do not really care. A piece of the answer, at least, is to establish a continuing outside presence beyond the strategic planning stage, lasting perhaps for a year or two.

Another key danger is that the team of outside experts will "know it all" and run roughshod over the community. After all, when the experts leave town, it is the community that must implement the redevelopment plan and live with its consequences. Therefore, community input into the redevelopment process is critical.

In short, the community's redevelopment plan must reflect the knowledge and insights of both the outside experts and the community. This is a difficult but important balance to maintain.

Balancing Act 2: Speed versus Thoughtfulness

Many involved at the federal, state, and local levels will want to move as quickly as possible to get an approved community redevelopment plan in place. The incentives for quick action are many and strong. First, the players will look decisive; this will be important for many, especially the politicians and the media, who love groundbreakings and pictures of new buildings going up. Second, as the weeks and months pass by, the focus on this community by those at the state and federal level will fade, so there's a desire to grab the attention and resources early when they are most readily available.

Third, at the community level, there is often a "let's get moving" attitude, with less concern about exactly what to do and more concern about getting something done.

However, the fast route is not always the best. We are talking here about a community redevelopment plan that may take five years or more to implement and that will likely shape in many significant ways the community for the next fifty years or more. The decision on whether to rebuild the destroyed high school in its old location on the edge of town or in a new location on the town square can have a major impact on the town's physical, social, and economic success over the next several decades. Such a decision should be given careful thought, with input from a wide variety of stakeholders and observers, including students, teachers, downtown merchants, and citizens from other towns with a downtown high school.

Again, the community redevelopment process must balance these competing demands for speed on the one hand and thoughtfulness and thoroughness on the other hand.

Balancing Act 3: Local versus Larger Perspective

Following a major disaster, both federal and state resources are brought into the picture. Whether explicitly acknowledged or not, providing these resources gives the state and federal government some control over the community redevelopment process. In many cases, the state or federal perspective on redevelopment will be virtually identical to the community's perspective. But, in some cases, significant differences will exist. For instance, the local community may desire to have its main commercial street rebuilt exactly where it was before disaster struck. But this location may be on a flood plain, and the state or federal government may see rebuilding in a different nonflood plain location as a better use of taxpayer dollars.

Nonetheless, some weight must be given to the local viewpoint. In New Orleans, for instance, locals point to the unique world-class culture—music, food, architecture—that would disappear from the face of the earth if much of the city is not rebuilt to resemble in most ways the pre-hurricane New Orleans.

Once again, the community redevelopment process must balance the perspectives and interests of the local community with those of the state and the nation as a whole.

Balancing Act 4: Certainty versus Flexibility

Every community, disaster or not, engaged in a redevelopment process must work in an environment with many unknowns. To move forward, reasonable assumptions must be made about resources, constraints, and opportunities; these assumptions can serve as a critical foundation for the redevelopment process. In the high intensity environment of the post-disaster community, the number and scale of unknowns can be overwhelming. In Louisiana, for instance, essential questions with no clear answers included

- What level of resources will FEMA, HUD, SBA, and other federal agencies provide to this community for redevelopment?
- How will federal agencies dictate the use of such funds as will be available? E.g., will funds be available to support any part of the community redevelopment plan, or only for certain purposes?
- How will the federal and state governments, and the private insurance industry, set their regulations and incentives to encourage or discourage (or even prohibit) reconstruction in certain locations (e.g., on flood plains)?
- What will be the timing on all of the above?

The resource providers and the regulators, including federal and state governments and key private sector players, will always want, of course, to retain some degree of flexibility, so that resources can be moved around from place to place or sector to sector in response to emerging opportunities or issues. But, nonetheless, the community redevelopment process is likely to be much more successful if communities are given more certainty much earlier than happened in Louisiana.

Balancing Act 5: Redevelopment versus Recovery

Throughout this chapter we have emphasized the importance of adhering to a redevelopment process, as compared with a narrower recovery process, in responding to the effects of a disaster. Some of the advantages of redevelopment are a greater comprehensiveness of the plans, stronger community participation, and a longer-term outlook.

However, in the wake of a disaster, it can be exceedingly difficult to hold the focus on the broader redevelopment concept. Many participants in the process, especially citizens and community leaders, may fail to see beyond restoring things to the way they were and may miss opportunities to rebuild a different and better community.

The FEMA/LRA Long-Term Community Recovery Planning process was intended to stimulate this longer-term broader perspective. However, the bulk of FEMA's focus was on its huge Public Assistance (PA) program for infrastructure reconstruction. Although the program is extremely flexible, the PA statutes support recovery, which tended to weight FEMA's overall efforts toward recovery rather than redevelopment. In short, then, the work in post-Katrina/Rita Louisiana has been largely aimed at recovery rather than redevelopment. This is, unfortunately, an enormous opportunity lost: the opportunity to begin building different—and better—communities in south Louisiana.

A hopeful sign is FEMA's creation of ESF14, which could be used to bring the broader redevelopment perspective to disaster response processes. As ESF14 resources are applied to other disasters and honed through experience, FEMA and the other ESF14 partners can, and should, assert leadership to assure that a community redevelopment approach is used in the aftermath of future disasters.

Conclusion

As we have emphasized throughout this chapter, however, the responsibility for creating a successful community redevelopment process (one that incorporates the core principles we have presented) must be shared across several key institutions, including federal, state, and local governments, and nonprofits. We are optimistic that, by carefully heeding the Louisiana lessons learned, the community redevelopment participants following the next big one will be more successful and effective in creating stronger post-disaster communities.

References

1. http://www.dhh.louisiana.gov/offices/page.asp?ID=192&Detail=5248.
2. http://en.wikipedia.org/wiki/Hurricane_Katrina.
3. http://en.wikipedia.org/wiki/Hurricane_Rita.
4. Long-Term Community Recovery, Emergency Support Function #14: Standard Operating Procedures, Final Working Draft (Washington: FEMA Recovery Division, June 2006).
5. Long Term Recovery Assessment Tool, Unpublished Excel spreadsheet (Baton Rouge: FEMA, 2005).
6. Long-Term Community Recovery Planning Process: A Self-Help Guide (Baton Rouge: FEMA, December 2005).
7. Long-Term Community Recovery Planning Process: A Guide to Determining Project Recovery Values (Baton Rouge: FEMA, February 2006).
8. Long-Term Community Recovery, Emergency Support Function #14: Concept of Operations (Washington: FEMA Recovery Division, June 2006).

PLANNING, PREVENTION, AND PREPAREDNESS

VI

Chapter 28

The Role of Training in Disaster Management: The Case of Hawaii

Ross Prizzia

CONTENTS

The role of training in disaster management is essential to an effective response before, during, and after natural and man-made disasters. In such crisis situations, emergency knowledge, skills, and abilities are especially important for first responders to disasters at the international, national and state, or local level regardless of type or size of the disaster. On the basis of a meta-analysis and review of documents from relevant government agencies and organizations and a survey of emergency managers in the State of Hawaii, this research describes the important role of training in the preparation for, response to, and recovery from disasters.

Disaster Preparedness Training at International Level

The United Nations Disaster Management Training Program (UNDMTP) is conducted by the United Nations Disaster Management Team (UNDMT) in collaboration and coordination with national governments and relevant affiliated national and international organizations. The UNDMT is composed of expert individuals and agencies in the field of emergency management. Its ability to respond effectively to disasters depends mainly on appropriate actions taken in advance that usually require a collective, team effort among the member agencies of the UNDMT. To the extent possible, preparedness arrangements within the United Nations Disaster Preparedness (UNDP) office and the UNDMT are integrated and designed to complement national preparedness arrangements. The UNDMT establishes working relationships with government agencies of each country responsible for disaster management, and is knowledgeable of the country's national and local government plans and capacities for responding to emergencies. The nature and extent of UNDMT preparedness arrangements depend on the disaster profile of the country and status of national preparedness. Similar arrangements are made with respect to interaction with international bilateral, multilateral, and NGO representatives most likely to be active in disaster response. Where national preparedness plans and systems are well-developed, the UNDMT's emphasis is on knowledge of

- Hazards and their typical effects
- National arrangements
- How the UN agencies, individually and collectively, should work with the national authorities in the event of an emergency
- Sources of supplies and services (including expertise) that may need to be provided by the UN agencies

Where sudden disasters constitute a major threat and national preparedness arrangements are in an early stage of development, the field office of the UNDMT must be ready to provide substantial management support to the government of the affected country. In addition, preparedness within the UNDMT includes compiling a wide range of relevant baseline data on the disaster-prone areas, and establishing arrangements to set up an emergency information and coordination center. The UNDMT compiles basic data on preparedness measures that exist or can be developed in advance of emergencies. This information includes the types of food, clothing, shelter, medical, and other supplies that are appropriate for local use, and communication and transport arrangements at ports, airports and airstrips, and all other facilities necessary for a rapid and effective response to emergencies. The UNDMT supports and implements standardization of supplies and equipment appropriate for the disaster area, giving priority to harmonizing communications equipment. The UNDMT also meets at regular intervals to

- Review prevention and preparedness arrangements within the country, including the progress of any relevant ongoing development projects.
- Review preparedness arrangements within the UN team of agencies.
- Discuss the analysis and interpretation of data from in-country and external early warning systems.
- Decide on any specific actions to be taken by members of the group individually or collectively.
- Get copies of national disaster preparedness plans. Keep up-to-date information on the disaster-prone areas and likely disaster scenarios, and baseline data on the most disaster-prone areas.
- Establish and maintain working relationships with government bodies responsible for disaster preparedness and response.
- Establish links with forecasting and warning systems for natural phenomena, and systematically monitor famine early warning indicators where there is a risk of famine.
- Establish links with the embassies, aid missions, and NGOs that are likely to furnish emergency assistance.

The UNDMT also develops a specific training action plan, which includes

- Defining the functional responsibilities of each member of the UNDMT in the event of a disaster.
- Establishing, in advance, the systems and procedures that will be needed to manage the UNDMT response to potential disasters, including arrangements for assessments, information management, communications, and coordination.
- Making arrangements to establish a UNDMT coordination center on short notice. This includes designating suitable offices and earmarking computers, communications, and other necessary equipment.
- Documenting all operating procedures fully and clearly, and making this documentation readily available to all concerned.
- Sending OCHA (the Office for the Coordination of Humanitarian Affairs) copies of government and UNDMT preparedness plans and any other relevant documents (UNDMTP, 2006).

The work of the UNDMT feeds into the Common Country Assessment (CCA) process. The CCA is a country-based process for reviewing and analyzing national development situations, including disaster-related issues. The objective is to achieve deeper knowledge of key development challenges among the partners involved in the CCA, based on a common analysis and understanding of development situations (CCA, 2006).

Monitoring of Warnings and Indicators

Ideally, warnings and indicators of impending or occurring potentially disastrous events are rapidly made available to national authorities, on whom rests the responsibility for alerting the populations and response mechanisms concerned. In practice this is often the case, but information may also reach the authorities slowly, in fragmented form, or not at all. However, to the extent possible, procedures are established for the UNDMT to receive promptly all forecasts and consequent public warnings of imminent floods, storms, volcanic eruptions, and tsunamis. These forecasts and warnings are obtained from the responsible national authorities, through the appropriate (and specifically designated) member agency. The UN Office for the Coordination of Humanitarian Affairs (OCHA) routinely receives warnings directly from international sources and contacts the UN Resident Coordinator for preliminary consultation (OCHA, 2006; Tadamori, 2005).

In any country where the food supply is uncertain, especially where crops are vulnerable to drought or pest attack, the UNDMT not only promotes the establishment of famine early warning systems, but also receives and reviews current condition data. These include official government channels, out-posted and traveling UN staff, and NGOs' and other observers' reports, including those from journalists and the news media. The UNDMT also determines who is responsible for obtaining particular data and bringing it to the attention of the team (Tadamori, 2005).

Electronic Sources of Information

Disaster preparedness at the international level utilizes Web-based sources such as ReliefWeb (ReliefWeb, 2006). ReliefWeb's purpose is to strengthen the response capacity of the humanitarian relief community through the timely dissemination of reliable information on response, preparedness, and disaster prevention. This includes access to time-critical reports, maps, consolidated interagency appeals and financial contributions for complex emergencies and natural disasters, and access to specific sections on emergency telecommunications, country and sectoral links, early warning, contact directories and site links, a training inventory, and library of reference, policy, and research documentation. Several hundred sources of information include UN agencies, governments, international and nongovernmental organizations, scientific and academic institutions, and the media.

Collecting and Interpreting Assessment Information

The UN Resident Coordinator and the UNDMT ensure that assessment and training activities are coordinated, well organized, and carefully planned. To obtain cross-country information that is consistent and comparable, only necessary disaster data is collected, with emphasis on avoiding duplication. There is also a special effort to focus the assessment on determining how to support local coping mechanisms and recovery processes and go beyond the simple listing of needs. The assessment must explicitly consider implementation means and capacities, and the possibilities of obtaining needed supplies and services locally. An initial assessment is completed rapidly in the disaster areas to identify immediate needs and criteria to be used in the detailed follow-up assessment. Moreover, all communities in the affected areas are covered systematically, and differences among areas and distinct population groups are identified. Information is shared as effectively as possible among all concerned parties, and the greatest possible consensus achieved among the national and local authorities, the donor community, and operational agencies concerning the situation, assistance requirements, and proposed interventions (UNDMTP, 2006).

A multi-sectoral approach to the assessment in which agencies and sectoral entities collaborate and agree on findings and response strategies is important. Sectoral assessments are undertaken independently and in isolation from each other and thus are likely to result in duplication of effort, and gaps in coverage and information. The training teams usually synthesize an overall assessment, reconcile different viewpoints, and determine intersectoral priorities. Similarly, consensus is pursued among national and local authorities, the donor community, and operational agencies. The UNDMT follows the objectives, assessments procedures, and standards for planning and providing assistance that have been defined by the various UN agencies in their respective areas of competence. Government agencies then apply the standards established by the UNDMT in their requests for international assistance. The UNDMT maintains close contacts with all embassies, bilateral agencies, and other institutions involved in making or evaluating assessments. Assessment information is analyzed carefully to ensure consistency and accuracy and to avoid possible biases and exaggeration, either erring on the safe side or underplaying needs. National or international vested interests and political pressures are watched for and resisted. Information provided from various sources is likely to vary in quality and precision, and is evaluated in terms of the experience and proven competence of the reporting organizations and individuals. Where necessary, information is cross-checked against other reports and available baseline data on the area.

The Importance of Coordination and Information

Coordination is critically important in emergency assistance operations. Lives are usually at risk, logistic and other resources are likely to be limited, and decisions are often made quickly. There are many possibilities for duplicating effort, wasting resources, and leaving gaps in geographic coverage. Timely, reliable information is crucial to planning and implementing emergency and postdisaster assistance operations, and to mobilizing national and international resources. The regular dissemination of relevant information is a precondition for effective coordination and cooperation at national and local levels among sectors and government, operational agencies, and donors.

Verifiable information must be collected, analyzed, interpreted, and used to make informed planning and operational management decisions. Detailed, up-to-date information is required about the impending crisis. The progress and status of assistance operations must be monitored, as well as the resources both on hand and expected. Similar information in summary form is necessary to support efforts to mobilize and direct the allocation of resources and encourage operational coordination. This includes identifying information gaps and unmet needs for assistance.

Effective management of national level coordination, information, and training is essential, and in the first instance, the responsibility of the national authorities. In many cases constraints to the effective management of coordination and information must be anticipated and minimized in the training phase at the local, national, and international levels by the UNDMT as part of operational preparedness and during response to disasters.

Disaster Preparedness Training at the National Level in the United States

The Bush administration began the process of coordination with the release of the National Strategy for Homeland Security. The strategy made several critical recommendations with regard to improving training, networking, and coordination

(Bush, 2002). First, the administration recommended increased collaboration and coordination in law enforcement and prevention, emergency response and recovery, and policy development and implementation. Second, the strategy promoted the use of the citizen corps to disseminate information on disaster preparedness techniques and train volunteer first responders. Other volunteer programs included training and would assist police departments, medical assistance programs, and counterterrorism surveillance. Third, the private sector was encouraged to conduct risk assessments to identify threats, vulnerabilities, and critical deficiencies in the national infrastructure. These assessments would support corporate governance and protect economic assets. Fourth, the president recommended the creation of state homeland security task forces to act as coordinating bodies and intermediaries between the federal government antiterrorism task forces in each federal judicial district and local first responders (CFR, 2002).

In practice, most of this coordination remains to be developed. Information sharing across levels of government is sporadic at best. State and local police officials have little access to the federal government's antiterrorism watch lists. Most of the border security effort remains focused on airline security, although recent initiatives have increased attention on cargo security (CFR, 2002). First responders have received little training for chemical and biological emergencies. In addition, much of the funding promised to first responders in the FY 2003 homeland security budget request was delayed by congressional failure to pass the budget. Most of America's energy infrastructure remains unprotected from terrorist attack. Moreover, legal barriers hinder the development of public–private partnerships to remedy many of these problems. Questions of anti-trust conflicts, proprietary information security under the Freedom of Information Act, and corporate liability all inhibit more extensive public–private collaboration.

At the local level, the U.S. disaster preparedness landscape includes 87,000 local governments that are mostly small, with volunteer officials among the 500,000 elected nationwide. More than 650,000 law enforcement officers, 1.1 million firefighters (75 percent volunteers), and 500,000 emergency medical personnel are first responders, who along with citizens are caught in disasters as victims or helpers. The private sector owns 85 percent of the infrastructure (e.g., 87,000 food processing plants, 6,000 chemical plants and 2,500 power plants) and there are thousands of nonprofits (Cigler, 2005).

Natural disasters such as floods, hurricanes, tornadoes, wildfires, drought, earthquakes, etc. lead to the greatest loss of lives and property in a typical year. After September 11, emergency managers have struggled to achieve a balance between the ever present threat of natural disasters and the need to protect and prepare for domestic terrorism and the likelihood of mass casualties. Katrina reminded emergency managers and policy makers that natural disasters can have catastrophic impact, and moreover that mitigation is the heart of emergency management and training is an integral part of mitigation. Mitigation minimizes loss of lives and property. For the Federal Emergency Management Agency (FEMA), mitigation has been about risk awareness; mapping flood-prone areas, relocating homes and sometimes communities away from harm, enforcing building codes for withstanding earthquakes and high winds, etc. The role of training in achieving these initiatives is essential. Unfortunately, FEMA's mitigation funding was reduced and first responders have complained that preparedness training has become more geared toward terrorist emergencies, at the expense of training for natural disasters. It appeared that the Department of Homeland Security (DHS) planned for FEMA to be a "response" wing of DHS through elimination of the directorate for emergency preparedness and response. However, it should be noted that the reorganization of FEMA in May of 2006 removed FEMA from DHS completely and set it up as an independent authority or agency (FEMA, 2006). Also, by June of 2006 a DHS undersecretary for preparedness was appointed to focus on all disaster types and to facilitate relevant preparedness training. DHS common operating procedures were updated, standardized, and validated (Newman, 2006). This approach has prompted some disaster management experts to suggest that adequate training and attention to mitigating natural disasters is unlikely because this is now viewed as a state or local role, despite the problems of limited capacity at these levels of government. Moreover, there are serious concerns about who will pay to prevent disasters with national economic implications and significant loss of life and prepare citizens for their roles as victims and helpers (Cigler, 2005).

Disaster Preparedness Training by FEMA

Disaster Field Training Opportunities

The quality of FEMA's response and recovery efforts is directly linked to knowledge and skills possessed by staff working at disaster sites. Keeping a well-trained field workforce is a great challenge. New disaster workers may be hired from the local community each time there is a disaster but most would have little or no disaster training. FEMA disaster employees may not have worked in months and many would not be current on disaster programs and policies that often vary from disaster to disaster. In catastrophic disasters, permanent full-time employees are sometimes deployed to work disaster assignments for which they have not been trained previously. These challenges create the need to provide quality on-site disaster training. The Emergency Management Institute (EMI) created the Disaster Field Training Operation (DFTO) to meet these field-training requirements. The mission of the DFTO is to

- Provide a professional training resource to ensure that all training requirements in the field are identified and met.
- Ensure that disaster staff has the skills and knowledge needed to provide effective and efficient services.
- Enhance the professional expertise of disaster staff to ensure they are prepared for future deployments (FEMA, 2006).

The DFTO is not intended to replace ongoing training that is conducted by FEMA or state and local governments. The DFTO is meant to provide on-site training opportunities to assist field staff in performing their job functions (FEMA, 2006).

EMI Courses

FEMA, through its courses and programs of the EMI serves as the national hub for the development and delivery of emergency management training to enhance the capabilities of federal, state, local, and tribal government officials; volunteer organizations; and the public and private sectors to minimize the impact of disasters on the American public. EMI curricula are structured to meet the needs of this diverse audience with an emphasis on how the various elements work together in emergencies to save lives and protect property. Instruction focuses on the four phases of emergency management: mitigation, preparedness, response, and recovery. EMI develops courses and administers resident and nonresident training programs in areas such as natural hazards (earthquakes, hurricanes, floods, dam safety), technological hazards (hazardous materials, terrorism, radiological incidents, chemical stockpile emergency preparedness), professional development, leadership, instructional methodology, exercise design and evaluation, information technology, public information, integrated emergency management, and train-the-trainers. Nonresident programs are sponsored by EMI and conducted by state emergency management agencies under cooperative agreements with FEMA (FEMA, 2005).

FEMA Higher Education Project

One of the goals of FEMA is to encourage and support the inclusion of emergency management-related training and education in colleges and universities across the United States. In the future, more and more emergency managers in government as well as in business and industry are expected to come to the job with a college education that includes courses in disaster/hazard-related topics.

To further this end of FEMA, the EMI, located in Emmitsburg, Maryland, focuses on skills-based training for existing emergency management personnel and the development of projects that promote college-based emergency management education for future emergency managers. Moreover, EMI devotes staff and time to the task of working with academics to develop and promote emergency management-related college courses.

EMI also instituted a higher education internship. Students enrolled at emergency management degree granting schools can intern at EMI for several weeks to several months under the sponsorship of their academic department. Roundtrip travel will be reimbursed; dorm-style housing will be provided, and a suitable assignment will be negotiated with the student and his or her faculty representative. No salary will be paid and interns are responsible for all their expenses, including meals. The student's school must agree to award credit hours (to be negotiated) for the internship and students will be evaluated on their performance (FEMA, 2005).

EMI compiled a list of college course syllabi and outlines of existing emergency management-related courses taught in academia. Over 70 course outlines or syllabi are now included in this compilation, which is available free of charge to any academic wishing to review the contents of an emergency management-related course. EMI also developed its own outline of a potential emergency management curriculum consisting of classroom-based, upper division (junior/senior), baccalaureate-level courses. EMI is now working with a variety of colleges and universities to develop emergency management curricula. The certificate program in Disaster Preparedness and Emergency Management (DPEM) at the University of Hawaii-West Oahu (UHWO) offers an emergency management curriculum (FEMA, 2005).

UHWO Certificate in Disaster Preparedness and Emergency Management

The University of Hawaii-West Oahu's Certificate in Disaster Preparedness and Emergency Management is designed to provide disaster preparedness and emergency management practitioners with a broad range of administrative skills and knowledge. The certificate can be self-standing or may be used as part of the bachelor of arts degree in public administration (BAPA) for those specializing in general public administration or justice administration.

Courses required for the certificate are

- PubAd 411 Emergency Management and Disaster Preparedness
- PubAd 460 Environmental Policy, Planning, and Administration
- PubAd 461 Social Dimensions of Disaster Response
- PubAd 462 Disaster Recovery and Business Continuation
- PubAd 463 Disaster Recovery and Hazard Mitigation
- PubAd 464 Terrorism and Emergency Management

The University of Hawaii-West Oahu is granted accreditation by the Western Association of Schools and Colleges (WASC) (FEMA, 2005).

Other training-related collaborations initiated between the U.S. Department of Homeland Security (DHS) and the University of Hawaii (UH) include a special grant from DHS's Office of Domestic Preparedness. In October 2004, the Office for Domestic Preparedness' Homeland Security Grant Program awarded the Department of Molecular Biosciences and Bioengineering in UH Manoa's College of Tropical Agriculture and Human Resources (CTAHR) a two-year, $300,000 grant. The grant is part of a $22,286,000 federal award the state received to enhance its ability to prevent, deter, respond to, and recover from threats and incidents of terrorism (UH News, 2004). Qiang Li, professor in the department and head of the environmental biochemistry laboratory, used the funds to purchase a liquid chromatograph-mass spectrometer (LC-MS) to enhance his laboratory's capability to identify unknown and threat chemicals present in environmental samples. He assured that, "Not only will we strengthen our research, we become part of the statewide homeland security infrastructure safeguarding Hawaii people and environment" (UH News, 2004). The Office for Domestic Preparedness (ODP) is the principal component of the Department of Homeland Security responsible for preparing the United States for acts of terrorism. In carrying out its mission, ODP is responsible for providing training, funds for the purchase of equipment, support for the planning and execution of field exercises, and technical and other assistance to states and local jurisdictions to prevent, respond to, and recover from acts of terrorism.

Training Programs in the State of Hawaii

The Hawaii State Civil Defense Agency (HSCDA) conducts and coordinates several ongoing training, exercises, and drills relevant to man-made and natural disasters in Hawaii. These include but are not limited to the following (HSCDA, 2006):

- FEMA EMI Courses:

To take a course at EMI, applicants must meet the selection criteria and prerequisites specified for each course. Participants may not take the same course more than once.

- Homeland Security Exercise and Evaluation Program:

The Homeland Security Exercise and Evaluation Program (HSEEP) includes both doctrine and policy for designing, developing, conducting, and evaluating exercises. HSEEP is a threat- and performance-based exercise program that includes a cycle, mix, and range of exercise activities of varying degrees of complexity and interaction.

- FEMA Independent Study Program: IS-800 National Response Plan (NRP), An Introduction

This course introduces you to the NRP, including the concept of operations upon which the plan is built, roles and responsibilities of the key players, and the organizational structures used to manage these resources. The NRP provides a framework to ensure that we can all work together when our nation is threatened.

- FEMA Independent Study Program: IS-22 Are You Ready? An In-depth Guide to Citizen Preparedness

"Are You Ready? An In-Depth Guide to Citizen Preparedness" has been designed to help the citizens of this nation learn how to protect themselves and their families against all types of hazards. It can be used as a reference source or as a step-by-step manual. The focus of the content is on how to develop, practice, and maintain emergency plans that reflect what must be done before, during, and after a disaster to protect people and their property. Also included is information on how to assemble a disaster supplies kit that contains the food, water, and other supplies in sufficient quantity for individuals and their families to survive.

- National Incident Management System (NIMS), An Introduction IS 700 (EMAC)

Provided as a public service by EMAC International, LLC, this Web-based independent study course introduces NIMS and takes approximately three hours to complete. It explains the purpose, principles, key components, and benefits of NIMS. Content, media, and images are provided by FEMA. You will have an opportunity to complete a FEMA administered online post-test upon the completion of this course.

- Makani Pahili 2006 Exercise Plan

Makani Pahili 2006 is a hurricane exercise scheduled over a two week period. During the week of May 15–19, 2006, the exercise focuses on pre-landfall preparedness activities, weather monitoring, testing communications, and addressing response and recovery actions following a catastrophic event. From May 22 to 26, 2006, exercise activities center on emergency management operations through workshops, roundtable discussion, and a tabletop exercise. The hurricane EXPLAN serves as a planning tool and guide for participating agencies.

An example of the HSCD local training schedule is provided below:

- Emergency Management Planning
- Emergency Medical Services Operations and Planning for WMD PER-211
- Emergency Response to Domestic Biological Incidents PER-220
- Hazardous Materials Technician Chemistry—2006
- Hazardous Materials Technician Refresher, Hawaii County
- Hazardous Materials Technician Tactics—2006
- Incident Response to Terrorist Bombings—Awareness
- Incident Response to Terrorist Bombings—Technician
- National Incident Management System (NIMS)
- Public Safety Response-Sampling Techniques & Guidelines
- Public Works: Preparing for & Responding to Terrorism/WMD
- WMD Incident Command Training Course/WMD Hands on Training Course

- WMD Radiological/Nuclear Awareness
- WMD Technical Emergency Response/Incident Command
- WMD: Defensive Operations for Emergency Responders
- WMD: Radiological/Nuclear Course for Hazmat Technicians

Emergency Preparedness and Response to Environmental Disasters in Hawaii

The State of Hawaii is required to be prepared to respond to natural and man-made disasters. As the only island state located in the Pacific Ocean, Hawaii is unique among the states in the United States to be prepared for a wide-range of natural disasters including tsunamis, volcanoes, hurricanes, earthquakes, floods, landslides, and brush and forest fires, all of which adversely impact the environment. Hawaii is challenged by man-made and technological disasters, which involve chemical spills, nuclear radiation, and transportation accidents (e.g., plane and ship crashes, etc.). Hawaii also needs to prepare for non-accidental man-made environmental disasters such as bioterrorism.

The State of Hawaii coordinates its activities relative to environmental preparedness in response to environmental disasters with National Center for Environmental Health and Health Studies Branch (HSB). The Health Studies Branch of the Division of Environmental Hazards and Health Effects is responsible for investigating the health effects associated with human exposure to environmental hazards, developing and evaluating strategies for preventing people's exposure to environmental hazards, and for minimizing the effect of such exposures when they do occur (NCEH, 2004). To accomplish this mission, the HSB identifies potential threats to health, responds rapidly to emergencies, recommends ways of reducing people's risk, and collaborates with local, state, national, and international governments and agencies. The HSB coordinated its activities with the State of Hawaii in assisting communities in Kauai and Oahu after Hurricane Iniki in 1992. The HSB sent response teams of experts to help government agencies on Kauai and Oahu to investigate the health consequences and provided epidemiologic and technical assistance. FEMA also coordinated its activities with HSB, the State of Hawaii, and county agencies in Kauai and Oahu to assess the health risks of the affected communities during Hurricane Iniki and subsequent natural disasters in Hawaii (NCEH, 2004).

The National Environmental Policy Act of 1969 (NEPA), the Council on Environmental Quality (CEQ) regulations implementing NEPA (40 CFR Parts 1500 through 1508), and FEMA regulations for NEPA compliance (44 CFR Part 10) are described. These laws, regulations, and statutes direct FEMA and other federal agencies to fully understand, and take into consideration during decision-making, the environmental consequences of proposed federal actions (projects) (FEMA, 2004).

The Oahu Civil Defense Agency (OCDA) is a department in the City and County of Honolulu and functions as the primary government agency for disaster response. The mayor acts as the CEO of OCDA. The mayor also has the power to declare a disaster. Disasters are county specific. Each county (i.e., Honolulu, Maui, Kauai, and Hawaii) individually determines what constitutes a disaster. For example, the island of Hawaii may have volcano eruptions listed as a natural disaster, whereas Honolulu would not. Disaster descriptions can also be localized to certain areas within a county and designated to the Local Emergency Planning Committee (LEPC), which is part of the city and county of Honolulu, as opposed to the State's Emergency Response Commission, which oversees the Hawaii State Civil Defense System. The State's primary responsibility is to provide leadership in rapid assistance during disasters with a full range of resources and effective partnerships. To advance this responsibility the State of Hawaii hosted leaders from the public and private sectors to meet and develop innovative response strategies at the Inaugural Asia-Pacific Homeland Security Summit in Honolulu in November 2003 (HSCDA, 2002).

There are also federal requirements for each state to establish a community emergency response plan and the primary responsibility for compliance for the city of Honolulu is through the OCDA and its Emergency Operations Plan (OCDA, 1997). The mayor must regularly report on the progress of various aspects of respective agencies such as the Environmental Protection Agency (EPA) and Occupational Safety and Health Agency (OSHA). Both OSHA and EPA have regulations to help protect workers with hazardous waste and emergency operations. The LEPC must develop a community emergency response plan (contingency plan) that contains emergency response methods and procedures to be followed by facility owners, police, hospitals, local emergency responders, and emergency medical personnel. The EPA generates these requirements and ensures that states implement emergency response planning programs. It should be noted that the State of Hawaii's Department of Labor and Industrial Relations is one of only 25 states to have an emergency response plan approved by OSHA (OCDA, 1997).

In May 2002, FEMA conducted a full-scale HAZMAT field exercise at Campbell Industrial Park to test Honolulu's Hazardous Materials Response Plan. This exercise named "Operation Kalaeloa," involved over 2,000 participants including 13 of 18 Oahu hospitals and was a successful test of Hawaii's emergency response procedures and system (Carter, 2002). Queen's Medical Center (QMC), the largest and oldest hospital and main trauma center in Hawaii, is instrumental in coordination of disaster response and plays an active role on Honolulu's Disaster Committee (Prizzia, 2004). QMC has developed a comprehensive emergency safety manual that contains detailed procedures for every unit of the hospital and for each kind of emergency. At the present time, employees must respond to a monthly hospitalwide drill that uses a randomly selected emergency code. Internally, the hospital's emergency preparedness plan is activated and everything usually goes as planned. The trauma center is prepared for the victims, and patients receive treatment as soon as they arrive. The results of the drills are reviewed by subcommittees and incorporated into the emergency preparedness recommendations they make to the board of trustees.

From an overall assessment by the author, the major factors contributing to QMC's excellent track record when handling emergencies can be identified as

- Continuous evaluation and improvement of the Emergency Preparedness Safety Manual
- High priority QMC places on continuous disaster preparedness training for all of its employees
- Competency of staff, and especially the Trauma Services Unit
- Highly effective coordination QMC has developed with outside agencies (QMC, 1999)

In 2002, the State of Hawaii developed the Hawaii State Multi-Hazard Mitigation Plan to address Hawaii's experience with and continued vulnerability to a wide range of climatic, hydrological, seismic, and geological hazards. This plan represents a long-term strategy for reducing the risks of natural disasters and was developed in response to the 2000 Disaster and Hazard Mitigation Planning Act, which established state and local hazard mitigation planning in accordance with federal standards required by FEMA (HSCDA, 2002).

Recognizing the importance of preparing citizens for a wide range of potential disasters at the community level, FEMA expanded training programs for the Community Emergency Response Team (CERT) from primarily fire to medical and eventually all hazards, natural and man-made. According to the OCDA Operations and Planning Director, many teams of Hawaii residents have participated in the various CERT training sessions since its beginning in 1997. More importantly, neighborhoods that have CERT-trained teams have not only been made more aware of how to respond to disaster but have been more effective and efficient in their response to actual emergencies (FEMA, 1999a). Communities that actively participate in the CERT and FEMA's Project Impact are provided assistance to develop strategies to become more disaster-resistant. The overall strategy involves coordination and a local partnership of government and business to reduce the human and financial costs of disasters. In Hawaii, the county of Maui and Hawaii county were selected by FEMA's Project Impact and are part of a growing list of specially designated "disaster-resistant communities" (WHT, 2001).

The Maui Civil Defense Agency (MCDA) has responsibility for administering and operating the various local, state, and federal civil defense programs for the county. In April 1999, FEMA welcomed the county of Maui to the agency's Project Impact initiative, a national effort to change the way America deals with disasters. The program encourages communities to come together, assess their vulnerabilities, and implement strategies to prevent or limit damage before disasters occur. Three common-sense principles are the basis of Project Impact; mitigation at the local-community level, participation by the private sector, and long-term preventive measures. FEMA also coordinates the federal response to environmental related disasters and provides communities, businesses, and individuals with technical support (MCDA, 2005).

The State Department of Health and the Hazardous Waste Branch coordinate with the Solid Waste Branch to protect Hawaii's lands from pollutants that endanger people and the environment prior to environmental related disasters. Through the coordination of training of personnel from these three agencies and with environmental laws and regulations, the state ensures the environmentally sound and economically cost-effective management of all solid and hazardous waste generated within the state through the promotion of pollution prevention and waste minimization activities and prevention of release of hazardous substances, pollutants, or contaminants into the environment (HSCDA, 2002).

Coordination Seminars

In August of 1999, FEMA representatives along with other federal agencies met with their Hawaii state counterparts to prepare and coordinate for any upcoming disasters. The nearness of Hurricane Eugene and Dora to Hawaii during the August seminar brought a sense of urgency and importance to the Regional Interagency Steering Committee (RISC) meeting. This meeting was designed to foster partnerships among all agencies and to coordinate interagency intergovernmental planning and response to disasters. As some predictions indicated a heavy hurricane season for the United States, and the two large systems of Eugene and Dora already made their presence known in the mid-Pacific, special emphasis was placed on hurricane preparedness and response.

"The two recent hurricanes have heightened our preparedness efforts," said Michael Lowder, Region IX Director of Response and Recovery. "We are using this meeting to provide a disaster preparedness forum to enhance the federal, state and local governments' ability to work in consent, so we are all on the same page when it comes to responding to disasters" (FEMA, 1999b).

Among the participants were representatives from FEMA and their state partner Hawaii State Defense who worked through scenarios in disaster preparation, response, and recovery. Other attending agencies included U.S. Army Corps of Engineers, Federal Aviation Administration, Coast Guard, U.S. Navy, and U.S. Army, along with the state and federal departments of transportation, health, commerce, agriculture, defense, public safety, highways, and numerous other state–federal counterparts. Also attending were some representatives from Kauai, Oahu, and Maui county civil defense agencies.

"By bringing all the entities together before a possible disaster occurs, critical working relationships and response planning will already be established," said Roy Price, Director of Hawaii State Civil Defense. "We all have memories of Hurricane

Iniki and the devastation such a force can bring with disasters, it's not a question of if, it's a question of when it will happen. Through seminars such as this, we will be prepared" (FEMA, 1999b).

Survey of Emergency Managers on Role of Training

The role of training in emergency management in Hawaii is of special importance. The impact of training on emergency management is a topic of great concern during all phases of a disaster, but is particularly critical during the final phase of disaster preparedness and the initial phase of disaster response. Training helps emergency managers to prepare and respond to disasters, especially in the immediate pre-impact and post-impact stage of a disaster. To obtain firsthand data on the role of training during the critical phase of final disaster preparedness and initial disaster response, a sample of 50 emergency managers, which represents about 20 percent of the emergency managers in the State of Hawaii, were surveyed during the months of December 2005 and January 2006. The emergency managers were contacted by e-mail and telephone and asked the following two questions:

- Do you feel that the existing disaster and emergency training is adequate for a major natural or man-made disaster?
- In your opinion, how best might the training be improved?

Results of the Survey
Adequacy of Training

In response to the question regarding the adequacy of existing disaster and emergency training among community, local, county, state, and federal agencies, to meet the challenge of major natural and man-made disasters, over 90 percent of the Hawaii emergency managers responded that they were adequately prepared. The main reasons given by respondents for the adequacy of training in Hawaii included the following:

- The city and county of Honolulu, in cooperation with the HPD, HFD, and Civil Defense, is ready and prepared to handle future man-made and natural disasters. Each organization has a specific plan in place to handle various events and are all interlaced for maximum efficiency. In addition, all staff go through department-specific training regularly, assuring that all procedures are updated with personnel. During the practical portion of the training, a scenario involving multiple factors (i.e., bombing, hazmat, etc.) must be handled. An Incident Command System is established and each agency follows through with its role.

- I do feel that Hawaii is prepared through existing training for a natural disaster. The problem is no one knows the strength of a natural disaster and the potential damage. People too often equate a major disaster with lack of training. A disaster that results in billions of dollar damage does not mean the state was not prepared.

- Current training in our division is adequate. Common and critical tasks are identified and capabilities are tested based on minimum acceptable performance standards. Staff cross-training is encouraged and, in some cases, required.

- The Honolulu Police Department takes their training very seriously especially after the 9/11 attacks that changed the way we live forever. Ever since then, training has been full-speed ahead and they are always looking for more training, whether it may be here or on the mainland with other emergency type organizations. He feels department personnel are well-trained and continuously train annually in all types of hazards. We work alongside with EMS and the military constantly and feed off each other.

- Training is important but just one portion of preparedness. Training leads to planning and then you must exercise the plans to ensure your plans work appropriately. Training is where you learn the methodology and are given the tools to develop your plans. But only by conducting field exercises do you ensure that your plans will work as you have designed them, which means you learned and understood the training.

- Currently first and second line responder training at the city and county of Honolulu is at a proficiency level to meet the response needs of those natural, human-caused, and technological disasters as identified by our current hazard analysis. Since 1997, the city and county of Honolulu has undertaken a major federally funded and supported effort to ensure that our city responders are trained and equipped to deal with a terrorist event involving a weapon of mass destruction. These efforts continue today supported by the Department of Homeland Security and the State Department of Justice.

- We have a very good system of training for disaster on Maui and in Hawaii for that matter for dealing with such emergencies and disasters. There is a good combination of preparedness training and procedures including district disaster plans to handle events ranging from an airplane crash to a hurricane to a terrorist attack. I guess the only way we will really know if the training is adequate is when we have a real attack. But we are probably as ready as can be. We have several training sessions each year dealing with a variety of scenarios that include all of the agencies who respond to such events including the volunteer organizations. These training events range from tabletop decision-making exercises for command personnel to full-blown exercises involving all first responder personnel. We have even had training on chemical or biological incidents using volunteers as victims to practice the distribution of medication needed in such an incident.

An experienced high-ranking emergency manager at the Honolulu Police Department responsible for the Bike Emergency Response Team gave a lengthy response that included the following important points:

■ This structure provides versatility to the response to natural or man-made disasters and at the same time provides for training from one large bike team with 52 police officers, or can be broken up into two platoons, 25 officers each, or even down to the basic unit of one sergeant and five police officers.

■ Training is specific to needs, so training is often done in the following areas: crowd control, response to civil disturbances, riot control, police mountain bike tactics, bike skills, first aid, or any other relevant training as needed.

■ The versatility that a bike emergency response team gives to law enforcement is only limited by the time and distance to the event. Officers are trained to ride 25 miles and can bring with them food and water to sustain themselves in an area of up to 24 hours without assistance.

■ One primary issue is that the officers assigned to the Bike Emergency Response Team are not assigned on a full-time basis. As such, training is on a limited basis, sometimes once a month or quarter. Due to personnel staffing issues, at times, overtime must be paid, which is difficult to do in fiscally challenging times.

■ Training, time, and money are always a challenge in any large organization and the Bike Emergency Response Team faces the same challenges.

Another high-ranking emergency manager with over 20 years experience in dealing with disaster training for tsunamis provided special insights on how Hawaii prepares for different kinds of tsunami threats.

■ There are two different kinds of tsunami threat. By far the most common and historically the most damaging is a tsunami from across the ocean. For these, we are confident that we can provide three hours' warning. The scarier (but rarer) threat is a tsunami generated within the Hawaiian Islands. The tsunami from a Big Island earthquake off the Kona Coast would reach Kailua-Kona in seven or eights minutes, South Maui in 20 minutes, and Honolulu in half-an-hour. Right now it would take us five or six minutes to issue a local tsunami warning, but we expect to cut that time down to two minutes in about a year.

■ So there are two distinctly different emergency plans, one for a distant tsunami, and one for a local tsunami. There is always room for improvement, but I think the plans are pretty good. Good plans alone are not enough, of course, so we have to train. Training exercises are twice a year and involve everyone in the warning and postdisaster response communities: the Pacific Tsunami Warning Center, state and county Civil Defense Agencies, the police, the Red Cross, the Civil Air Patrol, HI Department of Education, HI Department of Health, the Army Corps of Engineers, the Coast Guard, etc. All that is missing is the final link involving the public and in a practice evacuation. The arguments against going all the way have been predictable: an evacuation drill would scare off tourists; it would temporarily disrupt the economy, etc. These arguments have pretty much fizzled out since the December tsunami in the Indian Ocean, so I expect our next exercise will involve a limited practice evacuation of selected communities.

■ For a distant tsunami, the warning and evacuation plans are pretty good. We even have reason to hope that the public will behave correctly. Back in 1994, the last coastal evacuation, the public did very well (except for 40 surfers on the north shore). That was a long time ago, however, so practice evacuations would be a good idea.

■ During our last training for a local tsunami, exercises were designed to fit in with the monthly siren tests. There were a few minor problems, mainly involving communications, but we are fixing them. As we have never actually issued an urgent local tsunami warning we cannot be sure that we have anticipated every problem, but we keep tweaking the plans. For a local tsunami warning by far the greatest need now is to get the public more involved. They have to learn that unlike the usual tsunami warning, an urgent local tsunami warning means "Get moving immediately." To get that message across may require a publicity blitz.

Finally, a high-ranking emergency manager with military, civilian, and international experience responded to the question on adequacy of training for disaster as follows:

■ It is critical to both recognize and to articulate what category of disasters that you are referring to. I would prefer you start with stating whether this is either a conventional disaster or a catastrophic one, and secondly whether this is an international or domestic one. Personally, I have only been involved in large-scale disasters related to international war and conflict, never a domestic conventional disaster, so please accept my apologies upfront ... Many of the current domestic problems recently revealed have been issues also seen for years in the international humanitarian and disaster relief community where these concerns have been extensively studied, researched, and often solved ... unfortunately, this information has not always been transmitted well or digested by domestic disaster managers. Conventional disasters in the United States have been handled quite well overall. The response management approach has been protocol driven for the most part. If things occur that are not covered in the response protocols then the system freezes ... such as the response to Katrina when a hurricane became a public health emergency (which more often than not involves evacuation). U.S. disasters rarely have more than 40 casualties (before Oklahoma City), are rarely large scale, or rarely involve mass evacuation.

In both Okalahoma City and 9/11, secondary disasters occurred because there were too many health care providers ... in Oklahoma City there were 16 physicians for every victim and many created secondary medical problems because they were not disaster trained ... (e.g., caused wound care complications). Additionally, we have not had an epidemic in the United States in over 100 years nor do we have the necessary medical and public health training to deal with one.

■ Domestic disasters are for the most part responded to well in the United States However, with large-scale disasters ... Clearly, the United States and other countries are not adequately trained or managed.

Improving Training

In response to the question regarding how training might be improved, 93 percent of emergency managers responded that training, although adequate, could be improved and it is the most important means of improving coordination. All aspects of training were cited by emergency managers including increased frequency, increased funding for replacement emergency personnel while those in place are in training, more drills, more "hands-on" training, especially in the areas of tracking and enforcement. Typical responses from emergency managers on improving training included the following:

■ I believe that we can do more to educate the public about how to become more disaster prepared. As a county, we do train our responders to deal with emergencies. My thoughts are that we can always train more frequently. The more we practice/train, the better prepared we are to respond.

■ Improvement needed in the area of tracking and enforcement.

■ All training can be improved. I feel that additional drills are necessary.

■ Training can always be improved. The training given at Queen's Medical Center is adequate for natural disasters, and most of man-made disasters. Problem is: severity of the disaster will affect the organization's ability to respond. The best way to improve training is to ensure everyone participates in the drills. Also, currently, most training for hospital staff is "nonspecific." To better prepare our hospital staff, there needs to be more training in the areas of specialized triage and treatment of disaster victims.

■ As with any type of training, improvements can always be made. During a disaster, emergency personnel are obviously under intense stress. In these times, important information is relayed between agencies and is often lost or distorted. If staff were better trained to handle stressful situations, the efficiency of all agencies would increase.

■ As for improvements on all agencies, they are well-trained. As for our civil defense volunteers, we are trained monthly on all types of disasters.

■ I feel that the training which is provided is adequate. Of course, there is always the need for improvement and changes based on experiences of others and lessons learned in other disasters. Training is like muscle memory, but based on operating budgets not only in Hawaii but also nationwide, training can be sporadic.

■ Current training programs are well-supported and made available under most circumstances free of charge to county and state municipalities. Speaking for the agency I see no areas that currently need improvement.

■ Hurricane Katrina gave testimony that existing disaster/emergency plans failed due to surge capacity, lack of emergency equipment and life support systems, communication equipment failure, not being prepared for full evacuation, etc. Not because of training. We need to reexamine our hospital's preparedness for natural or man-made disasters with both training and emergency preparedness plans. I have recommended to our Hospital Executive Committee (HEC) for a more intensified training program devoted to emergency management and improving emergency equipment based on our recent external disaster drill.

Conclusion and Recommendations

The state of Hawaii seems prepared to respond to environmental related natural and man-made disasters in general. As the only island state located in the Pacific Ocean, Hawaii continues to require emergency management capability to respond to a wide range of natural disasters. Hawaii's emergency management and intergovernmental agency coordination at the federal, state, county, and even community level appear to be relatively effective in response to natural disasters such as tsunamis, hurricanes, earthquakes, and flooding. The effectiveness of disaster response coordination is supported and enhanced by environmentally relevant FEMA and other training programs and advanced technology that includes state-of-the-art warning systems at disaster centers and research facilities throughout the state. Interagency and inter-island disaster response training drills have also been extended to nongovernmental organizations including medical and other community facilities throughout the Hawaiian Islands to enhance cooperation and communication to minimize environmental damage at the point of impact during actual disasters.

Based on the research undertaken, the state of Hawaii should continue to maintain as a high priority the effectiveness of disaster preparedness training programs and technologically advanced disaster warning systems to minimize environmental damage. Existing disaster drills designed to improve communication and coordination during actual disasters should be ongoing and enhanced with the assistance of FEMA and other relevant environmental government agencies and nongovernment organizations. Finally, efforts to establish, maintain, and strengthen coordination and cooperation among emergency managers at the state, federal, county, and community level before, during, and after disasters should be common practice.

References

Blanchand, W.B., FEMA Emergency Management Higher Education Project. Emergency Management Institute, Emmitsburg, M.D., 2005, pp. 44–65.

Bush, G.W., *National Strategy for Homeland Security*, Washington, DC: White House, Office of Homeland Security, 2002, pp. 11–14, www.whitehouse.gov/homeland/book/nat_strat_hls.

Carter, D., *Oahu Civil Defense Agency Bulletin*, Vol. 22, March 1, 2002.

Cigler, B.A., Who's in charge: The paradox of emergency management, *PA Times*, Vol. 28, No. 5, 2005, pp. 7, 10.

Common Country Assessment (CCA), Common country programming, retrieved May 26, 2006 from the World Wide Web: http://222.undg.org.

Council on Foreign Relations (CFR), America–Still unprepared, still in danger. Report of an independent task force sponsored by the Council on Foreign Relations, Gary Hart and Warren B. Rudman, Co-Chairs, Stephen E. Flynn, Project Director, Washington, DC: CFR, 2002. www.cfr.org/pdf/Homeland_TF.

Federal Emergency Management Agency (FEMA), 2006, http://training.fema.gov/EMI-Web/Programs.

FEMA, Region IX, Environmental Information, Washington, DC, October 2004.

FEMA, Federal Response Plan, 9230, 1-PL., April, retrieved August 8, 1999a from the World Wide Web: http://www.fema.gov/r-n-r/frp.

FEMA, Region IX, Planning for Disasters in Hawaii, Washington, DC, August 1999b.

Hawaii State Civil Defense Agency, FEMA EMI Courses: http://www.training.fema.gov/emiweb, 2006.

Hawaii State Civil Defense Agency Bulletin, November 20, 2002, p. 2.

Maui Civil Defense Agency (MCDA), Local Hurricane: Mitigation Activities on Maui's Maui County, Kihei, Hawaii, 2005.

National Center for Environmental Health (NCEH), Prevention Strategies Related to Environmental Hazards and Disasters, Health Studies Branch, Atlanta, Georgia, 2004.

Newman, P., National Homeland Security Joint and Intergovernmental Education and Training Initiatives, panel presentation, Emergency Management and Homeland Security/Defense Higher Education Conference, National Emergency Training Center, Emergency Management Institute, June 5–8, 2006.

Oahu Civil Defense Agency (OCDA), Emergency Operations Plan, Honolulu: City and County of Honolulu, 1997.

Prizzia, R., Emergency management and disaster response in Hawaii: The role of medical centers and the media, *Journal of Emergency Management*, Vol. 2, No. 4, 2004, pp. 43–49.

Queen's Medical Center, Queen's Medical Center: General Information. [Brochure], Honolulu, HI: The Queen's Medical Center, 1999.

ReliefWeb, retrieved May 26, 2006 from the World Wide Web: http://www.reliefweb.int.

State of Hawaii, State Multi-Hazard Mitigation Plan, Hawaii, Civil Defense Agency, City and County of Honolulu, 2002.

Tadamori, I., JIU Review on Strengthening the Role of United Nations System in Humanitarian Assistance for Disaster Reduction and Response, Joint Inspection Unit of the United Nations Development Program, 2005.

UH Manoa receives $300,000 federal grant to enhance statewide, *UH News*, 1, 2004.

United Nations Disaster Management Training Program (UNDMTP), retrieved May 26, 2006 from the World Wide Web: http://www.undg.org.

United Nations Office for the Coordination of Humanitarian Affairs (OCHA), retrieved May 26, 2006 from the World Wide Web: http://www.humanitarianinfo.org/opt/.

West Hawaii Today, Daily Newspaper, June 14, 2001, p. 2.

Chapter 29

Disaster Management and Intergovernmental Relations

Pam LaFeber and Nancy S. Lind

CONTENTS

Introduction

As stated by President Woodrow Wilson, the United States is a system of shared government and responsibility, a system in which all levels of government are expected to cooperate to overcome a national challenge or disaster. This chapter will argue that disaster management is an area in which mutual aid and intergovernmental cooperation are integral to the mitigation, response, and recovery of natural disasters.

The study of disaster management, particularly with respect to natural disasters such as hurricanes, requires an examination of two key areas. First, intergovernmental cooperation in times of disaster is essential to a successful response. The three levels of government, federal, state, and local, must work together and complement each other's roles to achieve a successful response and a full recovery for the community. Federal organizations are only as strong as their state and local counterparts. When one or more links in this chain are weak, action and capacity to address the disaster are slow and inadequate. This leads directly into the second key area, the importance placed upon disaster management by state and local governments. Many subnational governments do not view disaster management as significant and therefore do not have comprehensive disaster management plans. When this is the case, the public is unaware of preparedness plans. Similarly, when a plan is not regularly revised and updated, the most advantageous response may not be utilized. Conversely, when subnational governments seriously address disaster management and prepare the public for the unpredictable, both response and recovery are likely to be more organized and effective.

This chapter examines the coordination and cooperation, or lack thereof, among the three levels of government and several private organizations in a time of disaster. Emergency management is popularly viewed as a federal problem because disasters present staggering economic losses in property, and sometimes life, each year. As one moves to the lower levels of government, the damages experienced become fewer from that level of government's vantage point (Charles and Kim, 1988, p. 10). This is because each state is only concerned with the disasters that occur within their boundaries. Local governments are least likely to perceive natural disasters as important problems because they extend far beyond their boundaries. The result is often a low priority for disaster management on the local level.

Problems in Disaster Management

One paradox with this scenario is that the governments least likely to perceive emergency management as a key priority, the local governments, are at center stage in terms of responsibility for emergency management (ibid.). Most first response functions in emergency situations fall to the local governments. Therefore, great importance should be placed upon the preparedness and mitigation programs by the local governments. Unfortunately, this is often not the case, and successful implementation is jeopardized.

An additional problem retarding successful disaster management policy implementation is government fragmentation. With more than 82,000 separate governmental units in the United States, the complexity of different structures complicates planning and the implementation of effective techniques (ibid.). The consequence of this fragmentation is a loss of cooperation, coordination, and the necessary communication between important actors. These aspects of disaster management will only be seen with the presence of strong leadership.

Disaster Management Policy Implementation

In spite of such obstacles, disaster management policies are successfully implemented. Implementation is an exercise that consists of four central actors: the local government, the state government, the federal government, and the private sector. These actors possess diverse components and have different organizational structures, sizes, and political mandates. Further, they are accountable to different publics with divergent interests (Perry, 1985, p. 8). To attain successful comprehensive disaster management activities, each actor must cooperate with the others and complement their duties. In reality, these actors have often worked against each other. To complicate matters, the absence of a universal disaster management philosophy serves as a great barrier to effective coordination between and within the levels of government.

Within the disaster management system each level of government not only has its specific roles and responsibilities, but also must share resources and activities with the other levels. Thus, the governmental system embodies the "shared governance" approach to intergovernmental policymaking (Schneider, 1990, p. 98). The overall framework works ideally from the bottom–up. As the localities first experience the disaster, the local government should logically be the first level to respond to the situation.

The Local Government Role

The local government plans a vital role in the development of disaster management policies. They have to develop and maintain a program of emergency management to meet their responsibilities of providing for the protection and safety of the public (McLoughlin, 1985, p. 165). Among their responsibilities are the making of land use decisions, the enacting of construction codes, and the duty of serving as primary managers of local preparedness, response, and recovery efforts (Perry and Mushkatel, 1984, p. 9). Most states require, or at least encourage, counties to establish and support emergency preparedness agencies and activities as a precondition for receipt of federal disaster preparedness funds (Schneider, 1990, p. 98). Once policies are written by either elected officials, such as the city council, or by appointed officials, such as a city manager, the policy implementation is commonly carried out by administrators or public safety department personnel. The administrators in a community tend to be most concerned with planning and coordination, though, rather than immediate response.

When local governments develop a disaster management plan, both citizens and officials must be aware that hazards exist and believe that the risk poses significant negative consequences. All hazards posing a potential threat need to be identified and addressed in the emergency management plan. This identification of possible hazards consists of two parts. The first part involves knowledge of the kinds of hazards that might threaten a community (McLoughlin, 1985, p. 168). This knowledge includes predicting the probability of the event occurring at varying levels and locations throughout the community. The second part consists of a basic knowledge of the community. This refers to having a familiarity with the area and the resources at risk to the damage, plus an assessment of the loss that would result from the occurrence of the event (ibid.). This knowledge includes such items as the number of people and the values of property that could be affected, as well as the communications, transportation, food supply, or other systems exposed to the hazard. When the data for each hazard is combined and analyzed, the community can assign priorities to its disaster management needs.

An additional requisite in disaster policy formulation is that local officials must believe that the hazard is manageable (Perry and Mushkatel, 1984, p. 11). Manageability refers to many activities that run the gamut from preventing the hazard altogether to altering human behavior by restricting building homes, for example, on floodplains.

The State Government Role

When the local governments can no longer successfully address the disaster, and resources are being delegated, state governments are engaged. The state plays a central role in disaster planning and response because the Tenth Amendment to the U.S. Constitution reserves to the states the power to conduct their internal affairs (Clary, 1985, p. 23). In exercising this power, the states have delegated the key first response duties to the local communities, and reserved as its primary role the coordination and support of all emergency and disaster relief activities, both interstate and intrastate. Ideally, the state should link the local government and their communities to appropriate federal aid sources as well as with other localities and private organizations for support. In most states this official responsibility is set forth in an emergency preparedness and response plan (Schneider, 1990, p. 98).

Perry and Mushkatel (1984) emphasize two aspects of the state government's role in disaster management. First, states engage directly in disaster management activities, particularly for hazards with a potentially broad scope of impact. Statutes and regulations are the tools that are most utilized by the states to implement policies and participate in its management. The second aspect is coordination. The National Governor's Association has stressed the importance of the state as a coordinator of the interactions between the federal government and localities in dealing with disasters. The reason for this is that the federal government sets basic requirements that must be included if a state wishes to receive federal assistance. Particularly emphasized is the notion of having one agency in charge of not only coordinating activities statewide, but also serving as a liaison between local and federal efforts (ibid., p. 14).

The Federal Government Role

The role of the federal government is much more extensive than that of the other two levels of government. As federal resources are more abundant, the federal government is involved in all phases of disaster management. However, direct federal involvement only begins with a formal request for assistance from the governor.

Gubernatorial authority to make this request is mandated by the U.S. Disaster Relief Act of 1974 (P.L. 93-288). This act limits federal involvement to instances in which "the situation is of such severity and magnitude that effective response is beyond the capabilities of the state and the affected local governments" (May and Williams, 1986, p. 7). It is at this stage that the Federal Emergency Management Agency (FEMA), now housed within the Department of Homeland Security, enters the picture.

FEMA must not only review the governor's request, but also must conduct its own investigation of the disaster. On the basis of the findings, FEMA then makes a recommendation to the president concerning federal aid.

It is the president, in conjunction with the secretary of homeland security, who must decide whether the crisis is beyond the capacity of state and local governments. If the president feels that the situation can no longer be handled successfully by the subnational governments, he issues a formal disaster declaration. When this declaration is issued, a federal coordinating officer (FCO), who serves as the presidential representative to the stricken area, is appointed and a field office is set up in the area. The field office traditionally is comprised of the FCO and a hazard mitigation team (HMT). The HMT usually functions as a regional, interagency, and intergovernmental team, and is required to prepare a report within 15 days of presidential declaration of a disaster (Rubin and Barbee, 1985, p. 59). This report recommends appropriate mitigation and response activities. This action has substantially improved intergovernmental relations, because all three levels of government are represented on this team. The efforts of the HMT have also improved the timeliness of response to disasters. The FCO bears the responsibility of coordinating all disaster relief and response activities of all three levels of government.

Working under the general direction of the FCO, FEMA organizes the federal response (Schneider, 1990, p. 99). FEMA and the affected state government contractually bind themselves with an assistance agreement. This agreement specifically states the manner by which federal aid is to be made available, and includes reference to items such as federal–state cost sharing, type of aid (i.e., temporary housing), and duration of the aid period (Clary, 1985, p. 23). Additionally, this document delineates the exact responsibilities of each level of government in the event of a disaster.

One of FEMA's key roles is to funnel aid to disaster-stricken areas. The chaos that typically follows a disaster leaves many people confused and not knowing where to turn for help. FEMA helps alleviate such anxiety by publicizing where to seek assistance and setting up disaster application centers. FEMA also administers several programs directly in the form of temporary housing, cash grants, and money to help restore or replace public facilities or property (ibid.). Implementation of these programs is a cooperative effort between all three levels of government. Here, FEMA relies greatly upon the lower levels of government. In fact, the state is actually responsible for determining program eligibility and for distributing funds to those who qualify (ibid.). The local government's role is to help finance such activities to the best of their ability and to assist the state in program implementation.

FEMA also matches people who are in need of assistance with the appropriate federal money. For example, it helps local businesses obtain loans from the Small Business Administration so they can repair or replace damaged facilities (ibid.). It is important to note, however, that FEMA only serves as a link to such agencies. FEMA is not responsible for the amount or type of aid received by the applicants.

FEMA also holds great influence over the subnational actors. FEMA's authority is based on legislation, executive orders, and regulations. This enables FEMA to change a state's actions by the establishment of new rules. If a state does not comply with such new rules, FEMA is in a position to withhold funding from the local government.

The above discussion illustrates that this system is intended to provide the most effective utilization of governmental resources with each level of government making its own unique contribution to the disaster management plan.

The Role of the Private Sector

The private sector, composed of various organizations, constitutes another sphere that may provide assistance to the local level government in times of disaster. Generally, private sector actors consist of two types of organizations. First are the organizations with the primary responsibility of fulfilling an emergency management role in the community. Examples include the American Red Cross and the Salvation Army. The second type of organization routinely pursues some private line of business, unrelated to emergency management, but has some equipment or expertise that is potentially useful in disaster management (Clary, 1985, p. 12). A common example of this type is the local construction company.

These private sector service organizations are very important in ensuring a smoother response to a disaster. There is an increased interdependence between the governmental actors and such private organizations to facilitate a local response to a disaster.

Conclusion

This chapter has stressed the importance of intergovernmental cooperation in the mitigation, response, and recovery of natural disasters. It has focused on the primary roles for each of the levels of government and explored the creation of the Federal Emergency Management Agency to strengthen the leadership of the federal government in the area of disaster management and abolish, or at least reduce, the existing fragmentation.

The state and local governments use their discretion when deciding whether or not to implement plans of action recommended by FEMA. When the local level governments choose to disregard FEMA's suggestions, and do not create a disaster management plan of their own, disaster management effectiveness suffers. Thus, it is clear that FEMA, and by extension the federal government's effectiveness, is influenced by the differentially prioritized disaster management techniques of local government.

Shared governance, in its most general form, embraces the notion that responsibilities can be shared among the layers of government (May, 1985, p. 41). Disaster management responsibilities are disbursed between the levels, beginning with the local level. Once this level of government has dealt with the situation to the best of its ability, the state level may be called upon for assistance. The state government serves as the facilitator of the monetary aid process, unemployment benefits, and shelter relocation information. The governor of the affected state has the authority to request from the president that the community be declared a disaster area, thus making it eligible to receive federal assistance. At this point, the federal government becomes an actor. This is where FEMA coordinates the activities of the other two levels and links individuals with the correct agencies and private organizations to meet their needs. It is important, however, to always remember that local level actors are the first to address the disaster management situation. When the local government is ill-prepared for the disaster, the appearance of the other levels of government is accelerated, and the response is severely hindered.

References

Charles, M.T. and Kim, J.C.K. *Crisis Management: A Casebook.* Springfield, Illinois: Charles C. Thomas, 1988.

Clary, B.B. The evolution and structure of natural hazards policies. *Public Administration Review*, 45: 20–28, 1985.

May, P.J. FEMA's Role in Emergency Management. *Public Administration Review*, 45: 40–48, 1985.

May, P.J. and Williams, W. *Disaster Policy Implementation: Managing Programs under Shared Governance*. New York: Plenum Press, 1986.

McLoughlin, D. A framework for integrated emergency management. *Public Administration Review* 45: 165–172, 1985.

Perry, R. *Comprehensive Emergency Management: Evacuating Threatened Populations.* Greenwich, Connecticut: Greenwood Press, 1985.

Perry, R.W. and Mushkatel, A. *Disaster Management: Warning Response and Community Relocation*, Westport, Connecticut: Greenwood Press, 1984.

Rubin, C.B. and Barbee, D. Disaster recovery and hazard mitigation: Bridging the intergovernmental gap. *Public Administration Review*, 45: 57–63, 1985.

Schneider, S.K. FEMA, Federalism, Hugo, and "Frisco". *The Journal of Federalism*, 20: 97–115, 1990.

Chapter 30

Issues in Hospital Preparedness

Robert Powers

CONTENTS

Introduction

Hospitals have traditionally lagged behind other public service providers in their disaster preparedness. There have been many causes of this from a lack of funding to a lack of understanding of the role of the hospital. Efforts have improved in the post 9/11 world as hospitals have become more aware of the criticality of their continued functioning during and after a disaster event. However, though improvements have been made, hospital preparedness is still far from where it should be to properly care for the community after a catastrophic event.

Obstacles to Preparedness

Hospitals' inconsistent willingness and ability to support disaster mitigation and preparedness programs are, first of all, linked to a lack of central oversight. There has been no one in the role of a disaster coordinator who could provide direction to any disaster initiatives. Various administrators or managers have traditionally piece-mealed the work together but it was just another task in a long list of tasks that needed their attention. There was no specialization and no one oversaw all aspects of disaster preparedness to give any definition or consistency to the program. Because of this, disaster programs rarely developed properly or at all. The Joint Commission on Accreditation of Healthcare Organizations (JCAHO) provides hospitals with standards for disaster preparedness that include the number of disaster drills that a hospital must perform each year; however, rarely have hospitals put the time and effort into these drills to make them anything more than a minimal-level drill to meet the requirement without any development of realistic scenarios and without any follow-up on issues discovered that could enhance preparedness. Even the hospitals that could realistically handle a mass casualty incident (MCI) could only handle one with a few patients and not anything near the volumes of patients that would be generated from a weapon of mass destruction (WMD) event [1]. Since 9/11, many hospitals have seen the increased need to be prepared for large-scale disaster events and have created a disaster coordinator position, but there must also be support from hospital administration to ensure the success of these initiatives.

Economic factors have also provided significant obstacles to hospital mitigation and preparedness efforts. First responders, such as EMS and fire services, operate without competition and are typically guaranteed their market by the state or local government. Costs of disaster mitigation initiatives for these services require approval but do not impact whether or not the service is able to continue operations. Hospitals, however, public or private, are businesses and hospital administrators must maintain a focus on the bottom line to ensure they maintain their hospital's competitiveness in healthcare's increasingly aggressive marketplace. Hospital administrators often opt against disaster mitigation measures because they are expensive and they are for items not normally needed [2]. Economic considerations for hospital preparedness involve the finding of funds to support the initiatives while, at the same time, maintaining competitiveness.

Hospitals have had varied results as they have individually weighed and assessed the risk of disaster events against the increased operating costs of structural changes and maintaining stockpiled supplies for events that may never happen. Without specific government requirements or mandates, hospital spending on mitigation and preparedness plans has developed at various levels. A hospital administrator could decide on the importance of various disaster-related programs and work to provide the budgetary funding to support them. But, without a mandate for the hospital's competition to spend the same amount, the disaster-focused hospital would find its increased operating costs to have created a disadvantage in competing against non-disaster-focused hospitals. This has been seen in some hospitals that made expensive seismic retrofits to their campuses while their competition found ways to avoid it in spite of the potential damage to their facility and to their ability to function after an earthquake. Hospitals noted it would be cheaper to rebuild post-earthquake than to perform the retrofits [3].

Government funding specifically targeting hospitals has helped alleviate some problems with nonfunded mandates. However, not all hospitals participate in these programs due to continued lack of vision and limitations on approvals of the grants themselves. Hospitals still must spend time focusing on developing the program and the application process takes time and effort that some still do not see the benefit of. Hospital administrators must change their attitudes regarding disaster preparedness. Administrators must understand that failing to make proper mitigation and pre-paredness measures is an act of irresponsibility to the community. Hospitals are a business but they are more than a business. They have a much larger role than merely providing a service.

Critical Function

The difference between other businesses and hospitals is that hospitals serve a critical function in the time of disaster. The United Nations Conference on Disaster Reduction noted that hospitals "are among the few facilities that must remain operational immediately after a disaster" [4]. Hospitals must sustain operations through the event to limit the impact of the disaster in loss of life. They have a criticality that other businesses do not. That is, if they fail to function during a disaster, they will contribute significantly to the impact of the disaster on the community.

Hospital administrators need to understand this public service duty has to remain functioning in a disaster event. Proper emphasis on mitigation and pre-paredness measures is crucial. A hospital that is closed because of structural damage post-earthquake, which could have been prevented with the proper seismic retrofits, or one that is closed because the risks detailed in the hazard vulnerability assessment were erroneously deemed low, is a disservice to the community and an act of irresponsibility. A prime focus of hospital administrators should be on ensuring their facility will maintain sustainability throughout a disaster event. Administrators, of course, cannot bankrupt their hospital with excessively lavish disaster preparedness. But, neither can they ignore the necessity of proper preparedness. There is no bottom line here that is bigger than making proper preparations to save human life.

Additionally, not only will hospital failure impact loss of life, but it will also impact the hospital's prestige. That is, failing to respond properly during a time of crisis will result in a loss of the hospital's reputation. Hospitals are dependent on their reputation in the community to attract business. Without that reputation, most of it word of mouth, patients will divert to another hospital. Just like patients remember that their relative died at hospital X, so they should go to hospital Y instead, they would remember that hospital X closed its doors at the time of the community's greatest need. Hospital Y will also be sure to capitalize on their sustainability during the disaster through local advertising that proudly, and rightly, announced that they are the one the community can count on.

Hospitals, however, are besieged on a normal day. Hospital bed closures over the last decade, coupled with limited staff, have led to chronically high bed censuses and delays in patient treatment. Emergency departments (EDs) routinely go on diversion status, diverting incoming ambulances because of ED overcrowding. If hospitals have a difficult time providing for the community's needs on a normal day, then the concern becomes how can hospitals possibly provide medical care for the community on a catastrophic day? The answer is by, first of all, giving mitigation, planning, and preparedness the priority they require; by making a point of devoting the time and attention necessary to make it happen; by obtaining the proper equipment and ensuring staff are well versed in its use; by utilizing available government funding to offset the costs; and by championing the cause to ensure that other people in the hospital are empowered to carry out implementation of the program.

Government Grants

With hospitals already operating at narrow profit margins, government assistance began with Metropolitan Medical Response System (MMRS) support and, in 2002, DHHS' Health Resources and Services Administration (HRSA) began providing hospitals with funding to enhance bioterrorism preparedness through its National Bioterrorism Hospital Preparedness Program (NBHPP). HRSA determined a critical benchmark list that detailed for hospitals what specific areas the funding should be used to improve [5].

Though there have been considerable improvements through the NBHPP program, there still remain significant shortcomings in hospital preparedness.

A GAO report to congressional committees found that 18 percent of responding hospitals had no emergency plan in place and that many lacked the necessary number of ventilators and other capacities to deal with a bioterrorism event [2].

Through NBHPP, funding is available but hospitals must take the initiative to see the value in the program and commit the resources needed to apply for the funding, process the grant paperwork, and then commit to upkeep of the obtained equipment. Some hospital officials still operate under the "it could never happen here" mentality; perhaps, because they are at a smaller hospital or a remote location their assumption is they will be bypassed in a disaster event. Although odds are against a WMD terrorist attack occurring in a small rural town, there are other events that could bring just as many casualties to the local ED, such as a chlorine gas leak or a chemical spill. These events, though not a WMD scenario, require some of the same materials for hospital response that would have been obtained through the HRSA grant funding. People are going to go to the closest hospital when an event happens [7]; they are not going to keep driving until they find the one that is properly prepared. Local resources must be available immediately to receive and care for the patients no matter what the causative agent of the event was.

Proper Planning

Hospitals need to focus on several items to ensure they are properly prepared. These mitigation activities need to result in hospital sustainability without any outside assistance for 72 hours post-event, the standard estimated time for how long it will take outside resources, such as FEMA response, to arrive in assistance of the area impacted. Even then, if the scope of the disaster is great, resources may initially be insufficient to provide assistance across the board to all impacted hospitals.

Hospital mitigation efforts begin with the hazard vulnerability assessment. This is the guide for hospital preparedness. Each hazard is rated by hospital personnel to determine which are more likely in their region and which will have the greatest impact on sustainability. An all-hazards approach is incorporated here that allows for mitigation and preparedness efforts that will encompass many hazards rather than just focusing on one. This allows the hospital to gain preparedness at a lesser cost. That is, rather than buying one type of supplies for a hurricane disaster and a different kind of supplies for an earthquake disaster, effort is made to make the plan globally apply to as many hazards as possible. This should also apply to the plans themselves; rather than having a different plan for each type of disaster, there should be only one plan with appendices as necessary for procedures that do not lend themselves well to the all-hazards approach. This also simplifies the response effort because staff are taught only one way to perform in a disaster and do not have to stop and make a determination of which way to respond. Thus, confusion is reduced and there is decreased risk of staff performing the wrong procedures for the event.

Impact of Disasters

There are two ways hospitals can be impacted from a disaster, either structurally or nonstructurally. Structural mitigation looks at the hospital as it is being planned or considers retrofits to improve the sustainability of an existing structure. These measures focus on such measures as seismic resistance to limit the damage to a facility from an earthquake or designing an emergency department entrance that has the capability to easily expand and handle a large influx of patients arriving in personal vehicles from a disaster event. Nonstructural systems include such systems as the HVAC (heating, ventilating, air conditioning) systems. Mitigation efforts here would include efforts to secure the air intake area with parameter fencing and security cameras as well as ensuring that air intakes are at the highest level possible and are fit with a high level of filtration to protect against airborne WMD agents.

Lifelines

Systems referred to as lifelines are also critical in maintaining the sustainability of the facility. Lifelines maintain needed links from the hospital to various outside entities or material suppliers. These include communications, utility, and transportation. Communication may be coming from local emergency management, emergency medical services, or the health department and is needed to keep hospital officials apprised of the current situation including numbers of continuing victims and possible causative agent. Communication is also necessary to replenish low running resources and discuss options regionally with other hospitals. Redundancy must be built into the communications systems to ensure at least one means of communication remains functional. Utilities, such as power and water, must be properly mitigated and planned for. Generators provide back-up power but flooding or long-term use can cause significant problems in sustaining hospital operations. Mitigation should provide protection of the generator system from adverse conditions such as winds or flood and coordinate contingency plans for ensuring delivery of fuel even during catastrophic events. Hurricane Katrina demonstrated the importance of this lifeline when nurses hand-ventilated patients, because mechanical ventilators had no power and put administrators in a difficult position of determining life or death for patients because of the failure of contingency planning. Additionally, transportation routes and transportation vehicles must be maintained for arrival of patients, supplemental supplies, and incoming staff to maintain hospital operation.

Surge Capacity

Sustainability requires mitigation and planning for surge capacity. Surge is the influx of patients to the hospital either immediately following a disaster or, in the case of biological agents, when the victims start becoming symptomatic. Mitigation for surge begins with structural considerations for this immediate surge to the emergency department and continues with planning for the flow of patients through triage, treatment, and admission or discharge. Surge capacity includes planning for isolation capabilities related to bioterrorism. Isolation areas must be identified that would accommodate the increasing number of patients and include alternate treatment areas, such as conference rooms or cafeterias. Proper mitigation has created these areas through designing the building with negative pressure availability in key expansion areas of the hospital and those areas more apt to become contaminated, such as the emergency department and the lobby.

In addition to creating the isolation areas themselves, there must be sufficient isolation supplies, such as masks and gowns, stockpiled to care for the victims. Staff may also receive prophylaxis, e.g., smallpox vaccine, before the event to ensure they can take care of the patients without concern of becoming infected or infecting their families. Mitigation efforts begin with simply enforcing personal hygiene practices and administration of various vaccines, such as the influenza vaccine. HRSA recommendations call for the ability to provide antibiotics not only for the biologically exposed patient but also prophylactically for staff and for staff's immediate family as well so that the staff member can work knowing that his family is being taken care of [6].

Decontamination capabilities are also needed, not only for WMD preparedness but also for incidents involving hazardous materials. Traditionally, hospitals have not been well prepared for response to patients exposed to hazardous materials. One CDC report details an ED that had three staff members become symptomatic after receiving just one organophosphate exposed patient [8]. With difficulties arising when receiving only a few patients, having hospitals capable of mass decontamination of large numbers of patients has been a difficult objective to obtain. HRSA funding has helped increase the decontamination equipment stockpiles of participating hospitals, but equipment alone does not make a functioning response. Those participating hospitals still must determine who to train and how to train them in addition to having plans that actually work rather than look good on paper. These decon capabilities must have quick implementation and not have so many hurdles that the facility is already contaminated before any of it can be activated. Proper preparedness involves staff members as well as administrators who understand their responsibility to the community and are committed to ensuring the success of these programs. The current capability of hospitals is far from adequate; one GAO study found that 40 percent of responding hospitals estimated they could decontaminate less than five patients an hour [2]. It would take an actual event or an extremely well put-together drill to determine if the hospitals with higher estimates in the GAO study were accurate or overly optimistic.

Disaster Drills

Hospital drills themselves are another important preparedness strategy. Drills vary from paper-based or tabletop to a full-scale simulation with actual patients. Hospital administrators, however, have long viewed disaster drills as simply fulfilling a JCAHO requirement. There has traditionally been little planning for drills and, overall, staff have been apathetic toward any participation. Also, drills often fail to simulate a real event because they are normally well announced to administration and staff, which causes the drill to not accurately reflect the hospital's true response capability. Properly run drills, however, are a critical strategy to gauging and improving hospital readiness. Excluding actual disaster events, it is only through the drill that paper plans come to life and create the opportunity to evaluate the live process. The drill evaluators should come from outside agencies, so there is more freedom to critique processes and procedures. A drill done with staff evaluators without sufficient background or experience to make proper evaluations or with evaluators who are merely checking boxes is counterproductive. Drill evaluations must provide relevant information that guides the hospital in what changes need to occur in their preparedness and response to be truly efficient in a real event.

Drills help illustrate the point that hospitals are in need of administration and staff that will champion the cause of disaster preparedness. Hospital readiness is dependent on proper preparedness and mitigation activities. The hospital disaster champion has a vision for the hospital's readiness and pushes through these activities and programs to ensure the hospital is ready for a disaster. The champion must ensure that others catch his vision for change because he cannot typically affect the change himself without the buy-in from executive administration. Post 9/11, the buy-in from upper administration has been easier to obtain but still lacks much in most hospitals. Areas where disasters have recently occurred tend to have a strong focus on disaster preparedness by senior administration. As noted earlier, in spite of their strong role as a public safety provider, hospitals are businesses and, as such, they do have to weigh purchases against budgetary considerations. They cannot spend themselves out of business in purchasing all the latest vendors' disaster preparedness items. However, they cannot turn a blind eye toward their responsibilities to the community. Administration must, at the very least, understand that disaster preparedness and mitigation efforts are as important as any other safety program.

In-Hospital and Out-of-Hospital Support

Disaster champions must also work to enlist and educate key players from throughout the hospital. These key players are the administrative leaders from such departments as the emergency department, radiology, infection control, laboratory, and engineering to obtain readiness throughout the hospital. The hospital safety committee or a specially created emergency management committee is the place to bring all these players together and ensure that they share the common vision for a hospital truly ready to respond to a disaster event.

Hospitals will not function alone in a disaster event and the disaster-focused hospital administrator must look beyond the hospital as well. Community interaction is essential because the hospital must know and help guide the community response to a disaster so that hospital operations fit seamlessly into other agencies' plans for optimum response and because a hospital's sustainability during a disaster event is directly dependent on the resources and support it receives from other community agencies.

A key component of this community interaction is regional response. Hospitals are using mutual aid plans and regional response planning to support each other. Hospitals outside of the disaster impact area could potentially send support personnel and equipment within a few hours to hospitals feeling the brunt of a disaster event. Regional response requires such mitigation efforts as agreeing on procedures for emergency credentialing, i.e., ways to verify incoming help are really physicians and nurses, and signing agreements on payroll and worker's compensation issues.

Conclusion

Hospitals must step-up to the plate. Hospital disaster champions must use their influence to gain support for measures that impact a hospital's ability to sustain operations during a large-scale disaster event. These preparedness and mitigation endeavors need administrative buy-in to ever become implemented. Hospitals have new disaster scenarios to prepare for that which were rarely mentioned in years past. Hospitals must not lag behind in their efforts to ready themselves for these hazards, to the detriment of the community. Hospital leaders should take up the torch and forward the cause of disaster preparedness not only in the hospital but also throughout the community. This is a time for hospitals to shine as innovators in efforts to safeguard the health and wellness of the community around them.

References

1. Barbara, J.A., Macintyre, A., and DeAtley, C. October 2001. Ambulances to nowhere: America's critical shortfall in medical preparedness for catastrophic terrorism. Assessed on March 28, 2006 on World Wide Web at http://www.e11th-hour.org/public/terror/ambulances2nowhere.html.
2. GAO-03-924. August 2003. Hospital preparedness: Most urban hospitals have emergency plans but lack certain capacities for bioterrorism response. United States General Accounting Office Report to Congressional Committees. Assessed on March 28, 2006 on World Wide Web at http://www.gao.gov/new.items/d03924.pdf #search='gao%20hospital%20preparedness'.

3. Connell, R.P. Disaster mitigation in hospitals: Factors influencing organizational decision-making on hazard loss reduction. Disaster Research Center Web site. Assessed on March 20, 2006 on World Wide Web at http://www.udel.edu/DRC/thesis/connell_thesis.DOC.
4. Pan American Health Organization. August 2004. Report on reducing the impact of disasters on health facilities. Assessed on March 20, 2006 on World Wide Web at http://www.paho.org/English/GOV/CD/cd45-27-e.pdf.
5. U.S. Department of Health and Human Services Website. Accessed April 20, 2006 on World Wide Web at http://www.hhs.gov/aspr/opeo/hpp/index.html.
6. SEMP Biot # 172. February 7, 2005. Hospital surge capacity standards and indicators. Suburban Emergency Management Project. Assessed on March 30, 2006 on World Wide Web at http://www.semp.us/biot_172.htm.
7. Auf der Heide, E. January 2006. The importance of evidence-based disaster planning. *Annals of Emergency Medicine.* 47 (1): 34–40.
8. CDC MMWR. January 05, 2001. Nosocomial poisoning associated with emergency department treatment of organophosphate toxicity. 49 (51): 1156–1158. Assessed on March 30, 2006 on World Wide Web at http://www.cdc.gov/mmwr/preview/mmwrhtml/mm4951a2.htm.

Chapter 31

Strategic Planning for Emergency Managers

Rhonda Sturgis

CONTENTS

Emergency management is a field that has for a long time been imbedded as an extra duty within the emergency response function. There has recently been a shift where many localities have placed more focus on emergency management and have begun moving toward a dedicated agency within their jurisdictions. This move has been made more evident with the September 11, 2001 terrorist attacks.

Traditionally, responders were trained to respond in the first hours of an event and to work the scene to save lives and protect property (GAO, 2005). After the terrorist attacks the role has expanded toward preventing emergencies and protecting public and property (GAO, 2005) through more detailed planning. Within this environment the role of the emergency manager has developed into a position, which is responsible for coordinating all components of the emergency management system (FEMA, 1995), and involves working with multiple agencies and jurisdictions. This role requires several tasks that become more work than one individual can feasibly do alone, resulting in a multiagency team environment.

This movement and increased responsibility has led to a slow development of a professionalized field within emergency management.

The benefit of separating emergency management into its own agency is that it allows for a complete focus on functions relating to disaster response. The one major disadvantage of the separation of the emergency management function is the lack of funding and resources provided to such a small agency within localities. Usually the importance of emergency management is realized at its fullest when an actual event takes place, and it is during this time that funding comes to the forefront. For example, between 2001 and 2003 the federal government increased monies for first responders by almost 1400 percent (Glasser, 2003). Fortunately, severe events such as September 11 seldom occur; nevertheless work continues to go on behind the scenes to prepare in case such a catastrophic event materializes again. Unfortunately, over time after a catastrophic event happens, funding and resources become scarce, limiting planning and preparedness abilities. Due to the importance of emergency management and the lack of funding and resources it is imperative that emergency managers develop strategic plans so that they can articulate their needs for funding and prioritize their work.

Strategic management planning is a process that helps organizations be responsive to the dynamic, changing environment of today's emergency management milieu. Strategic plans are an effective tool used to focus resources and efforts to address issues (GAO, 2004). A strategic plan provides direction in decision making and actions to shape and guide what an organization is and what it does. It provides a systematic process for gathering information from all possible sources and uses that information to establish a long-term direction that is broken down into goals, objectives (Poister and Streib, 2005), and measures. The strategic planning process involves a complex and complete set of planning steps that take into consideration many constituents and circumstances for current and future organizational decision making. It is important when developing a strategic planning process for emergency management that specific items are taken into consideration to necessitate the argument for funding and the ability to show proven success.

When beginning a strategic planning process, it is important to determine who should be involved in creating the organizational direction. Selecting a good strategic planning committee at the onset of the planning process will reduce gaps in the plan that would have to be addressed later due to lack of representation. The executive staff usually makes this determination of who will serve as the strategic planning committee. In an emergency management setting, this will depend on the structure and size of the agency. For example, for cities with a separate emergency management office this duty would fall to the coordinator, but in localities where this function is under the fire department it may be the responsibility of the fire chief. In an ideal setting, strategic planning should involve not only executive staff, but also frontline professionals and possibly some constituents that influence the organization's production.

Creating a strategic management planning committee from multiple levels provides for an outlook with broader organizational perspective (Sturgis, 2005).

The person responsible for creating the plan should be a good facilitator and be able to draw from the diverse representation to create a well-rounded strategic management plan that will address areas of concern and allow for creativity. In addition to a broader perspective, it is easier to get employees to buy into the strategic plan when they assist in its creation. For a plan to be successful it is imperative that employees are in agreement with the direction of the organization and that their actions are leading toward the vision. By including employees on the ground floor of creation, they are able to work with the team to develop a strategic plan that they feel is important for the agency. Through teamwork the plan will be brought to life and have a better chance of success. The selection of representatives to the strategic planning committee is an important first step for the development and success of an agencies strategic management plan.

Once a committee is established, it is vital that constituents and factors that influence the organization be determined before the strategic planning process begins. This allows the committee to become aware of internal and external factors influencing the decision-making process within the agency (Sturgis, 2005). Within an emergency management sector, these constituents and factors may include the following:

- City managers
- Mayors
- City council members
- State of the state address
- State of the city addresses
- Citizens and citizen groups
- Legislation
- Agency needs (police, fire, etc.)
- Employees
- Emergency management associations
- Regional emergency management functions
- Federal Emergency Management Agency (FEMA)
- National Incident Management System (NIMS)
- State Department of Emergency Management
- Budget constraints internally within the organization

The items listed above are just a few of things that may influence your plan. For example, FEMA and the State Department of Emergency Management many times mandate actions that will be required by an organization. The National Incident Management System (NIMS) is an item that has recently been placed at the forefront of emergency management and is now required for Department of Homeland Security (DHS) funding. The requirement of becoming NIMS-compliant for funding makes it important for it to be addressed somewhere within an emergency management strategic plan. In addition, many times governors will have a state address and mayors a city address that may specifically mention emergency management functions for developing a well-rounded state or city. These are important items to be aware of, as many times action items will be brought about to address the concerns in the speech. For example, if a governor wants to have a mass evacuation plan for his or her state that information will be worked through the state department of emergency management and will trickle down to the local agencies. By considering these types of items during the planning stage, agencies will be aware of their actual workloads and be able to utilize and manage resources better. These types of factors are essential in creating a strategic management plan. When the agency is able to determine what constituents and factors influence the decision-making process, a plan can be developed that will take into consideration all types of factors that may influence their responsibilities.

The strategic planning process begins by creating a mission. The mission defines the organization's purpose and tells everyone whom the agency is serving. The mission statement is necessary because it provides the overall direction of the organization. It elicits motivation and emotion, creating an environment where employees take pride in their organization. Finally, a mission statement is measurable, definable, and is reasonably actionable. The mission statement is a broad idea that will remain in effect for many years (Sturgis, 2005).

For emergency management the mission statement will need to include the five phases of emergency management. These five phases are important because emergency management has as its goal coordinating available resources to deal with emergencies, resulting in lives saved, avoiding injuries, and minimizing economic loss (FEMA, 1995). The five phases of emergency management (prevention, mitigation, preparedness, response, and recovery) assist and guide in making this possible. Due to their importance the five phases are briefly touched upon and will be expounded upon throughout the chapter.

1. Prevention is a sustained action to avoid or to intervene to stop an incident and to take actions to protect lives and property.
2. The mitigation phase involves activities that prevent or reduce the chance of an emergency occurring, or reduces the effects of unavoidable hazards that may occur.
3. The preparedness phase involves developing and providing plans, procedures, training exercises, and education for effective response to potential emergencies and disasters.
4. The response phase takes place during the incident. During this phase it is important to coordinate timely, rapid, accurate response and situation assessments, providing appropriate support to stabilize and control the emergency. This phase provides emergency assistance for causalities and reduces the probability of secondary damage.
5. Finally, in the recovery phase steps are utilized to stabilize and restore government, social, and economic infrastructure after the disaster (FEMA, 1995).

The mission sets the stage for the organization and in the emergency management field utilizes the phases of emergency management to address what the agency is in the business to do.

Once the agency determines what it is in business to do, it is very important to determine where they want to go. This statement relays to individuals what the organization wants to become, that is, its vision of the future. This process stretches the agency's capabilities, but is a realistic projection. The vision has a set time frame and is usually a five-year projection. Like the mission statement, the vision statement has to be measurable and definable. A good vision statement encourages employees to find pride and excitement in fulfilling the vision of the organization (Sturgis, 2005). The creative thinking of the strategic planning committee is critical at this stage.

By having a strategic executive committee that represents multiple agencies the group is diversified so that various resources, ideas, and skills to decision making are brought to the table (Bolman and Deal, 1997; Drucker, 1993). Through managing this diversity in a positive way, the strategic planning team is able to utilize healthy communication process resulting in maximum team creativity (Hughes et al., 1999; Moore, 1986). This creativity will allow for thinking outside of the box in creating a vision for the agency. The agency must realistically determine a direction for their future. For example, a vision may entail the idea of becoming accredited and being recognized as a leader in the emergency management field. It may consider the phases of emergency management and determine ways to expound upon these ideas, creating an environment where the agency strives to go beyond the services that they are currently providing. No matter what the agency determines to be important, the vision should be a motivational guide that will expand the current program and guide them into the immediate future.

Two additional items that are important in a strategic management plan are the creation of values and code of ethics. Values are the traits and behaviors that show how the organization values its customers, employees, and suppliers. The code of ethics provides a guideline for the conduct of its employees. These two items provide a guideline for acceptable behavior of reaching an organization's mission and vision (Sturgis, 2005). It is important that the leaders of the agency set a positive example and hold others accountable for abiding by the values and code of ethics. Emergency management deals with many outside factors and it is important that as a profession employees are representing themselves appropriately. For example, in the emergency management field employees are continually dealing with citizens. Many times this is through outreach mechanisms or may be in the aftermath of a disaster. No matter the forum, it is important that all citizens are treated fairly and with respect. Agencies should ensure that employees are made aware of how to deal with their customers and realize there are consequences if not done so appropriately. By establishing a set of values and code of ethics everyone in the agency is able to work toward the mission and vision with an understanding of what is expected of each employee.

Once the mission, vision, values, and code of ethics are created, it is of utmost importance to ensure that the organization is staying on track with what has been projected. All decisions made by the agency should be based on the mission and vision of the organization. The simplest way of staying on track is to create goals and objectives that are in alignment with the organizational direction. Goals are created as a general intention of the organization, and the objectives are a more specific path of how to accomplish the goal. Again, as with the mission and vision, goals and objectives must be realistic and measurable. The goal should align with the mission and vision so that it assists in achieving the overall organizational success (Sturgis, 2005). Goals and objectives need to be created at minimum for each phase of responsibility within emergency management. Individuals responsible for the action items should be held accountable for creating their own goals and objectives, ensuring they are in alignment with the mission and vision, and be held accountable for the successful completion of the items. Timelines of goals must be developed with projections of the steps taken to accomplish the goal and objective as well as completion dates. This allows the agency to determine if they are staying on track with meeting their vision in a timely fashion and allows for changes to be made as needed.

It is also important for goals and objectives to be created within budget constraints. If employees do not have the tools or money to perform the goal or objective, then it should not be created until such time resources are made available. For best results, it is good to establish goals and objectives during the budget process so that it aligns with what monies will be needed to meet the mission and vision of the organization. Well-created goals and objectives allow an organization to develop a plan for successful achievement of the mission and vision (Sturgis, 2005). In emergency management, these goals and objectives will at minimum relate back to the phases of emergency management. For example, a mitigation goal may be to develop and maintain a disaster mitigation plan, or a preparedness goal may be to increase citizen awareness. Additional goals and objectives can be developed based on anything that moves the agency toward meeting its mission and vision. For example, there may be a need to have an administrative goal, which deals with things such as developing and managing a strategic management plan or creating an agency's policy and procedure manual. By determining what the agencies' needs are and creating goals and objectives to meet the predetermined mission an organization should be moving toward their futuristic vision.

From the objectives created, performance measures should be developed. Performance measures allow the organization to determine its success in meeting the mission, vision, goals, and objectives. Measures should determine not only if the goal and objective have been met, but also if it has been a success (Sturgis, 2005). For example, if the goal is to increase citizen awareness, then it is imperative to document all the numbers and types of information released to the public. Did an agency speak to 15 school classes and do a presentation or did they run a video production about disaster preparedness on their local television channel that 10,000 households could watch? Documenting these types of items will substantiate that an agency has provided information through several different types of media avenues.

Another great example of success would be surveying citizens before and after an extensive advertisement campaign to see the percentage increase of the population that is aware of emergency preparedness.

Performance measures allow organizations to show success with activities being performed and also assist in determining when goals and objectives are not being achieved as originally envisioned. For example, it may be determined from the survey that more households were reached through mailings than through a video production. In a case such as this, it would be more productive for mailings to go out in the future instead of spending money on video productions. It is essential that measures be relayed back to the specific goal and easily analyzable. Goals and objectives can be influenced and manipulated by several outside factors, so it is important to ensure that when creating measures all potential factors are taken into consideration. Ultimately measures should track each goal and objective and provide a basis for accomplishing the mission and vision of the organization.

Once the strategic management plan is created it should be documented in a formalized report. This allows for the responsible parties to have a record of what achievements have been made and allow for areas of needed improvement to be easily analyzed. The document also allows for supervisors to easily review the type of work the agency is doing and can be utilized in assisting with state reports, budget reports, or other areas where specialized information is needed. Following is an excerpt of a sample report including a goal, objective, and performance measure, created based upon the mission and vision of the City of Newport News Office of Emergency Management.

Vision: The vision of the Office of Emergency Management is to save lives and property and reduce the effects of emergencies and disasters regardless of their cause. The office continuously strives to be the local, state, and nationally recognized leader in the emergency management profession. We seek to maintain a system build on a partnership of local, state, and federal governments, business and industry, volunteer agencies and individual citizens.

Mission: The mission of the Office of Emergency Management is to be the local public safety organization providing comprehensive, risk-based and coordinated emergency management prevention, mitigation, preparedness, response, and recovery for major emergencies and disasters affecting the City of Newport News and the Hampton Roads regional area. The office serves to protect the public peace, health, safety, lives, property, and economic well-being of the city and the citizens.

Goal: Preparedness—To develop and provide plans, procedures, training, exercises, and education for effective response to potential emergencies and disasters, and promote professional development of agency staff.

Objective: Develop an all inclusive outreach program that will increase citizen awareness and reduce the number and impact of emergencies and disasters.

Responsible Party: Dr. Rhonda Sturgis

Outcome: Citizen awareness through multiple sources.

Measure: Number and type of outreach functions performed. Number of outreach materials distributed. Number of video production special run.

Outcome: Creation of specialized outreach topics.

Measure: Number of outreach power points created. Number of brochures created related to specific topics.

Outcome: Awareness of Newport News Office of Emergency Management functions.

Measure: Number of newsletters distributed.

Timeline:

Outreach	
Task Item	Timeline Date
Develop an outreach matrix and keep track of all outreach activities.	January 2005
Develop a listing of all potential outreach topics. (Hurricanes, cold weather, floods, radiological, etc.)	March 2005
Develop a timeline for creation of each potential outreach possibility. (This includes developing handouts, creating power points, etc.)	May 2005
Develop a listing of all potential outreach candidates and avenues. (Media relations, city channel, schools, agencies, etc.)	May 2005
Update outreach matrix	June 2005
Create and administer an emergency management newsletter	June 2005
Update outreach matrix	September 2005

Outreach	
Task Item	*Timeline Date*
Update outreach matrix	December 2005
Update outreach matrix	March 2006
Create and administer an emergency management newsletter	May 2006

Status: Each quarter, a narrative of the status tells what is happening with the goal and if any changes need to be made.

Measures: This is what you should be tracking. For example, the graph shows number and type of outreach events attended.

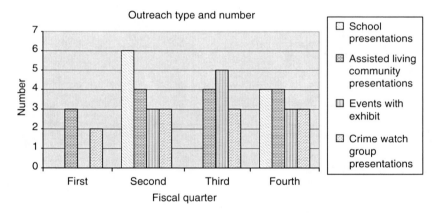

For best results, it is good to evaluate the goals, objectives, and performance measures on a quarterly basis. This allows the organization to report on the measures and make adjustments as necessary so everyone stays on track with the task at hand and ensures guidance on getting the organization to where they want to be. An annual review of the complete process should be performed to ensure everything is in alignment with the mission and vision of the organization. It is best to have this annual review completed just before time to prepare budgets so the agency knows what their needs are and can document those with measures. If major changes occur that could possibly change the organizational environment, then it is important to have an immediate review by the committee created to determine if changes need to be made. Strategic management planning is a continuous process that establishes and evaluates the direction of the organization. The following process, which has been used successfully by the Newport News Department of Emergency Management, is recommended for strategic planning.

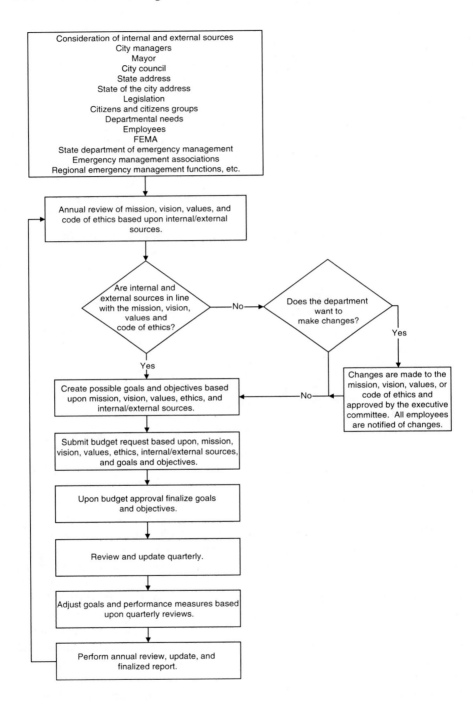

As a result of using a strategic planning process, an agency is able to set priorities and determine their future direction. This process allows the agency to set goals and objectives that will direct them toward success. In a successful strategic planning process, all employees buy into the direction of the organization and all work together with a common goal with a professed set of ethical standards and values. The development of this type of planning allows an agency to evaluate their success and make needed changes based on periodic reports. Strategic management planning is an important process for all organizations, especially emergency management agencies. A detailed plan will support financial request and show city management where areas are lacking. With a detailed reporting document, decisions can be made on the importance of emergency management functions and where local government should direct their attention. With the types of disasters, natural and man-made, that can potentially affect localities it is very important that they plan for the changing needs of the future and are able to prove they are being responsible steward. By following this direct process, strategic planning can be a simple success that provides many returns.

References

Bolman, L.G. and Deal, T.E. 1997. *Reframing Organizations, Artistry, Choice and Leadership*. San Francisco, California: Jossey-Bass.

Glasser, J. September 2003. Improving emergency response. *U.S. News & World Report*, 135 (8).

Drucker, P.F. 1993. *Management: Tasks, Responsibilities, Practices*. New York: Harper Business.

Federal Emergency Management Agency, July 1995. EOC's management and operations course, Independent Study, Emergency Operation Center, design, operations, management, exercises.

Hughes, R., Ginnett, R., and Curphy, G. 1999. *Leadership: Enhancing the Lessons of Experience*. Boston, Massachusetts: Irwin McGraw-Hill.

Moore, C.W. 1986. *The Mediation Process*. San Francisco, California: Jossey-Bass Publishers.

Poister, T.H. and Streib, G. January/February 2005. Elements of strategic planning and management in municipal government: Status after two decades. *Public Administration Review*, 65 (1).

Sturgis, R. December 2005. Strategic planning in a public works sector: Linking it all together. *APWA Reporter*, 72 (12).

Unites States Government Accountability Office, September 2004. Homeland Security, Effective regional coordination can enhance emergency preparedness, GAO-04-1009. Report to the Chairman, Committee on Government Reform, House of Representatives.

Unites States Government Accountability Office (GAO), July 2005. Homeland Security, DHS' efforts to enhance first responders' all-hazards capabilities continue to evolve. GAO-05-652. Report to the Chairman and Ranking Democratic Member, Subcommittee on Economic Development, Public Buildings and Emergency Management, Committee on Transportation and Infrastructure, House of Representatives.

Index

D

Damage assessment, for disaster rehabilitation, 481; *see also* Disaster management
Debswana mining company (Botswana), 326
Deccan Development Society (DDS), for local resilience, 346
December 26, 2004 tsunami (Asia), 5
Deep-Ocean Assessment and Reporting of Tsunamis (DART II), 489
Department of Defense (DOD)
role of, 406, 407, 409
subordinate to federal agency, 404–405
Department of Health and Human Services (DHHS), 85
Department of Homeland Security (DHS), 81, 536
emergency management requirement for, 573
FEMA removal, 536
training-related collaborations, 538
Disaster communications
future of, 395–396
and normal communications, 388–389
planning and preparation for, 393–395
principles for, 391–393
spokesperson role, 390–391
Disaster data collection and interpretation, 533
Disaster-development interface
development matrix, 487
futuristic perspective, 487
Yokohama strategy for, 488
Disaster Field Training Operation (DFTO)
Emergency Management Institute (EMI), 536
on-site training opportunities to, 537
professional training resource to, 536
Disaster-focused hospital, 563
Disaster management
community-based approaches, 431
complex logistical problems in, 428
definition of, 428–429
development by, 556
disabled and frail elderly populations, 430
disabled person handling, 431
disaster preparedness and mitigation, 478
disaster rehabilitation
convergence perspective of, 486
financial infrastructure, 482

noncompliance issues for, 485
physical rehabilitation, 479
psychological rehabilitation, 480
social rehabilitation, 479
stress management, 480
sustainable livelihood framework, 484
electronic sources of information, 533
federal government role, 557
FEMA role in, 557–558
global connotation, 488
local government plans, 555–556
mitigation, 431–432, 435
policy formulation, 555
policy implementation, 554–555
preparedness, 432–433, 435
private sector role in, 558–559
problems in, 554–555
role of training in, 530
state government role in, 556–557
strategic planning, 435–436
sustainable development, 486
sustainable disaster network (SDN) institutional framework, 485
timely and accurate information, 433
Disaster Medical Assistance Team (DMAT), 471–472
Disaster mitigation, 431, 432
Disaster policy and management
paradigmatic shift, 338–341
presidential performance on
Carter Administration's Reorganization Plan No. 3, 55–56
Clinton emphasis, 58, 67
Eisenhower on, 61
factors for, 55–56
Ford administration, 57
National Mitigation Strategy (1995) for, 66–67
President role in, 60–62
public and private agencies coordination for, 76–77
emergency managers role, survey on, 90–95
Katrina problems, 80–81
and organizational theory, 81–82
and strategic emergency planning, 84–87
and technology, 82–84
World Trade Center, terrorist attack, 78–80

T

U